Creative Writing

Edited by Linda Anderson

A Workbook with Readings

Taylor & Francis Group in association with The Open University

This publication forms part of an Open University course A215 *Creative Writing*. Details of this and other Open University courses can be obtained from the Student Registration and Enquiry Service, The Open University, PO Box 625, Milton Keynes, MK7 6YG, United Kingdom: Tel. +44 (0)870 333 4340, email general-enquiries@open.ac.uk

Alternatively, you may visit the Open University website at http://www.open.ac.uk where you can learn more about the wide range of courses and packs offered at all levels by The Open University.

To purchase a selection of Open University course materials visit http://www.ouw.co.uk, or contact Open University Worldwide, Michael Young Building, Walton Hall, Milton Keynes MK7 6AA, United Kingdom for a brochure. Tel. +44 (0)1908 858785; fax +44 (0)1908 858787; e-mail ouwenq@open.ac.uk

Published by Routledge; written and produced by The Open University

Routledge
2 Park Square
Milton Park
Abingdon
Oxfordshire
OX14 4RN

The Open University
Walton Hall, Milton Keynes
MK7 6AA

First published 2006

Edited and designed by The Open University.

Typeset by Tradespools – Typesetting Division of the Antony Rowe Group, Chippenham, Wiltshire.

Printed and bound in Malta by Gutenberg Press.

British Library Cataloguing in Publication Data: applied for

Library of Congress Cataloging in Publication Data: applied for

ISBN: HB 0415 372429
        PB 0415 372437

1.1

'For anyone getting going as a writer and even for those who have already made a start, this is an invaluable guide, full of useful tips, mind-freeing exercises, and inspiring wisdom from established authors.'

Blake Morrison, poet, memoirist and critic

'With so many angles covered and contributors' insights included, this workbook avoids imparting systematised guidelines for writing creatively. A valuable source for dipping in and out of.'

Russell Celyn Jones, novelist and critic, based at Birkbeck College, University of London

'A creative writing book as good as this is a rare event. It works across genres; it works outside the academy in the world of real people; and it places reading in its right and honourable place, for no writer can be any good without also being a great reader. But the chief reason it works superbly is because it is written by writers. It is informed by their precise experience of the practice of writing, and that means imagination and practicality are given an equal value.'

David Morley, poet and critic, Director of the Writing Programme, Warwick University

'This is a wonderfully heterogeneous workbook: thoroughly researched, it addresses a wide range of genres and is written by expert practitioners. The book is rich in stimulus, technical analysis, practical strategies and ideas about the linguistic imagination that resonate throughout a generous range of writing samples. It's a major contribution to the pedagogy of creative writing, an invaluable resource for anyone teaching or learning the craft.'

Graham Mort, poet and radio drama writer, Director of Postgraduate Studies, Creative Writing, Lancaster University

'A contemporary, no-nonsense approach to creative writing. The authors have distilled a mass of wisdom on the subject of writing, putting forward a workmanlike approach, demystifying the process.'

Monique Roffey, novelist and co-director of the Arvon Foundation's centre in Devon

'This is an excellent companion to the creative process.'

Justin Hill, novelist and travel writer

Contents

Contributors

Five of the contributors are current members of the Literature Department at the Open University. The author of Part 3, *Writing poetry*, is W.N. Herbert of Newcastle University.

Linda Anderson is an award-winning novelist (*To Stay Alive* and *Cuckoo*, both published by Bodley Head) and writer of short stories, poetry, performance pieces and critical reviews. Her work has been published in Britain, Ireland, USA and Australia. She has taught at Goldsmiths' College and at Lancaster University, where she was Head of Creative Writing from 1995–2002. She has designed several successful courses, including a training programme for new writing tutors and an MA in creative writing by distance learning. She has also worked as a producer and director for BBC Radio Drama. She has a PhD in creative writing.

Mary Hammond began her career as a writer/researcher in the US mass-market paperback industry in the early 1980s. She has a PhD in British publishing history and is the author of *Reading, Publishing and the Formation of Literary Taste in England 1880–1914* (Ashgate) as well as a number of articles on nineteenth- and twentieth-century publishing and book-selling. She has written and taught creative writing courses for the Open College Network, Middlesex University and the University of Southampton.

Sara Haslam completed her PhD, on Ford Madox Ford, in 1998 (University of London). She began her teaching career at King's College, London and the Roehampton Institute, and was lecturer in English at University College Chester, where she helped to establish creative writing provision. At the Open University she has written course material for the *Start Writing* suite of courses, as well as A215 *Creative Writing*. She has published essays and articles on Ford, Henry James, and modernism, a multimedia CD-ROM on Thomas Hardy's poetry, and her book, *Fragmenting Modernism: Ford Madox Ford, the novel and the Great War* was published by Manchester University Press in 2002. Current projects include an essay for the Blackwell *Companion to Modernist Literature and Culture*, and a study of Ford's autobiography.

W.N. Herbert is an award-winning poet, whose last four collections, all published by Bloodaxe, have attracted numerous accolades: *Forked Tongue* (1994); *Cabaret McGonagall* (1996); *The Laurelude* (1998); *The Big Bumper Book of Troy* (2002). In 2000 he edited the best-selling anthology *Strong Words: Modern poets on modern poetry* with Matthew Hollis. He taught in the Department of Creative Writing at Lancaster University (1996–2002), and currently teaches Creative Writing and Modern Scottish Poetry in the School of English at Newcastle University. He has a DPhil from Oxford on the Scots poet Hugh MacDiarmid, which was published by OUP in 1992 (*To Circumjack MacDiarmid*). His next book of poems, *Bad Shaman Blues,* is forthcoming from Bloodaxe.

Derek Neale is a writer whose short stories have appeared in various anthologies and periodicals. He has worked with the BBC on a number of radio and CD projects and has just completed his first novel, *The Book of Guardians*. He has taught fiction, stage, radio and film writing at the University of East Anglia since 1994; he also gained his MA and PhD from there. His research is concerned with the link between memory and writing, and the borderline that runs between fiction and life writing. He has taught writing in a prison and edited two collections of prison writing. He joined The Open University in 2003 to help design the *Start Writing* courses and to contribute to *Creative Writing*.

W.R. Owens has been teaching at the Open University since 1978, and is now Professor of English Literature. He has written teaching material for many courses, and is chair of the MA in Literature programme – the largest in the UK. His research interests are in seventeenth and early eighteenth century English literature, with a particular focus on the works of John Bunyan and Daniel Defoe. His publications on Bunyan include a Penguin edition of *Grace Abounding* (1987) and a new edition of *The Pilgrim's Progress* for the Oxford World's Classics series (2003). He has also published extensively on Daniel Defoe in collaboration with P.N. Furbank. They have written three books on Defoe together, and are currently General Editors of a 44-volume edition of *The Works of Daniel Defoe* (in progress, Pickering & Chatto, 2000–2008).

Introduction

LINDA ANDERSON

How do you become a writer? Many people hold to the notion that this is a glamorous fate mysteriously conferred. The writer is thought of as a 'genius' who must simply wait for the angel to tap his or her shoulder. There are several versions of this genius. One is a beady-eyed recluse who stands aloof from life, recording it with piercing accuracy. Another is a social outlaw who lives life to the hilt, sometimes recklessly, but who nonetheless manages to keep office hours to get the words out. There is also the writer who is stung into words by suffering. He or she has had an unhappy life or witnessed terrible events and has therefore developed unusual insight. This is backed up by statements like Henri de Montherlant's famous dictum, 'Happiness writes white'. If the writer is contented, nothing will show up on the page. Apart from the necessity of genius and/or suffering, the writer must be able to weather extreme solitude. Novelist Nadine Gordimer has called writing the most solitary of occupations, comparable only to that of a lighthouse keeper.

Fortunately, the truth is both more mundane and more reassuring. You do not have to be a genius or a trauma-survivor or a hermit. Even the most talented and experienced writers have to labour at writing, as you will see in the opening chapters of this book. Writing is a craft, the elements of which can be learned. Like every other art, writing requires practice, an idea taken for granted by musicians and painters but sometimes doubted by readers and aspiring writers alike. Nor is writing the exclusive preserve of the wounded or those who have had unusual lives. Imagination and empathy enable writers to enter experiences they have never had. The loneliness of the long-distance writer has also been exaggerated. Writing is indeed necessarily a solitary business but any writer as cut off as a lighthouse keeper might soon run out of subjects to write about.

There is a good solitude for writers and a bad one. The good one is when you become so immersed in your writing that you lose track of time and forget your normal worries. The bad one sometimes occurs afterwards when you doubt the value of what you have written or don't know how to progress it. This book seeks to counteract that form of loneliness by building your range of expertise and sense of possibilities at the same time as encouraging you to follow your own imagination.

How the book is organised

Creative Writing: A workbook with readings has been written by five published authors who are also experienced writing tutors. We have taught the subject in a wide range of institutions, including Lancaster University and the University of East Anglia, which both pioneered the teaching of creative writing in British higher education from the early 1970s.

The book is divided into two main sections: a Workbook followed by connected Readings. The Workbook is in five parts and is intended to provide a complete creative writing course from ways to jump-start your writing, right through to ways to present your work to agents and publishers. Three main genres are explored in depth: fiction, poetry and life writing, which includes biography, autobiography and travel writing.

Each chapter of the Workbook demonstrates aspects of writing which are illustrated by excerpts from contemporary or classical writings. These are located in the Readings section except in the case of poems or short prose sections, which are mostly included in the Workbook. We have deliberately chosen a very wide range of readings to show a variety of approaches and styles. Reading is one of the chief ways to train yourself as a writer. We have associated an activity with every reading. You are asked to consider some questions in relation to the text or to reflect upon what it might mean to you and your own writing strategies. Beyond this immediate function, the best way to use the Readings is to follow up on your enthusiasms and discoveries. If you feel a strong affinity with any authors or become fascinated by their writing methods, seek out more of their works and construct your own reading adventure.

How to use the book

The Workbook is highly practical. It is designed to help you engender your own abundant stack of material in response to suggestions and exercises. The keeping of a writer's notebook is a key strategy and should be begun early on. Your notebook is where you can store your observations, responses and experiments – it acts as a spur to both imagination and commitment.

Each chapter of the Workbook contains several writing exercises. Their purpose is to give you immediate practice in whatever aspects of writing are being discussed. They are not tests – they are meant to be enjoyable, doable, sometimes provocative or challenging. If you dislike an exercise, try it anyway. Sometimes irritation or resistance can mobilise creativity in surprising ways. You may find that some exercises will deliver more than an addition to your repertoire of techniques. You may come up with the seed of a poem or story, some fictional character who will lodge in your imagination, some scene that will start to suggest a whole story, or a personal memory that you can use in a new way. In these cases, the exercises are a scaffolding that falls away to reveal new work. The book contains a few exercises which are involved with producing longer projects but the majority of the exercises are designed to take between 10–45 minutes. If you enjoy a particular exercise, you may want to devote more time to it or return to it and try out variations. If you find yourself working on an exercise for several hours, rejoice – it's no longer an exercise but on its way to being a poem, story, or chapter.

This book forms one of the core components of an Open University writing course, A215 *Creative Writing*, and is also appropriate for use on other courses or by writers' groups or by individual writers working alone. It is suitable for aspiring writers who have begun to try things out as well as for more experienced writers who want to deepen their skills or seek new directions for their work. It may be worked through sequentially or used as a resource book for both writers and writing tutors to dip in to as needed. If you are a writer working on your own, you may wonder how to gauge the effectiveness of your writings. The discussion sections after each activity give some guidance on how to review what you've done. Put your work away for a while, and then read it with fresh eyes.

The most important aim of this book is to help you to discover and nurture your individual voice as a writer. In each chapter you will find lots of advice about writing but you do not have to take it. There are no 'rules' or prescriptions. There is no 'right' way to carry out the exercises, only your own best and truest way. In a letter to fellow novelist Jonathan Franzen, Don de Lillo wrote: 'Writing is a form of personal freedom. It frees us from the mass identity we see in the making all around us.' Whether you use this book in a class or working alone, we hope that you will make the book serve you and not the other way round.

Workbook

PART I

The creative process

1 Stimulating creativity and imagination: What really works?

LINDA ANDERSON

Writers speak a lot about the 'blank page' – usually the daunting emptiness of it or, sometimes, the lure of it. How do writers get started afresh each day, facing the pristine pages or the empty screen?

Let's look first at two opening sentences. These are the habitual starting points used by two novelists at the beginning of their daily practice. One of the novelists is a fictional character and the other is a real living writer.

Can you guess which sentence was written by an imaginary character and which by an actual author?

> One fine morning in the month of May an elegant young horsewoman might have been seen riding a handsome sorrel mare along the flowery avenues of the Bois de Boulogne.

> The quick brown fox jumps over the lazy dog.

The first sentence is one version of the constantly reworked opening of a novel by Joseph Grand, a somewhat comic figure in Albert Camus's *The Plague* (1960 [1947]), which explores the impact of an outbreak of bubonic plague on the inhabitants of the imaginary town of Oran. Joseph Grand is an aspiring novelist who devotes all of his spare time and energies to writing. He is impelled by the dream of a publisher reading his work and being so thunderstruck that he stands up and says to his staff, 'Hats off, gentlemen!' (p.98), which conjures the faintly surreal vision of publishers sitting in offices wearing their hats. But Grand can never progress beyond his first sentence. He worries at every detail of it, ponders the derivation and meaning of words, frets over the tastefulness, the rhythms, the factual accuracy. Is 'sorrel' really a colour? Are there really any flowers in the Bois de Boulogne? He makes minor alterations, never satisfied. And of course, the sentence doesn't work – we see the writer's fussy effort more than the scene itself.

The second sentence is the well-known line which uses all twenty-six letters of the alphabet. In volume two of her autobiography, New Zealand writer Janet Frame (1984) describes how she started her daily writing sessions by typing this sentence repeatedly when she was creating her first novel. After a long period of hospitalisation during which she endured over two hundred electro-convulsive shock treatments, 'each the equivalent, in degree of fear, to an execution' (p.112), she was living in the home of Frank Sargeson, an established author who took her under his wing. Each morning she went into a garden hut to write, while her mentor pottered about outside, tending his plants. Desperate to appear gratefully industrious she would type that line, alternating it with 'Now is the time for all good men to come to the aid of the party' (p.144). There was no 'theory' behind her strategy – she was acting out of timorousness and embarrassment. But it worked. She was safely at her desk, tap-tapping away. Eventually, the self-consciousness gave way to absorption; the mechanical lines to real work.

Frame's opening lines didn't matter at all; Grand's mattered far too much. The portrayal of Grand is exaggerated for satirical effect, of course, but he does show traits and motivations recognisable to many aspiring writers. He is ambitious and eager for success. He is also dogged by a paralysing perfectionism. His soaring ambition and crippled creativity seem to go hand in hand. Ambition and high standards are important, even essential at certain points, but they can obstruct and deaden writers in the production stages of work.

A researcher into creativity, Mihaly Csikszentmihalyi (1996), warned that artists must not start wondering how much their work will sell for or what the critics will think of it, not if they want to 'pursue original avenues'. He found that 'creative achievements depend upon single-minded immersion'. He introduced the concept of 'flow', that state of timeless-seeming happiness and concentration which comes when one's whole attention is absorbed.

Virginia Woolf has described this inspired state memorably:

> I walk making up phrases; sit, contriving scenes; am in short in the thick of the greatest rapture known to me.
>
> (Woolf, 1953, p.115)

The question for many writers is how to get to the 'rapture' without having to go by way of resistance. Some lucky people never have a problem but many will recognise this scenario:

You sit down to write and then run the gauntlet of self-sabotage: 'must have another coffee/wasn't that the phone ringing/should really check the electricity meter/maybe pop down town briefly/that three for two offer in the bookshop won't last forever/maybe ought to read something just to get the engine going/you'll never be a writer, anyway/who do you think you're kidding ...'

It may be comforting to know that even the most famous writers can be assailed by doubts and inner saboteurs. Here is Vladimir Nabokov:

> Just when the author sits down to write, 'the monster of grim commonsense' will lumber up the steps to whine that the book is not for the general public, that the book will never – And right then, just before it blurts out the word s, e, double – l, false commonsense must be shot dead.

> (quoted in Boyd, 1991, p.31)

How can we slay these lumbering monsters or at least shut them up? Let's explore some practical strategies commonly used by established writers.

Develop a writing habit

'Excellence is not an act, but a habit.'

Aristotle, quoted in Sher, 1999, p.18

Think again about Janet Frame's procedures. She established a habit of writing. Some new writers think that the correct thing to do is to wait for inspiration. They fear that if they try to write in a down-to-business mood or at routine times, the writing will not take flight. But inspiration will not reliably hunt you down at the supermarket or even on some idyllic country walk. Even if it did, you would need some practised skills and discipline to make the most of it. Court inspiration; make yourself available. Inspiration comes most often through the habit of work, unexpectedly, in the form of sudden ideas, ways and means, wonderful words and phrases, and sometimes complete breakthroughs. Kenzabura Oë, Nobel prize-winning novelist, said that it is 'accumulated practice' which enables the writer to 'reveal a landscape no one has ever seen before' (quoted in Sher, 1999, p.16). Writers practise regularly, just as musicians play and artists sketch.

<table>
<tr><td>**ACTIVITY 1.1**
Reading</td><td>Perhaps you're wondering how you could possibly fit regular writing practice into a busy life? In his essay, 'Fires' (1986 [1982]), Raymond Carver describes a decade of struggle to write while 'working at crap jobs' and raising two children. The essay is about his 'influences' as a writer but he subverts the usual listing of beloved literary antecedents. For him nothing could be more powerful than 'real influence' – the grinding daily responsibilities that obstruct literary work. Read the short extract from 'Fires', Reading 1 on p.413.</td></tr>
<tr><td>**DISCUSSION**</td><td>It can be consoling to know that most writers have to contend with obstacles to their work. The bitter radiance of Carver's moment of realisation in the laundromat also demonstrates that even the most mundane activities can be written about in an intensely interesting way.</td></tr>
</table>

Do you identify with any of Carver's difficulties? Or do you have your own problems? Make some notes to yourself about how you might be able to surmount any practical obstacles to your writing. You may wish to transfer these notes later into the writer's notebook which you will begin as you work through Chapter 2.

Can you carve out some time each day, even if it's just half an hour? It's the constancy that counts, the building of a habit, rather than the length of actual time you are able to spend each week.

Include consideration of times when you cannot actually be at your writing desk but can mull over and progress your ideas, or figure out ways of expressing some things. For example: late at night; when you're travelling by bus or train or even while driving (but don't take notes without stopping the car!); in the bath; in the middle of a boring meeting; during lunch breaks at work; in supermarket queues. In this way, you can keep the momentum going between your longer sessions. Start experimenting to find whatever suits you in terms of allocating time.

Experiment also with special rituals and different locations for your writing. Will it help if you play music? Stick inspiring mottoes on your computer or wall? Have a little shrine of favourite books propped on your desk? Where is the best place for you to write? Proust wrote in bed in a cork-lined chamber. Roald Dahl lay on the floor of a garden hut.

J.K.Rowling wrote the first 'Harry Potter' in an Edinburgh café. Find out what works for you.

Postpone perfection

The poet Louise Bogan once used the haunting phrase 'the knife of the perfectionist attitude' (quoted in Olsen, 1980, p.145). Perfectionism can kill writing, cutting it dead as it tries to emerge. There is a time for perfecting writing and it is not at the outset. Remember the hopelessly stalled Joseph Grand.

But what if you find it painful to produce clumsy, ineffective lines or sentences? You should understand that all writers, even the most experienced, can write badly. The gift of writing is a power that flickers – everyone has mediocre days as well as magical ones. Try to cultivate an attitude of curiosity. As Flannery O'Connor said: 'I write to see what I say' (1990 [1971], p.ix). Don't expect everything to be fluent or valuable. Virginia Woolf wrote about finding the 'diamonds of the dustheap' in her daily output (Woolf, 1953, p.7).

Most successful writers have a high tolerance of raw, messy first drafts and of a series of imperfect subsequent drafts. They know that stamina, the ability to stick with a poem or prose piece until it emerges as the best they can do, is as important as whatever talent they possess.

For example, the poet Ruth Padel has described the process of creating a poem as a sequence of stages (adapted from Ashby, 2003, p.16):

- Keep a file of interesting phrases and images – add to it when something engages you or has a charge.
- Block your poem out roughly, consulting your file to see if anything belongs. This is the modelling stage, when like a sculptor, you're gathering materials and working them up.
- Let yourself be led by how the words want to be. This is the initial stage when you let yourself pour out.
- Next, again like a sculptor, trying to see the image imprisoned in the stone, start chipping away and discarding.
- Learn the poem by heart; recite it to yourself to see if it sounds right.
- Finally, check every word, comma, line break, and ask yourself if they are absolutely necessary.

It can take many drafts to get the poem right.

Prose writers also need to build and revise their work through several drafts. One of the most prolific writers alive today, Joyce Carol Oates, is often thought of as an 'effortless' writer because of her vast output: over eighty books including novels, short story collections, poetry and essays. But she says: 'When people accuse me of writing easily, I can't imagine what they mean.' She writes by hand, starting stories countless times, making comments as she goes, often producing as many as a thousand pages of notes for every 250 printed pages (in Arana, 2003, p.11). The 'secret' of good writing is rewriting.

The most empowering right you can give yourself is the entitlement to write roughly, uncertainly, even badly.

Writing a first draft is like groping your way into a darkened room, or trying to catch a faintly overheard conversation. It is only when you have some kind of scaffolding down on the page that you will begin to glimpse the ultimate shape of your poem or prose piece.

Use techniques to free up your writing

The poet Paul Muldoon advises new writers not to think of themselves primarily as writers but as receivers (Open University, 2004). The writer acts as a kind of medium or channel, catching the words and organising them. You stay alert and 'listen' instead of bracing yourself for some hard test. If you cultivate an attitude of curiosity, trust, and receptivity towards writing, it will flow more easily.

There are several techniques that can help with this. They are often referred to as methods for 'harnessing the unconscious mind'. The idea is that our conscious mind contains only a fraction of our selves and we need to tap the huge fund of ideas, images, memories and emotions that make up our unconscious minds. All of the methods involve fast unpremeditated writing. This is in order to bypass the intellect or the internal 'censor', which is always trying to evaluate and direct the writing.

Freewriting

In freewriting – a term coined by Peter Elbow – we permit ourselves to associate freely, that is to write down the first words that occur to us, then whatever that makes us think of, following the train of thought wherever it goes. It can feel uncomfortable, especially at first. You may feel that what you are writing is silly or unseemly or banal. You may feel a strong urge to stop or control it. But don't. You will often be surprised, even delighted, by the liveliness and power of the ideas and words that emerge.

The method

How is it done? Let the words tumble out. Write anything at all, what's on your mind, what you notice:

> Like I'm now looking at the tree outside my window. Tangles of dark branches, spooky sometimes, but soon it will just explode into pink blossoms, fantastic pinkness for a few weeks before the wind shakes it all away. The sadness of trees, inherent sadness, but more mournful when there are no trees, like that place in Donegal, rocks and peat forever, no tree outlines against the sky. Remember V. after the stroke pointing at the cactus that had lost its flowers. Look, she said, it brings no more spoons. No more blooms. Her lost language and the new one she puts together and the way it makes sense.

ACTIVITY 1.2

Writing

Choose three or four of the following beginnings and freewrite for a few minutes about each one.

- The truth is ...
- I wish I had said ...
- I need proof ...
- I went outside and ...
- For the first time ever ...
- It surprised me when ...
- It was no use pretending ...
- A long time ago ...
- I turned the corner, and there, coming towards me was ...
- That smell reminds me of ...
- One summer's day ...

Read over your freewrites. Underline any words, phrases or lines that interest you. Start to build a stock of material for possible development.

DISCUSSION

Freewriting will often take you into your deepest ideas, feelings and memories. It enables you to amass material, some of which can be used and developed in your work. Writing in this way also trains you to be able to write breezily and with confidence as soon as you sit down to do it.

Clustering

Clustering is a technique developed by Gabriele Lusser Rico in her book *Writing the Natural Way* (1983). It is a method based on the distinctive functions of the brain's two hemispheres. The clustering method aims to rouse a generous flow of connected images and ideas and to bypass the ordering, analytical functions of the brain which might constrain writing at the outset.

Traditionally, it was thought that creativity comes from the right side of the brain and analysis from the left. But neuroscientist Antonio Damasio states that creativity requires interaction between both parts of the brain. A creative person needs 'a broad imagination' to produce 'a torrent of material'. Then they must have 'an educated emotional response to this flood of ideas'. Finally, they must have 'a good reasoning process to shape and communicate their ideas to others' (quoted in Wade, 2003).

Part of the trick of creativity is being able to move backwards and forwards between different areas of the brain as needed. Often, when we begin to think about writing something, we go into analytical mode, making lists, taking things step by step. Clustering, which is more like drawing or sketching than writing, helps to produce an initial wealth of material, all emotionally suffused, and reaching towards a tentative whole. It can enable us to begin writing more easily and coherently.

The method

To make a cluster, you take a fresh page and choose a word or phrase which represents the subject you wish to write about. For example, you might use single words like 'water', 'fire', 'India', or phrases like 'love at first sight'. Write this nucleus word or phrase in the centre of the page, circle it and then write down every connection that comes into your head. Let the words or phrases fan out from the nucleus like a branch. Circle each new word and join the circles with little lines or arrows. When you seem to exhaust a particular chain of associations, start another branch. When you come up with a very evocative word, you might start a new chain from that.

A cluster gives you a visual map of your thought. It helps you to organise your writing organically rather than sequentially. It can act as a blueprint of a whole poem or prose piece, or you may find most of it dreary but feel intrigued by one strand or one idea that crops up. Clusters are not an end in themselves. Use them to trigger writing. The simplest way is to launch into a 'focused freewrite', that is, one where you choose the subject.

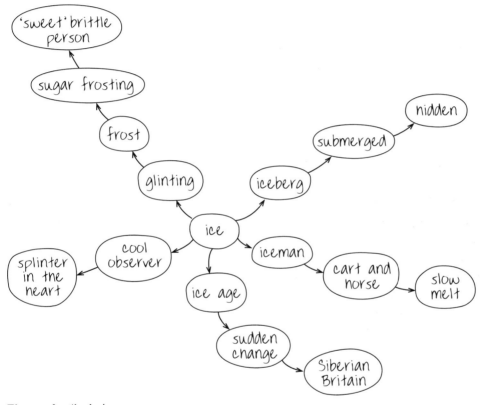

Figure 1   'Ice' cluster

Clusters are wholly personal and may seem partly impenetrable to someone else. In the ice cluster shown in Figure 1, one strand is connected to my mother's stories about her Canadian childhood, the weekly visits of the iceman who delivered blocks of ice for refrigeration on a horse-drawn cart. Another strand has 'splinter in the heart', which I recognise as Graham Greene's observation that writers have a 'splinter of ice in the heart'. The 'sugar frosting' line was the one that grabbed my interest. 'Sugar frosting' reminded me of a certain type of character: effusively friendly yet brittle and cold:

She has a sing-song voice and gushing manner like she's your best friend. But you know nothing about her and daren't ask. Her whole body looks clenched and her eyes are stony. You wonder what's behind the sugar frosting.

Remember that this kind of freewrite is 'focused' in the sense that you select the subject. You should still write them at a rapid pace, allowing the words to pour out.

Figure 2 'Grandmother' cluster

It is useful to create clusters for characters in stories or narrative poems. This is a character-cluster I made for a story called 'The Marvellous Boy' (Anderson, 1996, pp.70–89). The grandmother appears only through the memories of two characters in the story but she has a baleful influence. I wanted to get a better sense of her. The cluster gives a portrait of a stern matriarch and the suffocating atmosphere around her. One branch is a list of her favourite admonishments. Sometimes the lines spin into wordplay: 'judging, grudging' and the alliterative 'asthma/ ask for nothing', the kind of word design often obtained in clusters.

For me, the surprising leap in the cluster was from 'queen bee' to 'cockroach'. Then 'white cockroach' cropped up after 'whited sepulchre', the Biblical image for a pious hypocrite. I had no idea what these meant when I was doing the cluster. But I remembered later that the queen of a cockroach nest is white and the image fitted the story, which is essentially about an invincible unfeelingness, a numbing of the heart. The white cockroach queen represents that in the story and adds to its symbolic level. Without the cluster, I would never have come up with the idea.

ACTIVITY 1.3
Writing

Make four clusters followed by focused freewrites based on what interests you most in your clusters. Spend no more than 3 minutes on each cluster and the same amount of time on each of your freewrites. Choose your nucleus words from these lists, taking at least one from each:

- Family, friendship, the end of the affair, fame, rivalry, getting older, conflict.
- Afraid, angry, sad, hopeful, forgiving, suspicious, jealous, homesick.
- House, doll, photo album, flowers, gun, shoes, money.

DISCUSSION

Again, underline any parts of your freewrites which you feel you could develop further or use as they stand in a poem or story.

Which kind of nucleus word worked best for you – an object, feeling, or big abstract idea? Did you find yourself anchoring the abstract idea to specific, concrete details? If so, this could be a useful kind of cluster to make when you want to explore 'big' themes, which are best translated into the personal and specific. For example, 'war' is a soldier with post-traumatic stress syndrome; 'neighbourliness' is Marie looking after Sam's dog while he's in hospital.

As well as using clusters at the start of any writing, also try clustering any time you get stuck. When the sentences refuse to march across the page, clusters are much less daunting.

ACTIVITY 1.4
Writing

Practise clustering and freewriting for 20 minutes every day for a week. The objective is to begin your 'habit of writing'; become adept at the two techniques; and to turn up possible ideas and material for later use. You can choose your own 'triggering' words, or select from the suggestions below:

For freewriting, choose from these beginnings:

- Coffee, toast and three paracetamol ...
- She said it might put things in perspective ...
- I thought he would never change ...
- There was something unbelievable in the desk drawer ...
- They didn't even care ...
- I thought I heard a noise ...
- I love my new ...

You can choose clusters from any of these: heartache, spiders, skating on thin ice, fudge, purple, the best time ever, mirror, letting go.

Remember to move into a focused freewrite when you come up with exciting or revealing ideas.

Give yourself patient time

Unlike musicians or artists, who expect to undertake long training and practice, writers often feel impatient and unforgiving of themselves if they cannot swiftly produce accomplished work. This may be because our medium is the language we have already acquired and use incessantly. But it takes a long time to master the crafts of writing, to wrestle our ideas into the best arranged words, to find our special themes or to let them find us. 'Finding a voice', the writer's creation of a distinctive personal style or 'signature', also takes time and confidence to emerge. John Gardner, writing about this issue in connection with fiction writing in particular, thought it best illustrated by an example:

> Notice the careful, tentative quality of the opening paragraph of Melville's *Omoo*:
>
> > It was in the middle of a bright tropical afternoon that we made good our escape from the bay. The vessel we sought lay with her main-topsail aback about a league from the land, and was the only object that broke the broad expanse of the ocean.

There is, I think, nothing actively bad about this writing; but we get no sense of the speaker's character, no clear mood from the rhythm (we cannot tell how seriously to take the word 'escape'), certainly no sense of prose invading the domain of poetry. [...]

Compare what the same writer can do once he's found his booming authoritative voice:

> Call me Ishmael. Some years ago – never mind how long precisely – having little or no money in my purse, and nothing particular to interest me on shore, I thought I would sail about a little and see the watery part of the world ...

> (Gardner, 1985 [1983], pp.66–67)

The implication here is not that writers should necessarily seek a 'booming, authoritative voice'. Your particular voice might be sensuous, oratorical, tender, wisecracking, or whatever expresses you best. The point is that writing is a practice and a process. It requires patient time in abundance.

Avoid writer's block

It seems to be fashionable recently to deny the existence of writer's block. It is sometimes dismissed as a form of malingering; nothing that a bit of brisk determination would not cure. Just don't believe in it, seems to be the message. If it's not one of your articles of faith, then it won't happen to you. And perhaps some writers do talk about it too casually, claiming to be blocked when they are simply jaded or going through a period of silent renewal, that state which Keats called *agonie ennuyeuse* ('tedious agony' quoted in Olsen, 1980, p.6). In a fallow period, things are still growing out of sight.

But writer's block is a real condition and an oppressive one. Thomas Hardy stopped writing novels twenty-eight years before the end of his life, 'grated to pieces by the constant attrition' (ibid., p.122) of the censorship of his time. Gerard Manley Hopkins, torn between his vocations as both priest and poet, lamented to a friend in 1881 that 'every impulse and spring of art seems to have died in me ...' (ibid., p.129).

ACTIVITY 1.5

Reading

Read the extract from George Gissing's 1891 novel *New Grub Street* (1993), Reading 2 on p.415, which shows one of the most agonising attacks of writer's block ever described. Edwin Reardon is a writer of talent and high principles, who has enjoyed a modest literary success. He marries a socially ambitious woman, who expects him to achieve fame and money.

Is there anything surprising to you in this portrayal of writer's block?

DISCUSSION   It might be surprising that Edwin Reardon is a published writer, already building a reputation, but this does not protect him from writer's block. Even more surprising perhaps is that this writer's block is so very full of writing. Reardon is at his desk for almost ten hours daily and spurns companionship during his afternoon 'break' so that he can stay focused.

His self-persecution is brilliantly detailed. He moves straight from creation to punitive judgement. He abandons projects as soon as they present any difficulty. He is locked into a system of ferocious self-cancellation:

> 'What could I make of that, now?' 'Well, suppose I made him —?' 'But no, that wouldn't do,' and so on.

The particular causes of Reardon's plight are that he is fearful of not living up to his wife's expectations. Ambition and obligation rob him of the ability to achieve anything. He cannot write with 'the workhouse clanging' at his 'poet's ear' (Gissing, 1993 [1891], p.125).

How should we avoid this kind of calamity? Ted Solotaroff, editor of the *New American Review* for ten years, has written about this in his essay 'Writing In the Cold'. His magazine 'discovered' many new writers during his tenure, about half of whom later 'disappeared'. He speculated that the main thing which sustains writers who stick with it is a 'sense of necessity', a love of writing for its own sake. He quotes the novelist, Lynne Schwartz:

> Once I got started I wanted the life of a writer so fiercely that nothing could stop me. I wanted the intensity, the sense of aliveness that came from writing ... My life is worth living when I've written a good paragraph.

> (Solotaroff, 1985, p.279)

The enjoyment of writing, the pleasures of finding the precise word, of watching a fictional character unfold, of hitting on the right graceful rhythm for a poem: these are *intrinsic* rewards.

The desire for publication or for a good grade or for some stunned admiration from fellow-members of a writers' group – these are *extrinsic* rewards, potentially ensuing from the activity of writing but not part of the experience itself.

Researchers have found that creativity increases when a person's motivation is intrinsic. For example, T.M. Amabile carried out an experiment with seventy-two creative writing students in 1985 (Amabile, 1985). All of the students wrote a poem. Amabile then divided the students into two groups and distributed lists of reasons for writing. One group received a list emphasising intrinsic factors and the other received extrinsic motivations such as: 'You want your writing teachers to be favourably impressed with your writing talent' and 'You know that many of the best jobs available require good writing skills'. The students were then asked to write a second poem. External evaluators rated both poems from each student. Amabile found that there was a significant dip in achievement in the second poems written by students given the extrinsic list. Their writing was actually damaged by a focus on external rewards.

So, it seems best to leave our ambitions and obligations, our dreams and our deadlines, outside the door when we write; that way, we will find ourselves more often in the 'thick of the rapture' of writing.

References

Amabile, T.M. (1985) 'Motivation and Creativity: Effects of motivational orientation on creative writers', *Journal of Personality and Social Psychology*, No.48, pp.393–99.

Anderson, Linda (1996) 'The Marvellous Boy', in Lizz Murphy (ed.) *Wee Girls: Women writing from an Irish perspective*, Australia: Spinifex.

Arana, Marie (ed.) (2003) *The Writing Life: Writers on how they think and work*, New York: Public Affairs.

Ashby, Melanie (2003) 'The Padel Method', from 'Ruth Padel talks to Melanie Ashby', *Mslexia*, No.17.

Boyd, Brian (1991) *Vladimir Nabokov: The American years*, Princeton, N.J.: Princeton University Press.

Camus, Albert (1960 [1947]) *The Plague*, London: Penguin.

Carver, Raymond (1986 [1982]) 'Fires' in *Fires*, London: Picador.

Csikszentmihalyi, Mihaly (1996) *Creativity*, London: HarperCollins.

Frame, Janet (1984) *An Angel at My Table: An autobiography*, Volume 2, London: Women's Press.

Gardner, John (1985 [1983]) *On Becoming A Novelist*, New York: Harper & Row.

Gissing, George (1993 [1891]) *New Grub Street*, Oxford: Oxford University Press.

Lusser Rico, Gabriele (1983) *Writing the Natural Way*, Los Angeles: Tarcher.

O'Connor, Flannery (1990 [1971]) *The Complete Stories*, introduced by Robert Giroux, London: Faber and Faber.

Olsen, Tillie (1980) *Silences*, London: Virago.

Open University (2004) A171–6 *Start Writing*, Milton Keynes, The Open University.

Sher, Gail (1999) *One Continuous Mistake: Four noble truths for writers*, London: Penguin Arkana.

Solotaroff, Ted (1985) 'Writing In the Cold', *Granta*, No.15.

Wade, Dorothy (2003) 'You Don't Have to be Mad to be Creative ...', *Sunday Times Magazine*, 30 November.

Woolf, Virginia (1953) *A Writer's Diary*, London: Harcourt.

2 *Keeping a writer's notebook*

LINDA ANDERSON

In the previous chapter, we saw that Joyce Carol Oates makes voluminous notes in connection with each new work-in-progress. Ruth Padel keeps a file of phrases and images. She also calls this file her 'quarry' in keeping with her analogy of the writer as sculptor. Aptly, 'quarry' also means 'object of pursuit'. Writers are always on the alert for potential material and your own life – what you see, experience, think, and feel – will provide the principal source.

A notebook is an essential tool for any writer and has several functions. Sometimes you will see the terms 'writer's journal' or 'diary' used. These have the helpful connotations of daily discipline and absolute privacy, but in this chapter and throughout this book we will use the modest, down-to-business term writer's 'notebook' to encompass all the possible uses of such a record.

These range from the jotting down of observations while you're out and about to an account of daily events, your rants and raves, ideas for poems, single words, clippings from newspapers, responses to books or poems you've read, notes from research, all kinds of 'gathering'. Your notebook is for you, and it needs to contain whatever helps you or fuels your writing.

The way you organise it is also a matter of personal preference. You may decide to have separate sections, say, for writing exercises; a record of your thoughts and feelings; a section for memories; a section for story or poem ideas and drafts. Or you might like to simply add things in the order they occur, making a kind of creative compost heap. You might like to have one notebook for everything or keep separate ones, for example, a small unobtrusive notebook for carrying around with you and a larger one at home for fuller, more reflective writing.

The practicalities

First you need to think carefully about what sort of notebook will suit you. It will be a companion to you and your writing, and you need to be happy with it. It's up to you whether you prefer small bound notebooks or ones with tear-off pages; a loose-leaf file; sets of index cards; or even a hand-held computer.

Have a browse round a local stationery store. Only buy a beautiful hardback notebook if that would inspire you. If you think you might find it too forbidding to scribble in, choose something else. You need to allow yourself to write in a rapid, impulsive way. Get cheap school exercise books if that would give you the licence to write roughly and to score things out. Choose lined or blank pages according to preference. Remember that you may want to stick things into the book: newspaper cuttings, photographs, or letters. Buy a notebook that you can easily carry around. If you are attracted to an unwieldy one, use that one at home and carry a different one for note-taking outside.

Gathering

In this section we will look in more detail at the sorts of things that might go into your notebook and give you practice in some of them.

Observations of your environment

Carry your notebook wherever you go and get used to jotting down anything that strikes you as interesting: descriptions of people and places, snatches of overheard conversation, sudden insights and ideas. This practice of hopeful, purposeful looking will quickly sharpen your perception. The immediate capturing of your impressions will ensure that you write them when they are 'hot'. The notebook in your pocket or bag will also remind you that you are a writer even when other duties seem to marginalise the activity. You will soon find yourself automatically putting impressions into words. The biographer Michael Holroyd has written about his habit of taking long night-time walks in London as a young man, thinking about 'people, usually, and paragraphs' (2004).

ACTIVITY 2.1

Reading and writing

Here is Virginia Woolf's entry in her diary for 4 October 1934, a description of the impact of a storm on her garden pond at Asheham.

> A violent rain storm on the pond. The pond is covered with little white thorns; springing up and down: the pond is bristling with leaping white thorns, like the thorns on a small porcupine; bristles; then black waves; cross it; black shudders; and the little water thorns

are white; a helter skelter rain and the elms tossing it up and down;
the pond overflowing on one side; lily leaves tugging; the red flower
swimming about; one leaf flapping; then completely smooth for a
moment; then prickled; thorns like glass; but leaping up and down
incessantly; a rapid smirch of shadow. Now light from the sun;
green and red; shiny; the pond a sage green; the grass brilliant
green; red berries on the hedges; the cows very white; purple over
Asheham.

(Woolf, 1953, p.220)

Notice the urgency of this writing. Woolf is bent on capturing fleeting
change and motion and the result is cinematic and exact. The odd
punctuation (all those semi-colons), isolates each little change like single
snapshots. There is a sense of the writer's scrutiny and headlong
excitement in trying to convey the scene 'right here, right now'.

Try this the next time you are outside. Take a few minutes to stare at
your surroundings. Focus on weather, movement, colour, and detail.
Move from the small details to the larger surroundings as Woolf does –
in her scene, she moves gradually outwards from the rain on the pond
to the hedges, then to the cows and sky.

Concern yourself with atmosphere and exact pictorial detail rather than
correct sentence structure. You are trying to see things in a fresh,
immediate way. Spend about 10 minutes on this exercise.

Don't force comparisons but if anything reminds you of something else,
write it down. Woolf describes the driving rain as 'thorns' and then
compares the thorns to a porcupine's bristles and then to glass.

The search for similes (when something is *like* something else) and
metaphors (when something is said to actually *be* something else, for
example, 'his violence is a cooled volcano') can enhance writing, making
us see things in a new way. Practise seeing likenesses in unlike things
and collect possible images, similes and metaphors in your notebook.

Record of daily events

Many writers like to use their notebooks like a traditional diary,
recording small events, analyses of relationships, thoughts and feelings,
joys and gripes. This can be useful in several ways.

- It can act as a dumping ground for thoughts which might otherwise obsess you and get in the way of writing.

- It can increase your self-understanding. The examination of your own life can also help to deepen your knowledge of the rest of humanity.

- It can be a repository of possible raw material for fiction and poetry, even if you do not write autobiographically. There is rarely a direct transfer from real life to the page, in any case. As Katherine Anne Porter said, there is always a kind of 'paraphrase' operating when we use real events, places, or people in our work (in Moore, 1993, p.204).

Somerset Maugham published excerpts from notebooks which he kept from 1892 to 1949, in *A Writer's Notebook*. He explains his single-minded intention in keeping notebooks:

> I never made a note of anything that I did not think would be useful to me at one time or another in my work, and though, especially in the early notebooks, I jotted down all kinds of thoughts and emotions of a personal nature, it was only with the intention of ascribing them sooner or later to the creatures of my invention. I meant my notebooks to be a storehouse of materials for future use.
>
> (Maugham 2001 [1949], pp.xiv–xv)

He describes a kind of deliberate use of his own experience as a sort of laboratory, a dispassionate raiding of the self. In this way, a writer's private record of his or her own life has a purpose beyond itself.

ACTIVITY 2.2

Reading and writing

Read the extracts from Maugham's notebooks, in Reading 3 on p.417. Notice the random variety of what he records: observations of people; scenes from an abattoir; thoughts about social class; comments on Sinclair Lewis's novel *Main Street*; an obituary. Pay particular attention to his descriptions of people. His notebooks are full of these pen-portraits.

In '1922' he writes about the difficulty of portraying contradiction and complexity in fictional characters. He presents the problem in a dramatic way by listing a known woman's appalling faults and surprising virtues. 'There is real badness in her.'/'There is real goodness in her.'

Think of someone you know or remember who displays very contradictory traits. Write a description of the person, using Maugham's 'real badness/real goodness' dichotomy or use different co-ordinates, for example: wisdom/stupidity; meanness/generosity; cruelty/kindness;

prejudice/tolerance; refinement/vulgarity; beauty/ugliness. Write up to 150 words.

In Chapter 5 you will explore the issue of portraying complexity in characters in more depth. For this activity, simply describe the character conflict rather than show it in action.

Get into the habit of making character sketches or pen-portraits in your notebook. Sometimes you may only want to record a couple of details. Like someone's screeching, theatrical voice or habit of flicking away imaginary dandruff, anything that you might want to lend to one of your invented characters later.

Writing practice

If you read the published notebooks of famous writers, you will find that they often use them as the place where they 'limber up' for writing and where they reflect on their creative process.

For example, Virginia Woolf often reflected about her writing process in her diary. Because the diary did 'not count as writing' (1953, p.7), she was able to write it in a 'rapid haphazard gallop'. She found that this kind of unpremeditated and casual writing often yielded good 'accidents' and valuable discoveries:

> **20 January, 1919**
> Still if it were not written rather faster than the fastest type-writing, if I stopped and took thought, it would never be written at all; and the advantage of the method is that it sweeps up accidentally several stray matters which I should exclude if I hesitated, but which are the diamonds of the dustheap.
>
> (Woolf, 1953, p.7)

Later that same year, she realised that her habit of writing in this way just for herself was good practice, and had carried over into her professional writing and enriched it.

> **20 April, 1919**
> It has a slapdash and vigour and sometimes hits an unexpected bull's eye. But what is more to the point is my belief that the habit of writing thus for my own eye only is good practice. It loosens the ligaments. Never mind the misses and the stumbles. Going at such a pace as I do I must make the most direct and instant shots at my

object, and thus have to lay hands on words, choose them and shoot them with no more pause than is needed to put my pen in the ink. I believe that during the past year I can trace some increase of ease in my professional writing which I attribute to my casual half hours after tea.

(ibid., p.13)

Ultimately, on 23 February 1926, when she was working on *To the Lighthouse*, she wrote this gleeful entry:

I am now writing as fast and freely as I have written in the whole of my life; more so – 20 times more so – than any novel yet. [...] Amusingly, I now invent theories that fertility and fluency are the things: I used to plead for a kind of close, terse effort.

(ibid., p.84)

This bears out the importance of two strategies outlined in Chapter 1: the habit of daily writing ('my casual half hours after tea') and freewriting, the 'rapid haphazard gallop' that can turn up all kinds of surprises by outwitting the internal critic. From Woolf's account, it does much more than just turn over the soil. It can also help to develop fluency and richness in writing.

Morning pages

Dorothea Brande's *Becoming a Writer* is a classic inspirational guide, first published in 1934 and never out of print since. She advocates daily practice of freewriting (although she does not use this phrase), in the mornings as soon as you wake up. Her reasoning is that this is the time when we are still in touch with our dreams and our unconscious minds and can write in a half-reverie. We have not yet moved into the roles and tasks of the day.

ACTIVITY 2.3
Reading

Read Brande's chapter on 'Harnessing the Unconscious', Reading 4 on p.424, for her full instructions on how to write morning pages.

DISCUSSION

If you want to try this out, it may mean setting the alarm clock for half an hour earlier than usual and persisting for at least three weeks. You may enjoy it enough to go on for longer. Monique Roffey practised morning pages for two years, writing her first novel, *Sun Dog* (2002), during that period.

Part of the method is to be totally unconcerned with the worth of the material you produce. But paradoxically, this is a method that can lead not only to effortless writing but ultimately to better writing. For example, in her essay 'On Keeping a Diary', Nicole Ward Jouve (2001) gives this evidence:

> Some friends of mine, who were not writers, who wrote clumsily or naively in a magazine we edit together, started the practice of writing for twenty minutes every morning on waking. Anything that came into their heads, any which way, without any care for style ... I was doubtful: but I have found that their magazine writing has improved out of all recognition.
>
> (Ward Jouve, 2001, p.13)

Record of reading

It is hard to imagine a writer who is not also a keen reader. Melvyn Bragg said once that he 'gutted' novels as a preparation for his own writing. Reading is essential nourishment for writers and we get added-value from it. Not just for entertainment and inspiration but to add to our store of possible strategies by studying how writers obtain their effects. Books can be our best teachers. Even flawed or downright badly written material can help us if we diagnose the faults and think of how we might avoid them in our own work.

Read the extract from 'A Real-Life Education' by American novelist Susan Minot, Reading 5 on p.427, about her experience of reading and writing as allied activities.

ACTIVITY 2.4

Reading and writing

Think about your own early reading history and write up to 300 words about books that were important to you and why. If you were deprived of books for any reason, write about that and what it meant to you.

Minot traces the beginning of her literary ambition to an ecstatic reading experience when the 'power of the words rose up and whacked [her] on the forehead.'

Can you recall being similarly moved or amazed by something you've read? Write a few lines about the book or poem that affected you. How do you think the writer earned your response? Was it the beauty or truthfulness of the language? A dazzling style? An unexpected revelation or plot development? A deeply sympathetic character? Something else?

Spend about 5 minutes trying to pinpoint the elements that made an impact on you.

These two short pieces – about your childhood reading and one of your favourite books or poems – can be the start of your keeping a record of your reading. Make notes on the books you read. What works? What doesn't work? Why?

The more you do this, the more searching and purposeful your appraisals of your reading are likely to become. Reading *as a writer*, as an active apprentice or co-traveller, can not only inspire you but can also add to your expertise.

Daily haiku

You might like to try writing a haiku every day. A haiku is a Japanese lyric form which encapsulates a single impression of a natural object or scene in seventeen syllables arranged in three unrhymed lines of five, seven, and five syllables.

Here are two traditional haiku by the seventeenth-century poet, Bashô:

in the morning dew
spotted with mud, and how cool –
Melons on the soil.

(Bashô, 2002, p.125)

A chestnut falls:
The insects cease their crying
Among the grasses.

(Bashô, 2003, p.175)

(Notice the slight deviation here: the syllabic count is four–seven–five.)

And here's a contemporary one by Helen Kenyon:

Cat

Death on velvet paws.
Sleek assassin, razor clawed,
Purring by the fire.

(Kenyon, n.d.)

Spend half an hour now practising haiku. You might opt for traditional subjects (scenes in nature or seasonal change) or try to capture moments occurring in urban landscapes.

Focus on painting a picture in words and stick as closely as possible to the five–seven–five syllable structure. Don't exceed the seventeen syllables but you may sometimes make it slightly less. Don't sacrifice sound or sense to force a strict mathematical count. For example, if we add 'down' to 'A chestnut falls' in the second example above, we get the exact count but reduce the grace and drama of the poem.

Composing haiku can be an enjoyable discipline, something that can be practised on the bus home from work, for example. It trains your attention and your ability to capture a moment in a succinct form.

News items

Watch out for newspaper or radio items that intrigue you in some way or which yield powerful images. For example, during the week of writing this chapter, I heard a radio interviewer mention casually the 'obscenity of old age', a phrase which was received matter-of-factly by the writer being questioned. This set me fantasising about a story of a society in which old age is outlawed.

A chilling image from a newspaper article also lodged in my brain, got stored in my notebook, and will find its place in my work in some way. A reporter – investigating the allegation that human hair used in expensive hair extensions is obtained from impoverished Russian women and even from psychiatric patients or from corpses – was shown into a room in a hairdressing salon. This room was full of trays of human hair of every shade.

Spend 5–10 minutes scouring through a newspaper or magazine now, hunting for any likely material, which might include photographs as well as words. Or turn on the radio to a talk station and see if any topic or phrase grabs you. If you find anything evocative or highly charged, put it into your notebook.

Growing

Having experimented with various techniques and exercises, you may have accumulated lots of promising fragments. What should you do with them next? How do you move on to the developing and shaping stages?

Your notebook is a good place not only for initial ideas and sketches but for this elaboration stage of work. For example, let's go back to the pen-portrait you produced in Activity 2.2. You were asked to produce a description, rather than to show that character in action. Now let's release him or her into some action.

ACTIVITY 2.7

Writing

Give your character an invented address complete with house number, street, town or city and postcode and write this at the top of a fresh page. Now have him or her write a letter of about 300 words. The letter can be to anyone – a devoted parent, absconding lover, complaining neighbour, a child given away at birth, a member of parliament – you choose. It may be on any topic but it must be based on strong emotion, positive or negative: joy, relief, love, rage, scorn, vengefulness, and so on. Spend 15–20 minutes composing the letter.

DISCUSSION

You have now moved on from a basic character description to a sample of that character's written self-expression, the way he or she composes their voice to make a desired impact. Your letter will also have the germ of a story in it arising from the history (if any) and possible dynamic between the writer and the receiver of the letter.

If you would like to grow this character further, you could try creating other things that he or she writes: a shopping list, a diary entry, a sentimental verse. Or you could start imagining his or her history. What kind of upbringing has contributed to this character's dramatic contradictions? You might start fleshing out the other character, the recipient of the letter. Or dream up possible events or encounters which would challenge your main character.

Your notebook is a good place for this kind of playing and experimentation. Here you can 'interrogate' your writing, try out possible plotlines or verse forms, for example, without feeling that you are committing yourself too soon. The novelist Mary Gordon said: 'A writer uses the journal to try out the new step in front of the mirror' (in Shaughnessy, 1993, p.17).

Conclusion

Remember that you can use your notebook for all kinds of writing practice, whatever best suits you: freewrites, exercises and experiments, or diary keeping as a repository of raw material. (There will be a further exploration of diary keeping in Chapters 23 and 24 of Part 4, 'Life Writing'.) Use your notebook also to jot down those fleeting ideas and apt phrases that occur out of the blue and which might otherwise escape. You can also elaborate on initial ideas, using your notebook to plan ahead or explore possible ways forward.

The notebook will remain a key strategy throughout this book, and suggestions will be made for things to try out or include in it.

References

Bashô (2003) in *Haiku*, Peter Washington (ed.), London: Everyman Pocket Library.

Bashô (2002) in *Haiku, Poetry Ancient and Modern*, Jackie Hardy (ed.), London: MQ Publications.

Holroyd, Michael (2004) *Mosaic*, London: Little, Brown.

Kenyon, Helen (n.d.) 'Cat' [online]. Available from: http://www.baradel.demon.co.uk/haiku/index.htm (accessed 22 November 2004).

Maugham, W. Somerset (2001 [1949]) *A Writer's Notebook*, London: Vintage Classic.

Moore, Lorrie (1993) 'Better and Sicker' in Clare Boylan (ed.) *The Agony and the Ego: The art and strategy of fiction writing explored*, London: Penguin.

Roffey, Monique (2002) *Sun Dog*, London: Scribner.

Shaughnessy, Susan (1993) *Meditations for Writers*, London: Aquarian Press/Thorsons.

Ward Jouve, Nicole (2001) 'On Keeping a Diary' in *The Creative Writing Coursebook*, edited by Paul Magrs and Julia Bell, London: Macmillan.

Woolf, Virginia (1953) *A Writer's Diary*, London: Harcourt.

3 *Writing what you know*

DEREK NEALE

Creative writing courses and manuals often offer the advice 'write what you know'. This is undoubtedly good advice, yet what exactly does it mean? Many writers testify to using their life experiences – their memories and their everyday perceptions – as a source for their fiction or poetry, as well as for their autobiographies and memoirs. Yet these experiences aren't necessarily extraordinary in themselves. You don't have to have led an unusual or exotic life in order to write. You do, however, need to raise your level of perception above the ordinary. Writing what you know means being aware of your own world, both past and present, in as full a way as possible.

This chapter will introduce and briefly elaborate on some of the ways in which you might 'know' the world around you. By looking at the commonplace details of your life in a different way, using your sensory perceptions and learning to use your own memories, you will be exercising certain writing muscles, ones that need regular flexing. In this way you may discover you know more than you thought.

ACTIVITY 3.1
Writing

Write down a quick sentence in response to the advice 'write what you know'. What does it immediately suggest to you?

DISCUSSION

You may react positively to such advice; you may be able to go off happily and make use of every last ounce of your life experience, without doubt or consternation. Or you may think: 'I don't know anything'; 'all that I know is boring'; 'nobody would want to know what I know' or 'I know too much, how could I possibly get that down in words?'

Whatever your response, the aim of this chapter is to broaden the meaning of such advice, so it will act as a prompt the next time you hear it, reminding you that you have numerous ways of exploiting the raw materials of your own life.

The everyday

Writing is a perceptual art, one in which images are created via language in order for the reader to make meaning. It is therefore imperative that the writer's powers of perception are alert. Writing is a process of becoming aware, of opening the senses to ways of grasping the world, ways that may previously have been blocked. Often we take the world around us for granted, we are so immersed in habit. All of our lives contain relative degrees of routine. We go to sleep, we eat, we go to work. The things we may choose to write about will also contain repeated and habitual elements. How many times have you come across the word 'usually' in stories and novels, or phrases such as 'every day' and 'every year'? How many times do you read about meals, or other daily routines like dressing, looking in the mirror, going out, coming in? These are only a few of the many designators of habitual patterns of behaviour, giving the impression of life passing in a routine fashion. Taken out of context such details might be uninteresting, but in fact they are invariably the parts of the writing that build a world for the reader. This world is believable because it appears to have existed before the reader started reading about it and will continue on afterwards.

ACTIVITY 3.2
Writing

Close your eyes for a few moments and think of the room or place around you. Think of the details that you would include in any description and make a mental note of them. Open your eyes and, without looking around, write down what you thought of.

Now look at your surroundings and write a paragraph (no more than 150 words) describing them, picking out at least three things that you haven't noticed recently – things you didn't think of when you closed your eyes.

DISCUSSION

The details you noticed may have come in various guises. You may have seen some dirt on the floor, something that isn't usually there. You may have noticed an ornament that you haven't looked at for a while, an object that's always present but not always seen. You may have picked up on the colour of a wall, the handle on a door. Some of these things will have changed since the last time you noticed them – maybe the wall colour has faded. Some things will not be quite as you thought they were – maybe you didn't remember the door handle being made of metal. It is useful to do this sort of perceptual exercise at regular intervals. In this way you will revive the way you see the world – by de-familiarising your perceptions you will reinvigorate your writing.

Here are some similar follow-up exercises that you can try when you get time.

Try the same exercise on a different, but still familiar, place. You can also try it with familiar characters in your life – describe them in their absence and then take note of the things you didn't recall.

Think of the details of a short journey – say to the shops, to work or even to another part of your home – a journey that you make regularly. Jot these details down. Now make the journey, making a point of looking for things that you haven't noticed recently. Write a paragraph about the journey using the new details.

Write a paragraph describing a simple action that you do every day – for example, washing, cooking, shaving, putting on make-up, feeding the cat. When you next perform the action, notice everything about it and afterwards note down details that weren't in your original paragraph.

Collecting and selecting

As you have seen in Chapter 2, you should use your notebook to gather observations about your environment. It is important to go about your daily business with your eyes open and all your other senses similarly alert. Accumulate details about the world around you. For instance, using an imaginary scenario, you might notice how the man along the road twitches his curtains, how he wears colour co-ordinated clothes, usually but not always green. Note the melancholic tone of his voice and how he goes to the post office every Monday at 9.30 am, accompanied by his neighbour who often wears a purple sari. You might note how they walk faster as they pass the graffiti on the factory wall and often smile at the 'Elvis lives' slogan that someone has daubed on the adjoining fence. You might note how, at the post office, they both chat to a man with a white Scottie, a dog who snarls at most passers-by when he is tied to the railings outside the shop, but not at the man and his neighbour.

By noting such details you are collecting materials that you might use later in your writing. In the imaginary scenario above, we have almost formed a narrative. At times you might do this, at other times you might be more arbitrary and fragmented in what you gather, writing down a range of dissimilar observations: the weather, a character description, an overheard turn of phrase. You don't need to make complete sentences or connect it all into a sequence; you could make a list of bullet points. In whatever form, collecting serves to revive a certain detailed way of seeing the world: how you might have grasped the world as a child.

Perception is always a selective faculty. You will not be able to see all and everything anew each and every day. However, you can use tactics to keep yourself alert: cross over the road and walk on a different side, or sit in a chair that you don't usually use. It is important to develop an investigative attitude to your own environment, to look at things from a slightly different angle, and to search for the previously unnoticed. Eventually, when coming to write your story or poem, you will realise that, like perception, writing is also selective. You will pick the details to be included and excluded: which detail acts as a useful repetition, and which detail might be redundant. You can't pick and choose if you haven't gathered enough information in the first place.

In our scenario above, for instance: the man at the post office with the dog might have fluffy white whiskers just like his white Scottie – this is a relatively significant and amusing detail. The same man might wear a plain-coloured tie, which is less interesting information. Each piece of writing that you work on will demand its own level and type of detail. Details attain significance, for you and consequently for your reader, not just through being dramatic or unusual. Often they will attain significance because they are being noticed for the first time, because a usual or habitual perception has shifted. For instance, returning to the scenario above, every day you might walk past the graffiti on the factory wall, considering it to be an inane and messy scrawl, if you notice it at all. Then one day you see a sunrise painted behind the letters, or you might see 'Elvis lives' and realise for the first time that these words are formed from the same letters (anagrams), or that the yellow lettering matches the colour of the bedding flowers just planted by the council, or you might have a flashback of the bare concrete behind the graffiti and what the wall used to be like. It is these shifts in the way you see your familiar world that revive it. In this way writing is a process of scrutinising, looking closely at things, and then taking the observations onto a new level of perception, one in which you understand your world just a little more.

Some of the observational detail collected in your notebook might seem mundane and indiscriminate, its interest and significance not fully known even to you. Some of it might be more focused on something you are working on – an observation of a certain place or type of place. For instance, you may have set a story at a swimming pool and need to remind yourself of the smell of chlorine and the strange acoustics. Whether apparently insignificant or more focused, there is no prescription for the sort of observations you should make; they will always be personal to the individual writer, as you have seen from looking at the extract from Somerset Maugham (Reading 3) and the quotations from Virginia Woolf in Chapter 2.

Using your observations

The observations you make in your notebook might not always appear imaginative or pertinent to anything, but the mundane recording of events may have unlikely uses. Writing in my notebook on 15 December 1998, I observed the sky – at the coast on a murky winter's day, when the low cloud seemed to be lit by a churning, subterranean force:

> the earth comes to the surface, the soil muddies the sky, clouds the air – it even turns the sea into a sandy mix … the sea, the puddles, the rivers, the sky – all glow brown, glisten, shimmer – but not with the light of any sun.

On another occasion in the same notebook I observed a familiar river, and how the current flowed in 'one concerted way in the straights but was torn between two directions at the bends'. By struggling to express what I saw on those two separate days, the observations stayed with me, largely because I had taken time to write about them. I later combined parts of these two descriptions in a scene of a novel, *The Book of Guardians* (Neale, 2000), using the river setting to reflect the inner state of my main character, Philip Eyre:

> The swell of the river had caused the current to be perplexed, flowing concertedly in one midstream direction but torn between at least two, whirling between calm and rush, in the shallows and elbows. The rowing boat bobbed and turned uneasily like a gelding on its rope. The cigarette smoke smelt different – was it because we were outdoors? Fragrant, alluring, like woodsmoke in the night.
>
> It was one of those days: the earth rising to the surface, muddying the water, overflowing into the sky and air. The world in spate. The sandy mix, not brown or grey, black or orange. Illuminated, but not by the sun: the world glimmering with the density of its own substrata.

> (Neale, 2000)

What you put down in your notebook can act as a mnemonic, a memory aid, reminding you of the original observation, reviving certain thoughts and emotions. In this way your notebook – as well as being a writing 'gym' where you exercise perceptual and linguistic muscles – can also act as a future resource.

The senses

Becoming more aware of the everyday world around you involves more than just looking. If writing is a perceptual art then perception should involve all of the senses, not just the visual. You must also start to smell, feel, taste and hear the world you are trying to realise. So, in the made up scenario, when you see the man with the Scottie dog you might be too fearful to stroke his dog, but perhaps you could touch the cold metal bar where the dog was tied up – after he is gone, of course! You might feel the rough bark of the tree close at hand, smell the brash perfume of the washing detergent steaming out of the nearby launderette, taste the bitter dryness this causes in your mouth, and hear the wind whistle past the buildings. You might see the graffiti on the wall and appreciate that part of the street is always quiet, not even any traffic, and that there is a different smell: ammonia, it smells like fish.

By awakening your senses and becoming more conscious of the world around you, you will be enriching your grasp of that world. Once this heightened way of perceiving your environment has trickled down into your writing, your reader will benefit, getting a much fuller picture of the worlds you are creating.

ACTIVITY 3.3

Writing

In an indoor location write down three things for each of the following:
- sounds that you can hear;
- textures that you can feel;
- odours that you can smell;
- flavours that you can taste;
- objects that you can see.

These sensory perceptions will be used again in the next chapter, so make sure you know where to find them in your notebook.

DISCUSSION

Having the sensory perception is one thing; writing about it is quite a different matter. As you have seen in Chapter 2, with Virginia Woolf's 'thorns', we often need to use metaphor and simile to describe our perceptions. Even the most established writer struggles and strives to find phrases that can translate perception in an original and meaningful fashion. How do you write about feeling 'soaked to the skin' without using such a hackneyed phrase? How do you write about a rough surface or a bitter taste? The obvious solution is to find a comparison that fits the sensation. The rough surface becomes 'like gravel' or 'like sandpaper', the bitter taste becomes 'like lemon'. Some similes might seem a little too easy or too familiar and it is important to search for the metaphor or simile that fits your particular context.

For instance, in a story called 'The Barber's Victim' (Neale, 1995, p.68), I described a young lad, drenched by the rain, entering a new, grown-up world – a barber's shop – for the first time. After deciding against 'soaked to the skin' and several similes that seemed to me either too familiar or too odd ('drowned rat', 'dripping leaf') I wrote that he 'flapped through the red, white and blue fly strips like a grounded fish'. In this way the verb was working as hard as the simile. The use of 'flapped' revealed how awkward the character was in this setting, and the simile of the grounded fish reflected how he was being thrown into an unfamiliar and threatening world, and wasn't now in charge of his own actions.

Your writing will always benefit from exercising your sensory awareness. You can do more of these sorts of exercises, and in a variety of contexts. If you get time you might like to repeat this activity, finding three of each of the senses in an outdoor location.

Looking back over and revising your writing should become a habit. Look over your responses to Activity 3.2 and check for the sensory perceptions that you have used, add some relevant ones if you need to and redraft accordingly.

Contexts

On their own, sensory perceptions don't tend to mean that much. They depend on a context in which they can be brought to life: for instance, that of a character. Such sensory perceptions as you've just listed in Activity 3.3 might hold more meaning if the man who twitches the curtains was the character smelling the smells or touching the surfaces; if his neighbour in the purple sari was the character hearing the noises, tasting the flavours. Sensory perceptions offer dimensions that will enrich your writing, but generally they cannot operate in isolation.

Read Seamus Heaney's 'Death of a Naturalist' (below) and the opening of Laurie Lee's *Cider with Rosie*, Reading 6 on p.429. Think about the following questions:

ACTIVITY 3.4

Reading

- Which sensory perceptions are used, and how are they used?
- Do the perceptions belong to a character?
- Is a place realised through the sensory perceptions?
- How is time being organised?
- Are the perceptions from one moment or many?

Death of a Naturalist

All year the flax-dam festered in the heart
Of the townland; green and heavy headed
Flax had rotted there, weighted down by huge sods.
Daily it sweltered in the punishing sun.
Bubbles gargled delicately, bluebottles
Wove a strong gauze of sound around the smell.
There were dragon-flies, spotted butterflies,
But best of all was the warm thick slobber
Of frogspawn that grew like clotted water
In the shade of the banks. Here, every spring
I would fill jampotfuls of the jellied
Specks to range on window-sills at home,
On shelves at school, and wait and watch until
The fattening dots burst into nimble-
Swimming tadpoles. Miss Walls would tell us how
The daddy frog was called a bullfrog
And how he croaked and how the mammy frog
Laid hundreds of little eggs and this was
Frogspawn. You could tell the weather by frogs too
For they were yellow in the sun and brown
In rain.

Then one hot day when fields were rank
With cowdung in the grass the angry frogs
Invaded the flax-dam; I ducked through hedges
To a coarse croaking that I had not heard
Before. The air was thick with a bass chorus.

Right down the dam gross-bellied frogs were cocked
On sods; their loose necks pulsed like sails. Some hopped:
The slap and plop were obscene threats. Some sat
Poised like mud grenades, their blunt heads farting.
I sickened, turned, and ran. The great slime kings
Were gathered there for vengeance and I knew
That if I dipped my hand the spawn would clutch it.

(Seamus Heaney, 1980, pp.12–13)

DISCUSSION   In 'Death of a Naturalist', notice how the profusion of sensory detail is given the context of a personal memory. This locates it in an activity and place, which gives it significance. In terms of time, notice how the habitual, everyday action is realised in phrases like 'All year'; 'every spring'; 'Miss Walls would tell us how' – and how this is contrasted to the specific time of 'Then one hot day'. In this poem the sensory perception gets so rich and intoxicating that there seems to be some confusion in lines like 'bluebottles/wove a strong gauze of sound around the smell.' The senses (touch, smell, sight and sound) appear to merge. Heaney uses a rhetorical form called 'synaesthesia' – describing one sensory perception according to the terms of another.

Notice in *Cider with Rosie* too that all the senses are activated, and how happily the childlike perception – viewing the world as if for the first time – coincides with Lee's intention: realising this particular world afresh. Amid the flurry of sensory detail there is also a tight organisation of time. Even though Lee's recall of events must be fragmentary and confused, for the purposes of his narrative he has started arranging details in coherent and logical sequence. He is three years old, it is June, he gets deposited from a cart in the grass, feels lost, alone, overwhelmed, and consequently cries, before being rescued by his sisters. In your reading, look out for such temporal organisation, and be similarly aware of it in your own writing.

Memory and narrative

The philosopher John Locke made the assertion that individual identity is inextricably linked to memory – we are only what we remember being. Memory is a central part of how we think of ourselves, and indeed a central strand of what we might know. Memory is not simply a mechanical process. It works in various ways and you will use it in various ways in your writing. In Chapter 4 you will look at how to make the most of associations that arise from your memories. In Part 4, 'Life Writing', you will look in more detail at how memory works as a narrative, and how we tell ourselves stories about our own pasts. It will be useful to start thinking about memory and narrative now, as your memories will be of use in your poetry and fiction, as well as in your life writing.

Part of what a story does is organise events in time, as Lee has done. Memory often works like this – even when you aren't intending to write your memories down but are simply thinking. So when you try to remember what you did yesterday you start perhaps by recalling some fragments – a conversation, having breakfast, going to the park. The more you think about the fragments, the more you are likely to arrange them in some sort of temporal order – like a story. I had breakfast first, then I went to the park and when I returned, that's when my mother rang. Thinking of memory as a form of narrative or story is a great asset when you come to your own writing. But it's important to consider your memories to be narratives that you can use freely. Don't feel that you have to render them exactly in an 'as it really was' fashion.

ACTIVITY 3.5

Reading

Read Lesley Glaister's 'Memory: The true key to real imagining', Reading 7 on p.431. Look for the following things:

■ How is the memory realised and written about?

■ How is time organised in the memory?

■ In Glaister's version of this memory, what really brings it alive?

■ What use does Glaister make of her memory in her writing?

DISCUSSION

Notice how the memory is dramatised in the present tense, also how there is a shape to the telling of the memory, as if it were a fictional story with a starting point (father is invincible), a climax (father presumed dead) and a revelation (father is alive but flawed). Also note how the mix of precise detail and uncertainty ('I don't know where – Southwold perhaps') gives an authentic feel to the narration. Remember this in your own writing.

Also note that, according to this testimony, the content of the memory is only fleetingly used in Glaister's fiction. It is one small element, but something which is packed with resonance for her.

Raiding your past

The more you write, the more you will raid your own past. These incursions won't diminish or reduce your memories – rather those recollections can be enriched and become more fully realised. As Jamaica Kincaid says of her writing:

> One of the things I found when I began to write was that writing exactly what happened had a limited amount of power for me. To say exactly what happened was less than what I knew happened.

> (in Perry, 1993, p.129)

Writing using your memories can amount to more than just reciting the facts. You will look at a Jamaica Kincaid story in Part 2, 'Writing fiction', and can then consider what her particular mix of fiction and autobiography might look like. For now, it's important to realise that you will not betray the truth of any particular memory by failing to stick steadfastly to certain details, or by changing elements, or by not having a total recall of events.

There may be times when you will wish to use episodes or elements from your life experience more or less directly. Often you will use just fragments of your own past. You might like to use a single aspect of a character, or a place, for instance. You might like to use a turn of phrase that your grandmother used; you might focus on the feelings of being lost on the first day at a new school. There is no rule for how much or how little you can use.

ACTIVITY 3.6
Writing

Using the present tense, like Glaister does, write about a personal memory of either a place or a character in your notebook.

Make it brief, 250 words or so, but try to get as many sensory perceptions as possible going, and try to fix the memory in time, as Glaister does, so it is just one moment. Include everyday details and don't be afraid to admit one or two uncertainties.

DISCUSSION

This activity doesn't ask you to change anything from the way you remembered it, but you might have found yourself inventing things – some sensory perceptions, for instance. It is impossible to notice every little detail about an event or moment, let alone be able to recall such detail from the past. It is inevitable that you will invent even in this limited exercise. That invention should be welcomed, not resisted; it will always be guided by what you do know about the event.

Conclusion: You know many things

'Writing what you know' is a large and rich project, one that provides an endless resource, and one that can be undertaken in all the types of writing discussed in this book – poetry, fiction and life writing. The skill lies in reawakening your senses to the world around you, and then using what you find with discrimination. By realising the potentials of your own life experience, you will be collecting the materials necessary in order to write. 'Writing what you know' can amount to a lot more than you may have first bargained for. It doesn't mean that you are limited solely to your own life story, as the next chapter will illuminate further. Neither does it mean you have to be entirely true to your memories. Often a different kind of truth will emerge from the activity of writing about elements of your past and your everyday life. In this way, writing about what you know is a route to a different understanding of your own experience, and therefore also a route to finding out what you don't know.

References

Heaney, Seamus (1980) 'Death of a Naturalist' in *Selected Poems 1965–1975*, London: Faber and Faber.

Neale, Derek (2000) *The Book of Guardians*, PhD thesis, University of East Anglia.

Neale, Derek (1995) 'The Barber's Victim' in *Raconteur*, Graham Lord (ed.), No.6, London: Raconteur Publications.

Perry, Donna (ed.) (1993) *Backtalk: Women writers speak out*, New Brunswick, New Jersey: Rutgers University Press.

4 *Writing what you come to know*

DEREK NEALE

By using sensory perceptions and your own memories you are capitalising on your 'direct' experience of life. In this chapter you will do some more work with memory and using your imagination. You will look at the uses of research – or what might be called 'indirect' experience. We will step away from the literal gist of 'writing what you know', and look at the limitations of sticking too closely to such advice. If you only write about what is already known, then your writing might become tired and predictable. We will look at ways of reviving and reinvigorating it.

Memory and association

In Chapter 3, memory was viewed as a type of narrative. Of course, memory can be more than this – or less, depending on which way you look at it. Memory often works in a spontaneous manner, by way of association. You may catch a certain smell and all of a sudden you're cast back ten, fifteen or twenty years. You may feel a certain texture against your skin, hear a certain sound, and immediately think of another era. Pop songs offer an easy example of this. You may hear a certain song and be thrown back to your childhood, or to a time when, unlike now, the sun was shining and there wasn't a cloud in the sky, or to a time when you lived somewhere very different.

In Marcel Proust's *A la recherche du temps perdu* (*In Search of Lost Time*) there is a famous moment where a chance combination of sensory perceptions rekindles a memory:

> One day in winter, on my return home, my mother, seeing that I was cold, offered me some tea, a thing I did not ordinarily take. I declined at first, and then, for no particular reason, changed my mind. She sent for one of those squat, plump little cakes called 'petites madeleines' ... No sooner had the warm liquid mixed with the crumbs touched my palate than a shiver ran through me and I stopped, intent upon the extraordinary thing that was happening to me.

> (Proust, 2002, p.51)

The 'extraordinary thing' provoked by the taste of the cakes and tea is the memory of Combray, a central place in the novel and the setting for a crucial part of the narrator's past. The passage highlights the ordinary nature of the events leading up to the flashback, and how the recall was totally dependent on chance. In this type of recall the past returns through mundane coincidences, often a chance perception – a smell, a song, a taste.

These chance associations occur frequently in real life and in literature. Look back over 'Death of a Naturalist' (p.51) and the opening from *Cider with Rosie* (Reading 6 on p.429). See how the writing operates around a group of memories and associations that in the end form a constellation of recollection, not just one single moment. Memory often works like this: one perception leads to a memory, which in turn leads to another memory and so on. These associative and resonant memories seem at first glance to be mostly unconscious, serendipitous and hard to predict. There are, however, ways of prompting such thought processes.

You have already done some work on this with your clusters and freewriting. Now you will focus in more detail on associations and memories that are prompted by the senses.

Use the sensory perceptions that you gathered in Activity 3.3. For each perception write down an association from your own experience – a sentence for each at most.

ACTIVITY 4.1
Writing

Some of your perceptions might make you think of your childhood; they might remind you of something from yesterday or last week. Try to be specific. So, for instance, you might have listed the sound of a lorry driving past and it might make you think of the delivery driver who backed into the wall at the end of your street and how embarrassed he was. You might have listed the feel of the breeze through the window on your face and it might remind you of a different climate, a place you once lived perhaps, or a specific moment on holiday when the weather was especially good or bad.

Daydreaming

You may have found that by seeking one association other associations followed; your mind might have started wandering. For instance, you might have started with the sound of a plane flying overhead and thought of a particular destination you once visited, pictured the airport perhaps, then thought of a place you would like to go, and then a place your neighbour went to recently, and then thought about the colour of their front door and how it clashes with their curtains, and so forth.

Some might consider this rambling way in which memory and thought processes work to be a form of 'drifting off'. Sigmund Freud suggested this is what the act of writing was all about. In his essay 'Creative Writers and Day-dreaming' Freud describes one possible model of how creative writing is related to childhood play, memory and fantasising:

> A strong experience in the present awakens in the creative writer a memory of an earlier experience (usually belonging to his childhood) from which there now proceeds a wish which finds its fulfilment in the creative work. The work itself exhibits elements of the recent provoking occasion as well as of the old memory.
>
> (Freud, 1964 [1959], p.139)

Notice how both the elements of past and present are used by the writer according to Freud. In his opinion, the memory is usually connected to childhood, but this isn't always so. You aren't confined to a single part of your past; all of it can be used in your writing. Freud also notes how daydreams (and night dreams for that matter) can be boring and sometimes tiresome for those being forced to listen to them. The creative writer gets round this obstacle, according to Freud, by 'finding a suitable aesthetic form' – a story or poem – in which to express the daydream. In the preamble to finding that form, your notebook is the place to collect your perceptions and associations, where you have free rein to fantasise and wander (and wonder) aimlessly – or as Freud would have it, to daydream and to play.

The limitations of 'writing what you know'

'Write what you know' is good advice on the whole and, as we have seen, it can mean a variety of things. However, if taken too literally and interpreted in too limited a fashion, such advice can be restrictive:

- If you know something too well, there might be no sense of discovery or revelation in the writing. It might lack energy.
- If you can only write what you know, you might feel too inhibited, for instance, to write in the voice of a man instead of a woman and

vice versa, or unable to write of a place you've never visited, or of a profession in which you have never worked.

The two problems are connected in the way that you might solve them. For instance, you might want to write a story that pertains to characters or episodes from your own life, but you might feel too close to the material. The way to create a distance is to make shifts in the material – relocate the material in time, for instance, change a name or profession, change the sex of the biographical character, or relocate the material in terms of place. For example, Mr Patel, headmaster of South Street Primary School, might become Mr Pugh, manager of the local supermarket; Winston Valentine – the man who lived next door – might become Frank Churchill, the man your main character sits next to on a plane. Shifting the life experience revives your perception of it, lending the writing a sense of newness and discovery. It's important to remember that you have licence to make shifts like this; you are free to write about things you haven't experienced directly.

By way of example, when writing a short story called 'Violin Lessons' (Neale, 1993), I wanted to write about a man who worked with wood and who begins to make violins. My experience of working with wood had been at most fleeting and largely indirect, but I remembered vividly the woodwork classes from my school days. I recalled the smells, atmosphere, and a particular teacher who, because of the sharp instruments and power tools, enforced what I perceived at the time to be draconian rules in the classroom.

Rather than write directly about my own experience, I created the character of a boy waiting for his sister during her violin lessons, visiting a man's workshop while he waited. The man's rules in his workshop were very similar to the rules from my woodwork class – no ties to be worn, no sitting on seasoning wood. The man, at least in part, was based on my teacher; the lad, railing mischievously against the rules, was the schoolboy I wouldn't have minded being, if only for a little while.

Here a story has been created from a relatively ordinary memory – about school rules. The key is to reinvigorate your memories, to shift certain elements from their original context, so those elements are seen afresh by you, and consequently by your reader. This will be explored more later in this chapter and also in Chapter 6.

Cultural memory

Our memories are an infinite resource, but are not just made up of personal moments and individual detail. We all exist within particular cultures and there are historical episodes that run parallel to our own lives. When John Major was prime minister, a student of mine wrote a short story with the following opening sentence:

> I guess, just as with the Major assassination in the late 20th century, everybody can remember exactly where he was and what he was doing on the day the space people brought Jesus back to Earth.

> (Greenaway, 1994)

This dazzling start both embraces and imaginatively subverts shared cultural knowledge. John Major is referred to, but he is assassinated; Jesus is referred to, but he has been abducted by aliens. It also points to what has almost become a cliché – we knew where we were and what we were doing at certain historical moments: when JFK was killed; when Martin Luther King was assassinated; when Princess Diana died; when Bob Marley or John Lennon died; or on 9/11 when the twin towers were destroyed. Personal memories can often be associated with cultural memories and this shared knowledge can inform your writing. As well as historical events and characters, you can also use songs and films, and even TV programmes.

ACTIVITY 4.2

Reading

Read 'The Captain of the 1964 *Top of the Form* Team' below, by Carol Ann Duffy. Write down your responses to the poem, answering the following questions:

- What elements in the poem deal with a personal memory?
- What elements of the poem deal with cultural memory?
- How does the poem regard memories? Is it nostalgic?

For those who never saw it, *Top of the Form* was a television quiz programme along the lines of *University Challenge*, but for school-age contestants. Each team took along a mascot which sat in front of them during the programme.

The Captain of the 1964 *Top of the Form* Team

Do Wah Diddy Diddy, Baby Love, Oh Pretty Woman
were in the Top Ten that month, October, and the Beatles
were everywhere else. I can give you the B-side

of the Supremes one. Hang on. *Come See About Me?*
I lived in a kind of fizzing hope. Gargling
with Vimto. The clever smell of my satchel. Convent girls.
I pulled my hair forward with a steel comb that I blew
like Mick, my lips numb as a two-hour snog.

No snags. The Nile rises in April. Blue and White.
The humming-bird's song is made by its wings, which beat
so fast that they blur in flight. I knew the capitals,
the Kings and Queens, the dates. In class, the white sleeve
of my shirt saluted again and again. *Sir!... Correct.*
Later, I whooped at the side of my bike, a cowboy,
mounted it running in one jump. I sped down Dyke Hill,
no hands, famous, learning, *dominus domine dominum.*

Dave Dee Dozy... Try me. Come on. My mother kept my
    mascot Gonk
on the TV set for a year. And the photograph. I look
so brainy you'd think I'd just had a bath. The blazer.
The badge. The tie. The first chord of *A Hard Day's Night*
loud in my head. I ran to the Spinney in my prize shoes,
up Churchill Way, up Nelson Drive, over pink pavements
that girls chalked on, in the blue evening; and I stamped
the pawprints of badgers and skunks in the mud. My country.

I want it back. The captain. The one with all the answers. *Bzz.*
My name was in red on Lucille Green's jotter. I smiled
as wide as a child who went missing on the way home
from school. The keeny. I say to my stale wife
Six hits by Dusty Springfield. I say to my boss *A pint!*
How can we know the dancer from the dance? Nobody.
My thick kids wince. *Name the Prime Minister of Rhodesia.*
My country. *How many florins in a pound?*

DISCUSSION

Duffy's poem is full of cultural and historical detail pertinent to a
particular childhood. Yet notice how there is still reference to sensory
perceptions ('clever smell'; 'lips numb'). In many ways a poem reflects
the world around it – whether that world be full of golden daffodils (as
Wordsworth's evidently was on occasions) or television programmes and
pop songs (as in the case of Duffy's narrator).

Memory and nostalgia

The personal detail of Duffy's poem seems to revolve around one fictional character, although it can be safely presumed there are more than a few of Duffy's own memories contained in the poem. It is set in one specific year, which broadens into an era, one to which the narrator is rather conservatively attached. After celebrating that era in the first part of the poem, the voice takes on a rather bitter tone in the last stanza, still clinging to the old cultural perceptions ('I want it back'), challenging his own children with questions about old currencies, and still calling Zimbabwe 'Rhodesia'.

When you use your own cultural memories in your writing, it's important not to use them just for purely nostalgic or conservative reasons. Duffy has used such details here almost as a caution against nostalgia – while at the same time realising the warmth and energy of such memories. It's important to retain a focus and have a purpose when you use your past; beware of indulging your own nostalgia.

ACTIVITY 4.3

Writing

Using the Duffy poem as your model:

- write down in your notebook some cultural details (songs, singers, films, historical events) from a period of your own past;
- list some personal details from the same period (like the names of roads and friends such as Duffy includes);
- pick a specific year and an event – it could be a cultural event like a pop concert, sporting event or TV programme (as Duffy uses); it could be a more personal event like a school play, a homecoming, a wedding or a party.

Write either a poem (using no more than sixteen lines) or a piece of prose (up to 250 words) – which uses some of the cultural and personal details you've just gathered, and which focuses on the event you've chosen. This can be fiction, autobiography or a mix of both; the event can be a success or failure. For instance, you might write about the scoring of the winning goal in a cup final, or the school play in which you are humiliated by singing out of tune. Don't forget to use any pertinent sensory perceptions as well as cultural associations.

It is important that you make your memories dynamic and bring them alive rather than stick with staid perceptions. By changing key elements in your memory, you can sometimes learn more about what it is you are writing and what you want to write about. What would happen if I just shifted these people here, made them live in a different town, moved them to a different continent? What would happen if I set this story in the eighteenth century rather than the present day? What would the episode that I recall look like through the eyes of someone else, someone who was also there perhaps?

DISCUSSION

Asking these sorts of questions about what you remember, then shifting the recall, can lend a new energy or perspective to your subject matter, reviving an over-rehearsed memory, so you discover it anew as you reveal it. This is a vital strategy in all forms of writing, as you will now see.

Imagination

Writers have always found ways to overcome the difficulties presented by subjects beyond their direct experience. Pat Barker, for instance, wrote *The Regeneration Trilogy* of novels about the First World War and the plight of several male characters suffering from the effects of the war; the story largely covers their treatment by a male psychologist, Dr Rivers. The novels were written from the points of view of the various male characters. Yet Pat Barker is a woman and certainly didn't fight in the First World War. She has never worked as a psychologist. Barker evidently didn't experience any of her fictional events directly. Yet she did have a grandfather who survived being bayoneted during the war; she has talked publicly about how she remembers seeing his scar when she was a child and hearing her grandfather's explanation of how he had survived.

Some might draw the biographical link between her grandfather and the working-class character of Billy Prior, from whose perspective the second book in the trilogy is largely told. This link may not have been the only personal connection between the author and her material, yet in the novels she went well beyond that which she possibly could have known directly. Part of this came through research, which will be touched on a little later. Part of it came from using a tactic that is crucial to the creation of any textual world, whether that world is poetic, fictional or biographical – the use of the imagination.

'Use your imagination' is an imperative phrase that has come to be used in everyday conversation as a sort of mundane exhortation. It usually means something along the lines of 'think a bit harder'. In the context of the creative process, 'imagination' holds other connotations, many of them grander than this first assertion. It can suggest powers of invention, impersonation and also a semi-mystical process involving chance and inspiration whereby you wait for the bright idea to come along.

Although these connotations might be relevant sometimes, it's important to retain that first mundane definition, whether you're jotting something down in your notebook or preparing a final draft. Imagination *is* thinking harder. But remember, 'thinking harder' doesn't necessarily mean thinking in more difficult ways, it just means asking more questions. Imagination is a way of exploring possibilities, and going beyond what you immediately know. It is not necessarily mysterious, though it can undoubtedly be magical in terms of what it might produce. It isn't an exclusive skill possessed by a talented few. We all possess imaginative powers, but not all of us use them as fully as we might.

Pat Barker emphasises the use of imagination in converting material from her experience, but noticeably she doesn't call it 'imagination' or even 'being creative'. She talks of asking questions, the same sort of questions we have already considered as possible strategies for reviving tired and worn out knowledge:

> Quite often you are going off on a tangent – taking a fact in your own life and saying, 'What if? ...' and from that point you are going away from your own life at right angles, although the bedrock of the book was your own experience. For example, in *The Man Who Wasn't There* it's simply the sex of the child. What if you had been born into an all-female family as a boy rather than as a girl? ... If a boy were raised by these women, to what extent could he take strength from them and to what extent would it be a threat?

(Reading 8, pp.434–41)

ACTIVITY 4.4
Writing

Write down five facts about a person you know well. These facts can be just the straightforward details of their lives – their age, where they live, hair colour.

Now ask some 'What if ...?' questions about these facts and write them down. So, for each fact come up with at least one alternative. You might have chosen a friend who lives next door but your new version will live in New York; your friend might be tall and now is short; might be a woman and now she is a man!

You might have found that asking one question is enough to launch a whole new character and a stream of further questions that need answering about how this new character might live. Each and every life is surrounded by unfulfilled possibilities. By seeking out some of these possibilities you have started to use your imagination. This is not just something to be done with people. You can also do it with places – what if the village wasn't actually in Yorkshire but in Devon? What if the café was in the main street and not in a back alley? What if it was a Balti curry house instead of greasy spoon? You can do it with sets of relationships, as Barker does in *The Man Who Wasn't There*. You can do it with fictional characters, as Jean Rhys does in *Wide Sargasso Sea*, where the character of Bertha from *Jane Eyre* becomes the main protagonist rather than a peripheral figure. Indeed you can also do it with historical characters, as you will shortly see Barker does in *Regeneration*.

Research

John Fowles, whose novels are often set in specific historical periods, has said that every writer incorporates a 'wild man' and an 'academic'. The wild man gathers details of the story via associations, via the imagination and through the fickle, rambling process of trying to form a narrative of events. The academic tends to the pruning of what is produced, but also gathers other forms of knowledge, the elements that lie outside the writer's direct knowledge. This is something you will often need to do – research what you are writing about.

ACTIVITY 4.5

Reading

Read the interview with Pat Barker, Reading 8 on p.434, from which you read a quotation earlier in this chapter. Focusing on what she says about *The Regeneration Trilogy*, answer the following questions:

■ Which parts seem connected to her own life?

■ Which parts relate to her imagination?

■   Which parts are connected to research?

You can see from Barker's account of the sources for *Regeneration* that there was a definite biographical link but also an awful lot of research. Notice the number of real historical characters, such as Rivers, who have been used by Barker; how she has, according to this testimony, reinvigorated old memories that aren't necessarily personal to her. She has revived memories of a generation and a nation. By looking at the old case histories and then dramatising events she has deployed both historical fact and invention. As well as having a possible biographical source, the character of Billy Prior, it can be seen, was also 'very slightly based' on one of these real case histories.

What is research?

Doing research means investigating and, to a certain extent inhabiting, the world you want to realise – whether that world is a moment to be captured in a poem, a period of your own life story, or a scene in a fictional story. It doesn't mean that you stop using your imagination or what you know directly. When writing a story called 'The Revenge of Hannah Kemhuff', Alice Walker had originally intended to write about voodoo, but was torn between two possible settings. One involved an old, once 'crazy' aunt of Walker's and how she had been 'cured not by psychiatry but by powders and by spells' (1984, p.11). The other possible setting was part biographical and part imagined. It involved an episode her mother suffered during the Depression, when she was refused government surplus food by a woman in charge of the hand-outs. There was no voodoo involved in this tale but the woman in question grew senile and crippled, and Walker imagined a scenario whereby this rapid ageing was caused by voodoo. Walker became frustrated, however:

> I needed, instead of family memories, some hard facts about the *craft* of voodoo, as practiced by Southern blacks in the nineteenth century.
>
> (ibid., 1984, p.11)

Having done her research, the family story about the aunt, where voodoo was literally involved, wasn't used. The final version of the story instead combined biography, imagination and research. Walker used what she had found out about the nineteenth-century practices, and shifted this information into the twentieth-century scenario, based on the Depression and the episode of her mother in the food queue.

Family memories and even direct knowledge aren't always enough to go on and you may need to supplement 'what you know'. Alice Walker read some anthropology, particularly Zora Neale Hurston, to find out more about voodoo. Books will often be a vital source of information, but they aren't the only source. The internet will be a good source of further detail. Also, don't underestimate the value of field work. Sometimes you might like to take a trip to the local magistrate's court, to the Italian restaurant, to the pig farm or to sail on the ferry – to remind yourself of wherever you might be setting your story or poem.

ACTIVITY 4.6
Writing

Pick a brief item of news from your local newspaper or from the local radio or TV. Do some research about this item of news – using the internet, dictionaries or other reference books.

- Find out at least three further facts that you didn't previously know about the news article.
- Stick the original article in your notebook – or a summary of it, if it's a radio or television item.
- List underneath it or around it all the extra information you have managed to find.
- Write a fuller version of the item (in 200 words or less) including the information you have found.

For example, the news article might concern anglers catching fish in the local canal after a cleaning operation had countered pollution and years of neglect. The additional facts might include:

- the fish caught – carp – is bred for food in the Middle East (dictionary or encyclopaedia);
- where the canal runs to and from (local or national map);
- what the cargo carried on that particular canal used to be (internet or history book).

DISCUSSION

The type and depth of research you undertake will influence the course of your eventual writing. Sometimes research will not seem necessary, sometimes otherwise mundane events will be brought to life, made bigger, richer and more intriguing just by making a little effort and broadening 'what you know'. Sometimes this gathering of information will be included in your writing, sometimes it will be gathered and then discarded, having fulfilled its primary function – to convince you that you know what you are writing about.

Conclusion: The creative process

Most psychological models of the creative process include an unconscious stage, sometimes called the 'incubation period', where ideas hatch and develop beyond our conscious control or awareness. The work you do in your notebook will enable you to make the most of this 'unconscious' potential. As you have seen with Padel's model for writing poetry, part of the process is to let go, to allow the unconscious to come to the fore. Similarly with fiction, as Kurt Vonnegut attests: 'You can't really control a piece of fiction [...] Part of the technique is to lose control' (in Hayman, 1983).

Some writers engage in habitual behaviour while waiting for the hatching part of the process. Martin Amis is reputed to play darts, Kurt Vonnegut to play patience. Virginia Woolf invented a term for the state of mind needed in order to write – 'scrolloping' – a wonderful hybrid of 'scroll' or 'scribe' and 'lollop'. Other writers profess to learn what they are writing about during the physical act of writing. There is no one formula for how it will work for you. You will have to find your own working practice.

The writing process has many aspects. As most of the psychological models of creativity note, there is invariably hard work involved. You might persevere with an uncertain first draft, putting marks on the page for the first time. You might put in hours with the redrafting and editing. You might spend time mining your own past and present experience, and doing research to further your knowledge. You may come across ideas seemingly by accident or while asleep, or while occupied with something else entirely. To 'write what you know', or to write anything, is not a simple or straightforward matter. Yet it offers rich rewards. To finish a draft can be exhilarating. The feeling of just writing in your notebook can be utterly absorbing, and as you have seen with Woolf, sometimes rapturous.

It is important to remember that 'write what you know' is a liberating piece of advice, a route to discovery, not a limitation. Such advice invites you to explore what you know and therefore to understand it more fully. It reminds you to use every kind of knowledge at your disposal:

conscious, unconscious, sensory, accidental, researched, imagined. It reminds you to seek and to scrutinise at all times, whether working in your notebook or on a final draft. You are the conduit carrying the words, the stories, the poems, from thin air into the world. You are the only carrier. It will always be this link to you, the writer, which will lend a piece of writing its vitality and aura of believability.

References

Freud, Sigmund (1964 [1959]) 'Creative Writers and Day-dreaming' in *The Standard Edition of the Complete Psychological Works of Sigmund Freud*, Vol.9, London: The Hogarth Press, p.131–41.

Greenaway, Quentin (1994) 'Jesus Christ or a Better Class of Zoo', manuscript (unpublished).

Hayman, Ronald (1983) 'Interview with Kurt Vonnegut', *The Fiction Magazine*, Vol.2, No.1.

Neale, Derek (1993) 'Violin Lessons' in *Mafia*, with an introduction by Adam Mars-Jones, Norwich: CCPA at UEA.

Proust, Marcel (2002) *A la recherche du temps perdu*, translated as *In Search of Lost Time*, Scott Moncrieff and Terence Kilmartin (tr.), revised by D.J. Enright, London: Vintage.

Walker, Alice (1984) *In Search of our Mothers' Gardens*, London: The Women's Press.

PART 2

Writing fiction

5 *Character creation*

LINDA ANDERSON

If you have ever wanted to write fiction, chances are that you love to observe people and try to figure out what makes them tick. You're fascinated by their desires, histories and contradictions. But how do we create characters who will seem like living, breathing people, real enough to make our readers care about them?

Building characters is a gradual process. We will usually start with some glimmer of a personality which we need to flesh out. In fact, Elizabeth Bowen thought that the term 'creation of character' could be misleading:

> Characters pre-exist. They are *found*. They reveal themselves slowly – as might fellow-travellers seated opposite one in a very dimly lit railway carriage.
>
> (Bowen, 1948, quoted in Allen, 1958, p.179)

Finding your characters

How might you go about finding characters? There are four main approaches:

1 *Autobiographical method.* In this method you use yourself or aspects of yourself in the creation of character. Whether you want to write characters similar to you or not, don't underestimate yourself as a source. Everything that you understand or imagine about other people begins with your own experience. Your own consciousness is the only one to which you have direct access. You can create a multitude of characters from it.

2 *Biographical method.* The other main route to understanding people is through observation and intimate knowledge of others. In this method you base characters on people you know or have researched.

3 *Inventing characters from scratch.* You might start with a setting and imagine who would inhabit that place or own those objects. You might build characters from astrological signs or particular professions. Using the question 'What if ...?' as a prompt, you can start to build details. For example, what if a lawyer only became a lawyer to please her mother? What if she looks like her mother and accentuates it with similar clothes and hairstyle? What does she look like? Start getting the picture.

Or you might remember a stranger's face glimpsed on a bus or some striking portrait in a gallery may have lodged in your mind. You might cut out magazine photographs of faces that move or interest you. I still cherish a photograph which helped me to develop a male character for my first novel, a young school dropout who joins the army. I came across the picture in a magazine one day and thought 'That's him!' The man in the photograph had a complicated look, robust and open-faced but with something more withheld and knowing in the expression of the eyes and set of the mouth. Once I found the picture, my character became embodied, definite. Watch out for this kind of stimulus.

4 *Combination method.* This is the final method and the one most used. You mix aspects of known people with totally invented details. For example, take your own red hair and spendthrift habits, borrow someone else's low-carb diet and family feud, and donate the lot to a shop assistant nagged by stifled ambition. Or take your best friend's deadpan wit, make him handsome but with bad teeth, and turn him into a hopeless romantic who falls in love easily and often.

The combination method avoids some of the fears and pitfalls which can be associated with the autobiographical and biographical methods. If it makes you uncomfortable to base characters too recognisably on yourself or people close to you, then you can select a few features and behavioural styles but package them differently. As you have already seen in Chapter 4, this kind of reinvention can help to distance you from any stale, memorised feelings you may have about yourself or others.

When mixing and morphing your characters, you can do anything so long as you make it credible, which does not necessarily mean consistent. Although there are certain people who will never run a marathon, visit a nightclub in Bangkok, or own a cat, precisely because of who they are, remember that individuals are highly complicated, full of contradictions and capable of change.

Try out the third method now. Here is a list of ten random items:

- withered poinsettia;
- business card;
- dusty radio;
- silver locket with inscription;
- bottle of herbal medicine;
- auburn hair dye;
- fortune-telling cards;
- jar of sharpened pencils;
- brand new laptop.

Invent a character who owns these things. Write up to 250 words about the character, incorporating some of the objects into your description.

Flat and round characters

E.M. Forster distinguished between flat and round characters in *Aspects of the Novel* (1962 [1927], p.75). A round character is multidimensional, fully realised. A flat character is not rendered with such detail or complexity. These are often background or secondary characters, who sometimes play an instrumental role. They act as 'wheels to the coach', as Henry James expressed it (James, 1991 [1881], p.26). But you need to use specific, vivid details about flat characters too, however briefly they appear. Ford Madox Ford taught that you couldn't have a man appearing in a story long enough to sell a newspaper unless you put him there with enough detail to make the reader see him (quoted in O'Connor, 1970 [1957], p.92). Charles Dickens's novels abound with flat characters such as Uncle Pumblechook in *Great Expectations*: 'a large hard-breathing middle-aged slow man, with a mouth like a fish, dull staring eyes, and sandy hair standing upright on his head, so that he looked as if he had just been all but choked, and had that moment come to' (1953 [1861], p.21). Dickens always brings minor characters to life with loving exactitude.

Try to avoid using stereotypes or 'stock' characters even in your secondary characters, for example boring accountant, inarticulate footballer, vain film star, world-weary detective, old-fashioned elderly person, and so on.

Take one of the stereotypes mentioned above or use one of your own. Write a 250 word scene in which you portray that character in a complex way, going against the usual expectations.

Developing your characters

Be specific and particular when imagining your characters. New writers sometimes reach for abstractions and generalities, thinking that this is the way to indicate the wider or universal significance of a particular plight. But the more specific and grounded your stories are, the more they will illuminate the human condition.

To see the difference between the two approaches, let's say that we want to write a story about intergenerational conflict. We'll have a rich, possessive father who has indulged his only daughter. But she starts to forge a different set of values.

> **Example 1**
> He was a 38-year-old, public-school educated man of considerable wealth, who got very upset when his only daughter decided to do voluntary work overseas.

Packed with concise information but who cares? We can't see or feel anything. The characters are mere types. Everything is 'under wraps'.

> **Example 2**
> Nigel downed a tumbler of claret very fast. Emily was going to live in some dump of a country full of typhoons and terrorists for two whole years. He marched upstairs and yanked her designer clothes out of the wardrobe, making a mound on the floor. 'Won't need these, then, will you, Princess?' he thought.

Now we have subjectivity, action, and setting. Everything is personal and particular. But this version is more likely to make us feel and think about the implications of parent–child conflict and the impact of wealth than the generalised first example.

Character checklist

What sort of information should you collect about your characters? Some writers use questionnaires or checklists to devise characters in depth. Here are some of the main categories you should consider:

- *Physical/biological* – age, height, size, state of health, assets, flaws, sexuality, gait, voice.
- *Psychological* – intelligence, temperament, happiness/unhappiness, attitudes, self-knowledge, unconscious aspects.
- *Interpersonal/cultural* – family, friends, colleagues, birthplace, education, profession, hobbies, beliefs, values, lifestyle.
- *Personal history* – major events in the life, including the best and the most traumatic.

One of the most powerful ways to identify strongly with a character is to start with the body. Are your characters comfortable or unhappy in their own skins? Are they proud of one of their physical attributes? Do they draw attention to it in some way? Or do they try to conceal some aspect of their body? Do they have any physical difficulties or disabilities? Skin rashes, short-sightedness, a limp, impaired hearing? Think about the effect of any physical vulnerability on their self-image and behaviour.

Think about how a person's history is inscribed on his or her body. Signs of ageing, scars, stretch marks, loss of teeth. The body itself can be a storehouse of memory or a marker of identity. For example, Deirdre Madden's *One by One in the Darkness* (1996) is a story of three sisters. One of them, Cate, has striven to efface her Irish rural identity in her job as a journalist in London but lives there in a permanent state of homesickness. Her confident, glamorous exterior masks her deep uncertainties about identity and belonging. As the story opens, Cate is flying home to inform her family that she is pregnant. She is full of trepidation at the prospect of their rebuke. A glance in the mirror at her beautiful appearance fails to soothe her. She touches a tiny, invisible scar at her hairline, legacy of an accident with a hay baler when she was six. Touching this scar restores her sense of who she is, in a way that looking at her reflection does not.

Think about your characters' physical distinctions and the personal meanings invested in them.

Remember the wealth of influences that go into the making of characters. Think about the impact of age, gender, nationality, marital status, work, and religion on them. What is their attitude towards each one of these? Know your characters inside out. What they want, dream about, and fear. Their best and worst memories. How they react to strangers and surprises, to joys and embarrassments. Visualise them strongly – see how they stand, move, shake hands, or eat. Overhear their speech and how this may change in different contexts or moods. The more you know in advance about your characters, the more convincing your eventual stories will be.

Over the next week, in your notebook, start creating two or three characters you might use in stories later. Use any or all of the four methods described above to find your characters and then start fleshing them out with as much detail as possible. Work in short bursts of 10–15 minutes.

ACTIVITY 5.3
Notebook work

Credibility and complexity

Conflict is at the heart of stories and comes from within characters and not just between them. People all have desires, traits, and inclinations which are at war with each other. Sometimes the more closely we know people, the harder it becomes to sum them up because we see their contradictions. Think of the high-powered manager who is submissive at home, the person driven by ambition who also likes to vegetate, the lively, funny person with underlying sadness, the confident extrovert who feels secretly shy, the person who lavishes gifts and treats on friends but never leaves a tip, and so on. Aristotle called these conflicts within character 'consistent inconsistencies' (1996, p.24). We need to capture these in order to make our characters credible and complex. They are necessary to spark the 'engine' of our stories as it is these contradictions which generate dilemmas or obstacles for the characters to deal with.

Try this exercise which is based on the fact that most people's faces are faintly asymmetrical. Look at people's faces in some place like a doctor's waiting room, supermarket queue or café where you have a chance to study them for a couple of minutes. Be discreet, of course! See each face as two halves and try to detect a different character in each. For example, some pairings that students have found before are: artful dodger/serious student; romantic poet/traffic warden; wise child/

ACTIVITY 5.4
Writing

partygoer; warrior/playboy; dreamer/disciplined worker; joker/rescuer; practical mother/lone intellectual.

It can also be good to try this method with friends or family members, if you wish to base or partly base your characters on known individuals. But remember that whatever you find may not be 'true'. The point of the exercise is not detective work or uncovering secrets but to build a habit of seeing characters as made up of different, often surprising, component selves.

Take one of the 'dual' characters you have come up with and write up to 250 words of their current thoughts, allowing both aspects to filter through.

DISCUSSION   Here is an example using the 'romantic poet/traffic warden' pairing.

> I must be the only traffic warden who uses a gold-nibbed pen to write out these tickets. It's crazy, really – I have to wait for the ink to dry and that gives the irate punters a chance to pounce and tell me how blameless they are. But they know the score. Once issued, these tickets cannot be withdrawn. The most influential things I ever write.
>
> I don't usually care but sometimes I wish I could unwrite them. Like today – that young woman who caught me just as I was placing the ticket. She didn't protest at all, just looked defeated. She was beautiful but frail-looking. Her hair was fine, so fine it looked breakable, like dragonflies' legs. I wondered if that was a good simile. I wondered if she's ill. I walked round the corner and saw something strange. Flowers scattered in the gutter, twelve beheaded irises. I put one of the blooms in my pocket to think about later.

Notice how this character moves gently between his strict and sensitive sides. He is simultaneously tough and tender, practical and dreamy. In your own characterisations, aim for a similar interplay between contradictory aspects. Avoid violent or melodramatic switches, unless your story requires it, for example if you're writing in a horror genre.

Impersonation

For is biology destiny? Not for the writer or artist, it isn't.
      Joyce Carol Oates in *The Writing Life*, Marie Arana (ed.), 2003

Writers sometimes feel intimidated by the prospect of creating characters unlike themselves, especially in cases where a failed attempt might affront or even seem like a trespass to readers who know better. Can male writers invent convincing female characters? Can women write boys and men? Should a young person try to convey what it's like to be elderly? The answer is 'Yes' every time. Think of James Joyce's Molly Bloom soliloquy (which you will look at in Chapter 8); Pat Barker's portrayals of the impact of war on men; Rick Moody's searing portrayal of the infirmity of age in *Purple America*.

What about trying to imagine characters of a different ethnic origin from ourselves? This can be controversial but may be done successfully, provided that you do know a lot from observation and empathy. For example, Justin Hill spent years as a volunteer worker in small-town China before writing his prize-winning novel *The Drink and Dream Teahouse* (2001), a story full of Chinese characters, male and female, young and old.

In this matter of impersonation, boldness is everything. Writers who think they can imaginatively switch sex or age will probably find the belief self-fulfilling. But how exactly do you go about it?

Writers can learn from some of the methods actors use to help them identify with new characters. For example, the actor Harriet Walter has described a game called 'the hot seat', which is sometimes used in rehearsals. Actors take turns at being interviewed in character. They must answer probing questions like 'Are you satisfied with your job?', 'What are your hopes for your son?' (Walter, 2003 [1999], p.102). If they do not already know an answer, they have to reach for it then and there, and this can deepen their discoveries about the character. Walter says that writers could benefit from such a process and it would help to avoid situations where the writer's voice drowns out the character's own, as when a 'simpleton spouts elaborate philosophy' or a writer 'wrenches a character into a U-turn' in order to 'tie up ends' (ibid., pp.103, 104). If you have the opportunity to work with other writers, try playing the hot seat game. Alternatively, you can devise questionnaires and write the answers in your notebook. Or you might try writing a full history of your character as actors do in the Stanislavski Method as a way of identifying closely with them in order to produce a compelling performance. You can try out experiences you have not had and empathise with characters you don't know. With practice, you will be able to enter with conviction into the mind and voice even of characters you dislike or condemn.

For example, in Dostoevsky's *The Brothers Karamazov* Ivan is anguished by the fact of human suffering, especially that of children. He tells his brother Alesha a story about an aristocratic general who stripped a peasant boy naked and hunted him down with hounds who tore the boy to pieces in front of his mother. Ivan repudiates the Christian ideal of forgiveness for such extreme acts. He rejects God's creation because it incorporates unbearable cruelty. Ivan seems so noble and movingly eloquent that it comes as a shock to realise that Dostoevsky hated this type of scientific rationalist and thought him evil. But he was able to put his ego to one side and let the character call the shots.

Portraying your characters

There are five main methods of portraying characters:

- interpretation;
- appearance;
- action;
- thought;
- speech.

The first two methods rely on evaluation or description of characters. The final three are used to 'stage' characters, to show them directly through their behaviour.

Interpretation

A character may be interpreted by an author or by another character. In authorial interpretation, the writer tells us about the character, summarising or analysing his or her past, background, motives, mistakes, and so on. For example, here is a brief history and character summary of an archaeologist in Michael Ondaatje's *Anil's Ghost*:

> Palipana had not entered the field of archaeology until he was middle-aged. And he had risen in the career not as a result of family contacts but simply because he knew the languages and the techniques of research better than those above him. He was not an easily liked man, he had lost charm somewhere in his youth.
>
> (Ondaatje, 2000, p.80)

This kind of authorial interpretation can be a useful technique for when you need to condense facts or move the story on quickly.

A character may also be interpreted through the opinions and judgements of other characters. These interpretations provide a double vision, as we judge the judgement of the character who is speaking or thinking about the character in question. We have to decide whether to trust their analysis. For example, Zoë Heller's novel *Notes on a Scandal* (2004 [2003]) is narrated by Barbara Covett, a schoolteacher. Here is her verdict on one of her colleagues:

> Sue is terrifyingly dull. A living anthology of mediocre sentiments. A woman whose idea of an excellent *bon mot* is to sidle up to someone on a hot summer day and bark, excitedly, 'Hot enough for ya?'

> (Heller, 2004 [2003], p.34)

We learn as much about the narrator from this as we do about Sue. Barbara comes across as spiky, articulate, lethally observant, possibly snobbish.

Appearance

Sometimes writers neglect to convey the physical appearance of characters. They focus on their internal world as that is more 'important'. But characters can seem like ghosts unless vividly embodied. Physical details also act as an index to a character's psychology and values. In *The Book of Evidence*, by John Banville (2001 [1989]), the character-narrator says: 'This is the only way another creature can be known: on the surface, that's where there is depth' (p.62). Physical portrayals do not have to be static bits of information. They can be part of a scene or interaction, as in the following example from Leo Tolstoy's *War and Peace*:

> The princess smiled. She rose with the same unchanging smile with which she had first entered the room – the smile of an acknowledged beauty. With a slight rustle of her white ball-dress trimmed with ivy lichen, with a gleam of white shoulders, glossy hair and sparkling diamonds, she made her way between the men who stood back to let her pass; and not looking at any one in particular but smiling on all, as if she were graciously vouchsafing to each the privilege of admiring her beautiful figure, the shapely shoulders, back and bosom – which the fashionable low gown fully

displayed – she crossed to Anna Pavlovna's side, the living symbol
of festivity. Hélène was so lovely that not only was there no trace of
coquetry in her, but on the contrary she even appeared a little
apologetic for her unquestionable, all too conquering beauty. She
seemed to wish but to be unable to tone down its effect.

(Tolstoy, 1957 [1869], p.12)

By showing Hélène in a social context, Tolstoy makes her appearance
part of the action. He shows how burdened she is by her beauty. She
wears a forced smile and performs as an object of vision, both
triumphant and oppressed.

Action

Actions may be habitual behaviours which provide insight into character.
A story must also show decisive actions – ones that generate problems,
discoveries, and changes.

Thought

The ability to portray a character's thought is one of the assets of
fiction. Unlike film or drama where everything must be shown on the
outside (unless voiceover or soliloquy are used), fiction can render the
characters' mental and emotional processes. You may report a character's
thoughts or show them indirectly or directly:

She was afraid of what the doctor might say.

Why wouldn't he look up from his prescription pad?

Oh no, he looks like a hanging judge!

Speech

A character's speech reveals personality and opinions; attitudes and
beliefs; educational level; and economic or class background. The task of
the fiction writer is to get the right idiom and tempo for each character.
Sometimes when a character's voice doesn't ring true, or when all the
characters in a story sound the same, it means that the writer hasn't
fully carried out the groundwork of getting to know them well enough.

Choose two characters from the following list and develop their voices: a fitness fanatic; a disillusioned nurse; a bored, gifted student; a jovial social climber; a music-loving dentist. Make the voices different in rhythm, sentence-length, vocabulary, and degrees of eloquence. Write two monologues of up to 300 words each.

ACTIVITY 5.5
Writing

You may have found that you enjoyed creating one voice more than the other or that one came to you more easily. Experimenting with voices is a way of both discovering and extending your range of possibilities as a writer. Always read your monologues (and dialogues) aloud to check whether your characters' voices sound convincing.

DISCUSSION

Read the extract from Bernard MacLaverty's *Cal*, Reading 9 on p.442. Set in 1975 in Northern Ireland, this novel focuses on a single character destroyed by overwhelming political forces. Cal has been drawn into the IRA by local bully-boy Crilly to act as a driver for them. Guilt-stricken, he wants out. In the extract we see him taking part reluctantly in a robbery and bringing the proceeds to the home of the local IRA godfather, Finbar Skeffington.

ACTIVITY 5.6
Reading

In this dialogue-rich piece, study the way each of the three main characters speaks. Observe their personal styles and mannerisms. Are they terse or talkative? Formal or informal? Do they alter their speech with different people? Study their jokes, silences, and attempts at persuasion.

Write down in your notebook what you learn about their characters from what they say and the way they say it.

Each of the three men has a distinctive style of speech. Although both Cal and Crilly are terse, rarely speaking more than one clipped line at a time, Cal's speech is more emotionally expressive, and more caustic and witty. His speech alters in the different circumstances. Throughout the robbery his words are agitated and appalled. In the meeting with Skeffington he is sardonic and confrontational.

DISCUSSION

Crilly is a swaggering brute who gets high on violence. He is dim-witted, baffled by any slightly sophisticated utterance, like Cal's punning joke, 'The wit is off to his pit' or Skeffington's paradox, 'Not to act – is to act.' His silence reveals him too. Full of guffawing aggression in the car, he becomes subdued and deferential in schoolmaster Skeffington's presence, speaking only to back him up.

Set against the taciturnity of the other two men, Skeffington's long, self-regarding speeches indicate his sense of higher status. So does his tone: he speaks 'distinctly as if addressing one of his primary classes'. He reveals his father-fixation in his unwittingly comic attempts to present his mute parent as some charismatic figure. He spouts a rhetoric of blood sacrifice and martyrdom. He is sentimental, self-important, bullying, and ruthless.

We learn a great deal about these men from their words: we see who they are and what they stand for.

Dialogue does more than reveal character; it also furthers action. In the extract from *Cal* we see the beginnings of his mutiny, which will shortly lead to him hiding out on a farm where he finds work. Dialogue is also often haunted by the unspoken – what characters cannot or dare not say. These functions of dialogue will be explored in greater detail in Chapter 9.

ACTIVITY 5.7
Writing

Take one of the characters you have been developing in your notebook or one that has emerged from an earlier exercise. Now present him or her in five different ways in one scene. Include, in any order, an *interpretation* of what the character is like; his or her *appearance*; and a combination of *speech*, *thought*, and *action*.

DISCUSSION

Here is an example of the five methods used in one short scene:

> She was a 32-year-old lecturer who liked to be seen with younger men. They soon bored her but she enjoyed the feeling of triumph over her ex-husband, whom she hadn't heard from in three years. *[Interpretation]* No one seemed to find it strange that she wore nightclub clothes to work. It was part of her 'flamboyant' image, along with the abundant jet-black hair and glossy purple lipstick, which always looked freshly applied. *[Appearance]*
>
> Her latest conquest was a student, not something she usually risked, but he was not taking her course. In fact, he told her that he would never enrol for film studies – it was too fashionable, a soft option.
>
> You'll pay for that, she thought, you little know-all. *[Direct thought]*

She tugged his hair playfully. *[Action]* 'I'm sure you're right. I dare say I'll move on to something serious when I grow up.' *[Speech]*

The first two methods 'tell' us briefly about the character's history, personality and appearance. The latter three 'show' her in action and in relation to another character. In Chapter 9, you will explore more about 'showing and telling' and how to decide on the balance between them in particular stories.

Character and plot

It is a good idea to envisage character and plot as interlocking, rather than starting with a plot idea and then adding in characters. See how events emerge naturally from character. In *Letters to a Young Poet*, Rilke wrote 'the future enters into us [...] long before it happens' and went on to say 'we will [...] gradually learn to realise that that which we call destiny goes forth from within people, not from without into them' (Rilke, 1963 [1934], p.65).

This is not to say that what happens to characters is inevitable or predetermined. It is simply that particular characters seek or 'attract' certain events or encounters.

Henry James wrote a lengthy preface for *The Portrait of a Lady*, the story of Isabel Archer, a spirited young woman who gets entrapped in a loveless marriage with a cold-hearted aesthete. James describes in detail the genesis of the novel and the process of its creation. It began with no sense of plot or set of relations or even a situation 'but altogether in the sense of a single character, the character and aspect of a particular engaging young woman' (1991 [1881] p.15). He wonders why his grasp of the character was so strong despite the initial lack of context.

> Thus I had my vivid individual – vivid, so strangely, in spite of being still at large, not confined by the conditions, not engaged in the tangle, to which we look for much of the impress that constitutes an identity. If the apparition was still all to be placed how came it to be vivid?
>
> (ibid., p.19)

He concludes that the acquisition of such an imaginary figure is not to be retraced. What matters is that he began to see the character 'as bent upon its fate' (p.19). He asked himself: 'Well, what will she *do*?' In response, he seemed to wake up one morning with the full cast of characters surrounding Isabel Archer and so he began to have the 'concrete terms' of his plot (p.25).

It is an approach well worth trying. Start with a strong vision of your main character or characters. Ask then what they will do? Start seeing the kinds of dilemma, challenge, or conflict they might encounter and you will automatically be generating your plot. This may be expressed as a formula:

Character + conflict = plot

Apply this formula to the characters you have been developing in your notebook. Imagine your characters under pressure, forced to take risks or make choices or to stand up for themselves or someone else. What happens? Let the stories unfold.

References

Allen, Walter (ed.) (1958) *Writers on Writing*, London: Phoenix House.

Aristotle (1996) *Poetics*, London: Penguin Classics.

Banville, John (2001 [1989]) *The Book of Evidence* from *Frames Trilogy*, London: Picador.

Dickens, Charles (1953 [1861]) *Great Expectations*, Oxford: Oxford University Press.

Forster, E.M. (1962 [1927]) *Aspects of the Novel*, Middlesex: Penguin Books.

Heller, Zoë (2004 [2003]) *Notes on a Scandal*, London: Penguin.

Hill, Justin (2001) *The Drink and Dream Teahouse*, London: Weidenfeld & Nicolson.

James, Henry (1991 [1881]) *The Portrait of a Lady*, Preface, Everyman's Library, London: David Campbell.

Madden, Deirdre (1996) *One by One in the Darkness*, London: Faber and Faber.

O'Connor, Flannery (1970 [1957]) *Mystery and Manners*, Sally and Robert Fitzgerald (eds), New York: Farrar, Straus & Giroux.

Ondaatje, Michael (2000) *Anil's Ghost*, London: Bloomsbury.

Rilke, Rainer Maria (1963 [1934]) *Letters to a Young Poet*, New York: W.W. Norton.

Tolstoy, Leo (1957 [1869]) *War and Peace*, London: Penguin.

Walter, Harriet (2003 [1999]) *Other People's Shoes: Thoughts on acting*, London: Nick Hern Books.

6 *Setting*

LINDA ANDERSON

Thomas Hardy opened his novel *The Return of the Native* with an entire chapter describing the broody timeless landscape of Egdon Heath (1992 [1878], pp.3–7). Chapter 2 has the title: 'Humanity Appears upon the Scene, Hand in Hand with Trouble'. Although the opening chapter still has its passionate devotees, many readers nowadays feel a sense of relief when they get to Chapter 2, with its promise of characters in crisis. For them, dwelling on an unpeopled landscape for the length of a whole chapter may seem akin to staring for half an hour at a freeze-frame of the opening shot of a film.

But while lengthy 'still life' descriptions can be tedious, stories can also be boring and unconvincing because of a *lack* of setting. Stories about emotional problems, for example a woman's anger about her childhood, or a man trying to come to terms with his wife's desertion, can come across as case histories, if they focus on inward feeling without much external setting. But give us the unwashed cups, the framed photographs on the bedside table, the faint mothball smell in the wardrobe, the shrieks of children playing outside, the colour of the pavement after rain, the forlorn sound of a dog barking in the middle of the night, the strange mood of bleakness and solace induced by an all-night supermarket – the outside makes the inside real. If setting seems to be slowing down your narrative or if it seems dully informative, the problem may be that it is separated from character and action. Give us Humanity and Trouble and Scene together.

Setting and character

One of the most effective ways of revealing character is through details of the spaces they inhabit and the possessions they have chosen. A character's belongings can act as an index to his or her character. For example, here is a description of Alfred Lambert's special chair in the basement of his house in the 'gerontocratic suburb of St Jude', from the opening pages of Jonathan Franzen's *The Corrections*:

> To the west of the Ping-Pong table was Alfred's great blue chair.
> The chair was overstuffed, vaguely gubernatorial. It was made of

leather, but it smelled like the inside of a Lexus. Like something
modern and medical and impermeable that you could wipe the smell
of death off easily, with a damp cloth, before the next person sat
down to die in it. [...] [W]hen Alfred retired from the Midland
Pacific Railroad, he set about replacing the old cow-smelling black
leather armchair in which he watched TV and took his naps. He
wanted something really comfortable, of course, but after a lifetime
of providing for others he needed more than just comfort: he needed
a monument to this need. So he went, alone, to a non-discount
furniture store and picked out a chair of permanence. An engineer's
chair. A chair so big that even a big man got lost in it; a chair
designed to bear up under heavy stress.

(Franzen, 2001, pp.8–9)

At first the description is ironic. The chair is absurdly grand and
sinister-smelling. It's like a governor's chair, a vulgar status-symbol. We
might start off thinking that Alfred has delusions of grandeur and very
bad taste. But then we learn about the huge meaning he has invested in
this imposing chair, which is supposed to reward a lifetime's service and
self-denial. He does indeed crave status, some compensation for feeling
overlooked. We get a glimpse into a whole life through one particular
shopping trip. Possessions in themselves can hint at character but it is
when we understand what they *mean* to their owner that we get the
richest insights.

ACTIVITY 6.1
Writing

■ In up to 150 words, create a domestic setting for one of the
following characters so that we can imagine the absent person
vividly: a middle-aged recluse; a heart-throb actor in a television
soap; a foster child; a famous poet with writer's block.

■ Create a list of five cherished items belonging to the same character.
Now consider whether any of these objects could lead to a larger
story? For example, is there a significant memory or secret attached
to one of them? Is one of them deliberately concealed? Do any of
them belong to someone else? Jot down some plot ideas. The
objective is to practise seeing possible stories in settings.

Setting and emotion

The description of Alfred's chair is a kind of static character portrayal through setting. The *interaction* of character and setting can reveal character in a dynamic way and can also generate plot. While people may have their innate qualities, they are also the product of particular places. The reverse is also true. Places are the product of people and of people's imaginations. How we see the places in our lives reveals who we are and how we are at any given moment. A supermarket or a field or a church will look and feel very different to you on a day when you have just lost your job as opposed to a day when you've fallen in love.

ACTIVITY 6.2
Writing

Invent a character who visits a place of historical interest, one with a strong atmosphere of grief or light-heartedness or positive endeavour, for example a site of war graves, a museum of childhood, the former home of a writer. Or choose your own place.

- Write a 250 word version in which your character feels unwell and is worried about what the symptoms may mean.
- Write a second version in which the same character has just purchased a 'dream' house. Again use up to 250 words.

DISCUSSION

Check your two versions to make sure that the 'same' place changes with the character's mood. If you have chosen an inherently sad place, how does your 'happy' version work out? Or your 'worried' version, if you have a pleasant, positive setting? Have you shown the tension between place and person? Does your 'happy' character feel guilty or dragged down? Or buoyant despite the environment? Is your worried character uplifted or alienated by the cheerful setting?

For instance, imagine a woman visiting the home of the Brontë sisters in Yorkshire. In an anxious mood, she might think: 'How horrible to have that dark graveyard so near the house. I can see it from nearly every window.' In a hopeful mood, she might be enchanted by the Brontë children's tiny books full of their stories in minuscule handwriting. She might think: 'I'll have that – a big sunny place for my children to play and dream in.' Alternatively, her anxious mood could be allayed by the gloom ('They were so much worse off than me'); or her happiness undermined ('They had everything to live for, but look what happened.')

Setting and plot

So, characters may find settings either supportive or oppressive and either response can generate or advance a story. Where they are in tune with an environment, experiencing a sense of well-being or belonging, the writer will often introduce a disruptive element to shatter or test the harmony.

Shattered harmony

For example, Ian McEwan's *Atonement* opens in a big English country house where the Tallis family is gathering on the hottest day in the summer of 1935. Here is Cecilia Tallis, a recent Cambridge graduate, pausing in the doorway of the dining room:

> Dripping coolly onto her sandalled feet, the untidy bunch of rose-bay willow-herb and irises brought her to a better state of mind. The vase she was looking for was on an American cherry-wood table by the French windows which were slightly ajar. Their south-east aspect had permitted parallelograms of morning sunlight to advance across the powder-blue carpet. Her breathing slowed and her desire for a cigarette deepened, but she still hesitated by the door, momentarily held by the perfection of the scene – by the three faded Chesterfields grouped around the almost new Gothic fireplace in which stood a display of wintry sedge, by the unplayed, untuned harpsichord and the unused rosewood music stands, by the heavy velvet curtains, loosely restrained by an orange and blue tasselled rope, framing a partial view of cloudless sky and the yellow and grey mottled terrace where camomile and feverfew grew between the paving cracks. A set of steps led down to the lawn on whose border Robbie still worked, and which extended to the Triton fountain fifty yards away.
>
> (McEwan, 2001, p.20)

But this atmosphere of privilege and tranquillity is banished completely by the end of the day. Cecilia's life is changed forever by her younger sister Briony's misinterpretation of a scene she witnesses between Cecilia and her childhood friend, Robbie. Briony will spend the rest of her life trying to atone. The 'timeless, unchanging calm' (p.19) of the place proves utterly deceptive.

Antagonism

Where there is antagonism between character and place, there is already the potential for a story. For example, in Bernard MacLaverty's *Cal*, which is familiar to you from the previous chapter, Cal and his father Shamie are the only two Catholics living on a Protestant estate. They receive death threats posted through the door warning them to leave or be burnt out. This is Cal entering the enemy territory of his own street.

> As he turned into his street he felt the eyes on him. He looked at the ground in front of him and walked. The eyes would be at the curtains or behind a hedge as a man paused in his digging. He could not bear to look up and see the flutter of Union Jacks, and now the red and white cross of the Ulster flag with its red hand. Of late there were more and more of these appearing in the estate. It was a dangerous sign that the Loyalists were getting angry. The flags should all have been down by now because the Twelfth of July was long past. It was sheer cussedness that they were kept up. Even looking at his feet Cal couldn't avoid the repulsion because the kerbstones had been painted alternating red, white, and blue.

(MacLaverty, 1983, p.9)

Notice that the atmosphere of menace and exclusion is achieved by the focus on particular, concrete details: curtains with imagined watchers lurking behind them, a silent neighbour, fluttering flags, and painted kerbstones.

ACTIVITY 6.3

Writing

■ Write a 500 word scene in which a character feels trapped in his or her surroundings with no immediate prospect of escape. For example, the setting might be: a boarding school, a package holiday, a relative's house at Christmas, a hated job which is a financial necessity. Show the feelings through the descriptions of the place, not by naming the feelings.

■ Imagine a building (or use one you know) which has been changed dramatically but still bears traces of its former use, for example a restaurant that was once a church, a boarding school that used to be a family home, a modern house converted from a barn where animals were kept. Write about a character who, happily or unhappily, cannot stop being aware of the building's history. Use up to 500 words.

Defamiliarising the known

As writers we need to see our usual surroundings with a fresh eye. In Chapters 2 and 3 you started practices which are directly useful in the creation of believable fictional settings: noting down observations of your surroundings; using all of your senses; aiming for exact imagery. Keep on noting particulars of places you go – the works' canteen, the dentist's waiting room, a vandalised bus shelter, a holiday beach – so that you build up a handy resource of details and atmospheres. When creating your settings be specific. Instead of a flower, make it a bluebell; instead of a car, a battered Renault. Remember always to use all of your senses to recreate the full texture of existence.

For an example of a powerful evocation of place through the senses, read the first part of the extract from P.F. Kluge's *Biggest Elvis* (1996), Reading 10 on p.450, stopping before the paragraph which starts 'Chester Lane went out first'. This first part establishes the story's setting, a US naval base in Olongapo, Philippines. The narrator is Ward Wiggins, the oldest and fattest of a trio of Elvis Presley impersonators who entertain sailors and bar girls. (We will look at the whole extract in Chapter 7.)

ACTIVITY 6.4
Reading

- In your notebook, write down which senses the narrator uses to describe the setting.
- How do these descriptions convey his emotions about the place?

DISCUSSION

Wiggins conjures the place first through smell. When he closes his eyes, it is the memory of the overpowering mixture of odours which comes back first; then the sounds, the 'great river of noise'; and finally the sights. His nostalgia for Olongapo is conveyed by his tone of breathless excitement and his vivid use of language. Wiggins is a skilled orator who uses dazzling lists, shocking similes ('forests long gone, like the hair that falls out of a cancer patient's head'), rhythm and rhyme ('*what you want, baby we got it*, country western, hard rock, mud wrestling, foxy boxing, full-body massage, *what you need, baby we got it* ...'). The narrator's ability to stack up so many specific, richly atmospheric details lets us see and sense Olongapo. We are transported into that shimmering, stinky world.

Unexpected harmony

In *Biggest Elvis*, there is a tension between the seedy decay of the place and Wiggins's intense longing for it, which intrigues the reader. We could call this an example of *unexpected harmony* between character and setting, and this can be an exciting strategy. Think your town is drab and boring? Why not set a magnificent love affair in Dullsville? Or have a charismatic figure move into a soporific place and wake people up, to the delight or consternation of the inhabitants? Or take a generally despised setting and treat it as magical, a site of possibilities for your characters.

For example, *Eureka Street*, by Robert McLiam Wilson (1996), is set in Belfast just before and after the 1994 ceasefire. Wilson subverted conventional portrayals of the city as an immutably traumatised place, recasting it as a site of change and possible redemption. A whole chapter is devoted to a lyrical celebration of nocturnal Belfast.

> Belfast is Rome with more hills; it is Atlantis raised from the sea.
> And from anywhere you stand, from anywhere you look, the streets
> glitter like jewels, like small strings of stars.

> (Wilson, 1996, pp.213–14)

Terrible violence still occurs, jolting the main character, Jake Jackson, into experiencing Belfast again as a 'necropolis'. But the novel is packed with love stories.

Or, in *Long Journey Through a Small Town*, a novel-in-progress by Patrick Boyden, the setting is a 'Midlands town which epitomises dullness'. The story concerns the friendship between a grumpy man who looks after his invalid mother and a homeless young woman. Here is an extract from the beginning:

> Sunlight, even when dulled by thin cloud, brightens most things. It can pick out the subtle blues and greys in roof tiles, bring warmth to red brick, and form to chimneys and tower blocks. What it can do to buildings of more architectural merit can leave the spectator speechless. He may reach for his handkerchief to dab at the tear that arrives in the corner of his eye as the neo-Grecian columns on a town hall proudly puff themselves out as if to state 'We are tall, we are strong, we are timeless. Together we hold the roof up. Between our stems, you the people of this town wander, buying tickets for concerts. Behind us, you view the culture we contain, the visiting exhibition of traditional Dutch farming implements, or some sixties

pop group, unironically reprising their hits with all the style, dignity and edge of a middle-aged man playing *Twister*.'

And the sunlight will quizzically touch the golden onion atop the mosque, wondering where it came from and what happened to the brewery that was there, ooh, just a couple of years ago.

(Boyden, n.d.)

This opening dispels the stereotype of banal, rundown city. The narrator is affectionate and whimsical, even imagining the sunlight and the buildings as sentient. The story itself is entirely realistic but the opening primes us to expect promise as well as problems in the characters' situation.

Real or invented places

For every story, you need to decide whether to invent a location or use a real place, either already familiar to you or one that you can research.

One of the advantages of using a real location is that it anchors the story in a believable world. This is particularly effective in crime fiction, where part of the horror comes from frightening events occurring in ordinary places. It is possible to base a story in an identifiable location but make up aspects of it. For example, Ruth Rendell's *Adam and Eve and Pinch Me* is set mainly in Kensal Green in west London. Minty Knox lives there in 'Syringa Road', an invented street. Everything else seems based on real street names and locations.

> The morning was grey, misty, still. There was a queue for the 18 bus so she walked to the dry-cleaners past Fifth and Sixth Avenues, stepping over the joins. Minty had grown up with street names like that and couldn't see anything funny about it but it made Jock laugh. He'd only been in the area a few months and every time he saw the name he'd cast up his eyes, laugh that soundless laugh of his and say 'Fifth Avenue! I don't believe it.'
>
> Admitted, it wasn't a very nice part, but 'run-down' and 'a real slum', which were what Jock called it, were going a bit far. OTT, to use his own expression. To Minty it appeared grey and dreary but familiar, the background of her life for nearly thirty-eight years, for she'd been a baby when Agnes left her with Auntie for 'an hour at the maximum' and never came back. The row of shops ran from Second to First Avenue on the Harrow Road. Two of them had closed and been boarded up or they'd have been vandalised. The

> Balti takeaway was still there, a bathroom fittings shop, a builder's merchant, a unisex hairdresser and on the corner, Immacue.

(Rendell, 2002 [2001], p.12)

Minty Knox also dwells in a surreal world of her own, communing with ghosts. The diligent creation of locality and of the minutiae of her life and routine makes the derailing of her mind more convincing and more sinister.

Familiarising the unknown

Imaginary settings are important for certain types of narrative, for example science fiction or fantasy genres. Such settings are made plausible by embedding the exotic in the familiar. Elves speak English; wizards lose their temper; an outsider lands on a planet peopled by tiny hermaphroditic beings where the two nations are at war: the strange and the recognisable.

For example, Maggie Gee's *The Ice People* is set in the near future when the world is devastated by a new Ice Age. Men and women are segregated and use feathered robots as sexual partners. Europeans become 'the ice people', a mass movement of asylum-seekers clamouring to get into the relative warmth of Africa. The story is told by Saul, a divorced father.

> I sat in our flat like a man of stone and felt the world turning faster and faster. It was true, yes, it was definitely happening, but all of it seemed remote, unreal, I watched them on the screen, great swirls of black ants, crowding the airports, overloading the boats ... They were real people, though they looked like insects but I wasn't one of them. I was a ghost.

(Gee, 1999 [1998], p.120)

The story takes familiar tensions, sexual and ethnic, and shows them pushed to a logical extreme by catastrophic conditions. In details like the tables-turned asylum-seeking, it acts as much as a satiric commentary on the present as an apocalyptic vision of the future.

Setting as enclosed world

Institutions and workplaces can provide fascinating settings for fiction. Schools, factories, offices, army barracks, or prisons often operate like little islands with their own rituals, jargons, and systems of sanctions and rewards. Such settings can generate stories by having characters as initiates, power-grabbers, mutineers, victims, and so on.

Jed Mercurio's *Bodies*, about a young doctor's experience of working in a hospital, begins with a dramatic sense of entering a separate world 'with its own speed limits and language and even its own weather'.

Read the opening section of *Bodies*, Reading 11 on p.457. Study the choice of language, particularly the verbs, as the doctor goes further and further into the hospital environment. What kind of mood is created by this use of language?

ACTIVITY 6.5
Reading

The doctor's entry into the hospital is hurtling, almost hallucinatory. He is 'swallowed into' the place; his reflection 'slithers' over the panes. He 'plunges farther', and then is 'pointed deeper' into the multiplying straight, white corridors until he feels as if he is 'falling'. He is almost like an initiate being entombed in an underworld – a strip-lit, dazzlingly white underworld.

The mood is one of foreboding. We expect bad things. The rest of the novel shows how the character does 'fall' – into exhaustion and shame in the pitiless world of the hospital.

DISCUSSION

- Ask a relative or friend to describe his or her workplace to you, including any machines, special furniture or equipment used. Incorporate some of the details into a scene in which a character is tired of the same job and longs to leave it. Don't overload your piece with what you have learned – use just enough to give an authentic atmosphere: for example, the look of the post office sorting room at 4 am; the sounds of ailing rodents and Rottweilers in the vet's waiting room. Use up to 500 words.

- Write a story or beginning of a story about a new employee on his or her first day in a job. Show the character's response to the work environment and how much he or she is able to glean about the 'rules', hierarchies, how to fit in and become accepted. Give us a sense of whether the character will succeed in fitting in. Use up to 1000 words.

ACTIVITY 6.6
Writing

Setting as symbolic power

Sometimes setting can be more than backdrop to action or site of interaction between characters and place. It can take on symbolic power and act as a dynamic force in the story. For example, in Alex Garland's *The Beach* (1997 [1996]), a secret beach is a legend among young backpackers in Asia, who are lured by rumours of a select community living in an earthly paradise. The story enacts a modern-day 'fall', an expulsion from Eden.

Or in Barbara Kingsolver's *The Poisonwood Bible* (1999 [1998]), an arrogant Baptist missionary, Nathan Price, takes his wife and daughters to the Belgian Congo in 1959 in order to convert the natives. But it is the family who are challenged and changed utterly, tested to their limits by overwhelming forces of nature, culture shock, and politics.

From place to place

A word on moving characters around. Trains and boats and planes – who needs them? Writers sometimes dutifully record full details of characters' journeys, making the reader watch with them through the misty bus windows for the eventless miles until the story begins again. Unless the journey *is* the story (as in Conrad's *Heart of Darkness* or Melville's *Moby Dick*), or unless it contributes to plot, there is no need to include it. Like film-makers, we can *jump cut* from scene to scene. So, stick your backpacker in Goa; your honeymooners in their hotel; your prodigal son on the doorstep. Unless you have a special reason, don't *get* your characters there; just *put* them there.

Once upon a time ...

Stories are set in a particular time as well as in particular places. As you have seen in Chapter 4, research is sometimes necessary to enlarge your view even of the period of your own life story. For historical fiction your research will be more extensive again.

Sara Waters, author of *Tipping the Velvet* and *Fingersmith*, spends weeks researching things like locks, coins, shoes – what she calls the 'poignant trivia' of the period (quoted in Taylor, 2004, p.16). What does a dogskin coat smell like? How do you melt down a pewter cup on a kitchen fire? What is it like to share a bed with your servant?

Her method is to steep herself in the writing of the time – fiction, journalism, letters, diaries – and to continue this reading during the writing process to ensure that her mind stays saturated in the right atmosphere (quoted in Taylor, 2004, p.17).

This kind of research is enjoyable in its own right. Be careful about the temptation to cram it all into the fiction. Keep your story and your story's needs paramount.

Conclusion

Remember that what your characters own, and how they inhabit and furnish their 'spaces', will reveal them to your readers and will also help generate your stories. Make sure that you use the full range of sensory detail in your creation of place, not just the visual. Forget that you 'know' your own local area. Investigate it; find out the exact smell of the pavements after rain; how many stars you can see at night. Take walks; take notes. When you travel, consider taking photographs too. For the novel I'm currently working on, I've taken about a hundred photographs in Barcelona. They include a picture of two elderly women sitting in front of a café with their ancient dogs perched on their laps. Another is of a child in a confirmation dress standing on a park bench, her whole figure haloed and blurred in fierce sunlight. I also have pictures of isolated details: areas of pavement, graffiti tags, and market stall displays.

Even if you choose an imaginary setting for a science fiction story, you will need to realise it all in intense detail: its climate, laws, customs, cuisine, and so on. Whether you write about your own backyard or some outpost of the galaxy, make it real.

References

Boyden, Patrick (no date) *Long Journey Through a Small Town*, manuscript (unpublished).

Franzen, Jonathan (2001) *The Corrections*, London: Fourth Estate.

Garland, Alex (1997 [1996]) *The Beach*, London: Penguin Books.

Gee, Maggie (1999 [1998]) *The Ice People*, London: Richard Cohen Books.

Hardy, Thomas (1992 [1878]) *The Return of the Native*, Everyman's Library, London: David Campbell.

Kingsolver, Barbara (1999 [1998]) *The Poisonwood Bible*, London: Faber and Faber.

MacLaverty, Bernard (1983) *Cal*, London: Jonathan Cape.

McEwan, Ian (2001) *Atonement*, London: Jonathan Cape.

Rendell, Ruth (2002 [2001]) *Adam and Eve and Pinch Me*, London: Arrow.

Taylor, Debbie (2004) 'Sarah Waters Talks to Editor Debbie Taylor', *Mslexia*, No. 20.

Wilson, Robert McLiam (1996) *Eureka Street*, London: Secker & Warburg.

7 Point of view: Trying on voices

LINDA ANDERSON

Every story is told from a point of view, the perspective of a particular narrator. With each new piece of fiction that you write, you need to ask yourself early on: whose story is it? Who will tell it? Should the story be told by the main character? Or by a secondary character who witnesses the events? Should it be told by an anonymous witness who presents the action without comment? Or by an all-knowing power who can reveal the innermost thoughts and feelings of all the characters?

Choosing a point of view for a particular story can be a matter of 'intuition'. Perhaps you overhear a character's voice in your head and follow that. Or one character's connection to the story will appeal to you more than another's. But it is important to know what the choices are, what each one requires, and what are the advantages and limitations of each choice. Mastery of the basic techniques you can use to establish point of view is one of the most empowering things a fiction writer can learn. It gives you a range of possibilities to select from and increases your versatility and clarity as a writer.

To experience the impact of point of view, let's first look at two possible beginnings of the 'same' story. Jot down your impressions and responses to each version and think about the following questions:

ACTIVITY 7.1
Reading

- Who do you think is telling the story in each?
- To whom?
- How much does the teller know?

Version 1

My father says that our house is like a mini-industrial estate, what with all the cooking, laundering, violin-playing, pet-grooming (two tabbies and a Jack Russell), and the uproar of begging for the bathroom as we struggle to get to our busy-bee schedules outside the home. We all have 'schedules', even me, the 'baby' of the family. I'll be fourteen soon but there will be no amnesty. I'll probably be Baby when I'm thirty years old. Baby Middleton with her high heels, pink Porsche, and job on the twenty-fifth floor. A disappointment to her parents, who want me to be a moneybags all right but a doctor, lawyer, scientist, you get the picture. First, though, they're going to have to be disappointed by my eldest brother, Simon, when they get around to noticing. He has managed to fit some class A drugs into his schedule. I don't know where he gets the money but he sneaks out lots of times after everyone's in bed. Shows up at breakfast staring like a sleepwalker and nobody says a word.

Version 2

The Middleton family are the envy of their neighbours and friends. There are five offspring, all good-looking and 'gifted' in one way or another, and long-married parents who still send each other valentine cards. Susannah Middleton, the mother, runs the household with faultless organisation. No medical appointment is ever missed, no dry-cleaning abandoned and there is never a gap in the supply of teabags, bread, or shampoo. Her system of automatic replacement even extends to the household pets. When one of the animals exhausts its natural span, she buys a new puppy or kitten a few days later. This is not a sign of heartlessness, more like the opposite, a desire to fix everything, even sorrow.

In years to come, she will look back on this time and wish that she had paused to notice what was happening to her eldest boy.

DISCUSSION   These two openings are roughly the same length and deal with the same fictional material: a large, apparently happy and successful family in which the eldest son is secretly in trouble. Similar details are observed in each account: the zealous organisation of the household, the existence of pets, the value placed on achievement, the parents' 'blind spot' about impending trouble.

But the contrasting points of view or angles of vision produce startlingly different versions.

In the first version, I have written a first-person narration (an 'I' tells the story). The narrator is the 14-year-old youngest daughter of the family. The unmediated voice creates a vivid sense of intimacy. There is a direct address to the reader, who is seen as a kind of confidant ('... you get the picture'). We see through the girl's eyes and interpretations, getting an immediate impression of her character and her predicament on several levels: as an adolescent casting off her parents' values; as the youngest member in the family hierarchy; and as the only person aware of her brother's clandestine life. The silence and deception at the heart of this bustling little tribe come across worryingly, creating immediate suspense.

In the second version, I have adopted an omniscient (all-knowing) point of view, which uses the third person (using 'he', 'she', or 'they'). In this omniscient persona, my narrator knows what is happening now, what has happened in the past and what will happen in the future. She or he can make judgements about character which the characters themselves may be unaware of ('This was not a sign of heartlessness ...').

The fictionality of the second version is more obvious than in the first one, which aims to seem like a 'real' confessional voice. In the second version, we are aware of the narrator presiding over the story and controlling its telling. The language in this version is more formal and dispassionate. Whereas the first voice draws us in and confides in us, this voice is distant and authoritative, almost godlike. There is a faintly ironic tone in certain phrases which may reveal the narrator's attitude. For example, the quotation marks placed around 'gifted' seem to distance the narrator from this verdict. And why say 'exhausts its natural span' instead of 'dies'? Maybe the narrator is hinting at an evasive style of thought in the mother, an inability to face hard facts?

I'm the author of both these versions but my narrators have made-up voices. They may each have traces of my personal voice but their voices are invented for the purpose of the story. Jack Hodgins, in *A Passion for Narrative*, called the writer's own inescapable voice his 'voice-print' and the narrators he takes on, his 'voice-masks' (1994 [1993], p.193). With practice, it is possible to become a different sort of narrator every time, to try on many masks.

These methods of telling the story are just two possibilities among many. We will now look in detail at the main strategies used in first-person narrations. Chapter 8 will go on to explore third-person and second-person narrations.

First-person narration

A story is told in the first person when it is narrated by one of the characters. (An 'I' tells his or her own story.) The narrator may be the protagonist or central narrator, the person whose desires and decisions impel the action, and it is important to indicate this status quickly. For example, *The Butcher Boy* by Patrick McCabe opens with the vivid, disturbing voice of Francie O'Hagan:

> When I was a young lad twenty or thirty or forty years ago I lived
> in a small town where they were all after me on account of what I
> done on Mrs Nugent.
>
> (McCabe, 1993 [1992], p.1)

A first-person narrator may alternatively be a witness or peripheral
narrator, who observes the fortunes of a central character. We see and
understand that person through the filter of the witness's view and the
impact upon him or her. A recent example is Philip Roth's *The Human
Stain*, the story of the downfall of a university professor persecuted for
alleged racism. It is his neighbour who tells the story of the professor's
destruction and the narrator's status as witness is made clear from the
opening lines:

> It was in the summer of 1998 that my neighbour Coleman Silk –
> who, before retiring two years earlier, had been a classics professor
> at nearby Athena College for some twenty-odd years as well as
> serving for sixteen more as the dean of faculty – confided to me
> that, at the age of seventy-one, he was having an affair with a thirty-
> four-year-old cleaning woman who worked down at the college.
>
> (Roth, 2001 [2000], p.1)

ACTIVITY 7.2

Writing

- Going back to the scenario of the Middleton family (p.99), write
  another opening of that story from the point of view of the eldest
  son, Simon, in his private journal. Make sure he sounds different
  from his sister and that his writing comes across as for his eyes only.
  You might want to include some slang, jargon or abbreviations to
  make the voice authentic.

- Then write another opening from a witness's point of view, for
  example a concerned schoolteacher or a nosy neighbour. Use up to
  180–200 words for each version, as in the original examples.

Advantages of first-person narration

First-person narration is the most straightforward storytelling technique.
It has maximum subjectivity and passion and can therefore be
compelling. Access to the character's thoughts is smooth and immediate,
without the filter of another narrating voice. You are free to create
strongly authentic voices, using slang, faulty grammar, and colloquial

language where appropriate to the character. In the third person, these would be confined to dialogue.

First-person narration offers you the chance to make bold experiments in impersonation. You can pretend to be whatever you choose: judge, madwoman, vagrant, pop star, shopkeeper, wizard, ghost, anyone at all, even an animal or an object endowed with the power of thought. You may also, of course, use fictional versions of yourself in autobiographical stories, and this is often where new writers start.

... and limitations, with some possible remedies

There are certain hazards in the use of the first person. First-person stories can contain an over-concentration on the self with a tiresome repetition of 'I I I' like telegraph poles stalking the landscape. This can be avoided by having the narrator describe other characters, the action or the setting.

It is necessary to have your narrator centre-stage, as he or she must be able to relate all the significant events of the story. Therefore, your narrator must be in a plausible position to know or discover the whole story.

It is an odd fact that first-person narrators who are like yourself may not always come across convincingly, especially if you are still close to the events you are describing. The novelist Deborah Moggach has observed that some of her least successful characters have been women of her own age and background, maybe because they are too close to her, 'too blurred to get into focus' (Moggach, 1993, p.133). If you experience this problem, it would be a good idea to try a third-person narration to give yourself some distance.

There is also often the problem of partiality or limited vision with a first-person narration. Will the reader get fed up with a one-sided view? This possibility can be offset by including behaviour and dialogue which contradicts or undermines the narrator's version. This contradiction can provide a shadowy counter-narrative, allowing us the satisfaction of understanding more than the narrator. The character-narrator is telling the story but is unaware of other possible interpretations which we may be picking up.

ACTIVITY 7.3
Reading

Look again at the opening pages of P.F. Kluge's 1996 novel *Biggest Elvis*, Reading 10 (p.450–6). How has the writer avoided the pitfalls of a one-sided narration? Jot down your response.

DISCUSSION

The potential problem of partiality is managed by having another character challenge Wiggins's view. Albert 'Dude' Lane's stinging put-down of Wiggins's missionary zeal calls into question his claims to tap into a transcendent power in the show. After Wiggins's dazzling and persuasive narration, Albert's resistance is unexpected. We might start to wonder if his irritation is justified. Maybe Wiggins is a bit too po-faced, too grandiose? On the other hand, we may feel affronted by Albert's tone and become actively loyal to Wiggins. By setting up an opposition, the author complicates our view and possibly our allegiance.

ACTIVITY 7.4
Writing

- Create a character who is different from you in one or two basic ways: body type, sex, age, wealth, intellect, or morality. Or you might like to use a character you have already been working on. Write up to 250 words from the first-person viewpoint of this character as he or she prepares to deal with a problem.
- Write this same character's account of a past situation. Give the voice authority and panache by avoiding any tone of hesitation or defeat (as Kluge does with Ward Wiggins). Finally, introduce another character who opposes your narrator's view of the story either subtly or dramatically. Use up to 500 words.

The narrator's voice

The reminiscent narrator

In *Biggest Elvis*, Ward Wiggins recalls events that happened a few years ago, in 1990–91. First-person narrators often look further back, recounting stories from a distant past. Most of these narrators are endowed with astonishing memories, able to recall with exactitude every detail of conversations and events which may have happened decades ago.

Readers readily accept this convention and it is one that you may use. But it is also interesting to consider ways of acknowledging the unreliability of memory in such stories. Memory is fallible: we forget things or we make things up or believe what we were told. Our perspective shifts and we see our lives differently at different stages. We adapt our memories to support our current interpretations.

As you have seen in Lesley Glaister's story about her father in Chapter 3, it can be powerful to admit uncertainty about all of the facts recalled. This applies equally in fiction. In Margaret Atwood's *The Blind Assassin* Iris Griffin, now in her eighties, relates the story of her and her sister's entwined lives. She often doubts her own recollections and admits that she has forgotten some supposedly memorable occasions. Here is part of her account of her wedding day:

> There was champagne, of course. There must have been: Winifred would not have omitted it. Others ate. Speeches were made, of which I remember nothing. Did we dance? I believe so. I didn't know how to dance, but I found myself on the dance floor, so some sort of stumbling-around must have occurred.
>
> (Atwood, 2001 [2000], p.293)

Paradoxically, it is her struggle to remember and her partial retrievals of the past which inspire our trust.

ACTIVITY 7.5
Writing

Begin a story with the line:

> I thought I would always remember this, but over time it has become blurred.

Use a narrator who struggles to piece a memory together. The memory can be triggered by a chance meeting or the discovery of an old letter or photograph. Write up to 500 words.

The unreliable narrator

First-person narrators are inevitably fallible. You will have to decide how much your narrator can realistically know and understand. You must also choose whether they are truth-tellers or 'unreliable narrators', who can be either deliberate liars or self-deceivers.

The use of an unreliable narrator is a popular strategy in fiction. Bigots, madmen, innocents and liars address the reader directly. They can try to get us on their side or just assume values and views we don't share. Sometimes the unreliability is more subtle. Narrators may be ignorant of their own faults or motivations, usually in a way that causes disruption. Or they may be reliable in some ways but not in others. However florid or mild the unreliability, these kinds of stories force us to test the speaker's perspective against our own.

Given that we are inclined to trust first-person narratives, how do you signal unreliability? The author has to manipulate the narrator's tone to let us know that he or she is unreliable. The speaker says one thing but unwittingly reveals another. There may also be exaggerations, contradictions, obvious biases, or slips of the tongue.

For example, *The Yellow Wallpaper*, by Charlotte Perkins Gilman (1981 [1892]), shows a woman's mind derailing:

> Even when I go to ride, if I turn my head suddenly and surprise it – there is that smell!
>
> Such a peculiar odor too! I have spent hours in trying to analyze it, to find out what it smelled like.
>
> It is not bad – at first, and very gentle, but quite the subtlest, most enduring odor I ever met.
>
> In this damp weather it is awful, I wake up in the night and find it hanging over me.
>
> It used to disturb me at first. I thought seriously of burning the house – to reach the smell.
>
> (Gilman, 1981 [1892], p.29)

The Remains of the Day, by Kazuo Ishiguro (1990 [1989]), gives a picture of complete self-deception in the story of Stevens, a butler who wrecks his life through a kind of snobbish servility to Lord Darlington, owner of a stately home. In this scene, we see Stevens prioritising his work duties over his father's dying.

> Indeed, my father's face had gone a dull reddish colour, like no colour I had seen on a living being. I heard Miss Kenton say softly behind me: 'His pulse is very weak.' I gazed at my father for a moment, touched his forehead slightly, then withdrew my hand.
>
> 'In my opinion,' Mrs Mortimer said, 'he's suffered a stroke.' With that, she began to cry. I noticed she reeked powerfully of fat and roast cooking. I turned away and said to Miss Kenton:
>
> 'This is most distressing. Nevertheless, I must now return downstairs.'
>
> (Ishiguro, 1990 [1989], p.104)

The whole sad tale of Steven's abject deference to Lord Darlington, who turns out to be a Hitler appeaser and anti-Semite, and his driving away of Miss Kenton, who loves him, is told in a deadened and mirthless style. It would become tedious if it were not for our fascination with the gulf between that language and the reality of the events it attempts to describe.

ACTIVITY 7.6
Writing

- Write in the voice of a narrator who thinks of himself as deeply benevolent and generous. Show through his or her description of another person or group that he possesses a less charitable side. Use up to 150 words.
- Invent an unreliable narrator who is antagonistic towards a colleague. Again in up to 150 words, show that the narrator unknowingly envies or admires the other character.

DISCUSSION

Here is an example of a colleague-loathing schoolteacher who is an unreliable narrator:

> Thorpe is a pitiful specimen. Permanent shaving rash, whiny voice. He looks crumpled and pale as a parched mushroom. I used to have a fantasy about him living his eventless little life in the small cupboard under my stairs. Though I don't know how he managed to insinuate himself into my thoughts. I avoid the ordeal of trying to engage him in normal human conversation – it's hard enough with my pupils. Anyway, he would regard it a distraction from his seven-day working week. I suppose that's how he has collected all his promotions – by working constantly. No one seems to mind that his work is totally useless. I spotted at least twenty factual errors in his latest proposal, some nonsense about cutting truancy figures. Not that I will say anything. One dreadful day very soon, this charmless creature will become my boss.

Lots of clues about unreliability here: the narrator claims to dislike and avoid Thorpe but appears almost obsessed with him. Her fantasy and her notion that he is responsible for her thinking about him hint at a possible denied attraction. Her determination to belittle his work and achievements seems to indicate envy.

Alternating first-person narrators

Novels are frequently composed of a number of first-person narrators, who each have their own chapters, sometimes headed by their names to avoid confusing the reader. It is another method for countering the inevitable partiality of a single narration.

For example, *The Beet Queen* by Louise Erdrich is a novel told through several first-person narrators, including the cousins Mary Adare and Sita Kozka. The story opens with Mary's account of being suddenly abandoned by her mother who runs off with a fairground pilot, The Great Omar, leaving behind her three children, including a baby boy. When the baby wakes, screaming with hunger, Mary is tricked into handing him over to a stranger who offers to get him fed and return him but he disappears. Mary and her brother Karl then stow away on an overnight train, heading for their aunt and uncle's home in Argus. On the way, Mary and Karl get separated and she ends up alone on her relatives' doorstep, clutching a trinket box.

ACTIVITY 7.7

Reading

Read the first short extract from *The Beet Queen*, Reading 12 (pp.458–61). Make some brief notes about your response to Mary's account. Then read Sita's account (p.461–2).

- Does your view of the situation change?
- What about your feelings towards the characters – do they change?
- Why do you think the author chose this method of narration?

DISCUSSION

Mary's story could hardly be more involving or heart-rending. Dumped cruelly and without warning by her mother, suddenly responsible for herself and her brothers, and penniless, she shows great resourcefulness and courage. But she gets parted from both of her brothers and ends up on her relatives' doorstep utterly alone and bereft. She has reached a place of safety but with a resident enemy, Sita, the expert tormentor. The scene in which Mary presents the trinket box to her aunt and uncle, declaring that the contents will pay her way, ratchets up the anguish. As the box is wrenched open to reveal its worthless trinkets and pawnshop ticket, we witness the final stripping of Mary's pride and faith. The girl's mortification is complete and so is our sympathy ...

But then we read Sita's account of Mary's sudden arrival and her own sense of being ousted. We start to see that she is a child too, and suddenly not an only child any longer but someone propelled into a kind of sibling relationship without the usual years of learning how to share. We learn too that she sees Mary's mother, her aunt Adelaide, as a glamorous misunderstood figure, someone she identifies with. She does not believe Mary's accusations against her. Without losing sight of Mary's suffering, we can begin to see that Sita's spitefulness and resentment are understandable.

The author is likely to have chosen this method of alternating narrations precisely because of its jolting effect. It can cause us to switch our allegiance from one character to another, or at least to see things in a more complex way without the comfort of being able to label characters as 'goodies' and 'baddies'. The 'truth' is difficult to locate and cannot be fully delivered by one character's perspective. The presentation of more than one version of events honours this fact and also gives the reader the chance to work things out for themselves.

It is a demanding method, though, and one that is more appropriate for the novel than the short story, which has less room for multiple voices. The writer has to create a different voice for each narrator and try to make them equally interesting, otherwise the reader's attention will flag when their favourite speaker is 'offstage'.

ACTIVITY 7.8

Writing

Invent two characters who are in dispute, for example colleagues competing for a promotion, a father and daughter quarrelling over her choice of husband, an evangelist in debate with an atheist. Or choose your own scenario. Write alternating first-person accounts of the conflict. Try to make each version persuasive and sympathetic. They should both seem plausible, thereby complicating the issue. Use up to 250 words for each account.

Form of narration

First-person stories may be told in a variety of ways, chiefly through:

- *interior monologue* – the private self-communions of the character, which may be verbalised thoughts and reflections or, occasionally, diary writings;
- *dramatic monologue* – in which the character addresses another person or a particular audience in speech or sometimes by letter;

- *detached autobiography* – in which the narrator tells about his or her past life, the passage of time enabling him or her to achieve a fairly dispassionate stance.

The first two modes place the reader in the position of eavesdropper; the latter puts us in the position of acknowledged audience.

Biggest Elvis and *The Beet Queen* are both examples of detached autobiography addressed to a general reader in a highly self-conscious and constructed way. Diary writing and letters are worth experimenting with in stories where a more casual and intimate mode of revelation is appropriate.

The Bridget Jones's diaries are the most famous recent examples of 'private' journals. Notice the shorthand style in the opening of *Bridget Jones: The edge of reason*:

> **Monday 27 January**
>
> *9st 3 (total fat groove), boyfriends 1 (hurrah!), shags 3 (hurrah!), calories 2,100, calories used up by shags 600, so total calories 1,500 (exemplary).*
>
> **7.15 a.m.** Hurrah! The wilderness years are over. For four weeks and five days now have been in functional relationship with adult male thereby proving am not love pariah as previously feared. Feel marvellous, rather like Jemima Goldsmith or similar radiant newlywed opening cancer hospital in veil while everyone imagines her in bed with Imran Khan.
>
> (Fielding, 2000 [1999], p.3)

ACTIVITY 7.9
Reading

Read the opening pages of J.M. Coetzee's *Age of Iron*, Reading 13 on p.463, for an example of a first-person narration addressed to another character. In Cape Town, Elizabeth Curren has just learned that she has cancer. A destitute alcoholic sets up camp outside her house, waiting for her death.

- To whom is the story told?
- What effect does this have?

DISCUSSION

The narrator's story is in the form of a letter to her daughter. It also comes across partly as a private piece of writing, an unburdening prompted by sudden bad news:

> To whom this writing then? The answer: to you but not to you; to me; to you in me.

The effect is poignant and convincing. It seems more plausible that a woman told she will die soon would want to tell her dearest relative rather than some phantom general reader. The fact that her daughter is in America adds to the bleakness of the narrator's isolation.

Choosing a form

You will need to decide your approach at the outset. To whom is the story addressed? To the character-narrator's self, to another character, to a general reader? In what form? How much time has elapsed between the events of the story and its telling? There are stories told as the events are happening, stories told shortly afterwards, and stories recorded long afterwards. If your narrator is remembering events from long ago, how much has he or she changed? Is he still emotionally involved? What is her attitude to her younger self? Given that the narrator already knows the entire story, to what extent is he inclined to control the pace of revelations? For example, in *The Beet Queen*, Mary lets us know in the opening pages that she stayed at her aunt and uncle's house permanently: 'This was where I would sleep every night for the rest of my life' (Reading 12, p.458). Therefore there is no 'suspense' about the outcome; the fascination will come from seeing how the relationships worked out.

Conclusion

First-person narrative requires the creation of a compelling, single voice telling its own story in a way that produces a strong sense of realism. Of course, there is a great deal of artfulness and artifice in the production of this 'realism'. Such stories use the models of personal confession, the diary, autobiography, or memoir. Both first-person fictions and 'life writing' have enjoyed immense popularity in recent years and the boundary between them has blurred. For example, Andrea Ashworth's *Once in a House on Fire* (1998) is an autobiography which reads like a novel; Margaret Atwood's *Cat's Eye* (1990) is a novel which reads like an autobiography. Remember that the techniques you acquire for writing fiction will also enhance your 'life writing', which we will be looking at in Part 4.

References

Ashworth, Andrea (1998) *Once in a House on Fire*, London: Picador.

Atwood, Margaret (1990) *Cat's Eye*, London: Virago Press.

Atwood, Margaret (2001 [2000]) *The Blind Assassin*, London: Virago.

Fielding, Helen (2000 [1999]) *Bridget Jones: The edge of reason*, London: Picador.

Gilman, Charlotte Perkins (1981 [1892]) *The Yellow Wallpaper*, London: Virago.

Hodgins, Jack (1994 [1993]) *A Passion for Narrative: A guide for writing fiction*, New York: St. Martin's Press.

Ishiguro, Kazuo (1990 [1989]) *The Remains of the Day*, London: Faber and Faber.

McCabe, Patrick (1993 [1992]) *The Butcher Boy* Place: Picador.

Moggach, Deborah (1993) 'Fleshing my characters' in Clare Boylan (ed.) *The Agony and the Ego: The art and strategy of fiction writing explored*, London: Penguin.

Roth, Philip (2001 [2000]) *The Human Stain*, London: Vintage.

8 *Point of view: Degrees of knowing*

LINDA ANDERSON

Third-person narration

In a third-person point of view, the writer uses 'he', 'she', or 'they' rather than the first-person 'I'. There are three possible strategies to choose from:

- *Limited omniscience* – where the narrator knows everything that a particular character may see, feel and know but knows nothing more about other protagonists than the character-narrator.
- *Omniscience* – where the narrator knows everything about the events, places and all of the characters, even things which the characters themselves may be incapable of knowing.
- *Objective point of view* – where the narrator knows only what he or she can observe externally, as in a 'fly-on-the-wall' documentary, and recounts this neutrally.

Limited omniscience

This technique is the most commonly used because it enables the writer to capture in the fullest way both the inside and outside views of a character. It is also known as 'single character point of view' because the author allows us to see the world through the perspective of the chosen character. It combines the intimacy of the first-person point of view with a degree of distance as the hidden narrator is able to paraphrase the thoughts of the character, as well as to organise and comment on the story.

Here is an example from a novel-in-progress, *The Tree House*, by Amanda Hodgkinson. The story is about a Polish family who come to live in England after suffering terrible ordeals during the Second World War. The man, Janusz, tries to become an accepted member of his local community but his attempts are undermined by his wife and son. They have survived by hiding and living wild in the birch forests of the Polish countryside and cannot adapt to their new life.

> Gilbert grips the top of the wooden fence. He lowers his voice and Janusz steps closer. 'I've got a bottle of scotch in the garden shed.

> Come over when the women are out shopping on Saturday morning. We can talk about the war.'
>
> Janusz does not want to remember the war. Always go forwards, he says. You can't live in the past. What's the point of remembering things? It's all gone. The past is past. 'That would be nice,' he says, handing Gilbert back his matches.
>
> (Hodgkinson, n.d.)

An anonymous narrator reports everything from Janusz' perspective. It is as if the narrator and reader are confidants. The narrator's ability to convey the main character's inner thoughts, as well as to observe his behaviour from the outside, shows us the tension between Janusz's unexpressed and expressed feelings. In just a few lines, we get a poignant sense of the outsider's dilemma, how much he suppresses in order to fit in.

In first-person narration, we get direct access to the character's consciousness. In third-person limited narration, there is still intimate access to the character's consciousness through the method of 'free indirect style' a fusion of third- and first-person perspectives first developed at the end of the eighteenth century.

In the following example from Virginia Woolf's story, *Lappin and Lapinova*, Rosalind is a few days into her honeymoon. Notice the double vision at work. We get elegant reportage from an invisible narrator mixed with observations using the character's own sense impressions and chatty phrases.

> Ernest was a difficult name to get used to. It was not the name she would have chosen. She would have preferred Timothy, Antony, or Peter. He did not look like Ernest either. [...] But here he was. Thank goodness he did not look like Ernest – no. But what did he look like? She glanced at him sideways. Well, when he was eating toast he looked like a rabbit. Not that anyone else would have seen a likeness to a creature so diminutive and timid in this spruce, muscular young man with the straight nose, the blue eyes, and the very firm mouth. But that made it all the more amusing. His nose twitched very slightly when he ate. So did her pet rabbit's.
>
> (Woolf, 1949, in Lee, 1987, p.20)

ACTIVITY 8.1

Writing

■ Recall an argument you have had with someone. Write about the quarrel from your opponent's point of view, using third-person limited omniscience. The objective here is to practise empathy with points of view that antagonise you in reality. Empathy is not always easy to attain but it expands the fiction writer's imaginative range like nothing else. Write up to 300 words.

- Take one of your own memories and cast it in a third-person limited point of view. Don't aim to write it as a strictly 'truthful' account. Release it into a fictional story, feeling free to invent different details, deepen the drama or change the outcome. The aim is to give you practice in distancing yourself from your own experiences and using them as a fund of fictional material. Write up to 500 words.

Omniscient narrator

The third-person omniscient voice is the most wide-ranging and authoritative point of view. An omniscient narrator can enter the consciousness of any character; describe that character's appearance, speech, behaviour, thoughts, history, and motivations; know what has happened elsewhere or in the past and what will happen in the future; intervene in the narrative to make asides, such as comments on the action, forewarnings of future events, or wise reflections on life.

Notice the authoritative tone and summarising style of this extract from Anton Chekhov's *Lady with Lapdog*.

> He was not yet forty, but he had a twelve-year-old daughter and two schoolboy sons. He had been married off when he was still in his second year at the university, and his wife seemed to him now to be almost twice his age. She was a tall, black-browed woman, erect, dignified, austere, and, as she liked to describe herself, a 'thinking person'. She was a great reader, preferred the new 'advanced' spelling, called her husband by the more formal 'Dimitry' and not the familiar 'Dmitry'; and though he secretly considered her not particularly intelligent, narrow-minded, and inelegant, he was afraid of her and disliked being at home.
>
> (Chekhov, 1964 [1899], p.264)

Third-person omniscience was a popular choice in nineteenth-century novels where the author might even address the audience as 'dear reader' or 'gentle reader'. It became unfashionable as discoveries in psychology and science throughout the twentieth century eroded belief in the possibility of absolute 'truth' and impartiality. A.S. Byatt wrote recently about the prevalence of first-person narratives in modern historical novels and felt obliged to speak up for her own preference for 'the unfashionable Victorian third-person narrator' (2001, quoted in Lodge 2003 [2002], p.86)

But omniscience remains a standard method for certain 'genre' narratives, like science fiction, and it also appears to be making a comeback in literary fiction. For example, later in this chapter you will read the opening of Rick Moody's *Purple America*, a novel from the point of view of an omniscient narrator with a passionate, erudite voice and a lot to say about the treatment of the elderly and about the dangers of the nuclear power industry. Omniscience could be right for you or for certain stories you want to tell if you have a distinctive style or a lot to say about your characters, theme, or period of time.

Shifting third-person method

A lot of contemporary writers use omniscience in a modified form with minimal authorial intrusions. They use alternating third-person subjective viewpoints.

ACTIVITY 8.2
Reading

For a contemporary example, read the extract from Pat Barker's *Another World*, a novel with multiple points of view, Reading 14 on p.465.

■   What is the impact of the shift from the mother's mind to the son's?
■   How much authorial intrusion is there?

DISCUSSION

Fran's point of view is so involving and intimate, even making us privy to her bodily discomfort, that the sudden shift into Gareth's coarse, angry thought is dramatic. It is the sort of switch that could annoy or confuse a reader but Barker has established her method in this novel from the start. It is written as a series of limited omniscient voices alternating within the same chapters and linked by occasional authorial commentary, as here, giving us information about the school: 'But look at it he does. It's empty now, of course, in the middle of August, a long, low huddle of buildings, one of them with its windows boarded up, because last winter the pipes burst and flooded the labs and there's no money to get them repaired.'

If you want to tell a story using multiple characters' viewpoints without much direct intervention from an omniscient narrator, establish your method early on to accustom the reader. Signal each shift into another point of view by creating a slightly different tone and voice. It is also reader-friendly to use separate chapters or sections for each viewpoint, signalling changes by starting a new paragraph.

Objective point of view

The third-person objective point of view is impersonal. The writer is restricted to recording what may be witnessed from external appearances and facts. He or she will not enter the characters' heads or offer any interpretations or judgements. The technique is similar to that of film in that everything must be inferred from gestures, expressions, actions, dialogue, and silences. This technique can have a lot of appeal for writers and readers who enjoy a pared down, austere style. The reader has to ponder signs and clues in order to figure things out. On the other hand, such stories can also seem a little too spare and clinical. Try it out and see if this method suits you or might be right for some of your stories. It is an excellent discipline for writers who tend to explain too much in their stories.

ACTIVITY 8.3

Reading

Read Ernest Hemingway's 'The Doctor and the Doctor's Wife', Reading 15 on p.467. This is one of a series of stories featuring Nick Adams, a doctor's son.

■ Without access to the characters' thoughts and feelings, can you tell what they are thinking? How?

■ Why do you think the writer chose a neutral viewpoint for this story?

DISCUSSION

In each half of the story we see the doctor being humiliated and how he deals with it. Everything is indicated through physical gestures, actions, and the way the characters speak. Dick Boulton and the doctor's wife are overbearing in dramatically different ways. Dick confronts the doctor head-on in what seems to be a planned attack, teasing him edgily about stealing the logs. His speech is disrespectful and provocative. Notice particularly his frequent use of 'Doc' and the way he persists in his accusations while denying that he cares about them. The doctor is instantly and visibly shamed.

After this bruising encounter, the doctor returns home and is questioned by his invalid wife. She pleads with him not to keep anything from her but undermines what he says. The repetitions in her speech are revealing. She calls her husband 'dear' all the time even when she is scolding him. Her final pronouncement, 'Dear, I don't think, I really don't think that anyone would really do a thing like that', brooks no argument. She comes across as a sweet-voiced tyrant. The doctor defends himself with terse replies, the solacing action of cleaning his gun, and finally by going out for a walk. The story ends with the doctor and his son conspiring to ignore her summons of the boy in order to go off together. It seems that both of them want to escape her pious authority.

The story is very short and yet provides a strong sense of a harshly divided society and a bleak marriage. The doctor tends patients in the Indian camp but refers to Dick Boulton's wife as a 'squaw'. Boulton himself is casually referred to as a 'half-breed' in the vernacular realism of the narrative. The context helps us to understand why the row explodes so quickly. The doctor cannot stand being challenged by what he regards as a low-status male; Boulton rejoices in turning the tables. In the final two pages we get just one scene from a marriage but the chasm between the two people seems so huge and habitual that we feel the depth of estrangement between them.

Your own interpretation of the story and your speculations about the underlying emotions of the characters may be different from mine. With a story like this, each reader fills in the gaps for themselves and some things can only be guessed. This is precisely what Hemingway intended. His theory was that 'you could omit anything if you knew that you omitted it and the omitted part would strengthen the story and make people feel more than they understood' (Lodge, 2003 [2002], p.70).

Consistency of point of view

Once you have chosen a point of view for a particular story, it is important to stick to it with clarity and consistency. But this is a skill which requires practice. Try out the different points of view to find your own strengths. Each time you read a new novel, take a look at the point(s) of view chosen by the author. Make notes in your writer's notebook about how effective you think they are.

Point of view errors tend to occur with the use of third-person omniscience. Unlimited powers can be hard to handle! Because an omniscient author may enter the mind of any character, new writers sometimes dutifully report what is going on in everyone's mind, flitting back and forth from head to head. Here's an invented example:

> The restaurant seemed suddenly too noisy and hot. Robert wished they could be somewhere else, but he had promised Anthea this big celebration. She was secretly bristling with anger at his choice of venue as she ordered the most boring dishes on the menu. Their waitress hovered reluctantly, worrying about the ladder in her tights. It had already been a long shift.

A reader is likely to get baffled and annoyed by this sort of writing. It is impossible to tell who is an important character and who is secondary. Do we need to invest a lot of attention in the waitress or will she disappear soon from the narrative? The flitting from head to head is dizzying, like those films shot with a hand-held camera veering from one speaker to the next.

The way to make this example consistent is to lock in to one observing mind. Let's make Robert the viewpoint character here. We can indicate the same facts as he sees them or interprets them.

> The restaurant seemed suddenly too noisy and hot. Robert wished they could be somewhere else, but he had promised Anthea this big celebration. She didn't exactly look grateful, though, and was ordering dishes he knew she disliked. The sullen waitress wasn't helping to dispel his anxieties.

Sometimes a point of view shift happens in mid-sentence:

> She dreaded her teacher's response and braced herself for a stony-faced critique but he was impressed, even starting to wonder if she might be a star student.

This kind of shift is disturbing. Again, it works better if we lock in to the original observer and show the teacher's response through her viewpoint.

> She dreaded her teacher's response and braced herself for a stony-faced critique but he was clearly impressed, even saying that her essay was one of the best he had ever seen.

In the following example, we start off in a single character point of view but then in mid-sentence shift into an external view of him. As he cannot know how his own face changes or what effect it has, this is a jarring breach of the point of view.

He liked the look of his new tenant. A trainee solicitor! She would add a bit of class to the place. He caught the drift of her scent and smiled at her, transforming his pinched face into unexpected charm.

These kinds of slippages and muddles happen easily, even to experienced writers, especially in the creation of first drafts when you are trying to include as many significant details as possible. So don't worry about them but do look out for them. Mid-sentence shifts are particularly ugly and destabilising and should be avoided.

Multiple points of view and flitting from head to head *may* be used but must be handled cautiously. It is usually best to confine your viewpoint characters to a few and not to move around within the same page. But as with most general principles, this is not a 'rule'. You might decide that the power to move briefly into different minds suits a particular story you want to tell. The point is that you may do whatever you decide so long as you know what you're doing and stay in control.

ACTIVITY 8.4
Reading

For example, read part of the opening chapter of Tim Lott's, *Rumours of a Hurricane*, Reading 16 on p.471. This is a novel about the contrasting fortunes and failing marriage of Charlie and Maureen Buck who move to Milton Keynes during the Thatcher years. The extract begins just after an opening scene in which Maureen thinks happily about her divorce and looks forward to her day's work.

Track the omniscient viewpoint as it tells us the thoughts of different cameo characters.

DISCUSSION

On one level this is a story of two 'ordinary' lives and the novel does settle into their alternating points of view later. But the way they both change during the get-rich-quick eighties – the woman empowering and liberating herself, the man losing everything – is intended as a 'state-of-nation' picture, a study of the impact of Thatcherism on culture and morality. The author establishes this wider significance at the outset by including the thoughts of bystanders at the scene of an accident, ambulance men and a surgeon, none of whom will appear again in the novel.

ACTIVITY 8.5
Writing

Imagine a conflict between two characters. An elderly man meets his estranged son. A woman decides to call off her wedding. A parent confronts a teacher about school bullying. Or invent your own scenario.

Write about the situation three times from three different points of view, using up to 300 words for each version:

- third-person limited omniscient;
- third-person omniscient;
- third-person objective.

DISCUSSION

This exercise can help you to identify your own strengths and preferences. Did you enjoy presenting the workings of your main character's mind? Or did you prefer to keep the reader at a greater distance? Which version works best for your story and why? You might like to expand your favourite version into a completed story.

Some unusual points of view

First- and third-person points of view are the most commonly used. Once you have become familiar with them, it can be refreshing to try out more unusual strategies.

Second-person narration

In a second-person narration, the main character is referred to as 'you', which almost assigns the reader a role as player in the unfolding story. It is a provocative device, which can meet with resistance from the reader. 'You are standing watching the sunset ...' (*No, I'm not.*) ... 'when the door is flung open' (*No, it's not.*) ... 'and Amy is pointing a gun at your head' ... (*Wrong again!*) But when the method succeeds, it can involve the reader deeply in the story. It is best used for stories where the writer wants to convey the universality of an individual situation or for stories about lonely, obsessive characters. In that case, the 'you' seems to refer to a divided self, as if the character is so wounded or alienated that he has had to become his own confidant. This technique is difficult to sustain over a long narrative as it can become airless and tedious, so most writers alternate it with other points of view in long narratives.

ACTIVITY 8.6

Reading and writing

Read the two extracts illustrating second-person narration, Reading 17 on p.476 and Reading 18 on p.477.

The first is from John McGahern's *The Dark*, which is about a troubled adolescent boy. After a quarrel with his father, the narrator contemplates his father's boots and is overcome with compassion.

Jamaica Kincaid's *Girl* shows an inventive use of the second person. The girl's mind is saturated with a barrage of internalised orders from a controlling mother-figure:

' ... this is how you set a table for tea; this is how you set a table for dinner; this is how you set a table for dinner with an important guest ...'. Without resorting to obvious 'message', the piece seems to make a statement about female conditioning.

Now try this method out for yourself.

■ Invent a lonely character in some kind of confinement, for example a prisoner on remand, an infatuated person whose love is unrequited, or a homesick student at boarding school. Using the second person, describe a good memory from the character's past and compare it with their present predicament. Write up to 500 words.

■ Using *Girl* as a model, write a set of intimidating or satirical instructions in the second person about how to be a writer. Write 150 to 200 words.

Stream of consciousness

'Stream of consciousness' was the phrase first used by the psychologist William James to describe the ceaseless, random flow of thoughts, ideas, memories, and fantasies in people's minds. Dorothy Richardson, James Joyce, and Virginia Woolf were ground-breaking practitioners of stream-of-consciousness in fiction. These writers tried to mimic psychological reality, capturing the crazy paving of the human mind.

Here is a brief extract from Molly Bloom's famous 63-page, 1-sentence interior monologue which concludes Joyce's *Ulysses*.

> [...] what could you make of a man like that I'd rather die 20 times over than marry another of their sex of course hed never find another woman like me to put up with him the way I do know me come sleep with me yes and he knows that too at the bottom of his heart take that Mrs Maybrick that poisoned her husband for what I wonder in love with some other man yes it was found out on her wasnt she the downright villain to go and do a thing like that of course some men can be dreadfully aggravating drive you mad and

always the worst word in the world what do they ask us to marry
them for if were so bad as all that comes to yes because they cant
get on without us white Arsenic she put in his tea off flypaper wasnt
it I wonder why they call it that if I asked him hed say its from the
Greek leave us as wise as we were before she must have been madly
in love with the other fellow to run the chance of being hanged O
she didn't care if that was her nature what could she do besides
theyre not brutes enough to go and hang a woman surely are they
[...]

(Joyce, 1960 [1922], p.880)

Molly Bloom's thoughts are given in a rush of consciousness, in which
we can discern some coherence. She grumbles to herself about her
husband and men, and matrimony in general. Her thoughts about
husband-poisoner Mrs Maybrick veer from conventional disgust to
fascination and sneaking sympathy.

The advantage of this method is that it can seem very authentic and
alive. It has been influential in the way that writers now render
subjectivity, trying to capture the fluid nature of thought processes,
though this is usually done nowadays in a modified form, with
punctuation. This is because untrammelled stream-of-consciousness can
slow narrative pace since it is inevitably rambling and unfocused. But it
can be an effective technique to use in short bursts, particularly for
rants, intoxicated states of mind, or traumatised moments.

ACTIVITY 8.7
Writing

Take the situation of a clown putting on make-up before an illuminated
mirror. He has just been evicted from his flat. Write up to 250 words of
his thoughts, using stream of consciousness. You may omit punctuation
if you like or use some as in this example: 'Now for the application of
big red lips. I see red I see red I see red. Show must go on. Show
nothing to punters ...'

Voice: Tone and attitude

Whatever point of view you choose, it will deliver a particular voice. A
convincing narrative voice is a crucial element in achieving the
distinctive tone of a piece of fiction.

Writers often feel daunted about the possibility of writing anything
original. Everything about the human condition has already been

beautifully said. There have been billions of births, bereavements and betrayals in the world, and there is nothing new under the sun. But when something big happens to *you*, it feels new and personal. It is this freshness of experience, no matter how 'commonplace', that can be captured by creating an individual voice for a piece of fiction.

ACTIVITY 8.8
Reading

To see the impact of dramatically different narrative voices on the same theme, read the openings of Rick Moody's *Purple America* and Andrew Miller's *Oxygen*, Readings 19 and 20 (p.479; p.483).

- What is the shared theme?
- Which point of view has each author chosen?
- How would you describe the narrative voices in each?

DISCUSSION

Both stories are about the anguished sons of ailing mothers. They reflect the common plight of adult offspring having to come to terms with a parent's dying. The opening chapter of *Oxygen* uses a third-person limited viewpoint, bringing us close to Alec, the younger son. *Purple America* has an omniscient narrator who even uses one of the 'old-fashioned' devices of omniscience when he concludes with a final moral verdict in praise of carers.

The voices could hardly be more different. *Purple America* opens with a deliberately dazzling piece of rhetoric. It has one unbroken four-page sentence, which rises to a crescendo through the use of anaphora, the repetition of the same word at the beginning of successive clauses for rhetorical effect. As 'whosoever' is a word hijacked from the New Testament promise of victory over death,[1] this creates a kind of transgressive liturgy in which the narrator is claiming a sacramental value for the rituals of caring for an elderly parent. The voice is rousing and provocative, full of wit, rage, and tenderness. Ultimately, in his praise of carers everywhere, the narrator moves out from the almost unbearably intimate scene.

By contrast, *Oxygen* has a very restrained tone in keeping with the reticent coping behaviour of both mother and son. This understatement makes the moment of pure anguish, when it comes, all the more piercing: '[He] wondered to himself what could possibly comfort him. Where on earth he might look for consolation or ease.'

---

[1] 'Whosoever believeth in me, he shall never die.' (John 11, 26)

The effects of both pieces – stunningly tender and transgressive; or muted and moving – emerge from their respective authors' decisions about point of view and voice.

Conclusion

The critical element of any point of view is the narrative voice, a defining tone or attitude which filters through the story. Here is a summary of what this entails in relation to the viewpoints explored in this chapter and the preceding one:

- With a first-person narrator, the voice will be that character's distinctive language and phraseology, his or her way of thinking and writing.

- With second-person narration, the 'you' includes the reader as a player in the unfolding story or refers to the main character's divided self.

- With third-person limited omniscience, there will be a combination of the main character's personal voice and the narrator's reporting of that in free indirect style.

- With multiple viewpoints in the third person, there will be a subtle shift of tone each time you enter a different character's point of view.

- With third-person objective, the voice will be in a dispassionate tone, offering no interpretation of the events witnessed.

- With full omniscience, the tone will reveal the persona of your storyteller: majestic, barnstorming, forensic, elegiac, witty, unassuming, whatever you decide.

It requires practice to 'get' these various methods, so do refer back to the examples given. Also study the manipulation of point of view in every fiction you read, making notes in your notebook about strategies that impress you and that you would like to try.

References

Chekhov, Anton (1964 [1899]) *Lady with Lapdog and Other Stories*, David Margarshack (tr.), London: Penguin.

Hodgkinson, Amanda (no date) *The Tree House*, manuscript (unpublished).

Joyce, James (1960 [1922]) *Ulysses*, London: The Bodley Head.

Lodge, David (2003 [2002]) *Consciousness and the Novel*, London: Penguin Books.

Woolf, Virginia (1987 [1949]) *Lappin and Lapinova* in Hermione Lee (ed.) *The Secret Self 2: Short stories by women*, Everyman's Library, London: J.M. Dent & Sons.

9 *Showing and telling*

DEREK NEALE

What are showing and telling?

Having created a character or three, established a setting, and generally got the story moving, the new writer is often then given technical advice, such as 'show don't tell'. Yet what does this apparently simple instruction mean? On one level 'show don't tell' would seem an easy rule to follow. In practical terms it means that instead of writing 'He was angry' you describe the way 'He screwed the piece of paper into a tight ball and threw it so hard it bounced off the wall and the table before landing back at his feet.'

This is certainly one version of what is meant, but 'show don't tell' is an instruction that is interpreted and intended in a number of subtly different ways. In this chapter you will see different illustrations of what 'showing' and 'telling' might mean in practice.

First let's look at where the terms originated.

Read the essay by Lindsay Clarke, 'Going the Last Inch: Some thoughts on showing and telling', Reading 21 on p.487. In particular write down in your notebook your responses to these questions:

ACTIVITY 9.1
Reading

- What is the difference between the two versions of 'crying' talked of by Clarke, especially in relation to time?
- In what way might abstractions be a problem?

It's important to notice the equal emphasis given to both showing and telling: they each have their uses. Following on from James's exhortation ('Dramatize, dramatize, dramatize'), showing is often equated with a writing method that dramatises; telling is often seen as a writing method that summarises. Showing in this sense can be seen as a type of writing which unpacks the detail of a scene or episode; telling by contrast is a type of writing which tends to pass more fleetingly over the details.

DISCUSSION

The Golding passage, for instance where the crying goes on 'breath after breath', seems to unpack the action of crying, to stretch time, so the moment is expanded and more fully matches the significance of the tears. As Clarke suggests, showing and telling are relative methods. When you write 'he cried' it is in effect showing the emotional state of sadness in action, but it has only gone one step away from that abstract state, to a first basic action. It is a very brief summation of what the real life state of being sad usually entails. It hasn't attempted to imitate the duration of the crying or sadness.

Real time and fictional time are rarely aligned, but there is a proportionate relationship. Sometimes it will be appropriate to say 'he cried'; sometimes it will be necessary to spend longer with the scene, to breathe life into the moments of crying, the actual detail, the internal thoughts, and perhaps the causes and consequences. Remember that at climactic moments, fictional time can expand and have an even longer duration than the equivalent 'real' event, although often it will have a much shorter duration.

Showing

Sometimes you will have to cover events quickly because the small detail of those events will not be relevant to your story; sometimes you will have to pause over events because those particulars will be of great significance, either to the character or your story in general.

Avoiding abstractions

Telling, as Clarke suggests, sometimes summarises abstract emotions – such as love, sadness, or happiness – in a way that doesn't quite satisfy the reader. There are times when it will be appropriate to write 'She was irate' or 'He was sad', but there will be times when your reader will need more: they will need to see the crunched up paper bouncing off the walls; they will want to see your characters laughing or crying, and to be interpreting events for themselves.

ACTIVITY 9.2
Writing

'He was sad', if shown, might become: 'His shoulders heaved and he let out a long, frail sigh as he turned towards the door.'

'She was irate', if shown, might become: 'She glared through him, past him, stabbing the desk with her pencil.'

Using these as examples, for each of the statements below containing an emotional or physical state, write one or two sentences showing it in action:

■ He felt tired.

■ She loved him.

■ They loathed one another.

■ The children were bored.

■ Grandmother came home drunk.

DISCUSSION

As soon as you ask questions about how to bring a particular state to life, you also ask questions about who he was or who she was, and what might have made them tired or bored or whatever. You then start picturing scenarios and inventing details about the characters. Your reader will be doing this too. They feed off every scrap of information you give them, and soon become actively involved in recreating the causes and consequences of events.

In this way showing generates more vivid sensory pictures and arouses a more pressing intrigue than telling. You might show the grandmother falling over and the reader will be immediately intrigued. Why is she falling over? Is she ill? Has she been drinking? Why has she been drinking? Does she always do this? Did something happen that caused her to get drunk? You may not have got as far as answering these questions in your one or two sentences, but it is important to remember that this is the way the reader is working, and most readers like being active in the story in this fashion.

The role of your reader

Readers want to be involved; they want to ask questions and like to use their imagination in providing some of the answers themselves. If you give your reader too quick and full a summary of events you disengage their creativity and run the serious risk of sending them to sleep. David Lodge suggests that 'A novel written entirely in the mode of summary would [...] be almost unreadable' (1992, Lodge, p.122). Certainly if you have a predominance of telling in your writing, your style might veer towards reportage. Yet telling is importantly used to speed up the tempo, 'rushing us through events which would be uninteresting or *too* interesting – therefore distracting, if lingered over' (ibid., p.122).

For instance, in a simple passage of summary such as 'They went to the park and he said to her that it was going to be okay', we get the basic information about location, participants and what happened, all conveyed in matter-of-fact fashion, via the voice of the narrator.

In a 'shown' version of the same episode there would be more detail and it would be dramatised. It might read like this:

> The lights from the road reached the children's slide, but the swings where they were sitting were in almost complete dark. A dog sauntered past, sniffing briefly before running back off towards the road. The wind got up.
>
> > 'It will be alright you know,' he said.
> > 'Yeah,' she said, her hair falling over her eyes.
> > 'No, really – it will be alright.'
> > 'I said okay, didn't I,' she said, pushing off and swinging high into the starless night.

The information about the wind, the dog, the dark and the road provide a much fuller picture, as does the dialogue. The reader might even be delving into what isn't being said and starting to invent the dynamic between the two characters. If the incident in the park is an insignificant part of the story then all this detail and the level of invention, on the part of writer and reader, would be wasted and, what's more, misleading. The reader would be looking for significance where there was none.

ACTIVITY 9.3
Writing

Bearing in mind the scene in the park as an example, write a 'shown' version (using up to 100 words) of one of the following sentences:

- He went to see his father to make arrangements to move the furniture.
- They were all together in one room and she felt tired and claustrophobic.
- She waited with her sister, drinking tea, seeking reassurance.
- Back at the office the solicitor called with a new piece of evidence that had come to light.

DISCUSSION

Showing doesn't mean that you include all possible detail, but rather the pertinent detail. The scene in the park, for instance, includes the details about light and dark because that echoes the uneasy state between the two characters. Similarly, the dog's quick departure signals the unfriendly and private nature of the scene. When attempting to 'show' in this fashion, try to be concise and don't include unnecessary information. If you found that you went over the word limit, go back and cut. When editing, always ask the questions: 'Have I shown too much?' and 'Do I need to show that?'

If you get time, write in your notebook a 'shown' version for the three sentences that you didn't pick.

Telling

Now let's look at some stories where telling dominates.

Read 'The Artist' and 'The Dream', Readings 22 and 23 (p.492 and p.494).

ACTIVITY 9.4

Reading

As you read, in your notebook write down:
- any elements of the stories that 'show' rather than 'tell';
- how time is handled in the stories.

DISCUSSION

In terms of time and place these two stories never seem to pause. Swathes of time are covered – in 'The Dream' the merchant travels from Baghdad to Cairo in the blink of an eye; he sleeps through a robbery, which is summarised in a sentence. In 'The Artist' Jane gets married and proceeds to try various artistic endeavours at a rapid pace without any of them really being dramatised. Yet in both stories there are some shown elements, for instance when characters speak. Note, though, that in neither story do such exchanges have a real setting. All we know in 'The Dream', for instance, is that it is 'three days later' when the policeman talks to the merchant; we don't get the co-ordinates of a fully dramatised scene – a description of the room, what the characters looked like, or what they may have been thinking.

Exposition

You might have found 'The Artist' and 'The Dream' to be like fairy stories or parables. Such stories seem to have some other purpose than realising the particular details of a world. They operate in a simple, linear fashion, starting from point A and going straight to point B then C. Their respective plots dominate, suggesting that the overall shape and combination of events is more important than the small detail. The characters are types rather than real people. In 'The Dream', for instance, the main character is just 'a merchant'; he isn't even given a name.

These are perhaps not the sort of characters you wish to create in your fiction, but you can still use such summary techniques to help realise your peripheral characters or action, and to develop your main character, for instance, by giving them some history, what is sometimes called 'backstory'. Showing everything you know about your characters is neither possible nor desirable. Some information will be best left to summary.

One version of the fiction writing process has it that writing is all about information – withholding it and disclosing it. The writer is always doing one or the other – either keeping things unknown or drip-feeding the reader with details. Revealing information about certain aspects of your story is often termed 'exposition' – you are exposing the flesh and bones of it, what has happened, what is happening, what might happen. Ursula Le Guin suggests that all narratives carry some explanatory and descriptive load and that you can learn the skill of handling this 'expository freight' by making the information part of the story. For Le Guin, as for many other writers, the craft lies in breaking the exposition into small deposits so it doesn't come out as a lecture or an 'expository lump' (1998, p.119).

When writing summary passages that apparently 'tell' a lot, it's important to remember that they should also be leaving a lot out. Some of this omitted information will be irrelevant, but some of it can be the sort of detail that, by its very omission, will keep your reader awake and active. So, a summary of the drunken grandmother's backstory, for instance, might cover the fact that she has been drinking for twenty years, that she especially likes a certain kind of malt whisky, that she has two sons and five grandchildren, that she is divorced but still on amicable terms with her former husband, and that she once had a daughter. But this summary might then exclude crucial details about why the grandmother 'once had' a daughter. Has she been disowned? Is the daughter dead? Was there an argument and did the daughter leave home? Was this the cause of the drinking? The reader still needs to be asking questions when you are in telling mode; it should never be an excuse to overwrite or to give too much information.

You might use a telling technique when your narrative needs to move quickly in terms of location or time; between different eras of a character's life, for instance, or when they move from place to place, as you saw in Chapter 6. In most cases you might not want to detail the intervening action and events, but need nonetheless to make the reader aware of the shift. So, the story of the drunken grandmother might cover ten years, culminating in the grandmother being reunited with her errant daughter. It would be impossible to 'show' all of the intervening years, so you 'tell' just significant details, establish the passage of time, as with the merchant going to and from Cairo in 'The Dream'.

Picking a character either from your notebook or one you encountered and worked on in Activity 9.2 or 9.3, write a brief passage of backstory connected to the character. In your summary include a movement in time, that is the passing of years or days. Write up to 200 words.

ACTIVITY 9.5
Writing

Dialogue and stories

Writers have often experimented with the balance between showing and telling. Katherine Mansfield, for instance, in stories like 'The Black Cap', tries to dispense with telling altogether, by writing the narrative details in the form of stage directions; the rest of the story is written in dialogue. As you will see in the next activity, the story looks more like a play script.

Read Mansfield's 'The Black Cap', Reading 24 on p.496. Note in your notebook:

- how location and character appearance are realised;
- how the dialogue moves the story forward.

Take a particular moment from 'The Dream' or 'The Artist' and write it as a 'play script' story, as in 'The Black Cap'. Concentrate on just one sentence of the original story and produce only a brief adaptation (up to 200 words). When you have finished, in your notebook write some reflections on the following:

- what you consider to be the elements you lose by using this method compared to a more conventional narrative;
- what you consider to be gained.

ACTIVITY 9.6
Reading and writing

DISCUSSION   As soon as you begin inhabiting the characters and pausing over a dramatic event you start thinking about the story slightly differently. Showing events in this way may well mean that the story becomes different altogether. One of the potential gains from realising events in this way is the dramatic energy it harnesses in bringing the characters to life. However, you may have missed the power of description: the potential of certain details related to place and character, together with sensory details, to reveal the story. You might also have missed the ability to go into a character's thoughts. Mansfield achieves this to a certain extent with the woman's monologue, on the way to the station. Monologues and soliloquies are the way in which stage plays usually achieve the sense of a character's interior life.

You might find that this stage script method, as used by Mansfield in 'The Black Cap', seems strange because it isn't a conventional way of presenting dialogue in a story. It has, however, been used by other writers in sections of their novels – Samuel Richardson in *Clarissa* (1985 [1748]), James Joyce in *Ulysses* (1960 [1922]), and more recently Andrew O'Hagan in *Personality* (2003). The more widely known methods for presenting dialogue might place the speech within quotation marks and accompany the lines with a reporting clause – he said, she said, he asked, she replied. These clauses are sometimes left out, if the identity of the speaker is well established, and usually when the dialogue involves just two characters. It can get confusing otherwise. Whatever method of presenting dialogue you use, it is important for your reader that the identity of a speaker is unambiguous, and that your method is consistent throughout each individual story.

Mixing drama and summary

Even in stories relying heavily on dialogue and which are predominantly dramatised – such as 'The Doctor and the Doctor's Wife', read in the previous chapter – there is a fine balance between 'shown' and 'told' elements. Some parts of the story are still revealed through summary – such as the description of why the doctor got the logs cut up. This balance between showing and telling will vary according to the writer and the demands of a particular story.

Read 'I could see the smallest things' by Raymond Carver and 'The Dying Room' by Georgina Hammick, Readings 25 and 26 (p.501; p.505).

These are stories that 'show' a lot, yet also reveal themselves through telling. Write in your notebook:

■ any elements of showing and what these give to the stories;
■ any elements of telling and what these give to the stories.

Most noticeable in these stories is how the action is predominantly 'shown' through the use of detail and dialogue. It is left to the reader to interpret events as the narrator takes a back seat. Initially the Carver story details the actions and mundane preoccupations of a sleepless night, leading to the gate and the meeting with Sam. In this way it is showing the insomnia through action. The story uses telling when the backstory is summarised: the neighbours' relationship is given a concise history. This gives the reader the gist of the conflict, but still leaves them wanting to know more, and indeed imagining more. Notice also how showing isn't a licence to overwrite or crowd the reader out with unnecessary detail. The reader is most active in such stories; the balance of withholding and disclosing information is crucial to this. There are many details being offered, but there is less processed information; the reader is in charge of the interpretation. In 'The Dying Room' the story is largely made up of direct speech. Curiously it presents this using the reporting clauses – he said, she said – but it omits the quotation marks. The use of dialogue and the dramatic scene is its showing method, though it has some telling passages too – for instance when the mother's occupation of cook is summarised early on, so giving the reader background to the character. Such passages tend to be brief and isolated, but, as will be seen in the next chapter, have a crucial effect on the structure of the story.

Dialogue and subtext

If you sit around for a while in a café or a waiting room listening to conversations, you will notice it is fairly difficult, and often impossible, to recall such exchanges word for word after the event. Lines of real-life dialogue are often fragmentary; people don't finish sentences, and the overall conversation is often without shape. Such daily conversations can be mundane and insignificant. Yet the words will always be remembered in your fictional exchanges, and the conversations will always be shaped and hold a meaning, even if they are seemingly about mundane things. You will never be presenting dialogue just for the sake of itself; it will always have a purpose, for example illustrating things like character, action, atmosphere, mood, and plot.

Using dialogue allows you to develop a character, as you have already seen in Chapter 5. Once characters speak they seem to take on another level of creation, as if they have started breathing. Dialogue can also be useful when you have a major plot point to make. Going back to our story of the drunken grandmother, for instance, her missing daughter might come home. If you write 'then the daughter returned', this might seem too swift for such a significant moment. If you capture the return dramatically through dialogue, you make the event more plausible. It might read like this:

> As she reached for the light switch she felt a presence in the room.
> A voice said, 'Hello, Mum.' She knew the voice.
>
> 'H ... h ... hell ...' she stuttered, as she looked up.
> 'Well, am I worth a hug?'
> 'A hug?' she said.
> 'After all these years, aren't I worth even that?'

With the above dialogue and the dialogue between the man and the woman in the park, which we looked at earlier in the chapter, there is room for the reader to climb in between the lines and invent the dynamic between each set of characters. In each dialogue the reader is presented with the challenge of constructing and interpreting the scenario and what might be happening and what is really being communicated by the characters. The words spoken in any dialogue are only part of the exchange between people; often the unspoken elements can be louder, if less articulate. As seen in Chapter 5, these unspoken words may consist of the things that the characters cannot or dare not say, or may not even know. The dialogue you give your reader must offer an indication of this other, unspoken communication, what is often referred to as the 'subtext'.

The subtext can be to do with the atmosphere between characters; implied information about the participants; and implied information about the story and plot. David Mamet says:

> In the bad film, the fellow says, 'hello, Jack, I'm coming over to your home this evening because I need to get the money you

borrowed from me.' In the good film, he says, 'where the hell were you yesterday?' [...] The less you narrate [in the dialogue], the more the audience is going to say, 'wow. What the *heck* is happening here? What the *heck* is going to happen next ...?'

(Mamet, 1992, p.71)

The same is true for fiction writers trying to activate their readers. In the scene of the daughter's return, for instance, if her mother came straight out with: 'Oh, I've missed you, and I'm glad to see you, but I'm angry too. Where have you been all this time?' And if the daughter replied: 'I ran off with a boy. We had a baby together and I didn't want to tell you. Then he left me, but now I'm back. Have you got any money I could borrow?', it would be too straightforward for the reader. They would be left with nothing to imagine and the exchange would seem implausible – no one tends to talk that explicitly.

Similarly, with the exchange in the park between the man and the woman, the reader is left thinking: 'What will be okay? Why is she getting angry with him? Why is he trying to placate her? Is someone dying? Is she pregnant? What is causing the tension?' The reader is hooked. If the writer rushes into answering too many of these questions then the reader's sense of anticipation might be wasted.

Look back over the Carver and Hammick stories. Identify the following elements and detail them in your notebook:

ACTIVITY 9.8
Reading

- the parts of the dialogue that seem to be masking something and getting the reader to ask questions and imagine answers;
- the parts of the dialogue that are explicit and reveal information to the reader;
- what the subtext might be about in each story.

The sort of non-explicit dialogue that Mamet advocates is highly realistic. It attempts to imitate the unspoken exchanges between people, to use the spoken lines as a mask for what is actually being communicated. This sort of dialogue is often used in fiction writing – as you can see in the Carver story, where the dialogue covers over the cracks, barely disguising the strained atmosphere, ripe for reconciliation, between the two households.

DISCUSSION

The Hammick story is different. The subtext concerns the death of the father, and the tension between mother and son resulting from this. For a large part of the story this remains below the surface of the dialogue.

In the latter half of the story the dialogue becomes explicit (after 'Let me remind you of your father's childhood ... ') and the mother explains much of the backstory, telling the son (and the reader) about his father. The implausibility of this revelation – a character being told something he should already know – is avoided by the fact that the father died when the boy was too young to remember. Motivating and making such exposition plausible is most important, as it helps conceal the fact that information is being passed to the reader. This sort of dialogue is bearing the weight of exposition in a very different way from the Carver story.

ACTIVITY 9.9
Writing

Revisit Activity 9.2. Use the character that you created in that exercise (the tired, loving, loathing, bored or drunken character) and write a paragraph in summary of their backstory and key elements about them (using up to 150 words). For example, with the grandmother we have already imagined a possible backstory that includes details of how she has been drinking for twenty years, is divorced, and has a daughter who mysteriously left home.

Then write a page of dialogue involving the character (using up to 200 words). Try to create a subtext, an atmosphere or some implied information for your reader, beyond what the words of the dialogue explicitly say. For examples of this sort of dialogue look back over the shown version of the grandmother's reunion with her daughter or the dialogue in the park scene.

As a final stage combine the two passages, so the backstory and dialogue are mixed (using up to 250 words). This will mean you have to make crucial decisions on what stays in and what is less relevant and should be cut. Try to drip-feed the backstory into the narrative so it doesn't all come at once.

When to show and tell

Looking at your writing in terms of showing and telling should be an ongoing task, a part of the way you conceive a story and a part of the way you edit and redraft it. This will often mean unpacking something you have summarised: you will find yourself dramatising, setting scenes, using dialogue and characters' thoughts, and asking yourself what you really meant by describing characters and events in abstract terms. You will also, from time to time, realise that you have dramatised a section that really needs passing over quickly. 'Show don't tell' is such well-used advice because first drafts tend to be laden with telling, passages that are too condensed and need unpacking. But there are occasions when 'tell don't show' is the more appropriate advice. The craft of fiction writing combines both ways of revealing information. You should be hoping to strike a happy balance in any one particular story.

References

Joyce, James (1960 [1922]) *Ulysses*, London: Minerva.

Le Guin, Ursula K. (1998) *Steering the Craft*, Portland: The Eighth Mountain Press.

Lodge, David (1992) *The Art of Fiction*, London: Penguin.

Mamet, David (1992 [1991]) *On Directing Film*, London: Faber and Faber.

O'Hagan, Andrew (2003) *Personality*, London: Faber and Faber.

Richardson, Samuel (1985 [1748]) *Clarissa*, Harmondsworth: Penguin.

10 *Structure*

DEREK NEALE

What is structure?

According to David Lodge the structure of any narrative should remain largely invisible – 'like the framework of girders that hold up a modern high-rise building: you can't see it, but it determines the edifice's shape and character' (1992, p.216). As Lodge goes on to say, unlike a building, a narrative's structure has more to do with time than space. This chapter will explore the notion that a narrative's structure is made up of two connected elements:

■ dramatic action;

■ time and its arrangement within the story.

Dramatic action

The notion of a 'dramatic action', commonly associated with stage plays and films, has been acknowledged by fiction writers like Flannery O'Connor as a central plank of any narrative structure:

> A story is a complete dramatic action – and in good stories, the characters are shown through the action and the action is controlled through the characters, and the result of this is meaning that derives from the whole presented experience.
>
> (O'Connor, 1984 [1957], p.90)

It is important to note how the word 'action' here is different from the everyday usage. 'Action' in this instance refers not to some high adventure, no gunfights or thrilling battles, but to a movement which may be just a transition in time or a change in emotional state. In Charlotte Brontë's *Jane Eyre* (1996 [1847]), for instance, the character of Jane can be seen as the embodiment of a dramatic action. She begins the novel as an orphan with a burning but ill-defined ambition; she progresses through various ordeals and situations until she comes to realising her ambition, which has to do with finding a husband but on her own terms. This movement is sweeping – ranging from youth to maturity, from innocence to experience. The story is relatively straightforward in its development. It is a process of change witnessed by the reader – something happens and the reader sees the state of affairs before, during and after. It has:

- a beginning (Jane as orphan);
- a middle (Jane as young woman with romantic ideals which are challenged);
- an end (Jane as married woman yet independent, in terms of finance and status).

The dramatic action is a little less obvious in stories like Carver's 'I Could See the Smallest Things' or Hemingway's 'The Doctor and the Doctor's Wife'. In these stories something happens but it isn't as large in scale as a young person growing into adulthood. The Carver story consists of two neighbours going out in the night and talking by a gate. It begins with the narrator waking and restless; the middle is the conversation about slugs and other matters; the end is the return to bed. Yet what is the dramatic action? This is much harder to grasp, and seems to have to do with some move of reconciliation between the arguing neighbours (Sam 'used his hand to wave'), or the narrator's burgeoning realisation that her partner revolts her (his breathing at the end reminds her of the slugs Sam was trying to kill).

In Hemingway's 'The Doctor and the Doctor's Wife' the argument between the doctor, Henry, and Dick Boulton builds up to a sort of climax, yet they don't fight. Later the potential dispute between Henry and his wife never really reaches the level of an argument. There is no dramatic resolution to the conflicts in the story – even the slamming porch door is followed by a quick apology. The physical movement out to the woods, the third location in the story, echoes the emotional shift in Henry's character, though this shift is not easily pinned down. It is only now that Henry seems to be the main character in the narrative – in the first part Dick Boulton dominates the story, in the second part Henry's wife is dominant. The fact that Henry allows his son, Nick, to come with him at the end, rather than sending him back to his mother, could be seen as a shift towards defiance. Yet it is a relatively small matter, somewhat ambiguous, and not a grand, indisputable gesture.

You can see from these two examples that a dramatic action doesn't have to be tied in with something momentous like a death or a marriage. There doesn't have to be a fight for the conflict to become explicit; the movement involved can be really quite slight and may well defy definition.

Story, plot and action

E.M. Forster famously distinguished between the way a story works and the way a plot works. For Forster a story is a 'narrative of events arranged in their time-sequence' (1976 [1927], p. 87). His example:

> 'The king died and then the queen died.'

For Forster a plot is similar; it retains the time sequence, but with the addition of causality. So this is a plot:

> 'The king died and then the queen died of grief.'

Forster offers one further example:

> 'The queen died, no one knew why, until it was discovered that it was through grief at the death of the king.'

This, according to Forster, is a plot with mystery and therefore has great potential.

Plot is a relative element of any fiction – it can be negligible or it can be most prominent, depending on the story you wish to write. As Ursula Le Guin suggests:

> A story that has nothing but action and plot is a pretty poor affair; and some great stories have neither. To my mind, plot is merely one way of telling a story, by connecting the happenings tightly, usually through causal chains. [...] As for action, indeed a story must move, something must happen; but the action can be nothing more than a letter sent that doesn't arrive, a thought unspoken, the passage of a summer day. Unceasingly violent action is usually a sign that there is, in fact, no story being told.
>
> (Le Guin, 1998, p.117)

Whatever your regard for, or use of plot, what you need to remember is that there will always be at least two perspectives on the material you are working on:

- the whole story – the history of all the events found, imagined and researched – about which you might be writing;
- your version of the story – your eventual plotted representation of those events.

The first of these will have a certain sequential order and include all possible details. The second might have a different order and will almost certainly omit details. If you imagine the writing of a story to be like carving a figure out of wood, the 'whole story' is the lump of tree trunk that you cut from the forest, whereas 'your version' is the final shape of the carving once you've whittled away the wood you don't need.

For instance, the story might be about a woman who has reached a crisis in her life – perhaps her marriage has failed, perhaps she has always wanted to have a lot of children but her husband only ever wanted one, his precious daughter whom he idolises. Perhaps the woman is jealous of her daughter and doesn't realise it. As you can see from this rough scenario there is an enormous amount of usable conflict, material which raises structural questions. It appears to be the woman's story, so should the tale begin with the woman's birth and childhood and details of her own parents? Should it detail how the man and woman became husband and wife? These are the sorts of things that you might collect in your notebook, via your imagination and research, under the heading 'whole story'. This is the tree trunk you've cut down. But eventually you will have to choose the shape of your carving, to pick and choose which events and details you include in 'your version'.

ACTIVITY 10.1
Writing

Write a story (up to 300 words) using any or all of the details from the 'woman in crisis' scenario just described. If you find it difficult keeping within the word limit, try using one paragraph for the beginning, one for the middle and one for the end. Write in first person or third person and in whichever tense you wish, but write from one point of view, so it is one character's story. This character doesn't have to be the woman though – it can be the husband, or the daughter.

DISCUSSION

One of the decisions you will in effect have made (possibly without realising it) concerns the dramatic action. For instance, one possible action could be how the woman comes to realise that the relationship she has with her own daughter has been shaped by the resentment she feels toward her husband. This is a version of the story that has to do with her moment of crisis and realisation, therefore details of her own childhood might seem less relevant. Such an action would start halfway through her life story and finish before the end, before her death – you wouldn't bother including details about the piano lessons she used to have at school or her first boyfriend, though you might mention how she herself was an only child and always wished for siblings.

In trying to establish 'your version' of any story you will have to make many decisions about what to include and what to leave out; be aware that in many first drafts elements from the 'whole story' get included in 'your version', elements that you may later deem to be irrelevant. This is to be expected, but something always to be watched for in editing.

Time

One of the major decisions to make when arriving at 'your version' is about where to start and where to finish – marking out the parameters of the action. In making those decisions you are dealing with one of the main building blocks of structure – time.

Time works in many different ways within a narrative. It is used to establish a present in a story, and subsequently to establish a past and the possibility of time passing and moving towards a future. This is an obvious aid in establishing movement or action, but it is also a great aid in establishing what might be termed 'depth structure' – the richness of the text conveying a world which existed before the reader engaged with it and which will carry on existing after the reader leaves it. It is often this richness and depth that convinces readers that they are engaged with a believable world.

Emily Brontë's *Wuthering Heights* (1982 [1847]) begins when Lockwood, a visitor from the South, arrives at the bleak, northern farm. He is disturbed in the night by the apparition of Cathy knocking on the window, calling 'Let me in' (p.67). He also finds the names Catherine Earnshaw, Catherine Heathcliff and Catherine Linton scratched on the window ledge (p.61) These things are obviously connected to the backstory and events that happened long before the arrival of Lockwood, who is subsequently informed of those events by Nelly, the housekeeper. In effect the novel has begun nine-tenths of the way through the story's time-frame, yet Lockwood's arrival establishes a dramatic present immediately in the mind of the reader. It is one they can identify with as fellow newcomers into this world, and other time-frames can be organised around this arrival.

Similarly, when choosing the time-scheme for a particular story, you will need to establish a dramatic present, a fulcrum around which your backstory and any forward movement can be organised. For instance, with the scenario of the 'woman in crisis', you might have the woman looking out of the window at 8.30 am, watching the younger children going to school that particular morning is your dramatic present, though the woman may regularly look out of the window in this way. The establishment of repeated 'habitual time' is easily achieved in fiction, compared to film or stage plays where the emphasis is always on the dramatic present. In fiction events can happen daily, monthly or annually; habitual behaviour can be written in a line.

ACTIVITY 10.2
Reading

Look back over 'I could see the smallest things' and 'The Dying Room', which you read in Chapter 9, Readings 25 and 26 (p.501 and p.505). Also read Anita Desai's 'Pigeons at Daybreak', Reading 27 (p.515). In each story identify:

■ the elements that are establishing the dramatic present;

■ the elements that are establishing habitual time.

DISCUSSION

As you can see from these tales, a story can be many things; it is impossible to put a prescription on form or structure. There are common elements though. All three stories have a dramatic present, a 'now'. They all contain repeated behaviour that creates a sense of habitual time. The three stories establish a dramatic present fairly quickly – in the middle of a restless night; in a kitchen during a conversation; in cramped living quarters during the course of a hot, airless day and night. The dramatic present is all to do with the establishment of time and place, and is often achieved through showing.

The habitual time elements of a story are often related in a more telling fashion. So, as suggested in the last chapter, the 'The Dying Room' has an early summary of habitual behaviour – 'She cooks for her family [...]. She also supplies, on a regular basis, her local delicatessen with pâtés and terrines and tarts and quiches.' This gives backstory to the character of the mother. Yet not all these sorts of elements are revealed through telling. In 'I could see the smallest things', for instance, the habitual behaviour gets detailed in the lines of conversation, as Sam says 'I put bait out, and then every chance I get I come out here with this stuff'.

'Pigeons at Daybreak' proceeds from lunch-time on a certain day to dawn the next day. The story begins both with habitual behaviour and a dramatic present. Mr Basu is seen to hate his wife reading the newspaper to him, an action in the present but one which immediately suggests it has happened regularly before and that we are entering a pre-existing world. The reader hears the news stories, sees vistas of the city, catches descriptions of climate and types of food, getting a detailed indication of lifestyle and living arrangements, so getting a vivid impression of the habitual elements of such a life.

Either look through your notebook and find a character that you have noted and want to work on more, or write down in your notebook a sentence about a new character.

List five habitual things about the character in your notebook. So they might go to Scotland every year to visit family; they might have a tendency to scratch their head every few minutes. But it doesn't have to be something that the character does; it could be something that is just connected to the character's life. For instance, a delivery man might call at the shop across the road from your character's house once a week or a plane might fly overhead every day at the same time.

Taking your character and the five habitual elements, write the start of a story (up to 250 words). Establish a dramatic present in which your character is situated in a particular place at a particular time, but include the five habitual elements of your character's life. Try not to clump them all together – integrate them into the other elements of your story.

Starting in the middle of the action

It is often good practice, where possible, to start stories *in medias res*, that is in the middle of the action, so the reader gets the impression they are walking in on a pre-existing world. This can, and often does, mean beginning with an exchange of dialogue. Look, for instance, at the opening of 'The Dying Room', and how the conversation establishes character and place almost immediately, but also establishes the illusion that time is already in progress and events aren't just commencing for the reader's benefit. Beginning in the middle of the action can also mean simply establishing time and place. Look at this opening:

> My name is Lettice Pomfrey and I am thirty-four years old. I am sitting in the gynaecologist's waiting room waiting to see the gynaecologist. I tell you this now, at the beginning, in case gynaecology is not the subject for you; in case you find some aspects of it distasteful; in case you would rather be somewhere else than in this waiting room on a hot and sunny July afternoon.
>
> (Hammick, 1996 [1986], p.27)

This seems simple enough but places the reader, at a specific time and location, with a character, as well as launching an interesting rhetorical style and voice. The use of the second person pulls the reader straight into the situation, and even challenges them. Starting in the middle of the action, by this method or by using dialogue, usually means that there will be backstory to deal with later on in the narrative. You might have to tell the reader how your character got into a particular situation, for instance. Sure enough, the character-narrator, Lettice Pomfrey, soon tells the reader how many gynaecologists she has got through before arriving at this particular waiting room, though crucially omits any further information about why she might be there.

ACTIVITY 10.4

Writing

Look back through your notebook and find another character or scenario that you want to write about. As an alternative, you can use the 'woman in crisis' scenario again, but this time write from a different point of view (i.e. if you've already used the woman, choose the husband or daughter).

Write the start of a story (up to 250 words) which launches *in medias res* – in the middle of the action. So, you might start with some dialogue, for instance, or establish a dramatic scene.

Sometimes, as well as establishing a present and a past, you will also want to leap ahead to the future, anticipating events that will happen later in the narrative. This leaping ahead is often called foreshadowing.

Stories like 'I could see the smallest things', brief narratives based primarily in a dramatic present, contain barely any foreshadowing. Stories that are mainly dramatised do not use such devices. Neither is there any obvious foreshadowing in 'The Dying Room', though this has a foreshadowing device in the title – the word 'dying' – which anticipates something to be revealed later in the narrative. By juxtaposing the phrase 'dying room' next to the opening dialogue about the 'drawing room' the reader is pulled into a time loop, wondering how the room will change, who will die or has died, and if the rooms are the same. In this way the title becomes what some might call a 'plot hook'. If the reader knows in advance that someone is going to die or has died, they become imaginatively engaged trying to work out who and how and why.

This type of foreshadowing can sometimes be straightforward, as in 'This was how Mason lost his arm.', the first sentence from 'Sawmill' a short story by Adam Thorpe (1998, p.270),where the title and the words 'his lost arm' foreshadow the events of the story. Sometimes the foreshadowing can be more complex, as in this opening extract from *One Hundred Years of Solitude* by Gabriel Garcia Márquez:

> Many years later, as he faced the firing squad, Colonel Aureliano Buendía was to remember that distant afternoon when his father took him to discover ice. At that time Macondo was a village of twenty adobe houses, built on the bank of a river of clear water that ran along a bed of polished stones, which were white and enormous, like prehistoric eggs. The world was so recent that many things lacked names, and in order to indicate them it was necessary to point. Every year during the month of March a family of ragged gypsies would set up their tents near the village [...]
>
> (Márquez, 1978 [1967], p.9)

As this is the beginning of a novel, the world being launched has many dimensions and appears in one sense fantastical (with the lack of names and the simile about the stones – like 'prehistoric eggs'). The reader is strung between some mythic time and an era when guns existed. Yet the first line about the firing squad is full of foreshadowing. It acts as a plot hook – we don't know this character yet but wonder 'How did he get into that situation? Does he die? Who is firing at him?' This incident doesn't actually occur in the narrative for another hundred pages or so, but this early glimpse leaves the reader with the anticipation of what is to come and no further detail. Notice too how, even though this is the beginning, the narrative quickly establishes habitual time, with the gypsies coming every March. This way the reader is made to feel they are looking in on a pre-existing world.

ACTIVITY 10.5

Writing

Choose one of the following:

- find another character or scenario in your notebook that you want to write about;
- use the 'woman in crisis' scenario again, but this time write from the point of view of a fourth character; for instance a marriage guidance counsellor, or a solicitor.

Write the start of the story (up to 250 words), this time beginning with a plot hook which foreshadows events that will happen in the future. So, you may like to herald an event that will be crucial to the story. The event may be momentous, like a death, but it certainly doesn't need to

be. It could just be a departure, an arrival, or even a realisation. Give
this story a title.

Flashback and repetition

The art of storytelling consists largely of knowing where to leave holes
for readers to climb into the narrative. Time shifts and loops are part of
that process and an important way of structuring your story. Your
handling of time can give the narrative a real sense of depth. The
dramatic present acts as a stabilising force. The movement of a narrative
is worked out there, and from there the narrative can flit backwards and
forwards in order to push the action towards its fulfilment.

Yet the present of a story can be too fast or too dominant. Without
temporal variation the pace of a story can seem unrelenting. Look back
at 'The Dream' and 'The Artist', and specifically at their plots and how
events are sequenced. Events in these stories proceed, as you have seen,
in a straightforward, linear fashion, from one event to the next, at a
rapid pace. There doesn't appear to be any backstory or foreshadowing.

Stories vary in the amount they adhere to the forward drive of the
dramatic present. The form and style in *One Hundred Years of Solitude*
are such that the dramatic present is sometimes fractured both by
forward leaps in time (as with the firing squad) and also backward.
These latter, retrospective leaps towards dramatic moments in the
backstory are termed 'flashbacks', and are often associated with a
character's or narrator's memory. Some narratives rely more heavily than
others on this technique.

For instance, Toni Morrison's *Beloved* (1988 [1987]) is structured
around flashbacks. Ostensibly set in Ohio in 1873 after the abolition of
slavery, the novel is about Sethe, a former slave who killed one of her
children so the child wouldn't become a slave. The child comes back to
haunt the house where Sethe lives and acts as a catalyst for all the
characters' stories from the time before abolition. In this way the past is
seen to haunt the present and, in terms of form, the dramatic present of
Morrison's narrative is constantly ruptured by flashbacks of characters
and episodes from a time prior to 1873.

ACTIVITY 10.6
Reading
Reread 'Girl' by Jamaica Kincaid, Reading 18 on p.477, and in your notebook write down how it is structured and how time is working within the story. Take particular note of how repetition is used.

DISCUSSION   Some stories don't work in a straightforward progression or even have a dramatic present. 'Girl' seems to work on the basis of repetition. Habitual time and the creation of a world take precedence over the establishment of a specific time or location, or the movement through a dramatic episode. Certain elements are repeated at regular intervals – like 'benna' and 'Sunday'. Certain clauses and syntactical formations are also repeated so that, combined with the use of the second person, the story sounds incantatory. Variations in the repetitions and voice, such as the last line about touching the bread, are then most noticeable. They act as structural markers, as do the lines about 'becoming a slut', a strand which finds its culmination in this final line: 'you mean to say that after all you are really going to be the kind of woman who the baker won't let near the bread?' The narrative is ostensibly cyclical in form, though some might say that this final shift, coupled to the hint of rebellion in some of the 'answering back', constitutes a dramatic action.

Repetition can also be used in a less radical fashion. For instance, in 'The Dying Room', notice how the 'wireless' features at the start, then in the middle and again at the end, marking out the structure of the story. Repetition of certain features of a story can be used in this way as a deeper structural device to reinforce the action. If you recall, one of the suggested possibilities for the 'woman in crisis' scenario was that she herself was an only child and had wished for siblings when young. This echo could, in effect, act as structural reinforcement for the main action of the story. Habitual elements are also structurally useful in this respect. Stories can be built using the scaffolding of the daily plane flying overhead, or the annual trip to Scotland, or the weekly work routine.

In both the Carver and Desai stories you have looked at repetition can be seen to point up the main action and structure. In 'I could see the smallest things', Cliff's breathing is mentioned in the opening passage ('awful to listen to'), and then again at the end ('He cleared his throat'). The slugs appear in the middle of the story, in the conversation with Sam, and again at the end when Cliff's breathing difficulty and dribbling remind Nancy of the slugs. Sometimes the repetition can be the return of the exact same element; sometimes it can just consist of an echo, the appearance of something similar but not quite the same. In 'Pigeons at Daybreak' affliction is a structural and thematic element, which is repeated in different guises throughout the narrative – we get it in the first line about the newspaper reading, and then later in reference to Basu's chronic asthma. Crucially the omniscient point of view reveals both main characters at various times to be afflicted, though Otima is less liable to use that word.

ACTIVITY 10.7

Writing

Look through your notebook for characters or a location that you might want to develop (instead, if you need it, use 'tent' or 'pier' or 'hairdresser' as a prompt).

Then, again in your notebook, write a 'paragraph story' (up to 100 words) containing an element that is repeated at least once, and another element that is repeated with variation. For example:

> She stood on the bridge with her unfastened jacket billowing like a sail in the wind. In the distance she saw the island with its lighthouse and white cottages, and speculated about how long the ferry would take to cross the rough channel. He came up to her and said he wanted to go home. 'Why?' she asked, but he didn't answer, clinging with his gloved hands to the rails, buffeted by the swirling gusts. She took off her jacket and wrapped it around him, before leading him back towards the red brick houses on the quay.

Here the jacket is repeated and the housing varies – from being 'white cottages' on the island to 'red brick houses' on the quay.

DISCUSSION

You can see from the example that even in such a brief narrative, the paragraph appears to be a story because events are situated in time, and there is a beginning, middle and end. Repeated or echoed elements and motifs appeal to the reader's associative memory, allowing them to make more lateral connections. If used lightly, these can be fruitful devices that reinforce a structure, complementing the more logical and linear progression of a narrative. As with most devices though, if overused the echoes might seem implausible and clumsy, the writing can seem too planned or schematised. The craft lies in using such tactics judiciously.

ACTIVITY 10.8
Writing

Bearing in mind that you are trying to write a story with an element of repetition, pick a scenario from your notebook that you want to develop, or alternatively develop one of the following ideas:

■ an event repeated with the same or different participants – two dinner parties, for instance;

■ a repeated event which when repeated is on a different scale – a birthday spent alone and one spent with a group of friends, for instance;

■ a character who echoes another character – for instance, a teacher loath to admit he doesn't know something, echoed in a boy who won't admit he did wrong;

■ a location which is echoed – for example, the old people's home where a character is resident echoing the hotel where she worked as a girl.

Now write a story (up to 1000 words) which, as well as using repetition, also shows some or all of these technical elements:

■ a dramatic present;

■ a dramatic action;

■ habitual time;

■ flashback;

■ foreshadowing;

■ starting *in medias res*.

Because this story is longer than the paragraph story, the repetitions and echoes might be larger in scale.

Bringing the parts together

The structure of any narrative is arrived at through the organisation of time, from choosing where and how the narrative should start, to deciding upon the dramatic present. As a writer you have to sift through the 'whole story' in order to decide upon 'your version' – where you are going to end up, and the arrangement of the various components. In doing this you establish a dramatic action, a movement – things were one way, now they're different, however slightly, but something happens and you will have shown the transition. You may also use the device of repetition to help reinforce this movement and organisation of time. It is through these various techniques that your narrative will gain a sense of depth.

You don't necessarily need any or all of these elements in place before you start writing. Structural organisation is often arrived at during the writing. Eventually it will be the stability of your structure that reassures the reader. It is also the structure which invites the reader to be imaginatively active within a story. Those are the primary functions of your structure – getting your reader to trust you and then getting them to do some work.

References

Brontë, Charlotte (1996 [1847]) *Jane Eyre*, Harmondsworth: Penguin.

Brontë, Emily (1982 [1847]) *Wuthering Heights*, Harmondsworth: Penguin.

Forster, E.M. (ed.) (1976 [1927]) *Aspects of the Novel*, Harmondsworth: Pelican/Penguin.

Hammick, Georgina (1996 [1986]) 'A Few Problems in the Day Case Unit' in *People for Lunch/Spoilt*, London: Vintage.

Le Guin, Ursula K. (1998) *Steering the Craft*, Portland: The Eighth Mountain Press.

Lodge, David (1992) *The Art of Fiction*, London: Penguin.

Márquez, Gabriel García (1978 [1967]) *One Hundred Years of Solitude*, Gregory Rabassa (tr.), London: Picador.

Morrison, Toni (1988 [1987]) *Beloved*, London: Picador.

O'Connor, Flannery (1984 [1957]) *Mystery and Manners*, New York: Farrar, Straus & Giroux.

Thorpe, Adam (1998) 'Sawmill' in Carmen Callil and Craig Raine (eds) *New Writing 7*, London: Vintage.

11 *The story and the reader*

DEREK NEALE

What sort of story?

From these chapters on fiction writing it is possible to accumulate a list of elements that might, or even should, be included in any story that you write. A story should:

- have at least one character;
- be set somewhere;
- be written from a certain point of view;
- have a structure organised in time;
- have a balance between showing and telling in the way it is revealed to its reader.

Yet still there is a sense that something is missing, and that any list of ingredients will never be enough. Stories are more than this. There are no prescriptions for a story's content, for instance, as you can see from the stories we've looked at in Part 2, and no doubt have also seen from your own reading experience. A story can be about anything. Stories can also take many forms and while they have to give the reader the impression that this 'anything' is unique and worthy of their attention, the narrative has to be fashioned in a recognisable and comprehensible way.

ACTIVITY 11.1

Reading

Read over all the pieces of fiction you have produced so far in Part 2. Try to identify:

- the ones which you consider to be complete stories and why;
- the ones you consider to be part of much bigger stories and why.

DISCUSSION

Some stories will seem complete even though they are comparatively brief; some will appear to demand a novel-length narrative because of the content or theme. Some stories will be incomplete not because of their length but because some element or other just doesn't sit well with the other elements. On occasions you might be able to identify the element straightaway. Sometimes it will take a lot of editing before you realise that you have the order wrong, for instance, or that you've given too much prominence to a particular scene or character. The opinion of other readers is valuable in these instances, but in the end you're the final arbiter of a story's finishing point.

Long or short stories

One of the biggest decisions to be made about a piece of fiction is how long it should be. Often this decision seems to be made by what you are writing about. As Irish writer Frank O'Connor says: 'There is simply no criterion of the length of a short story other than that provided by the material itself' (1963 [1962], p.27). The same could be said of longer narratives. For instance, you might imagine a scene – with two people sitting on the shores of a lake. You might be able to picture immediately why the characters come to the lake every year, why the surrounding landscape has significance for these characters, and you might start picturing some moments in those preceding years, see some other characters and some of the causality surrounding events. Just from one scene you might find that you are getting involved in a web of connected elements that can't be contained in 1000, 5000 or 10,000 words: it would seem to demand a novel-length narrative.

Equally possible, you might picture the scene by the lake and not want or be able to do anything more with it. You won't want to develop the characters and take them to another location, to another moment in time and a wider fictional world. Some ideas have to be left small, though their effect isn't necessarily small. They are snapshots, captured moments in time that would lose something if they were elaborated upon.

The shorter variety of short stories are sometimes called 'sudden' fictions. These are usually under 2000 words long, and might include some of the stories you've considered in these chapters – those by Kincaid, Hemingway, Carver and Highsmith, for instance. Such narratives can be as brief as a paragraph long; they can read like poems or overheard conversations or anecdotes, as much as stories.

From the two alternative versions of the lake scenario, mentioned above, you might assume that there is a direct correlation between the passage of time within a story and the story's narrative length. This is not so. The decision about length of story isn't just about gauging narrative time; it is also connected to a decision about form and technique. For instance, consider two stories you've already read: 'I could see the smallest things' and 'The Dream'. As we've seen Carver's story is focused on a dramatic scene at a garden gate, a moment in time which is realised through a balance of showing and telling, though there is a predominance of the former. Its brevity matches the duration of time within it. 'The Dream', by contrast, moves over a considerable period of time, yet it is also a brief narrative. The form – telling the story as a form of parable – defines the length. James Joyce's *Ulysses* (1960 [1922]) covers the events of just one day but the extensively detailed narrative runs to almost 1000 pages. Both 'Pigeons at Daybreak' and 'The Dying Room' are based on relatively short periods of time yet are not quite as momentary as 'I could see the smallest things'. The length of a story is not just dependent on content and the duration of events, but also on your individual approach to those elements. The form you choose reflects your intention as a writer and your attitude to what you are writing about. So, for instance, the fact that Desai's story ends at dawn, not dusk, and with the beautiful image of the pigeons, 'like small pearls', transcending the city, rather than something bleaker, brings a note of hope to what might otherwise be seen as a claustrophobic tale.

Elizabeth Bowen writes:

> As to each new story, once it has been embarked on, a number of decisions have to be made – as to the size (or length), as to treatment (or manner of handling) and, most of all, as to what is this particular story's aim? What is, or should be, this particular story's scope? What is this particular story really about, and how best can what it *is* about be shown? To an extent, such decisions are made instinctively, but intellectual judgment must come in also. [...] Each new story (if it is of any value) will make a whole fresh set of demands: no preceding story can be of any help.
>
> (Bowen, 1965, p.8)

By asking these sorts of questions of your stories – especially 'What is the story really about?' and 'How best can this be shown?' – you will be more able to recognise when you have a novel on your hands, a sudden fiction, or something in between.

ACTIVITY 11.2

Reading

Read 'Writing Short Stories' by Flannery O'Connor, Reading 28 on p.523, an essay where she talks about her own stories and comments on seven stories by would-be writers. O'Connor is writing specifically about short stories. In your notebook reflect on what O'Connor suggests might be the important elements of a short story.

For O'Connor the short story is about people – characters who are realised through dramatic action and through the senses. Stories deal in what 'can be seen, heard, smelt, tasted, and touched'. This is a useful reminder of the approaches suggested in Part 1. The writer learns the habit of observing the world in this way, rather than in an abstract fashion; the writer learns to 'show' things rather than say them. The sort of detail that is shown should always have a purpose; it should always be central to the action of the story and is never there just for its own sake.

O'Connor suggests stories are made of two important qualities: 'the sense of mystery and [...] the sense of manners'. The latter means the imitation of something from real life – the way people behave and speak, for instance. This was explored in Chapters 5 and 6 on character and setting. 'Mystery' resembles Forster's notion of the plot with the most potential, the one that contains an unknown element (explored in Chapter 10). Mystery ('Why did it happen?') and suspense ('What might happen?') are certainly desirable qualities to have in any story, but should be there for a purpose. O'Connor talks about mystery in different contexts – 'the mystery of existence', the 'mystery of personality'. These all add a richer connotation to the term than the usual 'who-done-it' meaning. You might like to survey all the stories we have looked at so far and try to identify what the element of mystery might be.

Notice how O'Connor suggests form and structure are organic things – quite the opposite of how we might picture them (and how others have depicted them: remember Lodge's 'girders', for instance).

Endings and your reader

If you imagine a story about a funeral, the mystery could consist of a stranger attending the wake; it could consist of an unknown cause of death; or it could simply be a character not really knowing how they felt about the dead person. The mystery could be any number of things. Keeping something unknown is an important dynamic in any story. If everything is too obviously and too readily revealed to your reader, then the story is less likely to work. Your reader will need to be asking 'how' or 'why' at any one point in the narrative, in however small a fashion, and often they will be asking both questions simultaneously.

In each story you write your reader will go on a journey and will end up in a place which is both expected and surprising. The reader will be following every little crumb that you drop on the trail, asking and attempting to answer questions as they proceed. As Elizabeth Bowen suggests:

> Story involves action. Action towards an end not to be foreseen (by the reader) but also towards an end which, having *been* reached, must be seen to have been from the start inevitable.
>
> (Bowen, 1948, quoted in Allen, 1958, p.178)

In some narratives the uniting of expectation and surprise may not be easy, and a straightforward dramatic resolution may not be viable. The conventional endings for comedy (a marriage) and tragedy (a death), say, are often not suitable or even possible. Look at 'Pigeons at Daybreak', for instance, where the ending is one which finds the electricity supply restored and the light rising on a new day. Yet neither of the main characters dies or deserts the scene. There is an emotional shift, full of pathos, but one which is also strangely intangible. The mystery of their relationship isn't explained. In many ways Otima and Basu at the end are still perplexed within the predicament of their lives; the conflict doesn't reach a point of closure.

Each story you write will pursue its mystery in its own fashion. This doesn't mean it will be fully explained by the end. Often this would be undesirable. Charles Baxter says that one of the strengths of sudden fiction, for instance, is that it can end 'with a suggestion – a play of light – rather than an explicit insight' (1989, p.25). A complete closure in longer narratives might also be unrealistic and impossible to achieve. *Jane Eyre* provides a model of complete closure when Charlotte Brontë begins the concluding chapter with Jane's statement 'Reader, I married him' (1996 [1847], p.498). This is the culmination of the romantic quest, but novels aren't always resolved so conclusively. The modern sensibility often demands an emotionally realistic and, therefore, possibly more complex resolution. For instance, Tim Winton's novel *The Riders* (1995 [1994]) contains a central quest to find the protagonist's missing wife and to discover the reasons for her disappearance. The novel doesn't provide any satisfactory answers to this quest; however, by the end the protagonist has reached an emotional acceptance of his newly defined life but has not found his wife or fully explained her absence.

To plan or not to plan

Flannery O'Connor describes the evolution of her story, 'Good Country People', as though it just happened that way as she thought of the content (Reading 28, pp.528–9). Similarly Elizabeth Bowen says: 'The novelist's perception of his characters takes place *in the course of the actual writing of the novel*' (1948, in Allen, 1958, p.179). When writing novels Louis de Bernières says that he sees the individual chapters as self-contained short stories and leaves the ordering of these until the final stages of editing, when he lays the chapters out on the floor and shuffles them around (2004). On the other hand there are writers like Elizabeth George, the American author of the Inspector Lynley crime novels, who before starting a first draft goes through a process of questioning, listing and planning – what she calls 'expanding the idea', writing a 'step outline' and then writing a 'running plot outline' (2004, p.63). During this preparation she is trying to find out exactly what *kind* of story she wants to write (p.55).

ACTIVITY 11.3
Writing

Make a plan for a story, in note form, that is connected to one of the following topics (use up to two pages):

- moving house;
- door to door selling;
- the dawn;
- a funeral.

Don't use these topics as your title. Try inventing your own. You are planning for a 500 word story. In the plan list some of the elements you might need:

- character(s);
- setting;
- point of view;
- the dramatic present;
- backstory;
- habitual behaviour;
- some degree of mystery;
- where the narrative would end;
- where the narrative would start.

For example, your story might be about a house move that goes wrong in a seaside town. You might decide to begin when the removal people arrive and start loading the furniture, and finish just after they have left – having forgotten the washing machine! The characters of the story might be the house-owners and the three removal men. The mystery might be to do with the fact that the house-owners' teenage son was supposed to be around to help but didn't arrive and didn't even ring to say where he was.

In your plan, try to plot where and when in the narrative you might give particular packets of information to the reader. Draw a line with stations marked at intervals, at certain points bits of 'freight' will be added to the train of your story.

DISCUSSION   Some writers will be well suited to this sort of planning, but not every writer can plan in this fashion. It is a worthwhile exercise, on this occasion, to see if you can organise your thoughts in advance. There will be some level of planning and preparation involved in the writing of every story, but it might not always be as rational or visible as this. For many the act of writing is a process of revelation, where vital details of both content and form are discovered as they go along. The considerations suggested in this particular planning exercise are the sort of components you will in all likelihood have to consider at some point in the writing of any story. When and how you consider these is a matter of personal practice and often down to the particular demands of each individual story.

ACTIVITY 11.4   Now write the story you have planned in Activity 11.3 (up to 500
Writing   words). Keep as closely as you can to what you intended but feel free also to adjust as necessary.

DISCUSSION   A plan can liberate the blank page or screen. It can give you licence to start an idea, and also give you a helping hand. By thinking ahead you will have some idea of what to include in the first draft. By forcing yourself into some form of planning you are actually narrowing down the possibilities for a story and therefore honing its focus. It is important, though, to realise that the plan is part of your creation; it isn't something that should be imposed at all costs on the story. In most instances the plan will have to change as you proceed with the writing, as you discover what does and doesn't work. Sometimes it will have to be completely discarded.

Genre and the reader

In any story you communicate with your reader by building up a rhythm of disclosing or withholding information. By moderating what they know you are inviting your reader to use their imagination, to elaborate on the facts they are given and so help create the story. Genre is a parallel form of imaginative communication with your reader. By giving your reader hints that they might be reading a certain type of story, you are guiding their expectation.

From Aristotle onwards there has been a theory of writing which is all to do with the categorisation of literature into different types and forms. The three over-arching, modern day literary genres are fiction, poetry and drama. Within fiction there are also many sub-genres, such as science fiction, romance novels, and historical novels. The list is ever growing, and also includes types of fiction categorised according to the way it is written, as well as according to its content. So there are epistolary novels, written largely in the form of letters, such as Richardson's *Pamela* (2001 [1740]), or *Rites of Passage* by William Golding (1980), which deploys an epistolary journal. *Bridget Jones's Diary* by Helen Fielding is a popular descendant of this genre. In this way combinations are formed. *Bridget Jones's Diary* (1996), for example, is a 'journal' or 'diary' novel, but is also what has become known as a 'chick lit' novel, because it is written by a woman and is about the trials and tribulations of a modern, young woman.

Stories conforming to a specific genre are often regarded as a lesser type of writing, yet generic expectation within the reader is an important tool to be exploited. Most of the stories we have looked at so far lie outside the more obvious sub-generic headings and might be termed 'literary fiction'. Yet even amongst them there might be a scattering of generic labels. Raymond Carver, for instance, is often called a 'dirty realist' because of the subject matter and the nature of many of his characters – poor, sometimes alcoholic, and often suffering health and relationship problems. Also, as we have seen, 'The Dream' resembles a fairy story or parable, and 'The Artist' might be seen as a modern fairy story.

Genre is a dynamic aspect of writing and reading, not just a pejorative label placed upon certain types of writing. All readers are looking to spot what sort of narrative they're involved in at any one time. Readers aren't naïve creatures. Invariably they are aware of many genres of story; they are capable of picking up on certain clues which school their expectation.

They can understand such codes but don't necessarily need the expectation to be fulfilled. It is this play with generic expectations that often fuels their reading enjoyment.

ACTIVITY 11.5
Reading

Look at the three extracts of specific genres which follow. In your notebook detail what sort of writing each excerpt might be. Try to identify the features that drew you to this conclusion.

Extract 1

The pebbled glass door panel is lettered in flaked black paint: '*Philip Marlowe....Investigations.*' It is a reasonably shabby door at the end of a reasonably shabby corridor in the sort of building that was new about the year the all-tile bathroom became the basis of civilisation. The door is locked, but next to it is another door with the same legend which is not locked. Come on in – there's nobody in here but me and a big bluebottle fly. But not if you're from Manhattan, Kansas.

Extract 2

The year was 2081, and everybody was finally equal. They weren't only equal before God and the law. They were equal every which way. Nobody was smarter than anybody else. Nobody was better looking than anybody else. Nobody was stronger or quicker than anybody else. All this equality was due to the 211th, 212th, and 213th Amendments to the Constitution, and the unceasing vigilance of agents of the United States Handicapper General.

Extract 3

She didn't look crazy, Max decided. At a glance she seemed a rather ordinary, could-be-pretty-if-she-bothered country blonde. Only there was nothing ordinary about a slender young woman in a conservative navy blue suit sitting on a log at the edge of the ocean playing the banjo. Not when the yellow-tinged clouds overhead held promise of an April downpour, and the wind whistling past her ears was lifting her long hair so that it fell across her face like tangled silk.

She looked utterly incongruous. Prim conventionality gone mad.
Max found her enchanting.

DISCUSSION

It's surprising how it is possible to recognise certain signposts and linguistic features instantly, even though you may not be entirely familiar with a particular type of writing. These are some of the labels you might have come up with, along with the elements you might have picked up on:

Extract 1 – detective, thriller, crime

This is typified by its laconic, world-weary style, and its direct address to the reader, made famous by so many movie adaptation voice-overs. The name on the door rather gives it away. The place is 'shabby' and the general ambience, as illustrated by the fly, is seedy. One presumes there is a dingy crime about to land on Marlow's dingy desk. This is from Raymond Chandler's *Little Sister* (1955 [1949], p.5).

Extract 2 – science fiction, futuristic

This gives the futuristic year in which it is set straightaway, but the reader gets no other establishment of time or location. It focuses almost comically on a commonly held, present-day ideal (equality for all), while referring to present-day political language (for example 'Amendments', 'Constitution'). The sentences are short, full of rhythmic repetitions and ostensibly straightforward. This is Kurt Vonnegut's short story 'Harrison Bergeron' (1979 [1968], p.19). Interestingly it might provoke more generic labels. For instance, it might be classed as 'satire', or even 'dystopian', because it seems to be treating a possible utopian future with cynicism and irony.

Extract 3 – romance, love story

This is taken up completely with the description of a woman, and in particular details the woman's appearance in comparison to what might be deemed 'ordinary' or 'pretty'. The elemental forces of romance, the wind and the ocean, are also introduced here, together crucially with a man's approving gaze. This is Kay Gregory's *Man of the Mountains*, a Mills and Boon romance (Gregory, 1993, p.5).

Genre and the writer

The important thing for you as a writer is to be able to use some of these generic possibilities when and if you need to. You should be aware of such elements, and not use them accidentally. These are just three examples; there are many more genres that form part of our reading experience.

Now choose another of the starter topics from the list in Activity 11.3 and write the beginning of a story (up to 200 words) around this topic, choosing a particular genre. It doesn't have to be one of those exemplified above though; you might choose epistolary, historical, chick lit, or any number of different possibilities.

ACTIVITY 11.6
Writing

As an example, you might choose 'the dawn' in a science fiction genre. You might give a futuristic date, as Vonnegut does. Your characters might have breakfast, some tablets perhaps, and then wait for the purple sun to rise over the depopulated deadlands.

DISCUSSION   It is always a good question to ask: 'What sort of genre is this story?' Even if the answer is as general as 'It's about childhood – it's a childhood story', the question is still worth asking because it can help you gain a finer focus on your material. Sometimes the answer will be, 'This story isn't of any particular type' or 'It's a new genre.' You might think the story is about childhood but realise when you assess it in this way that there are some misleading generic signs, perhaps the hint of romance, or the suggestion of a thriller. You might like to cut these signs or you might like to make use of them, and keep your reader following that particular line of expectation. In this way genre is a potential strength in a piece of writing because it is another subliminal way in which you can commune with your reader. It's important to remember though that there are dangers from conforming too readily to generic expectations. If you reproduce a genre too conscientiously, rather than writing the story you want to write you are liable to produce clichéd action, characters and turns of phrase.

ACTIVITY 11.7
Writing

Revisit the story you wrote for Activity 11.4. Rewrite this story, subtly adding an element from a genre that you think might intrigue a reader. Don't conform fully to a genre as you did in the last activity (write up to 600 words).

For example, if you recall the moving house scenario where the son was missing and the washing machine was left behind in the move, the parents might see the shape of a gun in the overalls of one of the removal men. This might be combined with observations that the men are behaving suspiciously. This would give the story a crime or thriller element, even if the gun is later revealed to be just a tape measure.

Writer, reader and story

In writing stories you will constantly be trying out new techniques and exploring certain writing conventions. As you have seen throughout these chapters, it is important that you take your reader with you on these adventures. Have a consideration for the 'freight of exposition', and be aware of how much you are revealing and how much you are concealing as you proceed. The best form of exposition is motivated by the characters and action of your story, so it doesn't appear that you are giving out information at all. When honing your words into the shape of a story be aware of the way certain elements might be read in terms of genre, and be alert to the type of expectation you are generating.

Your readers like certain things. They like mystery and they like suspense; they like to be actively involved in the story. They also like to have key features of a world created for them – characters and setting, for instance – and these features need to be filtered through a consistent point of view. Yet these reader preferences are not parts that, once assembled simply produce an end product. There is always a synthesis involved, something beyond any possible formula; a coming together of form and content, structure and language, which makes any one story unique. As Flannery O'Connor says:

> A story is a way to say something that can't be said any other way, and it takes every word in the story to say what the meaning is.

> (Reading 28, p.527)

References

Allen, Walter (ed.) (1958) *Writers on Writing*, London: Phoenix House.

Baxter, Charles (1989) 'Introduction' in Robert Shapard and James Thomas (eds) *Sudden Fiction International*, NY and London: Norton.

Bowen, Elizabeth (1965) *A Day in the Dark*, Preface, London: Jonathan Cape.

Brontë, Charlotte (1996 [1847]) *Jane Eyre*, Harmondsworth: Penguin.

Chandler, Raymond (1955 [1949]) *The Little Sister*, Harmondsworth: Penguin.

de Bernières, Louis (2004) Interview with Mark Lawson, *Front Row*, BBC Radio 4, 1 July.

Fielding, Helen (1996) *Bridget Jones's Diary*, London: Picador.

George, Elizabeth (2004) *Write Away: One novelist's approach to fiction and the writing life*, London: Hodder & Stoughton.

Golding, William (1980) *Rites of Passage*, London: Faber and Faber.

Gregory, Kay (1993) *Man of the Mountains*, London: Mills and Boon.

Joyce, James (1960 [1922]) *Ulysses*, London: Minerva.

O'Connor, Frank (1963 [1962]) *Lonely Voice*, London: Macmillan.

Richardson, Samuel (2001 [1740]) *Pamela*, Oxford: Oxford University Press.

Vonnegut, Kurt (1979 [1968]) 'Harrison Bergeron' in *Welcome to the Monkeyhouse*, St Albans: Triad/Granada.

Winton, Tim (1995 [1994]) *The Riders*, London and Basingstoke: Picador.

PART 3

Writing poetry

12 Drafting

W. N. HERBERT

Writing a poem is a process, not a single action. Between the first inkling of a phrase or idea and the published work, there will be a succession of drafts. Each poem begins with a draft; each subsequent draft revises what has gone before. Learning how to revise, how to work through drafts to a publishable poem, is one of the key stages in a writer's development. It could even be said that the act of revision is where the life of a writer is at its richest. Certainly that would be the opinion of Don Paterson:

> It's taken me a pathetically long time to realise that the transcendental joy of poetry isn't getting your book published, reading to an audience of deeply-moved young women, getting your face on the box, winning a prize or anything else – it's the business of composition that blows you away, and the more you can do to savour it, the better.

> (Paterson, 1996, p.159)

What do poets mean by 'the business of composition'? Beginner writers sometimes assume that poetry comes about through a single event called inspiration, which results in a perfect draft. For them 'composition' equates with the first draft. But writing more usually consists of a series of actions, from five finger exercises that get us going (which you'll do shortly), through revisions, to the last correction to a proof. This expanded sense of the 'business' of being a writer is perhaps better termed the practice of writing. In this sense practice is or should be a daily habit, something the initial act of composition very rarely is. Nonetheless, composition can always arise from practice.

It is better to ready ourselves for this to happen, than to wait passively for inspiration. Inspiration is a problematic concept for the student writer, as a focus on its appearance or non-appearance can replace effort or conceal inhibition. Equally, over-attachment to the first draft is an impediment to developing the full richness of any text.

The aligned matters of titling the poem and the consideration of any necessary accompanying text, such as epigraph or footnote, help to frame the process of writing. They are important parts of drafting which we will also explore in this chapter.

Beginning to draft

We are going to begin without discussing our preconceptions about what a poem is, yours or mine. We won't even analyse how we determine what a line of poetry consists of, or whether a poem should rhyme or not. Don't worry, we will engage with all these things in due course, but to begin with we're simply going to start writing.

This is because these matters, important though they are, are essentially arguments, matters of opinion. All truly creative writing begins in the moment we go beyond opinions and arguments, into a territory we may know very little about, and poetry is no different.

This first exercise depends on external stimuli. Later, we'll work with internal stimuli, but it can be good to start with something outside our personal experience, as it focuses our attention on the act of invention, and it doesn't require us to reveal some personal truth (difficult), and to declare it significant (excruciating, if you have a shred of modesty).

The following instructions are quite detailed because I want you to be able to refer back to them in later chapters. Future exercises will assume you are pursuing this method or will clearly request you to depart from it.

When setting a writing exercise I tell people to write for 10–15 minutes without pausing. You can write down whatever you like as long as you keep writing – something you saw a few days ago that might be relevant, a list of possibly related rhymes, an older memory that's suddenly dislodged, an odd image that strikes you, a snippet of dialogue, a description of a person or place, or notes towards all of these. You might find yourself writing in some form of lineation or in a continuous prose block – either is acceptable.

Before you are two images. You can work with one of these, or provide one of your own. One of the things I do whenever I visit libraries, galleries or museums is look at the postcards. If any of them stands out enough to bring my eye back to it repeatedly, or to make me want to take it from a rack and read the back, then I frequently buy it. This is part of the process of building up the reservoir of images and ideas every writer must cultivate. Taking photographs can work in the same way. When selecting which image to use don't be too deliberate about your motives – the less set your goal in picking a picture, the more unrestrained your writing is likely to be.

Now I would like you to write for 10–15 minutes about your chosen image from any of the premisses listed below. (You may find it less distracting to set an alarm, rather than to keep looking at your watch.)

- Imagine what has happened immediately before this image, or what will happen immediately after.
- Focus on an object or person in the image: become that person or object and write in their voice.
- Imagine sending this postcard to someone – it can be anyone living, dead or imaginary – what would you write on the back?
- Imagine receiving this card from someone – living, dead or imaginary – what would they write on the back? Or would they be writing to someone else?

If you find yourself bending the rules – say, instead of becoming a character in the image, you start focusing on their story – go with it. If you start with one premiss, then move to another, fine. Remember: you are writing to find something which engages you creatively, not to produce a 'correct' response.

When the period of writing is over (be flexible: if taking another minute means you finish an important sentence, take another minute), then read what you have written. This may seem a trivial point, but it is in fact one of the more significant instructions I can give you. In itself, this action takes us from composition into revision.

Most people look at their writing in the sense of glancing over it – they **DISCUSSION** don't read it closely. What they see tends to be as much what they intended to write as what is actually on the page. Phrases and ideas which were never written down hover round the draft, becoming part of their reading experience but no one else's. Simply reading what you've actually written is by no means easy.

Mark those parts which you think might be worth working up later. Indicate those parts you're not sure are working. Write down why in both cases and make suggestions on the page. Ring words that aren't exactly what you want, but could be replaced. Underline rhythms you like the sound of. If your piece was getting interesting when you ran out of time, make a note now on the manuscript of where it might be heading. Don't assume you'll remember (you won't).

This experience of drafting for an exercise is similar to all drafting processes. In each case you are writing to discover: you are looking for a hook, something that engages you enough to keep on writing, to keep on exploring. This can be a draft of a whole poem, just a part of it, or even just a phrase or an image. Each is a valid and profitable result from any exercise.

It's important that you do all this searching on paper. We can have wonderful ideas for things we'd like to write, and it's tempting to daydream of these instead of getting something down on paper, which will always seem scrappy and inadequate in comparison. But the first suggestion I would make to you is: learn to think on paper.

Write down as much as possible of the process of approaching an idea, and especially the changes you want to make to it when you get a few phrases down. Thinking on paper is the beginning of drafting, and it's always easier to tidy up a messy set of notes than to touch a neat draft.

Go in fear of computers: they produce dangerously 'finished' versions, and they leave few traces of the process. Your previous drafts need to exist if you are to work on them. If you must use computers, save drafts, print out frequently, and get used to marking the page.

Revision

The first draft can be 'given', arriving in a single act of writing, or it can be assembled from a gradual accumulation of elements gathered in our notebooks. You will learn to work with both methods. These are, however, only the beginning of the process of revision. Poems can begin in self-expression, but revision is the means by which that expression is examined in order to arrive at its fullest potential. It is also the route by which we begin to consider and even address an audience. Revision is how a poem matures.

However, revision can also be an obsessive, retarding activity, in which we effectively prevent a poem from reaching its audience as we tinker beyond the point of refinement. It is important to gain a sense of when to stop. Revision can even move in the opposite direction. We may realise that an earlier draft (or a portion of it) is more vital than the current draft. Again, we have to learn through practice, through the act of reading (and listening) to the poem, how best to proceed.

ACTIVITY 12.2
Reading

Read Vicki Feaver on how she produced a draft of 'Ironing' (1994, p.10–11), in the extract from *'The Handless Maiden'*, Reading 29 on p.533. Are there any suggestions you can follow in your own drafts?

DISCUSSION

Notice how Vicki Feaver's notes for 'Ironing' contain both lines of poetry and lines about the poetry: her notes describe the process of writing and enact it. Notice how her notes are in shortish lines, so that whether a sentence is creative or descriptive, it has the appearance of a line of poetry. The concept of the line is helping her to focus on what the poem may eventually be like. Her notes, in themselves, give her a means of focusing, of meditating on specific words rather than nebulous ideas. This is why you must work on the page.

While you're digesting the process described by Vicki Feaver, I'm going to set you a second exercise. This may seem perverse: you may by now have a few ideas about how you could proceed with your first piece, but I have a simple reason.

Most poets have a number of poems on the go at once, at different stages of completion. This means there is a sense in which they're never blocked: as one piece is being finished, there is always another to polish up. This reduces the pressure the poet feels under to come up with solutions – a better image, a crucial rhyme, a new structure – to the problems of a given poem, until they are ready to turn to it.

It also has a far more important effect: it puts pieces of writing on the back burner. It ensures that the unconscious mind has time to play around with something before you look at it again. This means that when you look at a draft you may find your perspective on it has changed, and – possibly – some of those problems have found their own solutions.

ACTIVITY 12.3
Writing

Choose a piece of music lasting about 10 minutes. It is better if the music is unfamiliar, or you haven't played it in a while, so that you don't have a familiar series of associations for it. It can help if the piece is meditative or slow, but it doesn't have to be: experiment with this.

Listen to the music as far as possible without formulating any judgements: just allow it to suggest moods or settings, and to create a state of mind. You can make a few notes, but they should not be critical pronouncements on the type of music or performance. Let it produce an emotional or intellectual state – tranquillity or irritation are both acceptable.

Now write for 10–15 minutes from the mood created by the music. You can use it to conjure a physical setting, or recall a memory. Perhaps the different instruments suggested different characters, or a specific event. Perhaps they conjured a garment or a mode of transport. Write as far as possible to concretise what the music suggested.

And when you're done, read your writing and mark on the page how you feel about it and what you intend to do about it.

ACTIVITY 12.4
Revision

Now you have two pieces to work from. Pick one and copy the text again onto a new sheet of paper, taking account of all the comments you've made. Take 15–30 minutes, and produce a clean copy which follows your own directions.

Try to follow the phrases according to the physical layout of the first draft, whether you wrote in prose or in some form of lineation. In other words, write, as Vicki Feaver does, as though the piece is already in lines. Some of these may now appear as very long lines with any substituted or extra words you've decided to put in. Think about how you feel about these, even though you may not have originally written with any intention of putting phrases in lines. Do you want to break them into smaller units? Do other such lines now appear too short? If so, mark them, and begin to speculate why. This will prove valuable when we go on to consider why poems might be set out in lines.

Work through those instructions to yourself, and go further: produce that more precise description, include that phrase of dialogue, develop that further incident. Take it as far as you can in the time available, then once more write down on the sheet what you think requires to be done next. This will feed the next draft, and the next.

DISCUSSION   You may find revision takes more time than writing the piece in the first place. Perhaps you're still looking at what is essentially a series of half-ideas, or perhaps you found there was suddenly a new shape appearing. In either case you're uncovering a basic truth about revision: it is very much like writing the piece all over again. This can have all the mystery and excitement of a new piece of writing, but with this crucial difference: it's within a frame of reference you have already created. You have established some ground rules, and so the speculation, the surprise, is beginning to be directed towards a goal.

That goal, the final or publishable draft, may be a long way away, and there may be many issues of form and audience to consider, but you have begun a dialogue with a specific text. You've begun asking questions of it and allowing it to ask questions of you. In that process you can glimpse the life that other writers pursue for decades. This is the beginning of the same relationship with books – a life's work being shaped in poem after poem – which we intuit when we pick up a volume of collected poems.

At the end of each chapter, try and set aside time for revision. Perhaps in one exercise I'll have given you a choice of which piece of writing to develop – at the end of the chapter develop the others to the same degree. Perhaps something which remains fragmentary may change as the result of thinking about a later chapter. Revision is about finding time to carry these sorts of suggestions through.

Title

The title of a poem is of paramount importance in terms of its impact on the reader. When isolated on the title page of a collection or anthology, it can influence whether the poem is read or not. The space between a title and a first line is charged with anticipation; the moment after the last in which the title is reconsidered is a transformative, reflective zone. And yet it can often be under-considered or even tacked on last: the first thing a reader sees effectively an afterthought. By looking at titles much earlier in the creative process, we will pay them due attention.

There are two main categories of title: the descriptive and the evocative. One appears summative and direct, the other oblique and enticing. Each can in practice have the contrary effect. Each has its uses and subcategories. We will consider which to employ in relation to which poems. Some writers begin with a preponderance of descriptive titles; others may tend to produce more tangential, suggestive titles – if you discover a hitherto unexamined preference for one type, the other can offer new routes for exploration.

Here is a list of titles, some potential, some actual.

What the Cow Thought About the Rain

Otaku (Jap. obsessive)

Source Code

Anthropomorphisation for Beginners

The Shampoo

Between Two Nowheres

The Coral Mother

The Remark

Ghost Words

Things That are Early and Late

The Sea in the Seventeenth Century

Shoes in the Charity Shop

The Nutpacker Suite

The Secret Life of Life

'The Shampoo' would appear to be a descriptive title: this could be a poem about a specific type of shampoo, or an experience of being shampooed. There is an authoritative air about a title like this, a sense almost of definition. Of course the poem may do something very different, in which case there would be a kind of tension created by the type of title itself.

'The Sea in the Seventeenth Century' would also appear to be a descriptive title, but it raises an unresolved question: why the sea at that particular time? Was it noticeably different in that century? Presumably it was less polluted and contained more whales, but why not the sixteenth century, or better still the sea during the ice age? So we see that this title is provoking and intriguing us: it is actually a hybrid of the descriptive and the evocative.

'Ghost Words' would appear to be an evocative title, perhaps describing words said by ghosts, or appearing in a ghostly manner, like those at Belshazzar's feast. In fact it's a technical term for words which were printed wrongly in one text, and then taken up in that wrong form by other writers. Technical terms often have this evocative effect, precisely because they are precise terms, but in a specialism we do not recognise. Our response to them perhaps has to be slightly oblique.

'Between Two Nowheres' could be a straightforward evocative title: it suggests a territory that the poem may go on to delineate. It evokes a psychological state, and invites us to read a definition of that state. Of course it could be accurately describing the territory between two towns with the same unusual name.

ACTIVITY 12.5
Writing

Select one title from this list that attracts your attention and write for 10 minutes as though you are drafting a piece to be called by this title.

Now read your piece carefully in the usual way, marking any changes on the page. Ask yourself if this is really the title of the draft you have produced? If you were to rename it, thinking of the categories put forward above, what type of title would you give it? Think of two or three appropriate titles in this category and write them down.

Pick one and put it at the head of a new page and, using the principles of revision I've already outlined, write for another 10 minutes, redrafting your piece in order to align it with this new title.

DISCUSSION

Titles give your writing energy. Understanding the different appeal of different kinds of title begins a process of considering our poetry from the point of view of the reader. This perception of the reader becomes increasingly important as you present your work to an audience.

It's good to make lists of possible titles so that you get as used as possible to thinking about the particular energy they can give to a poem. See if you can come up with titles that fall into each of the above categories – or invent further categories. Keep adding to this list as new titles occur.

Epigraphs, glossaries, footnotes

It is a good discipline to write poems which require no exterior information in order to understand and appreciate them. Yet it is not an absolute rule. There are poems which need an obscure term glossed, or an arcane piece of information given as a footnote, and to omit such information would diminish our understanding if not our appreciation. Equally there are poems where the epigraph, that short quote appearing between the title and the first line, establishes a tone or an allusion that the poem then exploits.

Here's what Michael Donaghy says about the appearance of the text upon on the page: '... consider how any printed page of verse or prose, with all its paraphernalia of paragraphs, running heads, marginalia, pagination, footnotes, titles, line breaks and stanzas, can be understood as a diagram of a mental process' (Donaghy, 1999, p.11).

Every aspect of the text that appears on a page of poetry has a role to play in its reception, and to overlook elements which have a clear, if secondary, role is short-sighted. We will learn when and how to use these supportive elements and when they are better left off in favour of further revision.

This may seem rather an early point to look at finishing touches like these, but there are two reasons for doing so. As with title, the epigraph, footnote and glosses oblige the writer to consider the reader and what support they might need to understand a poem. This consideration for the reader can't be emphasised soon enough. The second reason is practical: writing from quotes can be a great deal easier than writing from experience. As you'll see in the next two activities, they generate exercises.

ACTIVITY 12.6

Reading

Read the list of quotes that follows below. They were harvested from my notebooks over a few months. You too should be copying quotes into your notebooks – if you haven't, begin now. Don't exert too much judgement over why you're copying something in. If it attracts your attention and intrigues you, whether because of what it's saying or how it's saying it, that's good enough for the time being.

> And he said, 'So is the kingdom of God, as if a man should cast seed into the ground; and should sleep, and rise night and day, and the seed should spring and grow up, he knoweth not how.'
>
> Mark, 4, 26

> The other half of half-afraid
> opens many a door.
>
> Brendan Kennelly

> I have been a thief, a liar, a beggar and a card cheat. I've ridden the Gitanjali Express to Mumbai to run on Chowpatty Beach. I've taken the Coromandel Express to Chennai to swim in the Bay of Bengal. I've sat on top of the Amritsar Mail all the way to the Golden Temple and jumped on the Dehra Dun Express to see the Himalayas, all before I passed ten years old. And I've never once paid for a ticket.
>
> Homeless boy, Howrah Station, *Guardian*, 16 November 2002

> The word itself is a musical sound.
>
> Pierre Bernac

> Certain sumo were handicapped by having a quince thrust down their loincloths.
>
> Source lost (but not invented!)

> He loved me more than he did not understand me. He loved me more than he wanted to control me.
>
> Pedro Almodovar on his father, *Guardian*, 17 August 2002

> Pandas often do handstands when urinating in order to spray their scent high on a tree trunk, say scientists in San Diego.
>
> *Scottish Sun*, 26 October 2002

> ... they know exactly what it was like in the old days you'll never be able to see.
>
> Sam Rowe (age 10) on old people, *Observer*, 1 December 2002

The silence became strict with absolutely focussed attention, cigarettes were unlit, and drinks stayed on the tables. And in all of the faces, even the most ruined and the most dull, a curious, wary light appeared.

James Baldwin, *Another Country* (describing the crowd during a sax solo)

Es verdad que lo ignoro todo sobre el.

(The truth is I knew nothing about him.)

Borges, 'Isidoro Acevedo'

Epigraphs can operate in three distinct ways in relation to the poem. They can place your new text in relation to a previously written work by quoting selectively from it, in effect saying 'my poem is a reaction to this: see if you can work out why'.

They can also provide a crucial piece of information, in which case their role overlaps with that of the footnote, and you must decide: do I want my reader to be aware of this before reading my poem, or shortly afterwards?[1]

The third use is harder to define: it is when a particular snippet of text, placed between the title and the first line, creates an atmosphere or tone which influences the reader, directing them to look at the poem in a certain way.

ACTIVITY 12.7
Writing

Pick a quote that catches your eye. Now go back to your list of titles and select one that might go with it. Now write for 10–15 minutes the piece suggested by the combination of title and quote, using any of the three devices: epigraph, footnote or gloss.

DISCUSSION

Be aware that not all poems will require this kind of accompanying material. Be careful of over-burdening a text which can stand up perfectly well by itself.

Sometimes a quote can be an inspiring device to get you into writing a poem, but you don't actually need to include it with the poem when you write it up – it's like the ladder that got you into a locked house, and now you can use the door. Keep collecting quotes, and explore what use you want to put them to. Used sparingly these devices can be highly effective.

---

[1] The footnote is, like the gloss containing an unusual word, slightly after the fact or even outside of the poem, which makes it a good place to store simple facts that are important to understanding the poem, but not a central part of the aesthetic experience.

Let the act of drafting become second nature to you. Every time you look at a poem, be prepared to scribble something on it, to reconsider the punctuation or the order of the ideas. Check if you can't think of a better title. Establish whether or not anything needs to be footnoted, or whether the footnote or epigraph could be dropped. When you find yourself putting something back in that you've already taken out five times (or vice versa), you'll know that it's time to stop fiddling. Up to that point, however, you're not only producing the best possible version of that poem, you're also training to become the best possible reader of your own work.

References

Donaghy, Michael (1999) *Wallflowers*, London: The Poetry Society.

Paterson, Don (1996) 'The Dilemma of the Poet' in Tony Curtis (ed.) *How Poets Work*, Bridgend: Seren.

13 *Line*

W. N. HERBERT

The line is the basic device which distinguishes poetry from prose. It does this by focusing on a different unit from the grammatical phrase. Whether a line forms a complete sentence or an incomplete one, whether it forms a musical phrase or strikes a harsh note, its purpose is clearly not limited to revealing sense. It is a unit of attention. The line momentarily removes a selection of words from the normal flow of language and suspends it for examination.

You might compare this to the instant of consciousness – approximately three seconds long – which neuropsychologists believe constitutes the present moment. In that brief space we can appreciate the language contained in the line on a number of levels: its rhythm, its sound, its ideas, its phrase-making or its metaphoric content. We can even relate it to previous lines and anticipate its relationship with subsequent ones.

At this stage we will consider the line firstly as a free verse unit, and then as a syllabic form. We will also look at the roles played by stress and alliteration in forming the line. More formal analysis of metre will be covered in Chapter 17.

The line break

Where we choose to break a phrase in order to begin a new line has consequences for the entire poem. If we break it at the end of a clause or sentence, then we reinforce grammatical sense with an unspoken emphasis. If we break within a phrase, then we introduce a sense of incompletion which can pull us forward through the poem, almost demanding that we make sense of the line by reading on. Conversely, if we break within a phrase and follow that with a space, whether an indentation or a stanza break, then we create a note of suspension, implying that the normal progression of a sentence can contain spaces where the reader can pause.

Let's look at what this might mean in relation to a poem, Liz Lochhead's 'Dreaming Frankenstein' (1984, p.11). Before I discuss this poem, I should just make a comment about the poetry I will be

ACTIVITY 13.1

Reading

presenting in Part 3. Each poem is there to illustrate a technical point. While it can be fascinating to explore the meanings of each piece, your primary focus must be on the issue under discussion. Don't feel you have to fully understand every nuance of a poem before you can proceed.

The technical point with this piece is its line breaks: can you find reasons for each line break Liz Lochhead makes?

Dreaming Frankenstein

for Lys Hansen, Jacki Parry and June Redfern

She said she
woke up with him in
her head, in her bed.
Her mother-tongue clung to her mouth's roof
in terror, dumbing her, and he came with a name
that was none of her making.

No maidservant ever
in her narrow attic, combing
out her hair in the midnight mirror
on Hallowe'en (having eaten
that egg with its yolk hollowed out
then filled with salt)
 – oh never one had such success as this
she had not courted.
The amazed flesh of her
neck and shoulders nettled
at his apparition.

Later, stark staring awake to everything
(the room, the dark parquet, the white high Alps beyond)
all normal in the moonlight
and him gone, save a ton-weight sensation,
the marks fading visibly where
his buttons had bit into her and
the rough serge of his suiting had chafed her sex,
she knew – oh that was not how –
but he'd entered her utterly.

This was the penetration
of seven swallowed apple pips.

Or else he'd slipped like a silver dagger
between her ribs and healed her up secretly
again. Anyway
he was inside her
and getting him out again
would be agony fit to quarter her,
unstitching everything.

Eyes on those high peaks
in the reasonable sun of the morning,
she dressed in damped muslin
and sat down to quill and ink
and icy paper.

That first line break alerts us to an unusual mind: 'She said she'. Many **DISCUSSION**
people would want to keep the verb with the subject by running those
first two lines together. But then they would have that funny line ending
'in' – in what? Ah yes, her head. And then we have the parallel phrase
'in her bed'. It might seem sensible to write these lines as:

She said she woke up with him
in her head, in her bed.

But think how reasonable that makes the phrasing sound. This is a
nightmarish event, and Lochhead's lineation follows that by cutting in to
our expectations. These are instances of broken phrases pulling us
onward, into the poem.

Later in the poem, we find the more normal usage of breaking the line
where the phrases naturally pause, using emphasis and strong nouns, but
notice how these line endings are suited to the more sober note the
poem is striking at this point:

Later, stark staring awake to everything
(the room, the dark parquet, the white high Alps beyond)
all normal in the moonlight ...

In fact the poem alternates between breaking the phrase up, and ending
neatly on it (as the whole poem ends), in order to reflect its subject
matter. That subject – the violence of an inspiration which changed
Mary Shelley's life, and entered popular iconography in the shape of
Frankenstein – is caught up with the gender of the speaker, and, like the
Vicki Feaver poem, contemplates how hard it can be for women to find
a voice. This means, when we glance back at the first line, that what

sounded fragmentary on first reading can now be said to hold an assertion: 'She said she' – she found a way of expressing herself.

The way the line can interrupt the run of sense to isolate and fleetingly suggest another meaning is one of the things only poetry can do. And it does this through exploitation of the line break.

It may seem a basic statement to make about the line that it must contain something, but this actually does a great deal of the hard work without going on to discuss metre. If we stick for now with just the idea of the line containing something, then perhaps we can see why many poets are keen on form.

Imagine a mother holding her child, then imagine a stranger holding the same child. One gesture has been built up from experience, it is caring and practical; the second is more spontaneous – it is equally careful, but less tutored, there is a threat that the child may be dropped, and slightly less emotional investment in it if it is. Imagine a fisherman holding a fish: his relation to the fish is much crueller, but it is also full of pride. It too is careful, but that is because it is the nature of the fish to be difficult to hold.

Each of these scenarios could describe the attitude of the poet towards a line of verse – the sure, loving crafter; the excited but uncertain beginner; the pure, almost cold technician. Each of them could describe the way that a poetic line holds words: the end-stopped, memorable unit; the tentative, could-be-different solution; the fluid, onward-driving, incomplete phrase.

ACTIVITY 13.2
Writing

Take one of the pieces you have been working on and spend 10–15 minutes breaking it into lines. By all means think about Lochhead's line breaks, and hold onto the idea that each line must contain something – but be prepared to break your lines on impulse and break them on feel. You will build up by this means a sense of what a line can be for you that will hold true whether you're writing in free verse or metrical poetry.

You should revise this draft after reading the next paragraph (or apply the same principles to one of your other drafts).

What is a line holding if not metrical beats? It could hold an image; an unusual word or phrase; a tone; a rhythm, whether analysed or not. It could hold a bit of alliteration; it could hold all you can say in a single breath; it could have a rhyme at the end of it you want the reader to notice. Lines in poems, whether free verse or metrically precise, will contain one or more of these. When you try justifying to yourself why one unit is a line, and why another isn't quite, ask yourself: 'What is it holding?' Is it holding enough to justify the reader looking on this for the whole three seconds of their present moment?

Syllabics

One of the consequences of limiting the length of a line is that we introduce a concept of duration. By weighing up how long a line should be relative to the other lines in a poem we begin calculating its actual length, and one of the simplest ways of doing this is to count the number of syllables it contains. The word 'sy-lla-bics' contains three syllables. The line 'all-nor-mal-in-the-moon-light' contains seven.

If we declared that all the lines in a poem should be seven syllables long, this would impose a shape, albeit one that took no account of the rhythm of a line. But it would offer a limit for the flow of the sentence to either meet or run over, and this gives us an important principle to work with. These two antagonistic principles – the flow of the sentence and the limit of the line – provide one of the bases of all form. From the tension between them arises the unique marriage of form and content that makes up a poem.

ACTIVITY 13.3
Writing

This exercise is in two parts, one consisting of freewriting in the manner you're accustomed to, and the other a slower piece of shaping.

I'd like you to write on the following theme: an animal you identify with. It can be a real animal you have owned, a family pet, perhaps; or a real animal you have seen in the wild or in a zoo or even on television. It can be an animal you've never seen, but have read about or seen pictures of; even an imaginary or mythic animal. The important thing is that you feel the animal embodies you in some way in its characteristics or behaviour – in the case of a pet, it could sum up a period of your life. Give yourself 10–15 minutes.

Afterwards, make your usual notes.

The second part of the exercise can be done immediately or later, depending on the time and energy you have available.

I'd like you to select one number between seven and eleven, and another between three and five. The first number is your syllable count, the number of syllables permitted per line of your redraft. The second is the number of lines per stanza, or verse paragraph. Yes, I know we're supposed to do stanzas later, but I want you to start wondering about these units within a poem – firstly so that some groundwork is done; and secondly because it gives you two things to work on within this draft. Trying to do more than one thing at a time in creative terms helps bring your unconscious into the process.

Now, take 10–15 minutes to rewrite your first draft, ensuring that each line fits your chosen syllable count, and that the poem is formed into regular stanza units.

DISCUSSION   One of the effects such an exercise is likely to induce is enjambment, or the running over of meaning from one line to another, and even from one stanza to another. You might even find yourself breaking some polysyllabic words in two to fit in with this artificially imposed shape. In all this there is a sense of transgression, that the containers, whether of the line, the stanza or even the word, have all been broken. Good. The issue about lineation which this exercise brings out is: purpose.

As we saw in the Lochhead poem, there is nothing inherently wrong with lines running on in this fashion, it's more a matter of determining why it's happening, and whether this furthers the sense of the poem – its intention, its drive, its rhythm – or runs counter to it.

This exercise underscores what has already been said about line: it is there to alert the reader to a sense of intent. It reinforces the meaning, the pace and the rhythm of what is being said. Depending on how the sense fits into the line, it can even help a statement become memorable. Syllabics run slightly counter to our instincts about line because they can feel arbitrary.

Of course a piece could be rewritten so that the phrases fall more exactly within the syllabic frame – and that frame can be altered to allow them to do so. But this doesn't address an underlying issue which the use of syllabics has to overlook. Syllabics just count, they can't measure, so to limit ourselves to them is to be insensitive to one of the dominant effects in poetry, the rhythm. Our language is stress-based, which means that every line contains a number of lighter or heavier stresses or beats. How light, how heavy, is an act of measurement, and this leads us on to the rudiments of metre.

Alliteration and other patterns

The oldest way of constructing a line in English poetry is by introducing alliteration, finding two or more words that begin with the same sound. The same principle is used in tabloid headlines to catch the reader's eye and ear. A regular pattern of alliteration causes us to count, to measure the line in some manner, and this imposes a shape, if not shapeliness.

Further, because English is a stress-based language, having a certain number of alliterative words will necessarily introduce a certain number of stresses. Consider the line 'Then the would-be assassin attacked me with an anglepoise.' There are several non-alliterating words in this sentence, some of which contain stresses, and so counting the alliterative terms only gives us a minimum number. But it is arguable, nonetheless, that alliteration helps to introduce a sense of rhythm.

In traditional alliterative verse the stress in the alliterating word is often focused on its opening syllable. This is to help the listener hear what's happening. The word 'anglepoise', being stressed '**ang**lepoise', emphasises the first syllable and therefore obviously alliterates on 'a'. The word 'at**tacked**', though it also begins with 'a', emphasises the second syllable, and so is less noticeably alliterating – the 't' of 'tacked', thanks to the stress, dominates. From counting alliterative words to noticing stresses in this way involves a small refinement of the ear, but it has enormous consequences.

If you can detect stresses then you can count them, and thus begin to think of lines as possessing beats. If you can regularise the number of strong beats in a line, then with or without alliteration, you have the metrical competence to write what is known as accentual verse, verse which is aware of the main accents or stresses which are distributed through English. Accentual verse is a category which includes both the medieval ballad and contemporary rap.

ACTIVITY 13.4
Reading

Read this section from the 'Age of Anxiety', by W.H. Auden, from *Collected Longer Poems* (1988 [1968], p.337). Identify the points at which Auden is alliterating.

If you blush, I'll build breakwaters.
When you're tired, I'll tidy your table.
If you cry, I'll climb crags.
When you're sick, I'll sit at your side.

If you frown, I'll fence fields.
When you're ashamed, I'll shine your shoes.
If you laugh, I'll liberate lands.
When you're depressed, I'll play you the piano.
If you sigh, I'll sack cities.
When you're unlucky, I'll launder your linen.
If you sing, I'll save souls.
When you're hurt, I'll hold your hand.
If you smile, I'll smelt silver.
When you're afraid, I'll fetch you food.
If you talk, I'll track down trolls.
When you're on edge, I'll empty your ash-tray.
If you whisper, I'll wage wars.
When you're cross, I'll clean your coat.
If you whistle, I'll water wastes.
When you're bored, I'll bathe your brows.

DISCUSSION

This is a deft piece of craftsmanship by a technical master: not only are there three examples of alliteration per line, but there is a clear repeated structure, an imposed shape of couplets beginning 'If' and 'When'. You can see this is as constructed a thing as, say, a poem rhyming in couplets.

Notice what he does in the line 'When you're ashamed, I'll shine your shoes' – 'ashamed' would appear to alliterate on 'a', but because the part of the word we stress most when we say it is actually the 'sh' sound, he can alliterate on that. Note also the licence he allows himself in 'When you're on edge, I'll empty your ash-tray' – two alliterations on 'e', then a word beginning with 'a'. Well, it is a vowel, and I suppose it sounds closer to 'e' than 'o' or 'u' would. But it just goes to show: don't box yourself into a corner if it means the poem can't proceed. Poetic rules are flexible, and sometimes the sign of a master is how he or she bends them!

Auden harks back in this poem to a use of alliteration which persisted in English poetry into the fourteenth century. Its last major practitioner was William Langland, the author of Piers Plowman. Pat Boran makes an interesting point about alliteration in relation to this poet:

> ... Langland was writing for listening audiences. He was 100% interested in sound. You might say that the invention of printing

relieved poets of some of that responsibility (or deprived them of some of those riches, depending on your point of view), but certainly once books began to appear, the whole shape and organisation of English poetry changed ... Chaucer was one of the first English poets to recognise 'the emerging literate mindset of his courtly audience', and his more complex sound and sentence structures confirm this. He wrote in the knowledge that if something was missed it could be returned to, re-read. It is believed Chaucer died the year Gutenberg was born. The invention of movable type revolutionised writing and printing, and therefore poem-making too, as has, to an extent, every major communications invention since.

(Boran, 1999, pp.80–1)

Chaucer, of course, rhymed. Arguably alliteration has an air of being an antiquated, almost crude device: poets use it, but it is not the dominant structural principle, more an occasional musical reinforcement. Nonetheless alliteration points us to the way poetry is older than most fiction – a form very happily married to the printing press. Poetry's reliance on music as an attention-grabber and an aide-memoire has survived into the computer age, and alliteration is still a primary building block in that musicality.

ACTIVITY 13.5
Writing

Write an alliterative love poem, but not to a human being. It can be domestic: to your favourite food, your favourite household appliance, or your car. It can be decidedly non-domestic, aspirational or even fantastical: to your favourite local monument, fictional character or planet.

What it must be is alliterative: I would go for two clear alliterative sounds in each line – three if you dare, or on an occasional basis. Try to keep the space between these sounds short enough for the relation between them to be audible. This doesn't mean writing in short lines: experiment with length and placement.

DISCUSSION

Depending on how concise your lines are, you can assume they will contain a minimum of three beats: one for each alliterating word, and probably at least one for the part of the sentence which separates them. Let's look again at two lines from Auden's poem:

When you're on edge, I'll empty your ash-tray.
If you whisper, I'll wage wars.

If we read this out loud, listening for emphasis, we can certainly say that, in the first line, we would stress the first syllable of each of the alliterating words: '**edge**', '**emp**ty', '**ash**-tray'. That's how we pronounce those words in ordinary conversation, and Auden has placed them in the line so that they form a little rhythm. This rhythm alerts us to another word he's stressing: '**when**'. So this line has four sounds in it we say with a little more emphasis than the others.

But when we say the second line aloud, we can say that, although it has three words beginning with 'w', the rhythm doesn't place equal emphasis on all three of them. '**Whisp**er' and '**wars**' seem to have a certain weight, but you have to emphasise '**I'll**' a little more than 'wage', both to make sense of the line, and to catch its rhythm. Of course, if we follow the pattern of the first line, and put some emphasis on '**if**' as we did on '**when**', then a pattern becomes clear:

When you're on **edge**, **I'll emp**ty your **ash**-tray.

If you **whis**per, **I'll** wage **wars**.

If we count syllables, we can see that the first line has one or two syllables between the stressed sounds; and the second has one. So the first line feels more expansive, and the second tighter.

So hearing beats has two components: finding where the main stresses are in a word in ordinary conversation, and finding how many more lightly stressed or unstressed syllables lie between them. In order to get a rhythm going, there has to be a fairly regular occurrence of beats with not too many of the less stressed or unstressed syllables in between.

If there is a regular number of beats in every line, then a certain pattern has been achieved, and you are, effectively, writing accentual verse. Later on, we'll discuss what happens when these beats combine with regular patterns of unstressed syllables. But for now, the important element is to begin listening and counting.

ACTIVITY 13.6
Revision

Look at your alliterative piece from the previous activity again. Check whether your alliterative words all have the main stress on the alliterating part of the word, and see if you can find the other words in each phrase which have a roughly equal stress. How many syllables apart are they, and how many syllables are there in each of your lines? Can you rephrase them to make the rhythm more audible?

The principle of containment alerts us to the line as a unit of attention. It enables us to present our phrases to a reader in such a way as to allow them to dwell on them momentarily and to notice and appreciate the particular linguistic effect that is going on. As writers, it enables us to begin to measure what we are saying rhythmically, to create pattern, and to build up music. It is not the case that none of these things would be going on if we were writing in prose, but it is certainly true that the line is a helpful unit when it comes to shaping what we have to say.

From this chapter on, experiment with writing your exercises in lines, reserving the right to sketch things out in prose if need be, but always revising towards a notion of the line.

References

Auden, W.H. (1988 [1968]) 'Age of Anxiety' in *Collected Longer Poems*, London: Faber and Faber.

Boran, Pat (1999) *The Portable Creative Writing Workshop*, Cliffs of Moher, Co. Clare: Salmon.

Lochhead, Liz (1984) 'Dreaming Frankenstein' in *Dreaming Frankenstein & Collected Poems*, Edinburgh: Polygon.

14 *Voice*

W. N. HERBERT

Many prospective poets consider themselves to be searching for their voice, which is seen as a recognisable combination of tone and subject. Together with the primacy of inspiration and the successful first draft, voice is felt to be another trait of the 'proper' writer. Like those, it can have a counterproductive role in a writer's evolution. It is better to grow into a voice, and to keep that voice flexible, than to seek to fix it at the earliest opportunity.

Voice is something to be discovered rather than imposed, and it is rarely a single entity: some poets argue there are as many voices are there are poems. It's more practical to begin by identifying the voice of the individual poem we are working on, and to build from that a sense of the range of voices we can successfully use.

ACTIVITY 14.1
Reading

Read Richard Hugo on 'public and private poets', in an extract from *The Triggering Town*, Reading 30 on p.537. Do you agree with these two categories?

DISCUSSION

Which type of poet do you think you are? Whenever I am asked a question like this, I always say 'Both' out of principle. Is it possible to be both types of poet at the same time? I would argue Walt Whitman is an example of this kind of writer, constantly reaching out to a whole nation, but in a language charged with inner meaning.

Hugo is asking you to focus on your relationship with language in a passionate way. Many people regard words as transparent means to an end: they contain a meaning, we speak or write the word containing the desired meaning, and that is the only meaning which is communicated. No account is taken of resonance, nuance or the irrational. I remember how I felt as a teenager when I first read Whitman's poem 'Eidolons' – I had no clear idea what an eidolon was, but it had a powerful effect, as though I was being shown a secret part of the mind – I almost didn't want to look the word up in a dictionary, in case it broke the spell. (It didn't: dictionaries are the biggest spell-books.)

Everyone has a way of speaking that's unique, and the same is true of how we write. Writers unaware of this produce an unusual mixture of styles: their work contains some unconsidered phrases which feel almost anonymous; and other phrases filled with – equally unconsidered – personal quirkiness. The former are things anyone would say, and indeed no one would notice. The latter are things only they would say, which only they can't hear. The search for a voice is often nothing more than bringing our attention to bear on how we already write, and filtering out that writing which conveys no individual charge.

Produce an alphabet of your favourite words. Twenty-six words which you find intriguing or delightful. They can be words from your childhood, words from the workplace, words from books. You can have loved them for years, or just be deciding to like them right now.

Here you might want to have recourse to an old writer's technique: it's called cheating. If when you get to a particular letter you can't think of a word that you like, go to the dictionary, open it at that letter, and put your finger down without looking. If you don't like that word, try the one above or below it. This is an old form of divination called the *sortes virgilianae* – people used to take their problems to Virgil's works, stick a finger in at random, and see if the quote helped them out.

Once you've assembled twenty-six, ask yourself: 'Why did I pick this word?' Was it because of its sound or its sense? Only rarely will it be fifty-fifty, more usually it's predominantly one or the other. But a writer's vocabulary must be a balanced unit, equally full of sound and sense. So pick another twenty-six words, and this time use the opposite category: if you picked 'abstract' because of its sense, pick 'abalone' because of its sound, and vice versa.

Now let's construct a simple acrostic: take the letters of your first name, and run them down the left column of a page. Mine would be:

B

I

L

L

Take your choices for each letter of your name. (As you can see, for mine I would have to find two more favourites beginning with 'l'.) Write a sentence for each letter, which must contain the two words. Keep it relatively brief, so there's a chance of picking up its rhythm, and try to make it make sense, but don't worry too much about that. See if you can count the number of beats it contains, but don't worry about regularising these.

This exercise generates a strange kind of self-portrait: it builds a picture of you out of letters and words, all of which are more or less intimately connected to you. Is it therefore in your 'voice'? Of course not, but there may be turns of phrase that strike you as characteristic. Note these. If there aren't any, do the same for your surname, or pick a theme word, a hobby you like, for instance 'bowling' or 'ikebana' (flower arranging), and do the same for that.

Notice I haven't asked you to make connections between each of the sentences, or indeed between all of the sentences and the name which forms the acrostic. You are of course at liberty to do so, but consider this: your voice is not just built up of what you say, it is also composed of what you don't say, the pauses or leaps between sentences or topics. Which feels right for you?

You may feel that poetic voice is something much more to do with tone or subject matter. But poets tend to be literal creatures when it comes to language: your voice, whatever it is, is made of specific words in specific combinations. My suggestion is: find the words, then look for the combinations. So pick a word summing up a tone you're after, or a subject – say 'licentious' or 'Luddite' – and try to explore that tone or subject in the sentences you construct.

This exercise creates a set of laboratory conditions where all these issues can be explored. Start keeping a record of changes to your favourite words: over a period of time it may settle down to Hugo's 'words you can own'.

The search for a voice is not something that will be resolved in the duration of this course, or even in years of writing. Sometimes the discovery of something we can classify as our voice coincides with a weariness with that voice, and the struggle begins to create a new voice. But the act of searching, concentrating as it does on reading and listening to our work, considering our feelings about words and tone with greater intensity, tunes our instrument, language, and polishes our technique.

Idiolect

Each of us clearly has an idiolect, a particular way of speaking derived from our upbringing and education. Our parents' and relatives' speech patterns and vocal tics and mannerisms; the way people speak where we were born; the way people speak where we live now; what we've read and when we read it: all these feed in to the way we unconsciously select one expression over another, one rhythm or one word as opposed to another. Poetry enables us to become as conscious as possible about the nuances of language, indeed to manipulate those elements to an aesthetic end.

For some writers, the task is to remain as authentic to those patterns as possible; for others, their idiolect is the basic template they will manipulate or even step away from to create new modes of expression. You will explore your voice to decide which tactic is right for which poem.

Michael Longley states:

> Poetry is mainly about putting the right word in the right place, a question of rhythm more than anything else. The ideal choice of word also decides tone of voice and verbal colour. This is where the idiomatic nature of English is invaluable. We can further enrich the argot by turning to dialect, though as one who speaks fairly standard English I would only do so when the dialect of my region, Ulster Scots, sets free a concept or phrase or line which would otherwise not be accessible to me.

> (Longley, 1996, p.115)

Notice how for Longley there is no sense that one type of language is superior to another. In creative terms there is no debate about whether one form of speech is 'proper' and another 'improper', there is only an issue about how naturally the language will fit in the poem in question.

You might like to have a look at that list of favourite words: Are any of them words which are local to your area or even family words like Paul Muldoon's term for a hot-water bottle, 'quoof'? (We'll look at his poem of this name in Activity 16.5.) If there's another language spoken in your home, are there words in that language which are used even when speaking English? Are any words there because they are used by your favourite writers?

ACTIVITY 14.3

Reading

Now read 'શેરડી *(Shérdi)'* by Sujata Bhatt, from *New British Poetry* (2004 [1998], pp.21–2). Do you feel her introduction of non-English terms is subtle or intrusive?

શેરડી *(Shérdi)*

The way I learned
to eat sugar cane in Sanosra:
I use my teeth
to tear the outer hard *chaal*
then, bite off strips
of the white fibrous heart –
suck hard with my teeth, press down
and the juice spills out.

January mornings
the farmer cuts tender green sugar cane
and brings it to our door.
Afternoons, when the elders are asleep
we sneak outside carrying the long smooth stalks.
The sun warms us, the dogs yawn,
our teeth grow strong
our jaws are numb;
for hours we suck out the *russ*, the juice
sticky all over our hands.

So tonight
when you tell me to use my teeth,
to suck hard, harder,
then, I smell sugar cane grass,
in your hair
and imagine you'd like to be
shérdi   shérdi   out in the fields
the stalks sway
opening a path before us

શેરડી (Shérdi): sugar cane

DISCUSSION

Sujata Bhatt cleverly plays intimacy off against what is, for some of us, an exotic setting. Notice how she places Gujarati before English and only glosses the title at the end of the poem. So there is a parallel between the delayed revelation of her sensual subject matter and the revelation (for an English-speaking audience) of her language. This delay is reflected in the choice whether or not to gloss words in the text: *chaal* is not glossed, while, later on, *russ* is. Of course, drawing out this line by adding this gloss also contributes towards the languorous atmosphere of the poem: 'for hours we suck out the *russ*, the juice.'

Despite this sophisticated layering of language, the tone of this poem is conversational until the lyric shift in the final part, where the repetition of the title takes on an incantatory feel. She convinces us that this mixture of language is entirely natural, even when she's clearly manipulating it towards her aesthetic end.

How natural do you think the voice we encounter in poetry should sound? What about a writer like Tom Leonard (1995) who abandons conventional spelling in order to represent the voice of a particular city and class? Are there certain ways of speaking that you personally find less suitable? Do you feel that it is part of the poet's task to present the best of the language?

These are not leading questions. Decorum – finding the most suitable language for a given poem – is an important standard for the poet to pursue. Our notion of what is natural or appropriate, however fraught, forms an inevitable part of the process of composition.

Can we always say a poem should sound natural in the sense that all of its language should appear as the ordinary idiolect of whoever we imagine to be speaking the poem? But what if there isn't a definite, single speaker of the poem? What if the speaker is a robot or an antelope?

The issue of idiolect and the associated matter of finding a suitable register for a poem are very like the issue of finding a voice. It opens us to a sense of the astonishingly diverse ways of writing at our disposal, some of which may well not sound particularly natural, some of which resoundingly will. The real issue remains: are they effective, and if so, what is that effect? Is it, as Michael Longley concludes, something that could not have been achieved by any other means?

ACTIVITY 14.4
Writing

Write for 10 minutes about an incident from your childhood where you were the centre of attention. It could be the time a relative showed you how to cook or garden; it could be a short performance you put on of your sporting or musical prowess. Write about what happened, where it happened, how everyone reacted.

Then write for a further 10 minutes about that incident from the point of view of the relatives or neighbours who witnessed it. See if there are any terms or modes of expression they would use but you would not. See if they would notice different things about what happened or its implications.

The exploration of idiolect is an exploration of resources. It is not incumbent on you to discover or learn a lost language, or to choose to write in the other language spoken in your family, or to put on an accent in your poetry that you wouldn't be comfortable speaking. But it is important that your poetry is not built out of a partial model of the range of Englishes and other languages that make up your linguistic consciousness.

Personae

Poetry is not always about self-expression in the sense that the 'I' who speaks in the poem is always the 'I' of the poet. Sometimes giving voice to others can be the most effective way we can find of expressing what we want to say. That other voice can be our polar opposite or a historical personage; it can be a character from someone else's fiction or even an object. Some poets have found that finding and fully inhabiting these other voices becomes the driving principle of their poetry.

By exploring the range of voices we can inhabit, we gain insights into ourselves. Sometimes we even gain insights into the constructed nature of the voice we employ when we attempt to speak as ourselves.

ACTIVITY 14.5
Reading

Read Edwin Morgan in interview on this issue, Reading 31 on p.539; and then read Jo Shapcott's 'The Mad Cow Talks Back', from *Phrase Book* (1992, p.41). Imagine a world in which literally everything had a voice: would it drive you as mad as Jo Shapcott's cow?

The Mad Cow Talks Back

I'm not mad. It just seems that way
because I stagger and get a bit irritable.
There are wonderful holes in my brain
through which ideas from outside can travel
at top speed and through which voices,
sometimes whole people, speak to me

about the universe. Most brains are too
compressed. You need this spongy
generosity to let the others in.

I love the staggers. Suddenly the surface
of the world is ice and I'm a magnificent
skater turning and spinning across whole hard
Pacifics and Atlantics. It's risky when
you're good, so of course the legs go before,
behind, and to the side of the body from time
to time, and then there's the general embarrassing
collapse, but when that happens it's glorious
because it's always when you're travelling
most furiously in your mind. My brain's like
the hive: constant little murmurs from its cells
saying this is the way, this is the way to go.

DISCUSSION

Some of you may have expected to get Browning's 'My Last Duchess' at this point. But that poem can make us think that adopting the voice of a persona is essentially a dramatic action; that your character has to have almost Shakespearean or at least novelistic stature. What Morgan is arguing is that voice is a way of perceiving and interpreting the world, and that the range of personae open to us is extraordinarily diverse, only bound by our sense of empathy. Real and imaginary people, yes, but also animals and inanimate objects.

Jo Shapcott's poem isn't exactly a dramatic monologue by a character you can imagine meeting. The Mad Cow isn't simply a cow with BSE; she also seems to be readable as a woman, and as a kind of allegorical figure, though she doesn't 'stand' unambiguously for Progress or The Dangers of Progress. She requires us to extend our idea of what the poetic voice can contain, which is what I was hinting at above when I said that 'natural' wasn't always a useful concept to describe diction. The cow speaks like a sensible, literate woman, but she embodies something that goes beyond both sanity and the human.

So when you explore personae, I suggest you start with an animal or an object. It can be good to start with the non-human, for the simple reason that it forces our attention on to issues of voice. It's hard to do an impersonation of an apple, whereas most of us would have a set response if we were asked to become a musketeer. The object obliges us to think as far as possible without preconceptions.

ACTIVITY 14.6
Writing

Earlier, in Activity 13.3, I asked you to write about an animal; and, in Activity 12.1, I gave you the option of writing in the voice of an object from a postcard. You can go back to one of these and revise them in the light of the following instructions, or you can choose another animal or another object.

If you opt for the latter, pick an animal you've observed recently, perhaps a dog that is frequently walked by your house, or a cat whose territory you appear to be in. It could be a bird or other creature you've seen out of your window. (One night I opened my window to watch a ship go down the Tyne, and saw that there was a fox loping along the deserted road. The streetlights seemed to bleach all the colour out of it, and I noticed that it was running with a limp.)

If you pick an object, why not select one already in your house, perhaps something you've not looked at for a while, or even neglected? Garden furniture can work as well as kitchen implements; old souvenirs have as much to say as items of clothing.

Write for 15 minutes in the voice of this animal or this object. Consider how it might sound: a hacksaw might make a wheedling noise, full of 's's and fricatives. Think about how it might construct its speech: would an onion's sentences be full of parentheses, one inside another? Imagine what it most wants to say: would that bottle of untouched plum brandy be like the genie in the Arabian Nights, its early eagerness replaced by bitterness after years of neglect?

DISCUSSION

How different was the voice you achieved in the last exercise to your own voice? Writing in voices is a way of looking back at ourselves. Sometimes we reveal more, catch more of a tone we recognise, by trying to go away from that voice. Sometimes not writing in our own voice helps us to define what that voice must therefore be.

The 'I' who appears in your poems is both intimately like and radically unlike you. It is a construct in the same way a poem in the voice of an onion is a construct. You can make it as like you as possible but, due to your selectivity and your invention, and the fact you're always creating a version of events, it's not exactly you. That doesn't make it a dramatic character exactly, but it means you can analyse this persona with the same degree of distance with which you analysed the object or the animal.

Narrative and other discourses

For most of literary history, poetry has been a way of telling stories. The lyric poem, in which a voice, more or less identified with the poet, speaks about experiences in the life of that poet, is just one form among many. When a story is told in verse, there is room to step away from this kind of verisimilitude and explore the act of storytelling. This may result in a narrative that feels less plot-driven than prose fiction, one that can experiment with pace or conventions of realism. Or it may result in the pared-down, super-real narration that we associate with ballads.

There are other ways of approaching the poetic act, some of which have a lineage extending over thousands of years, others being more the product of the last century's radical change and experimentation. Verse has been used to write about the nature of the universe; it has been written to appear on public art; and it has been collaged from the writing of others. Every mode should be examined for its possible expressiveness, and each way your voice can be extended should be examined.

In this section of the chapter we will look firstly at narrative in verse, and then experiment with moving away from conventional lyric subjects.

Read 'A Peculiar Suicide' by Matthew Sweeney, from *Cacti* (1992, p.13). Consider the implications of this narrative: what are we not being told?

ACTIVITY 14.7

Reading

A Peculiar Suicide

Begin with the note left on the table,
saying 'You'll never find me',
in a ring of photographs of sons.

Ask the moustached, diving policeman
how many river-holes he searched
where the salmon spawn in glaur.

Ask colleagues, ask the long one
who searched the farm – he'll tell you
he found nothing bar the note.

Ask the neighbour who played dominoes,
as usual, with him in the bar
the night before he disappeared,

and who saw the spade was missing
from its usual place, and got
the assembled police wondering why.

Got them scouring the grassland
around the house, until finally
they found it, and freshly laid sods

hiding planks and a bin-lid
with a rope attached, and a tunnel
that didn't go very far.

Ask what they found at the end –
just him, and the pill jar,
and the coldest hot-water bottle of all.

DISCUSSION   As with other Sweeney poems, this is a macabre account of what happened to an anonymous protagonist. His poetry can be full of names, particularly place names, and its register is carefully assembled to suggest setting, often his native Donegal (notice the muddy Celtic word 'glaur'). But frequently the subject of his poems remains nameless, so we feel that we are being let in to an account of awful events as outsiders, bystanders suddenly being given a shocking confidence. This is as deliberate a narrative device as Kafka telling us only the initial of his protagonist: K.

The genre this poem most resembles with its missing spade is the murder mystery – notice the instructions: 'Begin ... Ask ... Ask ...' We are drawn into the search for clues and encouraged to speculate about the elements we aren't given. Why has the man committed suicide? What has it to do with the 'ring of photographs of sons', for instance? But this is like the misdirection of the magician, and when teaching this poem I sometimes find myself reminding people: 'How did the suicidal man lay the sods after he'd put the bin-lid down?'

It is indeed a 'peculiar' suicide, and most of the peculiarity is generated by what the poet chooses to leave out, and how he focuses in like a tracking shot, finishing on that striking image, 'the coldest hot-water bottle of all.'

ACTIVITY 14.8   Think of the most unusual thing that's happened to you in recent
Writing   weeks, or something odd that you've witnessed or someone has reported to you. If you've been keeping your notebook going, then you should

have plenty such incidents to hand. Another resource is the newspaper or internet, which is continually reporting small 'human interest' stories.

If you can't think of anything, here are a couple of examples, one domestic, the other outré – it's better to think of these as the kinds of thing to look for: only use them as a last resort.

Once when I was teaching this exercise in a school near Falkirk, one of the pupils told the class how one morning she had seen her neighbour get into her car whilst her cat was sleeping on the bonnet. She drove off to work and neither neighbour nor cat noticed what was happening.

This article was torn out of a newspaper and inserted into my copy of *Cacti*:

> 'Police in central Shaanxi province arrested two brothers-in-law for digging up the corpses of two women last year and selling them as 'ghost brides' to the family of two men who died unmarried.'

Write about your incident for 15 minutes, recounting it as though it were part of a longer narrative. Keep it in third person (he or she) and concentrate on detail. Speculate about the motive for what's happening, and what might have happened just before and just after it. Now select which part you're going to focus on. Will it be the incident or its projected aftermath?

Rewrite the piece cutting out as much of the motivation as possible and just focusing on that event. Search for the details which make telling the reader about motivation irrelevant. Remember you can keep it mysterious. (Handy if you can't work it out yourself!) Give yourself another 15 minutes on this, then make the usual notes preparatory to revision.

As I said earlier, the poetic voice isn't simply lyrical or narrative. We'll now examine some very different approaches to subject matter and genre.

Look at this grid of the classical muses.

Name	Meaning of Name	Domain	Symbols
Calliope	The Fair Voiced	Epic Poetry	Writing Tablet
Clio	The Proclaimer	History	Scroll
Erato	The Lovely	Love Poetry	Lyre
Euterpe	The Giver of Pleasure	Music	Flute
Melpomene	The Songstress	Tragedy	Tragic Mask
Polyhymnia	She of Many Hymns	Sacred Poetry	Pensive Look
Terpsichore	The Whirler	Dancing	Dancing with Lyre
Thalia	The Flourishing	Comedy	Comic Mask
Urania	The Heavenly	Astronomy	Celestial Globe

The muses were the daughters of Apollo (intellect) and Mnemosyne (memory) – an interesting parentage for inspiration.

Modern culture has laid some solid barriers across the field of activity the Greeks would have recognised as the muses' domain. Astronomy is now considered a science, but should that mean the heavens need no longer inspire poetry? Not many people would regard themselves as writing 'sacred poetry' these days, though poets as different as R. S. Thomas, John Burnside and Pauline Stainer can be described as doing exactly that. And who writes historical poems or epics any more? (Well, Tom Paulin and Derek Walcott for two.)

Our society's conception of poetry is still largely shaped by a notion of the personal lyric – what the Greeks might see as Erato's territory – with a dash of tragedy in the mix for seriousness' sake. Births, (four) weddings and funerals are the points when we traditionally turn to verse, and the verse we traditionally turn to is what we half-digested at school – a Shakespeare sonnet, Wordsworth on daffodils, Masefield at sea – hearts, flowers and the lonely heavens. And yet for centuries poets have been writing about everything under and in those heavens in the widest possible variety of ways.

It can be good to shake our voice loose a little from dwelling on our immediate surroundings and our feelings. And it might help to have nine types of inspiration rather than (infrequently) one.

Write for 20 minutes on four or five occasions in which you could be regarded as encountering any of the muses. Interpret this rubric as generously or as cynically as you see fit. For instance, we all had a brush with Urania when they announced the discovery of Sedna, the tenth planet. You may not have seen much contemporary dance lately, but when was the last time you stood up suddenly (perhaps leaving a hostelry) and experienced 'The Whirler'? Would you like to invent a tenth muse? Should she be the muse of cookery or gardening? Pay particular attention to the language you encounter in these different fields of interest.

DISCUSSION

Types of the introspective lyric still fill most of the poetry books you will read, and it may be the case that your work too will tend to fall largely into this category. But the poetic imagination has always been capable of approaching the world from a number of different angles. Borrowing from the novel or the film, it can tell stories with intensity, strangeness or humour. By considering its own larger heritage, it can adopt and adapt other discourses, approaching different subject matters from love and despair, or bring those other areas to bear on traditional lyric concerns.

Keep your voice as open as your eyes, ears and notebook.

References

Bhatt, Sujata (2004 [1998]) શેરડી (*Shérdi*) in Don Paterson and Charles Simic (eds) *New British Poetry*, Saint Paul, Minn.: Graywolf.

Leonard, Tom (1995) *Intimate Voices: Selected work 1965–1983*, London: Vintage.

Longley, Michael (1996) 'A Tongue at Play' in Tony Curtis (ed.), *How Poets Work*, Bridgend: Seren.

Shapcott, Jo (1992) 'The Mad Cow Talks Back' in *Phrase Book*, Oxford: Oxford University Press.

Sweeney, Matthew (1992). 'A Peculiar Suicide' in *Cacti*, London: Secker & Warburg.

15 *Imagery*

W. N. HERBERT

The image appears to be a primary component both of language and indeed of how we conceptualise our world. We are constantly comparing one thing to another, or considering an idea as though it were a thing. As you'll see, many words and phrases are inherently metaphoric, and the imagery in others is clear enough from examining the roots of the word. 'Nostril', for example, combines 'nose' with 'thirl', or piercing, an old term for a window. So the nostril is the nose's window.

The image, then, is one point at which the practice of the poet would appear to be derived fairly naturally from universal habits. This makes it a powerful communicative tool.

Images can be used to familiarise the reader with unknown or exotic phenomena. Another perhaps more fruitful use for the image is to defamiliarise the overly familiar, to re-present the world to us as though we have never seen it before. In both cases it expands the range of our experience.

Read the extract from Julian Jaynes's *The Origin of Consciousness in the Breakdown of the Bicameral Mind*, Reading 32 on p.541. Were you aware of this many instances of imagery cropping up in your everyday conversation? Does it make you think of others?

ACTIVITY 15.1
Reading

Glance back and check how many times I and the poets I cite use images to explain one or another point. Notice how many of those metaphors or similes are drawn from ordinary life – for the simple reason that images surround us. Ah, you may reply, but that's only the case for poets who have trained themselves to think in this way. Not if Jaynes is right.

DISCUSSION

I was sitting by the local pool thinking about this chapter while my daughter attended a swimming class, when I suddenly realised that the swimming instructor was talking in images. First she divided the class into seals and dolphins, and got each unit to swim like those creatures. Then she said, 'Imagine there's a ladder ahead of you in the water. Now stretch out your hands and grab this ladder and pull yourself through the gap.' First she used simile (saying they were *like* those creatures), then she used metaphor (pretending the water *was* a ladder they could grip). And, because imagery is an easy and natural way of learning, all the children did exactly what she asked. For them imagery was something to be experienced at a bodily level. Similarly, a good image in a poem induces something more than a superficial recognition; it resonates through the consciousness.

On the drive home we saw a large seagull stride across the pavement as though it were going to cross the road, only to stop as we passed. My daughter laughed, and said it looked like one of those businessmen with briefcases and squinty eyes. I tell you this not to bore you with how wonderful my daughter is (that might be a regrettable side effect), but in order to demonstrate how 'normal' imagery is. It's primarily a question of attention.

ACTIVITY 15.2

Reading and writing

Read 'Ode to Salt' by Pablo Neruda, from *Elemental Odes* (1991, pp.366–9). Consider the order in which the images are presented.

Ode to Salt

This salt
in the saltcellar
I once saw in the salt mines.
I know
you won't
believe me,
but
it sings,
salt sings, the skin
of the salt mines
sings
with a mouth smothered
by the earth.
I shivered in those
solitudes
when I heard
the voice
of
the salt
in the desert.
Near Antofagasta

the nitrous
pampa
resounds:
a
broken
voice,
a mournful
song.

In its caves
the salt moans, mountain
of buried light,
translucent cathedral,
crystal of the sea, oblivion
of the waves.
And then on every table
in the world,
salt,
we see your piquant
powder
sprinkling
vital light
upon
our food.
Preserver
of the ancient
holds of ships,
discoverer
on
the high seas,
earliest
sailor
of the unknown, shifting
byways of the foam.
Dust of the sea, in you
the tongue receives a kiss
from ocean night:
taste imparts to every seasoned
dish your ocean essence;
the smallest,
miniature

wave from the saltcellar
reveals to us
more than domestic whiteness;
in it, we taste infinitude.

Now select an ordinary household object or substance, place it before you if it's moveable or place yourself before it if it's not. Write about it for 15 minutes focusing on attempting to produce as many images for it as possible.

Remember that although visual imagery may be your starting point, you have four other senses to consider – once you feel you've exhausted all the things it looks like, try finding images for its smell or feel. Don't go on to taste if it's a bottle of bleach or a carpet, but consider doing so if it's a slice of pizza or chocolate.

DISCUSSION   This exercise explores the assertion that poetry can be made from ordinary things, indeed from almost anything. As Natalie Goldberg says:

> Learn to write about the ordinary. Give homage to old coffee cups, sparrows, city buses, thin ham sandwiches. Make a list of everything ordinary you can think of. Keep adding to it. Promise yourself, before you leave the earth, to mention everything on your list at least once in a poem, short story, newspaper article.
>
> (Goldberg, 1986, p.100)

Neruda's vision gradually transforms the 'normal' world. By the time he asserts that salt is 'Dust of the sea' you may even find yourself looking on dust in a new way: it's not quite 'salt of the land', but it is a kind of sandy beach forming in all our houses.

Are there any images you've produced that have this kind of transformative feel, making you think 'I could develop this'? If so, are they near the beginning or the end? The order you wrote your images in is at present random; it's a list rather than an argument. But that can be changed.

Look at the way Neruda's images are ordered: saltcellar, salt mine, voice of salt, cathedral, then a prefiguring of the sea image: 'crystal of the sea', then it returns to the domestic scene to start again: powder, light, preserver, sailor, then the second crescendo: 'Dust of the sea'. Each of these patterns seems fairly associative, but the order allows the poem to build and recede and build again to a climactic image, from which it subsides to the expansive gesture of the last line: 'in it, we taste infinitude.'

Spend 10 minutes on the order of your images. Are there any that run together? Are there some that stick out too much? Do they work standing by themselves? If so, where should they go? See if you can find an order that gives your list of images some rhetorical flow.

Poetry is, in essence, a natural human response to being in the world, and having a language with which to express your reactions. The image is one of the means by which we respond to experience – everyone produces images, and indeed anyone could produce poems, but not everyone does, because it involves practice and effort to be good at it. A good poem is a formalised, almost ritual exchange between word and world, and the unit of currency is the image.

Received phrases

As I've said, one of the hardest things a writer learns to do is actually to read their own work. From first draft to proofing, we tend to see what we intend to write, rather than what appears on the page. A clear signal that this is happening is the appearance of received phrases, what people dismissively call clichés. Many received phrases are in fact tired images, and many mixed metaphors appear simply because the writer has overlooked the way that two phrases have metaphoric content and so clash with each other.

Attention to and elimination of the received phrase rejuvenates our writing at a basic level. Having to rethink the supposedly self-evident is not only good discipline; it ensures that we are concentrating on the fibre of our language. Paradoxically, many received phrases contain powerful images, but these have become worn away and invisible to us through over-use. Rethinking and rephrasing such expressions can lend our work a vernacular strength that an entirely new image sometimes lacks.

Read 'A Nutshell' by Simon Armitage, from *The Universal Home Doctor* (2002, pp.50–1). Can you identify the received phrases and proverbs this poem is using?

ACTIVITY 15.3

Reading

A Nutshell

It's too easy to mouth off, say
how this matchwood and cotton ship of the line
got where it is today.

how it put into port,
shouldered home through the narrow neck
of a seamless, polished-off ten-year-old malt,

came to be docked
in a fish-eye, bell-jar, wide-angle bottle,
shipshape and Bristol fashion.

See, the whole thing was rigged,
and righted itself at the tug of a string
or turn of a screw, main mast raised

to its full height,
every detail correctly gauged, taffrail
to figurehead, a model of form

and scale, right down
to the glow of coal, and the captain,
toasting himself in the great cabin.

It's the same kind of loose talk
that cost us dear, put fire in the chimney breast,
smoking the stork from its nest.

At the end of the day, couldn't we meet
half-way, in an autumn field,
in the stubble of hay,

hearing the chink, chink, chink
of cheers, prost, mud in your eye, and stumble
through gate or arch,

to emerge on an apple orchard
in full cry, where tree after tree bends double
with glass, where every growth

blows a bubble or flask of fruit-in-the-bottle –
Jupiter, James Grieve, Ashmeads Kernel –
branch after branch of bottled fruit,

there for the picking, preserved in light?

From the implied 'In' that could precede the title, this poem abounds with what we might think of as clichés, but, because the tone has a strange air of desperation to it, we may feel inclined to stick with it to its surreal conclusion. What do you think it's an image for, this orchard of bottled fruit? And what light does it cast back on the act of revealing how a ship gets into a bottle – a kind of visual cliché? The thickest grouping of familiar phrases occurs around a point of possible revelation:

It's the same kind of loose talk
that cost us dear, put fire in the chimney breast,
smoking the stork from its nest.

Here we glimpse that the subject of the poem may well be to do with fertility, or rather infertility. The stork which has been chased away makes us think again about the test-tube quality of those bottles of fruit. If this reading is right, then the poem is using its familiar phrases in a sharply ironic way: becoming pregnant as a commonplace event is described in language filled with commonplace expressions and images – except that being unable to conceive draws poignancy from those same expressions and images.

Make a list of the proverbial expressions commonly used in your family – the phrases that appear over-used to you. When I did this, they turned out to be rather unusual expressions: 'canna see green cheese but her een birl' (can't see mouldy cheese without her eyes rolling) was said of a jealous person; 'auld age disna come itsel' (old age doesn't come itself) accompanied my grandmother's every arthritic pang; 'Eh well' was the stock response whenever someone was challenged and saw no reason either to engage with the challenge or back down.

Spend 15 minutes in the attempt to rehabilitate these phrases. One tactic suggested by Matthew Sweeney and John Hartley Williams in their book *Writing Poetry* is to take these phrases literally (1997, pp.32–4): what happened to her eyes when the woman saw the green cheese and how did the cheese get green in the first place? What and who accompanies old age and where have they all just arrived at? What might we find down an 'Eh' well?

Another strategy, following Armitage, is to imagine a situation in which such phrases could reacquire their original force. This could mean writing in persona, or constructing a scenario in which the cliché is the only possible concluding line.

There is in a sense no such thing as a cliché, only inattention to language and clichéd thinking. That's why I prefer the term 'received phrase', implying that you've used something given to you by someone else without doing enough work on it to make it your own. With care, any expression can find its role in your writing. With attention, the received phrase need never appear, you'll be so busy conjuring your own.

Attentiveness

Powerful imagery is based in powerful observation, in the ability to perceive intensely and originally. It connects us with the world about us in an intimate and enlivening manner. It is above all an act of engagement. The poet attempts to bind phenomena together through his or her senses, to perform acts of linkage that enable readers to experience their environment in different ways.

Learning to work with images involves training the eye, the ear, touch and taste and scent, to apprehend and define particulars. From the search for precise language arise equivalents to those particulars, so we must try to catch fugitive impressions and the comparisons that can come from them. By cultivating a vocabulary of images, we begin to cultivate the faculty of image-making.

In your daily practice this means working with your notebook in the way an artist works with a sketchbook. Carry it with you everywhere, and always give yourself permission to stop what you are doing, whenever possible, to make a note in it.

Whenever you see something that intrigues you – and it can be an interaction between two people at a zebra crossing or a plastic bag blown against a wire fence – describe it, and say what it is like. Start to think in images.

The important thing is not to prejudge what you're noting down. Don't decide beforehand that it's too trivial or irrelevant to your aims as a writer – you may find your aims have to adjust to meet some apparently random comment. Regularly comment on or rewrite these entries.

ACTIVITY 15.5

Reading

Read 'Summer Farm' by Norman MacCaig (2000, pp.435–6). How many images does he employ?

Summer Farm

Straws like tame lightnings lie about the grass
And hang zigzag on hedges. Green as glass
The water in the horse-trough shines.
Nine ducks go wobbling by in two straight lines.

A hen stares at nothing with one eye,
Then picks it up. Out of an empty sky
A swallow falls and flickering through
The barn, dives up again into the dizzy blue.

I lie, not thinking, in the cool, soft grass,
Afraid of where a thought might take me – as
This grasshopper with plated face
Unfolds his legs and finds himself in space.

Self under self, a pile of selves I stand
Threaded on time, and with metaphysic hand
Lift the farm like a lid and see
Farm within farm, and in the centre, me.

DISCUSSION

MacCaig began writing under the influence of Dylan Thomas and the 1940s writers known as Apocalyptics. His acute image-making faculty preserved something of that period's surrealist power. Objects are seen with an intensity that's leavened by a deadpan wit: what on earth are 'tame lightnings'? What a great deal of energy to give to a piece of straw.

'A hen looks at nothing with one eye/then picks it up' is at first reading a witty line. Then we consider the implications of the speaker being 'afraid of where a thought might take [him]', and the picture gains an emotional intensity. That 'nothing' which the hen pecks at has more than a whiff of the void; and the alarming ease with which the grasshopper finds itself 'in space' prepares for the existential image in the last stanza.

MacCaig's imagery is not just for show. It helps to build the message of the poem, and it underscores its tone. It is doing imaginatively what the poem is saying, making us experience what, otherwise, might be a purely intellectual proposition. Some amateur poets just leave us with the thought, and fail to engage us on the level of the image. And plenty of professionals dazzle with imagery, but forget to align this to the message of the poem. You must learn to do both.

ACTIVITY 15.6
Writing

For a period of not less than twenty-four hours, keep your notebook to hand, open and ready to jot things down in. On the kitchen table, in the office, in the shopping trolley – on the bedside table beside you when you're asleep. Write things down whenever they occur to you – with one proviso. Only write down images. The top of my boiled egg sits on my plate like half a meteor. The paperclips lie on top of each other like sleeping ants. The uncooked chicken looks like a smacked bottom. My partner is snoring like an exhausted lumberjack.

For twenty-four hours, think in images, packs of them like timber wolves in a shopping mall. Give yourself over to a way of looking at the world, like an optician in a bath full of spectacles. And note them all down, like a special constable arresting a parrot.

DISCUSSION

Becoming good at imagery is primarily a matter of perfecting the technique of transmission: how efficiently you get your impressions down on paper. You must first become alert to the possibility of image-making, then give yourself space to pursue that possibility, and finally become adept at recording it precisely. Think of the difference between the amateur and professional photographer: one takes pictures only of those things they want to remember; the other photographs what they want everyone to remember. One takes a few pictures, the other shoots off reel after reel.

Formulae of imagery

A mixed metaphor is merely the incorrect form of a highly useful tool. More considered combinations of images can create interesting atmospheres and even rhetorical effects. Just as a single image gives tone, a succession of images can build up layers of resonance. A coherent progression of images has an almost argumentative force, and some poets construct poems almost as a formula of images which adds up to produce a specific effect in the reader. This is for many readers a glimpse of the further levels of meaning which poetry can manipulate.

For instance, look back at Chapter 14 on 'Voice'. In Activity 14.2 I suggested you wrote an acrostic based on your first name, then in the subsequent paragraphs I gave four sample words: 'bowling' 'ikebana' 'licentious' and 'Luddite'. These are, of course, an acrostic of my name.

My point is: while doing one thing, poetic language is usually doing another, and a chain of images is one means by which this is accomplished.

Glance back at that remark I made in Activity 15.2 in response to Neruda's line, claiming that dust was a beach in our homes. That reaction, inverting Neruda's image and checking it for sense, illustrates something peculiar to poetry. In a poem, metaphor is very much a method of thought. At the first level it's how observation is integrated with reflection: I see A, hmm, that reminds me of B. At the second level it's a method of generating ideas: if A is like B, then I can talk about A in the way I usually talk about B.

So, if dust is like the sand you find on a beach, then I can talk about my study or windowsill or mantelpiece, as though it is a beach. As Jaynes suggests, language is often there before us when it comes to metaphor: my bookshelf is echoed by the shelf of land that extends into the waves, off which I could dive into a sea of associations. But why?

One reason is certainly to be witty, showing yourself off to the reader as able to think nimbly in a pattern. Another more interesting reason is to allow the pattern to help you think, to use a chain of images to take you somewhere you might not have got to without them. And this touches on an important aspect of writing poetry.

Poetry as an art form invites us to go beyond our preconceptions, to invent, to be truly imaginative. One reason for this is because that action, of going beyond ourselves, is an effect of the form itself: the poem is a structure which helps us to think differently, and one of the ways it does this is through its focus on imagery, encouraging us to think through our images in rational or irrational patterns.

Read 'A Free Translation' by Craig Raine, from *Rich* (1984, pp.36–8). Again, look at the images, but this time consider the connections between them.

ACTIVITY 15.7

Reading

A Free Translation

for Norma Kitson

Seeing the pagoda
of dirty dinner plates,
I observe my hands

under the kitchen tap
as if they belonged
to Marco Polo:

glib with soap,
they speak of details
from a pillow book,

the fifty-seven ways
in which the Yin
receives the Yang.

Rinsed and purified,
they flick off drops
like a court magician

whose stretching fingers
seek to hypnotize
the helpless house ...

This single bullrush
is the silent firework
I have invented

to amuse the children.
Slow sideboard sparkler,
we watch its wadding

softly fray.
Your skein of wool
sleeps on the sofa,

a geisha girl
with skewered hair,
too tired to think

of loosening ends,
or fret forever
for her Samurai,

whose shrunken ghost
attacks the window pane –
still waspish

in his crisp corselet
of black and gold
hammered out by Domaru.

In coolie hats,
the peasant dustbins
hoard their scraps,

careless of the warrior class ...
It is late, late:
we have squeezed

a fluent ideogram
of cleansing cream
across the baby's bottom.

It is time to eat
the rack of pork
which curves and sizzles

like a permanent wave
by Hokusai,
time to bend

to a bowl of rice,
time to watch
your eyes become

Chinese with laughter
when I say that
orientals eat with stilts.

DISCUSSION

This is an instance of a Martian poem. Martianism was a short-lived literary phenomenon of the 1980s, in which clever use of metaphor was the dominant characteristic. It sometimes seemed clever for its own sake, but occasionally you felt the purpose of the re-visioning was to make you think differently.

Here Raine imposes an over-arching conceit: everything in this kitchen has an oriental aspect. (We note that this is also reflected at a structural level: the poem is in three-line, haiku-like stanzas.) The integration of the imagery serves a purpose, allowing the meditative exactitude of Chinese and Japanese poetry to reshape this very English scene.

ACTIVITY 15.8
Writing

Consider your list of images for objects from Activity 15.6, and the list of images for the household object you produced in Activity 15.2. Take one image from each that you think shows promise. Now apply that image to the other object. For instance, if you said that the paperclips in your office were like sleeping ants, and that a slice of pizza was like a town being covered in lava, now try those images out the other way round. In what sense is your office desk like a town beneath a volcano? What does a slice of pizza have to do with ants?

Well, the computer is continually emitting emails and print-outs: could they be like lava? Are the paperclips now the trapped population of Pompeii? As for that pizza, capers could well be ant heads and olives ant bodies, anchovies could be worms and Parma ham the wings of butterflies. Ew!

Write for 10 minutes on each possibility.

The effort of getting an image that 'should' apply to one thing to fit onto something quite different obliges us to think clearly about the rules of the image, those elements which enabled us to map it onto the object in the first place. A was like B because elements of A corresponded to elements of B; if C is also to be like B, then we must define those elements of B clearly enough to look for them in C.

One effect of this exercise it that it can produce unexpected and disturbing chains of imagery (insect pizza indeed!), which brings us on to my next point. Images don't have to make sense.

The image is also a profound source of irrational power within a poem. Instead of making a piece cohere, it can also be a way of disrupting habits of thought or casual assumptions. To return to the metaphor of the formula, sometimes the links between images aren't plus signs but minuses, and not every poem should reach a definite controlled conclusion. Through imagery we can glimpse the unconscious motives which drive us, and we must learn when to trust an unusual, mysterious or even destabilising image.

ACTIVITY 15.9

Reading and writing

Read Selima Hill's 'Portrait of my Lover as a Strange Animal', from *Portrait of my Lover as a Horse* (2002, p.67). How do these images make you feel?

Portrait of My Lover as a Strange Animal

Don't ask me why
but soon I started feeding it,
on caterpillars, chocolate drops, soft fruit –
anything as long as it was small.

Its mouth was as small and tight as a wedding-ring.
On moonlit nights it liked to watch the stars
and lean against me
like a giant jelly.
Then came the night I thought I heard it speak.
It said my name!
O Lord, it sounded beautiful! ...
But of course by then I was out of my mind with exhaustion.
I had sunk to my knees in the sand I was so exhausted.
And the sacks I had carried contained only roots.
And as for my name –
it was only the sound of its gums
crunching the body
of its final wren.

As the title of Selima Hill's collection suggests, this entire book is taken up with a series of portraits, very few of which can be said to be based on a visual stimulus. These images arise from a powerful concretising imagination, which can take quite abstract ideas and qualities, and find a way of embodying them.

Some of these images clearly refer to elements of a relationship: 'Its mouth was as small and tight as a wedding-ring.' Others are finding form for more amorphous, disturbing aspects of intimacy: the depersonalised 'it' of the lover leans against her 'like a giant jelly'. Still others seem inexplicable, but nonetheless carry a strong emotive charge, and Hill, significantly, chooses to end with the most unsettling of these:

... the sound of its gums
crunching the body
of its final wren.

Think back to the exercise I set you in Activity 14.2 in the chapter about 'Voice': you had to come up with a series of words you liked, half of which could be words you liked because of their sense. That's an abstract way of approaching language, so were any of these actual abstractions, such as Beauty or Horror, Boredom or Heartiness, Bemusement or Honesty? Either pick one from your list or select a new abstraction that you now feel sums up something of your interests as a writer. What quality or value might you be exploring recurrently in your work?

Now write for 15 minutes, concentrating on embodying this abstraction in a series of images in the following manner:

- Imagine the abstraction is in a box, and this box has a circular hole in the top, just big enough for your hand. Put your hand into the box and touch the abstraction: what does it feel like?
- Now put your nose to the hole and sniff: what precisely does it smell like?
- Listen to the abstraction: what does it sound like? Is it saying anything?
- Imagine putting your mouth to the hole and tentatively sticking out your tongue: what does it taste like?
- Now take the abstraction out of the box and hold it in your arms: is this even possible? What is it like to hold? Does it have feelings? Can you tell how it feels about you?
- Drop it: what does it do?

DISCUSSION

Sometimes images can seem contradictory and even inexplicable. Our task is to gauge the kind of energy they contain, and decide whether it's right for a particular poem. Sometimes this energy is so strong that it demands a poem of its own, or, in Hill's case, generates an entire book. Sometimes you have to trust what you don't quite understand. T.S. Eliot famously remarked that to appreciate a poem it wasn't necessary at first to understand it. The finest poetry yields up new meanings every time we read it.

A lot of people are put off poetry because they can't tolerate the fact they don't fully understand something the first time they read it. They read nuance as nuisance, complexity as confusion. Lovers of poetry learn patience because they know that the payback is usually far richer than any instant hit. Poetry is an attempt to find words for sensations, states of mind or perceptions which previously have had no words – this is what Pope meant when he said 'True wit' consisted of 'What oft was thought but ne'er so well expressed'. What helps people to tolerate the delay in gratification is often the music of the language, which is why we shall go on next to look at rhyme.

The image is one of the basic building-blocks of poetry, like line and rhyme. It is important because, like those devices, it focuses our attention on language and what language does. At a primary level, language conjures images: I say 'dog' to an English speaker, and they imagine some type of dog; I say 'chien' and they imagine some kind of poodle. Not only do they imagine the animal, they have an immediate, uncontrolled reaction to it: dogophiles see an Irish setter streaming across a field; dogophobes see a pit bull squeezing out something disgusting on a blasted pavement. The image, then, is your remote control to the reader's brain – they're usually in charge of this, but for the short time they consent to read a poem, you've got it. Press the buttons wisely.

References

Armitage, Simon (2002) *The Universal Home Doctor*, London: Faber and Faber.

Goldberg, Natalie (1986) *Writing Down the Bones: Freeing the writer within*, Boston: Shambhala.

Hill, Selima (2002) 'Portrait of My Lover as a Strange Animal' in *Portrait of my Lover as a Horse*, Tarset: Bloodaxe Books.

MacCaig, Norman (2000) 'Summer Farm' in Robert Crawford and Mick Imlah (eds) *The New Penguin Book of Scottish Verse*, London: Penguin.

Neruda, Pablo (1991) 'Ode to Salt' in *Elemental Odes*, Margaret Sayers Peden (tr.), London: Libris.

Raine, Craig (1984) 'A Free Translation' in *Rich*, London: Faber and Faber.

Sweeney, Matthew and Williams, John Hartley (1997) *Writing Poetry: and getting published*, London: Hodder Headline.

16 *Rhyme*

W. N. HERBERT

Poetry is always trying to achieve a perfect balance between sound and sense. It is as aware of the music of language as it is of its meaning. Rhyme involves an act of linkage, an awareness of pattern: it explores the associativeness of sound. As such it doesn't simply take place at the ends of lines, and it doesn't concern itself only with the full rhymes traditionally placed there.

Rhyme in its fullest sense is the attempt to integrate the sound of language with the particular shape, tone and sense of a poem. In order to do this rhyme must be free to occur throughout a poem in all its possible manifestations – as we'll see, assonance, consonance and slant rhyme are all part of the act of rhyming, as indeed is dissonance and the obtrusive patterns of comic rhyme.

You still occasionally hear the complaint during the questions that end poetry readings that modern poetry doesn't rhyme. I usually reply, 'Anglo-Saxon poetry and Middle English poetry doesn't rhyme either – and neither does most of Shakespeare and Milton and long stretches of Wordsworth. It's a disgrace!' What the complainer often means is that their impression of modern poetry doesn't rhyme, this impression being formed from a recollection of early modernism (around and after the First World War), and a partial awareness of the poetry of the 1960s and early 1970s. Of course, just as in the past, contemporary poetry doesn't have to rhyme, but, as Michael Longley tells us, that doesn't mean it doesn't want to:

> A lot of modern poetry, I insist, does rhyme. My own gifted contemporaries, Seamus Heaney and Derek Mahon, work with equal ease in free forms and in stricter conventional stanzas that use rhyme-schemes. A younger Ulster poet, Paul Muldoon, has taken the art of rhyme to new heights of subtlety and sophistication. A virtuoso deployment of rhyme has been a feature of Northern Irish poetry for more than three decades. Every line in my own first collection rhymes. I now rhyme only occasionally. Rhyme is one of the things that words do. In as much as poetry takes advantage of all those things, I regret not using rhyme more frequently (though receptive always to assonance, its clashes and chimes). When asked where he got his ideas from, Yeats sounded as though he was joking,

but he was in fact hinting at a mystery: 'Looking for the next rhyme,' he replied.'

(Longley in Curtis, 1996, p.118)

'Rhyme is one of the things that words do' is a statement I'm particularly fond of. Not just because of the implied 'just' appearing between 'is' and 'one', but also because of the sheer matter-of-factness of it. Imagery is also one of the things words do; so is metre. Basically, so is poetry. Poets tend to get on with it; it's people who aren't writing poetry who fret most about these things. So let's write.

ACTIVITY 16.1
Reading

Look at the diagram below. This is what I (using the power of metaphor) call a 'Rhymewell'. As you can see, I've dropped one of my keywords from Chapter 14, 'lascivious,' into the centre. Then I've filled the nearer 'ripples' with fuller rhymes, and the farther out ones with less full rhymes.

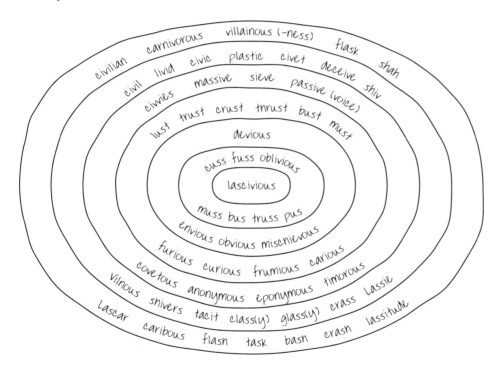

As you can see, apart from 'oblivious', the only truly full rhymes for 'lascivious' are concentrated on the very last syllable – even these aren't exact, as the 's' sound is softer in 'lascivious' than in 'muss'. As soon as we try to include two or more syllables in our rhyme, then the closest is 'devious' in which the vowel sound before the 'v' has changed slightly. If we abandon the 'v', more words come into play (including Lewis Carroll's nonsense word 'frumious'), but we're beginning to establish that English isn't a great language for unadulterated full rhyme. ('Passive voice', however, is an interesting near rhyme – remember that you don't have to match a single word to a single word when rhyming.)

What English is very good at is sounds that shade into each other, and those are the other words you'll find in this ripple. By adding the letter 't' to my monosyllabic 'truss' and 'muss' rhymes, I find a pack of suggestive terms highly appropriate to rhyme with 'lascivious': 'bust' 'thrust' and 'lust' don't seem to be in any doubt what they're about. By the time we move out to the next ripple, I've flattened that 'ious' ending to include rhymes like 'anonymous'. I've also extended my search to look for rhymes on the stressed sound 'lasciv' – the reader's ear will still be able to pick this up, so I can rhyme on 'sieve', and even (by shifting the stress a little) on 'massive'.

By the next few ripples there's a wide variety of possibilities, but some of them are starting to sound a bit remote ('shivers' – can you still hear that?) – I'm clearly approaching the rim of the well. There are still good rhymes out here, though, and even some surprising ones: 'carnivorous' is rhythmically a good match, and so 'obvious' I should have noticed it earlier. My favourite, though, is 'caribous' – its first two vowel sounds rhyme with 'lasciv' (this is what we call assonantal rhyme), but its last is only an eye rhyme for 'ous' (an eye rhyme is something that looks like it should rhyme, but doesn't when you actually say it). There's something about 'lascivious caribous' I find endearing.

There are a lot of words in this well, all more or less related to each other. If I'd stuck with the notion of full rhyme, I might have got two or three ripples out, but I wouldn't necessarily have happened upon 'carnivorous' and may never have noticed 'sieve'. The well method generates a lot of terms to throw into the mix when you're drafting something, and it's more organic than a rhyming dictionary. The other thing it does, as you'll have noticed at the end of my last paragraph, is create associations.

I may never write a poem about a carnivorous villainness and a curious shah in Vilnous, with guest appearances by an anonymous Lascar and, of course, two massive plastic (and crassly lascivious) caribous, but if I don't, it obviously won't be for lack of rhymes.

Pick a word from your original list of favourites or look for one in a draft you're already working on. Drop it in the Rhymewell and start listening. Try to get beyond the first few ripples and keep your ear alert for surprising terms. Do this for 10 minutes.

When you find yourself bumping up against the brickwork at the edge of the well, take the last term, the one you're least sure rhymes but are quite pleased to discover (mine would be 'caribous'). Drop it in a new well and start again. Give this another 10 minutes.

Now play with terms from both Rhymewells. Form associative patterns and see where they take you. Don't worry too much about making sense, and incorporate any other rhymes that occur to you as you write. Give this yet another 10 minutes.

Rhyme is all about the liveliness of your ear. The more attention you pay to the sounds of words, the more supple and responsive your own word selection becomes. Techniques like the Rhymewell shift us out of familiar habits of listening and help us to look into the hearts of words. Sometimes the things we find there are magical.

Look again at that last line by Neruda, or rather, at that line by Neruda's translator, Margaret Sayers Peden: 'in it, we taste infinitude'. Look in the words in the way the Rhymewell looked in 'lascivious'. Ah yes, repetition, the fullest rhyme of all: '*in it*, we taste inf *in it* ude.' Now there's a line that does exactly what it says on the label.

Full

If imagery is principally poetry's reclamation of the eye from disengaged, casual observation, then rhyme is how the poem reclaims our ear. The perfect rhyme can sometimes seem to point beyond itself, to contain sense in itself, though all the time we know it's the result of a happy coincidence of sounds. It can lend weight to utterance and strongly underscore conclusions.

It can also trivialise an idea by making it sound too pat. Full rhymes can sometimes feel expected, and even encourage facile composition, where the sense is being strung between uninventive sounds. Sometimes we can fall into accidental patterns of full rhyme in the same way as we occasionally employ received phrases and don't notice.

In other words the considered use of full rhyme is a powerful tool, and learning when to deploy it is a discipline we must acquire.

Read 'Leaving Inishmore' by Michael Longley, from *Selected Poems* (1998, p.22). What effect if any does the way the poem rhymes have on your reading?

Leaving Inishmore

Rain and sunlight and the boat between them
Shifted whole hillsides through the afternoon –
Quiet variations on an urgent theme
Reminding me now that we left too soon
The island awash in wave and anthem.

Miles from the brimming enclave of the bay
I hear again the Atlantic's voices,
The gulls above us as we pulled away –
So munificent their final noises
These are the broadcasts from our holiday.

Oh, the crooked walkers on that tilting floor!
And the girls singing on the upper deck
Whose hair took the light like a downpour –
Interim nor change of scene shall shipwreck
Those folk on the move between shore and shore.

Summer and solstice as the seasons turn
Anchor our boat in a perfect standstill,
The harbour wall of Inishmore astern
Where the Atlantic waters overspill –
I shall name this the point of no return

Lest that excursion out of light and heat
Take on a January idiom –
Our ocean icebound when the year is hurt,
Wintertime past cure – the curriculum
Vitae of sailors and the sick at heart.

This is a poem from Longley's first book, *No Continuing City*, in which, as he says in the passage quoted earlier in this chapter, every line rhymes. It marks a theme that recurs again and again in his poetry: the West of Ireland and its islands as a refuge, whether for his family, moral values, or the natural world, against traumas of all sorts – the First World War his father fought in, and the Troubles, which were to rock his subsequent work.

The poem focuses on the point of departure, so has an elegiac air, but performs a curious action: it freezes things at that point:

Summer and solstice as the seasons turn
Anchor our boat in a perfect standstill,
The harbour wall of Inishmore astern
Where the Atlantic waters overspill –
I shall name this the point of no return

The moment of solstice coincides with the moment of departure, and Longley poises the poem here, after departure but before arrival, since arrival involves change, threat, decay – note all those terms from illness in the last stanza: 'the year is hurt,/Wintertime past cure ... the sick at heart.'

Exploiting the way that a poem records a single event by emphasising that the poem will preserve that moment forever is an old literary trope, or tactic. It's what Shakespeare is doing when he tells his loved one in Sonnet 18 that 'thy eternal beauty shall not fade'. Why? 'So long as men can breathe, or eyes can see,/So long lives this, and this gives life to thee.' (in Allison, 1983, pp.186–7). Keats plays with a similar idea in the 'Ode on a Grecian Urn'. The figures on the urn can never finish what they are doing, and the poem contains the frozenness of that moment (ibid., pp.663–4).

In such a poem, you want the rhyme to be peaceful, clear, unthreatening, full. Even the rhyme scheme supports this notion of something being held and so preserved. If the first rhyme sound is designated A, and the next B, then we can see that Longley's stanzas rock gently between them before finishing where they began: ABABA. In the stanza above he reinforces this by rhyming on almost exactly the same word: 'turn' and 'return'. Remember what I was saying in the chapter on 'Line' about the fleeting sense we sometimes encounter, thanks to line breaks? Well here there is a similar effect through rhyme: we get the impression that the speaker of this poem would indeed like to 'turn' the boat and 'return'.

In the final stanza, rhyme is disrupted in order to demonstrate the disruption he fears will occur as a result of leaving the island: the A rhymes are far more distant. The first, 'heat', eye rhymes with 'heart', which is itself only a half rhyme for 'hurt', in that all its consonants are the same, but the vowel sound has changed. This latter rhyme is the opposite of assonance, by the way. These consonantal and assonantal rhymes are the mainstays of traditional Gaelic poetry, the sort we imagine would be known on Inishmore.

So Michael Longley's use of full rhyme plays an active part in the atmosphere, mood and purpose of this poem. And so, given the departure focused on in his title, does his departure from it.

ACTIVITY 16.4
Writing

Write for 10 minutes about a journey you took in childhood. It can be something you did regularly, or only once. Concentrate on the details of the mode of transport. It may be a bicycle you owned, or your parents' first car, or the method you took to visit a relative – train, ferry, plane. Write about its appearance, its smell, the details of the route, your surroundings.

Now put rings around the key words in the text you've produced: three or four will do. Spend 10–15 minutes on creating a Rhymewell for these, focusing on the first few 'full rhyme' ripples.

(This subsequent part can be done immediately or later, depending on how much time is available.)

Now revise the text to include as many of the rhymes as you feel fit. Try and write in lines if you haven't already done so. Don't make any special effort to put the full rhymes at the ends of lines, but don't resist if that's where they fall.

DISCUSSION

It's difficult to fit too many full rhymes in without everything starting to chime like a children's rhyme. Of course, this is about a childhood event, so that effect is not entirely inappropriate. How bunched were your rhymes? Did you find yourself fitting in all the rhyme sounds around your keywords, or did you spread them throughout the whole text? The broader the spread, the more chance there is of happening on a rhyme-scheme like Michael Longley's – not AAA, BBB, CCC, but something more blended.

When you compose with rhyme as part of your intention from the outset, you find that you often allow the search for a rhyme to guide your composition. This can be tricky – it's generally clear when the thought in a poem has been dominated by the search for a rhyme. Of course it can also be liberating when that search throws up a word you would never have thought of otherwise. That's why the Rhymewell can be a good way of exteriorising this process and providing a broad choice.

It can be good to decide roughly on what kind of rhyme scheme you want beforehand: relying on whatever pattern starts to appear can mean struggling to insert rhyme afterwards. We'll talk more about this in the next chapter; at the moment I just want you to observe the process of working with rhyme.

As we saw in the Michael Longley poem, full rhyme is not just a decoration. It, or its absence, can contribute to the meaning of a poem. This is a subtlety not available to those who only rhyme (and only rhyme fully) because poetry 'ought' to rhyme. That's a rather useless appendage to stick on a poem, however nice it sounds. A clear meaning behind your use of full rhyme won't happen all the time, but when it does it underscores an important point: rhyme, thoughtfully deployed, is an active technique.

Slant

Slant or half rhyme appears to be a phenomenon of the last hundred years or so. In fact it is a new definition for strategies poets have always used to build up musical patterns within and across lines. In Welsh poetry, for instance, where Wilfred Owen and Dylan Thomas encountered it, it's called *proest*. It widens the focus from full rhyme to consider the range of assonantal or consonantal shapes our ear can recognise as more or less distant relations of the original rhyme sound.

In so doing it broadens the range of English, allowing it to equal the rhyming resources of Italian or Russian by drawing on its native reserves of alliteration and vowel–patterning. It also reinforces the element of discovery which is an integral part of rhyme: the surprise of a good slant rhyme will invigorate the listener's ear just as much as a too-easily anticipated full rhyme tires it.

Read 'Quoof' by Paul Muldoon (1983, p.17). How many of these are full rhymes?

ACTIVITY 16.5

Reading

How often have I carried our family word
for the hot water bottle
to a strange bed,

as my father would juggle a red-hot half-brick
in an old sock
to his childhood settle.
I have taken it into so many lovely heads
or laid it between us like a sword.

An hotel room in New York City
with a girl who spoke hardly any English,
my hand on her breast
like the smouldering one-off spoor of the yeti
or some other shy beast
that has yet to enter the language.

DISCUSSION

This is a famous poem in which Paul Muldoon serves up another of his deft variations on the sonnet (we'll talk about the sonnet as a form in the next chapter – for now you only need to notice that there are fourteen lines divided 8:6, a standard division for this form). The play of images is nicely ranged between the vivid, the unexpected and the shocking, and so are the rhymes.

There are two full rhymes here, both in the first eight lines: 'bed' and 'heads', though the latter allows itself an extra 's', and 'word' and 'sword', though the vowel sound is slightly different. Notice how putting the latter two at the beginning and end of that unit helps to hold it together.

'Bottle' and 'settle' and 'brick' and 'sock' are consonant rhymes – the vowel sounds change, but the strength of the end sounds comes through clearly. So the first four rhymes are in roughly familiar territory, just as the sense is focused on the family, its language of the hearth.

But in the six-line unit we see what happens when you fish in the further-out ripples of the Rhymewell. 'City' and 'yeti' only involve a slight vowel shift, but what a surprising rhyme. It announces the increasing distance of the speaker from his origins. 'Breast' and 'beast' is (you'll recognise this by now) another eye rhyme. The most unusual rhyme, however, is the one Muldoon chooses to finish the poem with: 'English' and 'language'.

At one level this is a deeply satisfying rhyme: 'English' is after all the 'language' which has given its speakers so much poetry. But then we remember this is an Irish poet, from a culture which had its own language suppressed in favour of English. We note that the girl, whose breast is the focus of that bizarre imagistic leap whereby hot water bottle and yeti track confront each other, 'spoke hardly any English'. And we realise the eroticised absurdity of teaching a non-English speaker a purely private word. Of course by this point, 'quoof' no longer feels quite so strange to us, and so we realise that this is one way of describing the 'shy beast' we encounter in the act of '[entering] the language.'

The complexity of what is happening in this short poem is matched by the way the rhymes approach and recede from a 'standard' notion of full rhyme. Yet again, the sound of the poem reinforces its sense; the poem attempts the greatest possible harmony between form and content.

ACTIVITY 16.6
Writing

Since this exercise is related to the one you did in Activity 16.4, let's stick with the idea of travel. Write for 15 minutes about a journey that parallels the childhood one. This time, set it in adulthood, and write about a journey either frequently undertaken, or taken once that struck you forcibly. If you like you can try and find one that parallels the childhood journey in feel – perhaps it's even the same journey, but undertaken recently.

Again, select the three or four keywords, and, when you do your Rhymewells this time, look for those more distant, more surprising rhymes.

Again, rewrite the piece, setting it in lines and attempting to incorporate as many of the more slant rhyme words as you feel will enhance the sense. Think about how you distribute them, both in the line and throughout the poem.

DISCUSSION

Did you generate a lot of terms in each case, or did one search dominate? Was there a temptation to embellish the piece to include the more interesting rhymes, or were there rhymes you liked but just couldn't fit in?

Remember you don't need a lot of rhymes to bind a poem together – Muldoon uses just seven, each repeated once. So whether you're using full rhyme or not, you don't need to lather it on. Having said that, look at how many times within his lines you find words with '-y' or '-ly' endings: 'family', lovely', 'hardly', 'shy' – and these sounds go through the whole poem supporting it structurally.

Look at the two pieces you've written in these exercises. Do you feel that either one of them should be in full rhyme or slant rhyme? Do you feel they ought to rhyme at all? Perhaps a gentler, assonantal pattern would have suited better, or a robust, alliterative shape? At the end of this chapter look over all the pieces you've been working on, and start making notes about what sorts of sounds you'd like them to make.

Slant rhyme is to full rhyme what jazz chords are to standard guitar chords: it provides a richer texture if not the full resolution of a perfect rhyme. For this reason, it is a method of rhyming favoured by those drawn to subtlety and nuance.

Another strength slant rhyme provides is within the poem. Whether you rhyme overtly or not, these kinds of rhymes can recur, quietly, within the lines. They reinforce the framework of the poem.

Comic

When a poetic device signals its presence too strongly the effect is often comic. This is as true of rhyme as it is of far-fetched imagery or over-emphasised rhythm. Dwelling insistently on a single rhyme sound, or producing full polysyllabic rhymes, are devices a listener finds funny almost before a reader is aware of them. The impression that poetry always ought to be serious, or focused on 'important' feelings, means that some writers try to avoid such effects entirely (though over-seriousness too can bring on the giggles).

This is to overlook one of the great pleasures of poetry: that it entertains purely through its power to shape language. The listener is immediately aware when the rhythms and sounds of a poem are fresh and lively, and comic verse not only has as long a lineage as lyric poetry, if done well it communicates this liveliness in a highly direct manner.

Whether you think of yourself as funny or not, playing with language is in itself an invaluable learning process, and the comic rhyme is a powerful tool to that end.

ACTIVITY 16.7
Reading

Read the two poems 'The Shrimp' and 'The Axolotl' by Ogden Nash, from *Everyone but Thee and Me* (1968 [1963], pp.67 and 74). What impact does the rhyming have on the humour?

The Shrimp

A shrimp who sought his lady shrimp
Could catch no glimpse,
Not even a glimp.
At times, translucence
Is rather a nuisance.

The Axolotl

I've never met an axolotl,
But Harvard has one in a bottle,
Perhaps – and at the thought I shiver –
The very villain from Fall River,
Where Lizzie Borden took an axolotl
And gave her mother forty whaxolotl.

DISCUSSION

I know, they're deeply silly, but allow them to speak to you out of those absurd depths. Nash is a master of the polysyllabic rhyme, where it is the very exactness of the match, syllable for syllable, which draws your attention to its absurdity. That act of drawing attention to itself is very characteristic of comic verse: in terms of its shape and its sound it's always pointing out that it's just a construct, and a rather throwaway one at that.

(Or is it? Look at the limerick, which these Nash poems resemble – everyone knows where the rhymes go, but try scanning one to find out where the heavy stresses are. Here's one I prepared earlier:

Said I**sam**bard **King**dom Bru**nel**,
who **frequently visited Hell**,
'The **noise** and the **heat**
are **right** up my **street**,
but **what** they can't **get** is the **smell**.'

It's a highly complicated little form, and yet everyone seems to be able to make one up. Why? For the sheer delight of it, an important reason for writing often overlooked. Have a go.)

It's a particularly delightful anticipation we get on hearing the line 'Lizzie Borden took an axolotl', because we know what the next line will be, but we can't believe anyone would be so daft as to write it down. And yet that is the challenge we set ourselves every time we write. There's always a part of ourselves saying, 'This is daft,' and there's always another part of ourselves which has to find the gumption (courage is too serious a term) to write it down anyway. So comic poetry touches on something quite close to the heart of the compositional process.

Nash is clearly a writer deeply in love with language, with its quirks of expression and expectation. That is why he's able to turn the comic rhyme on its head in 'The Shrimp' and instead of a polysyllable, cut into a word for the exact term (you've never wondered, but now you know) for the sightings hoped for by a frustrated male shrimp who 'Could catch no glimpse/not even a glimp.'

And of course he demonstrates admirably that in poetry the structural equivalent of the punchline is the polysyllabically rhyming couplet: its role summative, its position delayed to just the right moment, its rhyme only too anticipate-able, and its effect excruciatingly absurd.

ACTIVITY 16.8

Writing

Look at your previous Rhymewells. There should be at least seven of them, and possibly as many as nine. I'd like you to pick from them the most incongruous words, the ones that have least in common with each other. Take two words from each well. These will resemble each other, but don't have to rhyme fully. Try to come up with one full rhyme for each word. You now have the rhyme words of at least seven four-line stanzas.

Pick a mode of transport you've always wanted to use, be that gondola or yak express. Your task, which you should spend at least 15 minutes on, is to describe a journey by this mode of transport in a poem which deploys as many of these rhymes as possible. You may end up with seven stanzas, or you could decide to use only a couplet from each Rhymewell (which would produce a sort of a sonnet), or you may end up with something shorter still.

DISCUSSION

As you've probably gathered, there's no particular need for this poem to make much sense. In this case as in many others, it's not the getting somewhere, it's the travelling that counts.

The need to bring in the seemingly irrelevant material generated by your rhyme words can create a bizarre narrative. That doesn't mean it'll be funny. Neither can the presence of odd rhymes alone guarantee a laugh – we can't all be cursed (blessed?) with the famously dreadful rhythmic sense of McGonagall.

Sometimes the material this exercise generates is more disturbing than comic. When you allow yourself to be almost entirely guided by rhyme it can be a little like free association: you're never sure what will come up next. That can be interesting. We don't always let ourselves open up when we're writing, and pursuit of the comic is one way around that restraint.

One issue that the attempt to produce comic verse usually throws up is the need for rhythmic control – jokes are all about timing, and a couplet won't have its maximum impact if you can't get both lines to move in a fluent pattern. In order to explore this, we need to move on to a study of what forms like the couplet are built out of: metre.

Comic verse encourages play with language, with ideas, and with your sense of the poet's role. It's a way of relaxing into that role, and it sometimes leads to more serious discoveries because we're relaxed: our sense of high purpose is off duty, and interesting material can slip under the radar. Playing with language is what all writers do when they're looking for new expressions; whether you're naturally funny or not, exploring such issues as complex rhyme, timing and the couplet can only have positive results.

References

Allison, A.W. *et al.* (eds) (1983) *The Norton Anthology of Poetry* (3rd edn), New York: Norton.

Curtis, Tony (ed.) (1996) *How Poets Work*, Bridgend: Seren.

Longley, Michael (1998) 'Leaving Inishmore' in *Selected Poems*, London: Cape.

Muldoon, Paul (1983) 'Quoof' in *Quoof*, London: Faber & Faber.

Nash, Ogden (1968 [1963]) *Everyone but Thee and Me*, London: J.M. Dent & Sons.

17 *Form*

W. N. HERBERT

By form I mean the related areas of metre and stanza. Together these constitute one of the most imposing aspects of poetry. Many people are suspicious of the assumed rigidity of a metric pattern, or the confines of often elderly stanza shapes. There is a natural tendency in the beginner to stick with free verse, and even to associate it with modernity, a relaxation of complicated rules supposed to be no longer necessary.

This is a valid position, if based on experience. We occupy a pluralistic era in which many types of poetry are possible. But if we are to be honest, then our decisions as to what forms we employ must result from open-minded examination of all the possibilities.

You may be nervous about form, but poetry is a matter of practice, not theory. By attempting it you can only strengthen your voice; by avoiding it, you only protect your writing from an unknown quantity. The unknown always tends to be more alarming than the familiar.

Certain rhythmic patterns are built into our literary heritage, but the reason to examine them is not that they are traditional, but because they enable us to do something with language that can only be approximated by other means. This is the same argument I've been advancing in relation to earlier chapters: formal issues are not dead weight, but living strategies for writing well. Feel free to disagree – cogently, giving reasons, in your notebook – after all, there are no absolute rules in poetry. But there are some very strong patterns. We ignore them at our peril, or rather at our art's peril.

These rhythmic patterns we group under the general heading of 'metre'. Metre isn't a metronomic structure we must adhere to, but something that grounds the rhythmic fluidity of the voice, something voice reacts against as well as with, something that enables sonority and stress to become measurable and memorable. We all have heartbeats, but all our hearts beat in different ways at different times. Nonetheless all these heartbeats correspond to a single governing principle: da **dum** da **dum** da **dum**.

Iambic pentameter

So, what exactly is an iambic pentameter? An old student friend who, as he was studying law, had little interest in poetic debate, would always cite the following: 'I think I'd rather like a cup of tea.' To put the stresses in:

I **think** / I'd **rath** / er **like** /a **cup** / of **tea**

Ten syllables and five little stress patterns, or feet, each going da **dum**. (The da **dum** is the iamb, and 'penta' is from the Greek for 'five'.) Try saying it any other way, or rather, try inverting the position of the stresses: '**I** think **I'd** rath**er** like **a** cup **of** tea.' You can get away with the first two, but the rest sound decidedly odd. So iambic pentameter follows the stresses that English naturally makes.

All those stressed sounds aren't equally weighted. Said with no particular emphasis, there is nonetheless a tendency to stress some words more than others – personally I'd stress '**rath**er' a little more than '**like**', and '**cup**' and '**tea**' more than '**think**'. But for the purposes of measuring the line we only need to find two categories: stressed and unstressed. In fact, that tends not to be the difficult bit: it's not hard to tell that both 'i**am**bic' and 'pent**a**meter' are stressed on the second syllable. The problematic part in writing pentameter is what we do with all the unstressed syllables in between.

Consider rephrasing the sentence 'English poetry is full of iambic pentameters' as an iambic pentameter. With its stresses in, it's

English / **po**etry / is **full** / of i**amb** / ic pen**ta**meters

That's got five beats, but it's not iambic. And it's fifteen syllables long, not ten. And the first stress goes **dum** da, the second goes **dum** da da. Then there's an iamb, da **dum**; and the next one goes da da **dum**. I don't even want to think what the last one is doing. (An important point to be made here is that if you can hear those beats and count those stresses, well done. As I've said before, this is called accentual verse, and these skills will take you a long way towards writing it.)

Another point to be made is that those first four patterns are perfectly respectable feet and much poetry has been written in each of them: **dum** da is called a trochee, **dum** da da is a dactyl; da **dum** you've already been introduced to, and da da **dum** is an anapaest. There are others, but recasting the phrase so that it forms an iambic pattern is the challenge here.

A useful tip is that it isn't unusual for the first foot to be 'reversed', i.e. a trochee, so in our example 'English' could stay. A less useful tip is: never reverse the second foot, it gives too strong an impression the whole line will be trochaic, so 'poetry' would have to go – except that's a far more important word here. Of course if 'English' went, the line could begin '**Poet** / ry'. The next sound would have to be stressed, though, to re-establish the da **dum** shape. What if 'is full' is contracted to '**Poet** / ry's **full**'? That's two feet out of five, but then of course you still have 'of **iamb**ic' to follow.

Perhaps you need to know another tip: elision. When you have two vowel sounds as close to each other as 'i' and 'a', you can elide one, or rather, treat a dipthong as though it's a single vowel. That would give us '**Poet** / ry's **full** / of **iamb** / ic ... ' – there's no way 'pentameter' is going to fit on the end of that, so there's a temptation to slap 'feet' on the end and be done. Except that's only four beats (or tetrameter). Of course you started out with fifteen, so perhaps you could allow yourself to fit it into two lines?

ACTIVITY 17.1
Writing

Turn the sentence 'English poetry is full of iambic pentameters' into iambic pentameter – give yourself 10 minutes. Feel free to rephrase it while preserving the essential message of the original phrase.

Once you've done that, spend another 10 minutes coming up with iambic pentameters to describe your daily habits, along the line of my pal James's 'cup of tea' line. These don't have to connect with each other: you're simply trying the shape on for size.

DISCUSSION

I've spent a long time looking at iambic pentameter, not just because it's the basis of a great deal of great poetry in English but because, frankly, it's difficult. Complicated from the outside, and no less complicated from the inside, but actually rather hands-on stuff. You just have to get down to it and cast and recast your lines till they sound like you.

Don't be tempted into distorting the way you would normally order a sentence. Don't worry if you have an extra unstressed syllable at the end. This, which is rather outrageously known as a feminine ending, is permissible. Just keep playing with the phrasing till you get something that will sit. Each pentameter is unique, individual, and will reflect your taste and personality if you infuse it with enough of yourself.

Here's what I ended up with:

Iambic ceilidhs **fill** our **Eng**lish **hall**

till **these** five-**foot**ed **danc**ers **climb** its **wall.**

The iambic pentameter is something you can spend the rest of your life mastering. It is much more flexible than its detractors give it credit for – usually because they haven't spend long enough trying to write it to qualify them to judge. And if you can get the hang of it, then writing in any other metre becomes far less difficult. One reason for acquiring competence is that you can then tackle a wide variety of stanza structures and poetic forms – the sonnet, the sestina, the villanelle – which are usually written in iambics.

The various tips I mentioned above contribute to that flexibility, so I'll recap them here:

- You can reverse the first foot – and the third or the fourth (though probably not all in the same line) – without disturbing the iambic beat too much.
- Reversing the second and the fifth make it harder for the reader to hear what's happening. So don't.
- You can elide vowels if they run together and are unstressed (in fact you can slip the occasional extra unstressed syllable in if you think you can get away with it – many do).
- And you can have an eleventh syllable at the end of the line if it's unstressed.

Of course you can decide to write in the more loosely stress-based line of accentual verse, and still work in complex forms; you can choose to write in free verse and work in them. But if you've got a notion of metre, you have a method of gauging what works or doesn't work at the rhythmic level. Look at the rhythmic pattern of the poems I've included in earlier chapters as examples. Look at the work you've produced so far.

Free

Many beginners' adoption of free verse is based on the misconception that it is not itself a form. In fact, each piece of free verse constitutes a unique form. Its rhythms, its line lengths, its shape, all demonstrate the rules of this particular form. One consequence of this is that the reader has to learn how each piece of free verse works through the act of reading. So good free verse is always simultaneously revealing its content and teaching us about its form.

This is an important skill for any writer to master. To consider the reader's reactions to this line-ending, or that indentation or spacing, to try to anticipate their thought processes, objectifies your methods and can help the process of communication.

Some free verse does not operate on these terms. Its intention is more to capture the movement of the poet's mind, in the belief that this is a more organic shape than established forms. As such, it is less concerned with its reader, and can be linked to a preference for the first draft, and a belief in inspiration. There are times when the results prove this to be an entirely valid approach, but it should not become the only model you employ. The apparently organic shape, when analysed, sometimes contains all the elements of formal verse, but in an unconsidered and even poorly-constructed state.

ACTIVITY 17.2

Reading

Read 'Mr and Mrs Scotland are Dead' by Kathleen Jamie, from *The Queen of Sheba* (1994, p.37). See if you can find a rhythmic pattern (NB if it exists, it might not be especially regular).

Mr and Mrs Scotland are Dead

On the civic amenity landfill site,
the coup, the dump beyond the cemetery
and the 30-mile-an-hour sign, her stiff
old ladies' bags, open mouthed, spew
postcards sent from small Scots towns
in 1960: Peebles, Largs, the rock-gardens
of Carnoustie, tinted in the dirt.
Mr and Mrs Scotland, here is the hand you were dealt:
fair but cool, showery but nevertheless,
Jean asks kindly; the lovely scenery;
in careful school-room script –
The Beltane Queen was crowned today.
But Mr and Mrs Scotland are dead.

Couldn't he have burned them? Released
in a grey curl of smoke

this pattern for a cable knit? Or this:
tossed between a toppled fridge
and sweet-stinking anorak: *Dictionary for Mothers*
M:— Milk, *the woman who worries* ...;
And here, Mr Scotland's John Bull Puncture Repair Kit;
those days when he knew intimately
the thin roads of his country, hedgerows
hanged with small black brambles' hearts;
and here, for God's sake, his last few joiners' tools,
SCOTLAND, SCOTLAND, stamped on their tired handles.

Do we take them? Before the bulldozer comes
to make more room, to shove aside
his shaving brush, her button tin.
Do we save this toolbox, these old-fashioned views
addressed, after all, to Mr and Mrs Scotland?
Should we reach and take them? And then?
Forget them, till that person enters
our silent house, begins to open
to the light our kitchen drawers,
and performs for us this perfunctory rite:
the sweeping up, the turning out.

DISCUSSION

In an interview in *Sleeping with Monsters*, Kathleen Jamie said she wasn't particularly interested in metrics (in Somerville-Arjat and Wilson, 1990, pp.93–4), and this is theoretically a free verse poem, ranging from very long lines ('And here, Mr Scotland's John Bull Puncture Repair Kit') to quite short ones ('in a grey curl of smoke'). There's no iambic pattern being adhered to, no rhyme scheme, but when we analyse the poem for stresses, we find that there's quite a strong recurrence of four beat lines:

On the **civic amenity landfill site** ...

hanged with **small** black **brambles' hearts** ...

and per**forms** for **us** this per**functory rite** ...

Some lines are longer, more are shorter (the three-beat line is probably the main secondary length), but the four-beat line, or tetrameter, occurs regularly enough to feel like the dominant structural element in this poem. It's argued that a lot of iambic pentameters rely on a slightly weaker fifth beat to get to their formal length, so can just as easily be analysed as more loosely patterned four-beat lines. Perhaps Jamie's poem is not that far from pentameter.

The point is that a notional rhythmic norm can be uncovered, and this norm contributes to the poem's effectiveness. When the poem stretches to a full five beats, 'and **here**, for **God**'s sake, his **last** few **join**ers' **tools** ...', there's a sense of the exclamation standing out rhythmically as well as rhetorically. And the last line, which is in iambic tetrameter, relies on both the expectation of four beats, and the more expansive rhythm of previous lines, in order to achieve its terse, elegiac concision (there's even a hint of a half rhyme to give us the closure of the couplet):

and per**forms** for **us** this per**func**tory **rite**:
the **sweep**ing **up**, the **turn**ing **out**.

ACTIVITY 17.3
Writing

Write for 15 minutes about an ending, but not a death or the end of a love affair. Write about when you had to get rid of some object you were very fond of – a car, a typewriter, a pair of shoes. Concentrate on describing the object and what happened to it, not on your feelings. See if your emotional response can be embedded in the description, in the imagery, or in what you did immediately after disposing of the object.

Now scan what you have written, look for the heavier beats among the unstressed syllables. Is there a dominant shape, as in Jamie's poem? Could some phrases be remade to sit with this shape? Is there a range of line lengths that seem appropriate to this piece? Consider where your line endings fall: is there any principle you can establish for these?

Spend 15 minutes revising your piece in the light of this analysis.

This way of looking at what we have written allows us to analyse something we have previously been trying to do on instinct. Most writers start with instinct, and gradually approach more formal analysis – some never feel the need to get there. The question is, how much of an instinct can someone have when they haven't actually written very much poetry?

The ability to scan your work gives you an objective tool. It also helps you to revise. (Remember, you don't have to change something to make it more regular: what if you decide you want the opposite effect?) It alerts you to what is happening structurally within your verse.

Free verse isn't exactly about doing anything you like; it's about being able to tell exactly what it is a particular poem requires, and working out whether that means it should or shouldn't conform to a historical norm. If it is to depart from that norm, how are you to do this? Certainly not by failing to notice when it's actually in a quasi-regular metre.

Free verse is not an easier form than metric poetry – sometimes it's just a less considered piece of writing. But at its best it is fully conscious, able to dip in and out of tradition as it pleases, producing a unique marriage between form and content that surprises and delights the reader whether they notice its radical shape or not.

Discovered

The discovered form frequently occurs because you create a shape you like in some section of a poem, and decide you want to repeat it elsewhere, or produce a variation based on it. You can repeat a syllable pattern or roughly duplicate a line length. You can put rhymes in the same places or just divide your poem into stanzas of a similar number of lines. Whatever you do, it points to an underlying truth about metre and stanza.

We all enjoy patterns in sound, and poets actively seek them out. Poets want to make patterns, not because they don't exist elsewhere, but because the elements of pattern are already present. Metric verse and stanzaic patterns are derived forms, not imposed ones, and engagement with them is part of the same impulse that drives poets to engage with language.

Read 'The Canonization' by John Donne, from *The Complete English Poems* (1971, p.47). How neatly do the sentences (and Donne's argument) fit firstly into the lines and then into the stanzas?

ACTIVITY 17.4

Reading

The Canonization

For God's sake hold your tongue, and let me love,
Or chide my palsy, or my gout,
My five grey hairs, or ruined fortune flout,
With wealth your state, your mind with arts improve,
Take you a course, get you a place,
Observe his Honour, or his Grace,

Or the King's real, or his stamped face
Contemplate; what you will, approve,
So you will let me love.

Alas, alas, who's injured by my love?
What merchant's ships have my sighs drowned?
Who says my tears have overflowed his ground?
When did my colds a forward spring remove?
When did the heats which my veins fill
Add one more to the plaguy bill?
Soldiers find wars, and lawyers find out still
Litigious men, which quarrels move,
Though she and I do love.

Call us what you will, we are made such by love;
Call her one, me another fly,
We are tapers too, and at our own cost die,
And we in us find the eagle and the dove,
The phoenix riddle hath more wit
By us; we two being one, are it.
So to one neutral thing both sexes fit
We die and rise the same, and prove
Mysterious by this love.

We can die by it, if not live by love,
And if unfit for tombs and hearse
Our legend be, it will be fit for verse;
And if no piece of chronicle we prove,
We'll build in sonnets pretty rooms;
As well a well wrought urn becomes
The greatest ashes, as half-acre tombs,
And by these hymns, all shall approve
Us canonized for love:

And thus invoke us; 'You whom reverend love
Made one another's hermitage;
You, to whom love was peace, that now is rage;
Who did the whole world's soul contract, and drove
Into the glasses of your eyes
(So made such mirrors, and such spies,
That they did all to you epitomize,)

Countries, town, courts: beg from above
A pattern of your love!'

This is the only non-contemporary poem I will ask you to consider, and I do so for a combination of reasons. Firstly, Donne is a great master of stanza forms, giving the impression he improvises his first stanza's shape, then effortlessly reproduces the same pattern. He has an almost unique ability to make the iambs fit his voice; his poetry is full of idiomatic energy, even if that idiom is from a different era. Secondly, when I was sixteen I was taught Donne by a very good teacher: this is a poem which made a huge impact on me when I began writing. Because of that I believe Donne is an excellent model to begin with when looking at formal verse. He thinks, brilliantly, and feels, intensely, and his form matches the movement of thought and the emotional range, precisely.

The poem opens with an outburst, which dismisses the whole of the go-getting world in a single sentence, ending with the same key word that ends the first line: 'love'. He then keeps that repetition up for four more stanzas, obliging himself to find ten rhymes for love (in fact he finds eight, and repeats two – nobody's perfect, or rather, not everyone needs to pretend they're perfect). In the course of this he considers sexual mores, myth and contemporary thought, ending with the outrageous conceit that he and his lover are sufficiently emblematic of Love to become saints. Let's look at the stanza form in which he does it.

The first four lines consist of pentameter (lines 1, 3 and 4), and tetrameter (line 2); they rhyme ABBA, an envelope rhyme (where the first rhyme envelops the second), which is found in the Italian sonnet. (A traditional British rhyme for this four-line unit (or quatrain) is ABAB, which is how Shakespeare rhymed in his sonnets. Ballads follow this pattern, but usually don't bother with the first rhyme: if we can designate a non-rhyming sound as X, then the ballad stanza rhymes XAXA.)

The next three lines are two tetrameters (lines 5 and 6), followed by another pentameter, and these rhyme CCC. This three-line unit is called a tercet. Finally we have another tetrameter (line 7) and, to finish, a three-beat or trimeter line, and these you'll recognise as a couplet: DD.

So each stanza rhymes ABBACCCDD, and the number of feet per line is 545544543. Sounds a bit bare. But this is notating the skeleton: to appreciate the shape we have to reread the poem: notice how many times Donne uses the fuller quatrain to establish the dominant idea for that stanza, then turns to a new idea or a variation in the next three lines, bringing each movement smartly to a temporary conclusion in his couplets.

These three units – quatrain, tercet, couplet – enable the poet to build a range of different verse shapes, each capable of containing the flow of very different thoughts and images. Varying the length of the lines allows you to be expansive or concise. These principles are as true of accentual and free verse as of metrical pieces.

ACTIVITY 17.5

Reading and writing

Don't worry, I'm not going to ask you to write a forty-five line poem in a stanza of your own devising that ranges across all of contemporary experience – you can do that later. What I am going to ask is that you attempt these building blocks: I'd like you to write three separate poems: one two lines long, one three, and one four. Try to write in metre, and rhyme, but the metre can be accentual or iambic, and the rhyme can be slant or full, as you or rather as the poem sees fit. Read the following, then give yourself 15 minutes for the exercise.

The couplet's strong summative note means it frequently ends up at the ends of poems: poems composed entirely of couplets have a hard job maintaining momentum unless each couplet is a stage in a developing argument or you don't pause the poem at every rhyme and let the meaning flow over. The couplet by itself must be conclusive. For this reason, poets like to write epigrams in it: short witty pieces which address a single issue or sum up a single person. Here's the Roman poet Martial as translated by Brendan Kennelly (2003, p.18):

You ask me why I like the country air.
I never meet you there.

The tercet takes things a step further, in that the first two lines can open up an argument the third can clinch: if you want to develop an image, then comment on it, you've more room. Rhyme-wise there are a few possibilities more than the single rhyme – CCC – we found in Donne: you can rhyme first and third AXA. The most famous tercet form in Western poetry, the *terza rima* of Dante's *Divine Comedy*, follows this pattern, though in Dante the middle sound is taken up in the next stanza: ABA BCB and so on. You can have a couplet followed by a third unrhymed line, AAX, or vice versa.

Probably the best illustration of the dynamics of the tercet is non-metrical, unrhyming, and non-Western: the haiku. Everyone learns the haiku as a syllabic form (5–7–5), though this is an approximate translation from an ideogrammatic language. What the haiku does perfectly is observe and turn: something is seen, then, with a little shift, it is reflected on. Here's Bashô (1985, p.75):

Small hut in
summer grove, untouched
by woodpeckers.

The quatrain is one of the most common stanza forms because it's big enough to develop an idea or image, and the even number of lines allows for a sense of balance. The number of possible rhymes is sufficiently diverse to lend some variety – not just ABBA and ABAB (or XAXA), but also two couplets, AABB, and three and one rhymes, AXAA, with the option of moving the position of the unrhymed line around, or of picking it up in a subsequent stanza (AABA BBCB). Many writers almost instinctually begin with some form of four-line stanza, usually following the ballad rhyme scheme.

The four-line poem can make a very satisfying unit for a short poem: there are many foreign examples of this, from the Rubaiyat to Rabindranath Tagore's *kabitika* to the four-line unit in traditional Chinese poetry. Here's one by the seventh century poet Wang Wei (1973, p.31):

I sit alone in the dark bamboos
Play my lute and sing and sing
Deep in the woods where no one knows I am
But the bright moon comes and shines on me there.

The discovered form, like the slant rhyme or the unexpected line break, can give a freshness and energy to a poem. You can arrive at a range of different forms by combining the couplet, tercet and quatrain, varying the length of the lines and the rhyme-schemes. You can also copy the different shapes poets have put together, including the Spenserian stanza, Burns's Standard Habbie, Byron's *ottavo rima*, Keats's ode stanza, and Arnold's Scholar Gypsy stanza (for examples see Allison *et al.*, 1983, p.110, p.511, p.592, p.660, p.783). The act of combining can leave you with elaborate shapes, so start simple and build gradually towards more difficult patterns.

Selected

Increased fluency with metre and stanza encourages writers to select more complex constructions. The various shapes which have emerged in British poetry over the centuries offer us a challenge which is a key part of the whole process of composition. This is the challenge of integrating content with form. Here we'll focus on one of the most durable short forms: the sonnet.

A poem is not a vessel into which we pour a previously prepared substance. On the contrary, by working within the particular restraints of a poem, we find that its laws alter our expression. An unexpected image or a surprising rhyme create new associations, and so too the demands of a stanza form reshape our thought. This is particularly true of the sonnet: we don't write to express ourselves, we write to discover what the sonnet is saying, how it expresses us.

By electing to write in an established shape, we firstly explore how that shapes us, but we also enter into a dialogue with all previous users of that form. We begin a larger dialogue than the beginner's conversation with him- or herself, or the address to a contemporary audience: we start to speak with the dead. By addressing a tradition, we place ourselves within it, and even consider how we may be read by future audiences.

The sonnet has a complicated history, which means it has come down to us in a number of forms. Two are commonly used in poetry in English: the Petrarchan (its name reflects the form's Italian origins, Petrarch being one of its first masters), and the Shakespearean (not that he was the only Elizabethan to pen a few, but history finds it easier to simplify). Each is fourteen lines long, and there is a division after the eighth line which gives us two main units, the octave and the sestet. The different ways the two kinds of sonnet rhyme affect the way ideas and arguments develop.

ACTIVITY 17.6
Reading

Read these two sonnets. The first, by Edwin Morgan, is Petrarchan; the second, by Eleanor Brown, is Shakespearean. Observe the different patterns of rhyme, and consider what impact these have on each poem's argument.

Glasgow Sonnets, i

A mean wind wanders through the backcourt trash.
Hackles on puddles rise, old mattresses
puff briefly and subside. Play-fortresses

of brick and bric-a-brac spill out some ash.
Four storeys have no windows left to smash,
but in the fifth a chipped sill buttresses
mother and daughter the last mistresses
of that black block condemned to stand, not crash.
Around them the cracks deepen, the rats crawl.
The kettle whimpers on a crazy hob.
Roses of mould grow from ceiling to wall.
The man lies late since he has lost his job,
smokes on one elbow, letting his coughs fall
thinly into an air too poor to rob.

(Morgan, 1990, p.289)

XLIII

He is a very inoffensive man;
a man without grave faults or dreadful tastes,
who need not be embarrassing; who can
tell an amusing anecdote; who wastes
less time than most on foolish flattery,
without descending into boorishness;
can pay a compliment quite prettily,
avoiding many kinds of clumsiness;

a very inoffensive man indeed;
an interesting man, and sensitive;
the sort that would be pleased to soothe a need,
if it were anything that he could give;
and I have sat with him this whole day through,
and hated him, because he is not you.

(Brown, 1996, p.40)

Morgan's sonnet, you may notice, has fewer rhymes in it than Brown's. **DISCUSSION**
Italian finds it far easier to rhyme than English, and this may well be
one reason why the form was changed. The structure of a Petrarchan
sonnet is built around repetition of two units you're familiar with: the
quatrain rhyming ABBA, and the tercet rhyming CDC. The first occurs
twice in the octave, the second twice in the sestet. Morgan has started
his sequence of ten sonnets with a bravura gesture: 'mattresses'
'fortresses' 'buttresses' 'mistresses' is no mean feat of rhyming from no
mean city.

(Notice that to scan this as a pentameter, the last syllable 'es' is being treated as stressed. This trick, treating an unstressed or more lightly stressed syllable as stressed in order to make up the pattern, is used quite often in metrical verse: my old bugbear 'pentameter' could be scanned as 'pen *ta* me *ter*' if need be.)

Of course you could allow yourself the luxury of introducing new rhymes in the second quatrain, and the sestet is sometimes rhymed CDECDE, which has the same result.

Eleanor Brown's sonnet breaks down into three quatrains, rhyming ABAB, then a couplet. The fact that you don't have to repeat the rhyme means that the quatrains can be more independent units, but Brown has chosen to run her first eight lines together syntactically and repeat her opening line at the opening of the sestet, demonstrating how a Petrarchan feel can be hinted at by the Shakespearean form. However, the emotive turn of the final couplet means the 8:6 division of the Italian sonnet is set against a 4:4:4:2 formation. Yes, I know I sound like a football pundit.

The effect of this shift of emphasis to the last two lines is to make the development of a Shakespearean sonnet feel more linear. The Petrarchan can abruptly shift around the end of the octave, an effect called the *volta* or leap, like the turn in a haiku. As we see the Shakespearean is at liberty to do this too – these are flexible forms which have evolved to follow patterns of thought, and indeed to guide thought into patterns.

ACTIVITY 17.7
Writing

Donne says in 'The Canonization' 'We'll build in sonnets pretty rooms'. I'd like you to write a sonnet about a room you've stayed in. It could be your childhood bedroom; your favourite room in your current house (even the room you're sitting in now); a room you once entered as a guest, a lover, a tourist.

Decide which sonnet form you'd like to try out, but don't trap yourself in it: remember both forms arguably consist of three quatrains up to the last two lines, when you have to decide whether to go for a couplet or complete a tercet. Try writing in pentameter, but allow yourself the luxury of lapsing into accentual verse: this isn't a penance or a workout. Don't feel you have to rhyme – the shape's the thing in the first instance. If you want to rhyme, don't worry whether you use ABBA or ABAB rhymes – plenty of poets have mixed and matched, and you're just experimenting.

My advice is to write freely for 10 minutes, generating descriptions, images and comparisons, and then do a little bit of planning. Treat the first two quatrains as introduction and development, and the sestet as reaction and conclusion. Consider including images for things in the room; comparisons of the room with other places; accounts of things that happened in the room; contrasts between how you felt once and how you feel now. Consider fitting those various ideas into the units you've already worked with: quatrain, tercet, couplet.

Give yourself 15–20 minutes to work on the sonnet (Shelley took fifteen for 'Ozymandias', quick work even for him, but it goes to show it can be done). Return to it as often as is necessary, but work in short, 15 minute bursts.

DISCUSSION

Sonnets can be hard to fill, or hard to squash everything into, or your thought can fit one as snug as a puffin in a burrow. How was yours? Some people say 'never again,' others 'I'll get it right next time'. In either case it can be years before the subject comes along that best suits both you and the sonnet.

But there's a huge satisfaction when the thoughts and the rhymes and the stanzas all cohere. There's a sense of having made something new out of an old design, and this goes close to the point of being a poet at all. The word is derived from *poesis* – making, in Greek. In my tradition, Scots poets have been known as 'makars' – makers – since before the sonnet entered the language. Poetry is about making something new out of words, something shaped, unique and sturdy.

The engagement with form is the point at which writing poetry begins to be a craft, rather than just a means of self-expression. Whether that engagement is with previous forms, or the search for a new form that will contain your voice, doesn't matter. The point is that something previously incoherent has gained substance.

People begin writing by hardly noticing words, just concerning themselves with what words say. Gradually, words become substantial to them as musical, rhythmic units. Similarly, patterns of words begin to be clearer, whether those of the line or of the larger units in a poem. It becomes possible that something can be built from word and line and stanza.

The word stanza comes from the Italian for 'room': *stanze* (which is why I set that subject for the sonnet). Rooms are part of a larger structure, and this notion of the poem as house, as something habitable, is probably the most important lesson form teaches us.

References

Allison, A.W. *et al.* (eds) (1983) *The Norton Anthology of Poetry* (3rd edn), New York: Norton.

Bashô, Matsuo (1985) Haiku No. 233 in *On Love and Barley: Haiku of Bashô*, Lucien Stryk (tr.), Harmondsworth: Penguin.

Brown, Eleanor (1996) *Maiden Speech*, Newcastle upon Tyne: Bloodaxe.

Donne, John (1971) 'The Canonization' in *John Donne: The complete English poems*, A.J. Smith (ed.), Harmondsworth: Penguin.

Jamie, Kathleen (1994) 'Mr and Mrs Scotland are Dead' in *The Queen of Sheba*, Newcastle upon Tyne: Bloodaxe Books.

Kennelly, Brendan (2003) 'The Reason' in *Martial Art*, Tarset: Bloodaxe Books.

Morgan, Edwin (1990) 'Glasgow Sonnets, i' in *Collected Poems*, Manchester: Carcanet Press.

Sommerville Arjat, G., Somerville, Gillean and Wilson, Rebecca E. (eds) (1990) *Sleeping with Monsters: Conversations with Scottish and Irish women poets*, Dublin: Wolfhound.

Wang, Wei (1973) 'Bamboo Grove House' in *Wang Wei: Poems*, G.W. Robinson (tr.), Harmondsworth: Penguin.

18 *Theme*

W. N. HERBERT

Theme in poetry arises from the sense that there is an area of concern to which the writer keeps returning. There may be a set of subjects we write about which, on examination, share an underlying theme. Like voice, this is better discovered than imposed, but this does not preclude the search. The attempt to address large issues or grand abstractions often occurs when a writer has little idea what they write well about. At such points they imitate the journalist searching for current or 'important' issues, rather than expressing what comes naturally to them – except that a journalist has a specific editor and audience to satisfy.

Often the subjects which engage us seem unlikely or slight, and we have to trust that inner compulsion which will eventually reveal the theme. Sometimes that theme may pass unnoticed until a reader or a fellow poet points it out. By engaging with such themes, the writer begins to move beyond the compass of a single poem, and starts to compose and revise in terms of the sequence or even the collection.

Read the extract from 'Proceedings in Palmersville' by Sean O'Brien. What is O'Brien's attitude towards his themes: precise, imprecise; matter-of-fact, respectful?

ACTIVITY 18.1

Reading

> I want to write poems which are places, in which paraphraseable meaning has been drawn back into the place itself, so that the reading of the poem resembles inhabiting or at any rate contemplating the place. The original landscapes of my life – Anlaby Road, Hull, in the mid 50s; the flat behind the butcher's shop, with its garden of lilacs; Salisbury Street, with its vast, lost orchard; the tenfoots between the avenues; the riverwide greenmantled drains before they were filled in the 60s; the goods line at the back of the houses; the bodily stink of purple furnace ash and free milk in the vast yards of St Winifred's RC Infants: these are not something to use but to enter, though I don't know why. They are sufficient.
>
> Politics is also inscribed in this material whenever I examine it, although I'm sometimes told I'm wrong by the pure in heart. This should ideally have been the sole item in this document. It would also contain railway arches, viaducts, junctions, cuttings, dead stations, torn-up lines, dockside buffers, lock-gates, estuaries, the

Ouseburn, statues of De La Pole and Collingwood, lighthouses, sea-lanes, ice-bergs, places which only exist as numbers on an Admiralty chart.

(O'Brien, 2000, pp.239–40)

DISCUSSION   Notice how O'Brien's impulse to compose is concerned with physical objects in a definite landscape – there is a strong sense of political engagement, and an effort to recover the past, and these two elements are linked. His work attempts to give value to the undervalued, but the method he chooses to give people and causes value is that delineated here: he records places with tender attention to detail; he describes them closely and lists their attributes. We might argue that if politics is his subject, place is his theme.

Of course these are not separate entities, and Sean O'Brien's poetry is very much about finding points of fusion between them, but theme is what arises through subject, and O'Brien's themes are identifiable, not just by the care he takes to capture them, but by the air of bafflement and reverence they induce: 'these are not something to use but to enter, though I don't know why. They are sufficient.'

ACTIVITY 18.2   Take that first phrase from this piece: 'I want to write poems which ...'.
Writing   Write for 15–20 minutes a series of sentences all beginning with this phrase. Allow yourself to range from grand themes ('I want to write poems which are edible and thus solve world hunger'), to the apparently trivial ('I want to write poems containing corn on the cob'), even if this causes you to suspect that not all your answers may be entirely true. The important thing with this exercise is to keep going, to be writing down the rest of the sentence almost before thinking.

The task here is to sort out the wheat from the chaff. Sometimes there isn't any wheat, in which case you should set yourself this as a daily exercise: 5 minutes before going to sleep or just after getting up.

DISCUSSION   What you are looking for is the same thing you were looking for in the first exercise in Chapter 12: a hook, something that catches your attention and niggles at you, so that you start wondering: 'Might that be true?' One question you should certainly ask yourself is: 'Are these potential themes reflected in anything I've actually written?' Sometimes they are, but when they're not, perhaps you need to adjust your subject matter.

Next time you go over your three lists – of favourite words, of titles and of quotes – have a look at this list too: do you see any links, any possible starting points?

Theme isn't something which you can impose on your writing; it's something that writing imposes on you. Theme is that thing beyond our present understanding that we embark on a piece of writing in the hope of discovering. Often it can sneak up on you, so that you gradually realise it's what you've already been writing about.

For years I supposed my writing was about recovering a sense of intensity located in language and in place I'd possessed as a child, because I equated this with belonging somewhere, with being acknowledged and being at home. Then it dawned on me that it was precisely the intensity with which I experienced these things which meant I didn't belong: it forced me out to a position where I can witness home and endure lack of acknowledgement.

This version of my theme will probably mutate in another few years because, like writing, theme evolves, it isn't stable. People tend to look for hard-and-fast 'rules' that will carry them through the difficult business of being a writer. As I've said, there aren't any, but when you catch a glimpse of a pattern, it is, as O'Brien puts it, 'sufficient'.

Subject

Subject is to theme as the line is to the poem. It is that single coherent point of focus which nonetheless relates to something beyond itself. Most writers find in time that there is a certain range of subjects within which they write well, because these subjects enable them to express a key theme. This does not of course preclude the search for new ideas and new modes of expression. It just confirms that, with subject as with language, we emerge from a particular territory that shapes our tastes and interests. For some writers, this realisation begins a continually deepening search for the perfect expression of a given subject. For others it sets them on a quest for variations or even radically contrasting new subjects.

How we respond to a sense of our subject range can tell us a great deal about what kind of writer we are. There is of course always the danger of hardening into repetition, of making a virtue of limitation. But equally, there is always the possibility of growth, of continually more radical redefinition.

As we work with a sense of the greater body of our work, we confront the issue of ordering, of how to group subjects in order to engage the reader with the underlying themes.

ACTIVITY 18.3
Reading

Read 'Assumptions' by Richard Hugo, from *The Triggering Town*, Reading 33 (p.544). How concrete are his examples? Do you feel he's describing real circumstances, or scenes from a film?

DISCUSSION

Notice how Hugo's description is as detailed as Sean O'Brien's. Almost everything is presented in concrete terms. And yet elements of this setting contradict each other: the composite nature of the triggering town, composed at once of many real and unreal towns, can quite happily contain contrary stimuli. The effect is both dream-like and cinematic, bobbing from grainy tracking shots to sudden documentary close-ups. It's not exactly a list of subjects, but it's certainly a list of those characteristics his potential subjects are likely to possess.

Because subject is a more objective area than theme, in that your work is always about something at a surface level, whereas theme may take several readings to emerge, it lends itself to these more graphic presentations. Can you tell from this list what Hugo's underlying theme is?

Notice the way he drifts in and out of the triggering town: sometimes he is present as a protagonist, sometimes he just records what's happening. Be aware that you may well be the subject of your poetry, but that doesn't mean it's all about you: other people, other voices, may define your subject as well as you do.

ACTIVITY 18.4
Writing

Look over everything you've written, the unfinished and less successful pieces as well as those you think might be starting to gel. Consider what you've been writing in your notebook. Everything is relevant at this stage. Take time to muse over all this – sleep on it and let your unconscious in on the process.

Then take 20 minutes to produce your own list of assumptions about your subject matter. As Hugo has done, don't go into why you're describing something, just describe it. You might be describing a particular place, as he does, or it may be a time of year or even an hour of the day, a particular point in someone's life – not necessarily your own.

Be detailed, evocative, persistent. Imagine you are a camera, or a journalist, or a tape recorder left whirring in a corner. Look at your subjects from close up; consider them through a telescope from sea.

What did you get? Look for those areas of concern that chime with what you're actually writing and hold most promise in terms of what you want to write. By separating your subjects from your conscious motivation (why you think you're writing about them), you start to allow them an autonomous existence. Perhaps another motive will appear, perhaps even a theme.   **DISCUSSION**

This is also a method of generating raw material. Are there any ideas here you could develop, by giving yourself 10 minutes to expand on something that you've just sketched out? The imagination has a remarkable capacity to put flesh on whichever bones you concentrate on.

Subject and theme are intimately interwoven: the more insight we possess into one, the more we can hope to possess into the other. The stronger a sense we have about those subjects which cause us the greatest creative excitement, the more definite we can be when embarking on a draft or a piece of reading – that this is our territory, somewhere we can thrive imaginatively.

We have to be alert to new subject areas when they are presented to us, and learning to identify that excitement can help us to distinguish between different possibilities. We can only test that, however, by being as open to new subjects as possible. It's only in the act of writing that we discover whether our intuition or lack of it was accurate.

Determining subject matter doesn't just affect the poems we might be going to write, it changes our attitude towards those we have already written. Pieces discovered to be within the area of our concerns become more central to any attempt to group our work and find an order.

Sequence

One of the difficulties writers often encounter arises from the attempt to completely cover a given subject in a single poem. Such poems can feel crammed and unfocused because there was an assumption that every aspect of that subject must be fitted in. The common perception that poetry is a pared-down art form can mean poets are reluctant to give themselves enough room to explore less predictable possibilities. The sequence is one way of allowing a subject to grow naturally.

By separating out different aspects of a subject and by trying different angles of approach, the sequence gives a writer a sense of perspective on how important a particular subject may be. It also provides insight into how poems interact with each other, a significant skill to develop as you move towards ordering large groupings.

ACTIVITY 18.5

Reading

Read 'Johann Joachim Quantz's Five Lessons' by W.S. Graham, from *New Collected Poems* (2004a, pp.228–31). Consider what the speaker's different subjects tell us about his student.

Johann Joachim Quantz's Five Lessons

The First Lesson

So that each person may quickly find that
Which particularly concerns him, certain metaphors
Convenient to us within the compass of this
Lesson are to be allowed. It is best I sit
Here where I am to speak on the other side
Of language. You, of course, in your own time
And incident (I speak in the small hours.)
Will listen from your side. I am very pleased
We have sought us out. No doubt you have read
My Flute Book. Come. The Guild clock's iron men
Are striking out their few deserted hours
And here from my high window Brueghel's winter
Locks the canal below. I blow my fingers.

The Second Lesson

Good morning, Karl. Sit down. I have been thinking
About your progress and my progress as one
Who teaches you, a young man with talent
And the rarer gift of application. I think
You must now be becoming a musician
Of a certain calibre. It is right maybe
That in our lessons now I should expect
Slight and very polite impatiences

To show in you. Karl, I think it is true
You are now nearly able to play the flute.

Now we must try higher, aware of the terrible
Shapes of silence sitting outside your ear
Anxious to define you and really love you.
Remember silence is curious about its opposite
Element which you shall learn to represent.

Enough of that. Now stand in the correct position
So that the wood of the floor will come up through you.
Stand, but not too stiff. Keep your elbows down.
Now take a simple breath and make me a shape
Of clear unchained started and finished tones.
Karl, as well as you are able, stop
Your fingers into the breathing apertures
And speak and make the cylinder delight us.

The Third Lesson

Karl, you are late. The traverse flute is not
A study to take lightly. I am cold waiting.
Put one piece of coal in the stove. This lesson
Shall not be prolonged. Right. Stand in your place.

Ready? Blow me a little ladder of sound
From a good stance so that you feel the heavy
Press of the floor coming up through you and
Keeping your pitch and tone in character.

Now that is something, Karl. You are getting on.
Unswell your head. One more piece of coal.
Go on now but remember it must be always
Easy and flowing. Light and shadow must
Be varied but be varied in your mind
Before you hear the eventual return sound.

Play me the dance you made for the barge-master.
Stop stop Karl. Play it as you first thought
Of it in the hot boat-kitchen. That is a pleasure
For me. I can see I am making you good.
Keep the stove red. Hand me the matches. Now
We can see better. Give me a shot at the pipe.
Karl, I can still put on a good flute-mouth

And show you in this high cold room something
You will be famous to have said you heard.

The Fourth Lesson

You are early this morning. What we have to do
Today is think of you as a little creator
After the big creator. And it can be argued
You are as necessary, even a composer
Composing in the flesh an attitude
To slay the ears of the gentry. Karl,
I know you find great joy in the great
Composers. But now you can put your lips to
The messages and blow them into sound
And enter and be there as well. You must
Be faithful to who you are speaking from
And yet it is all right. You will be there.

Take your coat off. Sit down. A glass of Bols
Will help us both. I think you are good enough
To not need me anymore. I think you know
You are not only an interpreter.
What you will do is always something else
And they will hear you simultaneously with
The Art you have been given to read. Karl,

I think the Spring is really coming at last.
I see the canal boys working. I realise
I have not asked you to play the flute today.
Come and look. Are the barges not moving?
You must forgive me. I am not myself today.
Be here on Thursday. When you come, bring
Me five herrings. Watch your fingers. Spring
Is apparent but it is still chilblain weather.

The Last Lesson

Dear Karl, this morning is our last lesson
I have been given the opportunity to
Live in a certain person's house and tutor
Him and his daughters on the traverse flute.
Karl, you will be all right. In those recent
Lessons my heart lifted to your playing.

I know. I see you doing well, invited
In a great chamber in front of the gentry. I
Can see them with their dresses settling in
And bored mouths beneath moustaches sizing
You up as you are, a lout from the canal
With big ears but an angel's tread on the flute.

But you will be all right. Stand in your place
Before them. Remember Johann. Begin with good
Nerve and decision. Do not intrude too much
Into the message you carry and put out.

One last thing Karl, remember when you enter
The joy of those quick high archipelagoes,
To make to keep your finger-stops as light
As feathers but definite. What can I say more?
Do not be sentimental or in your Art.
I will miss you. Do not expect applause.

DISCUSSION

The first of these poems originally appeared in Graham's 1970 collection, *Malcolm Mooney's Land*. By his next book it had developed into a group of poems. When his *Collected Poems* appeared, Graham chose to present both forms: the single poem, and, later, the sequence. He evidently felt these were two quite different things. The style of the first poem is indeed less intimate than the rest, and, in the 'certain metaphors' we can see some of Graham's general themes – language and the difficulty of communication, darkness and its equation with silence and isolation.

When the poem appears by itself, the 'you' addressed in it can be regarded as general, a trope Graham often exploits to mean the reader is being addressed. When it's read as part of a sequence, the 'you' evolves into Karl, the student.

The principal effect Graham gains by writing in sequence is transition: an indeterminate but significant period of time elapses between each poem: Karl's skills develop, and his attitude towards his tutor shifts, from impatience through arrogance to humility, whereupon he can become Quantz's peer.

It won't have escaped you that this is the journey any writer takes in relation to his or her influences, but what Graham does, by emphasising the independence of the first poem, is suggest that this is also the journey undertaken by a reader in relation to understanding a poem. First they find it forbidding, then they run through Karl's responses, arriving at an understanding which makes them equal to the poem's creator. The reader creates the poem by reading it imaginatively: Graham presents the dynamics of this process.

What the rest of the sequence adds to the first poem is drama and detail: it allows it to be a narrative rather than only or primarily a metaphor for poetry. This allows for tonal contrast as the sequence shifts from the odd formality of 'I am very pleased/We have sought us out ...' to the even colder austerity of:

Now we must try higher, aware of the terrible
Shapes of silence sitting outside your ear
Anxious to define you and really love you.
Remember silence is curious about its opposite
Element which you shall learn to represent.

There is quirkiness in 'Unswell your head' and pathos as well as insight into genuine vocation in the conclusion: 'Do not be sentimental or in your Art./I will miss you. Do not expect applause.'

ACTIVITY 18.6
Writing

Look at the drafts you produced in response to the exercise on the muses in the chapter on 'Voice'. Consider whether or not you could revise these to create a sequence – nine short poems on contemporary meetings with the muses.

Perhaps you've already worked up your drafts for these. In that case, pick up the suggestion I made at the end of another exercise in the chapter on 'Voice' where I said to think of animals that resembled you. Select four animals: one to represent you as a child, one for you as a teenager, one as an adult, and one which represents you in old age. (You may need to predict one or more of these.) The animal can be a pet from that period, a creature you encountered then, or simply a beast, real or imaginary which you feel sums up what kind of person you were or are or will be.

Write a poem about each of these four creatures, writing for 20 minutes on each over several days.

DISCUSSION

How did you write these poems? Were you present in them in some way, or did you depict the animals without much explanation? How little framing do you think they need? Did you take any formal decisions? Are the poems linked by their form or more diverse: how do they sit together in this sense?

Could any of them stand independently of the grouping? Are any less successful? (It wouldn't be terrible if you moved in the opposite direction to Graham, and came out of this with a single effective piece.) What is the progression of the sequence: do you feel the separate pieces add up to a kind of narrative, or are they simply a constellation, without any need to progress?

Do you feel any of the pieces you've worked on in this part ought to go together (even two poems make a kind of sequence)?

When you write a sequence you're making a statement about the interdependence of the poems within it. You're saying that, whatever sense they make individually, they make a greater whole when put together. This can come from narrative drive, or expansion to provide greater detail. It can also be a matter of thematic binding. Some poems may need to be gathered under a single title. Graham's last book contains a sequence of seventy-odd pieces, some very short, under the same title as the collection: *Implements in Their Places* (2004b, pp.240–57).

The sequence is a sign that you've spread your wings a little, and want to move beyond the confines of the short lyric. This in itself is not necessarily a good thing (think of your audience before writing five hundred sonnets on trout flies), but it can mark a stronger grasp of subject and perhaps even theme. If you develop your formal skills alongside these, it can indicate that you are ready to mature.

Pamphlet

When we place poems together, whether in a reading folder or in a draft for a collection, it soon becomes apparent that they speak to each other. The space between poems can be as charged as the space between lines or stanzas within a single poem. There is an accumulated effect that we overlook by dipping into a book and picking out a single poem. This effect is not quite the same as a narrative, but it can give a similar sense of a developing atmosphere, supported or disrupted by each successive piece. A level on which to explore this effect is the pamphlet.

Pamphlets can consist of anything from around twelve to about thirty poems. They allow us to select and reject pieces, to space out main themes, to consider the dynamics of sub-sections or sequences, and to decide on opening and closing poems. Like individual poems, they require titles and possibly epigraphs, which makes us contemplate the most important impression we wish to give from this grouping of our work.

They mark a significant transition point in how we see and present our poetry.

ACTIVITY 18.7
Reading

Read Helen Dunmore, 'An Unlikely Ambition' in *How Poets Work* (Curtis, 1996, p.84). Compare this approach to how you read all the pieces you've produced so far.

> Another part of the process of writing poems which I have come to appreciate more and more is the first stage of writing a way into a poem, making marks which can be as crude as they need to be in order to define the territory of the poem. This primitive map-making is often shot through with one or two fully-formed phrases which embody the essential music of the poem, the sound which the ear follows and seeks to shape. So these early drafts may offer a startling contrast between writing which is done for the sake of getting somewhere else, and perfect fragments of the poem as it will become. As collections of poems develop, something similar happens on a large scale. At a certain point I realise not just that these poems are beginning to form a collection, but what kind of collection it is going to be. The poems talk to one another. There's an exchange of ideas, and an intricate web of language: touched at one point, it vibrates at another. I grow more and more interested in the shaping of the collection, and again there's the question of discarding work. A good poem may sit uneasily in a particular book, just as an image can be beautiful, but fail to function in a poem.

DISCUSSION

Helen Dunmore neatly links the starting point and conclusion of these chapters on writing poetry: there is indeed a similarity between the way a draft develops into a poem, and how a group of poems evolves into a collection. The work you have done in this chapter on subject and theme should have started you on this process of, yet again, reading your own work, this time on the larger scale of assessing how poems might fit together.

You will already have begun the process of revising at least some of the pieces you have been asked to do in the exercises in Chapters 12 to 18. That process needs to be completed. Each exercise piece should be written up in the light of the work done across Part 3. That means considering each one in terms of its lineation and form, considering whether or not it should rhyme and in what way. Do any need to be gathered into a sequence? Are any still untitled? Would epigrams or footnotes enhance them?

Are there any suggestions I've made for other poems that you thought you could do something with? Have you made suggestions to yourself in your notebook about further pieces you could write? If so you need to set aside composition time as well as time to revise. When is the best time for you to compose, and when should you revise?

Throughout this process consider order. If you have been able to isolate a theme then this may help you to focus: what are most of your poems about? Are there some which, as Helen Dunmore suggests, don't seem to fit with the others?

Try and create a spine of poems which go through the pamphlet, each one of which relates in some way to that central theme. These don't have to succeed each other directly: you can intersperse them with more miscellaneous ones. But if the reader keeps coming back to another poem on the same or a similar theme, then they will understand that there is a structure to the pamphlet, just as there is a form to individual pieces. If your sequence expresses your theme, then perhaps it could form a spine by itself: could it go in the middle?

Otherwise there's a simple pattern you could try: establish which poems you think are most successful – three will do – put one of these at the start of your pamphlet, one in the middle, and one at the end. This apparently cynical advice in fact imposes a rhythm on the whole group – not everything is going to be as good as everything else, so you might as well ensure that the peaks are in the right place. Then you can concentrate on making the troughs as shallow as possible.

Look at your titles and epigraphs. Is there one title, one epigraph which encapsulates your theme better or more pithily than others? Is this your pamphlet's title or will you have to invent another? Will this epigraph work or do you need another for the whole thing?

With titles it can be good to look inside poems as well as at their titles: sometimes there's a phrase or part of one which would work well. Look at your lists of quotes – here's how Edwin Morgan came up with one of his best titles:

> ... the phrase actually came from a reviewer who had been looking at some of my poems and feeling that what I was doing was not so much variations on a theme, as it might seem on the surface to be, but rather the opposite – that it was really themes on a variation. And when I read this, my ears seemed to prick up somehow, and although it was a strange sort of reversal I began to think about it and thought that there was probably some truth in it. It seemed to me that it did apply (although I didn't want to work it out) – I just liked the phrase.

> (Morgan, 1990, p.289)

Notice how, like Sean O'Brien with theme, he doesn't investigate too much what he likes about the title. This can be one of the great impediments to completing any project: you may feel that you have to completely understand every aspect of what you are doing before you let it go. This equates with re-revising a poem till all the life has been revised out of it. As Pope says: 'Whoever thinks a faultless piece to see/ Thinks what ne'er was, nor is, nor e'er shall be'.

Both poets are determining instinctively when enough is enough. You must simply work as thoroughly and carefully on each poem and the collection as a whole as you have time. You're used to concentrating in bursts no longer than half an hour at a time. Not much will be gained by suddenly doubling or trebling this unit.

You have between twenty and thirty pieces of writing which you've been asked to produce in Part 3. Not all of these are going to have yielded poems (though you should exert as much ingenuity as possible in order to turn them into poems). Nonetheless that's enough to generate a pamphlet-length group of work.

Be clear about the ones that don't fit because they're not good enough, or not finished, as well as those which stand out too much because of subject or theme – and leave them out. Be serious about ordering: a chronological sequence is tempting, but until you try to integrate them with each other, poems done in response to the different chapters may remain somewhat sealed off from each other.

By letting the poems speak to each other, you can integrate the work you've done. By revising each piece in the light of work done in the others, you can assess how far the different principles you've studied might integrate into your practice. By titling the whole group, you can try to reach some conclusions about theme, about what kind of writer you are at this point.

Luxuriate in the process of selection and ordering: shuffle your poems frequently and take pleasure in re-reading them. After the hard work you've done, you deserve to enjoy its results.

References

Dunmore, Helen (1996) 'An Unlikely Ambition' in Tony Curtis (ed.) *How Poets Work*, Bridgend: Seren.

Graham, W.S. (2004b) *Implements in Their Places* in Matthew Francis (ed.), *New Collected Poems*, London: Faber and Faber.

Graham, W.S. (2004a) 'Johann Joachim Quantz's Five Lessons' in Matthew Francis (ed.), *New Collected Poems*, London: Faber and Faber.

Morgan, Edwin (1990) *Collected Poems*, Manchester: Carcanet.

O'Brien, Sean (2000) 'Proceedings in Palmersville' in W.N. Herbert and Mathew Hollis (eds) *Strong Words: Modern poets on modern poetry*, Tarset: Bloodaxe Books.

PART 4

Life writing

19 *Starting out*

SARA HASLAM

Introduction

You're now moving on from detailed attention to fiction and poetry, but many of the issues and writing practices that you've explored in previous chapters will remain live concerns in Part 4. Its subject is 'life writing', an umbrella term for biography and autobiography, which also covers popular sub-genres – like travel writing, for example.

Late in the seventeenth century, the poet and dramatist John Dryden defined biography as the 'history of particular men's lives' (quoted in Abrams, 1993 [1941], p.14). Now we would qualify his definition with the inclusion of women's lives (biographies of Madonna and Diana, Princess of Wales, outsell those of Dryden!). In this age of celebrity hunger, interpretation of the word 'particular' might well also be different from Dryden's. But we still expect a biography to give an account of a person's life, and times too. An autobiography is, of course, also an account of a person's life, but one written by the subject about him- or herself.

In what follows we'll investigate some of the ways in which biography and autobiography are generated and crafted – and as you'll see, creativity and imagination are as crucial to the life writing project as they are to fiction and poetry. We'll explore, and attempt, both autobiography and biography in Part 4, and in activities you'll be able to form your writing into poetry and/or prose.

Why write?

Chapter I: I am Born
Whether I shall turn out to be the hero of my own life, or whether that station will be held by anybody else, these pages must show. To

begin my life with the beginning of my life, I record that I was born (as I have been informed and believe) on a Friday, at twelve o'clock at night. It was remarked that the clock began to strike, and I began to cry, simultaneously.

(Dickens, 1966 [1850], p.49)

The extract you've just read is the beginning of *David Copperfield*, a novel by Charles Dickens. It may be fiction, but it raises issues crucial to the exploration of life writing and how it works. One of those issues concerns fact versus fiction, because how can anyone prove what they have only been told? Another is to do with the function of memory: incomplete memory doesn't prevent Copperfield from writing about himself. Both these issues will feature to a significant degree throughout Part 4. The extract is provocative in a further sense: it gets us thinking about why people might engage in life writing.

David Copperfield has been described as Dickens's 'veiled autobiography', so it is a form of life writing as well as a novel (Drabble, 1989, p.256). In its opening paragraph Dickens conjures with two of the most common reasons for writing autobiography, or biography, come to that. One is the desire to establish or record a series of truths, however that word is qualified. The other is the desire to tell a story about a developing self. It's a story which includes heroes, as Dickens says (and probably villains as well), recognised by the reader through his or her encounters with fiction. The emphasis on the word 'story' is important, though at first it might seem surprising in this context. But in one sense all anybody is doing when engaging in life writing is giving a narrative shape to a story of a life. 'I had long wanted to set down the story of my first twenty years', writes Simone de Beauvoir in the preface to her autobiography (1965 [1960], p.7). Though Dickens starts his story with birth, there are many other ways to begin. One biography of de Beauvoir opens when she's in her seventies, keeping vigil at the bedside of a dying Jean-Paul Sartre (Francis and Gontier, 1992 [1987], p.1).

The desire to record events, and to tell a story, may be among the more common reasons people write in this genre, but there are others. What might some of them be?

Consider life writing you have read or know about, and why these books might have been written. If it would be helpful, you could search your shelves, or those in the biography/autobiography sections of a bookshop or library for examples as you investigate this question – there is often a

ACTIVITY 19.1

Writing

clue early in the text. Make a list in your notebook of some of the reasons you come up with.

DISCUSSION   My list of reasons is given below, and I've also included some texts to illustrate them. It's not an exhaustive list, so you may have come up with further reasons of your own.

People may write auto/biography:

- To experiment with a new perspective on a life, perhaps by bringing increased subjectivity or objectivity to bear. A biographer of actor/ director Orson Welles claims that during her research Welles spoke to her 'freely and openly as I dare say he has never done before'. She was able then to communicate how 'Orson himself felt about it all' (Leaming, 1987 [1985], p.vii).

- To compete with other narratives on the subject, correcting, developing, or rebutting information they contain.
  Quotes from the cover of a John Lennon biography provide good examples: '*Lennon* is acknowledged as the definitive portrait of the complex, charismatic genius' and includes 'rare illustrations', we are told (Coleman, 1995 [1984]).

- To establish a particular narrative order over a life. Gore Vidal is concerned very much for the form of his autobiography, appropriately called *Palimpsest* (1996 [1995]). (A 'palimpsest' is a parchment that has been prepared for writing on more than once.) Vidal 'starts with life; makes a text; then a *re*-vision – literally, a second seeing, an afterthought, erasing some but not all of the original while writing something new over the first layer of text' (p.6). A revealed relationship between the past and the present is crucial to his approach.

- To look for answers to specific or more general questions, or to explore states of mind.
  'Writing this book [...] clarified for me Sexton's distinctive achievements as an artist', says Diane Wood Middlebrook of her biography of Anne Sexton (1992 [1991], p.xxi). Travel writer Bruce Chatwin demonstrates a similar approach in a journal: 'this book is written in answer to a need to explain my own restlessness – coupled with a morbid preoccupation with roots' (Chatwin, 1993, p.13).

- To get it off the chest, or to find some kind of peace. Writer Ford Madox Ford dedicated the first volume of his autobiography to his two daughters; he wanted to present to the next generation his knowledge of life (Ford, 1911, p.vii). My own great-aunt, Ethel Cox, who was childless, felt a similar urge when about to undergo an operation aged 95. She dictated some autobiographical notes to my mother.

■ To make money, or to enhance celebrity.
Model Jordan (Katie Price) begins her autobiography with a dramatic hook for potential readers, promising that 'I've held nothing back' (Price, 2004, p.ix).

Of course, things may well be more complex than this implies. Jordan, or Vidal, or Leaming, may have had more than one reason for writing (setting the record straight *and* making money, for example). The creative impulse must also have been involved – to varying degrees – too. But the reasons for writing seem pretty clear here nonetheless. In other examples of life writing they may be less apparent. We will explore this idea shortly.

Life writing authors often indicate some of their reasons for writing in the title that is chosen, so this can be a valuable place to start looking for clues.

Compare the following titles. What might they be saying about why each book has been written?

ACTIVITY 19.2
Reading

1 Kate Chisolm, *Hungry Hell: What it's really like to be anorexic: A personal story*

2 Agatha Christie, *An Autobiography*

3 David Jenkins, *Richard Burton: A brother remembered: The biography Richard wanted*

DISCUSSION

1 The title addresses the reader as an equal, or even a friend. Its hard-hitting red-top alliteration, and the extended subtitle with its conversational abbreviation make me feel as if I'm eavesdropping. Which in a way I am, because the title describes the telling of a 'personal story' in confessional form. It is carefully worded to avoid alienating any potential reader; it positions itself self-consciously 'on the level'. So the title indicates the desire to reach as wide a readership as possible with a story designed both to make an impact and inform. The strong implication in the word 'really' is that

readers will find awful details here about anorexia that may be missing from other similar narratives: Chisholm seems to want to attract even prurient attention. Here we have a multi-pronged, no holds-barred attempt to sell the book, at a time when anorexia occupies a powerful place in the cultural milieu (it was published in 2002).

2   The second title is curious. The choice of the indefinite article stands out: why should it not be *The Autobiography*? Possibly Christie is leaving room for the writing of a later, different narrative. But it's more likely that she's signalling her understanding of the fact that, as she wrote, she was able to tell only one of many possible stories about herself. She had to make narrative choices – where to begin and where to end, for example. Her memory and how she used it will have affected these choices, as will other likely variables (like her word limit). Overall the tone established by her title is hesitant, provisory, and creative, as opposed to definite and factual. Christie uses it to show that she is writing to provide the reader with information, even as she warns that she's not aiming at a complete or definite picture in narrative. She is strikingly different in approach from our final author.

3   In this title David Jenkins lays biological claim to his subject by calling him his brother – a fact Richard's stage name disguises – thereby self-consciously setting his narrative apart from others about Burton. As he is related to his subject, presumably he wants to persuade potential readers of his superior ability to produce an authoritative narrative. While Christie cultivates a sense of plurality with her title, then, he communicates a belief in a hierarchy of narratives with his own version at the pinnacle. He also seems to take another swipe at unauthorised versions (those written without the consent or assistance of the subject), by referring in the title to the subject's desire for his text. One inference a reader could make is that Jenkins is also writing in order to correct some wrong: there's a high level of defensiveness in the length of the title.

Reflect on this exploration into the reasons others may have for attempting life writing, or return to the initial list you made, as we now consider why you might want to practise this craft.

Write down in your notebook what some of your own reasons might be for creating a life writing narrative. Remember as you complete this activity that life writing can be shaped into poetry as well as into prose. A section of Alice Walker's poetry collection *Revolutionary Petunias* is devoted to autobiography (Walker, 1988 [1973], pp.1–25), for example. Remember also that creative processes are transformative: use of the first person in a poem does not necessarily mean it is exclusively autobiographical.

ACTIVITY 19.3
Writing

Whether you have one clear reason, or several, for your writing, do refer to them from time to time as you progress through this part. Reminding yourself of your reasons for writing may well assist you in the choices you will make as you complete activities and plan your writing. If you can't quite formulate an answer to this question, remember that all writing is in part an act of discovery: your reasons may become clear only as you progress.

DISCUSSION

In our discussion so far we have been exploring some of the more evident reasons why people may choose to create life writing narratives. Something like fame, or competition, or simply a need to set things down (or even a combination of all three), spurs writers into action. But earlier I said that other reasons why people may write are less apparent, or less specific. Many life writing narratives seem generated, for example, by the experience, or perception, of loss and perhaps this is something you listed when completing the first activity in this chapter.

You no doubt can recall texts in which loss is powerfully central. The loss that seems to drive the writer might be of a loved one, or of a place, like a home, perhaps. (So David Jenkins's narrative is relevant here too.) Stella Tillyard's biography of three eighteenth-century sisters, *Aristocrats*, opens forcefully, with destitute women queuing up to abandon their babies to the newly-formed Foundling Hospital in Hatton Garden in 1741 (1995, Tillyard, pp.1–3). The loss can also often relate to a concept, to an ideal, or to a state of happiness, health or innocence. In the sub-genre of narratives written by people who know they are suffering from life-threatening illnesses, the writer is one who is both doing the losing and anticipating being lost. Examples of these narratives, often searingly painful to read, are Oscar Moore's *PWA* [or Person With Aids] (1996), John Diamond's *C: Because cowards get cancer too* (1998), and Ruth Picardie's *Before I Say Goodbye* (1998).

These perceived or experienced losses seem to sting the author into a written attempt to account for, or to moderate, them. Creativity can be a way of countering and answering difficulty or suffering. We will explore some examples of texts like this in Chapter 21.

Into words

In the following activity you're encouraged to practise some of the ideas we have discussed so far, and the links between them.

ACTIVITY 19.4
Writing

Imagine you have a biographical subject, X, who was born somewhere in the world in 1914. In your notebook write two paragraphs, of up to 150 words each, on the following:

- In the first, invent four more facts about him or her, and then try to educate your reader about your subject.
- In the second paragraph, imagine that your subject has been forced by circumstance to leave a much-loved house. Describe this circumstance, and its impact on your subject.

DISCUSSION

You're dealing with a fictitious character here, rather than an actual biographical subject, but, as you know, imagination and creativity play a part in the construction of life writing narratives. In the discussion of Dickens's 'veiled autobiography' I drew your attention to the need to choose a place to start, for example, and the idea that readers look for stock characters from fiction as they read life writing.

For the second of your passages I gave you the basis of a plot with which to conjure: a cause and effect scenario with likely and imaginable emotional as well as physical consequences. (Think back to your work on plot in Chapter 10.) This brief outline meant that narrative considerations might have been to the fore as you wrote. The first paragraph demanded a more informative role, and you were working with a 'factual' framework which you may have enjoyed. But the development of the story will be important in this example too. If you come back to this activity later in Part 4, think how you might improve this aspect of it. A good place to start will be to consider the relationships you want to make between your facts.

As a conclusion to this introductory chapter, you're going to explore the role of imagination in autobiographical life writing. You will be writing about your birth, and when you do this you can't help but activate the relationship between fact and fiction (which you'll look at in detail in Chapter 23). To political thriller writer John le Carré his birth is one his 'imagination insists' on (le Carré, 2003, p.22).

Write a piece with the title 'Chapter 1, I am Born', or 'Poem 1, I am Born'. It can be either a 150 word prose piece or a 10–16 line poem.

When you have done this ask yourself the following questions about your paragraph or poem:

- Which elements are fiction/imagination, and which are fact?
- Does the paragraph/poem hint at your reasons for writing?
- What might make a reader want to read more?

Dickens used a combination of fact and fiction as he wrote his opening to *David Copperfield* – he was actually born on a Friday (Ackroyd, 2002 [1990], p.1) – and this is a common approach to take. As none of us can remember the occasion consciously, we must decide either to investigate in some way our unconscious minds as we research our births, or choose to rely on information passed on by others. Time and memory can combine to make that information less accurate, and more like fiction, than we might like to think. Feelings or memories that emerge from the unconscious must be treated with similar caution. But a blend of these processes may well prove fruitful and effective when translated into life writing. The best-selling *Road to Nab End* opens with a good example: 'the fierce rattling of my bedroom window-pane first roused me from the long sleep of birth' (Woodruff, 2002 [1993], p.9). In his poem 'The Fifth Philosopher's Song', Aldous Huxley sets the 'Me' he was born as against the 'million million' others he might have been instead (in Allott, 1962 [1950], p.125):

A million million spermatozoa,
All of them alive:
Out of their cataclysm but one poor Noah
Dare hope to survive.

And among that billion minus one
Might have chanced to be
Shakespeare, another Newton, a new Donne –
But the One was Me.

The blend of fact and fiction in this poem acts as a way of questioning the roots of identity and ideas of self-worth.

Compelling birth stories, you may think, and they are. Nonetheless there is another way to deal with this time of our lives: we can choose to acknowledge the lacuna (or missing part) which is at the beginning of our memory. Crime-writer P.D. James does just this in her autobiography, in which she avoids any fictionalising of her own birth: 'I seldom have a birthday without thinking back to that date which none of us can remember, at least not consciously; the moment of birth' (James, 2000 [1999], p.4). Her approach stands in stark contrast to that taken by Woodruff and Dickens. Here James admits to a general lack of memory, which all of us will recognise, but she also suffers from a more specific factual absence that may resonate with some readers too: 'I must at some time have been told the time of my birth, but I have forgotten it and, as those present are now dead, it is one of those facts I shall never know' (James, 2000 [1999], p.4). Basic information, like the time, and even the date – although this will be extremely rare – of your birth, may have been out of your grasp too. If that was the case, what choices in your paragraph or poem resulted from this? Did you decide to reconstruct that information, or to acknowledge its lack?

Your reflection on matters like this may help to ensure that your reasons for embarking on life writing, and your ways of interesting the reader, can merge in your text. If you need to find out what you think about your lack of memory, or information about some aspects of your life, and are using your writing to do so, your reader may well be able to identify with this process. Similar issues can apply when you're writing biography. You'll have the chance to come back to these ideas in Chapter 22.

References

Abrams, M. H. (1993 [1941]) *A Glossary of Literary Terms*, Orlando, FL: Harcourt Brace.

Ackroyd, Peter (2002 [1990]) *Dickens*, London: Vintage.

de Beauvoir, Simone (1965 [1960]) *The Prime of Life*, Harmondsworth: Penguin.

le Carré, John (2003) 'A sting in the tale', *Observer* Magazine, 7 December, pp.22–39.

Chatwin, Bruce (1993) *Photographs and Notebooks*, David King and Francis Wyndham (eds), London: Jonathan Cape.

Chisolm, Kate (2002) *Hungry Hell: What it's really like to be anorexic: A personal story*, London: Short Books.

Christie, Agatha (1993 [1977]) *An Autobiography*, London: HarperCollins.

Coleman, Ray (1995 [1984]) *Lennon: The definitive biography*, London: Pan Books.

Diamond, John (1998) *C: Because cowards get cancer too*, London: Vermilion.

Dickens, Charles (1966 [1850]) *David Copperfield*, Harmondsworth: Penguin.

Drabble, Margaret (ed.) (1989) *The Oxford Companion to English Literature*, Oxford: Oxford University Press.

Ford, Ford Madox (1911) *Ancient Lights and Certain New Reflections*, London: Chapman & Hall.

Francis, Claude and Gontier, Fernande (1992 [1987]) *Simone de Beauvoir*, London: Minerva.

Huxley, Aldous (1962 [1920]) 'Fifth Philosopher's Song' in Kenneth Allott (ed.), *The Penguin Book of Contemporary Verse*, Harmondsworth: Penguin.

James, P.D. (2000 [1999]) *Time to Be in Earnest: A fragment of autobiography*, London: Faber and Faber.

Jenkins, David with Rogers, Sue (1993) *Richard Burton: A Brother Remembered: The biography Richard wanted*, London: Random House.

Leaming, Barbara (1987 [1985]) *Orson Welles*, Harmondsworth: Penguin.

Middlebrook, Diane Wood (1992 [1991]) *Anne Sexton: A biography*, London: Virago.

Moore, Oscar (1996) *PWA*, London: Picador.

Picardie, Ruth (1998) *Before I Say Goodbye*, Harmondsworth: Penguin.

Price, Katie (2004) *Being Jordan: My autobiography*, London: John Blake.

Tillyard, Stella (1995) *Aristocrats: Caroline, Emily, Louisa and Sarah Lennox 1740–1832*, London: Vintage.

Vidal, Gore (1996 [1995]) *Palimpsest: A memoir*, London: Abacus.

Walker, Alice (1988 [1973]) *Revolutionary Petunias*, London: The Women's Press.

Woodruff, William (2002 [1993]) *The Road to Nab End*, London: Abacus.

20 *A preface*

SARA HASLAM

Introduction

In this chapter you will work towards writing a statement about a life writing text that you want to attempt, in poetry or prose. It might be helpful to think about this statement – which you will create as the final activity in the chapter – as being like a preface, or foreword, which a writer uses to explain the 'subject, purpose, scope and method' of a book (*Oxford English Dictionary*). There will probably be more than one narrative in this genre, shaped in more than one way, that you would like to write, but the first section of this chapter should help you to narrow this down to one that you can work with for now. It will also introduce you to a range of prefaces and the jobs that they do.

Prefaces

In Ruth Picardie's *Before I Say Goodbye* (1998), the preface is used by her husband to provide a brief biographical account of Picardie, as well as to explain how the rest of the book has been compiled (mainly from her columns in the *Observer Life* magazine, and emails to and from Picardie). The reader learns about Picardie's work as a successful journalist, and the breast cancer that ended her life prematurely, and is thus supported in the encounter with her own words. Max Arthur's *Forgotten Voices of the Great War* is a very different kind of life writing narrative. It's a collection of autobiographical sketches by men and women who fought on the Western Front and in Gallipoli during the First World War. He uses his preface to discuss the source of the material and the methods he has used to edit and to arrange it; he also makes links between the kinds of narratives involved and, perhaps most interestingly, reflects on issues of accuracy and the 'truth' of memory (Arthur, 2003 [2002], preface). Having read his preface, a reader is poised to engage with his book, and may well find it more useful or informative.

I've already used a brief example from the preface of Middlebrook's biography of poet Anne Sexton in the discussion of why people write. In it Middlebrook explains her aims, and also discusses the sources of her material: she tells us that she is writing with the full co-operation of Sexton's family, and was invited to undertake the task by Sexton's daughter (1992 [1991], pp.xx–xxii). Her preface establishes her credentials, then, as well as setting out that, for example, she intended to honour some of Sexton's attitudes to life by writing her book. Alice Walker's preface to *Revolutionary Petunias* is also thought-provoking. It reveals that the poems are 'about Revolutionaries and Lovers; and about the loss of compassion, trust, and the ability to expand in love that marks the end of hopeful strategy [...]'. Walker continues, 'They are also about (and for) those few embattled souls who remain painfully committed to beauty and to love [...]' (Walker, 1988 [1973]). While there are significant differences between these four examples of life writing, in style, content, and form, their prefaces perform a similar function: they prepare a reader for what is to come. This is what your preface should aim to do.

Your preface

The first decision to make before formulating your own statement is whether you intend to experiment with autobiographical or biographical writing. We're going to explore this choice. In each of the sections that follow I raise key issues which should stimulate your thinking, and help you to write your preface. Marge Piercy's pithy statement of the differences between biography and autobiography provides a productive starting point. She writes that 'autobiographers know everything; biographers never know enough' (Piercy and Wood, 2002 [2001], p.89). Your work in Chapter 19 – on memory and on birth, for example – means that you know that this statement requires substantial qualification, but its provocative nature might be useful too.

Autobiography

Though I consider this form in detail in Chapter 21, I want to introduce you to two ways of categorising prose autobiography. Think about which of the following categories you would like to find yourself in:

(a) writers who relish their subjectivity (the 'me-ness' of the narrative);

(b) writers who in the main use the autobiographical frame to comment on the world at large.

Read the following extracts from *Portrait of a Marriage* by Vita Sackville-West and *A Passage to Africa* by George Alagiah. Consider which illustrates a more objective and which a more subjective narrative position.

ACTIVITY 20.1

Reading

> Of course I have no right whatsoever to write down the truth about my life, involving as it naturally does the lives of so many other people, but I do so urged by a necessity of truth-telling, because there is no living soul who knows the complete truth; here, may be one who knows a section; and there, one who knows another section: but to the whole picture not one is initiated. Having written it down I shall be able to trust no one to read it; there is only one person in whom I have such utter confidence that I would give every line of this confession into his hands, knowing that after wading through this morass – for it is a morass, my life, a bog, a swamp, a deceitful country, with one bright patch in the middle, the patch that is unalterably his – I know that after wading through it all he would emerge holding his estimate of me steadfast [...].
>
> I start writing, having spent no consideration upon this task. Shall I ever complete it? and under what circumstances?, begun as it is, in the margin between a wood and ripe cornfield, with the faint shadows of grasses and ears of corn falling across my page.
>
> (Sackville-West, 1992 [1973], pp.9–10)

> In the aftermath of September 11, people were fond of saying that the 'world had changed'; that life would never be the same again. What they meant, of course, was that life in the rich world, and especially in America, had changed. In the poor world nothing much had changed at all, except that many more countries would be regarded with suspicion and many more of their citizens seen as potential terrorists. Very quickly, Somalia found itself on the list of those nations deemed to pose a threat to America's security. This is the country that the USA backed in the Cold War and then tried to save from famine in 1992.
>
> [...]
>
> *A Passage to Africa* has been a few months in the writing but literally a lifetime in the making. While the events it covers reflect the preoccupations of a conventional, Western newsroom – where I have worked since early 1989 – my response to what I have

witnessed is coloured by a much earlier experience. As a child, Africa was my home: my family moved from Ceylon, as it was then, to Ghana when I was six.

[...]

[This book] is, primarily, about Africa, but it is also about how I came to think about Africa in the way I do.

(Alagiah, (2002 [2001], pp.4–5)

DISCUSSION   It's probably fairly clear that I have chosen the Sackville-West extract as an illustration of a subjective narrative style. The Alagiah extract, though evidently still autobiographical, displays a dedication to wider subjects too. Contemporary politics and recent world history are foregrounded by Alagiah; they do not feature in the Sackville-West's writing. The back cover of Alagiah's text makes this disparity more clear; it describes the book as 'an autobiography not so much of George Alagiah, but of Africa itself'. Sackville-West's prose is, in contrast, dedicated to a self-reflexive journey through 'my life'. Other perspectives only intrude when they justify the need for the narrative; the 'I' is remorselessly repeated, circumscribing the world she wants to reveal. Although the Sackville-West extract is the shorter of the two, forms of 'I' ('I', 'me', 'my') occur more frequently, as you may have noticed.

Hilary Rodham Clinton's autobiography illustrates a further form of subjectivity – one that seems to combine these two approaches. Though the reader is very aware of the 'I' (look how many times it's used), her subjects are American history, politics and culture as well:

> I wasn't born a first lady or a senator. I wasn't born a lawyer or an advocate for women's rights and human rights. I wasn't born a wife and mother. I was born an American in the middle of the twentieth century, a fortunate time and place. I was free to make choices unavailable to past generations of women [...]. I came of age on the crest of tumultuous social change and took part in the political battles fought over the meaning of America and its role in the world.
>
> (Rodham Clinton, 2004 [2003], p.1).

Subjective it may be, then, but her *Living History* is about momentous and widely-relevant events too.

One textbook on creative writing suggests that autobiography, and I would guess especially the more subjective kind, can only be profitably indulged in when the writer is famous: 'successful autobiographies are usually written by people who have done something of outstanding significance' (Burton, 2003 [1983], p.173). I don't agree with this way of determining success. Life writing bookshelves often display autobiographies by people whose names are otherwise unknown, but which sell well. J.A. Cuddon writes that 'since the Second World War almost anyone who has achieved distinction in life – and many who have not – has written an account of his life' (1992, p.73).

I tend to agree with the approach Marge Piercy and Ira Wood take to this issue. They talk about the way it is helpful, when writing autobiography, to universalise individual experience, or render it in a more objective form – especially if fame isn't involved! Even if you do look inward, looking outward and finding ways of making your narrative engage your readers is necessary too (Piercy and Wood, 2002 [2001], pp.220, 89). And Nigel Nicolson, editor of the Sackville-West text (as well as being her son), provides an example of how one might go about this. '*Portrait of a Marriage* is a story of how love triumphed over infatuation', he writes in the introduction to the 1992 edition. Calling it a story offers his, and more importantly his mother's, readers one way of identifying with the text, making its subjectivity resonate more widely; this idea takes us back to our early thinking about *David Copperfield*. Offering a recognisable, universalising theme like love provides another way; as a theme it may well encourage readers to form a relationship with Sackville-West's text.

One final thought in this respect concerns the sub-genre of travel writing. Books like Bruce Chatwin's *In Patagonia* (1979 [1977]) are written in the first person, charting as they do individual experience, but they can be about a good deal else besides. Chatwin explored a part of the world that was seldom visited, and through observed or researched incident and anecdote he evoked its distinct character for his readers (from the adventures of Butch Cassidy to drilling for oil in Tierra del Fuego). *In Patagonia* offers a universalising theme in its representation of a largely unknown place, as well as, perhaps, in what it has to say about wandering and exile. If you have travelled, and are interested in experimenting with less obviously subjective autobiography, travel writing may be the form for you.

What might you offer a reader by way of a universalising theme in an autobiographical text? Write down some of your ideas in your notebook,

ACTIVITY 20.2

Writing

and remember to come back to them as you write your statement if you decide to opt for an autobiographical narrative.

DISCUSSION There is simply no right answer here, as you may imagine. Each life is different. *In Patagonia*'s offerings in this respect were discussed briefly above. In Pete Hamill's autobiography, *A Drinking Life* (1994), it is the contemporary New York culture of drink that offers a universalising theme. The back cover proclaims that 'Hamill learned early that drinking was an essential part of being a man, inseparable from the rituals of celebration, mourning, friendship, romance, and religion'. Further examples I can think of from autobiographies include:

- living and fighting through a war;
- experiences of migration, adoption and disability;
- dependency on drugs;
- losing a parent at a young age;
- employment in a particular field like education or health, which many people in the world encounter at some point in their lives.

More generally, most life writing narratives explore the sense of time and history moving on – issues associated with ethnicity or sexuality may be particularly relevant here. Focused exploration of one of these issues, perhaps in a way that ranges more widely than your own individual experience, would provide you with a way of stimulating recognition, and interest, in those reading your work. As a final suggestion in this respect, the act of memory itself can be a compelling and universalising component of autobiography. All autobiographies depend upon memory, though to varying degrees.

Biography

ACTIVITY 20.3
Reading

Read the extracts from *Paula* by Isabel Allende and *Funny Peculiar* by Mark Lewisohn. As you read them, consider the effect that is created by the emotional distance, or lack of it, between the writer and her or his subject. Which effect would you be more interested in emulating if you were to write a biographical narrative?

Epilogue
In December 1991 my daughter, Paula, fell gravely ill and soon thereafter fell into a coma. These pages were written during the

interminable hours spent in the corridors of a Madrid hospital and the hotel room where I lived for several months, as well as beside her bed in our home in California during the summer and fall of 1992.

Listen, Paula: I am going to tell you a story, so that when you wake up you will not feel so lost. The legend of our family begins at the end of the last century, when a robust Basque sailor disembarked on the coast of Chile with his mother's reliquary [a small box in which a relic is kept] strung around his neck and his head swimming with plans for greatness. But why start so far back? It is enough to say that those who came after him were a breed of impetuous women and men with sentimental hearts and strong arms fit for work.

(Allende, 1996 [1995])

Summon up an image of Benny Hill and chances are it will be of a moony, schoolboyish face with comfy-cushion cheeks, piercing, naughty blue eyes and a mischievous smile, leering at an under-dressed 'Hill's Angel' and speaking in a country-bumpkin's voice.

This is the man who became the world's most popular comedian in the television era. And indeed Benny Hill was a great comedian. His strength lay in comedy architecture, characterisation, mime, delightfully light vulgarity and a facility to redeploy jokes of all vintages.

(Lewisohn, 2003, [2002], Preface)

These narratives could hardly sound more different. The Allende extract is highly personal and emotionally charged, dealing as it does with the death of her daughter, encouraging the reader through empathy to situate him- or herself in the narrative. The other was also occasioned by a death but is, instead, distantly laudatory, light and conversational as it looks back at a figure many people in Europe would recognise by sight (and beyond – apparently Benny Hill is also big in Japan and the US). Both narratives may draw in their reader, therefore, but in the former this would probably be by way of a personally driven empathetic response. In the latter, Hill's television career, and the buoyant prose which describes it, establishes a greater sense of distance between reader and Lewisohn's subject even as he or she begins to read.

DISCUSSION

In the next activity we're going to explore these different approaches as life writers.

ACTIVITY 20.4
Writing

Choose one person from your own life, and one public figure. Identify an aspect of both lives you would like to research – a favourite pastime, perhaps, a characteristic behaviour pattern, or a typical day at work. Find out three or four relevant facts in each case and write them up into two paragraphs of up to 150 words each, or two poems (10–16 lines). This is an exercise in which you're simply practising some biographical skills, so don't go into too much detail. Research may include talking to friends or family, and using your bookshelves, or those in a bookshop or library, or the internet.

Reflect on the process once you have completed the writing, and produce a third paragraph of 250 words in which you assess your paragraphs or poems, and how you produced them. Questions you might explore in it include: did you find one flowed more easily than the other? Why? Does your writing sound as though you identify more closely with one subject than the other? Is this effect something you wanted to achieve?

DISCUSSION

In completing this activity you've explored two kinds of biographical writing, and the links between them. Research is necessary whatever form of biography you choose, though this will be undertaken in different ways. The last part of the activity encouraged you to think about your relationship with your subject, and how it might be made explicit in a piece of biographical writing. The results may have been surprising here – perhaps you feel there was a high level of imaginative identification with the public figure, for example? You may want to adapt this final paragraph when it comes to writing your preface in Activity 20.7.

The facts of the matter

Although you will consider fact versus fiction in more detail in the second half of Part 4, you need to be able to say something about it in your preface. You may be most aware of dealing with facts as a life writer, or you may not; what follows should help you to explore and to test this awareness.

Perhaps you think you may brazenly adopt Ford Madox Ford's attitude to fact in his biography of Joseph Conrad. He calls his biography a 'novel' and a 'work of art', then writes 'it contains no documentation at all; for it no dates have been looked up; even all the quotations but two have been left unverified, coming from the writer's memory' (Ford, 1989 [1924], preface). Ford wanted to preserve his sense of how things were, his impression of events, which for him represented important kinds of truth. He could not be challenged by his subject, who died before he wrote his biography, but Orson Welles's biographer recounts the potentially awkward appearance of 'inscrutable disparities between what Orson remembers and the data' she unearths (Leaming, 1987 [1985], p.2). Surprisingly, this does not prove to be a hindrance: Welles revels in this part of the process of being written about, though is adamant that the truth of the matter remains unresolved (ibid., p.3).

Such productively imaginative relationships with facts as those described above are truly engaging but are also, perhaps, rare. Ford's career in general suffered due to a reputation for a cavalier attitude to fact, and Welles is unusual in the strength of his positive, interested feelings towards being 'biographised'. Indeed, Welles applauds the consciousness-raising element of the whole process: 'one has organized one's life [...], and forgotten – perhaps deliberately and certainly unconsciously – what one wants to forget, and here is somebody coming up with the proof of things you're forced to remember or believe happened. I see the situation as a fascinating way to get into what a man's life is really like' (ibid., p.3).

Others may not display such an open, generous attitude to new or disputed 'facts'. My guess is you would have to choose the subject of your life writing narrative carefully to find one prepared, as Welles says he was, to be told things are not as they seemed. Bear in mind that there is a moral issue here too: what if something you discover may cause your subject or someone they know pain? True, to avoid this possibility you could make that subject yourself, and write autobiography. But active thinking and research can dislodge forgotten or buried memories and experiences in the autobiographer: you also would have to be prepared for them to come.

The status of your text

The first issue for your consideration here is whether the text you are writing may be one you could aim to publish, or whether it is something you are writing for yourself alone. Even if you already know that you are writing for yourself, the statement you are currently engaged in developing will prove an important part of your preparatory work. If you think you may have different plans for your text, further questions for your consideration under this heading include:

■ Will it be the only title on this subject, or one among many and therefore engaged in competition?

■ If the latter, how might it make its mark?

■ If the former, how might it appeal to a wide readership?

These issues can be explored using published books.

ACTIVITY 20.5

Reading

On a recent visit to my local bookshop, I counted seven different biographies of Diana, Princess of Wales. Below I describe the back covers and blurbs of two of these biographies. How is each used by the author and publisher to advertise the status of their text? (NB: This relates to the discussion of motives in Activity 19.1 and you might like to look back to that to help you.)

(a) *Diana: Story of a princess*, by Tim Clayton and Phil Craig (2001). The back cover describes the book as 'the acclaimed international bestseller, revised and updated, telling the full story of the quest for the truth about the life and death of Princess Diana'. Further quotations on the back cover include one from the *New Statesman* ('intelligent and well-researched ...') and the *Observer* ('good, plain, lucid, responsible').

(b) *Diana: In pursuit of love*, by Andrew Morton (2004). The back cover is a collage formed of photographs of audio tapes, and notes and letters to and from Diana. A publisher's note at the beginning of the text verifies the photographs (they are of the actual artefacts), and describes them as evidence of Morton's close relationship with his subject.

DISCUSSION

Both texts take their place as one among many books about Diana. The Clayton and Craig cover seeks to make its mark by stressing its learnedness and, perhaps, objectivity (although it can't resist the lure of the 'full story'). The Morton cover, on the other hand, goes unashamedly for the personal touch, with photographs of Diana's handwriting and tapes of her voice suggesting the mark it is making belongs to the subject herself.

Having practised negotiating some of the key issues associated with this genre in preparation for writing your own preface, we're now going to read one (nearly complete) biographical version.

Read the preface to Dennis Overbye's biography of Albert Einstein, Reading 34 on p.549. Make notes on its treatment of issues related to its genre, its use of fact, and its status as a text. If you need to, refer back to the discussion of these issues in this and the previous chapter.

ACTIVITY 20.6

Writing

DISCUSSION

Overbye makes a clear case for how his biography will make its mark, despite taking for its subject a much written about man. By focusing on the young Einstein, he finds original, untrodden ground; this may appeal to those who already know a great deal about the scientist, but will also provide non-specialists in the field with a gentle introduction to physics and to a great thinker via human and universalising concerns. Overbye may also be pitching his narrative towards a particular kind of reader or scholar: those who are interested in gender politics, and look to restore to women their rightful place in cultural and intellectual history. Finally, Overbye also has something to say about the interaction between fact and fiction in his text. He recognises the role his own interests have had in determining the direction of his narrative, but he also vouches for the extent of his research into original documents – research that is incorporated into his depiction of his characters.

Overbye's text provides a good example of how you can say something new about a famous subject. Remember, though, that you can also choose to write about someone known to you if you're going to opt for biography. The relationship between fact and fiction, research, and how your text will make its mark are issues for equal consideration should autobiography be your choice.

If you have not already done so, pick the subject for your preface. You also need to decide whether you are planning a text in poetry or prose. You will want to cover the issues set out throughout this chapter whoever your subject, and whatever your chosen form. Read back over the sections 'Autobiography', 'Biography', 'The facts of the matter', and 'The status of your text', if necessary. It might also be useful to go back to the definition of a preface (p.281), and to reflect again on Piercy's

ACTIVITY 20.7

Writing

statement too ('autobiographers know everything; biographers never know enough').

Write your prefatory statement, of about 750 words, in which you set out your reasoning for the choices you have made regarding the treatment of your subject, including use of fact, textual status and other issues related to biography/autobiography. Don't worry at this stage about publication; simply think of this exercise as describing what you are setting out to do with your life writing narrative.

DISCUSSION   You will return to this subject in Chapter 21 and you may decide that this narrative is one you would like to spend more time developing. If time permits, it may also be worth experimenting with the preface process again. Perhaps you might like to try writing a preface for a different subject – biographical if you went for autobiography in this activity, or for some travel writing, for example?

References

Alagiah, George (2002 [2001]) *A Passage to Africa*, London: Time Warner Books.

Allende, Isabel (1996 [1995]) *Paula*, Margaret Sayers Peden (tr.), London: Flamingo.

Arthur, Max (2003 [2002]) *Forgotten Voices of the Great War*, London: Random House.

Burton, Ian (2003 [1983]) *Teach Yourself Creative Writing*, London: Hodder Headline.

Chatwin, Bruce (1979 [1977]) *In Patagonia*, London: Pan Books.

Clayton, Tim and Craig, Phil (2001) *Diana: Story of a princess*, London: Hodder and Stoughton.

Cuddon, J.A. (1992) *The Penguin Dictionary of Literary Terms and Literary Theory*, London: Penguin.

Ford, Ford Madox (1989 [1924]) *Joseph Conrad: A personal remembrance*, New York: Ecco Press.

Hamill, Pete (1994) *A Drinking Life: A memoir*, New York: Little, Brown & Co.

Leaming, Barbara (1987 [1985]) *Orson Welles*, Harmondsworth: Penguin.

Lewisohn, Mark (2003 [2002]) *Funny, Peculiar: The true story of Benny Hill*, London: Pan Books.

Middlebrook, Diane Wood (1992 [1991]) *Anne Sexton: A biography*, London: Virago.

Morton, Andrew (2004) *Diana: In pursuit of love*, London: Michael O'Mara Books.

Picardie, Ruth (1998) *Before I Say Goodbye*, Harmondsworth: Penguin.

Piercy, Marge, and Wood, Ira (2002 [2001]) *So You Want to Write: How to master the craft of writing fiction and personal narrative*, London: Piatkus.

Rodham Clinton, Hilary (2004 [2003]) *Living History: Memoirs*, London: Headline.

Sackville-West, Vita (1992 [1973]) *Portrait of a Marriage*, Nigel Nicolson (ed.), London: Orion.

Walker, Alice (1988 [1973]) *Revolutionary Petunias and Other Poems*, London: The Women's Press.

21 Finding a form; writing a narrative

SARA HASLAM

Introduction

In this chapter, we are going to think more about the form (or, perhaps, forms) you might use in a life writing narrative. 'Form' simply means the organising principles of writing, as opposed to its substance or content. In this chapter, then, I discuss the various formal choices you will make as you construct your narrative, and offer examples from published texts. The activities encourage you to engage with and to practise a range of autobiographical and biographical forms.

ACTIVITY 21.1

Reading

In this introductory activity we're thinking about the effects of formal choices. What strikes you about the form of the quote below?

> I wake up in the night and there's a big dark shape leaning over me [...]. We live in a room in another woman's house, Mammy, Daddy and me and the baby. We are going out somewhere and my daddy is squatting on his hunkers in front of me tying my laces. He's swaying back and forth and this way and that and there's a queer smell about his breath and all at once he staggers back cursing, still on his hunkers, and nearly falls into the fire.
>
> (Boyle, 2002 [2001], pp.13–14)

DISCUSSION

I found the use of the present tense to be particularly striking as I read this passage from near the beginning of John Boyle's *Galloway Street: Growing up Irish in exile* (and this may remind you of your work on Lesley Glaister in Part 1). It creates a strong sense of immediacy, and also makes it easier for a reader to identify with the scene that is being described. Also of note is the way in which the passage combines the perception and language of a child ('he's swaying back and forth and this way and that'; a child can't identify the smell as that of alcohol) and those of an adult. It is a rich combination; time itself seems to become fluid in the way that his adult mind and memory give him some information, yet also withhold some from the child's persona which, for now at least, is narrating. Choices like this, about form, play a crucial part in the ways in which your narrative will take shape. Early consideration of the structural elements that underpin any piece of writing means greater freedom later on.

As further introduction to our in-depth work on form, I want briefly to offer a new way of dividing life writing into types. In the work you have done so far, you have mainly considered genre headings like 'biography' and 'autobiography' (sub-genres like 'diaries' and 'travel writing' have featured too and will do so more strongly in the remaining chapters of Part 4). But there are also categories of narrative method that it will be useful for you to address as you think about how you might like to write.

The first method is more fragmentary. In this category you might include autobiographical poetry, diaries, journals, letters, photographic records, and also narratives like John le Carré's memoir 'A sting in the tale', discussed below, or Jean Rhys's *Smile Please* (1981 [1979]). In *Smile Please*, an autobiographical text, Rhys simply collects a series of vignettes. Short chapters, for example 'Poetry', 'My Father', or 'St Lucia', grant Rhys a structure which means she doesn't have to provide a coherent, linking narrative. Horror writer Stephen King adopts a similar approach, stating matter-of-factly at the beginning of his book *On Writing: A memoir of the craft*, 'Don't bother to read between the lines, and don't look for a through-line. There are *no* lines – only snapshots, most out of focus' (King, 2001 [2000], p.4). There is a sense of liberation for King in the lack of 'through-line', and his visually suggestive word, 'snapshots', for what he provides instead may apply to aspects of Rhys's technique too. King's snapshots are short, numbered chapters that are often simply a page in length and relate, for example, a scene or memory to which he adds brief comment.

The second narrative method you might describe as being more continuous or connected. Here the more traditional kind of biography and autobiography might be found, in which prose links up sections of memories, and the appearance of a coherent and in some ways complete narrative is attained. Mary Benson's biography of Nelson Mandela reads more like a narrative without gaps, or with the gaps filled in, unlike the examples of Rhys and King:

> Nelson Rolihlahla Mandela spent his childhood in a fertile valley
> among the rolling hills of the Transkei. The family *kraal* of white-

washed huts was not far from the Mbashe River which flowed past maize fields and a wattle plantation, past grasslands where cattle grazed and on eastwards to the Indian Ocean.

In that setting Mandela's love for his country and for his people took root. He was born on 18 July 1918 at Qunu near Umtata, the capital village of the Transkei 'reserve'. As one of the royal family of the Thembu, his upbringing was traditional and a sense of responsibility was bred in him.

(Benson, 1986, p.15)

Although some life writing narratives may sound more complete than others, there is need for caution here. Anthony Trollope muses on the practice of writing autobiography in his own attempt. He suggests that producing a complete narrative – telling everything – is 'impossible'. 'Who could endure to own the doing of a mean thing?' he asks, let alone write absolutely everything down (Trollope, 1992 [1883], p.1). Trollope is right to ask these questions, and a complete narrative would be impossibly unwieldy, but a different answer to the moral question he raises had already been provided a hundred years earlier by Rousseau in his *Confessions*. Towards the beginning of his text, Rousseau writes that 'I have displayed myself as I was, as vile and despicable when my behaviour was such' (1953 [1781], p.17). Rousseau aimed to include shameful acts, hence the title of his autobiography (though he does not, in fact, present himself as completely 'vile'). His life writing narrative might then be said to be more complete in key respects than Trollope's version.

In the rest of the chapter you may find it useful to bear these methods – the more fragmented and the more connected – in mind, as a way of both helping you to make formal choices, and to make further links between some of the formal sub-genres that are discussed throughout the rest of Part 4.

ACTIVITY 21.2

Writing

Write about three separate incidents, memories or moments in your life or in someone else's. Each piece should be up to 50 words. Then try to identify a way of linking the three incidents, a 'through-line'. Did you relish the snapshot feel of the disconnected incidents, or did finding a through-line give you a stronger sense of narrative satisfaction?

My attempt at this exercise is given below.   **DISCUSSION**

> When I was 8 years old, I had a good friend at school called Sasha.
> A new girl, Stacey, joined our class and befriended me and Sasha.
> Gradually, Sasha and Stacey became better friends than I was with
> either of them. I lost touch with them both when I changed schools.

> We are planning our summer holiday this year. Brochures for
> holiday villas in France and Italy are collecting in the newspaper
> rack. But as we discuss it over a period of weeks we realise our
> thoughts are turning more and more to the cottage we often go to in
> Snowdonia, in the mountains, a place we love.

> I have been baking, as it is my daughter Maisie's first birthday
> tomorrow. We have planned games and invited some friends over
> for tea. A present we ordered for her was delivered this morning,
> and cards and gifts have been arriving for the past couple of days.

My through-line for these stories is the house in Snowdonia, and the
place of friendship that it represents. When I was a child I often wanted
to take Sasha there, as proof of friendship, though she never came. It is
a place to which I have since invited many friends, and I was married in
the valley. I want Maisie to take friends there as she grows.

Each of your three short paragraphs could be used as the basis for, or
even to form, separate sections of a more fragmented narrative of the
kind we discussed above. In fragmented form the paragraphs have
immediacy; they might be described as life writing snapshots of an
ordinary working mind on an ordinary day, or days. The mind, after all,
moves backwards, forwards, and around and about, not in precise
narrative order as it processes experiences and events. There is
something refreshing about this method and its effects for me. But a
through-line also offers satisfactions. It turns the paragraphs into the
beginnings of a plot with which to conjure. It suggests a way of
connecting the separate memories which means they can be investigated
in more depth.

Forms of autobiography

In this section we'll consider the characteristics of various forms of
autobiography and how you might employ them in a life writing text.
I'm going to discuss, in turn, memoir, travel writing, diary, journal, and
letters. Which might you like to write? Remember your version can be a

combination of forms, and of narrative methods too. Ruth Picardie's autobiography includes journalism, emails, and letters to and from the author. Susanna Kaysen's *Girl, Interrupted* (2000 [1995]), also an autobiography, incorporates photocopies of hospital admission forms, psychiatrist's reports, and case notes as well as more continuous reflective prose.

Memoir

The word memoir comes from the French for memory (la mémoire). As you might expect, writers of memoirs often foreground the act of memory in the record they are producing; a memoir therefore can sometimes be structured in a fragmentary, snapshot, fashion. John le Carré's memoir focuses on his relationship with his father, and although it does begin with the subtitle 'On being born and other adventures' it is revealingly and effectively structured as a series of key events or discoveries, not a 'begin at the beginning' narrative. Entertaining examples include 'In which I am talent-spotted for the monastic life and chastised by an Austrian night porter', and 'a Great Ambassador and a Grand Hotel Deprive Ronnie of his Golf Clubs' (le Carré, 2003, pp.36, 32). Between these key moments, there is little attempt to join the dots. The sense that is created is one of a life of episodes, without seamless transitions; the silence between episodes is intriguing, and, in some ways, accurately representative – who could write everything down?

Memoirs can also be written biographically – although they're usually fairly autobiographical biography – and the same kinds of characteristics may well apply. The extracts in the next activity, from John Bayley's memoir of his wife, Iris Murdoch, treat the memory of two swims in the Cherwell river outside Oxford. One takes place before they were married, and the other occurs many married years later, when Iris is suffering from Alzheimer's disease. In between, Bayley's narrative meanders through an account of some aspects of their life together, but it in no way has, or attempts, the feel of a 'complete' record.

ACTIVITY 21.3

Reading

Read the two extracts from John Bayley's memoir of Iris Murdoch, Reading 35 on p.551. Describe their tone, and style, and the comparative impact they have on you. How successful do you find Bayley's opening as a narrative technique?

Bayley opens his narrative in the time of the later swim, to which he returns in Chapter 2. In the later time, both at the start and in the second extract, it is the heat that he emphasises, a stagnant, oppressive heat which is successfully communicated initially by stark, short (breathless) sentences, and later by a slow drawn-out prose, which seems itself to be suffering under an oppressive force. By comparison, what stands out from his telling of their first swim is the swimming itself, their shared endeavour and excitement, and the implication of their nakedness. The sheer pace denoted in the 'tore our clothes off' and in the following sentence about the kingfisher struck me as the only times Bayley's prose gathers any speed at all. Later, Iris's costume signifies instead their increased distance from each other and from the sensuous pleasure the swim and nature used to afford. In the later time, too, Bayley is more alone: he struggles with her clothes; it is 'hard to persuade her'; she does not answer him and the sense of a shared jaunt really has gone. Although natural images provide continuity between the two periods (the water-rat and kingfisher, the moles and crows) it is significant that the flashing kingfisher is the emblem of forty-five years before, the flapping crow is that of the present.

I find this a successful technique, and its success is to do with the way in which it uses to full effect both the continuities and changes discernible in most lives. In fact it uses continuities to highlight the changes. Iris and John visit the same place, to do the same thing, but the experience is immeasurably different because of the physical, emotional and psychological changes wrought by the intervening years upon them both. The placed memories, separated in time but not by space, show more starkly than any more gradualist approach could do how much has changed. Transcendent, the river acts as a kind of through-line, joining times and experiences together so that they can be expertly and effectively compared. And so Bayley makes formal choices that are very different from King's, and although his memoir does not read like a complete record, it is far less fragmented than King's collection of shapshots. Life writers often make similar formal choices to Bayley: 'Through-lines' is the title of the penultimate section in this chapter, and these choices are investigated there.

Travel writing

Travel writers use examples of both the more connected and the more fragmented narrative methods that we have been exploring. (And note that they also write biographically too.)

ACTIVITY 21.4
Reading

Read the following extract, which begins at the end of Chapter 49 and continues with the opening of Chapter 50 of Bruce Chatwin's *In Patagonia*. Which narrative method seems most in evidence in this extract?

> The origin of the 'dog-heads' is to be found in the 'vizzards' or battle masks, such as worn by Genghis Khan's cavalry or the Tehuelches when they attacked John Davis at Puerto Deseado. Shakespeare could have picked them out of Hakluyt. But either way Caliban has a good claim to Patagonian ancestry.
>
> **50**
> In the British Club at Río Gallegos there was chipped cream paint and not a word of English spoken. The twin black smoke-stacks of the Swift Corporation's old freezer reared above the prison yard.
>
> (Chatwin, 1979 [1977], p.94)

DISCUSSION

Chatwin's chapters are, in general, short: often a page or two, sometimes only a paragraph (and are like King's in this respect). What is made clear in the above extract is the way in which the chapters can also dramatically switch subject and, as a result, tone. It is part of the appeal of Chatwin's text that his wide-ranging narrative means you are never quite sure what may be coming next.

While travel writing narratives do tend to share the wide range of Chatwin's text – often delving into history, human geography and the nature of travel itself, for example – some adopt a more focused approach. Colin Thubron's *In Siberia* (1999) has only nine chapters, as against Chatwin's ninety-seven. Thubron's are given titles which vary from the poetic ('Hauntings') to the specific ('To the Arctic'), but each covers a particular remit in some detail, though it may also make detours. Such a structure could be of use to the travel writer aiming to create a narrative which 'joins the dots'.

Diary

A diary is a record of daily events. It tends to be less detailed than a journal, which can also be defined in a similar fashion (though be aware of the fact that in the US, the word 'journal' means 'diary'). In respect of this sub-genre, and the two which follow, journal and letters, I would qualify the remarks I made earlier about acts of distinction not necessarily being required for publishing success in the genre of autobiography. Diaries, journals and letters, because of their intensely personal nature, are most often of interest to a wider reading public if they concern the life of someone who has made a name for him or herself in the public sphere, unless they emanate from an early historical period. Not everyone could expect to generate interest in the exclamation '5 December [1913]. How furious I am with my mother! I need only begin to talk to her and I am irritated, almost scream' (Kafka, 1992 (1910–23), p.244), or the observation 'Sunday 14 February [1915]. Rain again today. I cleaned silver, which is an easy & profitable thing to do' (Woolf, 1979 [1977], p.34).

In these sub-genres there is perhaps less place, too, for the universalising themes that can resonate in a general reader, as we explored in Chapter 20. If you decide to adopt one of these forms for a life writing narrative, I would suggest that you're also deciding not to aim at publication – unless, of course, you have performed that act of distinction likely to result in publishers' interest. Despite all this, novelist Susan Hill makes a clear case for what she thinks is demanded from a published diary, and she, in fact, does not mention the fame of its writer. She also suggests that universalising themes *can* find a place in this genre: 'If an insight into the human condition, wit, wisdom and a share in another's life and times are what most of us ask of a diary, the blessed ability to sketch a scene or sum up a person in a few perfectly chosen words must still come top. The best diaries are rich and yet succinct' (Hill, 2004, p.37).

Find the diary of someone who interests you, either on your bookshelf, in a library or bookshop, or on the internet. Judge the level of daily detail that they include in their narrative, and ascertain whether the book was published during their lifetime – the preface or introduction will give some clues here, as will the date of publication. Do you think your interest in them is fuelled or lessened by the things you learned about them from their diary?

ACTIVITY 21.5

Reading

DISCUSSION   The level of detail to which you have been treated will depend partly on where and when the book was published – as well as on who the subject is, of course. How you view this information will be a matter of personal choice: some will be bored, offended or shocked by certain kinds of behaviour, others will be captivated by the same material. In respect of this sub-genre, it is worth considering whether the personal things you learned merely helped to fill in the background to the image of the person that you already have, or whether they would have been enough to generate a dedication to the writer if you had not heard of them. If the latter is true, the minutiae of everyday life could well in themselves hold some level of fascination for you, and you should bear this in mind as you approach your own life writing.

I asked you to consider whether the diary had been published during the writer's lifetime or posthumously because writing with intent to publish – less common in diaries perhaps, with some notable exceptions, like those by former Prime Ministers – may alter the voice in which the diary is written, and lead to fewer personal events being recorded. The traditional view of the diary as something hidden from all eyes except those of the writer is, however, changing. Privacy is not what it was. In Hill's article Alan Clark's diaries provide an example of those written to be published (Hill, 2004, p.36).

Journal

A journal, as I indicated above, shares some important characteristics with a diary. It tends to focus on everyday events and experiences (and is etymologically related to the French word for 'day') as recorded by an individual subject. Journals can be associated with an anecdotal style, rather than the intimate tone or content that may be expected from a diary. (In other words, a journal may concentrate on striking events or thoughts.) In addition, a journal may provide substantial details about a specific project, perhaps, upon which the author is engaged. A journal can be a kind of workbook or notebook, like the one you have been using throughout this course. Writers often keep journals – useful critical tools showing the development of their work. Novelist Katherine Mansfield records in hers in 1916 that she wants in a new work to 'make our undiscovered country [New Zealand] leap into the eyes of the Old World. It must be mysterious, as though floating. It must take the breath' (quoted in Alpers, 1980, p.189).

Letters

This category is self-explanatory. Once more, published collections of letters are generally by men and women who are known to the public in some way. Though it may be tempting to place letters in a class of their own as they're written for a recipient, it is important to note that many diarists think of their text as a recipient (the 'dear diary' format). And as we know authors may write diaries or journals anticipating publication at a later date – and, therefore, a reading public. Theorists too might well make the point that when anything is committed to paper, an editor is at work, and thus the sense of a watchful, reading eye that is in some way separate from the writer's own is present (we'll come back to this in Chapter 25). So, letters too can be viewed as a form of autobiography. Malcolm Bradbury published *Unsent Letters* in 1988. On the back cover he says he hopes the book 'will spare him the trouble of ever having to write an autobiography' (Bradbury, 1988). In this collection he experiments with what he would have said to often imagined recipients, using the letter form as a targeted autobiography.

ACTIVITY 21.6
Writing

Find an example of a diary, or journal, or a collection of letters, that you think fulfils some of Susan Hill's criteria ('an insight into the human condition, wit, wisdom, and a share in another's life and times [...], the blessed ability to sketch a scene or sum up a person in a few perfectly chosen words'). This could be the same diary that you used for the previous activity. Choose an extract, about a paragraph in length, and write about that paragraph and the way in which it fulfils these criteria.

DISCUSSION

As you wrote about your paragraph I hope you had a sense of which aspect of its successes impressed you particularly. It may be this aspect that most obviously 'hooked' you as you were reading, and which you might like to think about emulating in a life writing narrative of your own.

Other formal possibilities

Now that we've explored the main autobiographical forms, we're going to open our frame of reference. In this section we'll deal with life writing forms more generally, encountering further options for structuring both autobiography and biography.

'Bildungsroman' is a literary term taken directly from the German. It refers to a novel which charts the education and development of its hero or heroine as he or she comes to maturity. Famous examples include Goethe's *Die Leiden des jungen Werthers* [*The Sorrows of Young Werther*] (1774), Austen's *Emma* (1816), and Dickens's *David Copperfield* (1850). We have already noted the autobiographical nuances of Dickens's novel, and critics have discerned autobiographical qualities in other Bildungsromans, so it may not come as a surprise that the term can provide a useful, general way of thinking about, or planning, the structure of a life writing narrative. The Bildungsroman is particularly closely related to a sub-genre of life writing: the conversion narrative, or spiritual account. Good examples of this sub-genre, such as those by Anna Trapnel and Hannah Allen, may be found in Graham *et al.* (1989, pp. 71–86; pp. 197–210).

Though Middlebrook's biography of Anne Sexton ends very differently from Copperfield's story (Copperfield muses in the penultimate chapter that 'my domestic joy was perfect, I had been married ten happy years' (1966 [1850], p.939)), she uses some aspects of the Bildungsroman form. Section I describes how her subject becomes Anne Sexton through marriage, having been born Anne Harvey; Section II charts her transformation from 'Housewife into poet', and the milestones in her poetic development along the way; Section III, 'The prizewinner', culminates in a chapter called 'Money and fame'. The final section, 'The performer', deals with her suicide, but also the bestowal of her third honorary doctorate, her success with a play, and her appointment as a professor. Middlebrook provides an abbreviated sketch of her structure in the preface: 'during her eighteen years as a writer, Sexton earned most of the important awards available to American poets. She published eight books of poetry [...] and she saw her play *Mercy Street* produced off-Broadway. She was a shrewd businesswoman, and she became a successful teacher; though skimpily educated, she rose to the rank of professor at Boston University, teaching the craft of poetry' (1992 [1991], p.xix).

Pete Hamill's autobiography, *A Drinking Life* (1994), might be classed as adopting the Bildungsroman form. At the beginning of *A Drinking Life* Hamill is a young child, deeply affected by poverty, and by the absence and then the drinking of his father. He learns at first that 'even the weakest human being could take a drink and be magically transformed into someone smarter, bigger, braver' (p.19). Later, his concern is to stop drinking, and the final chapter begins with the words 'One January afternoon, after five sober years, I went for another walk in the snow' (p.265). Placing the past alongside the present in this way (just as Bayley does in his memoir of Iris Murdoch), helps to show, through contrast, how far he has come in his moral development. Also emphasising this aspect of his narrative, a couple of lines later he writes, 'if I had not yet repaired some of the damage I'd inflicted on [the children] and others, I was trying, I was trying' (p.265). In expressing this sentiment, and perhaps anticipating success, he looks to the future too, and so all three tenses are employed, helping his narrative to resonate with the added power of recognisable fictional structure and form.

It is a relief to a reader to find that things can progress, and develop in positive directions: a life, so often a messy and chaotic affair, can be tamed and shaped like a novel. I am not suggesting that things were not as Hamill has written them, but rather that he has made a powerful choice in his narrative form, one that makes his story more than personal, closer to archetypal in that he moves forward out of ignorance and misery and towards happiness and freedom.

- Read the extract from Pete Hamill's *A Drinking Life*, Reading 36 on p.553. Identify aspects of the Bildungsroman form in the narrative.

- Write a 150 word paragraph or a 10–16 line poem in which you focus your attention on an aspect of development in a character. The character you choose can be yourself.

ACTIVITY 21.7

Reading and writing

Several things occurred to me in respect of the Bildungsroman form as I read this extract. The broken friendships, which may always be remade or replaced, seem crucial, as does the magical realism of a small boy's faith in his comic book hero father (despite the harsh intervention of the older narrator telling us that 'that never happened'). In the early stages, Hamill's character is shaped by violence and fantasy, then the opening of the new chapter illustrates how things are getting worse. It is as though he is taking a further step in the descent into a particular kind of hell. But the entrance 'into a harder, poorer world' simultaneously offers the possibility of an exit, a hope that at some stage the process will begin to be reversed. The extract ends with a mother's invocation to 'wait and

DISCUSSION

see' and, although this is said 'without much hope', her phrase ushers in the future, and focuses the reader's attention on how things will develop.

This activity focuses your ideas on transformations and turning points. If this way of shaping your writing appealed to you when you came to the second part of the activity, you might use it to make further decisions about structure as your thoughts for your life writing develop. Rites of passage, for example, could play a prominent part in your narrative or poem(s).

The past and the present

In *Watching the Tree* (2001 [2000]) Adeline Yen Mah uses childhood memories of her grandfather to begin a text which is part autobiography, part history of Eastern thought. But she soon makes clear that she didn't understand the full significance of her relationship with him, or the wisdom he imparted to her, until many decades later (p.2). The rest of her book is structured, highly effectively, as a way of achieving that understanding: remembered conversations with her grandfather and other family members are brought into the present so that she can explore and acknowledge their influence. Stories he told her are sourced in Chinese philosophical writings dating from 2000 years before. The book is also a kind of dialogue between the past child and the present adult self – as she comes to understand, and expound, Chinese wisdom and belief.

As I noted in the first example in this chapter, John Boyle's *Galloway Street: Growing up Irish in exile*, formal decisions related to use of past and present can have impressive consequences. Yen Mah usually employs the past tense – with the exception of recalled dialogue – as she reconstructs her memories. Boyle opts for the present tense as he seeks to turn the then into the now.

In the preface Boyle discusses his decision to use his boyhood self as narrator. It was not what he intended to do. 'For years', Boyle writes, 'I had been tinkering obsessively with reminiscences about my childhood in Scotland, as if some clue might lie there to my present confusion. It did not help, I began to understand, that these events were being recalled and enhanced by the middle-aged raconteur I had become. Now I felt the need to re-discover – truthfully, without embroidery – the boy I had been' (Boyle, 2002 [2001], Foreword, p.10).

In his planning, and perhaps even in early drafts, Boyle worked with what might be described as a dual narrator, his older self and the boyhood self both commenting on events and experiences. He abandoned this formal choice, though, in what he seems to consider the search for greater truth. Boyle was living in exile, away from Ireland, and, crucially, this meant that the boy he had been was not only from a different time and place, but spoke a different language too. The 'two distinct voices' Boyle refers to really were distinct. One, his adult voice, was for commercial voiceovers, probably in standard English and received pronunciation; he used the other to speak from the place he came from, to articulate an original self. This prior voice, once he had begun to listen to it, undermined and challenged Boyle's life at a distance, standing 'on the sidelines [...], watchful, reproachful' [...]: '"Cummoan", he says, "ye know fine there wis mair tae it than that"' (p.11). He decided, in the end, to use it to tell his story.

Think of a specific and significant event in your own life, or in the life of a subject you have done some research on already in Part 4. First of all write a 150 word paragraph about the event using the past tense. Then write about it again, also in 150 words, but use the present tense. Afterwards, consider which felt harder work, and which more suitable for the task.

ACTIVITY 21.8

Writing

This activity encourages you to experiment with the effects created by different tenses – effects you can replicate in your own narratives. A childhood voice, evoked in the present tense, can be highly effective, but Yen Mah and Boyle made different decisions, in the end, about whether the past or the present was most appropriate for their stories. A combination of the two can also work well.

DISCUSSION

In his autobiography, *Experience*, Martin Amis constructs a narrative that might be said to be like the one Boyle originally imagined. *Experience* is formally structured using a series of dualities, or parallels. As he takes his reader into his narrative, and explains his methodology (and his reasons for writing), he writes that 'My organisational principles [...] derive from an inner urgency, and from the novelist's addiction to seeing parallels and making connections' (Amis, 2001 [2000], p.7). (This addiction may apply to writers more generally, as we have seen.) Conversations he has with his father, Kingsley Amis, are recounted throughout the text, as are comparable conversations he has with his own sons. Extracts from novels, by him and by his father, provide another layer of comparison. Letters home from university allow the student Amis a narrative voice, though it is often qualified by the adult writer. Times collide as parallels show how much, or how little, has changed. (An important through-line is provided by Amis's disastrous teeth: you'll have to read the book to see how!)

It's a growing, but densely patterned, self that is emphasised here, then; Amis the child meets and challenges Amis the student and Amis the adult. It might be tempting to see this as a form of Bildungsroman, and yet as a whole the narrative is more chaotic than that. 'My life', Amis states towards the end of his autobiography, 'is ridiculously shapeless. I know what makes a good narrative, and lives don't have much of that – pattern and balance, form, completeness, commensurateness' (ibid., p.361). But some lives are written about as though they do have a shape, as we have seen, and in a way that *is* how he has addressed his own, bringing the past and the present into measured and productive encounters with one another. As we proceed we will consider one further formal characteristic of life writing, one that can help very much to enhance the sense of developmental pattern in a life.

Through-lines

Although Stephen King made it clear that his readers should not expect to find through-lines in his prose, such continuities can prove very useful as a way of structuring a text, both for the author and for the reader. They make up a crucial part of the writer's formal armoury, and can be particularly valuable to a life writer, in whom a sense of the relevance of echoes and resonances is often particularly developed.

In Chapter 19, in the discussion of reasons for writing, I talked about narratives that seem to owe their existence to the experience of some kind of loss. We're going to spend some time now thinking about loss as a through-line, and how it can structure a narrative.

Read the opening extracts by John Diamond, David Jenkins, and Gillian Slovo. What kinds of loss do they display, and what kind of impetus is that loss granting to the narrative as it begins?

ACTIVITY 21.9

Reading

In 20 years' time, if – touch wood, please God, all of that malarkey – I am still around, how will I feel about a bad back? I mean, a *really* bad back – the sort of ricked back I had a few years ago when I thought a kidney had burst and I couldn't move for a couple of days, and announced that things couldn't possibly get worse than this, and that this was the greatest medical indignity a man could suffer.

Or a cold – how will I feel about one of those colds when you can't breathe, or think, or write or imagine what it was like before the onset of the cold? Will I still feel about those everyday reasons for giving up as I did before 27 March 1997?

(Diamond, 1998, p.7)

The mountains have changed more than the village since we were children. Once bare of trees, a vast free playground for us, they are now thickly planted with conifers, gold Japanese spruce and Sitkas with sharp blue-green needles. Where we ran and chased one another, walkers and picnickers now dutifully observe the paths of the Forestry Commission.

(Jenkins, 1993, p.1)

An hour before she died my mother went shopping. In the company of one of her closest friends, Moira Forjaz, she left the house where they'd given lunch to fifteen. They were due to go their separate ways later that afternoon and so they drove in convoy. It was 17 August 1982 and Maputo's faded elegance glistened in the bright winter sun.

[...]

There is a photograph of her taken on the day before she died. I have it on my London wall – she stares at my back as I sit by my computer. I turn to look at her. I see her carefree, smiling, confident, at home and I conjure her up, as she must have been in those last hours, her feet clicking against the cobbled pavement, her neatly turned ankle lifted up into the ageing Renault 16 that she had shipped from England.

Turning away I close my eyes and am assailed by a different image: my mother as she had once been in England. I see a stylish, handsome woman who had never lost her passion for expensive clothes but who was showing the strain of an enforced exile, a husband who was constantly on the move and three angry daughters.

(Slovo, 1997, p.1)

DISCUSSION   In two of the narratives, Diamond's and Jenkins's, we are offered different experiences of terrible loss that might be compared if we read them as representing symbolic ejections from paradise. In Diamond's case, the date he was diagnosed with cancer forms an impermeable membrane between the innocent rage with which he used to greet a bad back or cold, and the appalling and new experience of the extremes of which illness is capable. We might imagine that the tension between his loss of innocence and the fact of his experience will now drive the narrative, as Diamond charts his new territory, without being able to forget the old. Indeed, the old is changed too by the new, for with experience alone does he know it as the innocent time that it was, by comparison, always and only by comparison.

Jenkins's narrative also opens by opposing the time before to the time after. He conjures up the Wales of his youth as a giant open playground, in stark contrast to the modern, constricting, capitalist adventure now sited there. In this case, we might imagine that the loss of the freedom of youth will form a significant theme throughout, and that Jenkins's sense of the pleasure and importance of home will, in later years, be compromised by what it had become. Another form of loss is yet more fundamental to this biography: that of his brother Richard.

Slovo's narrative has as its impetus a more complex experience of loss. Slovo's violent loss of her mother is the primary driver of the narrative. But loss features biographically here too. I am interested, in formal terms, by the images of her mother that feature on the first page of her text. One is a photograph of her mother, taken in Africa, showing her to be 'carefree, smiling, confident'. The other is a mental image of a 'handsome woman [...] who was showing the strain of an enforced exile' in London. Her mother was most herself, and most happy, in the more recent image – the photograph. This establishes a painful contrast. Ruth First was happiest when most in danger, when in Africa, rather than when in exile. Exile demanded too high a price for her, but being at home in Africa meant the risk of assassination, a risk that became reality in Mozambique in 1982. A pattern is constructed in the first page, then, that we might see developing throughout. We have two different representations of the same woman, which each evoke loss of self, of country, and of life, in powerful ways. Slovo's narrative pays attention to them both, as she in turn relates her own loss of her mother.

Make notes about whether your own explorations in narrative so far in Part 4 are rooted in loss of some kind.

ACTIVITY 21.10
Writing

DISCUSSION

If your focus has been primarily on autobiographical narrative as you have thought and written so far, it is to be expected that you have been particularly attuned to memories, of childhood perhaps, or of another previous time in your life. Memory is, of course, in some ways inseparable from the concept or feeling of loss (while it can also be experienced as restorative). But equally, perhaps, if you have seen yourself as a biographer of a more objective kind, loss may not fit with your idea of the basis for your narratives: discovery, or reclamation, may seem more appropriate roots.

Before moving on from this section, I would like briefly to outline for you some further ideas that provide through-lines in life writing narratives. These may help to give you ideas for your own writing:

- the desert – in Somalian writer Waris Dirie's autobiography, *Desert Flower* (2001);
- Englishness, and the way it affects character – in Sebastian Faulks's *The Fatal Englishman* (1997 [1996]);
- love – in examples including Sackville-West's *Portrait of a Marriage*, as we have seen in Chapter 20;
- houses in different countries – in Hilary Mantel's *Giving up the Ghost* (2003);
- ghosts – also in Mantel (2003);
- food – in Nigel Slater's *Toast: The story of a boy's hunger* (2003).

Return to the preface you wrote for a life writing narrative at the end of Chapter 20. Choose one of the through-lines from this list, or another that suits your chosen focus. Use the through-line to take this life writing a stage further. Write the first paragraph of the text (up to 150 words), or the first poem (10–16 lines), and then write some notes exploring how you will develop it using the through-line in some structural way.

ACTIVITY 21.11
Writing

When you go back to your writing from Activity 20.7 you may find that your thoughts have already moved on. Don't worry about this. Use this activity as a way of expressing that development. If you still like what you see by way of your preface, simply revisit the plans that you made and begin to bring the text to life with this initial paragraph of prose or poem.

DISCUSSION   Through-lines provide one way of establishing a formal structure for your life writing, and they are valuable in this respect. But you may also want to think of them as a unique aspect of your writer's imagination. As the previous list should have made clear, through-lines are diverse and wide-ranging. Even more common examples, like love, may prove to be an important way of you getting the most out of your particular creative energies and interests.

Poetic life writing

You may well have attempted some poetic life writing in response to activities earlier in Part 4. At this point I'd like to give you some examples of this form of life writing, to encourage you to think about whether you might be interested in exploring it further.

ACTIVITY 21.12   Read the poems by Elaine Feinstein, Reading 37 on p.556. In her
Reading   introduction to the poems in the anthology from which they are taken, Feinstein says that 'first and foremost, I wanted poems that were genuinely trying to make sense of experience' (Couzyn, 1985, p.115). As you read, think about the experience she is making 'sense of', and the poetic techniques she is bringing to bear to do so.

DISCUSSION   As suggested by her introduction, Feinstein often uses poetry to reconstruct, to chart and to reflect on autobiographical episode or incident, although she does so in different voices. In the five poems you have read she engages with a range of experiences: childbirth, dealing with taunting children, the challenges of marriage and family, the death of her father, thinking alone. Most striking to me, in terms of her poetic technique, is the way in which her images give life to the more fundamental rites of human existence incorporated in this list (birth, growing up, marriage, death). Appropriately, these images are powerful, sometimes archetypal: the Muse (Calliope is the Muse of eloquence and epic poetry, as you may remember from Part 3), the witch, the warrior. Such images resonate, so that her words may help to make sense of experiences beyond her own.

You may find that this form of life writing attracts you more strongly than prose. If so, then a combination of your work in Parts 3 and 4 will enable you to attempt a life writing narrative – perhaps via a sequence – in poetry. Your work later in Part 4 will provide you with other examples of autobiographical poetry. For a variety of verse forms and subject matter, you could also explore Ted Hughes' collection *Birthday Letters* (1998), or the poems of the nineteenth century poet Emily Dickinson (1830–1886) (Dickinson, 1999).

As you develop your life writing skills further in the chapter which follows, you will focus on a subject that is fundamental to all forms of autobiographical life writing, and to some forms of biography too: memory.

References

Alpers, Antony (1980) *The Life of Katherine Mansfield*, London: Jonathan Cape.

Amis, Martin (2001 [2000]) *Experience*, London: Vintage.

Austen, Jane (1966 [1816]) *Emma*, Harmondsworth: Penguin.

Benson, Mary (1986) *Nelson Mandela*, Harmondsworth, Middlesex: Penguin.

Boyle, John (2002 [2001]) *Galloway Street: Growing up Irish in exile*, London: Black Swan.

Bradbury, Malcolm (1988) *Unsent Letters*, London: Arrow.

le Carré, John (2003) 'A sting in the tale', *Observer* Magazine, 7 December, pp.22–39.

Chatwin, Bruce (1979 [1977]) *In Patagonia*, London: Pan Books.

Couzyn, Jeni (ed.) (1985) *The Bloodaxe Book of Contemporary Women Poets*, Newcastle: Bloodaxe.

Diamond, John (1998) *C: Because cowards get cancer too*, London: Vermilion.

Dickens, Charles (1966 [1850]) *David Copperfield*, Harmondsworth: Penguin.

Dickinson, Emily (1999) *The Poems of Emily Dickinson*, Cambridge, MA: Harvard University Press.

Dirie, Waris (2001) *Desert Flower*, London: Virago.

Faulks, Sebastian (1997 [1996]) *The Fatal Englishman: Three short lives*, London: Vintage.

Goethe, Johann Wolfgang von (1989 [1774]) *The Sorrows of Young Werther*, Michael Hulse (tr.), Harmondsworth: Penguin.

Graham, Elspeth *et al.* (eds) (1989) *Her Own Life: Autobiographical writings by seventeenth-century Englishwomen*, London and New York: Routledge.

Hamill, Pete (1994) *A Drinking Life: A memoir*, New York: Little, Brown & Co.

Hill, Susan (2004) 'Private lives', *Guardian* Review, 10 January, pp.36–7.

Hughes, Ted (1998) *Birthday Letters*, London: Faber and Faber.

Jenkins, David with Rogers, Sue (1993) *Richard Burton: A brother remembered: The biography Richard wanted*, London: Random House.

Kafka, Franz (1992 [1910–23]) *The Diaries of Franz Kafka 1910–23*, Max Brod (ed.), London: Mandarin Books.

Kaysen, Susanna (2000 [1995]) *Girl, Interrupted*, London: Virago.

King, Stephen (2001 [2000]) *On Writing: A Memoir of the Craft*, London: Hodder & Stoughton.

Mantel, Hilary (2003) *Giving Up the Ghost*, London: Fourth Estate.

Middlebrook, Diane Wood (1992 [1991]) *Anne Sexton: A biography*, London: Virago.

Rhys, Jean (1981 [1979]) *Smile Please: An unfinished autobiography* London: Penguin.

Rousseau, Jean-Jacques (1953 [1781]) *The Confessions*, J.M. Cohen (tr.), London: Penguin.

Slater, Nigel (2003) *Toast: The story of a boy's hunger*, London: Fourth Estate.

Slovo, Gillian (1997) *Every Secret Thing: My family, my country*, London: Little, Brown.

Thubron, Colin (1999) *In Siberia*, London: Chatto & Windus.

Trollope, Anthony (1992 [1883]) *An Autobiography*, Oxford: Oxford University Press.

Woolf, Virginia (1979 [1977]) *The Diary of Virginia Woolf*, Anne Olivier Bell (ed.), London: Penguin.

Yen Mah, Adeline (2001 [2000]) *Watching the Tree*, London: HarperCollins.

22 *Using memory*

DEREK NEALE

Remembering lives

Memory is important to biography and autobiography. In both the writer is recalling the habits, relationships and cultural setting of a life. In earlier chapters (in Parts 1 and 3 for instance), you were shown the advantages to be gained from using memory and details of your everyday world when writing stories and poems. It is especially important to realise this resource in life writing, and also to be aware that biography and autobiography aren't necessarily exclusive categories. Often when writing of your own life you will find yourself writing about the lives of other people – you might want to give outlines of your father's or mother's life history, for instance, or you may wish to detail the daily routine of a friend. On the other hand, when concerned with a biographical subject, one that doesn't have a personal link to your life, you might like to include yourself in the narrative, as many modern journalists do in magazine interviews and articles, and as some writers of biography also do.

It has already been mentioned that life writing doesn't necessarily have to follow a straightforward, start-to-finish chronology; you don't have to begin your narrative with a birth and end either with a death or in your subject's old age. The beginning of Dickens's *David Copperfield* is just one approach. For instance, you might just focus on a fixed period of time. Consider the start of J.D. Salinger's *Catcher in the Rye*, for the antithesis of Dickens's beginning:

> If you really want to hear about it, the first thing you'll probably want to know is where I was born, and what my lousy childhood was like, and how my parents were occupied and all before they had me, and all that David Copperfield kind of crap, but I don't feel like going into it, if you want to know the truth. In the first place, that stuff bores me ... I'm not going to tell you my whole goddam autobiography or anything. I'll just tell you about this madman stuff that happened to me around last Christmas just before I got pretty run-down and had to come out here and take it easy.
>
> (Salinger, 1994 [1951], p.1)

As with *David Copperfield*, this is the beginning of a novel, but it seems to be using and commenting upon the conventions of autobiography. It includes the reader, a second person addressee, as part of the narrative and establishes the boundaries of personal experience to be dealt with in the narrative; the memory is going to be finite. Also, two most pertinent points are made about the relationship between writer and subject matter: if you're writing about a life it is important not to be bored, and to inhabit the conventions of the genre in a personal fashion. Treat life writing like a bespoke garment, tailor-made for your subject matter, rather than something you've bought off the shelf which you have to fit into.

In this way your content will define the form of your writing. It can be a poem with little narrative, for instance, based around the memory of a moment; or it can be a dramatic scene involving many characters. As Richard Holmes says, 'Why should the biographer be limited to one kind of narrative voice, one kind of discursive prose?' (2000, Prologue, p.xi). His book *Sidetracks* includes pieces that are biography and autobiography, and which take the form of radio plays, travel pieces, essays, character-sketches, and short stories. All of them were 'written as different ways of investigating biographical material' (p.xi). In this call for the use of various narrative methods Holmes echoes the approach of Ruth Picardie and Susanna Kaysen, mentioned in Chapter 21. The suggestion is that your narrative voice and form will always arise from your purpose and the area of personal or biographical experience you are writing about.

Using your memory

Remember the advice offered in Chapters 3 and 4: think of memory as something that you can use to enrich your writing, not something you should feel obliged to adhere to. Recall as well the passage from *Catcher in the Rye*: if you are bored by an over-rehearsed episode from your past, then the chances are your reader will be bored too. You will need to reinvigorate it. The episode might be the first day in a new job, for instance, when you spilt a cup of coffee over yourself and felt embarrassed. You can revive the memory by looking at it from a different perspective perhaps; imagine a colleague watching what was happening. Ask some pertinent questions: who else was there? What sort of day was it? What were you wearing? Did you like the job? Who did you speak to on that first day? Asking questions like these, and answering just some of them while inventing answers to others (it would be impossible to remember all such details), is the way to revive the scene and events, for you and for your reader.

Looking back over your own life may flush out uncomfortable memories. The purpose of investigating your own life in these chapters is not necessarily therapeutic, though it may throw up therapeutic benefits. The activities are designed to improve your writing, not to spark wholesale re-evaluations of your life. If you find some of the autobiographical exercises too taxing or disturbing, it might be an idea to concentrate on biographical writing or a different era of your life.

When writing about your own life you will be calling on both your associative memory and your narrative memory, as discussed in Part 1. For instance, with a train of associative recall about the coffee incident you might think of flowers in a vase on one of the desks; the office and the type of work you did in the job; the big windows looking out onto the street; a painted brick wall on your route to work and a garage on the corner of the road and the smell of petrol; the mole on a colleague's forehead; another colleague, soon to become a friend, helping you to clean up the coffee and kindly pouring you another cup; perhaps you remember the friend's first name but can't recall more. These thoughts would all come in quick succession, and in no specific order.

With the second type of recall – narrative memory – you will have a less unruly train of thought. Events will be ordered in a time sequence, so you have in effect formed a story of events in your mind. You go to work on your first day and during the morning break you are drinking coffee and talking about the holiday you've just been on. A wasp comes in through the window and, in trying to avoid it, you spill your coffee. A colleague helps you to clean up, but for the rest of the day you feel clumsy and are conscious of the stain on your clothes.

Now let's try to get both kinds of memory – associative and narrative – working.

ACTIVITY 22.1

Writing

■ Draw a circle in the centre of a page in your notebook and in it write the word 'yesterday'. Create a cluster, as described in Chapter 1, writing down all the words and phrases that you can think of to do with what happened to you yesterday, circling them and linking them back to this central word.

- When you have finished, on a separate page write a single sentence about what happened to you yesterday.

These are two quite different ways of recalling your life. Writing the sentence meant that you had to arrange the words according to the conventions of grammar, so that they were being organised into some sort of sequence. While composing it you might also have thought of new words to put over in the associative cluster. On reflection the sentence might seem reductive as a version of the day, especially in comparison with the cluster version. Yet the cluster isn't entirely comprehensible to a reader, maybe not even to you; this too may seem dissatisfying as a version of the day. It will be important to harness and integrate both types of recall when writing about your life: to arrange your thoughts and memories as a narrative when needed, so that events appear in a time sequence with settings, characters and causalities; but also to capture the spontaneity of associative and resonant ways of remembering. Each way of remembering on its own may not provide a complete enough picture.

This is a useful exercise to return to, or to start a project. You might like to try it with different focuses. For instance:

- looking in the mirror and using your reflection;
- using an old photograph of yourself.

It is a useful exercise for writing biography as well as autobiography. When you are writing about another person's life you will need to make the most of all possible perceptions of that person. Try:

- a photograph of a friend or relative;
- a photograph of a celebrity you like;
- a photograph of a celebrity you dislike.

Storied lives

People's lives and their memories of those lives often read like constructed narratives, stories that have been in some way crafted. That is not to say that they are artificial; it is just a reflection of the fact that stories are a common way in which we actively think about and preserve our pasts. It is a pattern of thinking and representation we fall into even when we are attempting to be scientific, as Freud says about his patients' case studies:

> Like other neuropathologists, I was trained to employ local diagnoses and electro-prognosis, and it still strikes me myself as strange that the case histories I write should read like short stories [...] I must console myself with the reflection that the nature of the subject is evidently responsible for this, rather than any preference of my own.
>
> (Freud, 1955, p.160)

When the 'subject' is someone's life history, their sensibility and familial relationships, any representation is likely to resemble a story. Any attempt to remember all or part of a life involves ordering fragments, an editorial process of inclusion and exclusion, similar to the one you've just gone through with the cluster and the sentence. As Graham Greene says, 'An autobiography is only "a sort of life" – it may contain less errors of fact than a biography, but it is of necessity even more selective' (1974 [1971], p.9). Memories are a form of fiction-making and storytelling, and there is a fundamental difference between living a life and recalling that life.

Jean-Paul Sartre's novel, *Nausea* is written in the form of a journal. Its narrator, Roquentin, states his intention on the first page:

> ... to write down everything that happens from day to day. To keep a diary in order to understand. To neglect no nuances or little details, even if they seem unimportant ...
>
> (Sartre, 1963, p.9)

The premise of the novel is a metaphysical exploration of the discrepancies between living a life and recounting that life, either in thought and memory or in writing. Roquentin from time to time comes to some conclusions:

> ... for the most commonplace event to become an adventure, you must – and this is all that is necessary – start *recounting* it. This is what fools people: a man is always a teller of tales, he lives surrounded by his stories and the stories of others, he sees everything that happens to him through them; and he tries to live his life as if he were recounting it.
>
> (ibid., p.61)

This observation – that we think of our lives as stories – is most important when coming to write biography and autobiography; it means that you can use some of the skills you have gained in writing fiction. If writers like Sartre, Dickens and Salinger seem to be using the conventions of life writing in their novels, the reverse is also true. As Michael Holroyd says:

Biographers have learned a good deal from novelists – even from the writers of detective stories and thrillers. Though the biographer may not invent dialogue, he may use short quotations from letters and diaries, poetry and prose, which have the immediacy of dialogue.

(Holroyd, 2002, p.26)

Even the contention here, that the biographer can't use the fictional technique of writing dialogue as if recalled verbatim, has been challenged. In many of the examples of life writing that you will look at, dialogue is used to illustrate both typical and specific exchanges between characters. Also the use of the third person, a technique which would seem only suited to fiction or biographical writing, can also be used in autobiographical writing, as shown in such texts as Paul Auster's *The Invention of Solitude*, specifically the second part, 'The Book of Memory' (1988 [1982], p.71 ff.). Auster describes how he eventually came to use the third person:

When I started the next section, I assumed it would be written in the first person as well. I worked on it for six or eight months in that form but something wasn't right [...] What it came down to was creating a distance between myself and myself. If you're too close to the thing you're trying to write about, the perspective vanishes, and you begin to smother. I had to objectify myself in order to explore my own subjectivity.

(Auster, 1996, p.147)

This is another instance of life experience being revived by using a certain writing technique. Auster's novels and autobiographical writing are all concerned with exploring the 'shape of a life' (2004). For him lives are not scientific entities that can be easily verified. The recall of lives is a subjective affair, and often for the reader it is this personal regard for the past which holds the intrinsic appeal. Memory might be fallible but it is based on experience, a consciousness of life which is littered with elements that seem to offer themselves up as undeniably true. For instance, there is the sensory recall surrounding an event. As seen with the Proust example in Chapter 3, a smell or sound will sometimes be the trigger. Sometimes it will present itself as evidence of the truth of a memory. This is the case with Graham Greene, talking about his boyhood hide-away:

The danger of discovery lent those hours a quality of excitement which was very close to momentary happiness. Scent to me is far more evocative than sound or perhaps even sight, so that I become attracted without realizing it to the smell of a floor-polish or a detergent which one day I miss when I open my door and home seems no longer home. So in my sixties I seem able to smell the leaves and grasses of my hiding-place more certainly than I hear the dangerous footsteps on the path or see the countryman's boots pass by on the level of my eyes.

(Greene, 1974 [1971], p.56)

Here the sensory faculties seem to be governing the memory, and the emotional colour of the events is given priority over their sequence in time, their causality and arrangement into the form of a story.

ACTIVITY 22.2

Reading

Read the following:

- the first part of the extract from Hilary Mantel's memoir *Giving up the Ghost*, Reading 38 on p.560, ending at '... like the aftermath of a fire' (p.563);

- the extract from the first chapter from *Cider with Rosie* by Laurie Lee, Reading 6 on p.429, already read in Part 1;

- Seamus Heaney's 'Death of a Naturalist' on p.51, already read in Part 1.

In your notebook detail the different ways in which a memory of sensory perceptions is at work in these extracts. What 'associative' detail is being noted? How is the memory being ordered into story form?

DISCUSSION

As seen in Chapter 3, 'Death of a Naturalist' is full of sensory perception and seems to be composed of the associative memories from many occasions, yet also settles down into one specific time. Similarly, the *Cider with Rosie* extract is full of sensory detail based on memory; the detail accumulates effortlessly to realise time, place and event. Mantel's narrative is more self-conscious. Whereas Lee's passage confidently integrates the two kinds of recall, narrative and associative, Mantel directly addresses the issue of how the reality of past events is difficult to ascertain. First of all she admits the contemporary position from which the recollection is being made, by revisiting the 'carriage drive' as an adult and revealing what habitually rather than specifically happened to her as a child. She goes on to talk about the unreliability of memory and how she is unsure of the dateline, while describing the most vivid sensory recalls.

Think of a place from your past (not necessarily your childhood, it could be from your more recent past) – it might be a room, a street, or a garden, but not necessarily any of these. You choose. Spend ten minutes listing things about the place or creating a cluster for it in your notebook.

ACTIVITY 22.3

Writing

Then either write 250 words or write a 16 line poem about the place.

Whether writing prose or poetry use sensory detail, creating a sense of many occasions, but also situating yourself there at a certain time, possibly with other characters. For example, you might write about a field where you regularly played with your friends as a child; you might remember the smell of the newly cut grass and recall an occasion when you hurt yourself when playing there. Alternatively, it could be a street where you had to catch the bus to work, how the bus shelter smelt of stale cigarette smoke, and how you once saw an old friend in the queue.

DISCUSSION

Reflect for a moment on whether you have gained any new insight or had to invent any detail in order to write about the recall. The process of writing can often enrich a memory; detail can arise just from trying to focus on an event.

Unreliable memories

As Mantel illustrates with the talk of experiments with fake photographs, memory is notoriously susceptible to suggestion. For instance, the Swiss psychologist Jean Piaget had a vivid memory from when he was a very young child, of his nursery nurse being attacked by an assailant while walking him in the park. This memory of the event stayed with him for many years. He was convinced by the detail of the memory, even though he was only in a pram at the time. The nurse was awarded a watch as some sort of compensation for the ordeal. Years later the nurse returned the watch, saying she'd made the whole thing up. Piaget had believed the nurse's story so thoroughly that he'd invented images to go with it, yet it was an incident that never took place (Piaget, 1951, pp.187–8).

Certain memories will be clear to you and seem undeniably true; others will be shrouded in doubt. You may suspect some parts of your recall to be influenced by other people, or to be altered by the passage of time. Some narratives, like that from *Cider with Rosie*, admit less doubt; the dramatisation is presented as fact despite Lee being so young at the time. Mantel's approach is more circumspect, as you can see as she proceeds.

ACTIVITY 22.4
Reading

Read the second part of the extract from *Giving up the Ghost* by Hilary Mantel, Reading 38 on p.563, beginning at 'This is the first thing I remember.'

In your notebook identify the parts that are influenced by suggestion or which acknowledge the power of suggestion. What narrative techniques are being used to present the recall?

DISCUSSION

The memory of Bankswood seems to have been created by the photographs of that location seen at a later age. The photographs have helped create the scene of the photo shoot. Mantel's narrative acknowledges how the combination of fact and fiction is working, but this doesn't undermine the veracity of the account, in fact it adds to it. The vivid detail of the 'fast scudding clouds and the rush of sound over my head, the wind in the trees' combines with a later sensibility that can say 'as if the waters of life have begun to flow', and is also informed by the black and white photos of the 1950s. In this way memories are never a reflection solely of their moment of inception; they are continually influenced by different eras in their protagonist's life.

Mantel's narrative is structured in relatively short, sharp bursts of information, co-ordinated around certain recurring features – such as the narrator's age, and the numbers of certain houses which are key locations in her childhood. Such methods, as explored in Activity 21.1, create fragments which are linked by a not necessarily continuous through-line. Each burst narrates a concerted episode and seems almost self-contained; it isn't continuous with the preceding or subsequent passages. Yet when, for instance, a house number recurs the narrative connection is made between different passages. The use of the present tense lends the narrative immediacy; it declares to the reader that, although it is happening in the past, this narrative is coming from the present, the writer is still investigating the episode.

Imagination and memory

As Philip Roth says, 'the facts are never just coming at you but are incorporated by an imagination that is formed by your previous experience. Memories of the past are memories not of facts but memories of your imaginings of the facts' (1988, p.8). Imagination can play a big part in any reconstruction of events, as suggested in Chapter 20 and Ford Madox Ford's approach to writing the biography of Joseph Conrad. Personal impressions are an important form of information about a life, but they are notoriously difficult to verify. You may not be able to remember every detail about an event; your reader might need more detail than you possess in order for the event to be realised. You will have to make decisions as to how self-conscious you are going to be in the way that you admit this. It is important to remember that your version of the past, no matter the imaginative input, will not be just an arbitrary 'confabulation', as Mantel says; it will be grounded in the original experience. Imagination isn't just a whimsical activity, but often a necessary approach taken with material that is sometimes too close, or too distant in time, to see. Imagination is a way of opening up areas of life experience that otherwise would remain shuttered and confined; a way of widening the perspective we have on our own lives. This can be true with biographical subjects too.

Find a photograph of a character about whom you wish to write, someone other than yourself:

ACTIVITY 22.5
Writing

- Describe in your notebook the content of the photo (use up to 50 words).

- Then, again in your notebook, describe as much as you can of that which sits outside of the photo: who was taking it, what was just out of shot, who was present, the location, the time and other such details – some of which may be imagined, some researched (use up to 150 words).

- Now combine and integrate the two versions, so it reads like the story of the photograph being taken (use up to 250 words).

This task requires that you ask pragmatic questions about the evidence in front of you. You might not always know definite answers. By doing this you are gauging probability rather than following flights of fancy. The problem often arising when writing from visual stimuli, such as

DISCUSSION

photographs, is that the writer assumes that the reader knows something of the picture already. It's important that you make no assumptions about your reader in this respect. Using photographs can start exciting and unexpected narrative journeys that can explore both autobiographical and biographical subjects – as seen with Mantel and as will shortly be seen in the excerpt from Joan Didion's *Where I Was From* (Reading 39).

Research

When writing the previous exercise you might even have found it necessary to do some research and asked someone else questions about details you didn't know. You may have simply checked for a date printed on the back of the photograph. By doing this you are developing the detail in your writing, and enriching the description. As seen in Part 1, doing research can be an important part of writing fiction and poetry. This is no less true with life writing. Just because you may be writing about yourself, it doesn't mean you can rest assured that you have all the information you need ready at hand. The corroboration of facts is also an essential part of biographical writing; you will not be able to make certain claims without backing them up.

It might be necessary to locate the precise details about an episode from your own life or the life about which you are writing. This research may involve locating birth and marriage certificates, and other such historical documentation. On occasions it will be a case of looking in reference books and on the internet. Sometimes it will be more to do with contacting and talking to people, or it might even involve revisiting certain locations from your past, as Mantel does, to revive the sensory and emotional recall. The aim in your writing is to build up a substantial picture of events, and to convince your reader of the completeness of this picture. Memory is notoriously full of lacunae, gaps in description and detail. Your ambition, in using research and imagination, is to create as full a picture as possible so that, holes or no holes, the reader is convinced by the complexity of the world you are realising.

Read the extract from Joan Didion's *Where I Was From*, Reading 39 on p.567.

ACTIVITY 22.6
Reading

In your notebook write down what sort of narrative you think this is and detail the factual elements that have informed Didion's story of her family. What part do you think imagination has played in this narrative?

DISCUSSION

Although billed 'a memoir' just like Mantel's *Giving up the Ghost*, this extract reads more like a family history, one that leads into national history, detailing as it does the opening up of America's West in the mid-nineteenth century. It spans freely and quickly over a vast historical period, 1766 to 1957, using family possessions – photographs, testimony, quilts, recipes and pieces of appliqué – as through-lines to link the various strands. These in turn reveal the way of life and attitudes of the various eras. This is one thing that life-writing achieves almost incidentally. When working well it remembers the wider cultural context as well as an individual's situation. With Didion the issues of political and national identity are as prominent, if not more so, than the history of the individual identity; her memoir amounts almost to a political and historical memoir of California.

On a personal level it reads fluidly like a tour of family heirlooms; as if all of this information is at Didion's fingertips and she is merely turning like a tour guide from one artefact to the next. The truth is probably rather different, with considerable research and some imaginative venturing, as well as remembering – all of which are hinted at in the narrative. Look, for instance, at how she uses the photograph as a spur to recall the vocabulary inherited from her grandfather, to reveal the researched lineage of her grandmother, and also imagine the made-up stories of Indian blood.

Choose an object that has a connection either to your family or a friend. Don't choose a photograph this time, but something that somebody made, gave or wrote. For example, it could be the biscuit tin that is now used to store old Christmas cards, but which originally contained brandy snaps, given to you as a gift by an aunt who once emigrated to Australia with one husband but who came back with another.

ACTIVITY 22.7
Writing

In your notebook spend ten minutes listing the associations you have with the object. Then research one further thing about either the object or a person connected to the object. For instance, with the biscuit tin and the travelling aunt, you might ask a relative what happened to the husband she left in Australia; or you might try to find out what year and on what occasion the brandy snaps were given.

Then write the story of the object (use up to 500 words).

Conclusion

Memory often seems paradoxical – to be both rich and impoverished at the same time. On the one hand there are some memories that come complete with sensory detail. Such scenes can be smelt and touched and heard and tasted, as well as seen. These vivid memories tend to be well rehearsed; they're often thought about; some of them are even talked about and might be shared with others on occasions. The impoverished side of memory appears to be hard to get at, like a locked secret. It can sometimes feel as though you are struggling through the recurring, more vivid memories, trying to get to the rarer ones. Remember Mantel's model of memories laid side by side like seeds in the soil, which runs counter to the more conventional image of memories being buried more deeply the further away they are in time. It is more helpful to see your memories like Mantel suggests – as about to grow into something new. By actively exploring your memory, asking imaginative questions of 'what really happened' and maybe doing some research, you will be tending the soil, helping your memories to reveal themselves. In this way you will come to learn more about yourself and your subject as you write.

References

Auster, Paul (1996) *The Red Notebook and Other Writings*, London: Faber and Faber.

Auster, Paul (1988 [1982]) *The Invention of Solitude*, London and Boston: Faber and Faber.

Auster, Paul (2004) *Front Row*, BBC Radio 4, 31 May.

Freud, Sigmund (1955) *The Standard Edition of the Complete Psychological Works of Sigmund Freud Vol. 2: Studies on hysteria*, London: Hogarth Press.

Greene, Graham (1974 [1971]) *A Sort of Life*, Harmondsworth: Penguin.

Piaget, Jean (1951) *Play, Dreams and Imitation in Childhood*, C. Gattegno and F.M. Hodgson (trs.), London: Routledge & Kegan Paul.

Roth, Philip (1988) *The Facts: A novelist's autobiography*, New York: Farrar, Strauss and Giroux.

Salinger, J.D. (1994 [1951]) *Catcher in the Rye*, London: Penguin.

Holmes, Richard (2000) *Sidetracks*, London: Harper Collins.

Holroyd, Michael (2002) *Works On Paper: The craft of biography and autobiography*, London: Little, Brown and Co.

Sartre, Jean-Paul (1963) *Nausea*, Robert Baldick (tr.), Penguin: London. (Original French edition, published in 1938.)

23 *Versions of a life*

DEREK NEALE

This chapter will elaborate on some of the forms of life writing discussed in Chapter 21, looking at the techniques involved in trying different approaches – such as travel writing, diary writing and dramatic writing. Similarly we will be looking at some of the techniques used in writing fiction that might be of use to the life writer, and we will continue to consider how biographical and autobiographical approaches might sometimes cross over. Although you will ostensibly be dealing in facts and memories based on reality, you will still need to think of how to craft your writing. This chapter will focus on how you might go about producing particular versions of events.

Writing in diary form

Samuel Pepys's diary was one of the first diaries to be published. It is now regarded as a historical record and showed a move away from using diaries for business notations towards a more personal type of writing. The most notable modern day form of diary entry is a weblog, sometimes known as a blog, where the private diary entry is circulated via the internet, and can even invite comments and a level of interactivity. In this way blogging is often more than just a private record; blogs can read like testimonies, commentaries, journalism, or even pure fiction. They are conscious of their readership from the start.

Diaries lie on the cusp between private and public worlds. They are a form of writing that can be seen as a personal, secretive dialogue with the self, a form of isolated reflection, or alternatively as a pragmatic exercise in revelation. As mentioned in Chapter 21, diaries are sometimes written purely because of the possibility of publication, as with politicians, whose private and public identities are often under scrutiny. A diary promises insights into the most hidden corners of a character; it offers the potential to reveal a fully fledged identity, one with hopes, doubts, petty preoccupations and grand aspirations.

Sometimes diaries are written as a record of a journey, as with Dervla Murphy's *In Ethiopia with a Mule*, which you will be looking at shortly. Many writers, like the novelist Elizabeth George, see the writing of a novel as a 'journey' and start a new diary or journal for each new novel. Within the genre of diaries there are different degrees of acknowledgement or awareness that the reader might one day be peering into this private world. Many diaries that make it onto the book shelf are edited and redrafted so their appearance as spontaneous record is as much a question of craft as the well-honed stanza or the succinct short story.

You will shortly be looking at an extract from Anne Frank's diaries. Perhaps contrary to expectation, these diaries, covering a Jewish girl's wartime experiences under the Nazis, were written with a growing awareness of publication. After 1944 Frank started 'rewriting and editing her diary, improving on the text, omitting passages she didn't think were interesting enough and adding others from memory' (1997 [1947], Foreword, p.v). Before they came to publication, the diaries were also edited by Anne's father, Otto Frank, who chose to omit unflattering descriptions, especially of his dead wife, and details of Anne's nascent sexuality. The problem of censorship is most pertinent to diaries because, as a genre, they are known for revealing salacious detail. These are issues that every writer has to consider. What you might write in your meditative, private diary is not what you might want to reveal to a wider readership. You may well have already used your notebook as a diary, a place of quiet and secure reflection.

We will now explore the possibility of developing and using diary writing as a technique.

ACTIVITY 23.1

Writing

Start a diary for the duration of your work on the next two chapters – or two weeks, whichever is the longer. We will be coming back to this diary at the end of Chapter 24. The important thing is that you start it now; the first entry should be today. For the purposes of this ongoing exercise it would be better if you started a specially designated 'diary', separate from your notebook. This will attempt to be a daily record of your life, though there will be few prescriptions as to form and content.

Make sure you head each entry with at least the date, and possibly the time too (especially if you make more than one entry on any particular day). These entries should be more than a chronicle (a list of events), and more too than a calendar (a list of appointments). Make at least one entry a day. Record anything you wish – but write the first entry before you move on to the next activity. You may wish to record what you've done previously today, who you met with, the weather, your impressions of a person or a place – anything and everything. As a general rule try to keep your entries between 100–200 words.

| **ACTIVITY 23.2**
Reading | Read the extract from *The Diary of a Young Girl* by Anne Frank, Reading 40 on p.572. Note the sort of detail that is included and what, if anything, links the entries together. |

| **DISCUSSION** | In Frank's diary links are made between entries by introducing characters who might then recur. This in effect creates a through-line, a world and narrative with a sense of continuity, even though each entry is self-contained. As you can see from the last entry in this extract, Frank started to address her diary as 'Kitty' and wrote as if she were writing an informative letter, so engaging the reader as recipient. The reader gets to know Anne's personal attitudes as she writes character sketches, revealing her regard for the people who populate her world. When she speculates about who, if anyone, might read 'the musings of a thirteen-year-old schoolgirl', Frank shows she is aware of the possibility of a readership and how such writing is strangely positioned between the public and private domains. Note the way in which certain identities are protected by the use of arbitrary initials, as detailed in the footnote on the first page of the excerpt. Some of the effect of her editing and 're-visiting' can be seen here too, with the added comments. This form of reviewing illustrates how personal attitudes to experience can be re-evaluated, and how assessments of situations can change with time and a little reflection. |

There are always different versions

Your perceptions of life events will often alter over time. For instance, at the time you might have seen the dinner with friends the year before last as tedious, but now regard it warmly. This might be because the friends in question have moved away, or because your relationship with them has changed in some other way. Life is always shifting in this fashion, and it has an effect on how you see things. One event will often give rise to many different versions of what happened or what it was like, whether the different perspectives arise from one person over a period or whether they are the views various people hold of the same event. Sometimes the contrast between these different perspectives can be startling. Look at these two versions of the same event:

> (a) As the first mushroom floated off into the blue, it changed its shape into a flower-like form – its giant petal curving downward, creamy-white outside, rose-colored inside. It still retained that shape when we gazed at it from a distance of about two hundred miles.

> (b) My brother and sisters didn't get to the shelter in time, so they were burnt and crying. Half an hour later my mother appeared. She was covered with blood. She had been making lunch at home when the bomb was dropped. My younger sisters died the next day. My mother – she also died the next day. And then my older brother died.

The event was the dropping of the atomic bomb on Nagasaki, 9 August 1945. The first account, by William Laurence who viewed events through arc-welder's glasses in an 'observer' plane, was published three days after the event in the *New York Times*, and as an 'eye-witness' account was then syndicated worldwide (quoted in Pope, 1995, p.54, 55). The second version, by Fujio Tsujimoto, who was in the playground of his primary school at the time, was gathered through an interview some ten years later (quoted in Pope, 1995, p.54, 55).

You can see from these that the same event has produced not only two different perspectives but also two very different ways of representing that event in language. The first strives almost lyrically to paint a picture of what is happening, yet the identity of the narrator is not apparent. The second creates the family setting and the horrifying personal consequences of the event, and it does so in straightforward language, an edited interview, that produces a chillingly factual effect.

Exploring and detailing different perspectives of the same event can contribute a richness and complexity to your life writing. Yet it also presents a technical challenge. As with fiction writing, there is a need to orientate your reader through a stable point of view. Rather than switching from your own perspective, if writing of your life for instance, you have to find ways of incorporating other perspectives while maintaining the stability of the narrative's point of view. This can be done in a number of ways:

- By incorporating 'evidence', such as letters, testimony and diary entries, as a way of introducing other voices. This will also give the appearance of objectivity.

- You can dramatise certain scenes which will 'show' different perspectives through the dialogue.
- You can include interviews with people about certain events.
- You can narrate how you investigated and discovered that there was a different perspective of a particular event.

Through using some or all of these methods, and by using research and imagination, you can incorporate different versions of both your own life, when writing autobiography, and that of your subject, when writing biography. This sort of innovative approach is the way to revive and develop interest in your subject matter. Let's look at an example of how some of these strategies are used when approaching a biographical subject.

ACTIVITY 23.3
Reading

Read the transcript of the start of Richard Holmes's *To The Tempest Given*, Reading 41 on p.577, a radio play based on the poet Shelley's last days in Italy.

In your notebook, detail:
- what sort of 'evidence' you think is used by Holmes;
- what part you think imagination plays in the writing of this sort of biography.

DISCUSSION

Holmes's imagination is prominent here in the way the various testimonies are arranged – those of Percy Bysshe Shelley, Mary Shelley and the other characters. The exchanges all seem to be taken from letters, journals, poems, and other such testimonies. Holmes himself appears as the master of ceremonies, linking and interpreting all the researched and 'shown' elements. Holmes's interlocutions pursue his subject with a spirit of inquiry and a restless, imaginative approach to the facts, which incidentally aren't confined to what might be learned from books or from the internet. Evidently from his description of the present day Casa Magni, Holmes has done some ground research, as well as reading all the various testimonies. Contrary to what Holroyd suggests about dialogue not being available to the biographer, this docudrama method allows Holmes to use direct voices and objective summary together with factual 'evidence', so realising different perspectives.

Pick a celebrity, alive or dead, and research one or two facts about them. Choose someone you are familiar with and about whom you can easily check details. This doesn't mean you have to travel the world – use your existing knowledge, the internet, encyclopaedias and biographical dictionaries.

ACTIVITY 23.4
Writing

Write a dialogue between yourself and your subject using these facts. This can be a naturalistic exchange, as if you were meeting with them for a drink, or more of a documentary style commentary (as with Holmes), or it could even be an interview with them (use up to 300 words).

Each of the suggested methods – naturalistic dialogue, documentary, interview – offers a different benefit. The naturalistic dialogue serves to bring characters to life, as you will see shortly in an extract from Richard Holmes's *Footsteps*. The documentary style allows you, the commentator, to narrate a lot of background information. The interview allows for a little of both, the information being put in the mouth of the subject. Getting the character to speak in effect creates a docu-drama effect, which is a very familiar form on radio and TV.

DISCUSSION

Putting yourself in the picture

Sometimes in newspaper or magazine profile articles the interviewer will involve themselves in the narrative of the interview. They will not only ask the questions but also give their impressions of the interviewee's clothes and house, his or her manner, maybe even some personal recollection about the interviewee which lends a more intimate purpose to the article. In effect the writing, though ostensibly biographical, involves itself with two lives not just one.

A similar relationship between writer and subject can exist in travel writing. As suggested in Chapter 19, this is a form of autobiographical writing which is ostensibly focused on place and therefore less subjective. Yet travelogues like Jenny Diski's *Stranger on a Train* (2004 [2002]) illustrate how such narratives often concern themselves with people and personal memory. Diski's narrative describes her travels around the circumference of the USA; it is interspersed with personal memoir, and rather than being full of passing views of America, the features of landscape and place are subsumed by both the characters she meets on her journey and those from her past.

Let's look at a couple of other examples.

ACTIVITY 23.5
Reading

Read the extract from Dervla Murphy's *In Ethiopia with a Mule*, Reading 42 on p.581, and the extract from Richard Holmes's *Footsteps*, Reading 43 on p.586.

In your notebook, detail the following:

- In what way are these about place and travelling?
- What forms of life writing or other techniques do they use?
- In what way do they talk about the author?

DISCUSSION

Dervla Murphy's narrative, about a walking expedition to the highlands of Ethiopia in 1966–67, is presented as a journal, headed by dates and punctuated regularly with the details of place and sometimes by times, so the itinerary of the journey is laid out and always given prominence, as is the emotional and physical state of the traveller. Direct speech isn't used as it is in *Footsteps*; rather the narrative gives the writer's first impression of local customs and landscape. It is a more conventional travel format, but allows for occasional elaboration within the text. For instance, it gives information about numbers of American troops stationed in Ethiopia, information that the naïve traveller wouldn't have readily to hand. It also gives more researched information about certain aspects of the journey, as with the footnote about the history of Missawah. These are what could be considered to be the conventions of academic writing, often used in biographical writing, and here revealing Murphy's extensive pre- and post-journey research.

Though not included in these extracts both the Holmes and the Murphy books contain travel writing's common accompaniments – maps of the journey and occasional photographs. The Holmes extract is more than just the narrative of a journey though; it appears to use a number of different approaches. It traces the steps of Robert Louis Stevenson (RLS), and a journey undertaken by Stevenson in France almost a hundred years prior to Holmes's journey. JK refers to Jack Kerouac and the Beat generation's more contemporary (to 1964, when Holmes's journey was undertaken) vogue for travelling and sleeping rough. This has the feel of biography because Holmes is focused on Stevenson, but it is about an autobiographical journey as well, and gives the flavour of the place, specific to era. In this sense it also works as memoir because it is about Holmes at eighteen, his romantic quest and how he aspired to be a writer, even giving a sample from his journal. It 'shows' the exchanges between characters, so using fictional techniques and conventions to 'remember' dialogue and present it verbatim as direct speech, as in the exchange with Monsieur Crèspy.

Write about a holiday or journey you have taken in the last twelve months – it might be to a foreign destination, or just to the local supermarket (use up to 500 words).

ACTIVITY 23.6
Writing

Try to research some new facts about the place, give details about the people encountered, and your personal feelings about the place. Try to 'show' these feelings rather than stating them in abstract terms. Also, dramatise part of the scene with dialogue – even though you might not be able to remember what was said.

Place is as important to life writing as it is to fiction. As you have seen in the chapters on writing fiction, characters are often best realised through being shown to be involved with their surroundings. This is equally true of 'real' characters. They may be based on actual people but this doesn't mean they will by right spring vividly from the page. You still need to think of how you are representing them, and the elements of craft and technique involved in that representation.

DISCUSSION

One of these techniques is to do with dialogue. It is impossible to remember conversational exchanges verbatim even from yesterday let alone from ten or twenty years ago. Yet the novelistic convention of dramatising exchanges and giving direct speech to characters can invigorate your approach to a subject. Reproducing such unmediated voices will convince your reader that what they are reading is real. There are some, however, who would see this as beyond the bounds of true biographical writing. Remember when using the conventions of travel writing that the essential ingredient isn't the exotic location but the engagement with life and people. A trip to the laundrette can produce as good a piece of writing as a journey around the world. The reader will be engaged only if they feel they are being invited in to see the habits, thoughts and way of life of the characters on show, often including those of the narrator.

Diary reprise

In your daily diary entries started in Activity 23.1, try to include some
of the methods used so far in this chapter. Remember that in your diary
you can use fictional techniques to write about factual matters. So you
can write down some dialogue to record a character, exchange or
relationship. You can use your imagination and you can dramatise
events. You can write about little journeys, describe landscapes and
cityscapes, particular kinds of food, and cultural observations. The key is
to see the everyday from a new angle. Remember what Natalie Goldberg
says, as mentioned in Chapter 15: 'learn to write about the ordinary'.
This means writing about 'old coffee cups, sparrows, city buses and thin
ham sandwiches', but all seen in a new light. Look for the unfamiliar in
the familiar; try to treat each day as a journey.

Mixing fact and fiction

Holmes's willingness to incorporate many different writing techniques –
approaches that stretch the boundaries of biography and autobiography –
illustrates how the genre of life writing can be enriched, but also how
his content demanded that he improvise with form. The mixture of life
writing with other forms of writing can often be productive and
irresistible. The modern era has produced a wealth of hybrids which mix
fiction, memoir and biography, books which fruitfully explore the border
between fact and fantasy. For instance, Philip Roth's *The Facts: A
novelist's autobiography*, is addressed to Zuckerman, a recurring fictional
character from Roth's novels. As the opening of this autobiography
acknowledges, autobiography often contains fiction and fiction is often
autobiographical. At the end of *The Facts* Zuckerman responds to Roth:
'What you choose to tell in fiction is different from what you're
permitted to tell when nothing's being fictionalized ...' (Roth, 1988,
p.162).

Zuckerman's response to the autobiography amounts to a critique of the
'careful' memoir, which cares too much about people's feelings:

> I just cannot trust you as a memoirist as I trust you as a novelist
> because, as I've said, to tell what you tell best is forbidden to you by
> decorous, citizenly, filial conscience. With this book you've tied your
> hands behind your back and tried to write it with your toes.
>
> (Roth, 1988, p.169)

The paradox, of course, is that Roth's very method has admitted the fictional aspect of his autobiography, it is a testimony to the interdependence of fiction and life writing. There is deep irony and ambiguity in Roth's title, *The Facts*, because both types of writing, autobiography and fiction, are seen to be multiplying the possibilities about 'what actually happened' rather than pinning them down. You too might find this in your writing. By writing about your experience you can develop a deeper and richer picture of your own life, but one which is no longer simply reduced to a set of facts or straightforward anecdotes.

Often you will find that adhering too rigidly to the facts of your life can be limiting. Finding a fictional aspect on events can revive those events and make them in a strange way more truthful. As you have seen in Part 1, Jamaica Kincaid suggests 'To say exactly what happened was less than what I knew happened', in explanation of why she writes (autobiographical) fiction as opposed to a more conventional autobiography. This is testimony from a student writer:

> I found that when I started writing entries for the TooWrite [competition], which have to be true, simply writing down 'what happened' didn't work. I had to 'fictionalise' my own life, or at least remove myself from the equation and write as though I was dealing with someone else's story. I still wrote in the first person, but instead of just writing what happened I used symbolism ... such as a child's tea set, which I used to symbolise the domestic 'bliss' ... or a front door to symbolise how trapped I felt by the situation at home. In reality, neither the tea set nor the door were that [significant] in my life until I wanted to find a way of getting my stories across.
>
> (Hartshorn, 2004)

As seen in the last chapter, this is similar to what Auster says of using the third person in his autobiographical *The Invention of Solitude*. Notice how prior to writing about the memories, the tea set and the door were of no consequence. In this way these items, though based on fact, were used more like fictional devices, created in order to reveal the true complexity of the situation.

Inventing other lives

This attitude to life writing – using fiction techniques – can be extended to writing about other lives as well as your own. The sense of 'play' used in the writing of fiction is equally necessary to the writing of biography, and can often invigorate a subject. Virginia Woolf, for instance, wrote a biography of Elizabeth Barrett Browning's dog, *Flush* (1998 [1933]), a book which in one way was a parody of conventional biography and, as Woolf admits, of Lytton Strachey's *Eminent Victorians* (p.xvi). Yet by choosing this fictional approach Woolf succeeded in viewing her subject matter from a unique angle, one which lent her narrative a parallel: the subordinate or lowly viewpoint of the dog was akin to the lowly status of Victorian women poets, or at least how they were viewed in the 1930s when Woolf was writing. As she admits: 'yes, they are much alike, Mrs Browning and her dog' (p.xvii).

Julie Myerson's *Home: The story of everyone who ever lived in our house* (2004) is a biography of her own home, and all its former inhabitants. This project called for much research and verges on social history, but is still concerned primarily with lives. In this way the focus of the writing can shift radically when you choose your 'angle' and the range of your subject. Such unusual biographies could be said to have dual subjects, as with *Flush* where the subjects are the dog and Barrett Browning, or even multiple subjects, as with Myerson and the occupants of her house. It can take on even larger proportions if you choose a wider focus, for instance a city, as in Peter Ackroyd's *London: The biography* (2001), which views the city as a human body, and amounts to a vast historical and cultural guidebook. When considering your subject matter and your angle, you should be aware that there are many alternatives. A single person isn't the only option. You might write about a house or a dog, or you could write about a cricket team, or a village, or a street. Life writing potentially treads the path between social history and personal reflection. The important thing is that the writer is motivated with regard to his or her subject.

Philip Roth's '"I Always Wanted You to Admire My Fasting"; or Looking at Kafka' is interesting in this respect because its chosen angle makes it hard to classify. Written in two parts, it takes the combination of biography, autobiography and fiction to a new level. Its subject is the writer Franz Kafka, and the first part begins with a familiar life writing prop, a picture, and seems to be straightforward biography: 'I am looking, as I write of Kafka, at the photograph taken of him at the age of forty (my age) – it is 1924, as sweet and hopeful a year as he may ever have known as a man, and the year of his death' (1973, p.103). Noticeably the autobiographical first person is also prominent in this opening discussion, which then goes on to speculate about what might have happened had Kafka not died when he did, but instead emigrated to the US. It proceeds with elements of literary criticism, biography, and eulogy, giving many details about Kafka's life and punctuating the narrative regularly with dates. It is a literary hybrid, one on which the generic labels don't stick very easily. It shifts genres altogether in the second part.

Read the extract from the second part of Philip Roth's "'I Always Wanted You to Admire My Fasting'"; or Looking at Kafka', Reading 44 on p.590. List in your notebook what categories of writing you think it might fall under.

ACTIVITY 23.7
Reading

This second part would appear to be either an autobiographical account of Roth's schooling or a short story. The fantastical possibility suggested in the first part – 'What if the writer Franz Kafka didn't die in 1924, but emigrated to the US?' – has been incorporated as part of the narrative (Dr Kafka goes on to date the narrator's Aunt Rhoda). By using such an imaginative approach – both to the life of Kafka and to his own life – Roth has in effect rejuvenated the genres of biography and memoir, as well as broadening the range of fiction. This mixing of genres is something you might use in your life writing.

DISCUSSION

Use the celebrity you wrote about in Activity 23.4. Include this celebrity in a reminiscence about a real incident from your own past. Include some detail about the character's life in your account, as Roth does in 'Looking at Kafka'. (Use up to 350 words.)

ACTIVITY 23.8
Writing

By writing simultaneously in this biographical, autobiographical and fictional fashion you can find new ways to approach your subject matter. For instance, Roth reveals much about his own character in the way he writes about Kafka. Just by revealing your interest in the celebrity and by the way you write about them you will be showing a lot to your reader, information which would otherwise take much laborious explanation.

DISCUSSION

Conclusion

There are many ways in which lives can be imagined, remembered and investigated – and many ways in which they can be represented. Because elements within a life are 'real' and have a basis in fact, it doesn't mean those elements will automatically be apparent to your reader. By mixing biographical and autobiographical approaches you can sometimes invigorate your subject, so it becomes more than some flat thing to be described. The first person can be included in the narrative about the biographical subject; the third person can equally be used in the autobiographical narrative. Similarly, you can energise your writing through approaching your subject using a well chosen angle, one in which you have a strong interest. This is true whether the subject is your own life or that of someone else. You can dramatise scenes and use the techniques and conventions of other forms of writing, such as the diary, travel writing, academic writing, playwriting and, not least, fiction writing; by doing so you will be giving life to your writing.

References

Ackroyd, Peter (2001) *London: The biography*, London: Vintage.

Diski, Jenny (2004 [2002]) *Stranger on a Train*, London: Virago.

Anne Frank (1997 [1947]) *The Diary of a Young Girl*, Otto H. Frank and Mirjam Pressler (eds), Susan Massotty (tr.), London: Puffin.

Hartshorn, Tracy (2004) Private email to the Open University's A174 *Start Writing Fiction* tutor group conference.

Myerson, Julie (2004) *Home: The story of everyone who ever lived in our house*, London: Flamingo.

Pepys, Samuel (1970–1983) *The Diary of Samuel Pepys*, 11 vols, Robert Latham and William Matthews (eds), London: Bell.

Pope, Rob (1995) *Textual Intervention: Critical and creative strategies for literary studies*, London: Routledge.

Roth, Philip (1973) '"I Always Wanted You to Admire My Fasting"; or Looking at Kafka', *American Review*, No.17, May 1973, pp.103–126.

Roth, Philip (1988) *The Facts: A novelist's autobiography*, New York: Farrar, Straus & Giroux.

Woolf, Virginia (1998 [1933]) *Flush*, Kate Flint (ed.), Oxford: Oxford University Press.

24 *Life characters*

DEREK NEALE

Your life story is as much about the people you meet as about you. Life stories are made up of sequences of events, as in a novel, and those events always involve relationships between people. The interest for the reader, as with fiction, lies in the nature of the characters inhabiting a life. As Isaac Bashevis Singer suggests:

> When people come together – let's say they come to a little party or something – you always hear them discuss character. They will say this one had a bad character, this one has a good character, this one is a fool, this one is a miser. Gossip makes the conversation. They all analyse character. It seems that the analysis of character is the highest human entertainment ... The writers who don't discuss character ... stop being entertaining.
>
> (Interview with Richard Burgis, 1978, quoted in George, 2004, p.7–8)

Bashevis Singer's point illuminates the reader's appetite – we like to hear gossip about characters. Life writing's pre-eminent concern with human experience means that it often conjures up a whole raft of characters, both central and peripheral, some drawn at length over time and given great complexity, some painted succinctly in a page or two. It is the complexity of characters' histories and interactions that captivates, entertains and lends life writing its story. As with fiction, it is up to the writer to realise character through various techniques, giving characters certain attributes, such as an external appearance, a life history, behaviour, actions, thoughts, and dialogue.

Diary reprise

Don't forget the ongoing diary which you started in Activity 23.1. You might like to include gossip about characters in your diary. You might also like to include fantastical speculations about the lives of characters that interest you, as Roth does with Kafka. Your thoughts and fantasies can be as relevant and revealing to a potential reader as any material detail. They too are a part of your everyday life.

Teachers, witches and wild men

Childhood is full of characters who are not fully understood at the time and who can take on mythological status. The frightening, never-seen woman who lives in the 'witch's house' (how many childhoods have a witch's house!); the wild man who sleeps in the park; the mad PE teacher who once ran in a marathon and continually encourages his pupils to try it; the boy in the corner who is late for everything and who is always scruffy. Let's look from a child's perspective at an 'odd' character.

ACTIVITY 24.1

Reading

Read the extract from Wole Soyinka's *Aké*, Reading 45 on p.592. Concentrate on the various characters in the scene, and with regard to each character note what elements the reader is given. For instance, you might note details about:

- appearance;
- life history;
- behaviour;
- actions;
- thoughts;
- dialogue.

DISCUSSION

Aké is a memoir of Soyinka's childhood in Nigeria during the Second World War. In this extract Soyinka remains in the background, but with some telling moments that reveal his subordinate, child status, such as when he relishes the sweet biscuits and when he calls the man names, for which he would be slapped 'in other circumstances'.

The extract contains a number of characters who reappear throughout the memoir. One of these is Wild Christian, who is given a strong characterisation as a fearsome and fearless shopkeeper and guardian. Yet this episode is more about Paa Adatan. With the sword and scabbard we are given both his regular and his specific appearance – 'naked to the waist, his usual bulbous trousers had been pulled up from the calves'. His behaviour is generally described and then typified in the climactic scene. The episode is structured around him: he is introduced, seen in action and then does not die but makes his exit from the narrative. The general description gives him a 'backstory' and uses summary, as you might when creating a fictional character.

ACTIVITY 24.2
Writing

Write a scene about a character from your recent or distant past, someone with whom you no longer have dealings. Choose from the following:

- a friend you no longer know;
- an eccentric;
- a shopkeeper;
- a neighbour.

Make sure your scene introduces the character, involves an incident with the character and covers what happened to the character – this could be as simple as 'I never saw him again' as with Soyinka's portrait of Paa Adatan. (Use up to 350 words.)

DISCUSSION

When creating brief portraits like this, as with Monsieur Crèspy in the *Footsteps* extract, you will usually want to show the character in action. Dialogue can be part of that action. Showing such exchanges can enhance your main characterisation (yourself if it is autobiographical) and further develop a secondary character, as with Wild Christian in *Aké*.

Recall and character

Sometimes the recall of characters can be fragmentary; trying to remember more about them can induce digressions, trains of thought that take you away from what you're trying to focus on. In Graham Greene's *A Sort of Life*, for instance:

> My form master in the bottom form was called Frost. Later the school was reorganized and he was put in charge of the preparatory school which occupied a house in which my aunt Maud had once lived – it was there that I first read *Dracula* with great fear one long summer afternoon. The memory is salt with the taste of blood, for I had picked my lip while reading and it wouldn't stop bleeding – I thought I was going to bleed to death, one of Count Dracula's victims.
>
> Frost had the reputation of getting on well with very small boys, but I was a little afraid of him. He used to sweep his black gown around him in a melodramatic gesture, before he indulged his jovial ogrish habit of screwing a fist in one's cheek till it hurt.
>
> (Greene, 1974 [1971], p.46–7)

The narrative appears intent on giving the reader details about Greene's schooling but gets wonderfully distracted by a chance sensory and literary association. It still manages to give a fleeting but vivid picture of the character of Frost, who remains a mythic childhood perception, made up of rumour and one or two idiosyncratic mannerisms. Many life characters, not only from childhood, might appear in this archetypal and not-quite-fully-known fashion, as with Paa Adatan, who is not a fully rounded character, more of a fleeting visitor, in Soyinka's narrative. Yet the significance of such characters to the biographical or autobiographical subject can be great.

Also of note in Greene's narrative is the fact that the digressions are all to do with Greene, they aren't arbitrary or irrelevant; all contribute to the book's overall purpose, enlightening the reader about the character of Greene and his life experience. This is the essential through-line that orientates and reassures the reader when detours are taken to such fringe characters. They all link back to the main character's sensibility.

ACTIVITY 24.3
Writing

In your notebook list three teachers or employers that you can remember – they might be characters you liked or disliked. For each one, list some things you can remember about them. You might include:

- your regard for them;
- what they taught or what their job was;
- whether they were good at what they did;
- how they looked, acted, spoke;
- any associations you may have with them, with regard to other particular pupils, other employees or specific incidents.

Now write a brief summary of each (up to 100 words for each character). As this narrative is about you as much as the character, write in the first person and include any relative associations or digressions, but also remember to retain a focus.

DISCUSSION

This is always a useful exercise when struggling to capture a particular part of your life. You can set yourself the task of finding three or more people from that period and collecting memories about them. For instance, you could do the above activity with any one period of your life – old school friends, old colleagues, former neighbours.

Writing about your family

Family will inevitably form a large part of any autobiographical writing. Some writers even choose to write not about themselves but about particular family members. This is often the case when the family member is or has been famous, but this isn't the only reason for focusing in this way. For instance, Amos Oz has written a book about his mother (2004), Hanif Kureishi about his father (2004), and Blake Morrison has published books about both his father and his mother (1993, 2002).

As we saw with Anne Frank, when writing about family and friends there is often the need for discretion. You may not want to reveal certain details to the world about particular characters so as not to offend whoever you are writing about, for fear of incurring legal consequences, and because you may wish to keep certain elements of your life, or the life you are writing about, private. For instance, throughout *A Sort of Life*, Greene refers to 'my wife' but never names her and the narrative doesn't venture to give her a character or describe her in any great depth. This is partly to do with the fact that the narrative is concerned more with Greene's early years, but also it is a decision about who should be written about and who should be left out. In certain passages it was unavoidable that Greene's wife be mentioned, yet the level of inclusion was carefully gauged. As seen in the last chapter, another tactic is used by Anne Frank – with some characters who wished to remain anonymous being referred to by non-specific initials. In *Skating to Antarctica*, a travelogue and memoir, Jenny Diski changes the names of her childhood neighbours, at their request (1997). As characters they are essential to the narrative of how she investigates her childhood, and their inclusion helps realise a period in Diski's past, a particular way of living and thinking.

Now let's look at a characterisation that also reveals much about the way people thought in a particular era.

Read the extract from Lorna Sage's *Bad Blood*, Reading 46 on p.597. In your notebook, jot down how Grandma is portrayed, with particular regard to geographical, historical and cultural context.

ACTIVITY 24.4
Reading

Grandma is seen here to be a product of place – both Hanmer, an English village bordering North Wales, and the Rhondda valley in South

DISCUSSION

Wales. She is seen as a culturally specific character – the way she speaks, her taste in food (governed in part by rationing), and 'She shared her Edwardian generation's genteel contempt for sunburn and freckles'. This throws up some intriguing conflicts of class and status in the next generation, as Sage subsequently writes: 'My mother, however, got the worst of both worlds. She inherited the contempt for housework and she was also imbued with the notion that it was a sacred womanly duty' (2000, p.36). Practically all of Grandma's traits and characteristics are seen to have a cause and quite often also to have a consequence. It is this level of perception and portrayal, together, of course, with the narrator's personal regard for the character, that prevents Grandma from being seen as a stereotype.

Culture and character

In Part 1 you were invited to think of cultural associations as a way of remembering, and therefore as a source for creating and developing characters and scenarios for stories and poems. The culturally specific elements in *Bad Blood* are not just from one period and place but run across several historical eras, as do the generations of any family. For instance, in another extended portrait in Sage's memoir, that of her best friend, Gail, there is much reference to the popular culture of the 1950s, including film and music. Sage writes of Gail:

> Her eyes shone and she hummed a few bars of Paul Anka's number one hit, 'Diana', about a mythological older woman, which was written when he was fourteen and inspired by falling in love with his babysitter. Against all the odds she'd discovered in Whitchurch a Paul Anka lookalike – same high cheekbones and black, black hair – and although this one's eyes were blue and Paul's were brown (he was 'of Syrian extraction'), they were deep-set and inward-looking in just the right way. He was called Michael Price, a boy like a startled gazelle ...'

> (Sage, 2000, p.214)

Details about the cultural context can reveal much about characters, and such context should not be confined to the performing and popular arts. Revealing what a character reads, for instance, is a peculiarly private disclosure and can show a lot about a character's state of mind at any particular time in their life. Michèle Roberts, for instance, at the age of twelve or so, read stories of the *Knights of King Arthur*, over which she 'wept copiously: Gawain, Tristram, Percival were my heroes. I couldn't bear it when the book revealed that the fellowship of the Round Table came to an end through the involuntary agency of a woman, Guinevere' (Roberts, 1983, p.104). This conjures up the hopes and ideals of Roberts at a certain age, together with her level of innocence.

Coincidently, Sage writes, like Greene, of reading *Dracula*, but with a slightly different relish. She is talking in the context of how terrifyingly self-conscious and alien she felt in the adolescent world of pop music and boyfriends:

> It was different with books, I still hung on their every word. The night I finished *Dracula* was a lot more exciting than Saturday night at the Regal. Lying in my private pool of light with moths ricocheting between the bulb and the lampshade, and the wire from the radio aerial tapping on the window, I drifted into a pre-dawn trance while my little brother (not so little any longer, he was nine) slept soundly across the room in the shadows. Although I protested to our parents that I hated having to share a bedroom with Clive, his unconscious presence heightened my pleasure in my orgies of reading. I was sinning with an undead dandy while innocents wallowed in oblivion. The night was mine and Dracula's. How I yawned at the thought of common daylight's coffin.
>
> (Sage, 2000, p. 219)

It's important to bear in mind that you don't have to have read *Dracula*, or any particular type of book, for it to be of interest. Sage's enthralment and feeling of alienation are of interest not necessarily what she is alienated by or gravitates towards. You may have felt the reverse, been alienated by books and drawn towards popular music, for instance. *Star Wars*, U2 and *Countdown* will be as enlightening to your reader as Dickens, Woolf and Tolstoy, as long as their significance to the subject of your narrative is fully realised.

By disclosing details of what and how she read, Sage has revealed much of her teenage sensibility, but she does so with an adult's perspective and in a literary fashion. Writing about experience in this manner is very different from some of the immediate, present tense and more deliberately naïve evocations we have looked at. Compare it, for instance, to the Lesley Glaister extract looked at in Part 1, which narrates an episode on a beach from a child's perspective. This is a choice you will have to make in your life writing – how much will your narrative be affected by the wisdom and knowledge gained after the event; how much will you try to recreate the original response to the situation.

Compare, for instance, these two narratives of the same events. First, the start of James Joyce's autobiographical novel, *Portrait of the Artist as a Young Man*:

> Once upon a time and a very good time it was there was a moocow coming down along the road and this moocow that was coming down along the road met a nicens little boy named baby tuckoo ....
>
> His father told him that story: his father looked at him through a glass: he had a hairy face.
>
> He was baby tuckoo.

(Joyce, 1977 [1916], p.7)

Second, Anthony Burgess's parody of this in an adult voice:

> I remember I would be told infantile stories, altogether appropriate to my infantile station. One of them, I seem to recall, was concerned with a cow coming down the lane – which lane was never specified – and meeting a child who was called (I am embarrassed, inevitably, to recollect this in maturity) some such name as Baby Tuckoo. I myself, apparently, was to be thought of as Baby Tuckoo. Or was it Cuckoo? It is, of course, so long ago ...

(Burgess, 1973, p.63)

In Joyce's version we have the childlike words moocow and tuckoo, and naïve, uninterpreted sentences, simulating the child's perspective and world. In Burgess's version there are bigger words and more complicated paragraphs and sentences – though this version noticeably doesn't give the impression of having a more intelligent narrator, in fact quite the opposite. Both reveal gaps in the memory: the first version is written in fragments, like associated memories; the second version explicitly admitting that recall is uncertain. Both reveal very different but equally possible writing approaches to the same subject, which in itself involves a cultural item – a children's story about a cow.

ACTIVITY 24.5

Writing

Recall a book or a film or a TV programme or a song or a piece of music. In your notebook, jot down some memories surrounding it and why you liked or disliked it. Don't read it, watch it, or listen to it again to remind yourself – just operate from what you remember. Note:

- when you first came across the item;
- where you lived at the time;

- where you typically were when you were reading, watching, listening;
- if it reminds you of characters from your life;
- if it reminds you of aspirations now gone or still there.

Write up to 150 words about your original reaction to the book, film, programme or music, trying to realise all the things you have just noted; either use some of the diction and language usage you associate with the memory to try to recreate the era or write from the perspective of the present time, with appropriate use of language, acknowledging the vagaries of memory.

DISCUSSION

Showing what a character reads, watches, or listens to, and where and when they do it, are all great devices for helping you to reveal aspects about your characters' rational and irrational lives, as well as details about their life history. By showing such responses to cultural items you are creating depth in the characterisation. This is effective with biographical subjects as well as when the character is an autobiographical 'I'. Without 'telling' anything about her teenage turmoil, Sage, for instance, 'shows' excitement, fear and delight, just in her regard for one book. Books and popular music can offer exceptionally effective routes back to a particular period in your life, but the absence of such things might also be of significance. Perhaps there were no books on the shelf during your childhood; perhaps there was a piano but no other source of music; perhaps there was no radio or TV. Your cultural life and that of the characters you are writing about will always be of interest to your reader. The language and grammatical formations you choose to portray these characters will also reveal much about your present and past sensibility, and so create a character out of the narrative voice for your reader.

The heart of the family

In all forms of life writing there are certain characters who feature centrally, they lie at the heart of the narrative. In autobiographical writing one of these characters is obviously going to be the subject – the 'I'. But often in autobiographical writing there are one or more characters who hold almost as much importance as the subject, and upon whom the narrative can often be focused for long stretches. This is evidently the case, for instance, with Blake Morrison's narratives about his parents. Fathers and mothers are a commonly (but not always) used focal point in memoirs, and for a variety of reasons. Sometimes the reasons are to do with a positive regard for the character of the parent; sometimes they are to do with a fierce hatred. Often it is to do with a form of quest in the writer for a better understanding or a yearning to become reconciled to the nature of the writer's relationship with the parent.

Wanting to know a character from your own life better, and to explore that gap between how you see things and how things really are, is a quest commonly and profitably taken up in life writing. This is because it has both an objective and subjective purpose. In writing about one character from the outside you will always be revealing something both to yourself and your readers about who you are. It isn't necessarily estrangement or a difficult relationship with the character you're writing about that will make you want to write about them. Quite often it can be the paradox of their closeness and separateness that prompts the investigation. The need to understand more fully is motivation enough. As you have seen in Chapter 19, a sense of loss through death or absence can also be a strong prompt.

ACTIVITY 24.6
Reading

Read Tony Harrison's 'Long Distance' and Sharon Olds's 'Parents' Day'.

In your notebook detail how these poems portray a character, and how the writer's regard for the character is revealed. Also, what do you make of the form of the poems?

Long Distance
I
Your bed's got two wrong sides. Your life's all grouse.
I let your phone-call take its dismal course:

Ah can't stand it no more, this empty house!

Carrots choke us wi'out your mam's white sauce!

Them sweets you brought me, you can have 'em back.
Ah'm diabetic now. Got all the facts.
(The diabetes comes hard on the track
of two coronaries and cataracts.)

Ah've allus like things sweet! But now ah push
food down mi throat! Ah'd sooner do wi'out.
And t'only reason now for beer's to flush
(so t'dietician said) mi kidneys out.

When I come round, they'll be laid out, the sweets,
Lifesavers, my father's New World treats,
still in the big brown bag, and only bought
rushing through JFK as a last thought.

II
Though my mother was already two years dead
Dad kept her slippers warming by the gas,
put hot water bottles her side of the bed
and still went to renew her transport pass.

You couldn't just drop in. You had to phone.
He'd put you off an hour to give him time
to clear away her things and look alone
as though his still raw love were such a crime.

He couldn't risk my blight of disbelief
though sure that very soon he'd hear her key
scrape in the rusted lock and end his grief.
He *knew* she'd just popped out to get the tea.

I believe life ends with death, and that is all.
You haven't both gone shopping; just the same,
in my new black leather phone book there's your name
and the disconnected number I still call.

(Harrison, 1987 [1984])

Parents' Day

I breathed shallow as I looked for her
in the crowd of oncoming parents, I strained
forward, like a gazehound held back on a leash,
then I raced toward her. I remember her being
much bigger than I, her smile of the highest
wattage, a little stiff, sparkling
with consciousness of her prettiness – I
pitied the other girls for having mothers
who looked like mothers, who did not blush.
Sometimes she would have braids around her head like a

goddess or an advertisement for California raisins –
I worshipped her cleanliness, her transfixing
irises, sometimes I thought she could
sense a few genes of hers
dotted here and there in my body
like bits of undissolved sugar
in a recipe that did not quite work out.
For years, when I thought of her, I thought
of the long souring of her life, but on Parents' Day
my heart would band and my lungs swell so I could
feel the tucks and puckers of embroidered
smocking on my chest press into my ribs,
my washboard front vibrate like scraped
tin to see that woman arriving
and to know she was mine.

(Olds, 1996)

DISCUSSION   Harrison's poem appears motivated by affection and mourning, the character of his father and the dead mother are portrayed in a realistic fashion. So we get dialogue and Harrison's voice, but in a strangely fragmented form. The typeface and the stanzas are irregular but nonetheless bound tightly together, like the loving relationship between mother and father, by the alternate rhyme. The poem is formally bound in other ways as well, despite the dialogue, italics and dialect. Each section is written in Harrison's longer, sixteen line version of the sonnet form. In effect they read like elegies – songs of lament – capturing the pathos of old age and death through the magnificence of small detail. The lament grows into a celebration of these passing lives.

Olds's poem is focused on her mother and the recurring occasion of parents' evening, rather than one specific occasion. It is written in free verse and portrays the intense affection and pride the poet felt for her mother, hinting at how that regard dissipated in adulthood, but attempting really just to rekindle for the moment of the poem some of the details of the mother – the braids and her transfixing irises. The abiding sweetness of the first part of the poem – 'raisins' and 'undissolved sugar' – epitomises Olds's idolisation, and contrasts to the 'souring of her life' in later thoughts.

Write either a poem (up to sixteen lines) or a reminiscence (up to 250 words) about one of the following:

- someone who is dead who was known to you;
- a well known person who is dead;
- a person who is no longer known to you.

It should include some details of where and how the person appeared and/or lived.

ACTIVITY 24.8
Writing

Writing can be a way of reviving characters missing from your current life. By remembering their habits and the objects and mannerisms associated with them it is possible to further your understanding of your relationship with them. In this sort of writing it is especially important to remember that you have a reader, and that you need to balance sentiment and detail. While it is essential that you convey the emotional importance of a particular character, it is also important to avoid mawkishness. Remember that you are seeking to enrich your memory and to enlighten your reader; the quest is for further investigation, further understanding, not to celebrate in a purely nostalgic fashion.

DISCUSSION

Presenting yourself as the main character

In the narratives looked at over the last three chapters, the autobiographical 'I' has featured sometimes to the fore and sometimes it has taken a back seat. When the character at the front of the stage is the autobiographical 'I', the reader will need to see you more tangibly created as a character in your own right. You may have to give backstory for yourself (as Holmes does for himself in the *Footsteps* extract), you may have to give some indication of appearance, give thoughts, and present yourself in action. You may also wish to give evidence of your point of view, perhaps from a different period of your life. You can do as Holmes does, using his own journal to authenticate his particular state of mind at a particular age and moment in history, or by using other testimony like letters.

ACTIVITY 24.9
Writing

- Read over the diary that you have kept for the past two weeks. Select at least three and no more than five entries that you might use in a narrative of the two weeks. Preferably choose entries with linked elements, i.e. subject matter that recurs.

■ Edit these entries into a form that you think would be comprehensible to a reader, by cutting less interesting material and by adding to and correcting other parts.

■ Now write a version of your life over the past two weeks, using at least three of these edited diary entries, as illustrative testimony, like Holmes does with his journal extract. Don't forget to portray yourself as a character, perhaps include some backstory, some other characters perhaps, maybe some details of thought and details of what you have read, watched or listened to. (Use up to 750 words.)

DISCUSSION It is possible to look at all of your diary entries and edit them into some sort of shape. It is more likely though that, as with most writing, there are many entries that would be of use neither to you nor to your reader. Often the chronology of diary entries can help you to form a narrative. This way of juxtaposing narrative elements that aren't necessarily continuous can be similar to the way in which film scenes are 'cut' side by side. So for instance, in a film, you might see the image of a bird flying over woods, then suddenly cut to a hospital bed, then back to the woods. In the diary you can have an entry for Friday when you're happy and writing of a forthcoming trip to the coast, followed by Saturday's entry when you have a headache, and the car breaks down, then Sunday's entry when you've arrived at the coast and the sun is setting over the sea. Diary extracts are of particular use when trying to illustrate the past, and the immediacy of how you felt at a particular moment. Using diaries in this way is a key method of characterisation, either of yourself or your biographical subject.

Conclusion

Characterisation is as important in life writing as it is in fiction. The reader needs a point of identification with the life that is being written about. The reader wants to know about the complexity of relationships, to have the major characters well drawn and to be able to easily grasp the minor characters. Just as in a short story or novel, the reader needs to learn about motivations, conflicts and thoughts, and to see characters interacting with each other and within their setting. That is the sort of gossip your reader will be coming to the party for.

Life writing is often compared to portraiture. As Ben Pimlott suggests: 'A good biography is like a good portrait: it captures the essence of the sitter by being much more than a likeness. A good portrait is about history, philosophy, milieu. It asks questions as well as answering them, brushstrokes are economical and always to the subtlest effect' (2004, p.170).

This spirit of inquiry is essential to life writing, and the subtlety of effect is often achieved by being aware of the possible approaches – the fact that you can use diary techniques or methods from travel and fiction writing, to give just three examples. Writing about a life isn't merely a question of accumulating facts and then spilling them onto the page. It is often a question of asking: 'What most interests me about this life, this moment in a personal history? What is my focus? How can I make it more interesting?' As with writing fiction and poetry, writing well about a life is a question of craft. As Virginia Woolf says, the art of life writing can mix biography and autobiography, fact and fiction, and can potentially be: '... subtle and bold enough to present that queer amalgamation of dream and reality, that perpetual marriage of granite and rainbow' (Woolf, 1967 [1925], p.234–5).

References

Burgess, Anthony (1973) *Joysprick: An introduction to the language of James Joyce*, London: Andre Deutsch.

Diski, Jenny (1997) *Skating to Antarctica*, London: Granta.

George, Elizabeth (2004) *Write Away: One novelist's approach to fiction and the writing life*, London: Hodder and Stoughton.

Greene, Graham (1974 [1971]) *A Sort of Life*, Harmondsworth: Penguin.

Harrison, Tony (1987 [1984]) *Selected Poems*, London: Penguin.

Joyce, James (1977 [1916]) *A Portrait of the Artist as a Young Man*, London: Panther.

Kureishi, Hanif (2004) *My Ear at His Heart*, London: Faber and Faber.

Morrison, Blake (1993) *And When Did You Last See Your Father*, London: Granta.

Morrison, Blake (2002) *Things My Mother Never Told Me*, London: Chatto and Windus.

Olds, Sharon (1996) *The Wellspring*, London: Jonathan Cape.

Oz, Amos (2004) *A Tale of Love and Darkness*, London: Chatto and Windus.

Pimlott, Ben (2004) 'Brushstrokes' in Bostridge, Mark (ed.), *Lives for Sale: Biographers' tales*, London: Continuum.

Roberts, Michèle (1983) 'Outside My Father's House' in Ursula Owen (ed.), *Fathers: Reflections by daughters*, London: Virago.

Sage, Lorna (2000) *Bad Blood*, London: Fourth Estate.

Woolf, Virginia (1967 [1925]) 'The New Biography' in *Collected Essays, Volume Four*, London: Hogarth Press.

PART 5

Going public

Chapter 25 *Editing: The big changes*

SARA HASLAM

Introduction

This part of the book is about going public with your writing, an exciting stage for any developing writer – though probably a nerve-racking one too. It initially explores a number of the ways you will have to address your work before you do go public with it, in whatever sense. As you'll see in the first two chapters, editing processes are very similar whether you're showing your work to a friend, presenting it to a workshop, or thinking about trying to get it published.

Your first task as editor of your work is to find time for a 'cooling-off' period, and you'll investigate why it's important to do so in the first section of this chapter. You'll move on to consider first drafts, a critical process that will be familiar to you from earlier chapters in this book. The focus here though is on learning how to be an editor of those and subsequent drafts. It's the big issues that will concern you here: how and when to return to your writing; editing with your reader in mind; editing for structure, pace, or character, for example. In activities you'll develop and then practise a range of editing skills, from cutting words to dealing with a character who will not come to life. The end product to hold in mind throughout is a piece of your writing that is as effective, well-written, and professionally presented as you can make it.

Editing as you will be practising in these first chapters is primarily about you improving your story, life writing or poem. It can also be about you transforming that story, life writing or poem into something you might some day like to appear in print or on the web. Chapters 12 to 18 offered lots of guidance on how to edit your drafts of poems, and so, although some of what follows concerns editing generally, or editing poetry specifically, the activities in this part will be directed mostly towards editing prose. If you do decide to work on poetry here, you may wish to have advice from those earlier chapters alongside you too.

No writer, or teacher of writing, would disagree about the fundamental place of editing in the writer's life. Without it, there's no 'going public', but also perhaps no high-quality writing at all. 'There's no such thing as good writing, but only good rewriting' is how one editor puts it (Hill, 1977, p.10). Aspects of 'good rewriting' include: 'changing, correcting, adding, deleting, substituting, polishing'. We will return to all of these aspects of the editing process, but it's important to begin with the sense that writing really doesn't start out 'good'; it only becomes it.

> Interviewer: How much rewriting do you do?
>
> Hemingway: It depends. I rewrote the ending to *Farewell to Arms*, the last page of it, thirty-nine times before I was satisfied.
>
> Interviewer: Was there some technical problem there? What was it that had stumped you?
>
> Hemingway: Getting the words right.
>
> (quoted in Newman, 2000, p.163)

Writing that seems effortless often emerges from a great deal of labour. Thirty-nine edits is a lot, though it's possible some stages only involved more minor changes – Hemingway finding a different word or two, perhaps, or altering the punctuation.

ACTIVITY 25.1
Reading

Look at the extract on the next page, which gives an illustration of the editing writer at work. It's from the typewritten second draft of Virginia Woolf's novel *The Waves* (1976 [1931]). Which aspects of the editing process as defined above ('changing, correcting, adding, deleting, substituting, polishing') can you identify here?

DISCUSSION

There's certainly a great deal of change indicated here, and I imagine Woolf would have thought of it all as correction of her draft, or at least improvement. Specific processes are evident too: she adds words (like 'green'), deletes both lines and words throughout, and substitutes too ('neared' for 'approached', for example). Despite the extent of the changes indicated here, the published version is still far from view.

The Waves.

* The sun had not yet risen. ~~A black bar lay on the horizon~~. The sea ~~& the sky~~ was indistinguishable from the sky, except that the sea was slightly creased; _{as if a cloth had} ~~like a~~ grey

<small>wrinkles in it.</small>

~~like~~ a cloth. ~~As t~~ ~~Gradually,~~ ~~And~~ Gradually, the sky whitened; ~~& the creases deepened, & it seemed as if~~ they ~~moved~~ ~~something moved moved beneath, rolling them on; to~~ _{them ed}

~~Then~~ a   dark bar lay on the horizon; dividing the sea & the sky; ~~& then~~ the grey creased cloth became ~~slowly~~ deeper & deeper; & the bars which ~~stretched~~ across it were long backed ~~waves~~. barred with thick strokes. moving, one after another, across the breadth of the sea, regularly.   ~~The~~

In the colourless light they broke upon the beach & swept fanshaped filmy _{neared}   _{each wave}

As they ~~approached~~ the ~~bea~~ shore ~~they heaped~~ ~~themselves high~~, & became separate, ~~& the~~ heaped itself high, ~~& st~~ arched its back, curved, ~~& crashed~~ down on the ~~stones shaking~~ ~~throwing~~ up its spray lay fly a plume of spray & dashed itself down on the stones.   A fan of ~~thin~~ water ~~dashed~~ _[raised?] seething

~~onto~~ across the sand, filled hollows, bent the _{sea green   &   leaving   withdrew} sea holly; paused a second, & then slowly ~~with~~ drew. back. _{flung} the little [   ], ~~The little pebbles were turned over~~.   And then another fell;

& another fell. ~~In this d pa dim light,~~ the _{& each blow dealt   dealt by half seen waves} ~~sound was of~~ the blow ⋀ was tremendous;   ~~It was like~~ the ~~falling, from a half seen object~~ ~~heavy~~, like a was heavy

Figure 3 Woolf at work

Finding your editor within

Editing is what you do when, like Woolf, you work on something you have written. This type of work is closely related to redrafting or rewriting (we will discover just how closely over the next couple of pages). Some people may say that in every act of writing, unless you're deliberately cultivating the unconscious – writing when you have just woken up, say, or continuously with the pen not leaving the paper – the editing process has already been engaged. You will after all have selected the words you put on paper or on screen. True, but it's that initial act of writing that forms your first draft, not your thinking about it, and purposeful editing starts when it's in front of you.

Writers often suggest that when you have reached that stage, a transformation occurs inside the writer, and needs to. Time assists this transformation. The following activity will help you to think about what form it might take.

ACTIVITY 25.2   Return to one of your favourite short writing exercises from Chapters 5 to 24. It can be a poetry or prose exercise, but it needs to be one that asked you to write something new. Perform the exercise again and, when you have done so, find four adjectives to describe your writing self as you tackled this exercise (for example: inspired, agitated, compelled). Then leave it for a few hours if you can, and read over the piece slowly and critically, coming up with a couple of improvements. Find four more adjectives to describe the writing self you became as you worked on it to make it better.

DISCUSSION   Fay Weldon says that 'there have to be two personalities in every writer': A, who produces the first drafts, has to be 'creative, impetuous, wilful, emotional, sloppy'; B, who works on them, has to be 'argumentative, self-righteous, cautious, rational, effective' (quoted in Singleton and Luckhurst, 2000, p.305). Some of your adjectives describing your writing selves may match those she came up with, or be related to them. The important thing is that they register a similar kind of change. Other writers may be less dramatic in their conceptions of an A and B 'split' but they will all accept the need for this shift in the relationship between them and their words. Poet Rebecca Luce-Kapler suggests that when 'we return to rewrite' it is to 'write a poem rather than a cathartic draft' (1999, p. 157). The first draft is, for her, an emotional process (she's using cathartic to mean emotionally purifying or purging) that is all too easily discernible in the result. Later drafts fashion this raw material into a 'poem' that works and can be enjoyed by others.

This isn't a new idea. At the beginning of the nineteenth century, the poet Shelley provided a vivid image of the spontaneous phase: 'when my brain gets heated with thought it soon boils and throws off images and words faster than I can skim them off' (quoted in Marzano and DiStefano, 1981, p.112). What Frank Smith calls the 'secretary' that is part of any writer will then have organised and processed the results (Singleton and Luckhurst, 2000, p.303). Whether or not you sounded like Weldon or Shelley in your choice of words, the transformation you were exploring in this activity can be summarised as one of the following (or you can add your own formulation to the list):

- from spontaneity to care;
- from effervescence to craft;
- from creativity to shaping;
- from feeling to skill.

If it sounds as though the energising or liberating part of writing is over after the first draft, this isn't so. 'Through the work of rewriting', according to Luce-Kapler, 'the writer can discover the beauty of the piece' (1999, p.157). Remember too that Weldon spoke of the writer's reliance on both personalities: your first draft characteristics will still be present somewhere, though latent perhaps, as you edit. If while you're editing you feel the urge to exercise them again, you can always do so by trying something completely new in your draft, or by moving for a while on to a new piece of work.

Other ways of naming the differences between the writing and the editing self complicate the picture (of A and B personalities) as it has developed so far. In the end it might be difficult to make hard and fast distinctions between writing and editing, especially once other terms, like 'rewriting' and 'redrafting', get involved. *The Creative Writing Handbook* states that 'it is vital to make clear the difference between redrafting and editing' (Singleton and Luckhurst, 2000, p.303). By 'editing' it means only 'technical skills like spelling and punctuation'; 'redrafting' covers everything else – structure, content and word choice, for example. Useful and interesting as this chapter may prove to be in your further reading (and the approach is shared by *The Writer's Workbook*, an extract from which is included as Reading 49), this interpretation of the terminology is not shared by all practitioners. So for current purposes, and for simplicity's sake, editing will be the term I use to discuss all ways and means of working on a draft. Borrowing Weldon's terminology as we proceed, it's B personalities to the fore, but not to the exclusion of the A.

Returning to your writing: When and how?

In the following section you will find suggestions gleaned from a range of writers' tried and tested techniques. Trying some of them out for yourself will help you to determine what works in fostering your own editorial approach (in this, as in much else, writers vary).

When?

As I've already indicated, it's important to leave a good stretch of time after completing your first draft before you return to it. More than the few hours suggested in Activity 25.2, and in fact more than a couple of days, if possible, though each writer might adapt his or her practice in this respect. Marina Oliver thinks the editing part of the writing process is more difficult than completing the first draft. It is certainly more time consuming, especially if you have written first-off in the cathartic blur we explored above (Oliver, 2003, p.101). So you need to plan for, or at least anticipate needing, both the cooling-off period and then significant editing time too. Novelist Tim Pears says in the Open University course *Start Writing Fiction* that, broadly, he 'would expect to spend about eight months writing the first draft, and two years rewriting it' (The Open University, 2004). T.S. Eliot thought that the 'larger part of the labour of an author in composing his work is critical labour, the labour of sifting, combining, constructing, expunging, correcting, testing [...]' (quoted in Lodge, 1996, p.174).

ACTIVITY 25.3
Reading

Read the extract from 'Through a Tangle of Branches: Reworking the poem' by Rebecca Luce-Kapler, Reading 47 on p.602. What main benefits does a time-lag offer to the writer, according to Luce-Kapler?

DISCUSSION

The passing of time is the primary agent in the transformation of writer to editor. As time moves on, emotional ties are loosened, and the ability to see the work through the imagined eyes of others is quickened and fostered. Personal feelings are still at the forefront when a first draft is a recent creation. So it might seem a private affair – and hence unavailable for (even constructive) criticism. In the time-lag comes the remembrance of, and the desire to act on, the fact that she is 'writing for others'. Both the remembrance and the desire are necessary before you can edit. 'That "cooling off" period', writes Ursula K. Le Guin in no uncertain terms, 'is essential to revision' (1998, p.x).

How?

1   If you are working on paper, try editing with a pencil instead of a pen. The sense of impermanence and mutability that a pencil creates is a useful tool for the editing mind. It can encourage you to feel flexible in your approach to your work and to experiment with many variations: think back to your annotation of your poetic drafts in Part 3. Marks and comments can be layered with a pencil, by writing more or less purposefully; this palimpsest effect is appropriate for the task (a palimpsest is a parchment that has been written on in often still visible layers). This may not be the best method for you though. Michèle Roberts says that when she writes poetry, which she usually does in bed, she uses a pen and has all the drafts spread out around her (The Open University, 2004). Using different colour pens or pencils for different kinds of amendment is something else you can experiment with as you explore ways of editing your work.

2   A sense of impermanence has a value for the editing writer, but nonetheless keep all major drafts. You have to use your common sense here as to which you choose. You need to preserve a history of the most significant changes you made as you edited – these can be related to style (perhaps you decided each line of a poem needed new punctuation; keep the former version) or to content (perhaps you decided a character shouldn't have made a particular trip; keep the draft where she did). If you're working on a computer, print out drafts regularly and save files using different names. Using your working title plus D1, D2, D3 is one easy way of denoting drafts. If you're working on paper, date or number the significant drafts. This way you can track your changes and perhaps return to an earlier draft if you decide in the end that it's better. Knowing how you reached your final version could well be helpful in a discussion with a critical reader – it can be effective practice to go back and formulate an opinion as to how you got to where you are in your drafts. In addition all this means that you will have some alternatives up your sleeve, perhaps helping you to avoid new editing in the future.

ACTIVITY 25.4

Editing

Choose a poem or a piece of prose that you have worked on extensively at some point in the course. Find all the versions. Make sure you check your notebook too for re-worked odd lines. Put the versions in order and then number them. Decide which need keeping and why.

DISCUSSION

You may find that those drafts where you made small numbers of changes can have more of an impact on a piece than you would expect. If they are significant, you should keep them alongside those more dramatic looking annotated versions. Novelist Patricia Duncker says that the third editing stage is always a big one for her, where the most extensive changes are made, and as your practice develops you may discover a pattern emerges too (The Open University, 2004).

3   Use your writer's notebook as a place to plan and explore your editing progress: to exercise, in other words, your B personality. One way of doing this might be to test out as you're editing whether you can describe yourself using those same four adjectives that you came up with in Activity 25.2. Perhaps you can add new ones to your list? See how you fare if you try to become more like one of Weldon's descriptions instead ('cautious', 'rational', 'argumentative' ...).

4   You will need to decide what stage in the editing process writing onto a computer represents. For some writers, longhand is the only way to begin. You may, if you have seen copies of writers' notebooks, consider changes made to a longhand draft to be the most accurate representation of editing practice. To this way of thinking, work is transferred onto the typewriter or computer at a later stage. There is no doubt that transferring the work in this way can be a valuable way of fostering your editing self. But there are other methods. Mary Aswell Doll describes how her practice has evolved:

> Used to be I wrote longhand before I typed. I recall pages of scratched-out sentences, X's through entire paragraphs, suggestive of my terror of the white page. Now I work directly on the computer, trusting the flow within more than I did earlier.

> (Doll, 1999, p.3)

Novelist Jamake Highwater makes an even stronger case for the computer being part of the process from the start. He has never written his books in longhand and has 'no doubt [...] that the computer is an instrument capable of *connecting* with the body, facilitating the ability of the body to be the direct and vital transmitter of imagination and revelation' [his emphasis] (1999, p.26). Doll and Highwater both create and then edit onscreen, finding the transfer of longhand to computer isn't necessary for them. Whether the computer is part of your initial practice, or a valuable part of the editing process (the ability to track changes can be particularly useful), it is almost certain that you will need a version of your work on computer once you come close to giving it to someone else to read. If this does take the form of an editing stage, make it a useful one.

5   Reading your work aloud provides a very valuable way of stimulating the editor within. Many writers build this activity into their editing practice, perhaps by recording and then playing back sections of writing, as well as by reading it aloud. 'Speaking and hearing it', suggests Le Guin, 'may show up awkward bits and faults in the rhythm, and can help you make the dialogue natural and lively' (1998, p.x). She shows how it's possible to listen for 'what's awkward, unclear, excessive, what breaks the pace', as well as to read for these things (using eyes alone). In some cases the listening will pick up on weaknesses that the reading missed. Le Guin is talking about prose, but this process is extremely important for editing poetry too.

6   Start with the big changes, as you are in this chapter; move on to the little ones. The early stages of editing should be devoted to comprehensive alterations, to the pace and style of the piece, for example; later editing involves attention to detail, like spelling and other aspects of accuracy. Writer Gloria Anzaldúa describes herself as she returns to a second draft in Reading 48.

Read the extract from 'Putting Coyolxauhqui Together: A creative process' now, Reading 48 on p.603. What editing processes feature in the early stages for Anzaldúa?

ACTIVITY 25.5
Reading

First of all comes 'reacquaintance', a beautifully expressive term for the return to the draft having left it a while. Then she asks questions of her piece, as to its structure and the experience of an audience (of which more soon). When editing begins it is on 'large chunks' – paragraphs or a series of related paragraphs perhaps – and their relationship to one another. She moves them around as a way of answering her structural questions. More specific editing processes are involved too, like those we

DISCUSSION

saw in the example from Woolf's work: deletion, insertion, and attention to repetition and abstraction (both of which Anzaldúa has identified as her 'literary vices'). There's a lot involved then, at this stage – hence the need for time and energy. Factor this in when going through the early edits: later ones may be less demanding.

The idea of 'literary vices' will be a useful one as we move into the next sections. Spend a few minutes thinking now about what yours might be (inclination to stereotypical characters, for example, or to long-windedness). This should help you to decide where to concentrate your energies in the next activity.

Making the changes: First principles

A crucial first principle guiding your editing practice, as Anzaldúa indicated above, is your idea of your reader, who it is that will engage with your words. It can be a principle that you apply generally, covering for example the question of whether that reader 'will find pleasure in the imagery and language and be satisfied by the form' of your writing. Test this out by asking yourself this question from time to time as you edit (but remember it's sometimes your prerogative as a writer deliberately to delay or deflect that pleasure and satisfaction). Your idea of your reader can also be applied more specifically, because if you're writing for children it will help you to shape the kind of vocabulary you use, for example. Eventually, as you will see later, the imagined reader can be fundamental to the writer's decision-making process regarding agents and publishers.

A second principle that should guide your editing concerns the aim of your writing. What is its aim? In the case of creative writing, the obvious (though simplified) response is that your aim is to interest, to provoke or to entertain, or perhaps a mixture of the three. (Writing only to make money means your aim is unlikely to be realised!) You may agree, but there will be times when you're trying something different – perhaps to influence or inform instead. Know your work well enough to be able to answer to, and test out the success of, its aims. Even though they may be complex or subtly nuanced, you need to be able to edit it so that it fulfils these aims more effectively.

Editing practice

Readings 49 to 51, which you will look at in the next activity, offer some ways of developing and structuring your editing. Reading 49 covers several important points of focus (meaning, character, pace and style), and Readings 50 and 51 concentrate on one (repetition and cutting words). In the next activity you are given a choice as to which you want to practise now. One way of making the decision could be to use what you learned of your 'literary vices'. If you rely too heavily on stereotypical characters, choose the character focus. If you tend to be long-winded, go for the cutting words exercise. Remember to keep drafts as you complete these activities, and to work in the light of the two principles we've just been exploring (editing with your reader, and the aim(s) of your writing, in mind).

ACTIVITY 25.6

Editing

a) Read the extract from 'Redrafting and Editing' by Jenny Newman, Reading 49 on p.604. Choose a piece of your poetry or prose and identify one editing focus that you would like to apply to it (revising for meaning, character, pace or style). Of these, for example, meaning and character are probably more appropriate for prose, style for poetry or prose. Work on the piece in your notebook, or on the computer, using this focus.

b) Reading 50 on p.609, from *The Art of Fiction* by David Lodge, asks you to give your attention to effective use of repetition; in Reading 51 on p.613, from *Steering the Craft* by Ursula Le Guin, you are guided through the process of cutting words. Now choose to work with Lodge on Hemingway's use of repetition, or choose a further piece of your own writing to cut by half as Le Guin suggests.

DISCUSSION

a) If you identified meaning as your focus, make sure you can, in fact, answer the relevant questions as to what your piece is about. Keep a record of this in your notebook, as it may prove useful when you come to edit in other ways. The sections on character and pace both ask for specific attention to aspects of your work – though we'll be looking at dialogue in the next chapter so don't worry too much about this now. You may find that some of the style section is too detailed for early stages in the editing process, with the exception, perhaps, of poetry, so employ its advice when it seems most appropriate to do so. However, attention to your 'first interesting line or sentence' should certainly occur at this point. You need to grab your reader's attention as soon as you can – and then hold onto it.

b) The important thing to take from Le Guin's guidance through the often difficult cutting process is the sense of exploration as you work in this way. As you are keeping your drafts, any editing you do is reversible. You're seeing 'what the story [or whatever it is] looks like that way', that's all. If it's better, it can stay like that; if it's not, you can go back to an earlier draft. But for Le Guin, this process also teaches a necessary element of self-discipline for the developing writer. It will help you to come to know your own strengths and where, more precisely, the effectiveness of your words lies.

If you chose to work on Hemingway's use of repetition, you can apply what you learned to your own writing as you edit. This exercise will have helped you to explore how effective repetition can be. Many editing exercises will be dedicated to excising it from your writing (Le Guin mentions this too), but, as you'll now know, this isn't always the way to go.

Overall, your responses to all these aspects of editing practice will depend on your own writing and how it is developing. Return to these exercises, or to individually tailored variations, as often as you can.

Your work in this chapter has focused on the big changes likely to be necessary in early drafts. The next chapter will direct your attention towards the later stages of editing, when those big changes have been made and you can concentrate instead on the detail of your piece.

References

Doll, Mary Aswell (1999) 'The Web and the Work' in Marla Morris, Mary Aswell Doll, and William F. Pinar (eds) *How We Work*, New York: Peter Lang.

Highwater, Jamake (1999) 'The Fire Sermon' in Marla Morris, Mary Aswell Doll, and William F. Pinar (eds) *How We Work*, New York: Peter Lang.

Hill, Mary and Cochran, Wendell (1977) *Into Print: A practical guide to writing, illustrating, and publishing*, Los Altos, CA: William Kaufman.

Le Guin, Ursula K. (1998) *Steering the Craft: Exercises and discussions on story writing for the lone navigator or the mutinous crew*, Portland, OR: Eighth Mountain Press.

Lodge, David (1996) *The Practice of Writing*, London: Secker and Warburg.

Luce-Kapler, Rebecca (1999) 'Through a Tangle of Branches: Reworking the poem' in Marla Morris, Mary Aswell Doll, and William F. Pinar (eds) *How We Work*, New York: Peter Lang.

Marzano, Robert J. and DiStefano, Philip (1981) *The Writing Process: Prewriting, writing, revising*, New York, NY: D. Van Nostrand.

Newman, Jenny (2000) 'Redrafting and Editing' in Jenny Newman, Edmund Cusick and Aileen la Tourette (eds) *The Writer's Workbook*, London: Hodder Headline.

Oliver, Marina (2003) *Write and Sell Your Novel*, Oxford: How To Books.

The Open University (2004) A174 *Start Writing Fiction*, CD, Milton Keynes, The Open University.

Singleton, John and Luckhurst, Mary (2000) *The Creative Writing Handbook*, Basingstoke, Hampshire: Palgrave.

Woolf, Virginia (1976 [1931]) *The Waves: The two holograph drafts*, J.W. Graham (ed.), London: The Hogarth Press.

26 Editing: Later stages

SARA HASLAM

Introduction

The editorial changes that you have been making to your work so far are those that are likely to be more time consuming, and demand more energy too. As you have seen, Jenny Newman makes such a distinction when she discusses editing practices, and this should help you to plan your time as you edit. I am going to turn now to those other important issues that you will need to address as your final preparations before you show your work to someone, or send off your manuscript. These include: how you set out your text; dealing with dialogue; checking and correcting grammar and punctuation. Remember also that Reading 49 from Activity 25.6 included a section called 'Revising for Style'. Advice here – on redundant words, or adjective 'overkill', or predictable phrases, for example – is crucial for last checks and edits and you should return to this also when you can.

The second part of this chapter explores the next step and some of the many avenues that are open to you when you're ready to go public with your writing. (Later chapters will introduce further possibilities.) It addresses being edited. Here you will consider the process of having your work commented on critically, perhaps by colleagues in a workshop environment. In this part of the chapter you'll also have the chance to investigate more formal editing procedures, as we look at how professional editors work.

Final editing

Text layout

What follows applies to prose: your work on stanzas and line formation in Part 3 is the equivalent preparation of poetic text. This list of basic guidelines is based on one provided by Penny Rendall (2001, p.343):

- The first line of every paragraph should be indented, with the exception of the first in each chapter or section.
- There should be no space between paragraphs.

- A line space between paragraphs indicates a section break – a change of scene, of viewpoint or to show that time has passed.
- Asterisks can be used to draw attention to a section break that due to its position on the page might be missed by the reader.

In addition, the introduction of a new or different character usually means a new paragraph – indented of course. When dialogue is involved, the general rule is that each person's speech should begin a new paragraph: this makes it clear who is speaking and when. As effective dialogue is difficult to write, we're going to think about how you might successfully edit it in a little more detail.

Dialogue

Dialogue has three main functions. It advances the plot; it demonstrates character; it indicates relationships. It has important jobs to do, then, but has to go about doing them while sounding realistic. This combination is what can make effective dialogue difficult to write (a lot of everyday, and thus realistic, speech sounds anything but 'important'). Whether you're relying on your dialogue to do too much plot work is a major factor to consider when you're editing it: it's tempting to look to it to provide detail, and to advance the plot quickly and easily. Using too many adverbs when you're describing speech (like 'scornfully', 'loudly', 'emphatically') is also a common fault, because of what adverbs seem to reveal about character. Both faults make dialogue sound stilted and old-fashioned – so reading it aloud will help you to identify them as you edit.

The following example illustrates the three main functions of dialogue. However, it employs far too many adverbs, and it has a repetitive syntax and formal style which rob it of freshness:

'It is far too windy to take the boat out today,' Mother said with finality.

'The forecast promises fairer weather this afternoon,' Father responded aggressively as he put down the newspaper.

'May I be excused from the table please?' John said politely.

'The forecast is always wrong. It would be better to walk to Beachy Head instead,' Mother retorted impatiently, gathering the plates.

ACTIVITY 26.1
Editing   .

Think about how you might edit the passage, taking into account the advice above about telling and adverbs. You could add in some more actions to add weight to, or replace, characters' words, and perhaps report some speech rather than giving it directly. Before you look at a rewritten version, have a go at editing it yourself.

DISCUSSION

Here's one edited version, though yours may look quite different:

> Vera flipped the curtain aside. 'Not a chance,' she said. 'It's far too windy.'
>
> 'The forecast isn't bad,' Malcolm said, turning over the newspaper.
>
> She shot him a look. 'Since when did that count for anything down here?'
>
> 'I just thought ...'
>
> 'I've been sailing here for 25 years, sweetheart. Since I was six. In case you've forgotten.'
>
> John laid down his fork and asked if he might be excused.
>
> 'Beachy Head,' Vera said, gathering plates in noisy heaps. 'We'll go to Beachy Head instead.'

As you'll see, the addition of further actions means that lengthy explanation becomes unnecessary and the characters can take shortcuts in their speech, just as we do in real life when we have visual and aural signals to back up what we say. The added impact of their words means there's no need for adverbs telling us how they have been spoken. Also, John's rewritten character provides an example of how it can be more powerful not to give a character's speech directly. He is manifestly a marginalised figure in his parents' relationship as he's not allowed to speak for himself.

Returning to, or attempting, the 'revising for style' section from Activity 25.6 might well prove useful when you're editing your dialogue, so try and find 10 minutes to work with the advice there now. Concentrate on what it says about meaningless terms and weak intensifiers as this may be especially relevant.

ACTIVITY 26.2
Reading

What did you learn about presenting dialogue from the examples given above? Look at quotation marks, for example, and other punctuation.

Single quotation marks are used, not double. Also, commas and full stops are placed inside the quotation marks. You may have noticed that while each new speaker has a new line (so we know it's Malcolm speaking in line 4 even though there's no 'said Malcolm'), whenever that speech is preceded by an action performed by the speaker, it's the action that starts the new line ('She shot him a look'). Finally, each line of speech and its explanatory phrase is part of the same grammatical sentence ('Not a chance,' she said.)

DISCUSSION

Punctuation and grammar

Punctuation is there to help your reader understand your words. It is the means by which you indicate the intended grouping of your words, and so is also about attaining rhythm, and can be equated to pauses in speech. It is a fundamental aspect of good and effective writing. Your understanding of grammar and punctuation needs to inform your presentation of dialogue, but is also crucial in all other aspects of your writing:

> Theatres, magazines, production companies and publishing houses are bombarded with submissions from would-be writers. Who would struggle to read a badly laid-out script, or choose an ill-punctuated, misspelt novel over one which is comma-perfect?
>
> (Newman, 2000, pp.167–8)

This rhetorical question is one way of driving you to punctuate and spell your work correctly, so it communicates your ideas professionally, clearly and effectively.

Despite the importance of these aims for your poetry and prose, the notion of absolute 'correctness' in creative writing can be anomalous. Writing is also about making discoveries in words, stretching boundaries, and experimentation. Writers as diverse as James Joyce, Cormac McCarthy and Candia McWilliam subvert the rules of grammar, often to find new and different ways of representing subjective experience. You've looked at Georgina Hammick, who doesn't use quotation marks for speech, and Rick Moody, who often omits full stops. Poets, too, can choose to subvert grammatical rules as they bring an image to poetic life; as Newman has argued they tend to enjoy editorial autonomy in this respect. So perhaps think of what follows in this section not as rules in the main (though an apostrophe can certainly be used rightly or wrongly) but as guidelines which can be creatively interpreted in certain situations. Consistency of method will be key, and if you do choose to be creative with these guidelines in a piece of your own writing, it's crucial that you know why, and how, to the extent that you can justify it to yourself, and more importantly to others.

Before we go on to look in detail at using punctuation, we're going to edit two passages that contain many of the common mistakes made by new (and even not-so-new) writers.

Edit the following extracts, concentrating especially on punctuation and grammar. You may also want to pay some attention to style, identifying clichés and noting where you think you could improve on the technique.

a) The rain poured down rooftop's and gurgled into gutter's. "Its not a night for a dog to be out," DI Purkiss muttered, turning up his coat collar and squashing himself deeper into the smelly doorway of the long abandoned betting shop from which the faint odour of tobacco and body odour still permeated. Across the road he could just make out the faint figure of his partner Stanford lighting a cigarette, the faint glow came to him through the rain reflected in a puddle like a distant firework. He really ought to stop smoking, he reflected. He was a good cop though, even Montrose said so but then Montrose was a weirdo, weirder even than your average Super. He didn't like Montrose much and Mrs Montrose was even weirder with her obsession with rose's. He thought for a moment about his own wife and was unprepared for the stab of pain. She'd left him a mere three months ago and while it was'nt his fault he always felt guilty whenever he talked to Ann their daughter. Ann was now twenty-five and engaged to a man from the shipping industry who's only topic of conversation was usually perishable goods. "Purkiss!" Stanford hissed at him from across the road. "I'm going for a coffee. Want one?" "Yes please," Purkiss hissed back. "Any sugar or milk?" Stanford asked, approaching through the darkness. "Black, no sugar," Purkiss told him, and had a momentary vision of the shipping fiancé sitting behind his desk ticking off a mountain of sugar bags and milk cartons.

b) This was the last straw. Marilyn promised herself as she dropped the last pair of neatly folded trousers into her suitcase and snapped the lid shut, leaning on it with unnecessary force in order to shut it. There was a taxi waiting outside the hotel, it's meter was running but that didn't matter she would be paying for it with Andrew's credit card. That wasn't all she'd be taking from him either, she reflected, thinking about the last week and what a travesty of a marriage. She reflected back on the honeymoon bitterly, feeling the broken promises like a broken heart. The Malta sun shone bright and hot outside mocking her shattered dreams. If only I'd thought harder about what marriage to Andrew Da Silva was going to mean, she reflected bitterly, a tear collecting under her eyelashes, she wiped it away angrily. "I want my bags taken downstairs right away," she snapped irritably at the bellhop.

DISCUSSION

a) It's the misplaced apostrophes that probably stood out in the first extract. The first line alone contains two that shouldn't be there ('rooftop's', 'gutter's'), and omits one that should ('It's'). Double quotation marks are used instead of single for the dialogue, and the Inspector's first remark should begin a new line, as should each line of dialogue indicating a new speaker throughout. If you moved on to consider style, you may have focused on this cliché of a detective as well as the tired imagery, and misused words ('permeated'). Redundant words ('smelly' in the second sentence) and irrelevant information slow down the plot, helping to cause the plodding rhythm, and the dialogue between the two detectives is boring (surely they should know by now how each takes his coffee) and perhaps also ill-judged. It's unlikely that either an editor or a policeman would allow a coffee break at such a crucial moment in the plot.

b) Here you have a dreadfully contrived romance in which grammar and plot have been equally forsaken. The first sentence isn't a sentence, but belongs with the second and, in fact, the punctuation is flawed throughout: consider the first 'it's' and the absence of necessary punctuation in the same sentence. In style terms, the repetition of 'reflected' and other words is lazy, as is most of the clichéd imagery ('shattered dreams'). As a result, the heroine is difficult to visualise or sympathise with, and she also does strange things with her trousers (why fold then drop a pair?) as well as her tears. And where did the bellhop come from? Was he watching her pack? (In which case we *do* have the beginnings of a plot ...)

As you are editing for punctuation and grammar, it's important that you don't trust absolutely computer grammar or spell checks to make your text accurate. They can be useful, but they do not work contextually, and will accept mistaken variations of words and grammar, and suggest that you correct versions that are fine. For checking spelling, there is no substitute for a dictionary. Use one. And as we move now into the detailed consideration of full stops, commas, colons, semi–colons and so on, I am going to suggest you perform the exercises in Reading 52 as a self-diagnostic test. Answers are provided too, so you will be able to identify weak areas in your usage.

ACTIVITY 26.4

Grammar exercises

Complete the exercises in Reading 52 on p.615. Once you have done so, record in your notebook three specific aspects of your own usage that you need to keep an eye on.

DISCUSSION

Use what you have learned about your grammar competence as you edit. Return to the aspects recorded in your notebook and assess your progress too from time to time. Lynne Truss's bestselling book *Eats, Shoots and Leaves* (2003) provides an entertaining and fascinating account of the necessity of punctuation. If you're interested in seeing examples of how the same sentences can mean completely different things according to how they're punctuated, this book provides them.

Finally, before we turn to the topic of being edited, we need to address the question of when to stop editing. 'Writing on a piece never really ends', says Petra Munro, 'I could go on refining, editing, deleting, tightening...' (1999, p.215). But Munro did decide to end her work on this piece, as it is now in print. Knowing when to stop does take practice, but if you have worked carefully through all the stages of editing covered in this chapter, and if you feel the piece is as good as it can be, it may well be the right time to do so. Asking someone you know, a friend or relative perhaps, to read it aloud for you can be a useful way of performing a final edit. Remember though that you can edit your own work very effectively, and if you do decide to involve a third party choose carefully to elicit advice that's as useful and objective as possible. But the idea of bringing someone else into close contact with your work is also a way of bridging the gap to being edited, which is the subject of the second part of this chapter.

Workshops

One of the most common ways for a writer to go public, and to receive critical comments on their work, is through participation in a writers' workshop. Workshops can be open to anyone, or can require the submission of work before you join; they can be local weekly or monthly affairs, or residential weeks tutored by professional writers. They all share a crucial methodology, however, in that writers read their work aloud to their peers and then receive comments on it. Writer Julia Bell admits that workshops can be 'terrifying', but also believes that a good workshop will leave the writer feeling 'buoyant' and as though 'they know more about their own work than they did before they went' (Bell, 2001, p.292). Bell felt ill before her first experience of reading her pages of typescript, but recalls that the discussion that followed was 'gentle, pragmatic, encouraging'. So that discussion helped her to return to and to improve her work. She also explores why things might not go so well:

> Ultimately, a workshop is only as good as its members. A top-heavy group with one or two leading spokespeople runs the risk of splitting into factions and becoming too personality driven. The other members of the group may not be sympathetic to your type of writing, they may push you away from your original intentions.

And she offers ways forward from this (in advice which can be very usefully applied to any other experience of sharing your work):

> A good rule of thumb with workshop appraisals is to acknowledge the criticism that articulates a weakness in the work you had already feared to be true but hadn't quite expressed to yourself. If the comments seem irrelevant or off the wall or excessively negative, ignore them, steel yourself against them, not everyone is going to get what you are trying to do.

> (ibid., pp.292–5).

As you may already know if you have read or shown your work to anyone else, in a face to face encounter or in a group online, taking advice can be difficult – although it may become easier the further away you get from a first draft. It's worth thinking about how you might best listen and respond to criticism before you ask others to comment on your work. This will help you to get the most out of what they have to say, and to feel confident about distinguishing what is useful from what is not, an important distinction that Bell refers to above. Richard Aczel offers some pointers on the subject of listening to criticism, and believes that the most important issue is to be aware of exactly what is being criticised (2001, p.312). Don't make the mistake of thinking that it's all of your writing, or you personally, that are in the frame. He suggests that if you are used to editing and viewing your own work critically, it will become like second nature to recognise that there's nearly always another way of doing what you've already done. The more you foster the editorial approach to your writing, then the more easy you will find it to receive useful workshop criticism, and apply it to your drafts.

Editors

David Lodge's *The Art of Fiction* begins with the following dedication: 'To John Blackwell "genius among editors"'. While it doesn't tell us what constitutes an editor's genius, the dedication should alert us to an editor's influence and role in improving the work that writers submit. Lodge's gratitude and admiration are clear, but the relationship between a writer and an editor is one that can take some getting used to. In what follows we will explore some aspects of this relationship. Often the first contact a writer will have with an editor is through magazine publication, and it's worth being aware that poetry editors are in the main less interventionist than those of prose. If you have a poem accepted by a magazine, the editor is likely to print it as submitted, though he or she may have some suggestions for you to follow, or not, as you choose.

ACTIVITY 26.5
Editing

Choose a friendly critic or a critical friend (perhaps the same person that you asked, if you did this, to read your work aloud). It's important to choose wisely: you're looking for someone to offer criticism that's as objective and constructive as possible. Ask them to read carefully either that same piece, or another that you feel is well on its way to being completed, then comment on it. Once they have done so, take their comments seriously. Use your notebook to consider any recommendations that they have made. Make your decisions as to what you will change, and keep a record of why you are doing so. As you carry out this activity, bear in mind Bell's advice on judging the worth of an appraisal, and the recent discussion of how to deal with criticism.

DISCUSSION

In this activity your work has been commented on and in some ways you will have experienced what it is like to work with an editor. If you have gone through this process with other writing students too, so much the better. Knowing the person may well make the experience seem less daunting than working with a stranger, but by now you should be able to focus not on the identity of the commentator, but on the job that they are doing.

Comments an editor may make

Some forms of input from an editor are likely to be very simple and direct. The short story submitted may need to be 1000 words shorter (in which case activities like Le Guin's prove their value), or longer, to fill the space she or he has identified for it. The poem may benefit from a slight alteration to the title to make it fit more effectively with others in a magazine. Such changes are for the writer to implement, perhaps with the benefit of some further suggestions from the editor.

Other comments could involve more substantial thought and editing. An editor may consider one particular character is not drawn as effectively as she might be, or perhaps a couple of aspects need attention, as suggested in the following example of real feedback on a submitted story:

> We feel that the metaphor on which the story is built is not sufficiently clear to the reader, and would ask whether you could work on it to clarify the image of the lake in its psychological as well as its physical aspects, and perhaps shorten [the story] somewhat, and then resubmit it.

This is an example of a response that is ultimately encouraging, and is also very specific in its suggestions as to where reworking is necessary. In this kind of situation a writer's own editing should prove useful. Going back to drafts to see if there is any material that will help in clarification or development can also help to test why things are as they are in a draft, should a discussion with the editor seem like a positive way forward. Sometimes such discussions are welcomed (though they're not always to be advised), and can be very productive. As part of such a debate it can be worthwhile finding out how prescriptive the editor's comments are, and whether you are obliged to make changes in line with his or her suggestions, and not simply to take account of them. An editor is likely to be experienced, however, if employed by the publisher (whether staff or freelance), and has the impact and the readership of a writer's manuscript very much in mind. When they suggest changes, you need to take them seriously – which as I said above doesn't mean that a judgement cannot be questioned.

Copyediting

Once work with an editor has come to an end, a manuscript will be prepared for the author to proofread. The version that is proofread is the one that is to be published, barring any changes, so it is formatted and paginated as the final copy will be. Making substantial changes at this point becomes expensive and, if a contract has been signed (unusual for magazine publication), there is usually a clause which states at least some of the cost is passed on to the writer in this case. Reading 53 reproduces a table of proof correction marks, of the kind a writer uses as he or she checks over work for the last time. Some publishers have their own house guide, but the table shows you the kinds of symbols that are common to this late stage of the publishing process.

The chapter that follows will introduce you to further aspects of the publishing industry, and discuss some of the other avenues open to writers who want to take their edited manuscripts to the next stage.

References

Aczel, Richard (2001) 'Listening to Criticism' in Julia Bell and Paul Magrs (eds) *The Creative Writing Coursebook*, London: Macmillan.

Bell, Julia (2001) 'Workshops – Introduction' in Julia Bell and Paul Magrs (eds) *The Creative Writing Coursebook*, London: Macmillan.

Lodge, David (1992) *The Art of Fiction*, London: Penguin.

Munro, Petra (1999) 'A Truthful Tale about How I Work' in Marla Morris, Mary Aswell Doll, and William F. Pinar (eds) *How We Work*, New York: Peter Lang.

Newman, Jenny (2000) 'Redrafting and Editing' in Jenny Newman, Edmund Cusick and Aileen la Tourette (eds) *The Writer's Workbook*, London: Hodder Headline.

Rendall, Penny (2001) 'Final Revisions and Submission' in Julia Bell and Paul Magrs (eds) *The Creative Writing Coursebook*, London: Macmillan.

Truss, Lynne (2003) *Eats, Shoot and Leaves*, London: Profile Books.

27 *Exploring outlets*

MARY HAMMOND

> Oh you heavy-laden, who at this hour sit down to the cursed travail of the pen [...] Year after year the number of you is multiplied; you crowd the doors of publishers and editors, hustling, grappling, exchanging maledictions. Oh, sorry spectacle, grotesque and heart-breaking!
>
> (Gissing, 1982, [1903], p.54)

It may have been written over a century ago, but this passage probably touches a chord in most of us. Every writer at one time or another has probably asked him or herself the following questions. Is my work good enough for a wider readership? How can I make it stand out in a crowd? Who should I send it to? Will anyone even bother to read it when there's so much other good writing out there?

In fact George Gissing (1857–1903) had good reason to be bitter about publishers and the writing profession. In spite of his thorough first-hand knowledge of writer's block (which you came across in Chapter 1), in terms of output he was very successful, producing in his lifetime around fifteen novels and many volumes of essays, articles and short stories. But throughout his life he struggled constantly with poverty and self-doubt, becoming the archetype of the misunderstood artist starving in a garret, subsisting on weak tea and cigarettes. Despite what he says above, this was not just because there were simply too many writers in the nineteenth century. The market for novels, plays, poetry, newspapers, journals and non-fiction had never been so good. Many of the publishers whose names we recognise today started life in this period, and the national output of books and newspapers of all types more than tripled in the last half of the century. Not everyone could succeed, of course, but many of Gissing's contemporaries managed to achieve their goals and make a fortune, a very decent living, or at the very least a solid reputation.

The problem for Gissing was that he was blind to a series of huge and long-lasting changes that were sweeping through the publishing industry. This period saw the appearance of the first literary agents, the introduction of the literary prize, the emergence of niche publishers able and willing to cater for a wide variety of tastes, the introduction of the royalty system and the first effective international copyright agreements. Writers' clubs sprang up, providing forums for the exchange of drafts and ideas, and the Royal Society of Authors was founded to consolidate and protect the rights of professionals. In ignoring all these developments, Gissing made a series of catastrophic mistakes. All his life he maintained that writing was a solitary, mysterious, even spiritual activity rather than a craft that could be learned and improved. He tended to despise the critical opinions of others. For years he refused to consider employing an agent, sold most of the rights to his novels outright for an absurdly small sum instead of negotiating for a royalty, and lost out to foreign pirates while disdaining some of the most promising domestic markets for his work. Thankfully, nowadays more help is at hand to guide writers around these sorts of pitfalls.

You may not be ready to publish your work yet, and of course there are many types of writing which are naturally more suited to the private than the public domain. Autobiography, journals and notebooks are just some examples of the more personal types of writing which you have been practising as you've worked through this book. Whatever you write, you may be happy with what we have called the intrinsic rewards of writing – a sense of satisfaction at a turn of phrase or a well-chosen word, a sense of having improved, or simply the act of creation for its own sake.

But, as you have been finding out over the last two chapters, 'going public' is an important part of your development as a writer, helping you to find out whether what you have written is effective. It can mean a first step, such as sharing your work with family and friends, or with others over the internet. It can mean entering a competition. Eventually – though this may take years – there may come a time when you feel your work is of a type which warrants publication on a somewhat larger scale and is nearing a publishable standard, and you may feel you'd like to experience some of writing's more extrinsic rewards. Whatever stage you are currently at, you are likely to need some advice on how to go about getting your message across to your chosen audience. Even close friends and family need a clearly presented copy of your work which will not cloud what you have to say with errors. Even informal writers' chat rooms obey internet etiquette, and many websites have specific requirements in terms of genre. When it comes to larger scale publishing good advice is likely to be even more necessary. As in Gissing's time, there are many more authors, books and poems than there are gaps in the market. Not everyone who wants to get published can make it happen, and those who do often have to go through a frustrating apprenticeship first. Most of us have heard of writers who gathered enough rejection slips to paper their walls before getting their first break. But while rejection slips (and, indeed, other critical knocks) are something many of us have to get used to, most successful writers also feel that they wish they'd had some practical advice before they sent their first piece of work out into the world. I sent my first attempt, a three page hand-written children's story, out to Penguin Books wrapped up in pink wool. It was rejected with more kindness than it deserved, but apparently such naivety is not unusual. It is, however, avoidable.

The last two chapters of this book are designed to introduce you to some more of the issues and practices you will need to get to grips with as you move from editing your work towards its release into the wider world, whether you want to go public for commercial or personal reasons, in print or over the internet. Some of the information provided here might not be useful for some time to come. But having read and digested it you will be better informed, whatever stage of the writer's journey you have reached.

What kind of writer are you?

So how do you decide exactly what kind of work you are producing, and who might be willing to read, comment on or publish it? The chances are that by this stage you have found yourself enjoying or being more productive in one form of writing over another. You might, for example, have produced dozens of short stories, or enough sonnets to fill a bathtub. You might have done both, and also have a novel burgeoning away nicely on your computer at the same time. On the other hand you might only have managed one or two short pieces per chapter. But however prolific you are, or however slowly you write (and we all write at different speeds), sooner or later you will probably begin to feel something taking shape that you are particularly proud of. The extra effort spent on improving your style during the last chapters may have paid off. You may have received feedback on your work from an objective person whose opinion you respect, and realised that you have exceeded your own expectations. You may feel brave enough to want to share your work with a wider audience.

If you are convinced that you are still light years away from this moment, it's still worth working your way through the next couple of exercises. Understanding for whom you are writing is often a good way of clarifying your thinking. And in the long run it will make finding an outlet for your work – and getting useful feedback on it – that much easier.

ACTIVITY 27.1
Writing

■ Gather in front of you all the roughly finished pieces you have produced. Put away for the time being those you are not sure about, and keep out the ones you are the most proud of. If a clear favourite emerges from the group at this stage – perhaps as a result of the selections you made in Activities 11.1 and 25.4 – that's great. If not, you may need to do the following exercise for several pieces and base your final selection on the one with the strongest stylistic profile.

■ In your notebook, write down under the name of your piece the kind of writing it is (or you hope it will one day become). Single poem? Part of a sequence of poems? Autobiography? Short story? Novel? Sometimes this is obvious, sometimes less so. For example, as you discovered in Activity 11.1, something may have started life as a short story but you may now feel it has begun to evolve into the beginning of a novel. A single poem or a couple of poems may have begun to turn into a recognisable sequence.

■ Once you have decided on its basic form, write a fuller definition of the piece underneath. If it's to be a novel, state what type or genre. Is it literary fiction? If so, is there anything more specific you can say about it? Is it, for example, semi-autobiographical? Or is it fiction of a particular genre such as romance or horror? If it's a short story, think about whether it too is of a particular genre, whether it is of a literary or a popular ilk. If you have produced a poem or a series of poems, write a sentence describing the theme and subject matter.

■ Now jot down a rough list of the types of readers to whom you think this work might appeal, taking account of their age, gender, race, class, nationality, region or anything else you think might be relevant. You could write fairly general or quite specific descriptors or both (writing, for example, both the general phrase 'black British,' and the more specific 'British Caribbean women under 20', or writing both 'the middle-aged middle-classes' and 'all those belonging to a Wine Club').

If you found that you were unable to select a single piece but had two or three, that's fine. You can research one or all of them depending on the time available. You are not seriously looking for a publisher for your work at this stage: the important thing is that you have something concrete of your own to which you can start applying your research.

DISCUSSION

It's not uncommon to experience some difficulty in visualising a readership for your work. Sometimes, as the 'Endings and your reader' section in Chapter 11 suggested, it's important to keep a reader in mind as you plan and write. But sometimes a more specific sense of who might respond to your work comes much later. You discovered in 'Making the changes' in Chapter 25 that visualising a possible readership is an important way to start the process of going public; we are going to develop that process further now. When you have a stronger sense of the kind of writing you are producing and the kind of reader it might be aimed at, you can make a more directed choice about where you might be able to send it. At this stage, even if you feel your piece is likely to appeal only to 'other writers on the internet', you have made a good start.

- By keying the words 'writers' forums' or something similar into a search engine, compile a list of around six online writers' chat rooms or forums whose mission statements, welcome pages or contents seem to you to favour your kind of writing and your chosen readership, or which appeal to you in some other way. You will have plenty of choice: there are a large number of these ranging from the informal to the professionally focused. For example, at the time of writing the 'For Writers' forum describes itself as a laid-back place where writers discuss all types of 'writing (and cats ... and chocolate ...)'. The 'Writing Communities' forum, on the other hand, offers specific chat rooms for individual genres and advice on getting published, and urges you to contribute to an ongoing online novel. You will probably find that you initially prefer one kind to another.
- Make a list of their rules, noting in particular whether there are any kinds of writing which they don't encourage or refuse to post on the web.
- Make a list of their submission procedures and what they offer to subscribers. Do they, for example, have a facility for swapping drafts or do they seek merely to encourage discussion?

ACTIVITY 27.2

Research

DISCUSSION   It may be that you are already well accustomed to interacting with other writers in an online forum. In that case, use this exercise to find new forums which you've never explored before. Try to avoid getting 'cosy' with a particular forum: you will progress much more quickly if you keep searching for new, fresh feedback. Remember that your work is constantly developing, not just in quality but also in style. Within the space of a few months you might well outgrow the generic requirements of a particular forum. At the beginning of a given year you might feel you're a natural poet. By the end of it you might have a stronger leaning towards prose. You might develop from a writer of literary fiction into a crime novelist, or the other way around. The important thing is to keep searching for new outlets to keep pace with your own development.

This kind of research, like the decision to attend a writers' workshop which you encountered in the last chapter, forms a basic step in 'going public.' When you decide to post your work in a writers' forum you are no longer relying on the kindness (or, on some occasions, the tactlessness, untruthfulness or general unhelpfulness) of family and friends, but on the honesty of strangers. In addition, unlike the polite friendliness usually engendered by face-to-face contact with other writers, online forums represent a move towards letting your work go out into the world by itself, a world in which it must stand entirely on its own merits. This can be every bit as nerve-wracking as reading out loud – even when you're a forum veteran and are just posting your work on a new site. There's no doubt that some of the responses you'll get will be negative – sometimes unhelpfully so. Just remember Julia Bell's advice from Chapter 26, p.379: the chances are you'll get some constructive comments that will help you to develop, and any negative feedback that isn't helpful can be quietly dropped by the wayside.

Some writers spend a very short time getting feedback in this way before they become impatient to move on to bigger things. Some continue to post their work among amateurs, professionals and semi-professionals in forums long after they have had publishing success. The use you make of this outlet is up to you. It is, though, an excellent way to hone your skills, to pick up and try out new ideas, and to make contacts.

You will have noticed that some, if not all, forums and chat rooms contain a warning about the use of abusive language in messages or submissions. You should take this rule seriously. While no one wants to stifle your creativity, a wide and diverse audience such as the internet comprises is likely to include people who will be offended by strong language, explicit sex scenes or a derogatory tone. Sometimes it is enough just to post a warning about your submission below its title so that readers may avoid it if they choose. There are some sites, of course, which are specific to certain readerships and genres, and the rules on offensive material might be different for these. Horror is a good example. This is one more excellent reason to become aware of the requirements of particular genres and particular audiences.

Genres and readerships will become still more important as your writing career progresses. They are of crucial relevance when you enter competitions, which are often run by magazines with very specific audiences, or by committees who create distinct categories for submissions, with distinct rules and requirements. Eventually, you might feel ready to attempt a launch into a still wider market, and at that point you will certainly need to get to grips with the fact that publishers and agents take genre and readership very seriously indeed. There are a huge number of different types of publishing out there (reference and textbook, adult fiction and non-fiction, hardback and paperback, children's, educational, academic and so on), for an enormous, varied and ever expanding audience. Publishing houses don't all publish everything, and even the enormous companies that do are subdivided into departments (e.g. fiction, non-fiction, journals, multimedia) or imprints (e.g. contemporary fiction, children's literature, horror, romance, science fiction), each of which usually has its own specialist editor and production team. Most of us don't think about this much. We tend to take for granted the different sections in our local bookstore and the friendly staff who direct us to exactly the right spot. When we buy a book we may pay no attention whatsoever to who published it. But getting to know which publisher handles what kind of writing is extremely important for a writer. Every day many good pieces of work are needlessly rejected because they've been sent to the wrong publisher, or even to the wrong department within a single publishing house. So, at whatever point in your writing career you decide to dip a toe into professional waters, you can't just decide on an outlet – even if they describe themselves as 'general' – by sticking a pin into a page of *The Writer's Handbook* (Turner, 2005) or the *Writers' and Artists' Yearbook* (2005) (both updated annually). Whether you are entering a local competition or submitting work to an international company, you need to familiarise yourself with the rules and requirements in each case, and ask yourself some hard questions about your own material's suitability.

The following exercise is designed to encourage an awareness of the contemporary publishing industry, and to give you some practice at matching your work to the right outlet.

ACTIVITY 27.3
Research

- Make a list of around six or eight print publishers, large and small, which handle your type of work, or publish for your type of readers. Be as specific as you can; make sure that you are not just choosing 'general fiction' publishers, for example, if your story is a romance, or if you write poetry. Make a note of their postal addresses and, if appropriate, their web addresses too.
- Make a list of around six or eight current competitions, online or otherwise, which are open to your kind of writing.
- Make a list of around six or eight online publishers which handle your kind of work.

You can do these things using any or all of the following methods:

1   Using *The Writer's Handbook* or the *Writers' and Artists' Yearbook* (a very good method, but be sure you use an up-to-date copy as they are reissued annually – both are available in local libraries).

2   Browsing on the internet. This can be time consuming if you don't know exactly what you are looking for – at the time of writing the keywords 'writing competitions' brought up 690,000 hits, 'romantic fiction' brought up 1,560,000, and 'poetry publishing' brought up 2,600,000! But it's often worth the time it takes as you can usually find e-magazines willing to consider a single short story or poem. As a useful short cut to poetry outlets, go to James Wilson's listing of 'Poetry on the Internet' on Humbul Humanities Hub, for which you'll find the complete URL in the reference list (Wilson, 2004). For smaller or online publishers, try typing 'little magazines' or 'independent publishers' into your search engine. Again, you will come up with a huge number of hits but just the first couple of pages should give you enough information to make a start, whatever your type of writing.

3   Browsing in your local large bookstore or newsagent with a notebook at the ready, noting any publishers of books or magazines that seem to handle your type of work. Don't forget local newspapers and

journals! They will often take a single poem, and they are great for competitions.

4   Checking your local library. There should be a section of local interest publications from which you can get details of small local publishers. Also look in the 'Crafts' or 'Hobbies' section. Many amateur writers' groups publish small journals of local writing, and sometimes even helpful lists of independent outlets for new writing countrywide.

5   Looking through your own bookshelves and magazine rack for titles, stories or articles which are in a similar vein to your work. This can be surprisingly fruitful. We are often unconsciously influenced by work we have admired in the past, and there may be more similarities than you think.

■   Now, whenever you can make the time, do some narrowing-down research to find the best outlet for your work. You can do this by:

1   Visiting websites. Most publisher and magazine websites offer helpful advice to new authors, and list their current titles. These will give you an important clue as to whether the publisher is a good 'fit' with your work. If they provide printed guidelines for submitting manuscripts, download these or send for them, remembering to enclose a stamped self-addressed envelope.

2   Reading some examples of your chosen publishers' products. This is longer-term research but it is important. You should start building up a knowledge base of who publishes what. Pay close attention to length and style as well as form and genre. (Penguin rejected my three-page scribbled story not just because it was bad as well as badly presented – although it was both – but also because it was too short, and because they don't publish children's fiction under that imprint. They have the Puffin and Ladybird imprints for that). Where does your work fit in relation to those products? It's no good sending a literary short story to *Take a Break*. Buy a few of the books. Subscribe to a range of magazines. And read them.

■   Now, using one of these methods or a combination of them, decide on a single potentially suitable competition, publisher or imprint for your work. You may well find that more than one fits your criteria. This is good: just compile a shortlist of five or six and keep them handy. You can enter several competitions at once – though not with the same piece of work. If in the future you are conducting this kind

of research in order to find a publisher for real, and your first choice
turns you down, you will be ready to get back in the ring with the
next on your list.

■ Make a careful note of the advice provided on exactly how your
chosen publisher(s) prefer to be approached with new writing in the
first instance, and whether there are any special layout requirements
for competition entries.

DISCUSSION   Did anything strike you when you came to compare entries in the
reference books, or among the websites you visited? You probably
noticed that while some publishers proudly list the numbers of their
titles, the fame of their authors, the conglomerate which owns them and
their annual turnover, others state that they are interested in publishing
a small number of 'quality' or special interest titles or giving a chance to
writers who might be marginalised by more mainstream publishing.
Among the competition hosts, you will have noticed that some have very
specific generic requirements, while others are more open to stories,
articles or poems of all sorts.

Large or small?

There does sometimes seem to be a huge gulf between large companies
and small ones, and this can be confusing for the new writer. You might
well wonder which publisher, magazine, internet outlet or competition is
the most prestigious, who might be the most sympathetic to your work,
and perhaps at some point you may wonder who pays the most. It's
often claimed that large publishers dominate the marketplace to the
detriment of smaller ones, and they certainly take home more than their
fair share of accolades as well as profits. If you go to the Man Booker
Prize website and scroll down their list of previous winners, for example,
you will see the same publisher names appearing again and again (such
as Secker & Warburg, Macmillan, Chatto & Windus, and William
Heinemann), all of which are part of conglomerates. This can make it
seem as though literary prizes and big marketing drives are all part of
some cynical capitalist plot. But the big companies don't get it all their
own way. The 2002 Man Booker prizewinner, Yann Martel's *Life of Pi*,
was published by the small independent Edinburgh publisher
Canongate. They also published the US version of the 2003 Man
Booker winner, DBC Pierre's *Vernon God Little*. There are many other

examples of literary prizewinners and both moderate and runaway successes published by smaller firms who took a chance on new and untried authors.

It's roughly the same picture in the magazine industry. While most large magazine companies (such as IPC Media) have a wide range of titles which publish fiction and/or poetry, they often have a 'stable' of in-house or freelance writers who provide for most of their needs and it can seem very much a closed shop. While it's not necessary to rule these magazines out (first-timers do sometimes get their work accepted by one of IPC's publications), consider some of the smaller magazine publishers as well. Again, don't forget local publications or ones geared towards specific markets. There are magazines and journals devoted to almost every subject you can think of, and many you can't.

Simply put, there are pros and cons to each type of publishing. Large companies may seem unfriendly, profit-driven and unwelcoming to new authors but they tend to market their books more widely and handle them more quickly. Small ones may be constrained by ever-decreasing budgets and, because the staff is small, a piece of work might take a long time to appear. Or it might be less widely distributed or less well edited when it does. But small or local publishers could prove more willing to take on a less commercial project and their writers probably enjoy a closer and friendlier relationship with them. Richard Cohen, who has spent more than twenty years working for both types of publishing company, sums up their relative merits from an editor's point of view. Of conglomerates he says:

> [N]ew authors are acquired by the conglomerates all the time, but often it is an unhealthy Darwinism that prevails. Talent goes undernourished, and the general atmosphere can often be unfriendly, frantic, time-pressured and cynical: it is hard to have a sense of community when a company publishes over a thousand books a year.
>
> (Cohen, 1996, pp.44)

And of small publishers:

> One person ill can unbalance the entire office [...] But at least every book that is taken on gets attention. There are no orphans. Authors like dropping in, and despite the busyness there is time to see them. They *want* you to succeed, and feel themselves part of the attempt to do so.
>
> (Cohen, 1996, pp.46)

As for competitions, generally speaking the smaller the prize and the more local or specific the entry requirements, the better chance you will have. Some authors start small, say with a local newspaper, and work their way up. Some start at the top with the big nationals – and a very few succeed. You will need to decide which you think is best for you and for your work, based on an honest assessment of its qualities.

Internet versus conventional publishing

These sorts of hierarchies do not exist just between large companies and small ones. There is also a long-standing sense that internet publishing is something of an upstart, and that you can't really call yourself a writer unless you get published in print. So what is the truth of the matter?

ACTIVITY 27.4
Reading

- Read the extract on 'Opportunities for Poets' from Peter Finch's *How to Publish Your Poetry*, Reading 54 on p.638. Then read the extract on the role of the editor in conventional book publishing from Giles Clark's *Inside Book Publishing*, Reading 55 on p.643.
- In your notebook, make a list of what you judge to be the main differences between internet and hard copy publishing, and what implications these differences might have for your work.

DISCUSSION

Finch is concentrating on poetry, but his summary largely applies to other forms of e-publishing as well. These two extracts lucidly demonstrate how different the processes of print publishing and internet publishing really are. The internet has the advantages of speed, relative transparency, and a highly democratic approach that means anyone with access to the right technology can use it. As we have seen, you can post your work on the web for feedback from a discussion list or chat room, enter a competition, contribute to an established e-journal or start a magazine of your own. Print publishing on the other hand, as Clark demonstrates here, is a very long-established and skills-specific industry. That means it is often seen – somewhat debatably – as 'better' or more 'legitimate' than e-publishing. Relative durability might have something to do with this; we live in a world which tends to value longevity in literature. It is also considered more difficult to get your work accepted for publication in print publishing, and rightly or wrongly that tends to mean we value it more highly.

It is difficult to say which medium is the better, as so much depends on the needs of the individual writer and the character of his or her work. It is certainly no longer true that internet publishing is universally inferior to its conventional older cousin. There are now many excellent, prestigious e-journals edited by top-class professionals, for which subscribers must pay. On the surface it often seems as though internet publishers are more accessible, but the most prestigious e-journals are every bit as selective as any other publisher, and conventional publishers have to make an effort to be accessible too if they are to attract and keep good new writers. They sometimes go to some lengths to do so. In fact an excellent way to meet a publisher is to attend a writers' conference or literary festival. Publishers, agents and commissioning editors regularly attend the larger ones specifically to look for new talent. If you can't attend in person, many conferences and festivals run competitions, judged by professional editors or writers, which you can enter by post. Competitions are a great way to get your work noticed.

Conclusion

If you have crafted your work carefully and selected an outlet for it with the utmost care, some day you may see your work in print or on the web. But if you are to avoid becoming as bitter as George Gissing, you have to help your work to achieve its potential. The key is to do your homework using all the tools available to you. Get feedback from other writers. Have a go at some competitions and, even if you are unsuccessful, read the winning entries, taking note of what made them stand out. If and when you decide it's time to have a go at publication, research your market. Find out who publishes for it. Make sure you know whether your chosen publishing house or e-zine is willing to consider the work of new writers, and how much of your work they're willing to read. This is true even if you plan to approach an agent in the first instance. Agents, like publishers, want to know quickly whether they will be able to sell your work, and whether it will fit into a gap in their list. It's part of your job to tell them. Just as with drafting and editing, it is well worth the time it takes to go the extra mile.

References

Cohen, Richard (1996) 'Conglomerates versus Small Independents' in Peter Owen (ed.), *Publishing Now: A definitive assessment by key people in the book trade*, London: Peter Owen Publishing.

Gissing, George (1982 [1903]) *The Private Papers of Henry Ryecroft*, Brighton: The Harvester Press.

Turner, Barry (ed.) (2005) *The Writer's Handbook*, London: Pan Books.

Wilson, James (2004) 'Poetry on the Internet', Humbul Humanities Hub, Oxford, University of Oxford, http://www.humbul.ac.uk/topics/poetry.html (accessed 12 April 2005).

Writers' and Artists' Yearbook (2005) with foreword by Maeve Binchy, London: A&C Black.

28 *Presentation and proposal*

MARY HAMMOND

Now you have had some practice at finding a suitable outlet for your work, you need to know how to present it to an adequate professional standard. The onus is on you to make your work the best you are capable of. And that means one of your top priorities must be how it looks.

The manuscript

It may seem pedantic to insist that your work must be immaculately presented. After all, you may think, friends and non-professionals will not care what it looks like, and surely if the work is good enough, even editors and agents will look past the typing errors or the scruffy yellow paper. But the truth is, even good friends get irritated and have their judgement impaired by a piece of shoddy workmanship. And agents and editors won't get that far. As the quote by Jenny Newman in Chapter 26 (p.375) made clear, your work will be in competition with vast quantities of other submissions and if it falls below their standard it will not even get read. Consider the following passage:

> i) There is madness as well as magic in my family,. ~~which I~~ [first] learned this at the age of six, when I was visiting my Grand~~mother~~ma and caught the tail end of her conversation with a friend from the old ~~street days~~ street. They faced each other ~~slurping~~ across a turbulent landscape of meat paste sandwiches. Mrs Stone was chattering over a laden plate, jaws circling like a pack of hyenas. My Grand~~mother~~ma maintained a red brick privet hedge silence.

Were you irritated by the small print, the mistakes and the crossings out? No wonder. There's absolutely no point in sending out work that you've re-drafted and sweated over until it's stylistically perfect if you're going to jeopardise its chances with bad presentation. And presentation applies to every aspect of your work. To give just one example of how important presentation is, I know of a professional agent who, when sorting through new submissions, won't even open an envelope if it isn't a brand new one. He simply sends it back, believing that an author who sends out work in a battered, re-used envelope is not serious about his or her work and may well cut corners in other areas too. Your work must look the best it can – clean, fresh, error-free and easy on the eye. Use your spellchecker, when working on computer. But don't rely on it.

Follow the advice you were given in Chapter 25 and get someone you trust to check your manuscript through carefully for typos and spelling mistakes. We can get so close to our work that we read what we know is supposed to be there, rather than what's actually on the page.

Here are some golden rules, which should supplement the guidelines on text layout which you were given in Chapter 26 on p.371:

- Always use good quality standard plain white A4 paper. No colours and no tints. Expensive handmade sheets will not improve your chances.
- Type on one side of the paper only. You can economise by using both sides for drafts, but never for a submission.
- Always use a 12-point font, preferably Times New Roman. Fancy fonts won't improve your chances either; in fact they might reduce them. Editors would rather avoid eyestrain!
- Double-space your lines so that an editor can read the text easily and use the spaces to make notes to him or herself. (This is a good habit to get into for your own drafts too.)
- Set your margins at a width of at least 40 mm on the left, 25 mm top and bottom and about 13 mm on the right.
- Include a title page which adheres to the layout guidelines given below.
- After the title page, the first page of your manuscript should begin halfway down. It too should bear the title of your piece and have your name and contact details in the top right hand corner.
- Number your pages consecutively in the top right-hand corner.
- Make sure the title and your name appear at the foot of every page.

The title page

The title page might seem redundant, since it carries information you supply elsewhere, but it is important for a number of reasons. Even if you are just posting your work on a website, this page announces that you are serious about what you do.

You have automatic copyright in everything you write except for titles and ideas, and many new writers are anxious that someone will steal their best ones. In reality, theft is very rare. Stories abound of writers who sent their work to a publisher or posted it on a website only for it to turn up some time later under someone else's name. These stories are mostly apocryphal. But for your own peace of mind, there are some steps you can take. You can make sure your name and the title appear on each page, as described above. And you can provide a title page as shown in Figure 4. This will not protect your ideas legally, but it will indicate to readers that you claim authorship of the piece, that you are aware of your rights, and that you are likely to be alert to imitations.

The title page should stand alone, attached to but not an integral part of the rest of your manuscript. If you are sending the manuscript to a publisher and your work is accepted, the title page will be detached and sent to the accounts department. So important contact information needs to appear here, even though it also appears on your first manuscript page. Figure 4 shows the correct layout for a title page. The title page should have your name, address and contact details in the top right-hand corner. You should put the title halfway down the page, followed by your own name (or a pseudonym if you have a very good reason for using one). Put the approximate number of words at the bottom, rounded to the nearest hundred for short stories and the nearest thousand for novels. If this is a short story and you plan to offer it to a magazine in the UK, also write at the bottom the words 'First British Serial Rights Offered' (FBSRO). This will let the magazine know that you are not selling the copyright to them outright.
If you are mailing hard copies of your work, keep shorter manuscripts together by means of a paper clip, but for longer ones use an elastic band. Never staple the pages, and always pack them flat without folding. A manuscript should emerge from the (new!) envelope neat, crisp and crease-free, announcing itself as work that is professional and worth spending time on, inviting the editor or agent to pay attention.

About agents

I have mentioned agents several times in passing, but it is worth thinking a bit more about whether you should approach one first or not. George Gissing hated them and made a mess of his career as a result. The truth is there are many more pros than cons to employing an agent if you have a full-length novel or biography ready for publication. The cons are that you may find it difficult to find one: nowadays agents have a 'slush pile' of manuscripts to wade through just like editors, and can afford to be choosy. If an agent does take you on, he or she will take up to 15 per cent of everything you make in the UK, and up to 20 per cent

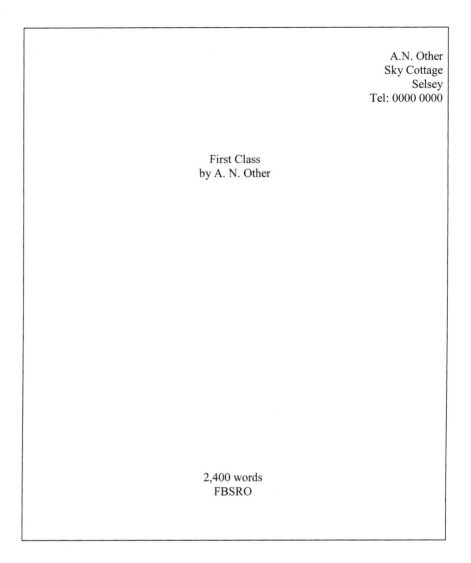

Figure 4 Layout of title page

of any foreign sales, and you may not feel this is worth it. Agents seldom take on short stories or poetry.

But the pros are many and attractive. The most important point in their favour is that increasingly, publishers and editors are saying that they simply will not consider work unless it comes through an agent. Quite apart from this fact, agents know more about the business than you do. They spend their lives courting editors and publishers, keeping up to date with developments by reading the trade papers and keeping their ears to the ground. They know who is looking for what, who has moved where, which trend is on the up and which coming to an end. They are acutely aware – as you should be – that publishers are always thinking up to two years ahead, and that today's hot news may be tomorrow's old chip paper. But unlike you, they have access to the trade gossip that alerts them to the specifics of such changes. They will therefore not only save you a lot of time and trouble in searching for the right publisher (though it's always worth doing a certain amount of the research yourself so that you can demonstrate in your initial proposal to an agent that you know what you are doing), but they will know things you can't possibly know that may positively influence the outcome. They will also do all the arguing and hard-nosed negotiating on your behalf when it comes to contracts and rights. If you are not the type of person who likes to handle this sort of thing then, when you reach the appropriate stage in your career, you should definitely consider employing an agent. It might be worth it even if you are. For more information on contracts, see Michael Legat's essays in the *Writers' and Artists' Yearbook* (Legat and Michaels, 2005, pp. 669–83) and on the web (Legat, 2001), and in his book *Understanding Publishers' Contracts* (2002).

So how do you find the right agent? Well, once more the *Writers' and Artists' Yearbook* and *The Writer's Handbook* are about as informative as it gets. There is, in addition, a useful website called 'UK editors and publishers' which, in spite of its name, lists several thousand agents, editors and publishers in the US and Canada as well as the UK, and provides addresses. But very occasionally a more personal approach is possible, and this will allow you to get some first-hand advice.

Agents sometimes put in an appearance at the larger writers' conferences and literary festivals, and in these cases it is worth doing some preliminary research, conference programme in hand, to find out who these agents are, which authors they have represented and for which publishers. Armed with this information, when you get there you should make an effort to attend their talks and to chat to them afterwards. Some agents even take part in running workshops at these events – and if so you should put your name down for one. It can be a bit terrifying to have your work critiqued by a professional who has no reason to be kind, but it is always valuable. And it is not unheard of for an unpublished writer to be taken on by an agent who has first encountered them in a workshop of this type.

Of course, some agents are better than others. Publishers know which agents are likely to send them the best material, and this can be a matter of degrees. As one busy publisher puts it, 'there are three types of agent.

At the top is the type for whom you will take a manuscript on holiday, then comes the type for whom you will take a manuscript home for the weekend, and finally the type for whom you will read a manuscript in your lunch hour if you've got nothing else to do.' Clearly, if you have an agent of any sort your manuscript will get read more quickly – and with considerably more attention – than it might if you sent it yourself. But this is not the only consideration. Some agents are able to sell nothing for their clients, while some seem to have the golden touch. Some are better at dealing pleasantly with publishers – and with authors – than others. The only way to find out these sorts of things is by asking someone who has had experience of them. If you know other writers who have been represented by an agent, ask them for some advice or a recommendation. If you don't, the internet is a good place to post such a question: you may well find a good agent through word of mouth in this way.

Writing a proposal

Agents, like publishers, need to be approached in very specific ways. Imagine this scenario. You have written something you are really proud of. You have polished and edited it to the best of your ability, and taken great pains to present it beautifully. You have done your homework, and found what you think might be a suitable publisher or agent for it. But the guidelines for submission state that you can't send your manuscript, you must send a query letter, synopsis or proposal first. What do these terms mean, and how do you write them?

The purpose of a proposal, simply put, is to convince a publisher that you have a good idea, that you can write and that there is a potential market for your work. In non-fiction (including much life writing) the proposal is often written before the work is complete (or even, on occasions, before it's even begun); a non-fiction proposal literally proposes a potential project to a publisher. In *Write the Perfect Book Proposal*, Jeff Herman and Deborah Levine Herman (2001 [1993], p.2) provide a few key points which a good non-fiction proposal should include. Among them are:

1   Title page

2   Overview

3   Author background

4   Competition section

5   Markets section

6   Promotions section

7   Chapter outline

8   Sample chapter(s)

Fiction and poetry do not work like this. New writers especially should finish the novel, story or at least six poems and polish them to the best of their ability before submitting them to a publisher or agent. Only proven, established writers are likely to be offered a contract before a work is finished. But the general principles outlined above hold good. Whether it is fiction or non-fiction, editors and agents want to know what your work is about, where it might fit in their list, and how qualified – or proficient – you are as an author. In a fiction proposal you won't need to give detailed coverage of competition, markets and promotion, but you will need to indicate that you recognise your work's potential audience, and make clear its strengths.

What should a proposal contain?

Generally speaking, a proposal might contain any or all of the following:

- a query letter;
- a synopsis;
- a sample of your work.

The format varies with the publisher and often also with the genre or form of writing. If you are submitting poetry to a magazine, for example, a query letter and around six medium-length examples of your best work is all you will need. If you are submitting a single short story, you will likewise probably just need a query letter and the well-polished story. For longer prose fiction, your proposal is likely to consist of a query letter, a synopsis and some sample chapters up to about thirty pages. The requirements may vary even more widely for internet publishers. You may well find that your chosen e-publisher is happy to look at a poem or short story either on spec or after a brief explanatory email. So how do you know what to send? Go back to your notebook and revisit the research you did for Activity 27.3, where you identified a suitable publisher for your style of work. During the process of that research you probably came across quite specific details of how that publisher wants to be approached, and you were asked to make a note of these. In starting to think about putting a proposal together, you must stick to these details to the letter.

Most conventional publishers say that they do not accept 'unsolicited manuscripts'. This does not always mean that you are barred from sending them your work unless it comes through an agent (though this is increasingly the case), but it does mean that they don't want you to send them a whole novel or a bunch of short stories or poems on spec. They want you to write them a query letter first telling them very briefly exactly what you are offering and why you think it is suitable for them. Many agents also now want to see a query letter before they agree to look at the work itself.

The query letter is therefore extremely important. It is the first contact publishers and agents have with you, with your ideas and your ability to express them clearly. If it is done properly, it not only makes a good first impression but also convinces them that you have done your homework and are not likely to waste their time. If they are attracted to your idea, they will write back to you asking to see either the complete manuscript or a sample of your work.

Some fiction publishers will want to see a sample of your work and a synopsis along with the query letter. And even for those that don't, if your letter has worked you will need to send a synopsis once they have asked for the material. Occasionally you might also be required to write a synopsis of a short story. So what is a synopsis? Very simply, it is a brief outline of the work, detailing its plot, characters and setting. And I do mean brief. However complicated your story, if it's a novel you should aim for a maximum of two pages, and for a short story about a third to half of a page. Some advice manuals advocate longer synopses, but the chances are if you write any more it quite simply will not get read.

We will be working on the specifics of how to write query letters and synopses in a moment, but whether you are a poet, a short story writer or a novelist it is a good idea to practise getting to the heart of your work before you start trying to pitch it to an editor or agent. Understanding – and clarifying succinctly on paper – what you are trying to do will help you when you come to write your proposal.

Look back at the piece(s) you have chosen to polish and research, and jot down answers to as many of the following questions as you can. In their original form they were compiled by the children's novelist Dianne Doubtfire (2003, p.123) as a good way of getting her students to think about what to put in a novel proposal, but whatever you write you may find them useful. You may also find it useful to refer back to your work for earlier chapters on point of view, characterisation, structure, form, theme, and setting.

■   What is the story or sequence of poems about?

■   Whose story is it?

■   What is the central problem?

■   Where does the story happen?

■   When does it happen?

■   What themes do your six poems explore individually, if they are not a sequence?

Now list each piece's strengths (based on your own honest opinion, or on the opinions of others). Is it, for example, particularly lyrical? Do you like the characters? Are you proud of the plot or the rhyme scheme? Is there a strong allegorical quality perhaps? Or is the piece a good example of a genre you are particularly fond of (such as crime, horror or romance)?

Finally, write a sentence or two (no more) stating why you think the piece or pieces are suitable for your chosen outlet. Based on your research, does the piece explore subject matter which has worked well in some of their previous publications? Is it suitable for a particular readership to which their publications tend to appeal? Does it offer a new approach which might appeal to their reputation for fresh new writing? If you find it difficult to specify exactly why your work is a good fit with your chosen publisher, you might need to do a little more research. Go back to their website, or to their publications. Take a long hard look at how they describe themselves and their products. Try to sum up the appeal of one of their published books before you start on an analysis of your own. Then write down how yours is similar, and how it is different. It does no harm at all to paraphrase their publicity (within reason) or to mention that your work has certain similarities with their successes, as long as you remember that you are a new, unique voice, not a spin-off.

ACTIVITY 28.1

Writing

If you found some of the questions irrelevant, that's fine. Just try to answer as many as you can, as fully as you can. You should now be a little better prepared to start thinking about what to say in your query letter, and how to angle a synopsis.

Writing a query letter

It is a good idea to send your query letter to a named commissioning editor (or named person in a literary agency) whenever possible. That way, it will quickly reach the person best qualified to evaluate it. Again, the research you have done on websites or in *The Writer's Handbook* and the *Writers' and Artists' Yearbook* should have provided you with the name of the agent or the editor responsible for commissioning new work in each department in your publishing house or magazine. These are usually listed as 'non-fiction editor', 'fiction editor', 'children's editor', 'poetry editor', and so on. If no name is given, address your letter to 'the commissioning editor' and do not assume that you can guess their sex.

A query letter should be no more than one side of an A4 page in length. It should include the following:

■ A short sentence explaining why you are writing to them.

■ A maximum of six lines describing what you have written. In the case of prose fiction say how long it is (approximate word count) and, drawing on your research, say why you think it is suitable for this publisher, magazine, imprint or agent. Stick to the facts! You can say that the novel is 'a thought-provoking exploration of single parenthood', for example, but it is best not to add that it will change the face of literary fiction. Leave that to the publicity department.

■ A maximum of two lines describing your own background and expertise. This section is to be used with caution: they don't want your life story, just an indication of your publishing experience and what might make you a valuable author to them. You could briefly mention any writing courses you have taken, competitions you have won, writing awards you have received, or special experience you have had connected to your writing. If, for example, your story is about nurses during World War Two in Burma and you yourself were there in that capacity, obviously you should include that information. If your poetry tends to focus on a particular autobiographical experience, you could mention that. But if otherwise important aspects of your life have no bearing on your writing, do not include them. As Peter Finch puts it: '"I've just completed an evening class in wine tasting" does not illuminate unless, of course, your work happens to be about drinking' (Finch, 1998 [1985], p.17). Do not be tempted to pad this section if you have never been published before and can't think of anything impressive to say. In that case it's best just to rely on the work's self-evident qualities.

- A concluding sentence offering the editor the first three chapters or around thirty pages, plus synopsis (if it's a novel and you haven't been asked to include it with your letter) or the entire short story (again, if the guidelines haven't asked you to include it with the letter).

- Your full, accurate contact details including email address.

That's a lot to get onto a single side of A4, and you will need to spend some time drafting and editing to get it right. Do not hurry the process. It's not always easy to get the balance absolutely perfect but it is crucial to give the editor or agent all the information he or she needs. Even if your publisher requests that a sample of your writing and a synopsis should accompany the letter, if you haven't managed to interest him or her on this first crucial page the rest may never get read. Remember to include a stamped self-addressed envelope (with correct postage by weight if you've sent work) for any reply.

Publishers' websites and e-zines, especially North American ones, sometimes provide an online proposal form which enables you to provide all this information electronically. These can mean a faster response, but there is a danger that you might be tempted towards informality when filling them out. It is a good idea to keep a hard copy draft of your query letter in front of you so that you can be succinct and still make the necessary impact. These forms must be completed with as much care and accuracy as any other initial approach if you are to arouse an editor's interest.

Writing a synopsis

This is a tricky thing for many writers. How do you boil down your carefully crafted work to just a page or two (which is the maximum you should allow yourself for a synopsis)? There is no simple trick to it, but practice does help. So does getting feedback from people who have never read your work. You might post your synopsis in your favourite writers' chat room on the web, or share it with your local writers' circle. Ask your readers whether their interest was piqued by your synopsis, whether it gave them enough information or left them with questions. You need to give an editor a full understanding of what your work is about. When asked for the secret of his success with readers, the nineteenth-century best-selling novelist Wilkie Collins apparently responded 'make 'em laugh, make 'em cry, make 'em wait!' This is all very well for the purchasing public, and not bad advice, but it won't do for a synopsis. If your story or novel has a surprise ending or a series of clever twists, all well and good, but you won't do yourself any favours by holding out on the commissioning editor in the hope that he or she will phone you, cheque in hand, to find out the ending. You need to make sure that all important plot points – including the ending – are covered in your outline.

We have already dealt with the crucial matter of presentation of your manuscript. Your synopsis should follow the same rules as to font and typeface. On the first page, type your title clearly in bold followed on the next line by the word 'Synopsis', and put your name and full contact details underneath. You might want to sum up the whole piece in a single pithy sentence before you start on the details. Some authors also like to include a list of principal characters, each accompanied by a sentence outlining their most important attributes (e.g. 'Luke McKenna: maverick American journalist in search of his mother's Polish past' or whatever). Some also put the names of principal characters in bold the first time they are introduced. There is really no hard-and-fast rule here. The important thing to remember is that your unique prose style and your skilful dialogue are not going to be shown to their best advantage except in the work itself. The synopsis is concerned only with demonstrating that you have a good story to tell about interesting characters, and that you know how to hang it together.

ACTIVITY 28.2
Writing

Look back at the answers you jotted down in response to the questions provided in the last exercise. In your notebook, remembering that this is for your eyes only at this stage, have a go at rewriting them as a half-page or so of continuous prose. If you're proposing a novel you can extend this to a page or more, asking yourself as you go what happens in each chapter and to whom. Write in the present tense – which is always used for synopses.

Did you find it difficult to write about your own work in this way? That's a common response, and shouldn't make you feel disheartened. Synopses are not easy for most people (though some lucky souls take to them naturally) but they are an important part of being a writer and they are worth persevering with. Whatever you have managed to scribble down in this exercise is a good place to start; now you just need to edit, correcting and adding and adjusting as you do so. Always try to open with a sentence describing who the story is about and what their problem is. Make sure you say soon afterwards where the main conflict of the story lies. After all, most readers want to read about how other people solve problems. If you are writing a novel you may find it helpful to break this early draft of the synopsis down into chapters, outlining what happens in each and to whom, before you put the whole thing together. (A non-fiction synopsis is usually submitted as a chapter-by-chapter outline, but for fiction it's best to present your work as a continuous whole).

Above all, even when you think you've got a viable draft you should get feedback on it from people whose opinions you respect (online writers' chat rooms are a great place for this.) You need to know if it flows, if it covers everything, if it's interesting. You know things about your story that may not be apparent to a fresh pair of eyes.

As a final tip, make sure you keep a clear and accurate record of exactly what you've sent, where you've sent it, and when. Once you get going you might have up to twenty manuscripts circulating at any one time, and it'll be impossible to remember what's gone where. As a simple rule, keep a 'mailing record' of each story or poem on a separate sheet. This should list the title of the piece, the name and address of the publisher, magazine or internet site you've sent it to, how much material you've sent, and the date you sent it, leaving some space free for the outcome.

Conclusion

Going public with your writing can seem incredibly daunting when you're first starting out. But it is possible to make it a positive experience, if you follow a few golden rules. Always make your work the best you are capable of, present it impeccably and research your outlet thoroughly. You may not reach your goal of publication this time, or maybe for the next hundred times. Rejection is a part of the writer's lot. Many writers (from Stephen King and J.K. Rowling to Raymond Carver) have stories about early struggles. But if you persevere and your work is good enough, some day you may find that you and your writing end up exactly where you want to be. At the very least, you will have learned some valuable lessons along the way.

References

Doubtfire, Dianne (2003) *Teach Yourself Creative Writing*, London: Hodder & Stoughton.

Finch, Peter (1998 [1985]) *How to Publish Your Poetry: A practical guide*, London: Allison and Busby.

Herman, Jeff and Herman, Deborah Levine (2001 [1993]) *Write the Perfect Book Proposal: 10 that sold and why*, 2nd edition, New York: John Wiley and Sons.

Legat, Michael (2002) *Understanding Publishers' Contracts*, London: Robert Hale.

Legat, Michael and Michaels, Amanda (2005) 'Copyright and Libel' in *Writers' and Artists' Yearbook*, London: A&C Black.

Legat, Michael (2001) 'Factsheets for Writers', http://www.writersservices.com/res/ml/r_factsheet_index.htm (accessed 12 May 2005).

Readings

With introductions by W. R. Owens

PART I

The creative process

| from 'Fires'

RAYMOND CARVER

Raymond Carver (1938–1988), short-story writer and poet, was born in Clatskanie, Oregon. His father was a saw-mill worker and his mother a waitress and retail clerk. He married young, and struggled to combine a writing career with his family responsibilities. It was not until 1976, when the collection *Will You Please Be Quiet, Please?* appeared, that his work attracted much attention. He gave up drinking the following year, and before his death published several more collections of stories, including *What We Talk About When We Talk About Love* (1981) and *Cathedral* (1983), describing in pared-down, colloquial prose the lives of working people. *Fires*, a collection of his stories, poems and essays (including the title essay), was published in 1982.

In the mid 1960s I was in a busy laundromat in Iowa City trying to do five or six loads of clothes, kids' clothes, for the most part, but some of our own clothing, of course, my wife's and mine. My wife was working as a waitress for the University Athletic Club that Saturday afternoon. I was doing chores and being responsible for the kids. They were with some other kids that afternoon, a birthday party maybe. Something. But right then I was doing the laundry. I'd already had sharp words with an old harridan over the number of washers I'd had to use. Now I was waiting for the next round with her, or someone else like her. I was nervously keeping an eye on the dryers that were in operation in the crowded laundromat. When and if one of the dryers ever stopped, I planned to rush over to it with my shopping basket of damp clothes. Understand, I'd been hanging around in the laundromat for thirty minutes or so with this basketful of clothes, waiting my chance. I'd already missed out on a couple of dryers—somebody'd gotten there first. I was getting frantic. As I say, I'm not sure where our kids were that afternoon. Maybe I had to pick them up from someplace, and it was getting late, and that contributed to my state of mind. I did know that even if I could get my clothes into a dryer it would still be another hour or more before the clothes would dry, and I could sack them up and go home with them, back to our apartment in married-student housing. Finally a dryer came to a stop. And I was right there when it did. The clothes inside quit tumbling and lay still. In thirty seconds or so, if no one showed up to claim them, I planned to get rid of the clothes and replace them with my own. That's the law of the laundromat. But at that minute a woman came over to the dryer and opened the door. I stood there waiting. This woman put her hand into the machine and took hold of some items of clothing. But they weren't dry enough, she decided. She closed the door and put two more dimes into the machine. In a daze I moved away with my shopping cart and went back to waiting. But I remember thinking at that moment, amid the feelings of helpless frustration that had me close to tears, that nothing—and, brother, I mean nothing—that ever happened to me on this earth could come anywhere close, could possibly be as important to me, could make as much difference, as the fact that I had two children. And that I would always have them and always find myself in this position of unrelieved responsibility and permanent distraction.

I'm talking about real *influence* now. I'm talking about the moon and the tide. But like that it came to me. Like a sharp breeze when the window is thrown open. Up to that point in my life I'd gone along thinking, what exactly, I don't know, but that things would work out somehow—that everything in my life I'd hoped for or wanted to do, was possible. But at that moment, in the laundromat, I realized that this simply was not true. I realized—what had I been thinking before?—that my life was a small-change thing for the most part, chaotic, and without much light showing through. At that moment I felt—I knew—that the life I was in was vastly different from the lives of the writers I most admired. I understood writers to be people who didn't spend their Saturdays at the laundromat and every waking hour subject to the needs and caprices of their children. Sure, sure, there've been plenty of writers who have had far more serious impediments to their work, including imprisonment, blindness, the threat of torture or of death in one form or another. But knowing this was no consolation. At that moment—I swear all of this took place there in the laundromat—I could see nothing ahead but years more of this kind of responsibility and perplexity. [...]

Source: Raymond Carver (1986) *Fires*, London: Picador, pp. 32–3.

2 from *New Grub Street*

GEORGE GISSING

George Gissing (1857–1903), novelist, was born in Wakefield, Yorkshire, the son of a pharmacist. He showed early promise as a classical scholar, but his academic career ended abruptly when he was expelled from Owens College, Manchester, for stealing money to help a young prostitute start a new life. He eventually married her, and became an obsessively hard-working and prolific novelist. He published nine novels before the publication of *New Grub Street* in 1891 earned him recognition as a major writer. The central character in *New Grub Street*, Edwin Reardon, suffers from agonising writer's block, as he tries to complete a novel that he knows is no good. Gissing himself went on writing up until his death (twenty-two novels in all), but never became rich.

For a week he got on at the desired rate; then came once more the crisis he had anticipated.

A familiar symptom of the malady which falls upon out-wearied imagination. There were floating in his mind five or six possible subjects for a book, all dating back to the time when he first began novel-writing, when ideas came freshly to him. If he grasped desperately at one of these, and did his best to develop it, for a day or two he could almost content himself; characters, situations, lines of motive, were laboriously schemed, and he felt ready to begin writing. But scarcely had he done a chapter or two when all the structure fell into flatness. He had made a mistake. Not this story, but that other one, was what he should have taken. The other one in question, left out of mind for a time, had come back with a face of new possibility; it invited him, tempted him to throw aside what he had already written. Good; now he was in more hopeful train. But a few days, and the experience repeated itself. No, not this story, but that third one, of which he had not thought for a long time. How could he have rejected so hopeful a subject?

For months he had been living in this way; endless circling, perpetual beginning, followed by frustration. A sign of exhaustion, it of course made exhaustion more complete. At times he was on the border-land of imbecility; his mind looked into a cloudy chaos, a shapeless whirl of nothings. He talked aloud to himself, not knowing that he did so. Little phrases which indicated dolorously the subject of his preoccupation often escaped him in the street: 'What could I make of that, now?' 'Well, suppose I made him——?' 'But no, that wouldn't do,' and so on. It had happened that he caught the eye of some one passing fixed in surprise upon him; so young a man to be talking to himself in evident distress!

The expected crisis came, even now that he was savagely determined to go on at any cost, to *write*, let the result be what it would. His will prevailed. A day or two of anguish such as there is no describing to the inexperienced, and again he was dismissing slip after slip, a sign of thankfulness at the completion of each one. It was a fraction of the whole, a fraction, a fraction.

The ordering of his day was thus. At nine, after breakfast, he sat down to his desk, and worked till one. Then came dinner, followed by a walk. As a rule he could not allow Amy to walk with him, for he had to think over the remainder of the day's toil, and companionship would have been fatal. At about half-past three he again seated himself, and wrote until half-past six, when he had a meal. Then once more to work from half-past seven to ten. Numberless were the experiments he had tried for the day's division. The slightest interruption of the order for the time being put him out of gear; Amy durst not open his door to ask however necessary a question.

Sometimes the three hours' labour of a morning resulted in half-a-dozen lines, corrected into illegibility. His brain would not work; he could not recall the simplest synonyms; intolerable faults of composition drove him mad. He would write a sentence beginning thus: 'She took a book with a look of——;' or thus: 'A revision of this decision would have made him an object of derision.' Or, if the period were otherwise inoffensive, it ran in a rhythmic gallop which was torment to the ear. All this, in spite of the fact that his former books had been noticeably good in style. He had an appreciation of shapely prose which made him scorn himself for the kind of stuff he was now turning out. 'I can't help it; it must go; the time is passing.'

Things were better, as a rule, in the evening. Occasionally he wrote a page with fluency which recalled his fortunate years; and then his heart gladdened, his hand trembled with joy.

Description of locality, deliberate analysis of character or motive, demanded far too great an effort for his present condition. He kept as much as possible to dialogue; the space is filled so much more quickly, and at a pinch one can make people talk about the paltriest incidents of life.

Source: George Gissing ([1891] 1993) *New Grub Street*, John Goode (ed.) Oxford: Oxford University Press, pp. 123–4.

3 from *A Writer's Notebook*

W. SOMERSET MAUGHAM

Somerset Maugham (1874–1965) was a prolific writer of plays, novels and short stories. He was born in Paris, but was orphaned and was brought up in England by an uncle. He studied medicine but never practised. Although his first publications were novels, he achieved greater success as a playwright. *Of Human Bondage* (1915) is usually regarded as his finest novel, but he is also reckoned to be among the best short-story writers in English, praised particularly for his merciless observation of life. He set out his views on life and art in *A Writer's Notebook* (1949) and *Points of View* (1958).

1919

They told him someone had said of him: 'He's smart, he doesn't give much away.' He beamed; he took it as a compliment.

She plunged into a sea of platitudes, and with the powerful breast stroke of a channel swimmer made her confident way towards the white cliffs of the obvious.

A married couple. She adored him with a selfish, passionate devotion, and their life was a struggle on his part to secure his soul and on hers to get possession of it. Then it was discovered that he had T.B. They both knew that this was her triumph, for thenceforward he would never escape her. He killed himself.

Jamie and his wife. Two stodgy people who do nothing but read novels. They live a perfectly monotonous life, but in the spirit, a life of romance. All their experiences are fiction. They had a baby and the baby died. Jamie hoped that his wife wouldn't have another. It disturbed the tenor of their lives. After the funeral they both settled down with a sigh of relief to the new novels that had just come from the library.

Arnold. For thirty years he had cultivated a pose till at last it became second nature to him. Then he was bored to death by it, but when he came to look into his heart for his real self he couldn't find it. Nothing was left but the pose. He went to France hoping to get killed, but he came back at the end of the war safe and sound, and there stretched before him then an illimitable emptiness.

Chicago. The hogs are driven into pens and they come squealing as though they knew what was before them; they are attached by a hind leg and swung from a moving bar which takes them to where a man in blue overalls splashed with blood stands with a long knife. He is a pleasant-faced young man. He turns the hog towards him and stabs it in the jugular vein; there is a gush of blood and the hog passes on. Another takes its place. Hog follows hog with a mechanical regularity which reminds you of the moving steps of an escalator. I was struck by the calm indifference with which the pleasant-faced young man killed them. It was like a grim caricature of the Dance of Death. They come, struggling and screaming, the poet, the statesman, the merchant prince; and no matter what ideals, what passions or high endeavours have been theirs, they are hurried on by a remorseless fate and none escapes.

The activity is intense as the hog is passed by a machine from one man to another; one scrapes off such hair as is left after the hog has gone through one machine, another cuts out the bowels, a third slices off the hams. There was not a moment's pause, and I wondered what would happen if a man fell out and missed his appointed task. There was one old man, grey-bearded, who lifted a huge chopper and mechanically cut off the hams. The movement of the chopper, so deliberate and regular, yet so unceasing, was strangely mysterious. They told me he had been doing that very same thing for thirty years.

Wabash Avenue. Many-storeyed buildings white, red and black, but dingy, with their fire-escapes like strange parasites on monstrous mushroom growths. Long lines of motors along the kerbs. The dull roar of trains on the elevated, the hurried, agitated string of street cars as they thunder along crowded with people, the sharp screech of motor horns and the shrill, peremptory whistle of the cop directing the traffic. No one loiters. Everyone hurries. Street-cleaners in their white uniforms, artisans in dingy overalls, brown or blue. The mixture of races, Slavs, Teutons, Irish with their broad smiles and red faces, Middle-Westerners, dour, long-faced, strangely ill at ease, as though they were intruders.

H. B. went down to stay in the country. His next-door neighbour was a very quiet prim little old lady; becoming acquainted with her, he gradually connected her with the heroine of a celebrated murder which had excited the world fifty years before. She had been tried and found not guilty, but the evidence was so damning that notwithstanding the verdict the general opinion was that she had in point of fact committed the crime. She discovered that he had found out her identity, taxed him with it and presently said to him: 'I suppose you want to know whether I did it or not. I did, and what's more, if it were all to happen again I'd do it again.'

An Italian, driven by hunger, came to New York and in due course got work on the streets. He was passionately attached to the wife he had left in Italy. Rumour reached him that his nephew was sleeping with her. He was seized with rage. He hadn't the money to return to Italy, but wrote to his nephew to come to New York, where he could earn good wages. The nephew came, and on the night of his arrival the husband killed him. He was arrested. The wife was brought over for the trial and in order to save him confessed what wasn't true, that the nephew had been her lover. The man was sentenced to a term of imprisonment and after no very long while paroled. His wife was waiting for him. He knew that she hadn't been unfaithful to him, but her confession was as great a burden on his honour as if she had been. It rankled. It shamed him. He made her violent scenes, and at last, hopeless, because there was nothing else to do, because she loved him, she told him to kill her. He drove his knife into her heart. Honour was satisfied.

When I have travelled through America I have often asked myself what sort of men those were whom I saw in the parlour-cars of trains or in the lounge of an hotel, in rocking-chairs, a spittoon by their side, looking out of a large plate-glass window at the street. I have wondered what their lives were, what they thought of and how they looked upon existence. In their ill-fitting, ready-made clothes, gaudy shirts and showy ties, rather too stout, clean-shaven, but wanting a shave, with a soft hat on the back of their heads, chewing a cigar, they were as strange to me as the Chinese and more impenetrable. Often I have tried to speak with them, but I have found no common language in which I could converse with them. They have filled me with timidity. Now that I have read

Main Street[1] I feel that I am no longer quite unfamiliar with them. I can give them names. I know how they behave when they are at home and what they talk about. I have enriched my knowledge of human nature. But the author of *Main Street* has done something more than depict with accuracy the inhabitants of a small town in the Middle-West, and I cannot make up my mind whether he has done it knowingly or by accident. He has described a very curious circumstance, the beginnings in America of the social distinctions which in Europe make up so important a part of life. And it is interesting to see this arise when in Europe the war is thought to have abolished so many distinctions of class. The story of *Main Street* is very simple: it is the description of the marriage of a lady with a man who is not a gentleman. He is an excellent fellow, but she suffers much because his ways are vulgar and the people among whom she has to live are common. In England a woman in such a case would have been at once conscious of the social difference and would have hesitated to marry. Her friends would have said to her: 'My dear, of course he's a dear good chap, but he's not a gentleman and you can't possibly be happy with him.' And much else of the story hangs on the various levels of village society; the tradesman looks down on the farmer and the farmer on the hired man. There could not be more class-consciousness in an English village; but in an English village each man knows his station and accepts it without rancour. It looks as though every civilisation as it grows complicated and stable gave rise to a minute difference of classes, and to acknowledge them frankly conduced to ease of mind. In the community described in *Main Street* every man allows with his lips that every other is as good as he, but in his heart he does not think it for a moment. The banker does not ask the dentist to his house and the dentist will not hobnob with the tailor's assistant. The lip-service which is given to equality occasions a sort of outward familiarity, but this only makes those below more conscious of the lack of inward familiarity; and so nowhere is class-hatred likely to give rise in the long run to more bitter enmity.

[1][Footnotes provided for clarification in this extract by W. R. Owens.] [*Main Street* is the title of a novel by the American writer Sinclair Lewis, first published in 1920.]

1921

Haddon Chambers.[2] I was told this morning that Haddon Chambers was dead, and I said: 'Poor chap, I'm sorry'; but it occurred to me immediately that I spoke according to a foolish convention. Haddon Chambers had made a successful job of life according to his own lights. He had enjoyed himself. His day was over and unless his jaunty spirit had found new resources of philosophy he had nothing much to look forward to that was attractive to a man of his temper. He died in a happy moment. If he is remembered at all it will be, not for his plays, but for his phrase: 'the long arm of coincidence'. That may well last as long as the language. He was a little man, shrivelled in his dapper clothes, who reminded you somehow of a dead leaf; and like a dead leaf he used to blow into the places he was used to frequent, tarry, without giving you the impression that he was settled even for a moment, and then with a singular aimlessness blow out again. He seemed to have no material attachments. He came and went without intention as though he were the sport of a perfectly indifferent chance. At the first glance he looked a youngish man, but presently you saw that in reality he was old, old; his eyes in repose were weary and he gave them brightness only by an effort of will; his face had an unnatural smoothness as though it were massaged and nourished with cold creams; he looked like someone who had been long buried and then dug up again. It made you think that he was much older than he really was. He never told his age. He clung to youth with a seriousness which he showed in no other of the affairs of life. He had the reputation of a Don Juan, and this he valued much more than any that his plays had brought him. One of his affairs at least had been notorious, and he rejoiced to the last in the fame of it. He liked to pretend that he was engaged in constant intrigues, and with innuendoes, hints, broken phrases, raisings of the eyebrow, winks, shrugs of the shoulder and waves of the hand would give you to understand that he was still pursuing his amorous career. But when he went out from his club, very spruce in clothes a little too young for him, ostensibly to a rendezvous, you had an inkling that it was in truth to dine by himself in the back room of some restaurant in Soho where no one he knew would be likely to see him. Since he wrote plays I suppose he must be counted as a man of letters, but surely there can have been seldom a man of letters who cared less for literature. I do not know

---

[2] [Charles Haddon Chambers (1860–1921), playwright.]

whether he ever read: certainly he never spoke of books. The only art in which he seemed at all interested was music. He attached no great importance to his plays; but it exasperated him to have his best play, *The Tyranny of Tears*,[3] ascribed to Oscar Wilde. For my part I cannot imagine how such a notion could ever have been as widely spread as it certainly was. No one could have had it who had any feeling for dialogue or any discrimination in humour. Oscar Wilde's dialogue was succinct and pointed, his humour well bred and urbane: the dialogue in *The Tyranny of Tears* is loose, pertinent rather than sparkling, and it has no epigrammatic quality; the humour smacks of the bar parlour rather than of the drawing-room. Its wit is due to its aptness rather than to any verbal ingenuity. It had the very stamp and idiosyncrasy of Haddon Chambers. He was a sociable creature, and when I seek for a characteristic impression with which to leave him I see him lounging at a bar, a dapper little man, chatting good-humouredly with a casual acquaintance of women, horses and Covent Garden opera, but with an air as though he were looking for someone who might at any moment come in at the door.

1922

Things were easier for the old novelists who saw people all of a piece. Speaking generally, their heroes were good through and through, their villains wholly bad. But take X, for instance. She is not only a liar, she is a mytho-maniac who will invent malicious stories that have no foundation in fact and will tell them so convincingly, with such circumstantial detail, that you are almost persuaded she believes them herself. She is grasping and will hesitate at no dishonesty to get what she wants. She is a snob and will impudently force her acquaintance on persons who she knows wish to avoid it. She is a climber, but with the paltriness of her mind is satisfied with the second rate; the secretaries of great men are her prey, not the great men themselves. She is vindictive, jealous and envious. She is a quarrelsome bully. She is vain, vulgar and ostentatious. There is real badness in her.

She is clever. She has charm. She has exquisite taste. She is generous and will spend her own money, to the last penny, as freely as she will spend other people's. She is hospitable and takes pleasure in the

---

[3] [This was a four-act comedy, published in 1899.]

pleasure she gives her guests. Her emotion is easily aroused by a tale of love and she will go out of her way to relieve the distress of persons who mean nothing to her. In sickness she will show herself an admirable and devoted nurse. She is a gay and pleasant talker. Her greatest gift is her capacity for sympathy. She will listen to your troubles with genuine commiseration and with unfeigned kindliness will do everything she can to relieve them or to help you to bear them. She will interest herself in all that concerns you, rejoice with you in your success and take part in the mortifications of your failure. There is real goodness in her.

She is hateful and lovable, covetous and open-handed, cruel and kind, malicious and generous of spirit, egotistic and unselfish. How on earth is a novelist so to combine these incompatible traits as to make the plausible harmony that renders a character credible?

In this connection it is instructive to consider Balzac's *Le Cousin Pons*.[4] Pons is a glutton. To satisfy his ignoble craving he thrusts his company at dinner-time on people who plainly resent it, and rather than go without good food and good wine will submit to the coldness, the acidulous greeting of his unwilling hosts and the sneers of their servants. He wilts when he has to eat at home and at his own expense. The vice is disgusting and the character can only excite aversion. But Balzac demands your sympathy for him and he gets it with ingenuity. In the first place he makes the people he sponges on vile and vulgar; then he dwells on his hero's faultless taste, for he is a collector, and on his love of beauty. He will deny himself not only luxuries, but necessities in order to buy a picture, a piece of furniture or of porcelain. Balzac again and again insists on his goodness, his kindness, his simplicity, his capacity for friendship, till little by little you forget his shameful greed and the abject sycophancy with which he tries to repay the good dinners he gets only to feel deep sympathy for him and to view with horror his victims, who after all had a lot to put up with but to whom Balzac has not allowed a single redeeming trait.

Source: W. Somerset Maugham (2001) *A Writer's Notebook*, London: Vintage, pp. 168–75.

[4] [Honoré de Balzac's novel, *Cousin Pons*, first published in 1848.]

4 from *Becoming a Writer*

DOROTHEA BRANDE

Dorothea Brande (1893–1948), literary editor and writer, was born in Chicago. She worked as associate editor of *The Bookman* from 1927 to 1932, and of the *American Review* from 1933 to 1934. In 1934 she published what was to be her most enduring work, *Becoming a Writer*, one of the earliest guidebooks aimed at aspiring writers. It has never been out of print. Her only full-length work of fiction, a detective story entitled *Most Beautiful Lady*, was published in 1935. The following year she published *Wake Up and Live*, an inspirational book of advice on how to succeed in life, which became a best-seller.

Harnessing the Unconscious

To begin with, you must teach the unconscious to flow into the channel of writing. Psychologists will forgive us for speaking so airily about 'teaching' the unconscious to do this or that. To all intents and purposes that is what happens; but less elegantly and more exactly we might say that the first step toward being a writer is to hitch your unconscious mind to your writing arm.

Wordless Daydreams

Most persons who are attracted by the idea of fiction at all are, or were in childhood, great dreamers. At almost any moment they can catch themselves, at some level, deep in reverie. Occasionally this reverie takes the form of recasting one's life, day by day or moment by moment, into a form somewhat nearer to the heart's desire: reconstructing conversations and arguments so that we come out with colors flying and epigrams falling around us like sparks, or imagining ourselves back in a simpler and happier period. Or adventure is coming toward us around the next corner, and we have already made up our minds as to the form it will take. All those naive and satisfying dreams of which we are the unashamed heroes or heroines are the very stuff of fiction, almost the *materia prima* of fiction. A little sophistication, a little experience, and we realize that we are not going to be allowed to carry off the honors in real life without a struggle; there are too many contenders for the role of leading lady or leading man. So, learning discretion and guile, we cast the matter a little differently; we objectify the ideal self that has caused us so much pleasure and write about him in the third person. And hundreds of our fellows, engaged secretly in just such daydreaming as our own, see themselves in our fictional characters and fall to reading when fatigue or disenchantment robs them of their ability to see themselves under any glamorous guise. (Not, thank heaven, that this is the only reason a book is ever read; but undoubtedly it is the commonest one.)

The little Brontës, with their kingdom of Gondaland, the infant Alcotts, young Robert Browning, and H.G. Wells all led an intensive dream-life which carried over into their maturity and took another form; and there are hundreds of authors who could tell the same stories of their youth. But there are probably thousands more who never grow up as writers. They are too self-conscious, too humble, or too solidly set in the habit of dreaming idly. After all, we begin our storytelling, usually, long before we are able to print simple words with infinite labor. It is little wonder that the glib unconscious should balk at the drudgery of committing its stories to writing.

Toward Effortless Writing

Writing calls on unused muscles and involves solitude and immobility. There is not much to be said for the recommendation, so often heard, to serve an apprenticeship to journalism if you intend to write fiction. But a journalist's career does teach two lessons which every writer needs to learn – that it is possible to write for long periods without fatigue, and that if one pushes on past the first weariness one finds a reservoir of unsuspected energy – one reaches the famous 'second wind.'
[...]

So if you are to have the full benefit of the richness of the unconscious you must learn to write easily and smoothly when the unconscious is in the ascendant.

The best way to do this is to rise half an hour, or a full hour, earlier than you customarily rise. Just as soon as you can – and without talking, without reading the morning's paper, without picking up the book you laid aside the night before – begin to write. Write anything that comes into your head: last night's dream, if you are able to remember it; the activities of the day before; a conversation, real or imaginary; an examination of conscience. Write any sort of early morning reverie, rapidly and uncritically. The excellence or ultimate worth of what you write is of no importance yet. As a matter of fact, you will find more value in this material than you expect, but your primary purpose now is not to bring forth deathless words, but to write any words at all which are not pure nonsense.

To reiterate, what you are actually doing is training yourself, in the twilight zone between sleep and the full waking state, simply *to write*. It makes no difference to the success of this practice if your paragraphs are amorphous, the thought vague or extravagant, the ideas hazy. Forget that you have any critical faculty at all; realize that no one need ever see what you are writing unless you choose to show it. You may, if you can, write in a notebook, sitting up in bed. [...] Write as long as you have free time, or until you feel that you have utterly written yourself out.

The next morning begin without rereading what you have already done. Remember: you are to write *before* you have read at all. The purpose of this injunction will become clear later. Now all you need to concern yourself with is the mere performance of the exercise.

Double Your 'Output'

After a day or two you will find that there is a certain number of words that you can write easily and without strain. When you have found that limit, begin to push it ahead by a few sentences, then by a paragraph or two. A little later try to double it before you stop the morning's work.

Within a very short time you will find that the exercise has begun to bear fruit. The actual labor of writing no longer seems arduous or dull. You will have begun to feel that you can get as much (far more really) from a written reverie as from one that goes on almost wordlessly in the back of your mind. When you can wake, reach out for your pencil, and begin to write almost on one impulse, you will be ready for the next step. Keep the material you have written – under lock and key if that is the only way to save yourself from self-consciousness. It will have uses you can hardly foresee.

As you take up the next exercise, you can return, in this morning task, to the limit that seems easy and natural. (But you should be able to write more words than when you began.) Watch yourself carefully; if at any time you find you have slipped back into inactive reverie, it is time to exert pressure on yourself. Throughout your writing life, whenever you are in danger of the spiritual drought that comes to the most facile writer from time to time, put the pencil and paper back on your bedside table, and wake to write in the morning.

Source: Dorothea Brande (1996) *Becoming a Writer*, London: Macmillan, pp. 63–8.

5 from *'A Real-Life Education'*

SUSAN MINOT

Susan Minot (b. 1956), novelist and short-story writer, was born in Boston, Massachusetts. She studied creative writing at Brown University and Columbia University, and began to publish short stories in 1983. These formed the basis of her first novel, *Monkeys* (1986), an immediate best-seller which dealt with the lives of a large Roman Catholic family in Boston, not unlike Minot's own. It was followed by the collection *Lust and Other Stories* (1989). Later novels have included *Folly* (1992), *Evening* (1998) and *Rapture* (2002). All her works are set in New England, and explore the precariousness of relationships, and the experience of women seeking for love.

You often hear stories of the incubating writer who never took her nose out of a book; you couldn't drag her out of the library. I wasn't like that. That burrowing came long after. I was not a particularly precocious reader, though I remember the power with which certain books struck me. *The Secret Garden*, by Frances Hodgson Burnett, read to me by my mother, was about a little girl discovering a walled-in garden where she makes a friend. It was like the experience of reading! One went into a hushed and private place, put oneself there and learned about other people. I didn't really like fairy tales—my mind was probably too much of a fairy already—but preferred stories of real life.

What went on out there in the world? As an 11-year-old I particularly liked biographies—Calamity Jane, Dorothea Dix, Geronimo, Helen Keller, Davey Crockett. It turned out there were more interesting men and women than one usually heard about in history class. Harriet the Spy left an indelible impression with her note-taking in her little book and her spying, both important qualities for a writer.

When I left home for boarding school I began to write on my own—prose poetry, journal writing. It was the first time I had a room of my own, and I found that writing was a way both of being alone and of finding out what was going on inside of my self. Instead of doing homework, I wrote pages of stream-of-consciousness long into the night.

The novelist Jim Harrison has said that he is suspicious of any budding writer who is not drunk with words. I was completely inebriated. I was compelled to write; it became a compulsion. I wrote out of desperation. In the great turmoil and gloom and euphoria of adolescence, I found there was nowhere to express the chaos of emotions I was feeling, nowhere but in words. I began to rely so much on writing that I was living a double life—one in the world and one on the page. The one on the page was more intense, more satisfying and for a long time much more real.

It was then that I was also beginning to be overwhelmed by the power of books. There was one moment I do remember when ambition entered into my feelings about writing. It was a spring day, and I was lying on the grass in front of the library in Concord, Mass., where I attended high school, reading William Faulkner's *The Sound and the Fury*. It was a book I had not been assigned but which had intrigued me when I heard some friends, boys from a nearby school, quote the line 'Caddy. She smelled like leaves.' Suddenly in the middle of a passage, the power of the words rose up and whacked me on the forehead. I felt the earth move as if a huge safe were being swiveled open and afterwards felt flushed and stunned as you are after sex. I'd had this reaction before—to other books, and to music and painting, but this time as I stared at the light-green blades of grass in front of me, vibrating, I was aware that it was the writer who had done something to me. And I thought, I'd like to do that to someone back.

When I started to publish stories and then books, in a strange way these events seemed like flukes, moments of luck or fortuity when my compulsion to write just happened to intersect with real activities in the world. Being a writer was never what drove me; writing did. In fact, though it's odd to say, I don't think of myself as a writer. I agree with Chekhov, who hated labels and said he wanted simply to be a free artist. 'Free artist'—now, that's a label I wouldn't mind.
[...]

I am very fortunate to make my living by writing, though I feel I got to this point through no more design than having followed an often bewildered instinct and by simply always writing. I believe that what an artist needs most, more than inspiration or financial consolation or encouragement or talent or love or luck, is endurance. Often the abstraction of using only words frustrates me—I write on paper with a dipped pen and ink, and type on a manual typewriter in order to have some three-dimensional activities with my hands—but again and again I discover how far words are capable of going, both in the world and on the page. The fact is, this side of the mind, nothing goes farther than words. With words I am able to do those things that first intrigued me when I was young, those things that made me feel most alive—I am able to paint pictures, collect things from muddy ponds, dissect insides, make things up, put on costumes, direct the lights, inspect hearts, entertain, dream. And, if it goes well, I might convey some of that vitality to others, and so give back a drop into that huge pool of what other artists have, as strangers, given me: reasons to live.

Source: Marie Arana (ed.) (2003) *The Writing Life: Writers on how they think and work*,
New York: Public Affairs, pp. 49–51.

6 from *Cider With Rosie*

LAURIE LEE

Laurie Lee (1914–1997), writer and poet, was brought up in rural Gloucestershire. He travelled in Europe from 1935 to 1939, and then worked in film. During the Second World War he was Publications Editor at the Ministry of Information. He published many collections of poetry, but his best-known book was, and remains, *Cider With Rosie* (1959), a lyrical and nostalgic description of a Gloucestershire childhood before the advent of cars, and modern farm and household equipment. It was followed by *As I Walked Out One Midsummer Morning* (1969), a memoir and travelogue describing his life in London and Spain in the 1930s.

I WAS set down from the carrier's cart at the age of three; and there with a sense of bewilderment and terror my life in the village began.

The June grass, amongst which I stood, was taller than I was, and I wept. I had never been so close to grass before. It towered above me and all around me, each blade tattooed with tiger-skins of sunlight. It was knife-edged, dark, and a wicked green, thick as a forest and alive with grasshoppers that chirped and chattered and leapt through the air like monkeys.

I was lost and didn't know where to move. A tropic heat oozed up from the ground, rank with sharp odours of roots and nettles. Snow-clouds of elder-blossom banked in the sky, showering upon me the fumes and flakes of their sweet and giddy suffocation. High overhead ran frenzied larks, screaming, as though the sky were tearing apart.

For the first time in my life I was out of the sight of humans. For the first time in my life I was alone in a world whose behaviour I could neither predict nor fathom: a world of birds that squealed, of plants that stank, of insects that sprang about without warning. I was lost and I did not expect to be found again. I put back my head and howled, and the sun hit me smartly on the face, like a bully.

From this daylight nightmare I was awakened, as from many another, by the appearance of my sisters. They came scrambling and calling up the steep rough bank, and parting the long grass found me. Faces of rose, familiar, living; huge shining faces hung up like shields between me and the sky; faces with grins and white teeth (some broken) to be conjured up like genii with a howl, brushing off terror with their broad scoldings and affection. They leaned over me one, two, three – their mouths smeared with red currants and their hands, dripping with juice.

'There, there, it's all right, don't you wail any more. Come down 'ome and we'll stuff you with currants.'

And Marjorie, the eldest, lifted me into her long brown hair, and ran me jogging down the path and through the steep rose-filled garden, and set me down on the cottage doorstep, which was our home, though I couldn't believe it.

That was the day we came to the village, in the summer of the last year of the First World War. To a cottage that stood in a half-acre of garden on a steep bank above a lake; a cottage with three floors and a cellar and a treasure in the walls, with a pump and apple trees, syringa and strawberries, rooks in the chimneys, frogs in the cellar, mushrooms on the ceiling, and all for three and sixpence a week.

I don't know where I lived before then. My life began on the carrier's cart which brought me up the long slow hills to the village, and dumped me in the high grass, and lost me. I had ridden wrapped up in a Union Jack to protect me from the sun, and when I rolled out of it, and stood piping loud among the buzzing jungle of that summer bank, then, I feel, was I born. And to all the rest of us, the whole family of eight, it was the beginning of a life.

Source: Laurie Lee (1962) *Cider With Rosie*, London: Penguin, pp. 9–10.

7 'Memory: The true key to real imagining'

LESLEY GLAISTER

Lesley Glaister (b. 1956), novelist, short-story writer and radio dramatist, was born in Northamptonshire and grew up in Suffolk. She took a degree with the Open University, and was 'discovered' as a writer when she attended a course at the Arvon Foundation in 1989. Her first novel, *Honour Thy Father* (1990), won both a Somerset Maugham Award and a Betty Trask Award. Other novels have included *Limestone and Clay* (1993), which won the *Yorkshire Post* Book Award, and, most recently, *As Far as You Can Go* (2004), a psychological drama about a young couple in a remote part of Australia. She teaches creative writing at Sheffield Hallam University.

I am on a beach. I don't know where – Southwold perhaps. I am very small and wearing a blue ruched swimming costume, which scratches the tops of my legs and fills with bubbles of water when I go in the sea. But I'm not in the sea. I'm sitting on a big striped towel, shivering. My dad is sitting beside me and I'm thinking how hairy his legs are, like gorilla's legs. Then I notice something: a hollow in the soft bulge of his calf, big enough to cup an egg in, not hairy like the rest but dull pinkish, fuzzy like newborn mouse skin. I want to put my finger inside and feel but I don't. Somehow I know I can't do that and I must not mention it. Then Dad gets up and hobbles down the shingle towards the sea. He breaks into a run when he gets to the flat bit before the sea begins. He plunges in and swims out and out and out. My mum is reading and my sister shovelling pebbles into a bucket. No one but me has noticed how his head gets smaller and smaller the further out he swims, until at last I can't see him between the waves. He has gone. But I don't shout or scream. I turn over and lie on my tummy on the towel, feeling my heart thudding against the lumpy pebbles. I have seen my daddy drown but I don't say a word. I lie there with the sea or my heart roaring in my ears.

I lie paralysed by fear and guilt for what seems hours until I hear the crunch of footsteps and feel the sprinkle of cold drops on my skin. Daddy is back and is standing above me waiting for me to get off the towel. He is fine, invigorated and oblivious to my terror, rubbing himself dry, slurping tea from the thermos.

That experience encapsulates for me a key moment of growing up: the sudden realization of my dad's vulnerability and his mortality – and by extension that of everyone including myself. An apparently insignificant moment when the bottom fell out of my safe child's world.

It wasn't until my father died, about twenty years later, that the seaside moment came back to me. Only then did it occur to me that the hollow in his leg was the scar of a tropical ulcer contracted during the war. He was one of the soldiers captured by the Japanese when Singapore was taken in 1941. He worked as a slave on the construction of the Burma/Siam railway, suffering cerebral malaria, cholera, dysentery, beatings, near starvation – an unimaginably traumatic time about which he never spoke. It was a deep area of silence. Not only was it never spoken of but there seemed an embargo even on wondering. It wasn't until years after his death that it even occurred to me why, as a naturally curious child, I never even *wondered*. About ten years after his death I became fascinated by the idea of that deeply layered silence – not unique to my family, I know – and began to plan the novel which became *Easy Peasy*. The seaside memory – only a tiny moment in the book – was the seminal one from which that novel grew, the true key to real imagining.

There are very few literally true moments like this in my own fiction, although naturally writers vary enormously in the way they process and utilize memory. Much of what I write feels as if it is made up – but that really means that it is memory refracted through imagination, often unconsciously, into something new. This might mean a scrap of a childhood memory is blended with something I heard yesterday and comes out as something unrecognizable as either. That, I think, is the real stuff of fiction – memory blended, refracted, transformed. That is why something that is apparently entirely imagined can have the real force of emotional truth.

For instance, my mild dislike of confined spaces was transformed into a potholing disaster in *Limestone and Clay*. And the queasy embarrassment I felt as a child at an accidental glimpse of my father's genitals (again on the beach!) dramatized into Jennifer's mortification at the spectacle of her naked grandparents in *Digging to Australia*. This latter was quite unconscious, indeed I didn't realize where it had stemmed from until years later.

And this unconscious salvaging is another and more fundamental way in which memory is employed in the making of fiction. Every impression ever made on a person from newborn babyhood onwards will contribute to the shape and texture of the imagination. And an individual's personality is largely shaped by early experience: unconditional love, disappointed hunger, rejection, displacement by a newborn sibling, star or scapegoat status within the family. These all affect the deep patterning of expectation, the rhythm of a unique world view. This affects the deep structure, the rhythm that becomes apparent within a piece of writing. This is why with many writers similar tropes recur, similar themes are visited and revisited. Whatever the actual consciously chosen subject – from true romance to sci-fi fantasy – that pattern or rhythm is very likely to recur.

The most exciting moment in the writing of a novel comes with the onset of the wonderful trance-like state when a book seems to begin to grow itself, seems there to be discovered rather than created. Some writers describe this as the moment when the characters take over. It seems that the writer has little choice but to let them have their way. It is thrilling and feels somehow *real*. That is because it is. It is simply the deep unconscious patterning rising up and taking over the conscious critical planning mind. The unconscious rhythm that dictates the shape of most deeply felt fiction that has its germ in the structure of the writer's personality; and which also bestows on each writer a unique and precious voice.

Would-be writers often object that they have no memories to draw on, or that nothing interesting ever happened to them. This is not possible. Memory can be hard to access, but it's a skill that can be learned. And it's not so much interesting things but unique ways of seeing ordinary things that makes the most original and satisfying fiction. Catching one little tail end of a memory and patiently teasing it out can be a way to start. And it doesn't matter if the memory is not complete, nor entirely true. Remember you are writing *fiction*. A little kick start from the memory can set off your imagination – and who knows where that might lead ...

Source: Julia Bell and Paul Magrs (eds) (2001) *The Creative Writing Coursebook*, London: Macmillan, pp. 75–8.

8 from *Backtalk: Women writers speak out*

PAT BARKER

Pat Barker (b. 1943), novelist, was born at Thornaby-on-Tees, near Middlesbrough, and was brought up by her mother and grandmother. Her first novel, *Union Street*, was published in 1982, and was awarded the Fawcett Society Book Prize. This, like a number of her subsequent novels, drew upon Barker's experience of life in the industrial north-east of England, describing how women, in particular, coped with hardship. In 1991 she embarked on a trilogy of novels set in the period of the First World War: *Regeneration* (1991), *The Eye in the Door* (1993), and *The Ghost Road* (1995), which won the 1995 Booker Prize. The trilogy draws upon the work of W. H. R. Rivers, a medical officer who treated shell-shocked soldiers, to explore the traumatic effects of the 'Great War'. Subsequent novels have included *Another World* (1998), *Border Crossing* (2001) and *Double Vision* (2003). Several of her novels have been adapted for the stage or the screen. In this extract Pat Barker is interviewed by the editor of *Backtalk*, Donna Perry.

Q: Before *Regeneration*, which seems thoroughly researched, did you do research for your novels?

A: No, I wrote about what I saw happening in depressed regions. We are becoming a much more deeply divided society. [...] There are people spending enormous amounts of money at Metrocenter, the largest shopping center in Europe, yet in Newcastle you see people queuing for day-old bread.

About research, I have never, ever gone out to try and meet someone who would be useful. I use women I know. I don't need to know an awful lot. I haven't been in a chicken factory, for example, but I have done bloody awful, monotonous jobs. In *Union Street* I wrote about something I had not done: working on an assembly line in a cake factory, where the women working the line can use the machine against one another by speeding the pace up.

Q: What is the relationship between your own life and these works?

A: It's probably different for the different books. I think the starting point is inevitably always something in your own life, just as the source of every single character you create has to be yourself. But quite often you are going off on a tangent—taking a fact in your own life and saying, 'What if? ...' and from that point you are going away from your own life at right angles, although the bedrock of the book was your own experience. For example, in *The Man Who Wasn't There* it's simply the sex of the child. What if you had been born into an all-female family as a boy rather than as a girl? Would you not have been debilitated by the same facets of your life which for a girl were sources of strength? Or perhaps you wouldn't be. Perhaps they would still be sources of strength. If a boy were raised by these women, to what extent could he take strength from them and to what extent would it be a threat?

Sometimes I've used a particular episode which actually occurred—like, for example, the hemorrhage in *The Century's Daughter* and *Union Street*. That's something that actually happened to me: I have had to pull clots of blood out of someone's throat. But, in each case, by giving it to a different person and making the relationship between the person watching and the person dying a different relationship, I've changed the significance of the episode. Basically, I'm not interested in writing autobiography in any way, shape, or form, although I think at the end of the day when you look at the books on the shelf they are—for every writer not just for me—the spiritual autobiography. And probably far more honest in their devious way than an actual autobiography would ever be, if you ever felt moved to write one.

Q: Is that painful birth certificate scene in *The Man Who Wasn't There* autobiographical?

A: That is very autobiographical. You could have a small birth certificate at a time when everyone had a large one. It meant either that you were adopted or illegitimate.

Q: Like Colin, were you the product of a wartime romance?

A: I never knew my father. He was in the RAF [Royal Air Force] where the death rate was very high.

Q: Besides Colin, whose life has parallels with your own, are any of your other characters like you?

A: Kath's [in *The Century's Daughter*] is the closest to my own experience, but even that is changed, mainly by leaving out a lot of things that happened. I was brought up by my grandmother and I had a whole string of great-aunts who used to get together and quarrel about things that happened when they were growing up in Victorian England.

Q: Were they storytellers?

A: They weren't telling stories so much as arguing about a past that was very much alive to them. They were always coming to blows about something that happened before the first world war, like was their father drunk or not the time he came home from the pub on a particular night and Mother said—no she didn't—this kind of thing. That was interesting for me growing up.

For *Regeneration* I had stories from my grandmother's second husband—who was my grandfather as far as I was concerned—about the first world war. He only told them towards the end of his life because they were so horrific that he didn't want to tell them before then.

Q: Can you give me an example of that kind of story?

A: I was thinking of the time that he was bayoneted. He had a bayonet wound in his side which I used to stick my finger into when I was a charming little girl [she laughs]. With his consent, of course. It was quite a horrific scar. He had been bayoneted and he was an officer's servant. And just as he was bayoneted, the officer got his revolver out and shot the German between the eyebrows, which meant that he didn't have the chance to twist the bayonet and pull it out, which is the bit that really does all the damage. So he survived, but he had to lie on the battlefield and he got flies all around and maggots in the wound. He lay on the floor of the hospital for hours and hours before he was treated.

Q: How did the wound form a hole?

A: Because he was a very thin young man and he became a very fat old man, the scar tissue didn't seem to grow out with him. The tragic thing was that when he was dying—I think it was of stomach cancer—the doctors, who were not very much into telling people the truth in those days, told him it was his bayonet wound that was killing him and he believed them. So he thought, 'Well, it's getting me in the end.'

[...]

Q: I notice that you have moved from writing about women in your first two books, to writing about an elderly woman and a male social worker in your third, to writing about a boy in your fourth and men in your fifth. Did you feel some pressure to create a male protagonist?

A: No, because I always knew I could. It's not a pressure. Fay Weldon says men are a different species. I don't feel that. I feel I could do either. I hope I will find a woman I want to write about. Some people may criticize me for deserting the cause, but I never thought for a second that feminism is only about women.

At the moment, I find more interesting what society does to men because I think I've gone as far along the road exploring what society does to women as I can. In a sense, you can't deal with one gender in isolation from the other. I'm more interested in looking at the pressures on men, which in wartime are specific and worse than those on women are, but not, I think, essentially different.

Q: Where did the idea for *Regeneration* come from?

A: Oh, several channels. I first read [Dr. William] Rivers's book, *Conflict and Dream*, when I was in my early twenties; I had read [poets] Wilfred Owen and Siegfried Sassoon in my teens. I had always wanted to write about Rivers and shell shock and about the first world war, too. That first thing I ever wrote was a terribly bad poem about the first world war when I was eleven. So the urge to write about it was there, but I wanted to wait until I could find a sufficiently original way of doing it because, obviously, it's one of the most overdone topics that has ever been. And it's been done brilliantly by people who were actually there.

Q: How did you find that angle?

A: Basically, by resolving not to write about the trenches themselves, but to put it on the home front. And to write about the treatment of shell shock, which has been done—Rebecca West did it—but I don't think it's one of her best books [*The Return of the Soldier*, 1918].

I would say that basically *Union Street* and *Regeneration* are both books about trauma and recovery. Everybody says, 'But those are upper-class men instead of working-class women,' but I think the feeling for the people involved is similar. I would say that Burns [in *Regeneration*], for example, is a similar character to Maggie in *Blow Your House Down*, the woman who is knocked on the head and has to sort out what she feels about it and behaves in a rather similar way to Burns, in fact. So I think the theme of trauma and recovery comes from my own background.

Q: Have people recognized the feminist perspective in *Regeneration*?

A: A lot of rather simple-minded people think that if you stop writing about women you have given up being a feminist. I must say that here in Britain men have tended to see this feminist perspective [in the novel] rather more than women.

I think the analysis of men's dependency and their lack of autonomy in that war, a study of why they suffered from hysterical symptoms rather than paranoia is a feminist analysis. But it's not any kind of feminist tract. And above all I'm not saying, as one woman suggested, that being a housewife in suburbia equals being a man in the front line. Anyone who believes that is so sunk in self-pity that there is no hope for them at all.

Q: How much is your portrait of Rivers like the real-life man?

A: He's as like as I could make him, which is a very enigmatic, a very mysterious sort of man. He's not easy to research. I think he is very like the real-life person.

Q: What about the historical basis for the other characters? We know about Owen and Sassoon, but what about the others?

A: They are all basically based on Rivers's case histories, with [the character] Prior very slightly based on Rivers. I needed Prior to bring out certain facets of Rivers's character that I couldn't bring out through Sassoon or any of the others. I needed someone basically to be fairly antagonistic to Rivers. Burns, the man who got his head stuck in a corpse and had all those terrible experiences, is very closely based on an actual case history. The young man who is treated by [Dr. Lewis] Yealland with electrodes is also entirely drawn from an actual case. The patient is hardly an individuated personality, but his problems and his method of treatment are entirely what happened.

Q: Was Yealland really this awful, treating enlisted men with shock therapy?

A: Yes, he was incredible. This very wooden dialogue is what he represents himself as having said. And he is clearly proud of having said it. [See his *Hysterical Disorders of Warfare*, 1918.]

Q: Rivers, treating officers, is compassionate; Yealland, treating enlisted men, is cruel. Which approach was more typical?

A: Neither Yealland nor Rivers was really typical, but the balance, at least for the [enlisted] men, was tilted more towards Yealland than Rivers. It was certainly tough treatment. As you say, officers and men were treated differently.

Q: What was the treatment for women suffering mental breakdowns at the time?

A: I think the treatment for female hysterics could be rough, but I don't think it was ever as rough as that. It could be quite hostile, but then I think psychiatrists tend to be hostile towards hysterics even today. I think hysterics are totally infuriating people, and they are manipulative.

Q: Well, it's about power and control, isn't it?

A: Yes, and it's about somebody who is evading responsibilities, and it's very hard for some people to go on being sympathetic. I think what made the treatment of the male hysteric during wartime so hostile was precisely that it was thought of as a female way of responding to stress, so the feeling was that he wasn't just shirking or being cowardly: He was also being effeminate. And this made them [the psychiatrists] very, very anxious. In the things Yealland says, he shows this: 'You must behave like the hero I expect you to be.' There is no shilly-shallying about it. You have to get back into line, and you will be prodded back by electrodes if you don't do it.

Q: Rivers has a theory that the men who were most like women were the ones in the observation balloons, who floated passively over the battlefields doing reconnaissance.

A: Yes, and in the observer's seat in the plane.

Q: That seems to be a remarkable insight into the reality of women's lives at the time.

A: He was asking the question, 'Why is hysteria so common in women in peacetime and so relatively uncommon in men?' The first answer he gave was that, in fact, women in peacetime have actually far more reason to be frightened than men. He was thinking about sexual assault, but he was also in that time thinking about the dangers of childbirth—that women just had reasons for being scared that men didn't have. They were helpless—just floating along till whatever might happen did, feeling that they couldn't control it.

But then he also got to the idea of women's lives being more passive and more circumscribed [than men's] and the paradox that when you sent men to the front thinking they were going off to do this great big, masculine, hairy-chested thing—no, they were actually going to sit in a hole and do as they were told and wait to be killed. It's total passivity. Far worse passivity than the majority of women would ever experience. And yet if you crack down under this total feminine passivity, you're told you're unmanly [she laughs]. So there's no way they can win.

Q: Prior introduces the class issue—he's a fish out of water because he comes from the working class and he is an officer.

A: There was a category of men in the first world war who were like that. Because the demand for officers was so great, the social qualifications for being an officer were relaxed. These people were known as not just temporary officers, but 'temporary gentlemen' was the phrase at the time. And they were held with great scorn, though with less scorn in the front line than behind the scenes.

Q: Rivers says at one point that he thinks that enlisted men don't have as complex a mental life as officers.

A: Yes, he did think that.

Q: So Rivers is a snob?

A: Yes.

Q: Is he less of a snob at the end?

A: Well, he is slightly less a product of his time by the end, but I think the class culture permeated everything in that time and nobody could hope to be free of it. You could tell whether somebody was a lady or gentleman simply by looking at them. It was as obvious then as race is obvious today. And it is true that the men presented different symptoms on the whole. It was the [enlisted] men who presented the mutism and paralysis and deafness, and the officers didn't present that. So, in a sense, it wasn't just that they were being treated differently; it is that they were responding to the intolerable situation in different ways. And this, too, has its modern parallels, where unskilled, unemployed people don't go to the doctor saying, 'I'm thoroughly depressed because society doesn't seem to have any use for me.' They go and say, 'My back aches,' or 'I've got headaches,' or 'I can't sleep.' Anything. It's acted out rather than verbalized.

And if you are into psychotherapy, of course, the patient who can verbalize in the way that is required by the treatment is a patient you can relate to. The patient who is just lying there saying, 'I cannot walk,' is that much more difficult to deal with.

Q: So it is significant that early on Prior isn't talking?

A: Yes, that's the point that Rivers makes and then Prior turns it on him and says, 'Well, if mutism is because you daren't say what you have to say, perhaps a lifelong stammer like yours is because there is something you daren't say that you want to say.' Prior makes the book, I think. It would be too bland without Prior.

Q: Silencing is central in the book, as it was in your earlier ones. I'm struck by Rivers's dream where he imagines that he is putting the bit on the patient, just as slaves were given the bit at an earlier time.

A: Yes, and the book actually ends, in a sense, with the silencing of Rivers. He comes to write the final word for now on Sassoon, and he says there is nothing more he wanted to say that he could say. So, in the end, Rivers is silenced, too.

Q: What other silencing is there in the book?

A: Oh, a tremendous amount. There's the mutism of Prior and Callan. When Prior is goading Rivers about his lifelong stammer being a result of his having been silenced, that is meant to be taken seriously, not just to be one of Prior's gibes. And the people, I think, who are not silenced, exactly, but not listened to very much, are the women in the factory. Somebody pointed out to me that what I had done was to establish two groups who find these men totally, outrageously laughable—one are the women in the factory and the other are the people [Solomon Islanders] on board the *Southern Cross*, who turn the tables on Rivers and laugh at the life of an Edwardian don and think that it is the most amazing, bizarre thing that ever was, too hilarious for anything.

Q: As a psychiatrist at that time, Rivers is supposed to 'cure' people who are homosexual. Why doesn't he do that with Sassoon?

A: [A pause.] I think, you see, that Rivers is homosexual, too. I think that he is in love with Sassoon. One of the things that can't be said, in fact, is the depth of the feeling he obviously has for Sassoon. Whether he even says it to himself I don't know. There is one time when Sassoon is talking about Owen's feelings for him and these amazing letters that Owen wrote to him. Sassoon thinks that Owen was in love with him and he hopes that he was kind enough, and Rivers simply says, 'It happens.' That is Rivers with everything hanging out.

Source: Donna Perry (ed.) (1993) *Backtalk: Women writers speak out*, New Brunswick, New Jersey: Rutgers University Press, pp. 45–7, 51–6.

PART 2

Writing fiction

9 from *Cal*

BERNARD MACLAVERTY

Bernard MacLaverty (b. 1942), novelist and short-story writer, was born in Belfast, Northern Ireland. He worked for ten years as a medical laboratory technician, and then went to Queen's University, Belfast, to study English. He is the author of four widely praised novels, *Lamb* (1980), *Cal* (1983), *Grace Notes* (1997), and *The Anatomy School* (2001), and four collections of short stories, *Secrets* (1977), *A Time to Dance* (1982), *The Great Profundo* (1987) and *Walking the Dog* (1994). Among his themes is the difficulty of remaining neutral in situations where communities are locked in violent opposition. He now lives in Glasgow.

Feeling clean on the outside, with his hair held back in a tail by an elastic band, Cal drove the van to Crilly's place. Crilly himself came to the door chewing and put him in the front room, switching on one bar of the electric fire. He said he would be with him in a minute. Cal sat slumped in an armchair, looking round him. The muted waves of unreal laughter from some show on the television rose and fell in the next room. There was a picture on the wall of a ragged child with one glistening tear-drop standing on his dirty cheek. Beside it was a plaque of wood and burned into it with a needle were the words MADE IN LONG KESH CONCENTRATION CAMP. It had a badly drawn clenched fist surrounded by barbed wire and the words IRELAND UNFREE SHALL NEVER BE AT PEACE.

There was a brass picture hammered out in some way so that the words and the figure were raised up from its surface. The figure was of an old woman sitting sideways wearing a bonnet and beneath her was a poem called 'A Mother'. It told of all the good things a mother ever did and ended with the line 'The only bad thing she ever does is to die and leave you'. Cal thought of Crilly's mother with her sagging breasts and her tight pink jumper the colour of her gums. He thought of his own mother and had to turn away and look at something else. He saw himself in a mirror above the fireplace. The edges of the mirror were laced with red and yellow roses. He turned his lip up in a sneer.

Crilly came in with a cup of tea and a slice of bread and jam. He sat down opposite Cal, folded the bread over and bit a half moon out of it. There were ticks of jam at the corners of his mouth. His voice was muffled with bread.

'Well?' he said.

'Well what?'

'Are you ready for tonight?'

'What are we doing?'

'You're driving, that's what. An off-licence in Magherafelt.'

'Guns?'

'Protection.'

Crilly finished his bread and jam and threw the hard crust into the empty fire-grate.

'Don't worry, Cal. It'll be easy.'

'What about a car?'

'I think I've that arranged. You like the Cortinas?'

Cal nodded.

'But there's no need to rush. The later we leave it the more takings there'll be.'

The door opened and Crilly's mother put her head in. There was something different about her.

'You never asked Cal if he wanted any tea,' she said to her son.

'No thanks, I'm just after some,' said Cal.

Mrs Crilly came right into the room and did a twirl in the middle of the floor, holding out her dress like a model.

'Do you like my new teeth?' she said. Then she smiled as if she was biting through steel. Cal said he thought they were lovely while her son sat and rolled his eyes to the ceiling.

At nine o'clock Crilly and Cal went out. Cal drove the van to an address at the other end of town. He stood with his back to the pebble-dash wall to one side of the door while Crilly rang the bell.

'Is your Dad in?'

Crilly turned and winked at Cal. A man's voice said,

'Oh, it's you, *a chara*.'

There was a jingle of keys and Cal saw a hand pass them out.

'Remember you didn't notice it gone until after eleven.'

'O.K.'

'If you do I'll break your legs, and if I don't somebody else will.'

The man laughed and Crilly smiled at him.

When the door was shut Cal moved down the path and got into the van. Crilly led in the white Cortina. Just outside Magherafelt Crilly indicated and turned off the road into a forestry plantation. The trees were black in the red brake lights. Crilly got out and began counting trees, then dodged in between the saplings. Leaning against the white car, Cal lit a cigarette. He held it between his lips as he pulled on a pair of thin leather gloves. His hands were shaking. He could hear the sound of Crilly thrashing and crackling about among the trees. Then he came out with a parcel. Cal slid behind the steering wheel of the Cortina and Crilly got in the other side.

'One for you and one for me,' he said.

'I don't want one,' said Cal. 'I'm driving.'

Crilly loaded his gun by the light coming from the open glove compartment. Cal pushed his aching back into the upholstery and adjusted his seat to suit his leg length.

'Do you wear stilts when you're driving?' he asked.

'I'll load yours just in case.'

'I'd only shoot myself.'

Crilly was wearing stylish driving gloves with holes in the backs of them. Cal wheeled the car round, the headlights probing deep into the dry brown forest floor. On the road there was no talk between them but Crilly hummed and clicked his tongue. Cal felt like screaming at him to stop it. He tried the car out for speed and handling and it responded well. As they drove towards Magherafelt he said,

'For Christ's sake, Crilly, don't use that thing.'

'It persuades people to hurry up.'

To get to the off-licence they did not need to pass through the security gates which blocked off the town centre. Cal parked on the opposite side of the road and they sat watching. A customer came out carrying a polythene bag in both arms. They could not tell whether the shop was empty or not because of its frosted-glass door.

'Do you know what it's like inside?' Cal asked.

'I've been in twice this week.'

Cal indicated and moved across the road, double parking directly in front of the shop. Crilly put on a pair of sunglasses and got out.

'Keep that engine running,' he said.

Cal turned up the collar of his coat. Crilly stood on tiptoe, looking over the dulled and lettered half of the door. Cal saw him flip up the hood of his anorak and pull his scarf over his mouth. He pushed the door open with his foot and stepped in. The door swung shut after him on its spring but in the instant that it was open, as if it was the shutter of a camera, Cal saw two women customers look up in fright. The door stayed shut and Cal began to count. Fourteen, fifteen, sixteen. He knew that to count accurate seconds he should say one thousand and seventeen, one thousand and eighteen. A man came round the corner and began walking towards the car. Was it the law? No double parking allowed here, sir. But the man had a dog on a lead. It kept stopping and sniffing at the bottoms of walls. After each bout of sniffing it lifted its hind leg and peed over the leavings of some other dog. One thousand and forty, forty-one, forty-two. He looked down at the tray beside the gear stick and to his horror saw that the pistol Crilly had left him was nakedly visible in the street lights. He covered it with a dirty cloth from the glove compartment. The man was now almost level with the car. Cal turned his head away, pretending to look for something in the back seat. Where the fuck was Crilly? Was he choosing a wine? The man stopped patiently for his dog again then moved off into the pool of the next street light. Cal rolled the window down to see if he could hear anything. A record on a jukebox played faintly farther along the street. Cal watched the door, trying not to blink, until his eyes felt dry. Where was the big bastard? Was it a thousand and ninety? He gave up the idea of counting. Crilly had been in there two or three minutes. Then suddenly the door sprang open and in its shutter-instant Cal saw the two women lying face down on the floor. He stuck the car in first and revved. Crilly, carrying a Harp polythene bag, thumped his shins and cursed getting between the two cars at the kerb. He jumped into the passenger seat. The gun was still in his hand. They were moving before he had time to shut the door.

'What kept you?' shouted Cal.

'I was like lightning.'

'What did you do to those women?'

'I told them to lie on the floor.'

'Jesus, I thought you'd killed them.'

Trying not to draw attention by squealing the tyres, Cal drove as fast as he could round the corner and out into the main road.

'It was easy – a cinch,' said Crilly. 'They were shaking in their fuckin high-heel shoes. Couldn't get the money into the bag quick enough.' He was laughing, but Cal put it down to nerves. He leaned forward and noticed the waft of nervous sweat – like onions – from beneath his own coat. He heard Crilly click the legs of his sunglasses shut and put them in his pocket.

'Sink the boot, Cal boy.'

But Cal already had his boot to the floor.

They dumped the car at the forestry plantation and got into the van.

'Are you sure you have everything?' said Cal. He turned the key in the starter. 'Oh Jesus, the other gun.' He leapt out and took the pistol from beneath the dirty rag and handed it through the window to Crilly. They drove off at speed as Crilly rewrapped the guns.

'We'll drop them at the manor house,' he said.

'The sooner the better,' said Cal.

An estate wall ran for some five or six miles along the right-hand side of the road. At several points it had become dilapidated and fallen down. Cal stopped when told at the first gap beyond the small bridge where they had turned off the main road. Crilly looked around and, seeing no headlights, left the van with his parcel. He returned almost immediately, staggering and laughing.

'What's up with you?' said Cal.

'I'm just remembering.'

'What?'

'The woman behind the counter. At first she refuses and I points the gun at her. Then she says, "Who's it for anyway?" As if it made any difference which side was robbing her.'

'You should have told her it was in aid of the Black Babies,' said Cal.

Crilly was still laughing quietly as they neared home, then Cal heard him scuffling in the Harp bag. He turned on the overhead light and sorted through the bundle of notes. Cal objected that he couldn't see to drive. Crilly switched the light out and put some of the money in his pocket.

'Do you want any fag money?' he asked. Cal said he didn't but Crilly threw some notes on his lap.

'You deserve it,' said Crilly. 'The Cause can afford it.'

He told Crilly that it didn't feel right, but when he stopped the van outside Skeffington's house he felt between his legs and put the money in his pocket.

'Are the pubs still open?' Crilly looked at his watch and nodded. 'Hurry up then.'

Skeffington lived in a big house with a gravelled driveway and as Crilly crunched his way up to the front door there was a frantic barking

from inside. The door opened a slit. Cal saw Crilly hand over the Harp
bag then turn and wave to the van. He cursed and got out.

'Cahal, *a chara*, come in,' come in,' called Skeffington.

'We were just off to the pub.'

'Sure, I'll give you a drink here.'

Crilly seemed to have gone dumb. Skeffington held an Alsatian by
its collar and motioned them in. Cal hesitated but then followed Crilly.
The house was luxurious, full of gilt mirrors and flock wallpaper.

'Besides, I'd like you to meet my father,' said Skeffington.

The Alsatian was snuffing at the crotch of Cal's jeans. Skeffington
smacked its nose, showed them into a room and led the dog away.

'Why didn't you tell him we were going to the pub?' said Cal.

'I didn't like to.'

'Arse-licker.'

They stood awkwardly in the centre of the room, uneasy about
sitting in the white armchairs. The door opened and old Skeffington
came in, followed by his son.

'This is my father, Cal. The man I've told you so much about.'

They were all introduced. He was small and bald, but the image of
his son. He even had the same facial tic, wrinkling his nose to adjust his
glasses. He wore a tweed sports jacket that looked too big for him and
Cal could see that the waistband of his trousers was as high as his
nipples. The old man nodded during the introductions but said nothing.

Finbar insisted that they all sit down and busied himself getting the
drinks. The old man seemed to disappear when he sat in the chair. His
son talked incessantly.

'Daddy was just telling me a great story before you came in.' Old
Skeffington nodded and smiled faintly. 'About going through the
barriers today. The transistor has been fading recently. Whiskey, Cal?
Some water? And Daddy was down getting some batteries. He got them
outside the security gates in Hanna's, and had to go on into town. What
about yourself, Daddy?' His father indicated with an almost closed finger
and thumb how much whiskey he wanted. 'And this young Brit frisked
him. He says, "What are those?" about the lumps in Daddy's pockets
and Daddy says, "Batteries," and, says your man, "Very good. On you
go."'

Because he was a Pioneer and used to orange squash, Finbar poured
very large whiskeys. They were in Waterford crystal tumblers. He
handed the drinks around and poured himself a tonic. Cal was still
waiting for the punchline of the story. 'You could have a bomb up your

coat and provided you declared it, I think they'd let you through. I'm a teacher, Cal, and I know that in England it is no different. It's all the boys at the runt-end of the school who are going to end up in the Army. The idiots, the psychopaths – the one class of people who *shouldn't* be given a gun.' Finbar sat down on the arm of the sofa with his drink. 'Daddy can spin a great yarn when he gets going.'

The old man smiled and sipped his drink.

'Do you remember the story, Daddy, of Dev in O'Connell Street?' His father nodded again. There was a long silence. 'Or the one about Patsy Gribben?' His father nodded yet again. Finbar turned to the other two. 'Patsy Gribben was this old boy who used to hang around my father's shop. Every day he'd be in betting. But the drink was his real problem. And then one day you decided to trust him, isn't that the way of it, Daddy?' His father agreed that that was the way of it. 'So you gave him – wasn't it a thousand pounds – to put in the bank. Well, Patsy Gribben didn't come back that day. Not surprisingly. This will make you laugh, Cal. He was picked up off the Embankment in Belfast, totally and utterly drunk. And do you know this, the police recovered nine hundred and ninety-seven pounds from his pocket. Poor Patsy.'

Old Skeffington finished his drink and smiled. He began to extricate himself from the chair. Finbar put one hand under his armpit to help him up. His father whispered something to him and then waved goodnight to Cal and Crilly. His son led him out, holding lightly on to his elbow.

'The wit is off to his pit,' said Cal.

'What?' Crilly leaned forward but Skeffington returned almost immediately. Cal looked at the clock and saw that the pubs had closed ten minutes ago.

'He says he's a bit tired tonight,' said Skeffington. 'But hasn't he such a wonderful fund of stories.'

The other two laughed politely. Skeffington slid down on to the seat of the sofa and asked,

'How much was there?' Cal shrugged. Crilly said that he hadn't counted it.

'Let's do that now then.'

Skeffington poured the contents of the bag on to the table and the others helped him sort the notes into piles. During the silence of counting Cal felt it on the tip of his tongue to say that he had got himself a job but he knew that the next question would be 'Where?' and he did not want to tell them. If Crilly knew that Cal was hanging around

Morton's farm he might want to break his legs – not only want to but might well do it. Skeffington might want to do worse. When they had finished counting there was seven hundred and twenty-two pounds. Skeffington congratulated them.

'I think, unofficially, we should slip a few quid of this to Gerry Burns's wife. He has four kids and things must be difficult.'

'What about Peter Fitzsimmons?' asked Crilly.

'His wife works.'

'Fair's fair.'

'O.K., let me think about it.' Skeffington stacked the different denominations of notes one on top of the other and folded them neatly into the bag. 'Well, Cahal, do you feel any better after tonight?'

'No.'

'Do you still want to – refuse to help?'

'I'm afraid so.'

'Not to act – you know – *is* to act.' Crilly looked confused. 'By not doing anything you are helping to keep the Brits here.'

Crilly nodded his head vigorously and said,

'If you're not part of the solution, you're part of the problem.'

'But it all seems so pointless,' said Cal.

Skeffington paused and looked at him. He spoke distinctly, as if addressing one of his primary classes.

'It's like sitting in a chair that squeaks. Eventually they will become so annoyed they'll get up and sit somewhere else.'

'How can you compare blowing somebody's brains out to a squeaking chair?' said Cal.

Skeffington shrugged his shoulders. 'That's the way it will look in a hundred years' time.'

'You have no feelings.'

'How dare you? How presumptuous of you, Cahal. You have no idea what feelings I have.' His voice calmed and he asked, 'Do you know Pearse's poem "Mother"?' Both the young men shook their heads. Skeffington began to recite,

'I do not grudge them: Lord, I do not grudge
My two strong sons that I have seen go out
To break their strength and die, they and a few,
In bloody protest for a glorious thing ...

'That poem ends, Cahal,

'And yet I have my joy:
My sons were faithful and they fought.

'Unlike you, Cahal.' [...]

Source: Bernard MacLaverty (1983) *Cal*, London: Jonathan Cape, pp. 64–73.

10 from *Biggest Elvis*

P. F. KLUGE

P[aul] F[rederick] Kluge (b. 1942), novelist, was born in New Jersey. He was a Peace Corps volunteer in the 1960s, and then worked as a reporter for the *Wall Street Journal* and as associate editor for *Life* magazine. He is the author of five novels, the earliest being *The Day that I Die* (1976), and the most recent *Biggest Elvis* (1996), his most successful book to date. His subjects encompass rock and roll and the experience of immigrants in America. He teaches at Kenyon College in Ohio, where he is writer in residence.

You should have seen us when we had our act together, top of our game, toast of the town, walking and talking miracles and—you'd better believe it—the real American thing. We were realer than real, if you ask me, more real than the Original because there were nights back then it felt like he couldn't have opened for us, couldn't have come close to us, not on the best night he ever had, not when you compared it to the nights we were having. I know it sounds crazy but I've got to say it. We went way beyond him. We crossed borders he never traveled, lived in a time he never saw, played in places he couldn't picture.

My name is Ward Wiggins and, though I'm not in that line of work anymore, I used to be an Elvis Presley imitator, one third of a trio of Presleys who played overseas for a while, 1990–1991. If you stayed home, you never saw us and you never will. Our time onstage is over now. There were three of us: the young Elvis, the middle Elvis, and the terminal Elvis, three ages of man, three lives in one, and also, I now realize, three versions of America, as it went out into the world. The youthful romantic, the jaded movie star, and the fat, doomed Las Vegas headliner. That last Elvis, that was me.

We showed up in a lot of places: Okinawa, Japan, Korea, Hong Kong and Macau, Guam and Saipan, all through the Philippines, down

to Singapore, Malaysia, Brunei, Sri Lanka. That was our territory, the
Pacific Rim. We played the military bases. That's where we started. We
entertained more troops than Bob Hope and ours were paying
customers, drunk and horny, not some captive audience grinning up at
television cameras. We played inside the gate, at officers' clubs and
baseball fields, and outside, at some of the roughest venues on the
planet. We played hotel resorts and convention centers, we opened
casinos, gambling ships, soccer fields, and cockpits, we pounded it out to
soldiers and sailors, high rollers and refugees, hookers and nuns, oh yes,
we did it all and we did it all over the place, but if I have to go back to
just one night, there's no escaping Olongapo, the Philippines city that
lived off the big naval base at Subic Bay. Used to live, I should say. The
base is gone now and the Americans have left, those twenty thousand
sailors who came romping into town, when the fleet was in. The party's
over, for better and for worse. But, in its time, it was something to see.
A kind of high watermark for America, our power, our party, our
mighty good times. The Americans went back where they came from
and it's just as well, I think. But I wouldn't have missed it for the world.

I can close my eyes this minute and still smell Olongapo, that mix of
spilled beer and barbecued meat, of talcum and cologne venting out of
barbershop air conditioners, diesel fuel belching out of jeepneys and
taxis, and underneath it all, that blend of shit and urine that the hardest
rain couldn't wash away, all of this in that hot, heavy Philippines air,
fecund, fog-thick stuff that invited you to drink and fornicate and sweat
and rot. I can smell it, all of it, and I can miss it too, right now, that and
the noises, the sidewalk hustlers, shoeshine boys, sellers of lottery
tickets, satay sticks, newspapers, *anything you want Joe*, and the shills
outside of nightclubs, *what you want, baby we got it*, country western,
hard rock, mud wrestling, foxy boxing, full-body massage, *what you
need, baby we got it*, money for honey, honey for money, quick pop, one-
night stand, local wife or partner for life, and the sounds that surged out
onto the street and into the traffic, horns, mufflers, and all, the music
from a dozen different nightclubs, each one a tributary spilling into that
great river of noise, sounds from Detroit and Nashville, New York and
Chicago, music from every time and everywhere.

Daytime, Olongapo was nothing to look at: tin roofs and rotting
wood, metal that rusted and concrete that grew moldy the day after it
got poured. Nothing stayed new in Olongapo and nobody stayed young.
It was crowded streets and poor, much-pissed-upon trees and if you
looked down at the river that separated the town from the base, it was

all gray and bubbly and fermented, a black hole of oxygen debt, like someone popped the lid on a septic tank. Beyond, the bay curved off into the distance, toward those brown, dead Zambales mountains, forests long gone, like the hair that falls out of a cancer patient's head once they start the chemo. Daytime in Olongapo was like a movie theater between shows, spilled popcorn, sticky floors, bad lighting. But at night, it made Manila look like a one-pump town, and especially those nights when the fleet was in and the town opened itself to those thousands of American kids, guilty, guilty, guilty of everything you charged them with and yet—you only had to look at them, six years out of Little League—they were innocent too, clueless and young, the best and worst of all of us, let loose in the greatest liberty port on the planet, paid and primped for Saturday night, stepping across that bridge and into Magsaysay Street, striding past the T-shirt shops—AS LONG AS I'VE GOT A FACE, BABY YOU'VE GOT A SEAT—the phosphorescent jackets with flags and logos and ports of call from Pusan to Diego Garcia; barbershops offering shampoo, haircut, manicure, pedicure, shave, facial, ear-cleaning, shoeshine, and in-chair massage; souvenir shops with whole flocks of carved, screaming eagles, herds of carabao, six-foot salad forks, women with bimbo bodies, men with porn-film hard-ons, all made out of the rarest rain forest hardwoods. Out they'd come into a town that wasn't America and it wasn't the Philippines but some gorgeous hybrid, some scabrous, misbegotten mongrel, anyway just one of a kind, dream and nightmare, and though there are moments when I look back in shame, I'd be a liar if I said I didn't miss it. It was our town. Our world. The burned-off mountains. The bay which swallowed fleets and a town which swallowed the men who came off the ships. Babylon and Fort Lauderdale. Sodom and Camelot. And now, show time! Show time at the ramshackle, pink-and-white-painted one-time movie theater that was known as Graceland.

Chester Lane went out first. He had the hardest job of all, or he would have if he weren't such a natural, if it weren't so effortless for him. It's not easy, stepping out in front of a house that's half hookers, half sailors. The girls had seen the show dozens of times, the sailors acted like they had. The girls were hustling drinks—those 300-peso margaritas that were tea and food coloring, you could drink a bucketful and never feel it—and the guys were noisily checking out women and walloping down San Miguel beers. This wasn't Carnegie Hall, these people weren't there to read the libretto by pocket flashlight and suck sour lemon balls, waiting for the fat lady to sing. You didn't get respect automatically, not in this town. The Original Elvis had been gone awhile now. He belonged to these kids' parents. Add to that the scattering of soul brothers in the house and you get an idea of what Chester was up against, stepping out in front of a bunch of people who figured our act was a joke, a clown show for used car lots. Or so they thought till Chester Lane knocked the shit right out of them.

Of the three of us, he least resembled the Original. But, with Chester, the look-alike question somehow never arose. He didn't imitate, he embodied, jump-sliding across the stage, jump-starting the evening, baggy pink slacks with black stitching, jacket to match, hair piled high. He could have been Ritchie Valens or Buddy Holly or—hell—Otis Redding, it wouldn't matter. Puck or Till Eulenspiegel. After five seconds, the crowd's show-me attitude was gone, replaced by openmouthed wonder. Before he finished 'Blue Suede Shoes' they'd gone from I-can't-believe-I'm-here to I-can't-believe-what-I'm-seeing. Chester walked onstage and Elvis lived, the drop-dead good-looking punk angel truck driver from Tupelo, the swivel-hipped whippersnapper working his way through the up-tempo early stuff, 'Tutti Frutti,' 'Hound Dog,' 'All Shook Up,' 'Ready Teddy.' Chester had all the early moves, the legs-spread backward lean, the one-foot swivel, the pumping hips, the fall-forward faint, the down-on-his-knees croon, even the sweat drops coming off the end of his chin, as if it were blood and tears, not perspiration.

Chester Lane did something I never talked to him about. If we'd discussed it, if he'd started thinking, it would have been gone. If I told Chester Lane to combine macho bravado with an air of youthful vulnerability—well, he'd be a lost ball in tall grass. But that's what he accomplished. You could see it when he shifted into a slow tune near the end of his act, 'Loving You' or 'True Love' or even 'Old Shep': out came that hurt boyish side of Elvis, the poet-in-spite-of-himself, the embarrassed romantic. 'From hard-on to heartbroken': that's how Albert Lane described Chester's act. That was Albert's way of talking.

Albert—'Dude'—came out next. He did the middle years, the movie years, the blandest patch in the Original's life, when he cranked out thirty mediocre movies while music passed him by. The rot was already there, the self-destructive games, the fawning entourage, the mother-love and self-loathing. Chester's Elvis was familiar and likable. Albert's Elvis made you uncomfortable. There was a sense of danger, of things getting out of hand. Maybe this was where the audience sensed that the life being enacted in front of them wasn't a happy one. Sure, it was Saturday night in the fun-town of Olongapo and, before long, everybody could get drunk and laid. But what unfolded in front of them was close to tragedy. They weren't counting on tragedy, on loss and death, not with all this fine stuff in easy affordable reach, not here of all places. But tragedy was what they got at Graceland. With music, beer, and girls.

Albert began with the movie stuff, even some of the novelty songs, and at first he came off as a bozo, a genial loafer, leering at starlets and laughing all the way to the bank. But then he did this slow, menacing version of 'Devil in Disguise.' You could just see the anger and cynicism take over, his shit-eating movie star grin turning into a snarl. Then Albert dashed off-stage, shed his aloha shirt, and came back as the Elvis of the famous 1968 comeback special, black leather jeans and jacket, reprising early hits with new energy, so that they sounded like different songs. Chester's 'Jailhouse Rock' was detention hall fun-and-games. Albert cut into 'Jailhouse Rock' and it was maximum security, three-time losers, throw-away-the-key. And 'Love Me Tender'! What Albert did with a microphone during that song would get him arrested in some states: the gasps, the groans, the timely stroking, the slow stride off of chairs in dark corners of the lounge. Albert's 'Love Me Tender' was good for business.

Now, me. My Presley, the final incarnation, bloated and sequined, spaced-out and psychic, druggy and delusional. I was the Presley people remembered. Chester's Elvis was a face on a postage stamp. Albert's Elvis came to you in faded Technicolor, film turning magenta with age. But my Elvis was the one they buried and mourned, the guy they still glimpsed from time to time at convenience stores around America. The demands placed on my third of the act were—well—heavier.

In the matter of appearances, I did not disappoint. At six-foot-one-inch and two hundred forty pounds, I had height and bulk. In my college-teaching years, smoking a pipe, wearing an oxford shirt, a corduroy jacket, jeans, and loafers, I was just another out-of-shape academic, sedentary and slack. Ah, but add those glaring sideburns, that hair all oiled and piled. Cast off those elbow patches and force-feed the whole package into a pair of white linen tights. Yes! And circle my belly with a bejeweled belt that might have been borrowed from the World Wrestling Federation. Then give me a shirt that billowed at the sleeves, a collar that peaked in back of my neck, and generous lapels that opened, like French doors, on my sweating, hair-matted chest. Yes! And then sprinkle me with sequins and with stardust and Elvis lived!

In truth, the Original wasn't so hard to imitate. Elvis was a common American type—possibly the most common—the gone-to-seed athlete, the aging hick, yesterday's wild youth, running to fat and trailing memories of some earlier, leaner, dreaming self. Those earlier selves intrigued me. I was the last stop in the transit from punk to hunk to hulk. An aura of imminent death surrounded me when I walked onstage, as if death were waiting in the wings and, on any given night, if it all came together—maybe when I reached down for those low notes in 'Suspicious Minds'—I might offer that final gift which the Original failed to deliver: public expiration. But it was more than the sense of death around the corner. In truth, I was the survivor. I was the last to die, because Chester and Albert had already passed on, only nobody noticed, because there was another Elvis coming along, a newer model. What that meant, unless I'd screwed this up entirely, was that their lives converged in me, they lived on in me. I contained them. I tried explaining this to the Lane brothers one time.

'You ... *contain* us?' Albert asked. Albert was the smart lazy student in back of the classroom, the guy with the baseball cap turned backward on top of his head and his legs stretched out on the chair in front, a show-me smirk on his face. He was the kid who rated your performance but rarely glanced at the books you assigned. Still, he could fire back at you when he felt like it.

'Youth dies first,' I said. 'So Chester's Elvis died about the time he went in the Army.'

'So we're like dominoes. One falls into the other....'

'I'm not wrong, am I? After, say, 1957, no one ever saw Chester's Elvis again. Because then your Elvis emerged. And that ended when—'

'I see where this is headed,' Albert said. 'And I think it's kind of sickening.'

'We all died. But you two went first. I was the last to die. Also the last to live. So if you lived on at all, you lived in me. See?'

'I'm going to say this once,' Albert said, shaking his head. 'And I'm going to put it into simple language that everybody can understand. Let's say you have a deer, a maybe ten-point buck, close to a hundred fifty pounds. This is a handsome damn beast. It runs like the wind, it jumps creeks, it flies off cliffs, and it's got big brown eyes besides. Okay?' Albert glanced at his younger brother, who was already deeply absorbed, waiting to see how the story came out, wide-eyed and wondering, like a kid around a campfire.

'Have I said anything you don't understand, so far?' Albert pressed. He had a smart-assed edge I often liked, but not now. 'If I have, stop me.'

I nodded. Go on, get it over with. I wasn't supposed to know, but Albert had been looking at Filipino movies, the action films they made here, rape and revenge films produced in three weeks. He figured that might be a way for him to get started, the way Jack Nicholson began in low-budget Roger Corman thrillers. He would leave the act someday and not look back, I guessed. Elvis was just a role he played. A role and not—as in my case—a fate.

'So you've got this beautiful deer,' Albert continued. 'A stag who gets shot on the first day of hunting season. End of act one. Shot, gutted, and strapped on the hood of some drunkard's Wagoneer. Skinned and butchered and marinated and turned into venison. Steaks, chops, sausages, and stew. And that's the end of act two. You with me, Chester?'

'So far,' Chester said. The kid was all ears. I wondered whether Dude would take Chester with him and whether he'd look after him, the way Chester needed looking after. Albert was cocky and arrogant. And he kept me honest, deconstructing my notion of the three Presleys, of continuous and cumulative time, of transcending and returning. Albert 'Dude' Lane didn't buy it.

'So this deer that becomes venison gets digested. It's attacked and broken down by all kinds of enzymes and acids. And this, music lovers, brings us to act three, end of show, last act, curtains, and I guess you could say it contains the deer and the venison, that it reincarnates them, but from where I sit it looks—and it smells—like a pile of shit. From which I—'

'Wipe ass and walk away!' Chester shouted, beaming. It was Albert's favorite line. He used it to end anything that bored him, a meeting, a meal, a movie, an affair. It was his philosophy of life.

'Nothing personal, old-timer,' Albert said. He clapped a hand on my shoulder, the kind of sympathetic pat a baseball manager gives a pitcher he's taking out of the game. 'We're doing fine right now and I appreciate what you've put together here. But listen—earth to Ward Wiggins!—this is an Elvis show. It's not the College of Cardinals. Chester is not a priest and I'm not a cardinal and you aren't the pope. Okay?'

'I hear you,' I said.

'I'm putting this in the nicest possible way but, with all due respect, I don't want to grow up to be you.'

Source: P. F. Kluge (1996) *Biggest Elvis*, London: Vintage, pp. 3–10.

11 from *Bodies*

JED MERCURIO

Jed Mercurio (b. 1966), television screen writer and novelist, grew up in Cannock. He trained as a doctor at the University of Birmingham Medical School, and worked for four years as a doctor in NHS hospitals in the West Midlands. He is best known for a number of highly successful television series, including the medical drama *Cardiac Arrest* (1994), the situation comedy *The Grimleys* (1997), and the science fiction series *Invasion Earth* (1998). *Bodies* (2002) is his first novel, and draws on his experiences as a doctor. He has also published a volume of children's stories, *The Penguin Expedition* (2003).

1:   *The Interior*

Leaving behind the outside world I turn off the perimeter road and on the First of August I pass under the metal arch of the hospital gates. Ahead towers of concrete and glass carve blocks out of cloudless blue sky under which I'm swallowed into a city within a city with its own speed limits and language and even its own weather.

As I enter the building my reflection slithers over panes of glass. Windows reframe the sky into blue squares while my heels click on hard flat floors and echo off corridor walls. The air turns dry and sterile and as I burrow deeper into the hospital it cools to a constant twenty-one Celsius. Sunshine fades to a trickle then in its place humming strip lights burn.

Bracketed to a high white wall a sign throws down directions for wards and departments. Each destination is coded a colour and a line of that colour is etched into the floor and it maps the route ahead.

Standing here under the sign looking lost I look like what I am. I slip into my white coat, the same one I wore in finals but with a new badge that puts 'Dr' in front of my name, and with the white coat stiff like armour I plunge farther into the hospital.

Some people ask me the way to Pharmacy. I think I might be able to remember from the sign but I can't and I blush and I have to shake my head.

I say, 'It's my first day.'

They laugh. It's a nervous laugh. If a doctor doesn't know the way round his own hospital then maybe there are other things he doesn't know.

Ahead of me a straight white corridor drops away to a set of doors and through the glass of the doors I see another straight white corridor stretching to another set of doors. In the glass of those second doors I make out a third straight white corridor and all together the corridors and the doors are an ever diminishing series of arrows pointing me deeper in and I feel like I'm falling.

I'm falling through layers of brick, concrete and glass. In the weatherless vaults of corridors and stairwells outsiders dwindle. Here come only the sick, those who love them and those who look after them. From the perimeter road I've travelled inwards three-quarters of a mile. This is the interior.

Source: Jed Mercurio (2003) *Bodies*, London: Vintage, pp.5–6.

12 from *The Beet Queen*

LOUISE ERDRICH

Louise Erdrich (b. 1934), short-story writer, novelist and poet, was brought up near Turtle Mountain Chippewa Reservation in North Dakota. Her mother was a Chippewa Indian, and her father was a German-born teacher. This mixed ancestry forms an important theme in her writing. In *Love Medicine* (1984) she explores the complicated cross-cultural pressures on the lives of members of the Kashpaw and Lamartine families in a sequence of fourteen linked stories. In *The Beet Queen* (1986) she also uses several narrators in a story about survival against the odds. *Tracks* (1988) explores similar themes, this time set back in 1912 among Native Americans ravaged by tuberculosis and cheated out of their lands. *The Bingo Palace* (1994) takes the stories of some of the characters in *Love Medicine* into the late twentieth century.

Mary Adare

Uncle Pete was tall and blond and wore an old blue denim cap the same color as his eyes. His smile was slow, sweet for a butcher, and hopeful.

'Yes?' he asked. He did not recognize me even after I told him who I was. Finally his eyes rounded and he called out for Fritzie.

'Your sister's girl! She's here!' he shouted down the hall.

I told him I was alone, that I had come in on a boxcar, and he lifted me up in his arms. He carried me back to the kitchen where Aunt Fritzie had been frying a sausage for my cousin, the beautiful Sita, who sat at the table and stared while I tried to tell Fritzie and Pete just how I'd come to walk in their front door out of nowhere.

They watched me with friendly suspicion, thinking that I'd run away. But when I told about The Great Omar, and how Mama held up her purse, and how Omar helped her into the plane, their faces turned grim.

'Sita, go polish the glass out front,' said Aunt Fritzie. Sita slid unwillingly out of her chair. 'Now,' Fritzie said. Uncle Pete sat down heavily and pressed his fists together under his chin. 'Go on, tell the rest,' he said, and so I told all of the rest, and when I had finished I had also drunk a glass of milk and eaten a sausage. By then I was so tired I could hardly sit upright. Uncle Pete lifted me. I remember sagging against him, then nothing. I slept that day and all night and did not wake until the next morning.

I lay still for what seemed like a long while, trying to place the objects in the room, until I remembered they all belonged to Sita.

This was where I would sleep every night for the rest of my life. The paneling was warm stained pine. The curtains were patterned with dancers and musical notes. Most of one wall was taken up by a tall oak dresser with fancy curlicues and many drawers. On it there was a wooden lamp in the shape of a wishing well. A full-length mirror hung on the back of the door. Through that door, as I was taking in my surroundings, walked Sita herself, tall and perfect with a blond braid that reached to her waist.

She sat down on the edge of my trundle bed and folded her arms over her small new breasts. She was a year older than me and one year younger than Karl. Since I'd seen her last, she had grown suddenly, but her growth had not thinned her into an awkward bony creature. Sita grinned. She looked down at me, her strong white teeth shining, and she stroked the blond braid that hung down over one shoulder.

'Where's Auntie Adelaide?' she asked.

I did not answer.

'Where's Auntie Adelaide?' she said, again, in a singsong furious voice. 'How come you're here? Where'd she go? Where's Karl?'

'I don't know.'

I suppose I thought the misery of my answer would quiet Sita, but that was before I knew her.

'How come she left you? Where's Karl? What's this?'

She took the blue velvet box from my pile of clothes and shook it next to her ear.

'What's in it?'

I snatched the box with an angry swiftness she did not expect. Then I rolled from the bed, bundled my clothes into my arms, and walked out of the room. The one door open in the hallway was the bathroom, a large smoky room of many uses that soon became my haven since it was the only door I could bolt against my cousin.

Every day for weeks after I arrived in Argus, I woke slowly, thinking I was back in Prairie Lake and that none of this had happened. Then I saw the dark swirls in the pine and Sita's arm hanging off the bed above me. The day started. I smelled the air, peppery and warm from the sausage makers. I heard the rhythmical whine of meat saws, slicers, the rippling beat of fans. Aunt Fritzie was smoking her sharp Viceroys in the bathroom. Uncle Pete was outside feeding the big white German shepherd that was kept in the shop at night to guard the canvas bags of money.

I got up, put on one of Sita's hand-me-down pink dresses, and went out to the kitchen to wait for Uncle Pete. I cooked breakfast. That I made a good cup of coffee at age eleven and fried eggs was a source of wonder to my aunt and uncle, and an outrage to Sita. That's why I did it every morning until it became a habit to have me there.

I planned to be essential to them all, so depended upon that they could never send me off. I did this on purpose, because I soon found out that I had nothing else to offer. The day after I arrived in Argus and woke up to Sita's accusing questions, I had tried to give them what I thought was my treasure—the blue velvet box that held Mama's jewels.

I did it in as grand a manner as I could, with Sita for a witness and with Pete and Fritzie sitting at the kitchen table. That morning, I walked in with my hair combed wet and laid the box between my uncle and aunt. I looked from Sita to Fritzie as I spoke.

'This should pay my way.'

Fritzie had my mother's features sharpened one notch past beauty. Her skin was rough and her short curled hair bleached platinum. Her eyes were a swimming, crazy shade of turquoise that startled customers.

She ate heartily, but her constant smoking kept her string-bean thin and sallow.

'You don't have to pay us,' said Fritzie. 'Pete tell her. She doesn't have to pay us. Sit down, shut up, and eat.'

Fritzie spoke like that, joking and blunt. Pete was slower.

'Come. Sit down and forget about the money,' he said. 'You never know about your mother. ...' he added in an earnest voice that trailed away. Things had a way of evaporating under Fritzie's eyes, vanishing, getting sucked up into the blue heat of her stare. Even Sita had nothing to say.

'I want to give you this,' I said. 'I insist.'

'She insists,' exclaimed Aunt Fritzie. Her smile had a rakish flourish because one tooth was chipped in front. 'Don't insist,' she said.

But I would not sit down. I picked up a knife from the butter plate and started to pry the lock.

'Here now,' said Fritzie. 'Pete, help her.'

So Pete got up, fetched a screwdriver from the top of the icebox, sat down and jammed the end underneath the lock.

'Let her open it,' said Fritzie, when the lock popped up. Pete pushed the little round box across the table.

'I bet it's empty,' Sita said. She took a big chance saying that, but it paid off in spades and aces between us growing up because I lifted the lid a moment later and what she said was true. There was nothing of value in the box.

Stickpins. A few thick metal buttons off a coat. And a ticket describing a ring and the necklace set with garnets, pawned for practically nothing in Minneapolis.

There was silence. Even Fritzie was at a loss. Sita nearly buzzed off her chair in triumph but held her tongue until later, when she would crow. Pete put his hand on his head. I stood quietly, my mind working in a circle. If Sita had not been there I might have broken down and let the tears out again, like in the rooming house, but she kept me sharp. [...]

Sita Kozka

My cousin Mary came in on the early freight train one morning, with nothing but an old blue keepsake box full of worthless pins and buttons. My father picked her up in his arms and carried her down the hallway into the kitchen. I was too old to be carried. He sat her down, then my mother said, 'Go clean the counters, Sita.' So I don't know what lies she told them after that.

Later on that morning, my parents put her to sleep in my bed. When I objected to this, saying that she could sleep on the trundle, my mother said, 'Cry sakes, you can sleep there too, you know.' And that is how I ended up that night, crammed in the trundle, which is too short for me. I slept with my legs dangling out in the cold air. I didn't feel welcoming toward Mary the next morning, and who can blame me?

Besides, on her first waking day in Argus, there were the clothes.

It is a good thing she opened the blue keepsake box at breakfast and found little bits of trash, like I said, because if I had not felt sorry for my cousin that day, I would not have stood for Mary and my mother ripping through my closet and bureau. 'This fits perfectly,' my mother said, holding up one of my favorite blouses, 'try it on!' And Mary did. Then she put it in her drawer, which was another thing. I had to clear out two of my bureau drawers for her.

'Mother,' I said, after this had gone on for some time and I was beginning to think I would have to wear the same three outfits all the next school year, 'Mother, this has really gone far enough.'

'Crap,' said my mother, who talks that way. 'Your cousin hasn't got a stitch.'

Yet she had half of mine by then, quite a wardrobe, and all the time it was increasing as my mother got more excited about dressing the poor orphan. But Mary wasn't really an orphan, although she played on that for sympathy. Her mother was still alive, even if she had left my cousin, which I doubted. I really thought that Mary just ran away from her mother because she could not appreciate Adelaide's style. It's not everyone who understands how to use their good looks to the best advantage. My Aunt Adelaide did. She was always my favorite, and I just died for her to visit. But she didn't come often because my mother couldn't understand style either.

Source: Louise Erdrich (1987) *The Beet Queen*, London: Pavanne/Pan Books, pp. 17–21, 27–28.

13 from *Age of Iron*

J. M. COETZEE

J[ohn] M[ichael] Coetzee (b. 1940), novelist and literary critic, was born in Cape Town, South Africa, the son of a lawyer father and schoolteacher mother. English was his first language, and was spoken at home, though with other relatives and friends he used Afrikaans. After graduating from the University of Cape Town, Coetzee worked for a few years in England as a computer programmer, and then taught in the USA before returning to Cape Town. His first novel, *Dusklands*, was published in 1974, and he has since gone on to win many prestigious literary prizes. He is the only writer to have won the Booker Prize twice – for *Life and Times of Michael K* (1983) and *Disgrace* (1999) – and in 2003 he was awarded the Nobel Prize for Literature. Although in general resistant to the dominance of realism, preferring instead a complex reworking of allegory or moral parable, in *Age of Iron* (1990) he took as his subject the unrest in Cape Town in 1986. He is Professor of General Literature at the University of Cape Town.

There is an alley down the side of the garage, you may remember it, you and your friends would sometimes play there. Now it is a dead place, waste, without use, where windblown leaves pile up and rot.

Yesterday, at the end of this alley, I came upon a house of carton boxes and plastic sheeting and a man curled up inside, a man I recognized from the streets: tall, thin, with a weathered skin and long, carious fangs, wearing a baggy grey suit and a hat with a sagging brim. He had the hat on now, sleeping with the brim folded under his ear. A derelict, one of the derelicts who hang around the parking lots on Mill Street, cadging money from shoppers, drinking under the flyover, eating out of refuse cans. One of the homeless for whom August, month of rains, is the worst month. Asleep in his box, his legs stretched out like a marionette's, his jaw agape. An unsavoury smell about him: urine, sweet wine, mouldy clothing, and something else too. Unclean.

For a while I stood staring down on him, staring and smelling. A visitor, visiting himself on me on this of all days.

This was the day when I had the news from Dr Syfret. The news was not good, but it was mine, for me, mine only, not to be refused. It was for me to take in my arms and fold to my chest and take home, without headshaking, without tears. 'Thank you, doctor,' I said: 'thank you for being frank.' 'We will do everything we can,' he said, 'we will tackle this together.' But already, behind the comradely front, I could see he was withdrawing. *Sauve qui peut*. His allegiance to the living, not the dying.

The trembling began only when I got out of the car. By the time I had closed the garage door I was shaking all over: to still it I had to clench my teeth, grip my handbag. It was then that I saw the boxes, saw him.

'What are you doing here?' I demanded, hearing the irritation in my voice, not checking it. 'You can't stay, you must go.'

He did not stir, lying in his shelter, looking up, inspecting the winter stockings, the blue coat, the skirt with whose hang there has always been something wrong, the grey hair cut by a strip of scalp, old woman's scalp, pink, babyish.

Then he drew in his legs and leisurely got up. Without a word he turned his back on me, shook out the black plastic, folded it in half, in quarters, in eighths. He produced a bag (Air Canada, it said) and zipped it shut. I stood aside. Leaving behind the boxes, an empty bottle and a smell of urine, he passed me. His trousers sagged; he hitched them up. I waited to be sure he had gone, and heard him stow the plastic in the hedge from the other side.

Two things, then, in the space of an hour: the news, long dreaded, and this reconnaissance, this other annunciation. The first of the carrion-birds, prompt, unerring. How long can I fend them off? The scavengers of Cape Town, whose number never dwindles. Who go bare and feel no cold. Who sleep outdoors and do not sicken. Who starve and do not waste. Warmed from within by alcohol. The contagions and infections in their blood consumed in liquid flame. Cleaners-up after the feast. Flies, dry-winged, glazen-eyed, pitiless. My heirs.

With what slow steps did I enter this empty house, from which every echo has faded, where the very tread of footsole on board is flat and dull! How I longed for you to be here, to hold me, comfort me! I begin to understand the true meaning of the embrace. We embrace to be embraced. We embrace our children to be folded in the arms of the future, to pass ourselves on beyond death, to be transported. That is how it was when I embraced you, always. We bear children in order to be mothered by them. Home truths, a mother's truth: from now to the end that is all you will hear from me. So: how I longed for you! How I longed to be able to go upstairs to you, to sit on your bed, run my fingers through your hair, whisper in your ear as I did on school mornings, 'Time to get up!' And then, when you turned over, your body blood-warm, your breath milky, to take you in my arms in what we called 'giving Mommy a big hug,' the secret meaning of which, the meaning never spoken, was that Mommy should not be sad, for she would not die but live on in you.

To live! You are my life; I love you as I love life itself. In the mornings I come out of the house and wet my finger and hold it up to the wind. When the chill is from the north-west, from your quarter, I stand a long time sniffing, concentrating my attention in the hope that across ten thousand miles of land and sea some breath will reach me of the milkiness you still carry with you behind your ears, in the fold of your neck.

The first task laid on me, from today: to resist the craving to share my death. Loving you, loving life, to forgive the living and take my leave without bitterness. To embrace death as my own, mine alone.

To whom this writing then? The answer: to you but not to you; to me; to you in me.

Source: J. M. Coetzee (1991) *Age of Iron*, London: Penguin, pp. 3–5.

14 from *Another World*

PAT BARKER

> For biographical details, see Reading 8, p. 434.

Fran's car is so hot she has to open all the windows to cool it down before they can get in. She swings one door to and fro out of a vague feeling that this will help. Jasper's trying to throw handfuls of gravel, but his coordination's so poor he topples over and lands on his bottom. One whimper, and he's on his feet again, this time throwing the gravel at Gareth, who thumps him on the arm.

'Gareth!'

'He started it.'

'He's just a baby, he doesn't understand.'

'He started it.'

'Just get in, will you?'

Gareth sits in the front passenger seat.

'Not there. In the back.'

'Why?'

'Because it's the law. You're not allowed in the front till you're twelve.'

'Nick lets Miranda.'

'Miranda's thirteen.'

'I'm nearly twelve.'

'And when you are twelve then you can sit in the front.'

Gareth gets in the back. Fran's not inclined to congratulate herself. In dealing with Gareth, there's nothing more ominous than a small, early victory.

Jasper, who hates the hot plastic car seat, stiffens his legs till they're like planks. Fran, holding a heavy toddler at arm's length, back aching, stomach getting in the way of everything, pendulous breasts each with a swamp of sweat underneath, thinks, This is stupid. She stops, lets Jasper get out, and plays with him for a while, pretendy chases and tickling and incey-wincey-spider-climbed-up-the-spout, then when he's curled up and helpless with giggles she slips him quickly into the seat and clicks the buckle. He opens his mouth to scream, but she crashes the gears, turns the radio on full blast, starts to sing 'Incey Wincey Spider' at the top of her voice, until Jasper, bowling along the open road, breath snatched out of his mouth, deafened by the noise, forgets what he's crying about, and points at the shadows of leaves flickering across the roof. ''Ook, 'ook.'

'Yeah,' says Gareth sourly. ''Ook.'

Fran slips one hand into her blouse and surreptitiously rubs the sweat, flaps the cotton, does what she can to dry off. When she was a girl – back in the middle Jurassic – she'd been one of the last in her class to hold a pencil under them. Get pencil cases in there now. Be a pencil factory soon if she doesn't do something about this bloody saggy bra. 'Look, Gareth,' she says, trying to keep the lines of communication open. 'There's your new school.'

And why the fuck would anybody want to look at that? Gareth thinks.

But look at it he does. It's empty now, of course, in the middle of August, a long, low huddle of buildings, one of them with its windows boarded up, because last winter the pipes burst and flooded the labs and there's no money to get them repaired. Though Digger says it wasn't burst pipes, it was his brother Paul and a gang of lads broke in and left the taps running. Gareth doesn't know whether to believe him or not.

Source: Pat Barker (1999) *Another World*, London: Penguin, pp. 130–2.

15 'The Doctor and the Doctor's Wife'

ERNEST HEMINGWAY

Ernest Hemingway (1899–1961), novelist and short-story writer, was born in Illinois and spent much of his youth in the Great Lakes region. He served with an ambulance unit of the Red Cross in the First World War and was seriously wounded in 1918. He worked as a journalist and in 1921 moved to Paris as a foreign correspondent. There he met famous literary figures such as Gertrude Stein, Ezra Pound and Ford Madox Ford. In the early 1920s he began to publish short stories, among them 'The Doctor and the Doctor's Wife' (1926). He achieved wide recognition with *The Sun Also Rises* (1926), a novel about the disillusionment of young Americans and Englishmen in the aftermath of the War. Other famous novels include *A Farewell to Arms* (1929), *For Whom the Bell Tolls* (1940) and *The Old Man and the Sea* (1952), but he is almost equally famous for his short stories, of which there were many collections. In 1954 Hemingway was awarded the Nobel Prize for Literature.

Dick Boulton came from the Indian camp to cut up logs for Nick's father. He brought his son Eddy, and another Indian named Billy Tabeshaw with him. They came in through the back gate out of the woods, Eddy carrying the long cross-cut saw. It flopped over his shoulder and made a musical sound as he walked. Billy Tabeshaw carried two big cant-hooks. Dick had three axes under his arm.

He turned and shut the gate. The others went on ahead of him down to the lake shore where the logs were buried in the sand.

The logs had been lost from the big log booms that were towed down the lake to the mill by the steamer *Magic*. They had drifted up on to the beach and if nothing were done about them sooner or later the crew of the *Magic* would come along the shore in a rowboat, spot the logs, drive an iron spike with a ring on it into the end of each one and then tow them out into the lake to make a new boom. But the lumbermen might never come for them because a few logs were not worth the price of a crew to gather them. If no one came for them they would be left to waterlog and rot on the beach.

Nick's father always assumed that this was what would happen, and hired the Indians to come down from the camp and cut the logs up with the cross-cut saw and split them with a wedge to make cordwood and chunks for the open fireplace. Dick Boulton walked around past the cottage down to the lake. There were four big beech logs lying almost buried in the sand. Eddy hung the saw up by one of its handles in the crotch of a tree. Dick put the three axes down on the little dock. Dick was a half-breed and many of the farmers around the lake believed he was really a white man. He was very lazy but a great worker once he was started. He took a plug of tobacco out of his pocket, bit off a chew and spoke in Ojibway to Eddy and Billy Tabeshaw.

They sunk the ends of their cant-hooks into one of the logs and swung against it to loosen it in the sand. They swung their weight against the shafts of the cant-hooks. The log moved in the sand. Dick Boulton turned to Nick's father.

'Well, Doc,' he said, 'that's a nice lot of timber you've stolen.'

'Don't talk that way, Dick,' the doctor said. 'It's driftwood.'

Eddy and Billy Tabeshaw had rocked the log out of the wet sand and rolled it toward the water.

'Put it right in,' Dick Boulton shouted.

'What are you doing that for?' asked the doctor.

'Wash it off. Clean off the sand on account of the saw. I want to see who it belongs to,' Dick said.

The log was just awash in the lake. Eddy and Billy Tabeshaw leaned on their cant-hooks sweating in the sun. Dick kneeled down in the sand and looked at the mark of the scaler's hammer in the wood at the end of the log.

'It belongs to White and McNally,' he said, standing up and brushing off his trousers knees.

The doctor was very uncomfortable.

'You'd better not saw it up, then, Dick,' he said, shortly.

'Don't get huffy, Doc,' said Dick. 'Don't get huffy. I don't care who you steal from. It's none of my business.'

'If you think the logs are stolen, leave them alone and take your tools back to the camp,' the doctor said. His face was red.

'Don't go off at half cock, Doc,' Dick said. He spat tobacco juice on the log. It slid off, thinning in the water. 'You know they're stolen as well as I do. It don't make any difference to me.'

'All right. If you think the logs are stolen, take your stuff and get out.'

'Now, Doc—'

'Take your stuff and get out.'

'Listen, Doc.'

'If you call me Doc once again, I'll knock your eye teeth down your throat.'

'Oh, no, you won't, Doc.'

Dick Boulton looked at the doctor. Dick was a big man. He knew how big a man he was. He liked to get into fights. He was happy. Eddy and Billy Tabeshaw leaned on their cant-hooks and looked at the doctor. The doctor chewed the beard on his lower lip and looked at Dick Boulton. Then he turned away and walked up the hill to the cottage. They could see from his back how angry he was. They all watched him walk up the hill and go inside the cottage.

Dick said something in Ojibway. Eddy laughed but Billy Tabeshaw looked very serious. He did not understand English but he had sweat all the time the row was going on. He was fat with only a few hairs of moustache like a Chinaman. He picked up the two cant-hooks. Dick picked up the axes and Eddy took the saw down from the tree. They started off and walked up past the cottage and out the back gate into the woods. Dick left the gate open. Billy Tabeshaw went back and fastened it. They were gone through the woods.

In the cottage the doctor, sitting on the bed in his room, saw a pile of medical journals on the floor by the bureau. They were still in their wrappers unopened. It irritated him.

'Aren't you going back to work, dear?' asked the doctor's wife from the room where she was lying with the blinds drawn.

'No!'

'Was anything the matter?'

'I had a row with Dick Boulton.'

'Oh,' said his wife. 'I hope you didn't lose your temper, Henry.'

'No,' said the doctor.

'Remember, that he who ruleth his spirit is greater than he that taketh a city,' said his wife. She was a Christian Scientist. Her Bible, her copy of *Science and Health* and her *Quarterly* were on a table beside her bed in the darkened room.

Her husband did not answer. He was sitting on his bed now, cleaning a shotgun. He pushed the magazine full of the heavy yellow shells and pumped them out again. They were scattered on the bed.

'Henry,' his wife called. Then paused a moment. 'Henry!'

'Yes,' the doctor said.

'You didn't say anything to Boulton to anger him, did you?'

'No,' said the doctor.

'What was the trouble about, dear?'

'Nothing much.'

'Tell me, Henry. Please don't try and keep anything from me. What was the trouble about?'

'Well, Dick owes me a lot of money for pulling his squaw through pneumonia and I guess he wanted a row so he wouldn't have to take it out in work.'

His wife was silent. The doctor wiped his gun carefully with a rag. He pushed the shells back in against the spring of the magazine. He sat with the gun on his knees. He was very fond of it. Then he heard his wife's voice from the darkened room.

'Dear, I don't think, I really don't think that anyone would really do a thing like that.'

'No?' said the doctor.

'No. I can't believe that anyone would do a thing of that sort intentionally.'

The doctor stood up and put the shotgun in the corner behind the dresser.

'Are you going out, dear?' his wife said.

'I think I'll go for a walk,' the doctor said.

'If you see Nick, dear, will you tell him his mother wants to see him?' his wife said.

The doctor went out on the porch. The screen door slammed behind him. He heard his wife catch her breath when the door slammed.

'Sorry,' he said, outside her window with the blinds drawn.

'It's all right, dear,' she said.

He walked in the heat out the gate and along the path into the hemlock woods. It was cool in the woods even on such a hot day. He found Nick sitting with his back against a tree, reading.

'Your mother wants you to come and see her,' the doctor said.

'I want to go with you,' Nick said.

His father looked down at him.

'All right. Come on, then,' his father said. 'Give me the book, I'll put it in my pocket.'

'I know where there's black squirrels, Daddy,' Nick said.

'All right,' said his father. 'Let's go there.'

Source: Ernest Hemingway (1993) *The Essential Hemingway*, London: Arrow Books, pp. 312–16.

16 from *Rumours of a Hurricane*

TIM LOTT

Tim Lott (b. 1956) was born in Southall, Middlesex. After leaving school he worked on a local newspaper, and then as a writer on pop music, and in publishing. He went to university in 1983 and studied history and politics. After spells as a magazine editor and television producer, he became a writer. An autobiographical work dealing with his mother's depression and eventual suicide, *The Scent of Dried Roses*, was awarded the 1996 J. R. Ackerley Prize. His first novel, *White City Blue* (1999), a comic account of the lives of a group of young men, won the Whitbread First Novel Award. A second novel, *Rumours of a Hurricane* (2002), follows a couple living in Milton Keynes during the Thatcher years, and a third, *The Love Secrets of Don Juan*, was published in 2003.

As she opens the ledger, fifty or so miles away to the south a man stands under a flyover in London, swaying slightly back and forth from the balls of his feet to the flat of his heels. He keeps this rocking movement going for five, maybe six minutes. There is no sunshine here, only a steady dull downpour.

People hurrying by on the way to the nearby underground station entrance avoid looking at him. The pointlessness, the giant inappropriateness of his smile, the rock, rock of his ruined body put them on guard, register him as mad, render him invisible. His smile widens; something like a laugh emerges, but is obliterated by the rumbling of the tube train.

The smile dissolves. He takes a long, deep draught from a can that is clutched in his left hand. Then he crushes the can and lets it drop to join the five or six empties that he has previously let fall there. He stops rocking. His face is still, at rest. He closes his eyes.

His face, now expressionless, exposes clearly the topography of its damage. Thin, vermilion blood vessels snake across his cheekbones and nose. There is the remnant of a serious bruise there, and his hair, of which there is a thick mass, stands up with caked grime as if gelled and set. The effect is that of broken feathers on the back of an injured pigeon. His mouth is thin and inclines down heavily at either end. The impression is not so much of sadness but of anaesthesia. There is not the animation any more to drag the lips up at the extremities, to continue the pantomime of a private joke being shared with the battering rain.

His eyes are still closed. People hurry past. The rain strengthens and the wind that drives it pulls sheets of water whipping under the flyover. Yet still the man does not move. Another train arrives.

His clothes are soaking now, on every side. The damp seems to neutralize their colour, so that they appear not colourless but unidentifiable as any shade of any hue in particular. It is the colour of that which has fallen from the secret edge of the world.

A pale flicker of the smile reappears. Then the eyes open once more. They are shot. They were once cornflowers but now have come to resemble the damp non-colour of the man's clothes. Yet briefly they seem to blaze with some light, a light that is somewhere at the dark end of the blue-green spectrum and that sends out messages nobody is there to read. The lids widen slightly. Then the man closes them again. And takes a step forward. The flow of pedestrians redirects itself to avoid the obstruction, forced now to momentarily recognize the man's existence and thus recalibrate their own.

The traffic boulders down the main road at an urgent pace, each pair of windscreen wipers battling the downpour, the moment-by-moment flicking between clarity and opacity. When the trains pass and the traffic is growling, the sounds combine to make a thick, tumbling wall of noise that blocks a human voice pitched at the normal level. Car and train, train and car, the systematic indifference of machines. The man takes another step forward. The pedestrian flow redirects automatically.

The man reaches the kerb and he stands there, steadily, waiting until the trains and cars combine to create the necessary duet of obliteration. The quality of the noise is the cue he has given himself, pointless and nonsensical. He considers this apt. The 8.03 is late. A mechanical failure at Stratford is responsible.

Eventually, however, the man hears the train approach. He swallows. And again, then blinks, once. Although very drunk – he has been very drunk now for one and a half years – he feels, unexpectedly, a subterranean bolt of fear. This means he muffs his step slightly when he leaves the kerb, the ghost of a second thought hobbling him. So the lorry, when it hits, does not take him full on, but propels him from the shoulder, at an angle, twenty feet into the distance. It is not enough. Instead of the warm darkness which he hoped for, there is a cacophony of world-obliterating pain.

As if the rain were adrenalin, the crowd, a moment ago so united, so careful in its indifference, so discerning in its chosen horizons, flows undammed towards him. He hears himself screaming, and he hears voices babble around him, words that are rendered meaningless and incomprehensible by his agony.

The pain has not merely failed to kill him. It has brought him vibrantly alive, made him aware of the oldest edict coded into his genes: to survive. His cry sounds from somewhere he had not previously understood to have existed. The deadness of his spirit is in momentary retreat. For the first time that he can remember, at the chosen moment of his death, he wants to live. He is beyond registering the irony.

It is some time before an ambulance arrives. After the first excitement of the incident, which will be translated into a hundred anecdotes, each of them inaccurate in its own particular way, each inadequate to the size of the event, people are embarrassed. Many have moved on, refusing to let a wino's fate admit entropy into the grooved regularities represented within their loose-leaf appointment books. Others are fascinated by the blood which still pours in extraordinary quantities from several wounds on the man's head, chest and what is left of his right leg, and their initial shock has been replaced by an irrepressible voyeurism. A third group are paralysed by a need to do something and, countervailing that, a complete inability to do anything at all.

But to move on seems more callous than staying. So they shuffle from foot to foot, and they chatter concernedly, in lieu of more positive action. The dying of this man is too extraordinary a spectacle to leave; and yet now they want to be released from it, to glide back into their lives and consign this to memory, and then forgetfulness.

Some few of this third group try to talk to the man out of whom life is leaking, but their words emerge as diminished, shrunken by the dimensions of this event. *Where does it hurt? The ambulance won't be long. Can you move your leg? You'll be OK.*

This last, tender lie is the most profound of the deceits woven into the scene, so violently does it disagree with the remnant that is prostrated on this cracked and bloodied pavement. The words are uttered by the lorry driver, whose eyes are wide with surprise, who never expected to kill a man today. He is delivering plastic canisters to a feed manufacturer in Wakefield. Despite his upset, he worries that he will be late. He takes out a cigarette and lights it, and almost immediately puts it out again. The point is in the doing.

The consoling sound of an ambulance can be heard now. A wash of relief begins to crest above the spectators; they want their responsibility for this event to end now. But the siren turns out to be a police car, on another mission entirely. It passes by and the siren fades.

The right leg is almost severed below the knee. Corals of bone, shocking white, have appeared. One spectator finds it too much and the sound of retching joins the chorus of anxious muttering, motor engines, seagulls, descending planes. Another train arrives. Traffic is moving as before, drivers sequentially irritated by the hulk of the lorry stopped on zigzag lines.

Now the ambulance really is coming. Announcing itself by sound and light, sad cavalry approaching through the rain, it screeches towards the site of what will be logged in the driver's record book as an 'incident'. Neutral, painless-sounding.

The ambulance pulls up behind the lorry. Two men emerge, wearing yellow reflective vests over their uniforms. They take in the sight without registering shock or revulsion. They are both experienced; carnage is banal.

They go through the routine. A glance is enough to trigger the first part. One man, who is big, red-faced and naturally angry-looking, radios the hospital, ensuring that surgeons will be at the ready at the anticipated arrival time of around fifteen minutes. He speaks calmly, even delicately, despite the fury of his face. The fury is an illusion; he is a kind man who finds his work taxing and doleful.

The other man, smaller and younger, is attending to the shivering heap on the pavement. He mutters some words to him; takes various appliances from a bag, prepares an injection and administers it. The patient quietens down somewhat. He whimpers now, instead of screaming, but he remains frightened; the drug is not strong enough to erase this primal directive.

Within minutes he is loaded on to a stretcher, his half-severed leg, now tourniqueted, loaded on almost separately, nearly an afterthought. It is obvious to both the ambulance men that the leg is beyond repair. It is obvious to them also that the man they are now guiding into the small holding cell that is the rear of the ambulance will not be needing it

anyway in a short while. A day, maybe two. Perhaps not even that long
– a DOA.

The possibility of organ donation automatically crosses the mind of
the older ambulance man, but he almost laughs at himself for making
such a slip. The parts of a wino are detritus, particularly one of this age;
early sixties, he guesses, subtracting ten years from what the face shows
to allow for the wear and tear of street life.

No donations. The beating heart, the grey filter of kidneys, the soft
sponge of lung are always too hardened, too softened, too punctured and
fatty and gristled. And the liver of course ... No. These are not prime
cuts. No patient, even a dying, desperate, breathless, dialysis-tethered
one, would embrace such maimed offerings.

The journey to the hospital is uneventful. In the wake of the
ambulance, a few of the abandoned pedestrians are still staring at the
brown penumbra of blood, are still guiltily enjoying the excitement. The
paramedics are thinking about how long is left on their shift. The man
on the stretcher is delirious. His thoughts are like scattered, broken
glass, each containing a reflection connected, yet unconnectable, with a
larger picture. He thinks of a wide boulevard dotted with yew trees. He
thinks of a woman with auburn hair removing a plucked and trussed
bird from a microwave oven. She is smiling, but unhappy. He thinks of
an overheated room and a barometer shaped like a Spanish guitar. He
hears the sound of cascading orchestral strings.

At the hospital doctors and nurses crowd around him as he is
unloaded. Something in him is grateful for the attention, even flattered
by it. He thought he had forgone such privileges long ago. Injury is
elevating. People grant you respect.

Soon after the unloading, the man loses consciousness. He has been
given a general anaesthetic. The surgeon, a cynical, hunched-over
sexagenarian with a hatred of life that has somehow been generated by
its endless sluicing through his hands, can hardly find the wherewithal
to operate. He has taken his saviour's knife to too many street roughs
and drunks and hopeless cases with their ruined insides, keeping him
from spending valuable time on those he thinks of as more valuable
people, those he believes misfortune, rather than personal weakness, has
laid low. He hates what he tries to save; a futile drain on resources.

He immediately forms the conclusion that this man is probably going
to die. The vital functions are too far gone. It is a waste of time. He
removes what is left of the leg, out of a sense of propriety and tidiness.
Then he closes the man up again, half hoping for a flat line there and

then on the screen. But a weak pulse continues producing its sharp green hills. Another misuse of a hospital bed.

Source: Tim Lott (2003) *Rumours of a Hurricane*, London: Penguin, pp. 3–10.

17 from *The Dark*

JOHN MCGAHERN

John McGahern (b. 1934), novelist and short-story writer was born in Dublin and brought up in Cootehill, County Cavan, where his father was the local police sergeant. He worked as a primary schoolteacher in Clontarf, Dublin from 1955 to 1964. His first novel, *The Barracks*, was published in 1963. His second, *The Dark* (1965), an account of adolescent sexual awakening, aroused much controversy when it was first published. It was banned under Ireland's censorship legislation, and McGahern was dismissed from his teaching post. He was forced to leave Ireland and went to work in London, not returning until 1974. His later novels have been widely acclaimed. They include *The Leavetaking* (1974), *The Pornographer* (1979), *Amongst Women* (1990), which was shortlisted for the Booker Prize, and *That They May Face the Rising Sun* (2002). His *Collected Stories* was published in 2002.

He went muttering and complaining that way to bed. And then, when he was gone, the wave of remorse that came. You'd troubled him, and for what? Did it matter what was prayed for? If it gave him satisfaction to pray for success why not let him, it would make no difference except he'd not be upset as now. Stupid vanity had caused it all. The house had gone to bed. You were alone in the kitchen. You wanted to say to him you were sorry but you weren't able.

His boots, wet from the grass, stood drying by the raked fire. They started to take on horrible fascination.

They were your father's boots, close to the raked fire. They'd been put there to dry for morning. Their toes touched where the ashes spilled out from the fire on the concrete, boots wet from the grass. Your father's feet had been laced in their black leather, leather over walking flesh. They'd walk in his hopes, be carried over the ground, till they grew worn, past mending, and were discarded for the new pair from Curley's, on and on, over the habitual fields, lightly to the football matches in Reegan's field on Sundays, till the feet themselves wore, boots taken off his dying feet. Corns of the flesh against the leather. All the absurd anxiety and delight and heedlessness the boots carried. They stood so utterly quiet by the fire, the feet that they'd cover resting between sheets to wear them through another day. The boots were so calm there. They would not move. You touched them in fascination, they did not stir, only the rough touch of wet boot leather against the finger-tips. One lace was broken, replaced by white twine.

How could you possibly hurt or disturb anyone? Hadn't the feet that wore the boots, all that life moving in boot leather, enough to contend with, from morning to night to death, without you heaping on more burden, from sheer egotism. Did it matter to the boots, moving or still, whether your success was prayed for or not? Why couldn't you allow people to do the small things that pleased them? In this same mood you did what you had never done and went and knocked on his door.

'Who's that? What do you want?'

'I'm sorry over the prayers.'

'It's a bit late in the day to be sorry now, easy to be sorry when the harm's done, such heathen rubbish, easy to know why you're sorry. It's more than sorry you ought to be———'

Anger rose as the voice continued to complain out of the darkness of the bedroom. The same boots could kick and trample. You couldn't stand it, you'd only meant well, that was all.

'Forget it for God's sake. I just said I was sorry,' you said and closed the door sharply to go troubled and angry through the kitchen to your own bedroom.

Source: John McGahern (1983) *The Dark*, London: Faber & Faber, pp. 130–2.

18 *'Girl'*

JAMAICA KINCAID

Jamaica Kincaid (b. 1949), novelist and short-story writer, was born Elaine Potter Richardson in St. John's, Antigua, in the West Indies. She never knew her biological father, and her mother soon remarried. After school she migrated to New York, where she went to college and began writing. Her first book, *At the Bottom of the River* (1983), a collection of stories, won the Morton Dauwen Zabel Award of the American Academy of Arts and Letters, and she went on to publish a widely admired semi-autobiographical novel, *Annie John*, in 1985. In 1988 she published *A Small Place*, a highly polemical indictment of Antigua's colonial history and an attack on the harmful consequences, as Kincaid saw it, of tourist development on the island. A second semi-autobiographical novel, *Lucy*, was published in 1990, and was followed by *The Autobiography of My Mother* (1996), the story of a mixed-race girl whose mother dies in childbirth. Her most recent novel, *My Brother* (1997) describes in harrowing detail the sufferings of her brother, Devon, who died of AIDS in Antigua at the age of 33.

Wash the white clothes on Monday and put them on the stone heap; wash the colour clothes on Tuesday and put them on the clothes-line to dry; don't walk barehead in the hot sun; cook pumpkin fritters in very hot sweet oil; soak your little cloths right after you take them off; when buying cotton to make yourself a nice blouse, be sure that it doesn't have gum on it, because that way it won't hold up well after a wash; soak salt fish overnight before you cook it; is it true that you sing benna in Sunday school?; always eat your food in such a way that it won't turn someone else's stomach; on Sundays try to walk like a lady and not like the slut you are so bent on becoming; don't sing benna in Sunday school; you mustn't speak to wharf-rat boys, not even to give directions; don't eat fruits on the street—flies will follow you; *but I don't sing benna on Sundays at all and never in Sunday school*; this is how to sew on a button; this is how to make a button-hole for the button you have just sewed on; this is how to hem a dress when you see the hem coming down and so to prevent yourself from looking like the slut I know you are so bent on becoming; this is how you iron your father's khaki shirt so that it doesn't have a crease; this is how you iron your father's khaki pants so that they don't have a crease; this is how you grow okra—far from the house, because okra tree harbors red ants; when you are growing dasheen, make sure it gets plenty of water or else it makes your throat itch when you are eating it; this is how you sweep a corner; this is how you sweep a whole house; this is how you sweep a yard; this is how you smile to someone you don't like too much; this is how you smile to someone you don't like at all; this is how you smile to someone you like completely; this is how you set a table for tea; this is how you set a table for dinner; this is how you set a table for dinner with an important guest; this is how you set a table for lunch; this is how you set a table for breakfast; this is how to behave in the presence of men who don't know you very well, and this way they won't recognize immediately the slut I have warned you against becoming; be sure to wash every day, even if it is with your own spit; don't squat down to play marbles—you are not a boy, you know; don't pick people's flowers—you might catch something; don't throw stones at blackbirds, because it might not be a blackbird at all; this is how to make a bread pudding; this is how to make doukona; this is how to make pepper pot; this is how to make a good medicine for a cold; this is how to make a good medicine to throw away a child before it even becomes a child; this is how to catch a fish; this is how to throw back a fish you don't like, and that way something bad won't fall on you; this is how to bully a man; this is how a man bullies you; this is how to love a man, and if this doesn't work there are other ways, and if they don't work don't feel too bad about giving up; this is how to spit up in the air if you feel like it, and this is how to move quick so that it doesn't fall on you; this is how to make ends meet; always squeeze bread to make sure it's fresh; *but what if the baker won't let me feel the bread?*; you mean to say that after all you are really going to be the kind of woman who the baker won't let near the bread?

Source: Jamaica Kincaid (1983) *At the Bottom of the River*, New York: Farrar Straus Giroux, 1983, pp. 3–5.

19 from *Purple America*

RICK MOODY

Rick Moody (b. 1965), novelist and short-story writer, was born Hiram F. III Moody in New York City. His parents divorced when he was a child, and he went to a boarding school in New Hampshire. He worked in publishing for a time, but finding a publisher for his own first novel, *Garden State* (1992) was difficult. His second novel, *The Ice Storm* (1994), was made into a highly successful film. He has published many short stories, the most acclaimed collection being *Demonology: Stories* (2000), and a memoir, *The Black Veil* (2002). His novel *Purple America* (1997) attracted a great deal of attention, and something of a cult following, for its highly experimental form and use of language.

Whosoever knows the folds and complexities of his own mother's body, *he shall never die*. Whosoever knows the latitudes of his mother's body, whosoever has taken her into his arms and immersed her baptismally in the first-floor tub, lifting one of her alabaster legs and then the other over its lip, whosoever bathes her with Woolworth's soaps in sample sizes, whosoever twists the creaky taps and tests the water on the inside of his wrist, whosoever shovels a couple of tablespoons of rose bath salts under the billowing faucet and marvels at their vermilion color, whosoever bends by hand her sclerotic limbs, as if reassuring himself about the condition of a hinge, whosoever has kissed his mother on the part that separates the lobes of her white hair and has cooed her name while soaping underneath the breast where he was once fed, whosoever breathes the acrid and dispiriting stench of his mother's body while scrubbing the greater part of this smell away with Woolworth's lavender soaps, who has pushed her discarded bra and oversized panties (scattered on the tile floor behind him) to one side, away from the water sloshing occasionally over the edge of the tub and choking the runoff drain, who has lost his footing on these panties, panties once dotted with blood of children unconceived, his siblings unconceived, panties now intended to fit over a vinyl undergarment, who has wiped stalactites of drool from his mother's mouth with a moistened violet washcloth, who has swept back the annoying violet shower curtain the better to lift up his stick-figure mother and to bathe her ass, where a sweet and infantile shit sometimes collects, causing her both discomfort and shame, whosoever angrily manhandles the dial on the bathroom radio (balanced on the toilet tank) with one wet hand in an effort to find a college station that blasts only compact disc recordings of train accidents and large-scale construction operations (*he should be over this noise by his age*), whosoever selects at last the drummers of Burundi on WUCN knowing full well that his mother can brook only the music of the Tin Pan Alley period and certain classics, and whosoever has then reacted guiltily to his own selfishness and tuned to some lite AM station featuring the greatest hits of swing, whosoever will notice in the course of his mission the ripe light of early November as it is played out on the wall of the bathroom where one of those plug-in electric candles with plastic base is the only source of illumination, whosoever waits in this half-light while his mother takes her last bodily pleasure: the time in which her useless body floats in the warm, humid, even lapping of rose-scented bathwater, a water which in spite of its pleasures occasionally causes in his mother transient scotoma, ataxia, difficulty swallowing, deafness, and other temporary dysfunctions consistent with her ailment, whosoever looks nonetheless at his pacific mom's face in that water and knows — in a

New Age kind of way — the face he had before he was born, whosoever weeps over his mother's condition while bathing her, silently weeps, without words or expressions of pity or any nose-blowing or honking while crying, just weeps for a second like a ninny, whosoever has thereafter recovered quickly and forcefully from despair, whosoever has formulated a simple gratitude for the fact that *he still has a mother*, but who has nonetheless wondered at the kind of astral justice that has immobilized her thus, whosoever has then wished that the bath was over already so that he could go and drink too much at a local bar, a bar where he will encounter the citizens of this his hometown, a bar where he will see his cronies from high school, those who never left, those who have stayed to become civic boosters, those who have sent kids to the same day school they themselves attended thirty years before, whosoever has looked at his watch and yawned, while wondering how long he has to let his mother soak, whosoever soaps his mother a second time, to be sure that every cranny is disinfected, that every particle of dirt, every speck of grime, is eliminated, whosoever steps into a draining tub to hoist his mother from it, as if he were hoisting a drenched parachute from a stream bed, whosoever has balanced her on the closed toilet seat so that he might dry her with a towel of decadent thickness (purple), whosoever has sniffed, lightly, undetectably, the surface of her skin as he dries her, whosoever has refused to put his mother's spectacles on her face just now, as he has in the past when conscripted into bathing her, as he ought to do now, though in all likelihood she can only make out a few blurry shapes, anyway (at least until the cooling of her insulted central nervous system), whosoever wishes to prolong this additional disability, however, because when she is totally blind in addition to being damn near quadriplegic she faces up to the fact that her orienting skills are minimal, whosoever slips his mother's panties up her legs and checks the dainty hairless passage into her vulva one more time, because he can't resist the opportunity here for *knowledge*, whosoever gags briefly at his own forwardness, whosoever straps his mother's bra onto her, though the value of a bra for her is negligible, whosoever slips a housedress over her head, getting first one arm and then the other tangled in the neck hole, whosoever reaches for and then pulls the plug on the radio because the song playing on it is too sad, some terribly sad jazz ballad with muted trumpet, whosoever puts slippers on his mother's feet, left and then right, fiddling with her toes briefly first, simply to see if there is any sensation there, because her wasting disease is characterized by periods in which *some* feeling or sensation suddenly returns to affected extremities (though never all sensation), and likewise periods in which sensation is precipitously *snuffed out*, whosoever notes the complete lack of response in his mother when he pinches her big toe, and whosoever notes this response calmly, whosoever now finally sets his mother's glasses on her nose and adjusts the stems to make sure they are settled comfortably on her ears, whosoever kisses his mother a second time where her disordered hair is thinnest and takes her now fully into his arms to carry her to the wheelchair in the doorway, whosoever says to his wasting mom while stuttering mildly out of generalized anxiety and because of insufficient pause for the inflow and outflow of breath, *Hey, Mom, you look p-p-p-p-p-pretty fabulous t-t-tonight, you look like a million b-b-bucks*, whosoever says this while unlocking the brake on the chair, whosoever then brings the chair to a stop in the corridor off the kitchen, beneath a cheap, imitation American Impressionist landscape that hangs in that hallway, just so that he can hug his mom one more time because he hasn't seen her in months, because he is a neglectful son, because her condition is worse, always worse, whosoever fantasizes nonetheless about lashing her chair to a television table on casters so that he can just roll her and the idiot box with its barbiturate programming around the house without having to talk to her because he's been watching this decline for two decades or more and *he's fed up with comforting and self-sacrifice, the very ideas make him sick*, whosoever settles her in the kitchen by the Formica table and opens the refrigerator looking for some mush that will do the job for this evening, some mush that he can push down her throat and on which she will not spend the whole night choking as she sometimes does, so that he will have to use that little medical vacuum cleaner thing, that dental tool, to remove saliva and food particles from her gullet, tiny degraded hunks of minestrone and baby food, whosoever trips briefly over his mother's chair trying to get around it on the way to the chocolate milk in the fridge and jams his toe, *shit, shit, shit, sorry, Ma*, whosoever then changes his mind and fetches out a six-pack of the finest imported beer that he brought himself from a convenience store in town, and pops open one can for himself and one for his mother, whosoever then dips into his mother's beer a weaving and trembling plastic straw, whosoever then carries this beverage to his mother and fits the end of the straw between his mother's lips, exhorting her to *drink, drink*, whosoever then tilts back his own head emptying a fine imported beer in a pair of swallows so that he might move on to the next, whosoever then hugs his mom (again) feeling, in the flush of processed barley and hops, that his life is withal the best of lives, full of threat and bounty, bad news and good, affluence and penury, the sacred and the profane, the masculine and the feminine, the present and the repetitions of the past, whosoever in this instant of sorrow and reverence, *knows the answers* to why roses bloom, why wineglasses sing, why human lips, when kissed, are so soft, and why parents suffer, *he shall never die.*

Hex Raitliffe. And if he's a hero, then heroes are five-and-dime, and the world is as crowded with them as it is with stray pets, worn tires, and missing keys.

Source: Rick Moody (1998) *Purple America*, London: Flamingo, pp. 3–7.

20 from *Oxygen*

ANDREW MILLER

Andrew Miller (b. 1960), novelist, was born in Bristol and brought up in the West Country. He has lived in Spain, Japan, Ireland and France, as well as in England. He studied creative writing at the University of East Anglia, and completed a PhD in creative writing at Lancaster University in 1996. His first two novels, the prize-winning *Ingenious Pain* (1997), and *Casanova* (1998) were set in the eighteenth century. His third novel, *Oxygen* (2001), is set in England in the 1990s, and has two narrative lines, one concerning two brothers who return home to nurse their dying mother, the other the story of a Hungarian playwright living in Paris who becomes involved in the Kosovo conflict.

Inside the house his father's clocks were striking the hour. Faintly, the chimes carried to where he stood in the garden, a lank young man in a summer sweater and shapeless blue trousers, wiping the lenses of his glasses with the corner of a crumpled handkerchief. He had spent the last hour with the hose watering the flower-beds and giving the ground around the younger trees a good soaking, as he had been instructed to. Now, having carefully coiled the hose, he made his way back towards the house, his progress shadowed by a cat that pushed through the stems of delphiniums and peonies and oriental poppies. At the top of the house, the light in Alice's room shone dully from between half-open curtains.

It was the dusk of his third day back at Brooklands, the house in the West Country with its grey stone walls, brown-tiled roof and rotting summerhouse, where he had spent the first eighteen years of his life. His own small flat in London was shut and locked, and his neighbour, Mr Bequa, whose clothes carried their own atmosphere of black tobacco and failed cooking, had agreed to forward the mail, though there would not be much. Bequa had even come down into the street to wave him off, and knowing where he was going and why, had done so with gestures of extravagant melancholy, – 'Goodbye, Alec friend! Good heart! Goodbye!'

Wandsworth Bridge, Parsons Green, Hammersmith. Then west along the M4 past out-of-town superstores and fields of rape. A journey he had made so many times since Alice was first diagnosed he often completed the entire trip in a daze of inattention, startled to find himself rounding the last corner by the poultry farm, the sky ahead of him falling in luminous sheets towards the estuary and Wales. But this time, as each familiar landmark had dwindled in the rear-view mirror, then passed out of sight, it had seemed irretrievable, and carrying his suitcase into the hallway at Brooklands he had known with utter certainty that it was his last true homecoming, and that one half of his life was about to slough off like tons of earth in a landslide. For fifteen minutes he stood there surrounded by the soft weight of coats and hats, old boots, old tennis pumps, staring at the over-vivid snap on the wall by the door into the house – himself, Larry and Alice; Stephen must have taken it – arm in arm in the snowy orchard twenty years ago. And he had bowed his head, hearing from upstairs the chatter of his mother's radio and the rasping of her cough, and had wondered to himself what could possibly comfort him. Where on earth he might look for consolation or ease.

Coming from the garden, the house was entered by descending a short flight of mossy steps from the lawn to the terrace, and opening the glass doors into the kitchen. Here, by the worn mat, Alec slipped off his shoes and went through the house to the stairs, hoping that Alice would already have fallen asleep and would not need him. She had refused to have a room made up for her on the ground floor, despite everyone – Dr Brando, the visiting nurse Una O'Connell, and even Mrs Samson, the woman who for as long as Alec could remember had come in one morning a week to clean the house – saying how much better it would be, how much easier on good days to get into the garden. Wasn't there a perfectly suitable room downstairs, undisturbed for years other than by the daily swipe of sunlight across the mirror? But Alice had smiled at them all like a child made special and irreproachable by illness, and said that she was too used to the view, to the potato field, the church, the line of hills in the distance (like a boy, she once said, lying on his belly in the grass). And anyway, her bedroom had always been upstairs. It was too late to start 'rearranging the entire house'. So the subject was dropped, though for an angry moment Alec had wanted to tell her what it was like to watch her, that twenty-minute ordeal, hauling herself a step at a time towards the landing, her fingers clutching at the banister like talons.

Some measures she had agreed to. She took sit-down showers instead of baths, had a raised plastic seat on the toilet, and on Alec's last visit he had rigged up a bell, running the wire down the stairs from the bedroom and screwing the bell-housing to a beam by the kitchen door. There had even been some laughter when they tested it, Alice pressing the white knob by her bed (complaining that it sounded like the dive klaxon on a submarine) while Alec moved around the house to check the bell's range, and then went out to the garden, giving the thumbs-up to Una, who leaned dashingly from the bedroom window. But by evening, Alice had decided that the bell was 'a silly thing', and 'quite unnecessary', and she had looked at Alec as if its installation had been tactless, yet another item among the paraphernalia of her sickness. More inescapable proof of her inescapable condition.

She was not asleep when he went in. She lay propped against the pillows in her nightgown and quilted robe, reading a book. The room was very warm. The heat of the sun was in the timbers of the roof, and the radiator was on high, so that everything sweated its particular smell, a stuffiness half intimate, half medical, that hung in the air like a sediment. Vases of cut flowers, some from the garden, some from friends, added a note of hothouse sweetness, and there was a perfume she sprayed as a kind of luxurious air-freshener, which masked very little, but which Alec could always taste in his mouth for an hour after leaving the room.

Cleanliness – even the illusion of it – was an obsession with her now, as though the sickness were something, some lapse in hygiene, that might be hidden behind veils of scent. For an hour each morning and evening she washed herself with catlike attention in the en-suite bathroom, the only real physical work she still did. But no soaps or night creams or lavender shower gel could entirely hide what filtered out from the disasters inside of her, though nothing would ever be quite as disturbing as that first course of chemotherapy the winter of two years ago, when she had sat wrapped in picnic rugs on the sofa in the living room, alien and wretched and smelling like a child's chemistry set. When her hair had grown again, it had sprouted brilliant white, and was now a weight of frost-coloured locks that reached to the mid-point of her back. This, she said – the one thing remaining to her she could still be vain about – was the reason she had refused more treatment when she came out of remission, and of all the people who attended on her now, it was her long-time hairdresser, Toni Cuskic, who had the greatest power to soothe. They had a new arrangement: there was no question of Alice making the twenty-minute trip into Nailsea, so once a week Toni drove out from the salon to pull her heavy brush the length of Alice's hair, while Alice tilted her face to the light, eyes shut, smiling as she listened to the gossip from the shop. Sometimes Toni brought her poodle, Miss Sissy, a show bitch with tight black curls, and Alice would stroke the animal's narrow skull and let it lick her wrists, until it grew bored of her and wandered off to sniff at some stain or savoury relic around the fringes of the bed.

'Everything all right, Mum?' He was standing just inside the door, hands in pockets, very slightly rocking on the balls of his feet.

'Fine, dear.'

'Need anything?'

She shook her head.

'Sure?'

'Thank you, dear.'

'Cup of tea?'

'No, thank you.'

'I've done the garden.'

'Good.'

'How about some hot milk?'

'No, thank you.'

'You haven't forgotten your Zopiclone?'

'No, dear, I haven't. Do try not to fuss.'

She frowned at him, the old headmistress again, bothered by some wittering pupil. A go-away look.

'I'll let you read,' he said. 'Look in later.'

She nodded, the movement triggering off a fit of coughing, but as he moved towards her (what was he going to *do*?) she waved him away and he went out, listening from the landing until she was quiet, then going slowly down the stairs, blushing from an emotion he could not quite identify.

Source: Andrew Miller (2001) *Oxygen*, London: Sceptre, pp. 9–14.

21 'Going the Last Inch: Some thoughts on showing and telling'

LINDSAY CLARKE

Lindsay Clarke (b. 1939), novelist and radio dramatist, was born in Halifax, West Yorkshire. He worked in education for many years in Africa, America and the UK, before becoming a full-time writer. He is the author of three novels, *Sunday Whiteman* (1987), *The Chymical Wedding* (1989), which won the Whitbread Fiction Prize, and *Alice's Masque* (1994). He has a particular interest in mythology, and among his other books are *Essential Celtic Mythology* (1997) and *Parzival and the Stone from Heaven* (2001), a re-telling of the Grail romance.

A novel is a game for two players. The book may get written in solitude but it kicks into life only when a reader's imagination collaborates with that of the writer, so in working out how best to secure and sustain that collaboration, writers might usefully recall what most engrosses them as readers. In the early drafts of a piece, you are still working out what you are trying to say to yourself, and too much mental trafficking with an audience at that stage can inhibit the flow of your imagination. But if you mean to go public, then sooner or later you have to consider the legitimate needs of your readers, and a large part of the process of revision will be about making sure that you have given their imagination all the room it needs to work.

In this respect Henry James offered the novelist three key words of advice: 'Dramatize, dramatize, dramatize.' His disciple Percy Lubbock turned the recommendation into a rule by insisting that 'the art of fiction does not begin until the novelist thinks of his story as a matter to be shown, to be so exhibited that it will tell itself', and the cry of 'show, don't tell' still rings across writing workshops. To understand why, you need only ask which is more immediately engaging – to witness an event for yourself or to be told about it afterwards by someone else?

A brief example will *show* what the distinction between showing and telling can mean for fiction. If, in a first novel, an author had written, 'The boy broke down and began to cry so wretchedly that the other small children started howling too,' he would, rather dully, have told us something. When, in *The Lord of the Flies*, William Golding wrote that 'his face puckered, the tears leapt from his eyes, his mouth opened till they could see a square black hole … The crying went on, breath after breath, and seemed to sustain him upright as if he were nailed to it,' he has unforgettably *shown* us something. By which I mean that he has brought us so closely into the presence of the weeping child that we can see him and hear him and feel our own inconsolable portion in the sense of universal grief he disturbs in the other 'littluns'. Who could prefer the told version to the shown?

Yet forty years after Lubbock's book on *The Craft of Fiction*, Wayne C. Booth pointed out in *The Rhetoric of Fiction* that showing is itself only one among the diverse strategies of telling, and that direct telling can work potent magic, too. Consider, for instance, the opening of Paul Auster's *Moon Palace*, with its recklessly overt resume of the story we are about to read – all telling, every word of it, but told to magnetic effect.

What's more, if we insist on showing everything, especially things that might more effectively be told, then it won't be long before we start to bore the reader. The error shows itself in the common tendency of young writers to begin in the wrong place, so that we must watch the leading character get out of bed, stare in the mirror, eat breakfast and so on, to the point where we begin to lose interest long before some intriguing encounter seizes our attention. In those dull circumstances, the collaboration with the reader will end before it's properly got started. So what seems to be in question is the right choice of narrative strategy *at any given moment*. Do I tell the readers this or should I show it? Which approach will most effectively draw them into the dream of the novel, and keep them there till the dream is done?

Reading and dreaming have much in common. In both we generate images out of a limited visual field. These images move and disturb us because we feel that we are immediately involved with them, at times more intensely than with our everyday experience, yet they arrive without overt explanations and require us to work for meaning. Also, unlike those of film, the images we find in books and dreams are unique to each of us, the work of our own imagination. So my Heathcliff does not look like yours, and when either of us tries to tell someone else about a dream we've had, or a book we've read, we know just how much gets lost.

Now dreams remain a great mystery, but their vocabulary of images seems to allow the oldest, pre-verbal parts of the brain to speak to the neocortex, thus opening a channel of communication between the conscious and unconscious minds. By flexing all the inward senses of the imagination, fiction can tap us into that hotline, too, and when that happens, good writing literally works like a dream. And what may most deeply excite us about it is the fact that we have been set free to dream the story for ourselves.

This freedom of the imagination is of profound, countervailing importance in a time when we are so often the passive recipients of information and reportage. So there may be more than just literary reasons for the emphasis on showing over telling in most fiction workshops. But what matters here is the recognition that, if we are to create and sustain a lively dream in the imagination of the reader, then much of our revision will be about questioning our choices of narrative strategy, altering them where necessary, then fine-tuning their effects.

In practice this means hunting down those moments that unintentionally tip the reader out of the dream. They can be considered under two broad headings: problems that arise from underwriting, when the author hasn't done enough imaginative work to secure the collaboration of the reader, and those of overwriting, when the reader is crowded out by the author trying to do too much.

Merely telling the reader something that's crying out to be dramatized is a form of underwriting. William Blake once wrote that 'he who does not imagine in minute particulars does not imagine at all', and it seems clear that if we don't bring the focused energy of the imagination to bear on the scene we're writing, then we're unlikely to activate its full potential for exciting the reader's interest. The result is inert wordage that
leaves the reader cold, so it's as well to keep an eye out for the symptoms.

Prominent among them is the retreat into abstraction. Watch out for a reliance on abstract nouns in your writing, particularly those to do with states of feeling. Simply to announce that a character is 'filled with fury' or 'rotten with jealousy' is the weakest way to make your reader feel the impact of their emotions. We have your word for it but little else. However, if you show us the children wincing as Harriet throws the curry she's just cooked across the kitchen, or we see Ken straining to overhear a telephone call through a closed door, then we draw our own conclusions. It's a useful exercise to forbid yourself the use of keynote words such as 'fury' or 'jealous' when dramatizing an emotional condition. Similarly, when you find yourself writing *about* an important conversation, ask whether your readers might not prefer to hear the exchanges for themselves, particularly as characters are revealed through the different ways they use the language, and dialogue can subtly move the narrative along.

Of course, this kind of dramatized showing is much harder than straight telling, and in good writing there's no distinction between language and content, so the success of a piece will depend on how skilfully your words perform the show. When you come to revise a draft, ask yourself, for instance, how many details have been blurred by the broad-brush adjectives you've used to depict a scene. Is there a more limber way of conjuring the characters into the reader's presence than merely attaching descriptive tags? Does your use of adverbs short-circuit energy out of your sentences by labelling actions that a sharper movement of the syntax might quicken into life? And when you come across a cliché, take it for what it is – a sign that you've nodded off and it's time to recharge your imagination. Somewhere behind that prefabricated block of language lies a living moment. Close your eyes, activate your inward senses, then write and rewrite till you've hit a pitch of high fidelity. After all, if you don't care enough about the characters and events of your story to do them imaginative justice, why should the reader stay inside the dream?

Overwriting indicates a failure to trust the imagination of the reader. Consider how much of the pleasure of reading comes from inferring that which has nowhere been explicitly stated. A writer who pre-empts such moments of realization by obtrusive winks and nudges soon becomes a bore. The same is true of any lack of economy and concision in your prose. By making a careful selection of details from a scene that you've imagined for yourself 'in minute particulars', you free your readers to visualize it, too. But if you pile on the adjectives, or double the contents of your sentences through the loose use of similes, you are more likely to crowd them out.

Often enough you'll find that less can do more. A marvellous letter written by Conrad in 1899 demonstrates what this principle means in practice. A friend had asked his opinion on some stories he had written, one of which contained these sentences: 'When the whole horror of his position forced itself with an agony of apprehension upon his frightened mind, Pa'Tua for a space lost his reason. He screamed aloud, and the hollow of the rocks took up his cries and hurled them back mockingly.' Conrad sharpened the passage, to powerful effect, simply by cutting out a quarter of the words. Bearing in mind his general admonition that the author hadn't left enough to the reader's imagination, you might like to work out which words he cut.

Sometimes we overwrite out of the desire not so much to show as to show off; and sometimes, less exuberantly, out of anxiety to make sure that our meaning gets across. Either way we have to learn to 'murder our darlings' for the greater good of the book, and this can come hard. I was so infatuated with a sentence in one of my own novels that it passed unscathed through every draft, right through to the galley proofs, when my wife declared that she had always hated it. I woke up and saw that either the whole story dramatized what the sentence had to say – in which case it was redundant – or it didn't in which case that sentence alone wasn't going to save the book from failure. It was an edgy moment, but I knew that in the end the finished work had to speak clearly on its own terms, uncluttered by the author's attachments. That sentence might have helped to keep me on track throughout the writing of the book, continuously reminding me what it was supposed to be about, but the reader had no use for it. So I struck it out, and have long since forgotten it except as a happy reminder of the satisfactions of revision.

Alexander Solzenhitsyn celebrates the importance of such moments in his novel *The First Circle*, where one of the characters, a prisoner in the Gulag, speaks movingly of 'the rule of the last inch'. It's a rule that applies near the end of a project when you sense that, despite all your efforts, the quality you were after is not yet quite attained, and there's still more to be done before the long journey of the work is over. The rule of the last inch is simply not to neglect it. It's a rule that all writers who care for their craft will strive to take to heart.

Source: Julia Bell and Paul Magrs (eds) (2001) *The Creative Writing Coursebook*, London: Macmillan, pp. 256–61.

22 *'The Artist'*

PATRICIA HIGHSMITH

Patricia Highsmith (1921–1995), novelist and short-story writer, was born Mary Patricia Plangman in Fort Worth, Texas. Her parents, both commercial artists, separated before she was born and she was given the name of her stepfather, Stanley Highsmith, another commercial artist. It was an unhappy childhood. After a brief attempt at painting, Highsmith turned to writing for a living. Her first novel, *Strangers on a Train* (1950) was instantly successful and was made into a film by Alfred Hitchcock. She went on to produce about twenty novels, usually classified as crime fiction because of their focus on the criminal and criminal psychology. Collections of her short stories include *Little Tales of Misogyny* (1977) and *The Animal-Lover's Book of Beastly Murder* (1975).

At the time Jane got married, one would have thought there was nothing unusual about her. She was plump, pretty and practical: she could give artificial respiration at the drop of a hat or pull someone out of a faint or a nosebleed. She was a dentist's assistant, and as cool as they come in the face of crisis or pain. But she had enthusiasm for the arts. What arts? All of them. She began, in the first year of her married life, with painting. This occupied all her Saturdays, or enough of Saturdays to prevent adequate shopping for the weekend, but her husband Bob did the shopping. He also paid for the framing of muddy, run–together oil portraits of their friends, and the sittings of the friends took up time on the weekends too. Jane at last faced the fact she could not stop her colours from running together, and decided to abandon painting for the dance.

The dance, in a black leotard, did not much improve her robust figure, only her appetite. Special shoes followed. She was studying ballet. She had discovered an institution called The School of Arts. In this five-storey edifice they taught the piano, violin and other instruments, music composition, novel-writing, poetry, sculpture, the dance and painting.

'You see, Bob, life can and should be made more beautiful,' Jane said with her big smile. 'And everyone wants to contribute, if he or she can, just a little bit to the beauty and poetry of the world.'

Meanwhile, Bob emptied the garbage and made sure they were not out of potatoes. Jane's ballet did not progress beyond a certain point, and she dropped it and took up singing.

'I really think life is beautiful enough as it is,' Bob said. 'Anyway I'm pretty happy.' That was during Jane's singing period, which had caused them to crowd the already small living-room with an upright piano.

For some reason, Jane stopped her singing lessons and began to study sculpture and wood-carving. This made the living-room a mess of dropped bits of clay and wood chips which the vacuum could not always pick up. Jane was too tired for anything after her day's work in the dentist's office, and standing on her feet over wood or clay until midnight.

Bob came to hate The School of Arts. He had seen it a few times, when he had gone to fetch Jane at 11 p.m. or so. (The neighbourhood was dangerous to walk in.) It seemed to Bob that the students were all a lot of misguided hopefuls, and the teachers a lot of mediocrities. It seemed a madhouse of misplaced effort. And how many homes, children and husbands were being troubled now, because the women of the households – the students were mainly women – were not at home performing a few essential tasks? It seemed to Bob that there was no inspiration in The School of Arts, only a desire to imitate people who had been inspired, like Chopin, Beethoven and Bach, whose works he could hear being mangled as he sat on a bench in the lobby, awaiting his wife. People called artists mad, but these students seemed incapable of the same kind of madness. The students did appear insane, in a certain sense of the word, but not in the right way, somehow. Considering the time The School of Arts deprived him of his wife, Bob was ready to blow the whole building to bits.

He had not long to wait, but he did not blow the building up himself. Someone – it was later proven to have been an instructor – put a bomb under The School of Arts, set to go off at 4 p.m. It was New Year's Eve, and despite the fact it was a semi-holiday, the students of all the arts were practising diligently. The police and some newspapers had been forewarned of the bomb. The trouble was, nobody found it, and also most people did not believe that any bomb would go off. Because of the seediness of the neighbourhood, the school had been subjected to scares and threats before. But the bomb went off, evidently from the depths of the basement, and a pretty good sized one it was.

Bob happened to be there, because he was to have fetched Jane at 5 p.m. He had heard about the bomb rumour, but did not know whether to believe it or not. With some caution, however, or a premonition, he was waiting across the street instead of in the lobby.

One piano went through the roof, a bit separated from the student who was still seated on the stool, fingering nothing. A dancer at last made a few complete revolutions without her feet touching the ground, because she was a quarter of a mile high, and her toes were even pointing skyward. An art student was flung through a wall, his brush poised, ready to make the master stroke as he floated horizontally towards a true oblivion. One instructor, who had taken refuge as often as possible in the toilets of The School of Arts, was blown up in proximity to some of the plumbing.

Then came Jane, flying through the air with a mallet in one hand, a chisel in the other, and her expression was rapt. Was she stunned, still concentrating on her work, or even dead? Bob could not tell about Jane. The flying particles subsided with a gentle, diminishing clatter, and a rise of grey dust. There were a few seconds of silence, during which Bob stood still. Then he turned and walked homeward. Other Schools of Art, he knew, would arise. Oddly, this thought crossed his mind before he realized that his wife was gone forever.

Source: Patricia Highsmith (1995) *Little Tales of Misogyny*, London: Penguin, pp. 16–20.

23 'The Dream'

ANON

'The Dream' comes from Tales from *the Thousand and One Nights*, or *Arabian Nights Entertainments*, a collection of ancient stories written in Arabic, first introduced into Europe in the early eighteenth century and often translated thereafter. The framework is that the Sultan Schahriah has each of his wives strangled on the morning after the consummation of their marriage. The clever young Scheherazade, however, amuses him for a thousand and one nights by telling him tales, as a result of which he revokes his cruel decree. One of the most famous sequences in the collection concerns the adventures of Sinbad the Sailor.

There lived once in Baghdad a merchant who, having squandered all his wealth, became so destitute that he could make his living only by the hardest labour.

One night he lay down to sleep with a heavy heart, and in a dream a man appeared to him, saying: 'Your fortune lies in Cairo. Go and seek it there.'

The very next morning he set out for Cairo and, after many weeks and much hardship on the way, arrived in that city. Night had fallen, and as he could not afford to stay at an inn he lay down to sleep in the courtyard of a mosque.

Now as the Almighty's will would have it, a band of robbers entered the mosque and from there broke into an adjoining house. Awakened by the noise, the owners raised the alarm and shouted for help; then the thieves made off. Presently the Chief of Police and his men arrived on the scene. They entered the mosque and, finding the man from Baghdad lying in the courtyard, seized him and beat him with their clubs until he was nearly dead. Then they threw him into prison.

Three days later the Chief of Police ordered his men to bring the stranger before him.

'Where do you come from?' asked the chief.

'From Baghdad.'

'And what has brought you to Cairo?'

'A man appeared to me in a dream, saying: "Your fortune lies in Cairo. Go and seek it there." But when I came to Cairo, the fortune I was promised proved to be the blows your men so generously gave me.'

When he heard this, the Chief of Police burst out laughing. 'Know then, you fool,' he cried, 'that I too have heard a voice in my sleep, not just once but on three occasions. It said: "Go to Baghdad, and in a cobbled street lined with palmtrees you will find such-and-such a house, with a courtyard of grey marble; at the far end of the garden there is a fountain of white marble. Under the fountain a great sum of money lies buried. Go there and dig it up." But would I go? Of course not. Yet, fool that you are, you have come all the way to Cairo on the strength of one idle dream.'

Then the Chief of Police gave the merchant some money. 'Here,' he said, 'take this. It will help you on the way back to your own country.'

The merchant recognized at once that the house and garden just described were his own. He took the money and set out promptly on his homeward journey.

As soon as he reached his house he went into the garden, dug beneath the fountain, and uncovered a great treasure.

Thus the words of the dream were wondrously fulfilled, and Allah made the ruined merchant rich again.

Source: N. J. Dawood (tr.) (1973) *Tales from the Thousand and One Nights*, Harmondsworth: Penguin, pp. 328–9.

24 'The Black Cap'

KATHERINE MANSFIELD

Katherine Mansfield (1888–1923) was born in Wellington, New Zealand, as Katherine Mansfield Beauchamp (she adopted her beloved grandmother's maiden name as her pseudonym). Her father was a self-made man who ended up as chairman of the board of the Bank of New Zealand. She was sent to finish her education in London, and although she went back briefly to New Zealand, she returned to England determined to become a writer. She began publishing stories in avant-garde literary magazines in 1910. Her first volume of stories, *In a German Pension* (1911) dealt with sexual relationships and the position of women in society. Later collections – *Bliss and Other Stories* (1920) and *The Garden Party and Other Stories* (1922) – centred on her childhood in New Zealand. She died of tuberculosis.

(A lady and her husband are seated at breakfast. He is quite calm, reading the newspaper and eating; but she is strangely excited, dressed for travelling, and only pretending to eat.)

SHE: Oh, if you should want your flannel shirts, they are on the right-hand bottom shelf of the linen press.

HE (*at a board meeting of the Meat Export Company*): No.

SHE: You didn't hear what I said. I said if you should want your flannel shirts, they are on the right-hand bottom shelf of the linen press.

HE (*positively*): I quite agree!

SHE: It does seem rather extraordinary that on the very morning that I am going away you cannot leave the newspaper alone for five minutes.

HE (*mildly*): My dear woman, I don't want you to go. In fact, I have asked you not to go. I can't for the life of me see....

SHE: You know perfectly well that I am only going because I absolutely must. I've been putting it off and putting it off, and the dentist said last time....

HE: Good! Good! Don't let's go all over the ground again. We've thrashed it all out pretty thoroughly, haven't we?

SERVANT: Cab's here, m'm.

SHE: Please put my luggage in.

SERVANT: Very good, m'm.

(*She gives a tremendous sigh.*)

HE: You haven't got too much time if you want to catch that train.

SHE: I know. I'm going. (*In a changed tone.*) Darling, don't let us part like this. It makes me feel so wretched. Why is it that you always seem to take a positive delight in spoiling my enjoyment?

HE: I don't think going to the dentist is so positively enjoyable.

SHE: Oh, you know that's not what I mean. You're only saying that to hurt me. You know you are begging the question.

HE (*laughing*): And you are losing your train. You'll be back on Thursday evening, won't you?

SHE (*in a low, desperate voice*): Yes, on Thursday evening. Good-bye, then. (*Comes over to him, and takes his head in her hands.*) Is there anything really the matter? Do at least look at me. Don't you – care – at – all?

HE: My darling girl! This is like an exit on the cinema.

SHE (*letting her hands fall*):   Very well. Good-bye. (*Gives a quick tragic glance round the dining-room and goes.*)

(*On the way to the station.*)

SHE: How strange life is! I didn't think I should feel like this at all. All the glamour seems to have gone, somehow. Oh, I'd give anything for the cab to turn round and go back. The most curious thing is that I feel if he really had made me believe he loved me it would have been much easier to have left him. But that's absurd. How strong the hay smells. It's going to be a very hot day. I shall never see these fields again. Never, never! But in another way I am glad that it happened like this; it puts me so finally, absolutely in the right for ever! He doesn't want a woman at all. A woman has no meaning for him. He's not the type of man to care deeply for anybody except himself. I've become the person who remembers to take the links out of his shirts before they go to the wash – that is all! And that's not enough for me. I'm young – I'm too proud. I'm not the type of woman to vegetate in the country and rave over 'our' own lettuces. . . .

What you have been trying to do, ever since you married me is to make me submit, to turn me into your shadow, to rely on me so utterly that you'd only to glance up to find the right time printed on me somehow, as if I were a clock. You have never been curious about me; you never wanted to explore my soul. No; you wanted me to settle down to your peaceful existence. Oh! how your blindness has outraged me – how I hate you for it! I am glad – thankful – thankful to have left you! I'm not a green girl; I am not conceited, but I do know my powers. It's not for nothing that I've always longed for riches and passion and freedom, and felt that they were mine by right. (*She leans against the buttoned back of the cab and murmurs.*) 'You are a Queen. Let mine be the joy of giving you your kingdom.' (*She smiles at her little royal hands.*) I wish my heart didn't beat so hard. It really hurts me. It tires me so and excites me so. It's like someone in a dreadful hurry beating against a door. . . . This cab is only crawling along; we shall never be at the station at this rate. Hurry! Hurry! My love, I am coming as quickly as ever I can. Yes, I am suffering just like you. It's dreadful, isn't it unbearable – this last half-hour without each other. . . . Oh, God! the horse has begun to walk again. Why doesn't he beat the great strong brute of a thing. . . . Our wonderful life! We shall travel all over the world together. The whole world shall be ours because of our love. Oh, be patient! I am coming as fast as I possibly can. . . . Ah, now it's downhill; now we really are going faster. (*An old man attempts to cross the road.*) Get out of the way, you old fool! He deserves to be run over. . . . Dearest – dearest; I am nearly there. Only be patient!

(*At the station.*)

Put it in a first-class smoker. . . . There's plenty of time after all. A full ten minutes before the train goes. No wonder he's not here. I mustn't appear to be looking for him. But I must say I'm disappointed. I never dreamed of being the first to arrive. I thought he would have been here and engaged a carriage and bought papers and flowers. . . . How curious! I absolutely saw in my mind a paper of pink carnations. . . . He knows how fond I am of carnations. But pink ones are not my favourites. I prefer dark red or pale yellow. He really will be late if he doesn't come now. The guard has begun to shut the doors. Whatever can have happened? Something dreadful. Perhaps at the last moment he has shot himself.... I could not bear the thought of ruining your life.... But you are not ruining my life. Ah, where are you? I shall have to get into the carriage.... Who is this? That's not him! It can't be – yes, it is. What on earth has he got on his head? A black cap. But how awful! He's utterly changed. What can he be wearing a black cap for? I wouldn't have known him. How absurd he looks coming towards me, smiling, in that appalling cap!

HE: My darling, I shall never forgive myself. But the most absurd, tragic-comic thing happened. (*They get into the carriage.*) I lost my hat. It simply disappeared. I had half the hotel looking for it. Not a sign! So finally, in despair, I had to borrow this from another man who was staying there. (*The train moves off.*) You're not angry. (*Tries to take her in his arms.*)

SHE: Don't! We're not even out of the station yet.

HE (*ardently*):   Great God! What do I care if the whole world were to see us? (*Tries to take her in his arms.*) My wonder! My joy!

SHE: Please don't! I hate being kissed in trains.

HE (*profoundly hurt*): Oh, very well. You *are* angry. It's serious. You can't get over the fact that I was late. But if you only knew the agony I suffered....

SHE: How can you think I could be so small-minded? I'm not angry at all.

HE: Then why won't you let me kiss you?

SHE (*laughing hysterically*): You look so different somehow – almost a stranger.

HE (*jumps up and looks at himself in the glass anxiously*, and *fatuously, she decides*): But it's all right, isn't it?

SHE: Oh, quite all right; perfectly all right. Oh, oh, oh! (*She begins to laugh and cry with rage.*)

(*They arrive.*)

SHE (*while he gets a cab*): I must get over this. It's an obsession. It's incredible that anything should change a man so. I must tell him. Surely it's quite simple to say: Don't you think now that you are in the city you had better buy yourself a hat? But that will make him realise how frightful the cap has been. And the extraordinary thing is that he doesn't realise it himself. I mean if he has looked at himself in the glass, and doesn't think that cap too ridiculous, how different our points of view must be.... How deeply different. I mean, if I had seen him in the street I would have said I could not possibly love a man who wore a cap like that. I couldn't even have got to know him. He isn't my style at all. (*She looks round.*) Everybody is smiling at it. Well, I don't wonder! The way it makes his ears stick out, and the way it makes him have no back to his head at all.

HE: The cab is ready, my darling. (*They get in.*)

HE (*tries to take her hand*): The miracle that we two should be driving together, so simply, like this.

(*She arranges her veil.*)

HE (*tries to take her hand; very ardent*): I'll engage one room, my love.

SHE: Oh, no! Of course you must take two.

HE: But don't you think it would be wiser not to create suspicion?

SHE: I must have my own room (*To herself.*) You can hang your cap behind your own door! (*She begins to laugh hysterically.*)

HE: Ah! thank God! My queen is her happy self again!

(*At the hotel.*)

MANAGER: Yes, Sir, I quite understand. I think I've got the very thing for you, Sir. Kindly step this way. (*He takes them into a small sitting-room, with a bedroom leading out of it.*) This would suit you nicely, wouldn't it? And if you liked, we could make you up a bed on the sofa.

HE: Oh, admirable! Admirable!

(*The Manager goes.*)

SHE (*furious*): But I told you I wanted a room to myself. What a trick to play upon me! I told you I did not want to share a room. How dare you treat me like this? (*She mimics.*) Admirable! Admirable! I shall never forgive you for that!

HE (*overcome*): Oh, God, what is happening! I don't understand – I'm in the dark. Why have you suddenly, on this day of days, ceased to love me? What have I done? Tell me!

SHE (*sinks on the sofa*): I'm very tired. If you do love me, please leave me alone. I – I only want to be alone for a little.

HE (*tenderly*): Very well. I shall try to understand. I do begin to understand. I'll go out for half an hour, and then, my love, you may feel calmer. (*He looks round, distracted.*)

SHE: What is it?

HE: My heart – you are sitting on my cap. (*She gives a positive scream and moves into the bedroom. He goes. She waits for a moment, and then puts down her veil, and takes up her suitcase.*)

(*In the taxi.*)

SHE: Yes, Waterloo. (*She leans back.*) Ah, I've escaped – I've escaped! I shall just be in time to catch the afternoon train home. Oh, it's like a dream – I'll be home before supper. I'll tell him that the city was too hot or the dentist away. What does it matter? I've a right to my own home.... It will be wonderful driving up from the station; the fields will smell so delicious. There is cold fowl for supper left over from yesterday, and orange jelly.... I have been mad, but now I am sane again. Oh, my husband!

Source: Katherine Mansfield (1984) *The Stories of Katherine Mansfield*, Antony Alpers (ed.) Oxford: Oxford University Press, pp. 207–11.

25 'I could see the smallest things'

RAYMOND CARVER

For biographical details, see Reading 1, p. 413.

I was in bed when I heard the gate. I listened carefully. I didn't hear anything else. But I heard that. I tried to wake Cliff. He was passed out. So I got up and went to the window. A big moon was laid over the mountains that went around the city. It was a white moon and covered with scars. Any damn fool could imagine a face there.

There was light enough so that I could see everything in the yard – lawn chairs, the willow tree, clothesline strung between the poles, the petunias, the fences, the gate standing wide open.

But nobody was moving around. There were no scary shadows. Everything lay in moonlight, and I could see the smallest things. The clothespins on the line, for instance.

I put my hands on the glass to block out the moon. I looked some more. I listened. Then I went back to bed.

But I couldn't get to sleep. I kept turning over. I thought about the gate standing open. It was like a dare.

Cliff's breathing was awful to listen to. His mouth gaped open and his arms hugged his pale chest. He was taking up his side of the bed and most of mine.

I pushed and pushed on him. But he just groaned.

I stayed still awhile longer until I decided it was no use. I got up and got my slippers. I went to the kitchen and made tea and sat with it at the kitchen table. I smoked one of Cliff's unfiltereds.

It was late. I didn't want to look at the time. I drank the tea and smoked another cigaret. After a while I decided I'd go out and fasten up the gate.

So I got my robe.

The moon lighted up everything – houses and trees, poles and power lines, the whole world. I peered around the backyard before I stepped off the porch. A little breeze came along that made me close the robe.

I started for the gate.

There was a noise at the fences that separated our place from Sam Lawton's place. I took a sharp look. Sam was leaning with his arms on his fence, there being two fences to lean on. He raised his fist to his mouth and gave a dry cough.

'Evening, Nancy,' Sam Lawton said.

I said, 'Sam, you scared me.' I said, 'What are you doing up?' 'Did you hear something?' I said. 'I heard my gate unlatch.'

He said, 'I didn't hear anything. Haven't seen anything, either. It might have been the wind.'

He was chewing something. He looked at the open gate and shrugged.

His hair was silvery in the moonlight and stood up on his head. I could see his long nose, the lines in his big sad face.

I said, 'What are you doing up, Sam?' and moved closer to the fence.

'Want to see something?' he said.

'I'll come around,' I said.

I let myself out and went along the walk. It felt funny walking around outside in my nightgown and my robe. I thought to myself that I should try to remember this, walking around outside like this.

Sam was standing over by the side of his house, his pajamas way up high over his tan-and-white shoes. He was holding a flashlight in one hand and a can of something in the other.

Sam and Cliff used to be friends. Then one night they got to drinking. They had words. The next thing, Sam had built a fence and then Cliff built one too.

That was after Sam had lost Millie, gotten married again, and become a father again all in the space of no time at all. Millie had been a good friend to me up until she died. She was only forty-five when she did it. Heart failure. It hit her just as she was coming into their drive. The car kept going and went on through the back of the carport.

'Look at this,' Sam said, hitching his pajama trousers and squatting down. He pointed his light at the ground.

I looked and saw some wormy things curled on a patch of dirt.

'Slugs,' he said. 'I just gave them a dose of this,' he said, raising a can of something that looked like Ajax. 'They're taking over,' he said, and worked whatever it was that he had in his mouth. He turned his head to one side and spit what could have been tobacco. 'I have to keep at this to just come close to staying up with them.' He turned his light on a jar that was filled with the things. 'I put bait out, and then every chance I get I come out here with this stuff. Bastards are all over. A crime what they can do. Look here,' he said.

He got up. He took my arm and moved me over to his rosebushes. He showed me the little holes in the leaves.

'Slugs,' he said. 'Everywhere you look around here at night. I lay out bait and then I come out and get them,' he said. 'An awful invention, the slug. I save them up in that jar there.' He moved his light to under the rosebush.

A plane passed overhead. I imagined the people on it sitting belted in their seats, some of them reading, some of them staring down at the ground.

'Sam,' I said, 'how's everybody?'

'They're fine,' he said, and shrugged.

He chewed on whatever it was he was chewing. 'How's Clifford?' he said.

I said, 'Same as ever.'

Sam said, 'Sometimes when I'm out here after the slugs, I'll look over in your direction.' He said, 'I wish me and Cliff was friends again. Look there now,' he said, and drew a sharp breath. 'There's one there. See him? Right there where my light is.' He had the beam directed onto the dirt under the rosebush. 'Watch this,' Sam said.

I closed my arms under my breasts and bent over to where he was shining his light. The thing stopped moving and turned its head from side to side. Then Sam was over it with his can of powder, sprinkling the powder down.

'Slimy things,' he said.

The slug was twisting this way and that. Then it curled and straightened out.

Sam picked up a toy shovel, and scooped the slug into it, and dumped it out in the jar.

'I quit, you know,' Sam said. 'Had to. For a while it was getting so I didn't know up from down. We still keep it around the house, but I don't have much to do with it anymore.'

I nodded. He looked at me and he kept looking.

'I'd better get back,' I said.

'Sure,' he said. 'I'll continue with what I'm doing and then when I'm finished, I'll head in too.'

I said, 'Good night, Sam.'

He said, 'Listen.' He stopped chewing. With his tongue, he pushed whatever it was behind his lower lip. 'Tell Cliff I said hello.'

I said, 'I'll tell him you said so, Sam.'

Sam ran his hand through his silvery hair as if he was going to make it sit down once and for all, and then he used his hand to wave.

In the bedroom, I took off the robe, folded it, put it within reach. Without looking at the time, I checked to make sure the stem was out on the clock. Then I got into the bed, pulled the covers up, and closed my eyes.

It was then that I remembered I'd forgotten to latch the gate.

I opened my eyes and lay there. I gave Cliff a little shake. He cleared his throat. He swallowed. Something caught and dribbled in his chest.

I don't know. It made me think of those things that Sam Lawton was dumping powder on.

I thought for a minute of the world outside my house, and then I didn't have any more thoughts except the thought that I had to hurry up and sleep.

Source: Raymond Carver (1985) *The Stories of Raymond Carver*, London: Picador/Pan Books, pp. 204–7.

26 *'The Dying Room'*

GEORGINA HAMMICK

Georgina Hammick (b. 1939), short-story writer and poet, was born in Hampshire, the daughter of an army officer. She began as a teacher of English and art, and then worked as a director of Hammicks Bookshops Ltd. She now teaches creative writing. She has published widely in literary magazines, and her first collection of short stories, *People for Lunch*, was published in 1987. Other books include *Spoilt* (1992) and *The Arizona Game* (1996).

I think I left my wireless in the drawing room, his mother said. Could you get it? I'd be grateful.

His mother and he were in the kitchen. He took a big breath. He said, You can't use that word any more, I'm sorry, we've decided.

What word are you talking about? his mother said. She took a tray of cheese tartlets from the oven and put them on the table. His mother is a cook. She cooks for her family when they're at home and she cooks professionally: for other women's freezers and other women's lunch and dinner parties. She also supplies, on a regular basis, her local delicatessen with pâtés and terrines and tarts and quiches. Blast, these look a bit burnt to me, his mother said. Do they look burnt to you? What word can't I use?

'Drawing room', he said. It's an anachronism, it's irrelevant. It's snobbish. It has associations with mindless West End theatre. It's embarrassing.

His mother said nothing for a minute. She looked thoughtful; she looked thoughtfully at her feet. Then she said, Who are 'we'? 'We' who have decided?

My sisters and I, he told her. Your children. All of them.

I see, his mother said. First I've heard of this, I have to say.

The point is, he said, our friends, the ones we bring here, find it offensive – or a joke. And so do we. It is offensive, and ridiculous, to continue to use a word that means nothing to ninety-nine per cent of the population, that ninety-nine per cent of the population does not use.

Hang on a minute, his mother said, I just want to get this straight. You're at university, and most of the people you bring here, from whatever background, are students too. Are you saying that this doesn't make you an elite of some kind? Are you telling me that the words you use in your essays are the words ninety-nine per cent of the population uses? Don't look at me like that, his mother said. If you want to know, I don't feel that strongly about 'drawing room'; it's what your father called it, it's the habit of a lifetime, but you can break habits. I have wondered about it. The room in question is rather small for a drawing room. What word would you like me to use instead? 'Lounge'?

There were other words, he told his mother.

Are there? his mother said. What's wrong with 'lounge'? I bet 'lounge' is what ninety-nine per cent of the population uses. But if you don't like it, if its airport and hotel connotations bother you, how about 'front room'? Will that do?

The room his mother calls the 'drawing room' is at the back of the house and looks on to the back garden. It looks on to a square of lawn with three apple trees on it, two mixed borders either side and, beyond the lawn and divided from it by a box hedge, the vegetable garden: peasticks and bean poles and a rusty fruit cage and a potting shed. A cottage garden, his mother has always described it as.

I can't call it the 'morning room', his mother murmured, more to herself than to him, because we tend to use it mostly in the evenings. I can't call it the 'music room' because none of us plays an instrument, and because all those gramophones – those CD and tape-deck affairs – are in your bedrooms. To call it the 'smoking room', though when you're at home accurate, would be tantamount to encouraging a health-wrecking practice I deplore.

His mother was mocking him. She was, as usual, refusing to address the issue, a serious and important one. She was declining to engage with the argument. He said so.

Address the issue? Engage with the argument? His mother turned the phrases over and weighed them in invisible scales. Engage with the argument. Is that an expression ninety-nine per cent of the pop ....? Well, no matter. Where was I? I know, in the 'parlour'. I like 'parlour', I rather go for 'parlour'. It's an old word. It conjures up monks in monasteries having a chinwag, it conjures up people in ruffs having a tête-à-tête. Then there's the ice-cream side of it, of course – oh, and massage, and nail buffing and leg waxing .... Which reminds me ....

Oh for God's sake, he said.

I like 'parlour', his mother said. I think I like 'parlour' best. But on the other hand – *parlare, parlatorium* – a bit too elitist, don't you think? On the whole?

Look, he said, there are other names for rooms, ordinary ones, not jokey or archaic or patronising, that you haven't mentioned yet, that you seem to be deliberately avoiding.

If you mean 'sitting room', his mother said, I did think of it, it did occur to me, and then I thought, No, too safe, a compromise choice, with a whiff of amontillado about it.

It's less offensive than 'drawing room'. And it's more exact – people do tend to sit in rooms.

Probably it is for you, his mother said. You and your siblings and friends are great sitters. Great loungers and withdrawers too, I might say. But I don't have that much time for sitting. In the room that for the moment shall be nameless I tend to stand.

His mother was standing as she said this. She was standing by the stove, lifting the lid from the saucepan, giving the soup a stir. He was sitting on a chair at the table, lounging perhaps. He sat up. He stood up.

You haven't got an ashtray, his mother said, here, use this. By the way, his mother said, did I ever tell you about the misprint your father found in the local paper once? In an estate agent's advertisement? 'Five bed, two bath, kitchen, dining room, shitting room'? Or perhaps it wasn't a misprint, who can say? This soup doesn't taste of anything much, his mother said, come and try it. Come and tell me what you think it needs.

He took the spoon from his mother's hand and tasted her soup. It's okay, he said, it's fine, could do with more salt. The name you're avoiding, he said, the name we use, as you must have noticed, that we want you to use, is 'living room'. A room for living in. The room where people live. Graham Greene wrote a play about it. No, he said (for he could see his mother was about to interrupt him), there are no jokes to be made. I defy you to be satirical about this one. 'Living room' is accurate. And it's classless, it embraces all. The pathetic thing is (and he banged his fist on the table) it'd be impossible to have this argument anywhere else but here! It'd be meaningless anywhere but in Little England. Christ, what a shower!

Nineteen fifty-three, was it? his mother said, or nineteen fifty-four? The year I saw *The Living Room*. Dorothy Tutin was made a star overnight – don't think that sort of thing happens any more, does it? I'd seen her in *Much Ado* at the Phoenix, but .... Look, it's accuracy I want to quiz you about, his mother said. Pass me that colander, would you. No not that one, the red one. Think for a moment – where are we having this conversation? If we can be said to live anywhere, it's the kitchen – except for your grandfather, poor man, who lives in the lavatory. No, we live in the kitchen and we make occasional forays – withdraw, if you like – into –

You're so clever, he said, you think everything can be reduced to a clever, silly, word game.

No, his mother said, no I don't, I just want to understand your motives, which I suspect are suspect.

Our motives, our motive, is clear, he said. There's nothing eccentric about it. We're egalitarians and we want to live in an egalitarian world. Drawing rooms – withdrawing rooms, as no doubt you'd prefer – have no place in that world. They have nothing to do with the real world as it is now. They have to do with privilege and power. They have to do with tribalism in the worst sense.

His mother took a bunch of parsley from a jam jar on the windowsill. Do come and see what these sparrows are up to! she said. Damn, you're too late, she said. She put the parsley on a chopping board. Then she took five soup bowls off the dresser and put them in the bottom oven. She straightened up.

He said, Look, doesn't it embarrass you when you say 'drawing room' to Mrs Todd, for example? Doesn't it make you feel uncomfortable? Doesn't it? It does us, I can tell you.

His mother looked astonished. She said, You astonish me. Why ever should it? It doesn't embarrass her. I'll tell you how it works. I say to her, Oh Mrs Todd, the children were down at the weekend, and you know what that means, so I think the drawing room could do with some special attention ... or she'll say to me, Thought I might do the lounge through today, Mrs Symonds – kids home Sunday, were they? Point is, we have our own language, a language we feel comfortable in, and we stick to it. Both of us. Not just me. Don't think it's just me. But we understand each other. We do. And – though you may not believe this – we're fond of each other. We've got a lot in common. We're both working women, we're both widows. We've been seeing each other twice a week now for what? – fifteen years. I know a lot about her life, I know

all about our Malcolm and our Cheryl and our Diane and our Diane's
baby Gary – who's teething at the moment incidentally – and she knows
even more about my life. I remember her birthday, and she – unlike
some I could mention – always remembers mine. I went to see her when
she was in hospital, and she came to see me when I was. She came on
the bus the day after my op, and then later in the week she got Malcolm
to drive her over after work. Malcolm's pick-up is very unreliable, you
know. He spends all his Sundays working on it, but even so it invariably
fails its MOT. If it isn't the gear box it's the brakes, and if it isn't the
brakes it's the exhaust … I'm very much afraid Malcolm was sold a
pup.

If you're such good friends, he said, if you know everything there is
to know about Mrs Todd's life, how come you don't call her by her first
name? How come she doesn't call you by your first name?

Ah, you can't catch me there, his mother said. The answer is
because she doesn't want it. I asked her once. She'd been here about a
year, and I said, Mrs Todd, don't you think we've known each other
long enough to call each other by our Christian names? Mine's
Elizabeth, as I expect you know. And she said, Think I'd rather leave
things the way they are, if it's all the same to you, Mrs Symonds. So we
did. I did feel crushed at the time, I did feel a bit snubbed, but I don't
think she meant to snub me. I really don't think she did.

About 'living room', he said.

Oh that, his mother said. If that's what you're set on, I'll give it a
try. But if you want to bring Mrs Todd into line, I fear you've got
problems – she's a 'lounge' person, definitely. 'Definitely' is another of
her words. She says 'definitely' very often when I'd say 'yes'. Do you
find your microwave has made life easier, Mrs Todd? I'll ask her, and
she'll say, Oh definitely, definitely. It definitely do, definitely. Mrs Todd
is a very definite person. If you think you can get her to turn her lounge
into a living room, well, good luck.

I never said I wanted her to alter anything, he said. You're putting
words into my mouth. I never said that. Of course she can keep her
lounge. We want you to get rid of your drawing room, which is quite
different. He hesitated. He said, We won't bring our friends here unless
you do.

Can I have that in writing? his mother said. Joke, she said, when she
saw his frown. Could you pass me that baking tray please. Actually, Kit,
I don't like your tone. Dictatorship and blackmail seem to be the names
of your game. Why? Couldn't you wait for evolution to do the job? You

won't have to wait long. 'Nurseries' – in houses large enough to have a
nursery – are mostly 'playrooms' now. 'Studies' have turned themselves
into 'telly rooms'. 'Drawing rooms' are dying even as we speak. By the
time my generation is under the sod, the only 'drawing rooms' left will
be in palaces and stately homes. Truly, you won't have to wait long.

If you want to make yourself useful, you could lay the table, his
mother said.

What I don't understand, his mother said, is why you have to be so
heavy about all this. If your friends don't like the vocabulary I use,
couldn't you make a joke of it? Couldn't you just tell them your mother
is an eccentric old bat? That sort of confession would improve your
street cred no end, I should've thought.

There isn't any point in going on with this, he said. There isn't any
point in trying to have a serious discussion with you. You're the
personification of the English disease, the English upper class disease, of
superciliousness. Everything you've said this morning, and the way
you've said it, is offensive, but you can't even see it, you can't even hear
it. If you knew the way you sound to ordinary people! 'Our Malcolm'
and 'our Joanne' – mocking and superior, that's how you sound.

Diane, his mother said, Diane, not Joanne. I wasn't mocking, I
assure you, I was borrowing. I was repeating. And who's calling who
ordinary? No one's that ordinary. In my experience most people, when
you get to know them, are extraordinary. Look, if you're not going to
lay the table, d'you think you could stop hovering and sit down?

I didn't mean 'ordinary', he said, I meant 'other'. Other people. You
mentioned palaces and stately homes a minute ago, he said. What you
don't seem to understand is that this place is a palace to some of the
friends I bring here. In fact that's exactly what Julie said the first time
she came down. She walked in the door and said, God, it's a palace!
You never told me your mother lived in a fucking palace, Kit.

I don't get this, his mother said. First it's 'drawing room', then it's
the way I talk, now it's this house. You keep moving the goal posts. Are
you saying people shouldn't be allowed to live in five-bedroomed
houses, in five-and-a-half- – if you count the box room – bedroomed
houses in case other people, who live in two-bedroomed houses or flats,
might think of them as palaces? Is that what you're saying? I happen to
know that Julie liked this house. She came down early one morning that
first visit – you were still in bed – and had breakfast with me. She said,
I really love this place, Elizabeth – it's magic. I'm going to live in a place
like this one day. We went round the garden and she knew the names of

everything. Monkshood! she said, my dad won't have monkshood in the garden ... I was fond of Julie. She was a very nice girl. I was sorry when you gave her the push.

Martin found you frightening, he said. D'you remember Martin?

That's okay, I found Martin frightening, his mother said.

When I say 'frightening' I mean 'posh', he said. I met Martin in the pub the other night and he seemed a bit down and fed up with life – well, with his job really – and I asked him if he'd like to get away to the country this weekend. He wanted to know if you were going to be there. I said probably you would, it was your house. And he said, Well, think I'll give it a miss then. No offence, but your mother and her 'drawing rooms' and 'wirelesses' and 'gramophones' are a bit posh for me. He pronounced it 'poshe'.

Well that hurts certainly. Yes it does, his mother said. Could you come here a minute, I can't read this without my specs, does it say two ounces or four?

Martin spent a lot of his childhood in care, you know, he said. Four ounces, he said. He was shunted from council home to council home. From the age of seven, that is. Before that he lived in a one-room flat with his parents. They ate in it and slept in it and his parents screwed in it. A lot of pain went on in that living room. His father beat his mother up in it – night after night after night. Dreadful, bloody beatings. If Martin tried to stop him he got beaten up too.

That is very dreadful, his mother said. Poor child. Poor Martin. I didn't know that. I am very sorry indeed about that.

So you can probably see why 'drawing rooms' and such would put him off, he said. Piss him off. I mean, what the fuck have they got to do with his life, or with anything he knows about? Like fucking nothing.

Yes I do see, his mother said. I understand now why he's on the defensive. What I don't understand is, why, if you're so fond of him, you didn't warn me about all this before he came down here. It would have saved me asking him all sorts of tactless questions about his life and family, and him having to skate round them – which is what he did do.

How patronising can you be! he said. Martin doesn't need explaining, or explaining away, by me or anyone. He is himself, he is a valuable human being.

His mother took her mixing bowl and egg whisk to the sink and ran the tap over them. She turned the tap off, twisting it hard. Remind me to get something done about this washer, she said. She said, Why do I get the feeling that, for you, only one sort of person, from one sort of background, is a valuable human being? Why do I get the impression that, in your view, a person has to have been brought up in an obviously deprived environment to know anything about pain?

I haven't said that, he said.

So much so that I feel I've failed you, that you'd have preferred to have had Martin's childhood, that kind of misery being the only passport – as you would see it – to full membership of the human race.

You're silent, his mother said. She tapped him on the shoulder. Hey, look at me.

He looked out of the window.

Let me remind you of your father's childhood, his mother said. It was a very comfortable, green-belt childhood. There was a cook, Inez I think, and a maid. Two maids. There was a nanny until your father went away to school. There was a big garden with a shrubbery one end to play in – though he had to play by himself most of the time, of course, being an only child. There was all that. There were also your grandparents who hated each other. They slept at different ends of the house, but in the evenings when your grandfather came home from his office they sat together in the drawing room in their own special chairs and tormented each other. Your grandmother had the edge, she was the cleverer. She was frustrated. Nowadays, I suppose, she'd have been a career woman, and perhaps not married. From all the evidence she despised men. While this ritual was going on, while they goaded and persecuted each other, your father was made to sit in a corner and play with his Meccano or read a book. He was not allowed to interrupt and he was not allowed to leave the room. At six-forty-five on the dot your grandmother would take a key from the bunch on the thin leather belt she always wore and unlock the drinks cupboard, and the serious whisky drinking – and the serious torturing – would begin.

I know about that, he said, you've told me about that.

There was no blood, his mother said, there were no visible bruises, just –

I've got the point, he said, you've made your point.

When your father was dying I thought about the nightmare he'd had to endure while he was growing up. I wondered if it might have been responsible in some way for his illness, if the stress of it had made him vulnerable, damaged his immune system. D'you think that's possible?

Could be, he said. Could be. I don't know.

I wish you'd known him, his mother said. That's the worst of it, your never knowing him, or rather being too young to remember him. That photograph on my dressing table, the one of you aged eighteen months or so with Daddy. You're looking up at him and you're hugging his knees. Now I remember that occasion – I took the photograph. I remember the way you ran, well, staggered up the garden – you were a very late walker, you know, very slow to get yourself off your bottom – and threw yourself at him. You nearly toppled him. And then I pressed the button. I remember that afternoon very well. I remember your father telling me there was no point in taking any photographs, the light was too poor ... well, I remember it all. I remember how tired your father was. He was already ill but we didn't know. I remember that you had a tantrum about ten minutes before I took the photograph. You lay on the grass and kicked and screamed. But you don't remember. You don't remember him, and you don't remember you – or any of it. It's just a photograph to you.

Cass and Anna remember him, he said, they say they do. They've told me things.

He did his dying in the drawing room – as it was then called – his mother said. He wanted to be downstairs so he could see into the garden – walk into it to begin with. When he was given his death sentence, at Christmas, he set himself some targets. The start of the cricket season – on telly – was one. The peonies and irises out was another. We had wonderful irises in those days, the proper rhizomatous sort, the tall bearded ones, a huge bed of them your father made. He was passionate about his irises, quite boring about them. Irises are tricky things, they like being by themselves, they don't like being moved, they have to have full sun, you're supposed to divide them every three years immediately after flowering – it's quite a performance. It takes patience to grow good irises, and your father was not a patient man. He was a quick-tempered man. I was quite jealous of his irises and all the patient attention they got. Every weekend spent in the garden – or the bloody potting shed. Graham Greene has got a lot to answer for, if you ask me.

He had not known about the irises. He said, Did he see them? Were they out in time?

Some of them were out, the ordinary white flags, and the blue ones. The red peonies were out, the *officinalis*, but the pale ones weren't – you know, the Chinese ones. The ones he liked best weren't.

I don't think I knew he died in the living room, he said. I don't think you ever told me that.

He didn't die in it, his mother said. About three weeks before he died we moved him upstairs. It had become impossible to look after him properly downstairs, and it was too noisy. Small children – you were only two and obstreperous – kept bursting in. When they carried him upstairs, which was difficult because he was in agony, I waited at the top, on the landing; and when he saw me he said, Next time I go down these stairs, folks, it'll be feet first. He said it to make me laugh, to make the doctor and the nurse – who'd made a sort of chair for him out of their hands – laugh. It was brave to make that joke, but it was cruel too, because three weeks later when he did go down the stairs, in his coffin, I kept remembering him coming up, I kept hearing him say, Feet first.

If I don't talk about it much, his mother said, it's because I don't like thinking about it. I prefer to remember your father before he got that bloody disease. He was a different person before he got it. I don't mean just because he looked different – obviously if someone loses six stone in a short time he's going to seem different, he's going to feel unfamiliar – I suppose because we tend to think of a person's shape as being part of their personality, of being them – but that wasn't the real problem. The real problem I discovered was the gap there is between the living and the dying. An enormous, unbridgeable gap.

We're all dying though, aren't we, he said. From the moment we're born you could say we're dying.

Don't give me that, his mother said, don't give me that claptrap. Could you move your elbow please, I'm trying to lay the table. I want to give you a knife and fork.

Sit down, he said, stop working and sit down and talk to me. Just for five minutes. You never sit down and talk. You never tell me anything. You never tell me anything about you.

It's lunch time, his mother said, we can't talk now. Grandpa will be starving. Could you go and tell him it's ready and give him a hand down the stairs. I fear we're going to have to have a lift put in, you know, or –

What is lunch? he said. What are we having? Fish fingers and peas? he said hopefully, beefburgers and beans, sausage and chips?

I wish you hadn't mentioned sausages, his mother said, why did you have to mention sausages? Okay, I'll tell you, his mother said (as though he'd asked her to, which he hadn't, he hadn't said a word), why not? I'll tell you. When your father was dying, before he got to the point of not wanting anything to eat at all, the only thing he wanted was sausages. I'd put my head round the door and ask him, What d'you fancy for lunch today, darling? and he'd say, Bangers and mash. Then I'd go away and cook him something quite other – something I thought would be nourishing and easy to digest, that would slip down. I'd bring in the tray – he'd be sitting with his back to me, shoulders stooped, head supported by a hand, looking out at the garden – and he'd say, without turning his head because turning and twisting were very painful for him, Doesn't smell like bangers. And I'd say, You just wait and see. I'd put the tray down on a chair, and tuck a napkin under his chin and adjust the invalid table and wheel it up over his knees, and put the plate on it and whip the cover off and say, There! Doesn't that look delicious? And he'd stare down at the plate. I asked for bangers, he'd say eventually. I was expecting bangers.

I don't think I let him have bangers more than twice in the whole of that five months, the whole time he was dying, his mother said. I don't know why I didn't give him what he asked for. I've tried to work out why I didn't.

He said nothing for a minute. Then he said, You thought they'd be hard for him to digest, you thought they'd make him uncomfortable.

Did I? his mother said. What would a bit of discomfort have mattered? He was dying, for God's sake! He wanted bangers.

Say something! his mother said. I've shocked you, haven't I? I can tell.

No. No, you haven't, he said. Look, I'd better go and get Grandpa, I'd better go and find the girls.

Could you bring me my wireless at the same time? his mother said, I want to hear the news. I'm not sure where I left it, downstairs I think, in the – in some room or other.

Source: Georgina Hammick (1996) *People for Lunch/Spoilt*, London: Vintage, pp. 368–80.

27 'Pigeons at Daybreak'

ANITA DESAI

Anita Desai (b. 1937), novelist, short-story writer and children's author, was born in India, the daughter of a German mother and a Bengali businessman. Her family spoke German at home and Hindi to friends. It was only at school in New Delhi that she learned English, the language in which she writes. Among her many novels are *Fire on the Mountain* (1977), winner of the

Winifred Holtby Memorial Prize, and *Clear Light of Day* (1980), *In Custody* (1984) and *Fasting, Feasting* (1999), each of which was shortlisted for the Booker Prize. *The Village by the Sea* (1982) won the Guardian Award for Children's Fiction. Although she now spends some of her time in the USA, where she teaches creative writing at Massachusetts Institute of Technology, Desai's novels are almost all set in northern India, and deal mainly with the lives of women. She is noted for the clarity and brilliance of her style, achieved, she says, by 'the conscious labour of uniting language and symbol, word and rhythm'.

One of his worst afflictions, Mr Basu thought, was not to be able to read the newspaper himself. To have them read to him by his wife. He watched with fiercely controlled irritation that made the corners of his mouth jerk suddenly upwards and outwards, as she searched for her spectacles through the flat. By the time she found them – on the ledge above the bathing place in the bathroom, of all places: what did she want with her spectacles in *there*? – she had lost the newspaper. When she found it, it was spotted all over with grease for she had left it beside the stove on which the fish was frying. This reminded her to see to the fish before it was overdone. 'You don't want charred fish for your lunch, do you?' she shouted back when he called. He sat back then, in his tall-backed cane chair, folded his hands over his stomach and knew that if he were to open his mouth now, even a slit, it would be to let out a scream of abuse. So he kept it tightly shut.

When she had finally come to the end of that round of bumbling activity, moving from stove to bucket, shelf to table, cupboard to kitchen, she came out on the balcony again, triumphantly carrying with her the newspaper as well as the spectacles. 'So,' she said, 'are you ready to listen to the news now?'

'Now, he said, parting his lips with the sound of tearing paper, 'I'm ready.'

But Otima Basu never heard such sounds, such ironies or distresses. Quite pleased with all she had accomplished, and at having half an hour in which to sit down comfortably, she settled herself on top of a cane stool like a large soft cushion of white cotton, oiled hair and gold bangles. Humming a little air from the last Hindi film she had seen, she opened out the newspaper on her soft, doughy lap and began to hum out the headlines. In spite of himself, Amul Basu leaned forward, strained his eyes to catch an interesting headline for he simply couldn't believe this was all the papers had to offer.

'"Rice smugglers caught"' she read out, but immediately ran along a train of thought of her own. 'What can they expect? Everyone knows there is enough rice in the land, it's the hoarders and black-marketeers who keep it from us, naturally people will break the law and take to smuggling ...'

'What else? What else?' Mr Basu snapped at her. 'Nothing else in the papers?'

'Ah – ah – hmm,' she muttered as her eyes roved up and down the columns, looking very round and glassy behind the steel-rimmed spectacles. '"Blue bull menace in Delhi airport can be solved by narcotic drug—"'

'Blue bulls? Blue bulls?' snorted Mr Basu, almost tipping out of his chair. 'How do you mean, "blue bulls"? What's a blue bull? You can't be reading right.'

'I am reading right,' she protested. 'Think I can't read? Did my B.A., helped two children through school and college, and you think I can't read? Blue bulls it says here, blue bulls it is.'

'Can't be,' he grumbled, but retreated into his chair from her unexpectedly spirited defence. 'Must be a printing mistake. There are bulls, buffaloes, bullocks, and *bul-buls*, but whoever heard of a blue bull? Nilgai, do they mean? But that creature is nearly extinct. How can there be any at the airport? It's all rot, somebody's fantasy—'

'All right, I'll stop reading, if you'd rather. I have enough to do in the kitchen, you know,' she threatened him, but he pressed his lips together and, with a little stab of his hand, beckoned her to pick up the papers and continue.

'Ah – ah – hmm. What pictures are on this week, I wonder?' she continued, partly because that was a subject of consuming interest to her, and partly because she thought it a safe subject to move onto. '*Teri Meri Kismet* – "the heartwarming saga of an unhappy wife". No, no, no. *Do Dost* – winner of three Filmfare awards – ahh ...'

'Please, please, Otima, the news,' Mr Basu reminded her.

'Nothing to interest you,' she said but tore herself away from the entertainments column for his sake. '"Anti-arthritis drug" – not your problem. "Betel leaves cause cancer." Hmph. I know at least a hundred people who chew betel leaves and are as fit—'

'All right. All right. What else?'

'What news are you interested in then?' she flared up, but immediately subsided and browsed on, comfortably scratching the sole of her foot as she did so. '"Floods in Assam." "Drought in Maharashtra."

When is there not? "Two hundred cholera deaths." "A woman and child have a miraculous escape when their house collapses." "Husband held for murder of wife." See?' she cried excitedly. 'Once more. How often does this happen? "Husband and mother-in-law have been arrested on charge of pouring kerosene on Kantibai's clothes and setting her on fire while she slept." Yes, that is how they always do it. Why? Probably the dowry didn't satisfy them, they must have hoped to get one more ...'

He groaned and sank back in his chair. He knew there was no stopping her now. Except for stories of grotesque births like those of two-headed children or five-legged calves, there was nothing she loved as dearly as tales of murder and atrocity, and short of his having a stroke or the fish-seller arriving at the door, nothing could distract her now. He even heaved himself out of his chair and shuffled off to the other end of the balcony to feed the parrot in its cage a green chilli or two without her so much as noticing his departure. But when she had read to the end of that fascinating item, she ran into another that she read out in a voice like a law-maker's, and he heard it without wishing to: "'Electricity will be switched off as urgent repairs to power lines must be made, in Darya Ganj and Kashmere Gate area, from 8 p.m. to 6 a.m. on the twenty-first of May." My God, that is today.'

'Today? Tonight? No electricity?' he echoed, letting the green chilli fall to the floor of the cage where other offered and refused chillies lay in a rotting heap. 'How will I sleep then?' he gasped fearfully, 'without a fan? In this heat?' and already his diaphragm seemed to cave in, his chest to rise and fall as he panted for breath. Clutching his throat, he groped his way back to the cane chair. 'Otima, Otima, I can't breathe,' he moaned.

She put the papers away and rose with a sigh of irritation and anxiety, the kind a sickly child arouses in its tired mother. She herself, at fifty-six, had not a wrinkle on her oiled face, scarcely a grey hair on her head. As smooth as butter, as round as a cake, life might still have been delectable to her if it had not been for the asthma that afflicted her husband and made him seem, at sixty-one, almost decrepit.

'I'll bring you your inhaler. Don't get worried, just don't get worried,' she told him and bustled off to find his inhaler and cortisone. When she held them out to him, he lowered his head into the inhaler like a dying man at the one straw left. He grasped it with frantic hands, almost clawing her. She shook her head, watching him. 'Why do you let yourself get so upset?' she asked, cursing herself for having read out that particular piece of news to him. 'It won't be so bad. Many people in the city sleep without electric fans – most do. We'll manage—'

'*You'll* manage,' he spat at her, 'but I?'

There was no soothing him now. She knew how rapidly he would advance from imagined breathlessness into the first frightening stage of a full-blown attack of asthma. His chest was already heaving, he imagined there was no oxygen left for him to breathe, that his lungs had collapsed and could not take in any air. He stared up at the strings of washing that hung from end to end of the balcony, the overflow of furniture that cluttered it, the listless parrot in its cage, the view of all the other crowded, washing-hung balconies up and down the length of the road, and felt there was no oxygen left in the air.

'Stay out here on the balcony, it's a little cooler than inside,' his wife said calmly and left him to go about her work. But she did it absently. Normally she would have relished bargaining with the fish-seller who came to the door with a *beckti*, some whiskered black river fish and a little squirming hill of pale pink prawns in his flat basket. But today she made her purchases and paid him off rather quickly – she was in a hurry to return to the balcony. 'All right?' she asked, looking down at her husband sunk into a heap on his chair, shaking with the effort to suck in air. His lips tightened and whitened in silent reply. She sighed and went away to sort out spices in the kitchen, to pour them out of large containers into small containers, to fill those that were empty and empty those that were full, giving everything that came her way a little loving polish with the end of her sari for it was something she loved to do, but she did not stay very long. She worried about her husband. Foolish and unreasonable as he seemed to her in his sickness, she could not quite leave him to his agony, whether real or imagined. When the postman brought them a letter from their son in Bhilai, she read out to him the boy's report on his work in the steel mills. The father said nothing but seemed calmer and she was able, after that, to make him eat a little rice and fish *jhol*, very lightly prepared, just as the doctor prescribed. 'Lie down now,' she said, sucking at a fish bone as she removed the dishes from the table. 'It's too hot out on the balcony. Take some rest.'

'Rest?' he snapped at her, but shuffled off into the bedroom and allowed her to make up his bed with all the pillows and bolsters that kept him in an almost sitting position on the flat wooden bed. He shifted and groaned as she heaped up a bolster here, flattened a cushion there, and said he could not possibly sleep, but she thought he did for she kept an eye on him while she leafed through a heap of film and women's magazines on her side of the bed, and thought his eyes were closed genuinely in sleep and that his breathing was almost as regular as the slow circling of the electric fan above them. The fan needed oiling, it made a disturbing clicking sound with every revolution, but who was there to climb up to it and do the oiling and cleaning? Not so easy to get these things done when one's husband is old and ill, she thought. She yawned. She rolled over.

When she brought him his afternoon tea, she asked 'Had a good sleep?' which annoyed him. 'Never slept at all,' he snapped, taking the cup from her hands and spilling some tea. 'How can one sleep if one can't breathe?' he growled, and she turned away with a little smile at his stubbornness. But later that evening he was genuinely ill, choked, in a panic at his inability to breathe as well as at the prospect of a hot night without a fan. 'What will I do?' he kept moaning in between violent struggles for air that shook his body and left it limp. 'What will I do?'

'I'll tell you,' she suddenly answered, and wiped the perspiration from her face in relief. 'I'll have your bed taken up on the terrace. I can call Bulu from next door to do it – you can sleep out in the open air tonight, eh? That'll be nice, won't it? That will do you good.' She brightened both at the thought of a night spent in the open air on the terrace, just as they had done when they were younger and climbing up and down stairs was nothing to them, and at the thought of having an excuse to visit the neighbours and having a little chat while getting them to come and carry up a string bed for them. Of course old Basu made a protest and a great fuss and coughed and spat and shook and said he could not possibly move in this condition, or be moved by anyone, but she insisted and, ignoring him, went out to make the arrangements.

Basu had not been on the terrace for years. While his wife and Bulu led him up the stairs, hauling him up and propping him upright by their shoulders as though he were some lifeless bag containing something fragile and valuable, he tried to think when he had last attempted or achieved what now seemed a tortuous struggle up the steep concrete steps to the warped green door at the top.

They had given up sleeping there on summer nights long ago, not so much on account of old age or weak knees, really, but because of their perpetual quarrels with the neighbours on the next terrace, separated from theirs by only a broken wooden trellis. Noisy, inconsiderate people, addicted to the radio turned on full blast. At times the man had been drunk and troubled and abused his wife who gave as good as she got. It had been intolerable. Otima had urged her husband, night after night, to protest. When he did, they had almost killed him. At least they would have had they managed to cross over to the Basus' terrace which they were physically prevented from doing by their sons and daughters. The next night they had been even more offensive. Finally the Basus had been forced to give in and retreat down the stairs to sleep in their closed, airless room under the relentlessly ticking ceiling fan. At least it was private there. After the first few restless nights they wondered how they had ever put up with the public sleeping outdoors and its disturbances – its 'nuisance', as Otima called it in English, thinking it an effective word.

That had not – he groaned aloud as they led him up over the last step to the green door – been the last visit he had paid to the rooftop. As Bulu kicked open the door – half-witted he may be, but he was burly too, and good-natured, like so many half-wits – and the city sky revealed itself, in its dirt-swept greys and mauves, on the same level with them, Basu recalled how, not so many years ago, he had taken his daughter Charu's son by the hand to show him the pigeon roosts on so many of the Darya Ganj rooftops, and pointed out to him a flock of collector's pigeons like so many silk and ivory fans flirting in the sky. The boy had watched in silence, holding onto his grandfather's thumb with tense delight. The memory of it silenced his groans as they lowered him onto the bed they had earlier carried up and spread with his many pillows and bolsters. He sat there, getting back his breath, and thinking of Nikhil. When would he see Nikhil again? What would he not give to have that child hold his thumb again and go for a walk with him!

Punctually at eight o'clock the electricity was switched off, immediately sucking up Darya Ganj into a box of shadows, so that the distant glow of Cannaught Place, still lit up, was emphasized. The horizon was illuminated as by a fire, roasted red. The traffic made long stripes of light up and down the streets below them. Lying back, Basu saw the dome of the sky as absolutely impenetrable, shrouded with summer dust, and it seemed to him as airless as the room below. Nikhil, Nikhil, he wept, as though the child might have helped.

Nor could he find any ease, any comfort on that unaccustomed string bed (the wooden pallet in their room was of course too heavy to carry up, even for Bulu). He complained that his heavy body sank into it as into a hammock, that the strings cut into him, that he could not turn on that wobbling net in which he was caught like some dying fish, gasping for air. It was no cooler than it had been indoors, he complained – there was not the slightest breeze, and the dust was stifling.

Otima soon lost the lightheartedness that had come to her with this unaccustomed change of scene. She tired of dragging around the pillows and piling up the bolsters, helping him into a sitting position and then lowering him into a horizontal one, bringing him his medicines, fanning him with a palm leaf and eventually of his groans and sobs as well. Finally she gave up and collapsed onto her own string bed, lying there exhausted and sleepless, too distracted by the sound of traffic to sleep. All through the night her husband moaned and gasped for air. Towards dawn it was so bad that she had to get up and massage his chest. When done long and patiently enough, it seemed to relieve him.

'Now lie down for a while, I'll go and get some iced water for your head,' she said, lowering him onto the bed, and went tiredly down the stairs like some bundle of damp washing slowly falling. Her eyes drooped, heavy bags held the tiredness under them.

To her surprise, there was a light on in their flat. Then she heard the ticking of the fan. She had forgotten to turn it off when they went up to the terrace and it seemed the electricity had been switched on again, earlier than they had expected. The relief of it brought her energy back in a bound. She bustled up the stairs. I'll bring him down – he'll get some hours of sleep after all, she told herself.

'It's all right,' she called out as she went up to the terrace again. 'The electricity is on again. Come, I'll help you down – you'll get some sleep in your own bed after all.'

'Leave me alone,' he replied, quite gently.

'Why? Why?' she cried. 'I'll help you. You can get into your own bed, you'll be quite comfortable—'

'Leave me alone,' he said again in that still voice. 'It is cool now.'

It was. Morning had stirred up some breeze off the sluggish river Jumna beneath the city walls, and it was carried over the rooftops of the stifled city, pale and fresh and delicate. It brought with it the morning light, as delicate and sweet as the breeze itself, a pure pallor unlike the livid glow of artificial lights. This lifted higher and higher into the dome of the sky, diluting the darkness there till it, too, grew pale and gradually shades of blue and mauve tinted it lightly.

The old man lay flat and still, gazing up, his mouth hanging open as if to let it pour into him, as cool and fresh as water.

Then, with a swirl and flutter of feathers, a flock of pigeons hurtled upwards and spread out against the dome of the sky – opalescent, sunlit, like small pearls. They caught the light as they rose, turned brighter till they turned at last into crystals, into prisms of light. Then they disappeared into the soft, deep blue of the morning.

Source: Anita Desai (1978) *Games at Twilight and Other Stories*, London: Penguin, pp. 98–107.

28 from *'Writing Short Stories'*

FLANNERY O'CONNOR

Flannery O'Connor (1925–64), short-story writer and novelist, was born in Savannah, Georgia. For much of her adult life she suffered from an inherited terminal illness, lupus erythematosis. Her strong Roman Catholic faith was an important influence on her writing, as was her upbringing in the southern states of America. She studied at the prestigious writing workshop at the University of Iowa, graduating from there in 1947. Her first novel, *Wise Blood* (1952) explores issues of religious belief through the highly disturbing story of Hazel Motes, a self-blinding prophet who tries to set up a 'Church of Christ Without Christ'. *The Violent Bear it Away* (1960), also about religious fanatics in backwoods Georgia, was described by O'Connor as 'a very minor hymn to the Eucharist'. Her stories were collected in *A Good Man is Hard to Find* (1955), *Everything that Rises Must Converge* (1965), and *Complete Stories* (1971). A collection of her non-fictional prose and lectures was published as *Mystery and Manners* in 1969.

I have heard people say that the short story was one of the most difficult literary forms, and I've always tried to decide why people feel this way about what seems to me to be one of the most natural and fundamental ways of human expression. After all, you begin to hear and tell stories when you're a child, and there doesn't seem to be anything very complicated about it. I suspect that most of you have been telling stories all your lives, and yet here you sit—come to find out how to do it. [...]

A story is a complete dramatic action — and in good stories, the characters are shown through the action and the action is controlled through the characters, and the result of this is meaning that derives from the whole presented experience. I myself prefer to say that a story is a dramatic event that involves a person because he is a person, and a particular person—that is, because he shares in the general human condition and in some specific human situation. A story always involves, in a dramatic way, the mystery of personality. I lent some stories to a country lady who lives down the road from me, and when she returned them, she said, 'Well, them stories just gone and shown you how some folks *would* do,' and I thought to myself that that was right; when you write stories, you have to be content to start exactly there—showing how some specific folks *will* do, *will* do in spite of everything.

Now this is a very humble level to have to begin on, and most people who think they want to write stories are not willing to start there. They want to write about problems, not people; or about abstract issues, not concrete situations. They have an idea, or a feeling, or an overflowing ego, or they want to Be A Writer, or they want to give their wisdom to the world in a simple-enough way for the world to be able to absorb it. In any case, they don't have a story and they wouldn't be willing to write it if they did; and in the absence of a story, they set out to find a theory or a formula or a technique.

Now none of this is to say that when you write a story, you are supposed to forget or give up any moral position that you hold. Your beliefs will be the light by which you see, but they will not be what you see and they will not be a substitute for seeing. For the writer of fiction, everything has its testing point in the eye, and the eye is an organ that eventually involves the whole personality, and as much of the world as can be got into it. It involves judgment. Judgment is something that begins in the act of vision, and when it does not, or when it becomes separated from vision, then a confusion exists in the mind which transfers itself to the story.

Fiction operates through the senses, and I think one reason that people find it so difficult to write stories is that they forget how much time and patience is required to convince through the senses. No reader who doesn't actually experience, who isn't made to feel, the story is going to believe anything the fiction writer merely tells him. The first and most obvious characteristic of fiction is that it deals with reality through what can be seen, heard, smelt, tasted, and touched.

Now this is something that can't be learned only in the head; it has to be learned in the habits. It has to become a way that you habitually look at things. The fiction writer has to realize that he can't create compassion with compassion, or emotion with emotion, or thought with thought. He has to provide all these things with a body; he has to create a world with weight and extension.

I have found that the stories of beginning writers usually bristle with emotion, but *whose* emotion is often very hard to determine. Dialogue frequently proceeds without the assistance of any characters that you can actually see, and uncontained thought leaks out of every corner of the story. The reason is usually that the student is wholly interested in his thoughts and his emotions and not in his dramatic action, and that he is too lazy or highfalutin to descend to the concrete where fiction operates. He thinks that judgment exists in one place and sense-impression in another. But for the fiction writer, judgment begins in the details he sees and how he sees them.

Fiction writers who are not concerned with these concrete details are guilty of what Henry James called 'weak specification.' The eye will glide over their words while the attention goes to sleep. Ford Madox Ford taught that you couldn't have a man appear long enough to sell a newspaper in a story unless you put him there with enough detail to make the reader see him.

I have a friend who is taking acting classes in New York from a Russian lady who is supposed to be very good at teaching actors. My friend wrote me that the first month they didn't speak a line, they only learned to see. Now learning to see is the basis for learning all the arts except music. I know a good many fiction writers who paint, not because they're any good at painting, but because it helps their writing. It forces them to look at things. Fiction writing is very seldom a matter of saying things; it is a matter of showing things.

However, to say that fiction proceeds by the use of detail does not mean the simple, mechanical piling-up of detail. Detail has to be controlled by some overall purpose, and every detail has to be put to work for you. Art is selective. What is there is essential and creates movement.

Now all this requires time. A good short story should not have less meaning than a novel, nor should its action be less complete. Nothing essential to the main experience can be left out of a short story. All the action has to be satisfactorily accounted for in terms of motivation, and there has to be a beginning, a middle, and an end, though not necessarily in that order. I think many people decide that they want to write short stories because they're short, and by short, they mean short in every way. They think that a short story is an incomplete action in which a very little is shown and a great deal suggested, and they think you suggest something by leaving it out. It's very hard to disabuse a student of this notion, because he thinks that when he leaves something out, he's being subtle; and when you tell him that he has to put something in before anything can be there, he thinks you're an insensitive idiot.

Perhaps the central question to be considered in any discussion of the short story is what do we mean by short. Being short does not mean being slight. A short story should be long in depth and should give us an experience of meaning. I have an aunt who thinks that nothing happens in a story unless somebody gets married or shot at the end of it. I wrote a story about a tramp who marries an old woman's idiot daughter in order to acquire the old woman's automobile. After the marriage, he takes the daughter off on a wedding trip in the automobile and abandons her in an eating place and drives on by himself. Now that is a complete story. There is nothing more relating to the mystery of that man's personality that could be shown through that particular dramatization. But I've never been able to convince my aunt that it's a complete story. She wants to know what happened to the idiot daughter after that.

Not long ago that story was adapted for a television play, and the adapter, knowing his business, had the tramp have a change of heart and go back and pick up the idiot daughter and the two of them ride away, grinning madly. My aunt believes that the story is complete at last, but I have other sentiments about it—which are not suitable for public utterance. When you write a story, you only have to write one story, but there will always be people who will refuse to read the story you have written.

And this naturally brings up the awful question of what kind of a reader you are writing for when you write fiction. Perhaps we each think we have a personal solution for this problem. For my own part, I have a very high opinion of the art of fiction and a very low opinion of what is called the 'average' reader. I tell myself that I can't escape him, that this is the personality I am supposed to keep awake, but that at the same time, I am also supposed to provide the intelligent reader with the deeper experience that he looks for in fiction. Now actually, both of these readers are just aspects of the writer's own personality, and in the last analysis, the only reader he can know anything about is himself. We all write at our own level of understanding, but it is the peculiar characteristic of fiction that its literal surface can be made to yield entertainment on an obvious physical plane to one sort of reader while the selfsame surface can be made to yield meaning to the person equipped to experience it there.

Meaning is what keeps the short story from being short. I prefer to talk about the meaning in a story rather than the theme of a story. People talk about the theme of a story as if the theme were like the string that a sack of chicken feed is tied with. They think that if you can pick out the theme, the way you pick the right thread in the chicken-feed sack, you can rip the story open and feed the chickens. But this is not the way meaning works in fiction.

When you can state the theme of a story, when you can separate it from the story itself, then you can be sure the story is not a very good one. The meaning of a story has to be embodied in it, has to be made concrete in it. A story is a way to say something that can't be said any other way, and it takes every word in the story to say what the meaning is. You tell a story because a statement would be inadequate. When anybody asks what a story is about, the only proper thing is to tell him to read the story. The meaning of fiction is not abstract meaning but experienced meaning, and the purpose of making statements about the meaning of a story is only to help you to experience that meaning more fully.

Fiction is an art that calls for the strictest attention to the real—whether the writer is writing a naturalistic story or a fantasy. I mean that we always begin with what is or with what has an eminent possibility of truth about it. Even when one writes a fantasy, reality is the proper basis of it. A thing is fantastic because it is so real, so real that it is fantastic. Graham Greene has said that he can't write, 'I stood over a bottomless pit,' because that couldn't be true, or 'Running down the stairs I jumped into a taxi,' because that couldn't be true either. But Elizabeth Bowen can write about one of her characters that 'she snatched at her hair as if she heard something in it,' because that is eminently possible.

I would even go so far as to say that the person writing a fantasy has to be even more strictly attentive to the concrete detail than someone writing in a naturalistic vein—because the greater the story's strain on the credulity, the more convincing the properties in it have to be.

A good example of this is a story called 'The Metamorphosis' by Franz Kafka. This is a story about a man who wakes up one morning to find that he has turned into a cockroach overnight, while not discarding his human nature. The rest of the story concerns his life and feelings and eventual death as an insect with human nature, and this situation is accepted by the reader because the concrete detail of the story is absolutely convincing. The fact is that this story describes the dual nature of man in such a realistic fashion that it is almost unbearable. The truth is not distorted here, but rather, a certain distortion is used to get at the truth. If we admit, as we must, that appearance is not the same thing as reality, then we must give the artist the liberty to make certain rearrangements of nature if these will lead to greater depths of vision. The artist himself always has to remember that what he is rearranging *is* nature, and that he has to know it and be able to describe it accurately in order to have the authority to rearrange it at all.

The peculiar problem of the short-story writer is how to make the action he describes reveal as much of the mystery of existence as possible. He has only a short space to do it in and he can't do it by statement. He has to do it by showing, not by saying, and by showing the concrete—so that his problem is really how to make the concrete work double time for him.

In good fiction, certain of the details will tend to accumulate meaning from the action of the story itself, and when this happens they become symbolic in the way they work. I once wrote a story called 'Good Country People,' in which a lady Ph.D. has her wooden leg stolen by a Bible salesman whom she has tried to seduce. Now I'll admit that, paraphrased in this way, the situation is simply a low joke. The average reader is pleased to observe anybody's wooden leg being stolen. But without ceasing to appeal to him and without making any statements of high intention, this story does manage to operate at another level of experience, by letting the wooden leg accumulate meaning. Early in the story, we're presented with the fact that the Ph.D. is spiritually as well as physically crippled. She believes in nothing but her own belief in nothing, and we perceive that there is a wooden part of her soul that corresponds to her wooden leg. Now of course this is never stated. The fiction writer states as little as possible. The reader makes this connection from things he is shown. He may not even know that he makes the connection, but the connection is there nevertheless and it has its effect on him. As the story goes on, the wooden leg continues to accumulate meaning. The reader learns how the girl feels about her leg, how her mother feels about it, and how the country woman on the place feels about it; and finally, by the time the Bible salesman comes along, the leg has accumulated so much meaning that it is, as the saying goes, loaded. And when the Bible salesman steals it, the reader realizes that he has taken away part of the girl's personality and has revealed her deeper affliction to her for the first time.

If you want to say that the wooden leg is a symbol, you can say that. But it is a wooden leg first, and as a wooden leg it is absolutely necessary to the story. It has its place on the literal level of the story, but it operates in depth as well as on the surface. It increases the story in every direction, and this is essentially the way a story escapes being short.

Now a little might be said about the way in which this happens. I wouldn't want you to think that in that story I sat down and said, 'I am now going to write a story about a Ph.D. with a wooden leg, using the wooden leg as a symbol for another kind of affliction.' I doubt myself if many writers know what they are going to do when they start out. When I started writing that story, I didn't know there was going to be a Ph.D. with a wooden leg in it. I merely found myself one morning writing a description of two women that I knew something about, and before I realized it, I had equipped one of them with a daughter with a wooden leg. As the story progressed, I brought in the Bible salesman, but I had no idea what I was going to do with him. I didn't know he was going to steal that wooden leg until ten or twelve lines before he did it, but when I found out that this was what was going to happen, I realized that it was inevitable. This is a story that produces a shock for the reader, and I think one reason for this is that it produced a shock for the writer.

Now despite the fact that this story came about in this seemingly mindless fashion, it is a story that almost no rewriting was done on. It is a story that was under control throughout the writing of it, and it might be asked how this kind of control comes about, since it is not entirely conscious.

I think the answer to this is what Maritain calls 'the habit of art.' It is a fact that fiction writing is something in which the whole personality takes part—the conscious as well as the unconscious mind. Art is the habit of the artist; and habits have to be rooted deep in the whole personality. They have to be cultivated like any other habit, over a long period of time, by experience; and teaching any kind of writing is largely a matter of helping the student develop the habit of art. I think this is more than just a discipline, although it is that; I think it is a way of looking at the created world and of using the senses so as to make them find as much meaning as possible in things.

Now I am not so naïve as to suppose that most people come to writers' conferences in order to hear what kind of vision is necessary to write stories that will become a permanent part of our literature. Even if you do wish to hear this, your greatest concerns are immediately practical. You want to know how you can actually write a good story, and further, how you can tell when you've done it; and so you want to know what the form of a short story is, as if the form were something that existed outside of each story and could be applied or imposed on the material. Of course, the more you write, the more you will realize that the form is organic, that it is something that grows out of the material, that the form of each story is unique. A story that is any good can't be reduced, it can only be expanded. A story is good when you continue to see more and more in it, and when it continues to escape you. In fiction two and two is always more than four.

The only way, I think, to learn to write short stories is to write them, and then to try to discover what you have done. The time to think of technique is when you've actually got the story in front of you. The teacher can help the student by looking at his individual work and trying to help him decide if he has written a complete story, one in which the action fully illuminates the meaning.

Perhaps the most profitable thing I can do is to tell you about some of the general observations I made about these seven stories I read of yours. All of these observations will not fit any one of the stories exactly, but they are points nevertheless that it won't hurt anyone interested in writing to think about.

The first thing that any professional writer is conscious of in reading anything is, naturally, the use of language. Now the use of language in these stories was such that, with one exception, it would be difficult to distinguish one story from another. While I can recall running into several clichés, I can't remember one image or one metaphor from the seven stories. I don't mean there weren't images in them; I just mean that there weren't any that were effective enough to take away with you.

In connection with this, I made another observation that startled me considerably. With the exception of one story, there was practically no use made of the local idiom. Now this is a Southern Writers' Conference. All the addresses on these stories were from Georgia or Tennessee, yet there was no distinctive sense of Southern life in them. A few place-names were dropped, Savannah or Atlanta or Jacksonville, but these could just as easily have been changed to Pittsburgh or Passaic without calling for any other alteration in the story. The characters spoke as if they had never heard any kind of language except what came out of a television set. This indicates that something is way out of focus.

There are two qualities that make fiction. One is the sense of mystery and the other is the sense of manners. You get the manners from the texture of existence that surrounds you. The great advantage of being a Southern writer is that we don't have to go anywhere to look for manners; bad or good, we've got them in abundance. We in the South live in a society that is rich in contradiction, rich in irony, rich in contrast, and particularly rich in its speech. And yet here are six stories by Southerners in which almost no use is made of the gifts of the region.

Of course the reason for this may be that you have seen these gifts abused so often that you have become self-conscious about using them. There is nothing worse than the writer who doesn't *use* the gifts of the region, but wallows in them. Everything becomes so Southern that it's sickening, so local that it is unintelligible, so literally reproduced that it conveys nothing. The general gets lost in the particular instead of being shown through it.

However, when the life that actually surrounds us is totally ignored, when our patterns of speech are absolutely overlooked, then something is out of kilter. The writer should then ask himself if he is not reaching out for a kind of life that is artificial to him.

An idiom characterizes a society, and when you ignore the idiom, you are very likely ignoring the whole social fabric that could make a meaningful character. You can't cut characters off from their society and say much about them as individuals. You can't say anything meaningful about the mystery of a personality unless you put that personality in a believable and significant social context. And the best way to do this is through the character's own language. When the old lady in one of Andrew Lytle's stories says contemptuously that she has a mule that is older than Birmingham, we get in that one sentence a sense of a society and its history. A great deal of the Southern writer's work is done for him before he begins, because our history lives in our talk. In one of Eudora Welty's stories a character says, 'Where I come from, we use fox for yard dogs and owls for chickens, but we sing true.' Now there is a whole book in that one sentence; and when the people of your section can talk like that, and you ignore it, you're just not taking advantage of what's yours. The sound of our talk is too definite to be discarded with impunity, and if the writer tries to get rid of it, he is liable to destroy the better part of his creative power.

Another thing I observed about these stories is that most of them don't go very far inside a character, don't reveal very much of the character. I don't mean that they don't enter the character's mind, but they simply don't show that he has a personality. Again this goes back partly to speech. These characters have no distinctive speech to reveal themselves with; and sometimes they have no really distinctive features. You feel in the end that no personality is revealed because no personality is there. In most good stories it is the character's personality that creates the action of the story. In most of these stories, I feel that the writer has thought of some action and then scrounged up a character to perform it. You will usually be more successful if you start the other way around. If you start with a real personality, a real character, then something is bound to happen; and you don't have to know what before you begin. In fact it may be better if you don't know what before you begin. You ought to be able to discover something from your stories. If you don't, probably nobody else will.

Source: Flannery O'Connor (1984) *Mystery and Manners: Occasional Prose*, Sally and Robert Fitzgerald (eds), London: Faber & Faber, pp. 87–106.

PART 3

Writing poetry

29 from *'The Handless Maiden'*

VICKI FEAVER

Vicki Feaver (b. 1943), poet, was born in Nottingham. She has degrees in music and English from Durham University and University College, London, and has taught creative writing at University College, Chichester, where she is Emeritus Professor of Poetry. She has published two collections of poetry: *Close Relatives* (1981), and *The Handless Maiden* (1994) which won the Heinemann Award. *The Handless Maiden* includes the poems 'Lily Pond', winner of the Arvon Foundation International Poetry Competition in 1992, and 'Judith', winner of the Forward Poetry Prize for Best Single Poem in 1993. Her work has been included in many anthologies, and a selection was included in the Penguin Modern Poets series (1995). She has also published essays on the process of writing, and on twentieth century women poets.

[...] I had read Lorca's lecture on *duende* (printed at the back of the Penguin *Selected Poems*) and found exciting the idea of art originating in a power 'that has to be roused in the very cells of blood'. I made a conscious decision to try and draw on this energy in my writing. The words 'wound' and 'death' that appear disconnectedly in the first draft of 'Lily Pond' may be references to Lorca's identification of *duende* with death and suffering: 'The *duende* does not appear if it sees no possibility of death ... [It] likes the edge of things, the wound'.

But women have also identified with the need for violence and ferocity in their writing. Virginia Woolf felt that she had to 'kill' the Angel in the House before she could write uncensored. Sylvia Plath spoke of the 'blood jet' of poetry, Emily Dickinson of a 'loaded gun', and Stevie Smith, in the most violent images she could muster, of 'an explosion in the sky ... a mushroom shape of terror', of the human creature 'alone in its carapace' forcing a passage out 'in splinters covered with blood'. Poetry, she wrote, 'never has any kindness at all'.

It has been so difficult for women — the soothers and carers and comforters — to be good poets. Every term at my all girls' school we were read the beautiful passage from Proverbs: 'The price of a good woman is above rubies ... She walks behind her husband in the gates ... She clothes her family in scarlet'. It entered my consciousness so deeply I bought scarlet flannel to line my children's duffle coats. It was a long time before I found the necessary anger and distance to express my ambivalence at such seductive but potentially imprisoning images.

I managed it finally in a poem called 'Ironing'. Its structure is based on George Herbert's poem 'The Flower'. The conjunction of seventeenth century priest and twentieth century feminist is not as unlikely as it might seem when you think of the angry dialogue with God in his poem 'The Collar' ('I struck the board, and cry'd, No more'). A Freudian might even see an unconscious link in the word 'board'.

A spiritual autobiography in miniature, Herbert's poem uses the cycle of a flower through winter into spring as a metaphor for the death and regrowth of the soul. My poem is a mini-autobiography too: only I take my metaphor not from nature but from my life as a woman — my relationship with ironing.

> I used to iron everything:
> my iron flying over sheets and towels
> like a sledge chased by wolves over snow,
>
> the flex twisting and crinking
> until the sheath frayed, exposing
> wires like nerves. I stood like a horse
>
> with a smoking hoof
> inviting anyone who dared
> to lie on my silver-padded board,
>
> to be pressed to the thinness
> of dolls cut from paper.
> I'd have commandeered a crane
>
> if I could, got the welders at Jarrow
> to heat me an iron the size of a tug
> to flatten the house.
>
> Then for years I ironed nothing.
> I put the iron in a high cupboard.
> I converted to crumpledness.
>
> And now I iron again: shaking
> dark spots of water onto wrinkled
> silk, nosing into sleeves, round
>
> buttons, breathing the sweet heated smell
> hot metal draws from newly-washed
> cloth, until my blouse dries

to a shining, creaseless blue,
an airy shape with room to push
my arms, breasts, lungs, heart into.

Just before I began writing the poem, I had jotted down two notes about pieces in *The Guardian*. One was by the art critic Tim Hilton on a Holbein portrait of a woman with a pet squirrel and starling. 'She has such a lovely face — serious, studious,' I wrote. Then:

Tim Hilton says the painting is not symbolic — but I wonder.

Squirrels and starlings are fierce. The squirrel — woman's feelings on a chain. The starling — her squawking voice.

The second was a quotation from Saul Bellow on how Mozart's music was produced without effort:

What it makes us see is that there are things which must be done easily. Easily or not at all — that is the truth about art.

'If that is true,' I added, 'I ought to give up trying to be a poet.'

In retrospect, both these jottings relate in a significant way to the poem. They show that I was already thinking about two opposing aspects of a woman: the lovely calm madonna's face in contrast to the fierceness of her feelings (symbolised by the squirrel) and jarring voice (symbolised by the starling).

I was also worrying about the idea that art should come easily. Keats said it, too, even more categorically: 'If poetry comes not as naturally as leaves to a tree it had better not come at all'. Because I've always had such a battle with poems, his words have stuck in my mind, internalised as a rebuke that on the one hand makes me want to give up writing, and on the other to rage against them. After all, giving birth is natural — and how many babies are born easily? It is another reason why I was drawn to Lorca. *Duende* celebrates the idea that art involves a struggle.

One way I defeat the critical voices that tell me to give up even before I've started is to keep a notebook. I fill it with shopping lists, student marks, quotations, fragments of a diary, resolutions to lead a more organised life, and, before I commit myself to the terror and potential failure of actually writing a poem, with 'notes' for poems. This is the page headed 'IRONING (notes for)':

Soothing/smoothing/smell/steam
Weight of my hand & arm & shoulder
push into sleeve, the crumpled fabric,

a blouse, silk, purple, violet, crumpled
smooth heat/dampness, the smell of
washed clothes which I know is synthetic
but I am deceived by its smell to believe its natural,
like in a bluebell wood
(Look Back in Anger/Dashing Away with a Smoothing Iron —
I used to sing with my father — he stole my heart away.)
For the years of my children's childhood
I ironed everything (the good mother) even for six months
starch tea-towels (tv ad for spray on starch).
Then for years I ironed nothing.
'Your clothes always look as if they've just come out of
the laundry basket,' a woman whose husband fancied me
told me.
The iron itself — like a mechanical mouse with a long tail.

Only the seeds of the finished poem are in this first draft: but among them is the antithesis that provides the poem's argument — 'For years ... I ironed everything' and, the only line to have survived intact, 'Then for years I ironed nothing'.

Various elements have been disposed of altogether. 'The good mother' I must have rejected because it was too obvious and because I was more interested in the revolt against domesticity. The synthetic bluebell smell of the detergent was too banal, a distraction from the central idea of the poem. The song I sang with my father, 'Dashing Away With a Smoothing Iron', went too. The emotion was too soft for what I wanted. The anecdote about the woman who said my clothes looked as if they had come out of a laundry basket must have seemed too exposing and confessional. The idea stays with 'I converted to crumpledness'.

The anger in the finished poem is fairly muted in the first draft, expressed only in the title of John Osborne's *Look Back in Anger* — a play which, of course, begins with a woman ironing while the men sit and read the Sunday papers. It is certainly not in the simile of the iron as a mouse.

I don't usually go in consciously for 'Martian-style' similes. But I wanted to make the iron a real physical presence in the poem; to create a series of dream-like and slightly menacing pictures, rather like Paula Rego's nursery-rhyme illustrations. But I rejected the mouse, for its associations with timidity. I replaced it with a whole string of visual similes — a 'sledge chased by wolves over snow', 'wires like nerves' and a 'smoking hoof' — that are not only closer graphically to an iron but that also reflect more effectively the stress and anger of the narrator's emotions. The further images of paper dolls and an 'iron the size of a tug' were added both for their emotional weight and because they came from my life at the time. Like lots of mothers I helped my children cut strings of skirted and trousered figures out of folded paper. Living in Newcastle, I had visited Jarrow to see a ship being launched.

The 'notes' for the poem were actually written after ironing a blouse. Though greatly worked on, the sensual details of colour and smell have remained, moved from the opening of the poem to the end in the interests of the argument. This section of the finished poem, beginning 'And now I iron again ...', draws directly on Herbert's

> And now in age I bud again
> After so many deaths I live and write;
> I once more smell the dew and rain
> and relish versing.

Ever since I first read them, these lines have affected me powerfully. It is partly because of the subject — the possibility of new life and renewal after what I imagine as a series of depressions. But it is also because they break out of the poem's controlling metaphysical metaphor — the flower — into describing, simply and directly, Herbert's own pleasure in sensual experience: in dew and rain and writing.

I wanted my poem to do something similar: to mark the emotional journey from ironing as a metaphor for the constriction of domestic life to ironing as a celebration of domesticity — of its sensual pleasures and, when there's a choice, its freedoms.

Source: Tony Curtis (ed.) (1996) *How Poets Work*, Bridgend: Seren, pp. 146–50.

30 from *The Triggering Town*

RICHARD HUGO

Richard Hugo (1923–1982), poet, was born in Seattle. He was brought up by his mother's parents after his father left the family while Hugo was still an infant. During the Second World War he served in the United States air force, reaching the rank of first lieutenant before leaving service in 1945. After studying creative writing at the University of Washington, he worked for about thirteen years as a technical writer for Boeing. His first book of poems, *A Run of Jacks*, was published in 1961, and in 1964 he began teaching creative writing at the University of Montana. He went on to publish about ten volumes of poems, many of them celebrating the towns, landscapes and people of his native Northwest, but some also drawing upon his wartime experiences.

[...] Please don't take this too seriously, but for purposes of discussion we can consider two kinds of poets, public and private. Let's use as examples Auden and Hopkins. The distinction (not a valid one, I know, but good enough for us right now) doesn't lie in the subject matter. That is, a public poet doesn't necessarily write on public themes and the private poet on private or personal ones. The distinction lies in the relation of the poet to the language. With the public poet the intellectual and emotional contents of the words are the same for the reader as for the writer. With the private poet, and most good poets of the last century or so have been private poets, the words, at least certain key words, mean something to the poet they don't mean to the reader. A sensitive reader perceives this relation of poet to word and in a way that relation—the strange way the poet emotionally possesses his vocabulary—is one of the mysteries and preservative forces of the art. With Hopkins this is evident in words like 'dappled,' 'stippled,' and 'pied.' In Yeats, 'gyre.' In Auden, no word is more his than yours.

The reason that distinction doesn't hold, of course, is that the majority of words in any poem are public—that is, they mean the same to writer and reader. That some words are the special property of a poet implies how he feels about the world and about himself, and chances are he often fights impulses to sentimentality. A public poet must always be more intelligent than the reader, nimble, skillful enough to stay ahead, to be entertaining so his didacticism doesn't set up resistances. Auden was that intelligent and skillful and he publicly regretted it. Here, in this room, I'm trying to teach you to be private poets because that's what I am and I'm limited to teaching what I know. As a private poet, your job is to be honest and to try not to be too boring. However, if you must choose between being eclectic and various or being repetitious and boring, be repetitious and boring. Most good poets are, if read very long at one sitting.

If you are a private poet, then your vocabulary is limited by your obsessions. It doesn't bother me that the word 'stone' appears more than thirty times in my third book, or that 'wind' and 'gray' appear over and over in my poems to the disdain of some reviewers. If I didn't use them that often I'd be lying about my feelings, and I consider that unforgivable. In fact, most poets write the same poem over and over.

Wallace Stevens was honest enough not to try to hide it. Frost's statement that he tried to make every poem as different as possible from the last one is a way of saying that he knew it couldn't be.

So you are after those words you can own and ways of putting them in phrases and lines that are yours by right of obsessive musical deed. You are trying to find and develop a way of writing that will be yours and will, as Stafford puts it, generate things to say. Your triggering subjects are those that ignite your need for words. When you are honest to your feelings, that triggering town chooses you. Your words used your way will generate your meanings. Your obsessions lead you to your vocabulary. Your way of writing locates, even creates, your inner life. The relation of you to your language gains power. The relation of you to the triggering subject weakens.

Source: Richard Hugo (1979), *The Triggering Town: Lectures and essays on poetry and writing*, New York and London, W. W. Norton & Company, pp. 14–15.

31 from *Nothing Not Giving Messages*

EDWIN MORGAN

Edwin Morgan (b. 1923), poet, playwright and translator, was born in Glasgow and has lived there most of his life. During the Second World War he served in the Middle East in the Royal Army Medical Corps. After the war he was appointed to a lecturing post at Glasgow University, eventually becoming titular Professor of English from 1975 until his retirement in 1980. A prolific author, Morgan's first book, *The Vision of Cathkin Braes and Other Poems*, was published in 1952. His output is marked by an extraordinary variety of style, form and subject matter. He has translated poetry and drama from several European languages and in 2001 received the Weidenfeld Prize for his translation of Racine's *Phaedra* into Scots. In 2000 he was awarded the Queen's Gold Medal for Poetry, and in 2004 the Scottish Executive appointed him 'Scots Makar', or Scottish poet laureate ('makar' being the ancient Scots word for poet).

Your 1973 collection is called From Glasgow to Saturn. *Your selected translations carry the title* Rites of Passage. *The idea of constant translation*

— linguistic, cultural, and geographic — seems central to your work as a whole. Do you feel that that's the case?

Translation in all senses! Well, maybe so. I like translation itself as an activity, the challenge of translation, of trying to do it as well as I can. Yes, also I like various kinds of confrontation, I suppose — like going back to these old encyclopaedias that I mentioned, the different kind of subjects being brought together. I like the idea, say, in *From Glasgow to Saturn*, of living in a place, like Glasgow, acknowledging that as your base, seeing the place where you have your being as it were, but at the same time feeling that you're not by any means bound to be only writing about that; you're quite entitled to think of Saturn or some other place outside our world and as far as you can to have ideas or feelings about it and to bring that into your writing too. And the whole business of communication — I suppose that comes into translation — always interested me a lot and it was partly the difficulties of communication (I suppose that's often a theme in what I write) or even imaginary communication, but again the idea of bringing things together and of giving things a voice through what I write, even if they don't have an actual voice — giving animals or inanimate objects a voice — that attracts me a lot, and I suppose that is a kind of translation in a way. If I write a poem called 'The Apple's Song', the apple is being translated if you like into *human* language. Who knows what an apple thinks! We don't really know — it doesn't give signs of thinking, but because we don't get signs of what an animal or a plant or a fruit really is thinking, I don't think we're entitled to just switch off and say it's not feeling or thinking. I like the idea particularly that in a sense we're surrounded by messages that we perhaps ought to be trying to interpret. I remember in 'The Starlings in George Square' I brought in the bit about 'Someday we'll decipher that sweet frenzied whistling', which in a sense I suppose I believed actually — although it seems just a fantastic idea.

Messages from the past and the future also?

I think probably also. Yes, yes, yes. The writer or the poet being in *receipt*, if you like, of messages, just like people listening for stars' messages, astronomers listening for that. I think the writer too does that kind of thing. He does his best. He tries to decode, if you like, the messages that he thinks he gets from everything that surrounds him. Nothing is not giving messages, I think.

Source: Edwin Morgan (1990) *Nothing Not Giving Messages: Reflections on work and life*, Hamish Whyte (ed.), Edinburgh, Polygon, pp. 130–1.

32 from *The Origin of Consciousness in the Breakdown of the Bicameral Mind*

JULIAN JAYNES

Julian Jaynes (1920–1997), psychologist, was born in West Newton, Massachusetts. He studied at Harvard and Yale, and taught psychology at Princeton University from 1966 until 1990. His earlier publications focused on the study of animal behaviour, but he later became interested in human consciousness. This led him to write his most famous and controversial book, *The Origin of Consciousness in the Breakdown of the Bicameral Mind*, first published in 1977. This presents the theory that ancient peoples were 'unconscious': the right hemisphere of the brain was dominant, which meant that they could not 'think' as we can but followed the dictates of what they perceived as gods. Modern, problem-solving human beings 'learned' consciousness about four thousand years ago, when they faced cataclysmic change. Consciousness is therefore a product of human history and culture which is still developing, and which issues from the brain's left hemisphere.

Metaphor and Language

Let us speak of metaphor. The most fascinating property of language is its capacity to make metaphors. But what an understatement! For metaphor is not a mere extra trick of language, as it is so often slighted in the old schoolbooks on composition; it is the very constitutive ground of language. I am using metaphor here in its most general sense: the use of a term for one thing to describe another because of some kind of similarity between them or between their relations to other things. There are thus always two terms in a metaphor, the thing to be described, which I shall call the *metaphrand*, and the thing or relation used to elucidate it, which I shall call the *metaphier*. A metaphor is always a known metaphier operating on a less known metaphrand. I have coined these hybrid terms simply to echo multiplication where a multiplier operates on a multiplicand.

It is by metaphor that language grows. The common reply to the question 'what is it?' is, when the reply is difficult or the experience unique, 'well, it is like —.' In laboratory studies, both children and adults describing nonsense objects (or metaphrands) to others who cannot see them use extended metaphiers that with repetition become contracted into labels. This is the major way in which the vocabulary of language is formed. The grand and vigorous function of metaphor is the generation of new language as it is needed, as human culture becomes more and more complex.

A random glance at the etymologies of common words in a dictionary will demonstrate this assertion. Or take the naming of various fauna and flora in their Latin indicants, or even in their wonderful common English names, such as stag beetle, lady's-slipper, darning needle, Queen Anne's lace, or buttercup. The human body is a particularly generative metaphier, creating previously unspeakable distinctions in a throng of areas. The *head* of an army, table, page, bed, ship, household, or nail, or of steam or water; the *face* of a clock, cliff, card, or crystal; the *eyes* of needles, winds, storms, targets, flowers, or potatoes; the *brow* of a hill; the *cheeks* of a vise; the *teeth* of cogs or combs; the *lips* of pitchers, craters, augers; the *tongues* of shoes, boardjoints, or railway switches; the *arm* of a chair or the sea; the *leg* of a table, compass, sailor's voyage, or cricket field; and so on and on. Or the *foot* of this page. Or the *leaf* you will soon turn. All of these concrete metaphors increase enormously our powers of perception of the world about us and our understanding of it, and literally create new objects. Indeed, language is an organ of perception, not simply a means of communication.

This is language moving out synchronically (or without reference to time) into the space of the world to describe it and perceive it more and more definitively. But language also moves in another and more important way, diachronically, or through time, and behind our experiences on the basis of aptic structures in our nervous systems to create abstract concepts whose referents are not observables except in a metaphorical sense. And these too are generated by metaphor. This is indeed the nub (knob), heart, pith, kernel, core, marrow, etc. of my argument, which itself is a metaphor and 'seen' only with the mind's 'eye'.

In the abstractions of human relations, the skin becomes a particularly important metaphier. We get or stay 'in touch' with others who may be 'thick-' or 'thin-skinned' or perhaps 'touchy' in which case they have to be 'handled' carefully lest we 'rub' them the wrong way; we may have a 'feeling' for another person with whom we may have a 'touching' experience.

The concepts of science are all of this kind, abstract concepts generated by concrete metaphors. In physics, we have force, acceleration (to increase one's steps), inertia (originally an indolent person), impedance, resistance, fields, and now charm. In physiology, the metaphier of a machine has been at the very center of discovery. We understand the brain by metaphors to everything from batteries and telegraphy to computers and holograms. Medical practice is sometimes dictated by metaphor. In the eighteenth century, the heart in fever was like a boiling pot, and so bloodletting was prescribed to reduce its fuel. And even today, a great deal of medicine is based upon the military metaphor of defense of the body against attacks of this or that. The very concept of law in Greek derives from *nomos*, the word for the foundations of a building. To be liable, or bound in law, comes from the Latin *ligare*, meaning to bind with cord.

In early times, language and its referents climbed up from the concrete to the abstract on the steps of metaphors, even, we may say, created the abstract on the bases of metaphors.

It is not always obvious that metaphor has played this all-important function. But this is because the concrete metaphiers become hidden in phonemic change, leaving the words to exist on their own. Even such an unmetaphorical-sounding word as the verb 'to be' was generated from a metaphor. It comes from the Sanskrit *bhu*, 'to grow, or make grow,' while the English forms 'am' and 'is' have evolved from the same root as the Sanskrit *asmi*, 'to breathe.' It is something of a lovely surprise that the irregular conjugation of our most nondescript verb is thus a record of a time when man had no independent word for 'existence' and could only say that something 'grows' or that it 'breathes.' Of course we are not conscious that the concept of being is thus generated from a metaphor about growing and breathing. Abstract words are ancient coins whose concrete images in the busy give-and-take of talk have worn away with use.

Source: Julian Jaynes (1993) *The Origin of Consciousness in the Breakdown of the Bicameral Mind*, London: Penguin Books, pp. 48–51.

33 from *The Triggering Town*

RICHARD HUGO

For biographical details, see Reading 30, p.537.

ASSUMPTIONS lie behind the work of all writers. The writer is unaware of most of them, and many of them are weird. Often the weirder the better. Words love the ridiculous areas of our minds. But silly or solid, assumptions are necessary elements in a successful base of writing operations. It is important that a poet not question his or her assumptions, at least not in the middle of composition. Finish the poem first, then worry, if you have to, about being right or sane.

Whenever I see a town that triggers whatever it is inside me that wants to write a poem, I assume at least one of the following:

The name of the town is significant and must appear in the title.

The inhabitants are natives and have lived there forever. I am the only stranger.

I have lived there all my life and should have left long ago but couldn't.

Although I am playing roles, on the surface I appear normal to the townspeople.

I am an outcast returned. Years ago the police told me to never come back but after all this time I assume that either I'll be forgiven or I will not be recognized.

At best, relationships are marginal. The inhabitants have little relation with each other and none with me.

The town is closely knit, and the community is pleasant. I am not a part of it but I am a happy observer.

A hermit lives on the outskirts in a one-room shack. He eats mostly fried potatoes. He spends hours looking at old faded photos. He has not spoken to anyone in years. Passing children often taunt him with songs and jokes.

Each Sunday, a little after 4 P.M., the sky turns a depressing gray and the air becomes chilly.

I run a hardware store and business is slow.

I run a bar and business is fair and constant.

I work in a warehouse on second shift. I am the only one in town on second shift.

I am the town humorist and people are glad to see me because they know I'll have some good new jokes and will tell them well.

The churches are always empty.

A few people attend church and the sermons are boring.

Everybody but me goes to church and the sermons are inspiring.

On Saturday nights everyone has fun but me. I sit home alone and listen to the radio. I wish I could join the others though I enjoy feeling left out.

All beautiful young girls move away right after high school and never return, or if they return, are rich and disdainful of those who stayed on.

I am on friendly terms with all couples, but because I live alone and have no girlfriend, I am of constant concern to them.

I am an eleven-year-old orphan.

I am eighty-nine and grumpy but with enormous presence and wisdom.

Terrible things once happened here and as a result the town became sad and humane.

The population does not vary.

The population decreases slightly each year.

The graveyard is carefully maintained and the dead are honored one day each year.

The graveyard is ignored and overrun with weeds.

No one dies, makes love, or ages.

No music.

Lots of excellent music coming from far off. People never see or know who is playing.

The farmers' market is alive with shoppers, good vegetables, and fruit. Prices are fixed. Bargaining is punishable by death.

The movie house is run by a kind man who lets children in free when no one is looking.

The movie house has been closed for years.

Once the town was booming but it fell on hard times around 1910.

At least one person is insane. He or she is accepted as part of the community.

The annual picnic is a failure. No one has a good time.

The annual picnic is a huge success but the only fun people have all year.

The grain elevator is silver.

The water tower is gray and the paint is peeling.

The mayor is so beloved and kind elections are no longer held.

The newspaper, a weekly, has an excellent gossip column but little or no news from outside.

No crime.

A series of brutal murders took place years ago. The murderer was never caught and is assumed still living in the town.

Years ago I was wealthy and lived in a New York penthouse. I hired about twenty chorus girls from Las Vegas to move in with me. For a year they played out all of my sexual fantasies. At the end of the year my money was gone. The chorus girls had no interest in me once I was poor and they returned to Las Vegas. I moved here where, destitute in a one-room shack on the edge of town, I am living my life out in shame.

One man is a social misfit. He is thrown out of bars and not allowed in church. He shuffles about the street unable to find work and is subjected to insults and disdainful remarks by beautiful girls. He tries to make friends but can't.

A man takes menial jobs for which he is paid very little. He is grateful for what little work he can find and is always cheerful. In any encounter with others he assumes he is wrong and backs down. His place in the town social structure is assured.

Two whores are kind to everyone but each other.

The only whore in town rejected a proposal of marriage years ago. The man left town and later became wealthy and famous in New York.

Cats are fed by a sympathetic but cranky old woman.

Dogs roam the streets.

The schoolhouse is a huge frame building with only one teacher who is old but never ages. She is a spinster and everyone in town was once in her class.

Until I found it, no outsider had ever seen it.

It is not on any map.

It is on a map but no roads to it are shown.

The next town is many miles away. It is much classier, has a nice new movie house, sparkling drive-ins, and better-looking girls. The locals in my town dream of moving to the next town but never do.

The town doctor is corrupt and incompetent.

The town druggist is an alcoholic.

The town was once supported by mining, commercial fishing, or farming. No one knows what supports it now.

One girl in the town is so ugly she knows she will never marry or have a lover. She lives in fantasies and involves herself in social activities of the church trying to keep alive her hopes which she secretly knows are futile.

Wind blows hard through the town except on Sunday afternoons a little after four when the air becomes still.

The air is still all week except on Sunday afternoons when the wind blows.

Once in a while an unlikely animal wanders into town, a grizzly bear or cougar or wolverine.

People stay married forever. No divorce. Widows and widowers never remarry.

No snow.

Lots of rain.

Birds never stop. They fly over, usually too high to be identified.

The grocer is kind. He gives candy to children. He is a widower and his children live in Paris and never write.

People who hated it and left long ago are wealthy and living in South America.

Wild sexual relationships. A lot of adultery to ward off boredom.

The jail is always empty.

There is one prisoner in jail, always the same prisoner. No one is certain why he is there. He doesn't want to get out. People have forgotten his name.

Young men are filled with hate and often fight.

I am welcome in bars. People are happy to see me and buy me drinks.

As far as one can see, the surrounding country is uninhabited.

The ballpark is poorly maintained and only a few people attend the games.

The ballpark is well kept and the entire town supports the team.

The team is in last place every year.

People sit a lot on their porches.

There is always a body of water, a sea just out of sight beyond the hill or a river running through the town. Outside of town a few miles is a lake that has been the scene of both romance and violence.

Source: Richard Hugo (1979), *The Triggering Town: Lectures and essays on poetry and writing*, New York and London, W. W. Norton & Company, pp. 19–25.

PART 4

Life writing

34 from *Einstein in Love: A scientific romance*

DENNIS OVERBYE

Dennis Overbye (b. 1944), science journalist and writer, was born in Seattle. He studied physics at the Massachusetts Institute of Technology and astronomy at University of California, Los Angeles. After working for some years on scientific journals such as *Discover* and *Sky and Telescope*, he published his first book, *Lonely Hearts of the Cosmos* (1991), a study of scientific exploration of the origins, structure and fate of the universe. It was a finalist for the National Book Critics Circle Award for nonfiction, and won the American Institute of Physics Science Writing Award. His second book, *Einstein in Love*, a portrayal of the private life of the young Einstein, was published in 2000. He is now Deputy Science Editor of *The New York Times*.

As of this writing Albert Einstein has been dead for forty-five years, but in his absence he seems more present than ever. He remains the scientist most likely to make front-page newspaper headlines[.] [...] The hottest thing in physics labs these days is Einstein-Bose condensate, an exotic new form of matter whose existence Einstein first predicted in 1932; the substance itself was first created only in 1995.
[...]

From a distance, the trajectory of Einstein's life looks mythic. The one-time humble patent clerk, with his corona of white hair and the haunted eyes; who overturned the universe and gave us the formula for God's fire, who was chased by war and Promethean guilt to wander sockless like a holy fool through the streets of Princeton, making oracular pronouncements about God and nature, has become an icon not just of science but of humanity in the face of the unknown.[...] Behind the iconic face, however, was a human being, one capable—as all human beings are—of behaving in distinctly un-iconic ways.

I first made the acquaintance of this lesser-known Einstein in 1990, in New Orleans, during a meeting of the American Association for the Advancement of Science.[...] A small clique of revisionist historians was advancing the notion that Einstein had cheated Mileva, who became his first wife, out of her proper share of credit for the theory of relativity. One slow afternoon at the meeting, I stumbled into a heated debate on this subject and was mesmerized.[...] In my naiveté about history, I'd always presumed the key questions about Einstein—how he invented his theories, the nature of his relations with lovers and loved ones—had long since been answered.

[...]

The claim that Mileva had a part in the authorship of relativity came largely from a selective reading of passages in letters, recently published for the first time, that Albert had written to her during their student years. In their correspondence, he had talked about the scientific issues that relativity would ultimately resolve, as well as about details of their courtship, Albert's fights with his mother, and, most spectacularly, the birth of the couple's illegitimate daughter, Lieserl in 1902. (Mileva's half of the correspondence for the most part seems not to have survived.) When I began to look further into the alleged controversy over relativity's authorship. I found that the letters, fifty-one in all, were only the most sensational part of an avalanche of newly uncovered material about Einstein, material that had the potential to transform our whole understanding of the man, his life, and his science.

[...]

Strictly speaking, this is not a biography of Einstein—there is already an abundance of those on the bookstore shelves. Instead, my goal has been to bring the youthful Einstein to life, to illuminate the young man who performed the deeds for which the old man, the icon, is revered. Over the last seven years I've gone through five eyeglass prescriptions, reading hundreds upon hundreds of published and unpublished letters.[...] I've followed him as he discusses everything from the details of space-time metrics to how his children should brush their teeth. I've tracked down every place Albert and Mileva lived, separately or together, and have walked the streets of their neighborhoods.[...] I've read Einstein's high school transcripts and his divorce papers. I've clambered on the razor-edged Säntis Mountain where Einstein almost lost his life as a teenager.

[...]

No history, especially a narrative one, can escape the charge that it is, on some level, a fiction, an inexact blending of a writer's subjective choices, interests, and prejudices with the data of the documentary record. While the Albert Einstein portrayed in this book is of necessity partly my own creation, thoughts or feelings that I attribute to Albert or Mileva are drawn from letters or other of their writings. When I speculate about what someone's thought processes might have been, I've taken pains to clearly signal in the text that I'm out there alone on the thin ice of history. [...] [N]o exposition of Einstein could pretend to completion if it did not explore both the sacred and the profane aspects of his existence.[...] As much as he may sometimes have wished it were otherwise, physics was not all of Einstein's life. He lived on the Earth, with a belly and a heart.[...]

Source: Dennis Overbye (2003) *Einstein in Love: A scientific romance*, London: Bloomsbury, pp. x–xiii.

35   from *Iris: A Memoir of Iris Murdoch*

JOHN BAYLEY

John Bayley (b. 1925), teacher, literary critic and novelist, was Warton Professor of English at Oxford University from 1974 until his retirement in 1992. He is the author of studies of a number of Russian, English and American writers, and of several novels. He was married to the novelist Iris Murdoch, and when she developed Alzheimer's he looked after her for five years. Following her death, he wrote *Iris* (1998), an account of their life together, and the onset and progress of her illness. It attracted enormous attention, became a best-seller, and was awarded the PEN Stern Prize. Bayley went on to write two further books of memoirs, *Iris and Her Friends: A memoir of memory and desire* (1999), and *Elegy for Iris* (1999).

A hot day. Stagnant, humid. By normal English standards really hot, insufferably hot. Not that England has standards about such things any more. Global warming no doubt. But it's a commonplace about growing old that there seem to be no standards any more. The Dog Days. With everything gone to the dogs.

Cheerless thoughts to be having on a pleasure jaunt, or what used to be one. For years now we've usually managed a treat for ourselves on really hot days, at home in the summer. We take the car along the bypass road from Oxford, for a mile or two, and twist abruptly off on to the verge – quite a tricky feat with fast moving traffic just behind. Sometimes there are hoots and shouts from passing cars who have had to brake at speed, but by that time we have jolted to a stop on the tussocky grass, locked the car, and crept through a gap in the hedge.

I remember the first time we did it, nearly forty-five years ago. We were on bicycles then, and there was little traffic on the unimproved road. Nor did we know where the river was exactly: we just thought it must be somewhere there. And with the ardour of comparative youth we wormed our way through the rank grass and sedge until we almost fell into it, or at least a branch of it. Crouching in the shelter of the reeds we tore our clothes off and slipped in like water-rats. A kingfisher flashed past our noses as we lay soundlessly in the dark sluggish current. A moment after we had crawled out and were drying ourselves on Iris's waist-slip a big pleasure boat chugged past within a few feet of the bank. The steersman, wearing a white cap, gazed intently ahead. Tobacco smoke mingled with the watery smell at the roots of the tall reeds.

[...] We trailed slowly over the long field towards the river. The heat seemed worse than ever, although the sun, overcast, did not beat down as fiercely as it had done earlier in the day. The hay had been carried away some time before, and the brownish surface of the field was baked hard and covered incongruously with molehills. The earth in them was like grey powder, and I wondered how the moles ever managed to find any sustenance as they tunnelled within it. A pair of crows flapped lazily away as we approached the river bank. Crows are said to live a long time, and I wondered idly if they were the same birds we had seen there on our bathing visits for many years past.

I wished we had managed to come earlier, before the hay was cut, and when wild flowers – scabious, white archangel, oxeye daisies – stretched over the whole field among the grass. It was not a lush river field, probably because a bed of gravel lay just below the surface. There were big gravel ponds not far away, by the main road, but this field was a protected area, a plant and bird sanctuary of some kind. Not a fish sanctuary however: there were sometimes a few fishermen about, who kept themselves to themselves and remained almost invisible among the reeds.

Our own little nook was seldom occupied however, and it was empty as usual today. Once we would have got our clothes off as soon as possible and slid silently into the water, as we had done on that first occasion. Now I had quite a struggle getting Iris's clothes off: I had managed to put her bathing dress on at home, before we started. Her instinct nowadays seems to be to take her clothes off as little as possible. Even in this horribly hot weather it is hard to persuade her to remove trousers and jersey before getting into bed.

Source: John Bayley (1998) *Iris: A memoir of Iris Murdoch*, London: Duckworth, pp. 11, 33.

36 from *A Drinking Life: A memoir*

PETE HAMILL

Pete Hamill (b. 1935), journalist and novelist, was born in Brooklyn, New York, the eldest of seven children of Irish immigrant parents. He left school at sixteen to work in the shipyard as a sheetmetal worker, and then served in the US Navy. He studied painting and writing at Mexico City College, and worked first as a graphic designer and then as a journalist for the *New York Post* and a number of other newspapers and magazines. He has published eight novels and two collections of short stories, as well as other books, and in 1994 his memoir, *A Drinking Life*, became a best-seller.

One day I ran into Brother Foppiano again. He was nastier now, because he had bloodied me and made me cry and run. *Your old man's an Irish drunk, your old man* ... I realized I was being watched by other kids, including my former friend Ronnie Zellins, and I knew that this time I couldn't run. So I piled into Brother, frantic, afraid, but determined not to cry, not to 'give up.' He hit me and hit me, but I held on to him, tripped him, fell upon him, hit him, then felt his hard wiry arms lock around my neck. I struggled. I jerked. But I couldn't get free.

So I whispered the word: *Shazam.*

Nothing happened. Brother Foppiano tightened his grip and I tightened mine on him.

We might be locked in that violent embrace to this day if Ronnie Zellins's beautiful mother hadn't come along and ordered us to stop. I watched Brother walk away, his green striped shirt as dirty as mine.

There was a sneer on his face, but he didn't say anything; he didn't speak badly about my father. I felt better for another reason: the humiliation of public crying and loss was erased. Then Ronnie Zellins came over to me.

Want to go down the Alley? he said.

No.

What about comics? Want to go trading?

No, I said. I don't want to do anything with you.

One Sunday afternoon, a week after my second fight with Brother Foppiano, my father ordered me out of Gallagher's. His face was loose and bleary again, the way it had been the day I first saw him drunk. I imagined him leaving the saloon, helped by one of the men, staggering down the street to our house, and Brother Foppiano emerging from hiding to start his cruel chant. I asked him to come home. Maybe I whined. Maybe I was annoying. I know I was holding on to his coat. He jerked the coat out of my grip, looked down at me, and ordered me in a harsh voice to go home to my mother. Hurt and angry, I ran outside.

But I didn't go home. I went directly to Foppiano's candy store. I was desperate now, even willing to fight Brother again to be sure that he wouldn't see my father drunk. I could punch him. I could tease him. Or I could talk to him, argue with him, maybe even try to make friends with him. I just didn't want him to see my father being helped down the block. But Brother wasn't around, not behind the counter, not in the back room. His father sat there, reading a newspaper and smoking a cigarette. And with a sense of relief, I looked at the comic book racks near the door. I had read most of the new comics and was not interested in the books about funny animals or high school girls. Then I found the very first issue of Master Comics. I began to read the story of Captain Marvel, Jr., and was lifted out of Brooklyn.

Hey, Mister Foppiano said, ya gonna read or ya gonna buy?

I handed him a dime and rushed home, clutching my copy of Master Comics. Back at 435, I read this issue over and over, watching a crippled boy named Freddy Freeman hobble on his crutches. Suddenly he said *his* magic word — 'Captain Marvel,' the name of his hero — and was transformed into a lithe, strong hero in a sleek blue gold-trimmed costume. After my fight with Brother, I knew that 'Shazam' didn't work for me; it probably was just a lie. But maybe it could work for others. Maybe words, like potions, were also capable of magic. And I wished that my father had a secret word too. He would come home from Gallagher's and sit in the kitchen and whisper ... *Captain Marvel.*

A lightning bolt would split the sky and there he would be: two legs, young, whole, like the man in that old photograph, his eyes sharply focused. He would smile at me and reach over and hug me and off we would go together to play ball.

That never happened.

After two years in the first floor right, we moved again.

The new flat was only a few blocks away, but it was another descent, into a harder, poorer world.

Seventh Avenue was a wide avenue with trolley cars of the 67 line moving in both directions. The steel wheels of those sleek green-and-silver 'streamlined' cars ran on steel tracks, and we would hear their squealing clattering sounds through the night; some of us heard those trolleys for the rest of our lives. The power lines were hidden in steel poles that made a deep bonging sound when you hit them with bats or pipes; from the tops of these poles cables fed the lines that ran above the trolley tracks. Those poles and lines and the steel tracks gave the avenue the look of an artist's exercise in perspective, with diminishing lines flowing away into infinity, or its equal: Flatbush Avenue at one end of the avenue, Greenwood Cemetery at the other. In the mind of an eight-year-old, both were as far away as Madrid.

Our building was 378, a tenement rising four ominous stories above the street. It was in the middle of the block, between Eleventh and Twelfth Streets, with a butcher shop on one side of the doorway and a fruit and vegetable store called Teddy's to the right. That first day, it was a place in another country.

I stood on the sidewalk with my mother and Tommy and Kathleen, who was bundled in a red snowsuit in a stroller and bawling. My mother moved the stroller back and forth, shushing Kathleen, while I gazed around at this new piece of geography. There was a barbershop across the street, with a red, white, and blue pole turning slowly outside. On one side of the barbershop was a dry cleaner's, the windows opaque with steam, then a notions shop, a variety store, a fish store, and a diner. To the left, filling the corner of Eleventh Street, was Rattigan's Bar & Grill, dark inside, with men going and coming through the front door. Nobody used the side door.

Across the street, on a diagonal from Rattigan's, there was one glimmer of the familiar: the red, white, and blue sign of still another Roulston's store. But otherwise I felt like a stranger as we waited outside for the large men from Gallagher's to arrive in a truck with our furniture and our stuffed cardboard boxes. My mother said, You'll like it here. But I looked up and saw fire escapes climbing the brick face of the building, as if drawn with rulers, and a strange canopy hanging over the edge of the roof, and a flock of pigeons circling against the hard sky. I shivered in the cold, and my mother told me to wait in the hallway. But I was afraid to go through that door. I didn't think I would like it here at all. I wanted to go back to 471 Fourteenth Street, my real home.

Do they have roaches here? I said.

My mother laughed. I hope not, she said.

I don't want to live here if they have roaches, I said.

Well, she said without much hope, let's wait and see.

Source: Pete Hamill (1994) *A Drinking Life: A memoir*, Boston, New York, Toronto, London: Back Bay Books, pp. 23–5.

37 *Five Poems*

ELAINE FEINSTEIN

Elaine Feinstein (b. 1930), poet, novelist, biographer and translator, was born in Liverpool, brought up in Leicester and educated at Cambridge. In 1980, after a career in university teaching and journalism, she became a full-time writer. She has travelled widely in Russia, Europe, India, USA, and South East Asia. She is the author of fourteen novels, a number of them exploring her Russian-Jewish roots, and a dozen volumes of poetry. Her *Collected Poems and Translations* won a Poetry Book Society Special Commendation in 2002. She has also written for television and radio, and has won awards for her translations of the poems of Marina Tsvetayeva. Among her five biographies are lives of Tsvetayeva, Pushkin, D. H. Lawrence and Ted Hughes.

Calliope in the labour ward

she who has no love for women
married and housekeeping

now the bird notes begin
in the blood in the June morning
look how these ladies are
as little squeamish as
men in a great war

have come into their bodies
as their brain dwindles to
the silver circle on
eyelids under sun
and time opens
pain in the shallows to wave up and over them

grunting in gas and air
they sail to a
darkness without self
where no will reaches

in that abandon less
than human
give birth
bleak as a goddess

Song of Power

For the baiting
children in my
son's school class who
say I am a witch:
black is the
mirror you give me

drawn inward at siege
sightless, mumbling:
criminal, to bear three
children like fruit
cannot be guarded
against enemies.

Should I have lived sterile?
The word returns me.
If any supernatural power
my strangeness earns me
I now invoke, for
all Gods are

anarchic even the Jews'
outside his own laws, with
his old name
confirms me, and I

call out for the
strange ones with wild hair

all the earth over to
make their own coherence
a fire their children
may learn to bear at last
and not burn in.

Marriage

Is there ever a new beginning when every
word has its ten years' weight, can there be
what you call conversation between us?
Relentless you are as you push me
to dance and I lurch away from you
weeping, and yet can we bear to lie
silent under the ice together like
fish in a long winter?

A letter now from York is a reminder of
windless Rievaulx, the hillside moving through
limestone arches, in the ear's liquid the
whir of dove notes: we were a fellowship of three
strangers walking in northern brightness, our
searches peaceful, in our silence the
resonance of stones only, any celibate
could look for such retreat, for me
it was a luxury to be insisted on
in the sight of those grass-overgrown dormitories

We have taken our shape from the
damage we do one another, gently as
bodies moving together at night, we amend
our gestures, softly we hold our places:
in the alien school morning in the
small stones of your eyes I know how
you want to be rid of us, you were
never a family man, your virtue is
lost, even alikeness deceived us
love, our spirits sprawl together
and both at last are distorted

and yet we go toward birthdays and other
marks   not wryly   not thriftily
waiting, for where shall we find it, a
joyous, a various world? in fury
we share, which keeps us, without
resignation: tender whenever we touch   what
else we share   this flesh   we
bring together   it hurts to
think of dying as we lie close

Dad

Your old hat hurts me, and those black
   fat raisins you liked to press into
my palm from your soft heavy hand:
   I see you staggering back up the path
with sacks of potatoes from some local farm,
   fresh eggs, flowers. Every day I grieve

for your great heart broken and you gone.
   You loved to watch the trees. This year
you did not see their Spring.
   The sky was freezing over the fen
as on that somewhere secretly appointed day
   you beached: cold, white-faced, shivering.

What happened, old bull, my loyal
   hoarse-voiced warrior? The hammer
blow that stopped you in your track
   and brought you to a hospital monitor
could not destroy your courage
   to the end you were
uncowed and unconcerned with pleasing anyone.

I think of you now as once again safely
   at my mother's side, the earth as
chosen as a bed, and feel most sorrow for
   all that was gentle in
my childhood buried there
   already forfeit, now forever lost.

Night thoughts

Uncurtained, my long room floats on
   darkness, moored in rain,
my shelves of orange skillets
   lie out in the black grass.
Tonight I can already taste
   the wet soil of their ghosts.
And my spirit looks through the glass:
   I cannot hold on for ever.

No tenure, in garden trees, I
   hang like a leaf, and stare
at cartilaginous shapes
   my shadow their visitor.
And words cannot brazen it out.
   Nothing can hold for ever.

Source: Jeni Couzyn (ed.) (1985) *The Bloodaxe Book of Contemporary Women Poets: Eleven British writers*, Newcastle upon Tyne: Bloodaxe Books, pp. 117–23.

38 from *Giving Up the Ghost: A memoir*

HILARY MANTEL

Hilary Mantel (b. 1952), novelist, was born in Glossop, Derbyshire. She studied law at the London School of Economics and Sheffield University, and became a social worker. She lived in Botswana for five years and in Saudi Arabia for four, before returning to England in the mid-1980s. She was film critic for *The Spectator* from 1987 to 1991, and her first novel, *Eight Months on Ghazzah Street*, was published in 1988. Her second novel, *Fludd* (1989) won three prizes, and a later novel, *An Experiment in Love* (1995) won the Hawthornden Prize. Her memoir, *Giving Up the Ghost* (2003), includes an account of some of the processes that led her to writing.

You come to this place, mid-life. You don't know how you got here, but suddenly you're staring fifty in the face. When you turn and look back down the years, you glimpse the ghosts of other lives you might have led. All your houses are haunted by the person you might have been. The wraiths and phantoms creep under your carpets and between the warp and weft of your curtains, they lurk in wardrobes and lie flat under drawer liners. You think of the children you might have had but didn't. When the midwife says 'It's a boy,' where does the girl go? When you think you're pregnant, and you're not, what happens to the child that has already formed in your mind? You keep it filed in a drawer of your consciousness, like a short story that wouldn't work after the opening lines.

In the February of 2002, my godmother Maggie fell ill, and hospital visits took me back to my native village. After a short illness she died, at the age of almost ninety-five, and I returned again for her funeral. I had been back many times over the years, but on this occasion there was a particular route I had to take: down the winding road between the hedgerows and the stone wall, and up a wide unmade track which, when I was small, people called 'the carriage drive'. It leads uphill to the old school, now disused, then to the convent, where there are no nuns these days, then to the church. When I was a child this was my daily walk, once in the morning to school and once again to school after dinner – that meal which the south of England calls lunch. Retracing it as an adult, in my funeral black, I felt a sense of oppression, powerful and familiar. Just before the public road joins the carriage drive came a point where I was overwhelmed by fear and dismay. My eyes moved sideways, in dread, towards dank vegetation, tangled bracken: I wanted to say, stop here, let's go no further. I remembered how when I was a child, I used to think I might bolt, make a run for it, scurry back to the (comparative) safety of home. The point where fear overcame me was the point of no turning back.

Each month, from the age of seven to my leaving at eleven, we walked in crocodile up the hill from the school to the church to go to confession and be forgiven for our sins. I would come out of church feeling, as you would expect, clean and light. This period of grace never lasted beyond the five minutes it took to get inside the school building. From about the age of four I had begun to believe I had done something wrong. Confession didn't touch some essential sin. There was something inside me that was beyond remedy and beyond redemption. The school's work was constant stricture, the systematic crushing of any spontaneity. It enforced rules that had never been articulated, and which changed as soon as you thought you had grasped them. I was conscious, from the first day in the first class, of the need to resist what I found

there. When I met my fellow children and heard their yodelling cry –
'Good mo-or-orning, Missis Simpson,' I thought I had come among
lunatics; and the teachers, malign and stupid, seemed to me like the
lunatics' keepers. I knew you must not give in to them. You must not
answer questions which evidently had no answer, or which were asked
by the keepers simply to amuse themselves and pass the time. You must
not accept that things were beyond your understanding because they
told you they were; you must go on trying to understand them. A state
of inner struggle began. It took a huge expenditure of energy to keep
your own thoughts intact. But if you did not make this effort you would
be wiped out.

Before I went to school there was a time when I was happy, and I
want to write down what I remember about that time. The story of my
own childhood is a complicated sentence that I am always trying to
finish, to finish and put behind me. It resists finishing, and partly this is
because words are not enough; my early world was synaesthesic, and I
am haunted by the ghosts of my own sense impressions, which re-
emerge when I try to write, and shiver between the lines.

We are taught to be chary of early memories. Sometimes
psychologists fake photographs in which a picture of their subject, in his
or her childhood, appears in an unfamiliar setting, in places or with
people whom in real life they have never seen. The subjects are amazed
at first but then – in proportion to their anxiety to please – they oblige
by producing a 'memory' to cover the experience that they have never
actually had. I don't know what this shows, except that some
psychologists have persuasive personalities, that some subjects are
imaginative, and that we are all told to trust the evidence of our senses,
and we do it: we trust the objective fact of the photograph, not our
subjective bewilderment. It's a trick, it isn't science; it's about our
present, not about our past. Though my early memories are patchy, I
think they are not, or not entirely, a confabulation, and I believe this
because of their overwhelming sensory power; they come complete, not
like the groping, generalised formulations of the subjects fooled by the
photograph. As I say 'I tasted', I taste, and as I say 'I heard', I hear: I
am not talking about a Proustian moment, but a Proustian cine-film.
Anyone can run these ancient newsreels, with a bit of preparation, a bit
of practice; maybe it comes easier to writers than to many people, but I
wouldn't be sure about that. I wouldn't agree either that it doesn't
matter what you remember, but only what you think you remember. I
have an investment in accuracy; I would never say, 'It doesn't matter,

it's history now.' I know, on the other hand, that a small child has a strange sense of time, where a year seems a decade, and everyone over the age of ten seems grown-up and of an equal age; so although I feel sure of what happened, I am less sure of the sequence and the dateline. I know, too, that once a family has acquired a habit of secrecy, memories begin to distort, because its members confabulate to cover the gaps in the facts; you have to make some sort of sense of what's going on around you, so you cobble together a narrative as best you can. You add to it, and reason about it, and the distortions breed distortions.

Still, I think people can remember: a face, a perfume: one true thing or two. Doctors used to say babies didn't feel pain; we know they were wrong. We are born with our sensibilities; perhaps we are conceived that way. Part of our difficulty in trusting ourselves is that in talking of memory we are inclined to use geological metaphors. We talk about buried parts of our past and assume the most distant in time are the hardest to reach: that one has to prospect for them with the help of a hypnotist, or psychotherapist. I don't think memory is like that: rather that it is like St Augustine's 'spreading limitless room'. Or a great plain, a steppe, where all the memories are laid side by side, at the same depth, like seeds under the soil.

There is a colour of paint that doesn't seem to exist any more, that was a characteristic pigment of my childhood. It is a faded, rain-drenched crimson, like stale and drying blood. You saw it on panelled front doors, and on the frames of sash windows, on mill gates and on those high doorways that led to the ginnels between shops and gave access to their yards. You can still see it, on the more soot-stained and dilapidated old buildings, where the sandblaster hasn't yet been in to turn the black stone to honey: you can detect a trace of it, a scrape. The restorers of great houses use paint scrapes to identify the original colour scheme of old salons, drawing rooms and staircase halls. I use this paint scrape – oxblood, let's call it – to refurbish the rooms of my childhood: which were otherwise dark green, and cream, and more lately a cloudy yellow, which hung about at shoulder height, like the aftermath of a fire. [...]

This is the first thing I remember. I am sitting up in my pram. We are outside, in the park called Bankswood. My mother walks backwards. I hold out my arms because I don't want her to go. She says she's only going to take my picture. I don't understand why she goes backwards, back and aslant, tacking to one side. The trees overhead make a noise of urgent conversation, too quick to catch; the leaves part, the sky moves, the sun peers down at me. Away and away she goes, till she comes to a halt. She raises her arm and partly hides her face. The sky and trees rush over my head. I feel dizzied. The entire world is sound, movement. She moves towards me, speaking. The memory ends.

This memory exists now in black and white, because when I was older I saw Bankswood pictures: this photograph or similar ones, perhaps taken that day, perhaps weeks earlier, or weeks later. In the nineteen-fifties photographs often didn't come out at all, or were so fuzzy that they were thrown away. What remains as a memory, though the colour has bled away, is the fast scudding of clouds and the rush of sound over my head, the wind in the trees: as if the waters of life have begun to flow.

Many years later, when there was a suspicion about my heart, I was sent to hospital for a test called an echocardiogram. A woman rolled me with a big roller. I heard the same sound, the vast, pulsing, universal roar: my own blood in my own veins. But for a time I didn't know whether that sound came from inside me, or from the depth of the machines by my bed.

I am learning, always learning. To take someone's picture, you move away from them. When you have finished, you move back.

The results of the test, I should say, were satisfactory. My heart was no bigger than one would expect.

I learn to walk in the house, but don't remember that. Outside the house, you turn left: I don't know it's left. Moving towards the next-door house: from my grandmother (56 Bankbottom, Hadfield, Near Manchester) to her elder sister, at no. 58. Embedded in the stonework on the left of my grandmother's door is a rusty iron ring. I always slip my finger into it, though I should not. Grandad says it is where they tied the monkey up, but I don't think they really ever had one; all the same, he lurks in my mind, a small grey monkey with piteous eyes and a long active tail.

I have taken my finger from the ring, and tasted it for metal. I am looking down at the paving stones beneath the window. I have to pass the length of that window before I arrive at no. 58. I keep my eyes on the narrow stones which, placed edge to edge, form a kerb. One, two, and the third is a raised, blueish stone, the colour of a bruise, and on this stone, perhaps because it is the colour of a bruise, I will fall and howl. Because I know I always, always cannot get past; and because howl is my stage of life, it is indulged in me. This goes on, till one day the consciousness of self-fulfilling prophecy enters my head. I decide I will not fall; I will not fall, and see what happens. I negotiate the bruise stone. It is the first time. Only once is needed. Now I can walk outside the house. I jump into the arms of my grandfather, George Foster, and I know I have nothing to fear.

At no. 58 the top of my head comes to the outermost curve of my great-aunt, Annie Connor. Her shape is like the full moon, her smile is beaming; the outer rim of her is covered by her pinny, woven with tiny flowers. It is soft from washing; her hands are hard and chapped; it is barely ten o'clock, and she is getting the cabbage on. 'Hello, Our Ilary,' she says; my family have named me aspirationally, but aspiration doesn't stretch to the 'H'. Rather embarrassed for her, that she hasn't spotted who I am, I slip her my name of the day. I claim I'm an Indian brave. I claim I'm Sir Launcelot. I claim I'm the parish priest and she doesn't quibble. I give her a blessing; she says, thank you Father.

My head comes above the keyboard of the black piano. When you press a key the sound is bronchial, damaged; the piano at no. 56 has a more mellow note. I know how to find middle 'C' because on the piano at no. 56 this key has a brown stain on the ivory, and a frill chipped out of it, as if some tiny animal has nibbled it. I am fond of the pianos, their two different voices and smells: the deep, disdainful, private aroma of their wood. Nobody has told me yet that I am disastrously unmusical and had better leave the pianos alone. If someone will play I will stand at the side with my fingers on the wood and feel the resonance, the piano breathing and purring like a cat. I do not know a cat. Tibby is Mrs Clayton's cat. He lives at no. 60, and flees along the wall. I do not know him. He is a Protestant cat. George Clayton is the first in the yard to rise in the morning, winter and summer long before dawn, treading from his house to the lavatory. I see him in the afternoon, coming home in broad day: a bulky figure in blue overalls, with a bulky blinkered head. One day he dies. Mrs Clayton, people say, is 'taken to Macclesfield': that is to say, she is mad. When she returns, the cat Tibby still flees along the wall. Instead of George, Mrs Clayton gets a blunt-headed dog called Shula. The dog's kennel name, she tells me, is Shula Ballerina. It snaps and snarls and hurtles about the backyard. This does not prevent her going mad again.

In no. 58, Annie Connor starts a game. You go into a corner of the room. She into another. You both shout, very loud:

The wind blows east,
The wind blows west,
The wind blows o'er yon cuckoo's nest.
Where is he
That has to go
Over yonder fields?
Hi Ho!

Then you just run about the room, screaming. So does she.

Two things not to believe: the monkey. People who say, 'I have eyes in the back of my head.'

I sit on the stairs, which are steep, box-like, dark. I think I am going to die. I have breathed in a housefly, I think I have. The fly was in the room and my mouth open because I was putting into it a sweet. Then the fly was nowhere to be seen. It manifests now as a tickling and scraping on the inside of my throat, the side of my throat that's nearest to the kitchen wall. I sit with my head down and my arms on my knees. Flies are universally condemned and said to be laden with filth, crawling with germs, therefore what more sure way to die than swallow or inhale one? There is another possibility, which I turn and examine in my brain: perhaps the tickling in my throat is the sweet itself, which is a green sweet from a box of assorted candy called Weekend. Probably I shouldn't have eaten this one, but a jelly kind or fudge, more suitable to a child, and if I had hesitated and said I want that marzipan someone would have said 'That's bad for you,' but now I'm on the stairs not knowing whether it's green sweet or fly. The fear of death stirs slowly within my chest cavity, like a stewpot lazily bubbling. I feel sorrow; I am going to miss seeing my grandparents and everyone else I know. I wonder whether I should mention the fact that I am dying, either from a fly or a green sweet. I decide to keep it to myself, as there won't be anything anyone can do. It will be kinder for them if they don't know; but I feel lonely, here on the stairs with my future shortening. I curse the moment I opened my mouth, and let the fly in. There is a rasping, tickling sensation deep in my throat, which I think is the fly rubbing its hands together. I begin to wonder how long it will take to die . . .

After a while I am walking about in the room again. My resolve to die completely alone has faltered. I suppose it will take an hour or so, or I might live till evening. My head is still hanging. What's the matter? I am asked. I don't feel I can say. My original intention was not to raise the alarm; also, I feel there is shame in such a death. I would rather just fall over, and that would be an end of it. I feel queasy now. Something is tugging at my attention. Perhaps it is a sense of absurdity. The dry rasping in my throat persists, but now I don't know if it is the original obstruction lodged there, or the memory of it, the imprint, which is not going to fade from my breathing flesh. For many years the word 'marzipan' affects me with its deathly hiss, the buzz in its syllables, a sepulchral fizz.

Source: Hilary Mantel (2003) *Giving Up the Ghost: A memoir*, London and New York: Fourth Estate, pp. 20–5, 27–33.

39 from *Where I Was From*

JOAN DIDION

> Joan Didion (b. 1934), novelist, journalist, essayist and screenwriter, was born in Sacramento, California. While a student of English at the University of California, Berkeley, an essay she submitted in a competition won a prize sponsored by *Vogue* magazine, and she subsequently spent eight years in New York working for *Vogue*. Her first novel, *Run River*, was published in 1963, and the following year she returned to live in California with her husband. Although she wrote a further four novels, Didion is more famous for her essays analysing contemporary American life and culture, collected as *Slouching Toward Bethlehem* (1968) and *The White Album* (1979). She is also the author of a memoir, *Where I Was From*, published in 2003.

My great-great-great-great-great-grandmother Elizabeth Scott was born in 1766, grew up on the Virginia and Carolina frontiers, at age sixteen married an eighteen-year-old veteran of the Revolution and the Cherokee expeditions named Benjamin Hardin IV, moved with him into Tennessee and Kentucky and died on still another frontier, the Oil Trough Bottom on the south bank of the White River in what is now Arkansas but was then Missouri Territory. Elizabeth Scott Hardin was remembered to have hidden in a cave with her children (there were said to have been eleven, only eight of which got recorded) during Indian fighting, and to have been so strong a swimmer that she could ford a river in flood with an infant in her arms. Either in her defense or for reasons of his own, her husband was said to have killed, not counting English soldiers or Cherokees, ten men. This may be true or it may be, in a local oral tradition inclined to stories that turn on decisive gestures, embroidery. I have it on the word of a cousin who researched the matter that the husband, our great-great-great-great-great-grandfather, 'appears in the standard printed histories of Arkansas as "Old Colonel Ben Hardin, the hero of so many Indian wars."' Elizabeth Scott Hardin had bright blue eyes and sick headaches. The White River on which she lived was the same White River on which, a century and a half later, James McDougal would locate his failed White-water development. This is a country at some level not as big as we like to say it is.

I know nothing else about Elizabeth Scott Hardin, but I have her recipe for corn bread, and also for India relish: her granddaughter brought these recipes west in 1846, traveling with the Donner-Reed party as far as the Humboldt Sink before cutting north for Oregon, where her husband, the Reverend Josephus Adamson Cornwall, was determined to be the first Cumberland Presbyterian circuit rider in what was then called Oregon country. Because that granddaughter, Nancy Hardin Cornwall, was my great-great-great-grandmother, I have, besides her recipes, a piece of appliqué she made on the crossing. This appliqué, green and red calico on a muslin field, hangs now in my dining room in New York and hung before that in the living room of a house I had on the Pacific Ocean.

I also have a photograph of the stone marker placed on the site of the cabin in which Nancy Hardin Cornwall and her family spent the winter of 1846–47, still short of their destination in the Willamette Valley but unable to get their wagons through a steep defile on the Umpqua River without abandoning Josephus Cornwall's books. (This option seems to have presented itself only to his daughters.) 'Dedicated to the memory of Rev. J. A. Cornwall and family,' the engraving on the marker reads. 'They built the first immigrant cabin in Douglas County near this site, hence the name Cabin Creek. The family wintered here in 1846–1847, were saved from extreme want by Israel Stoley, a nephew who was a good hunter. The Indians were friendly. The Cornwalls traveled part way westward with the ill-fated Donner Party.'

My mother was sent the photograph of this marker by her mother's cousin Oliver Huston, a family historian so ardent that as recently as 1957 he was alerting descendants to 'an occasion which no heir should miss,' the presentation to the Pacific University Museum of, among other artifacts, 'the old potato masher which the Cornwall family brought across the plains in 1846.' Oliver Huston's letter continued: 'By this procedure, such items can then be seen by all Geiger and Cornwall heirs at any time in the future by simply visiting the Museum.' I have not myself found occasion to visit the potato masher, but I do have a typescript of certain memories, elicited from one of Nancy Hardin Cornwall's twelve children, Narcissa, of those months on what would later be called Cabin Creek:

> We were about ten miles from the Umpqua River and the Indians living there would come and spend the greater part of the day. There was one who spoke English, and he told Mother the Rogue River Indians were coming to kill us. Mother told them if they troubled us, in the spring the Bostons (the Indian name for the white people) would come out and kill them all off. Whether this had any effect or not I don't know, but anyway they did not kill us. But we always thought they would come one day for that purpose. One day Father was busy reading and did not notice the house was filling with strange Indians until Mother spoke about it. ... As soon as Father noticed them he got up and got his pistols and asked the Indians to go out and see him shoot. They followed him out, but kept at a distance. The pistols were a great curiosity to them. I doubt if they had ever seen any before. As soon as they were all out of the cabin Mother barred the door and would not let them in any more. Father entertained them outside until evening, when they got on their ponies and rode away. They never returned to trouble us any more.

In another room of this house I had on the Pacific Ocean there hung a quilt from another crossing, a quilt made by my great-great-grandmother Elizabeth Anthony Reese on a wagon journey during which she buried one child, gave birth to another, twice contracted mountain fever, and took turns driving a yoke of oxen, a span of mules, and twenty-two head of loose stock. In this quilt of Elizabeth Reese's were more stitches than I had ever seen in a quilt, a blinding and pointless compaction of stitches, and it occurred to me as I hung it that she must have finished it one day in the middle of the crossing, somewhere in the wilderness of her own grief and illness, and just kept on stitching. From her daughter's account:

> Tom was sick with fever the first day of the crossing, no chance for a doctor. He was only sick a day or two when he died. He had to be buried right away, as the train of wagons was going right on. He was two years old, and we were glad to get a trunk to bury him in. A friend gave a trunk. My aunt, the following year, when her baby died, carried it for a long time in her arms without letting anyone know for fear they would bury the baby before coming to a station.

These women in my family would seem to have been pragmatic and in their deepest instincts clinically radical, given to breaking clean with everyone and everything they knew. They could shoot and they could handle stock and when their children outgrew their shoes they could learn from the Indians how to make moccasins. 'An old lady in our wagon train taught my sister to make blood pudding,' Narcissa Cornwall recalled. 'After killing a deer or steer you cut its throat and catch the blood. You add suet to this and a little salt, and meal or flour if you have it, and bake it. If you haven't anything else to eat, it's pretty good.' They tended to accommodate any means in pursuit of an uncertain end. They tended to avoid dwelling on just what that end might imply. When they could not think what else to do they moved another thousand miles, set out another garden: beans and squash and sweet peas from seeds carried from the last place. The past could be jettisoned, children buried and parents left behind, but seeds got carried. They were women, these women in my family, without much time for second thoughts, without much inclination toward equivocation, and later, when there was time or inclination, there developed a tendency, which I came to see as endemic, toward slight and major derangements, apparently eccentric pronouncements, opaque bewilderment and moves to places not quite on the schedule.

> Mother viewed character as being the mainspring of life, and, therefore, as regulating our lives here and indicating our destiny in the life to come. She had fixed and settled principles, aims and motives in life. Her general health was excellent and in middle life she appeared almost incapable of fatigue. Winter and summer, at all seasons and every day, except Sunday, her life was one ceaseless round of activity. The care of her family, to provide for hired help, to entertain visitors, and to entertain preachers and others during meetings which were frequent.

That was the view of Nancy Hardin Cornwall taken by her son Joseph, who was thirteen years old during the crossing. Nancy Hardin Cornwall's daughter Laura, two years old during the crossing, took a not dissimilar view: 'Being a Daughter of the American Revolution, she was naturally a brave woman, never seeming afraid of Indians or shrinking from hardships.'

A photograph:

A woman standing on a rock in the Sierra Nevada in perhaps 1905.

Actually it is not just a rock but a granite promontory: an igneous outcropping. I use words like 'igneous' and 'outcropping' because my grandfather, one of whose mining camps can be seen in the background of this photograph, taught me to use them. He also taught me to distinguish gold-bearing ores from the glittering but worthless serpentine I preferred as a child, an education to no point, since by that time gold was no more worth mining than serpentine and the distinction academic, or possibly wishful.

The photograph. The promontory. The camp in the background.

And the woman; Edna Magee Jerrett. She is Nancy Hardin Cornwall's great-granddaughter, she will in time be my grandmother. She is Black Irish, English, Welsh, possibly (this is uncertain) a fraction Jewish through her grandfather William Geiger, who liked to claim as an ancestor a German rabbi but was himself a Presbyterian missionary in the Sandwich Islands and along the Pacific coast; possibly (this is still more uncertain) a lesser fraction Indian, from some frontier somewhere, or maybe, because her skin darkens in the sun as she was told not to let it, she just likes to say that. She grew up in a house on the Oregon coast filled with the educational curiosities of the place and period: strings of shells and seeds from Tahiti, carved emu eggs, Satsuma vases, spears from the South Pacific, an alabaster miniature of the Taj Mahal and the baskets her mother was given by the local Indians. She is quite beautiful. She is also quite indulged, clearly given, although she knows enough about mountains to shake out her boots for snakes every morning, to more amenities than could have been offered in this mining camp in the Sierra Nevada at the time in question. In this photograph she is wearing, for example, a long suede skirt and jacket made for her by the most expensive tailor in San Francisco. 'You couldn't pay for her *hats*,' her father, a ship's captain, had told her suitors by way of discouragement, and perhaps they had all been discouraged but my grandfather, an innocent from the Georgetown Divide who read books.

It was an extravagance of spirit that would persist through her life. Herself a child, she knew what children wanted. When I was six and had the mumps she brought me, as solace, not a coloring book, not ice cream, not bubble bath, but an ounce of expensive perfume, Elizabeth Arden 'On Dit,' in a crystal bottle sealed with gold thread. When I was eleven and declined to go any longer to church she gave me, as inducement, not the fear of God but a hat, not any hat, not a child's well-mannered cloche or beret, but a *hat*, gossamer Italian straw and French silk cornflowers and a heavy satin label that read 'Lilly Dache.' She made champagne punch for the grandchildren left to sit with her on New Year's Eve. During World War II she volunteered to help salvage the Central Valley tomato crop by working the line at the Del Monte cannery in Sacramento, took one look at the moving conveyer belt, got one of those sick headaches her great-grandmother brought west with the seeds, and spent that first and only day on the line with tears running down her face. As atonement, she spent the rest of the war knitting socks for the Red Cross to send to the front. The yarn she bought to knit these socks was cashmere, in regulation colors. She had vicuña coats, hand-milled soap, and not-much money. A child could make her cry, and I am ashamed to say that I sometimes did.

Source: Joan Didion (2003) *Where I Was From*, London: Flamingo, pp. 3–11.

40 from *The Diary of a Young Girl*

ANNE FRANK

Annelies Marie 'Anne' Frank (1929–1945), diarist, was born in Frankfurt-am-Main. Her parents were Jews, who fled from Germany to Holland in 1933. After the Nazi occupation of Holland in 1942 the family, with four other people, hid in a sealed-off annex of rooms above an office in Amsterdam until their betrayal on 4 August 1944. They were all taken to concentration camps, and the following year Anne died of typhus at Bergen-Belsen. From her thirteenth birthday, on 12 June 1942, until 1 August 1944, she had kept a diary, which was preserved and published in 1947 by her father, the only member of the family to survive. It was translated into English in 1952 and into many other languages thereafter, and was subsequently dramatised and filmed. Through her diary, Anne Frank has become the best-known symbol of the suffering of Jewish people during the Holocaust.

Monday, 15 June 1942

I had my birthday party on Sunday afternoon. The Rin Tin Tin film was a big hit with my classmates. I got two brooches, a bookmark and two books.

I'll start by saying a few things about my school and my class, beginning with the other children.

Betty Bloemendaal looks rather poor, and I think she probably is. She lives on an obscure street in West Amsterdam, and none of us knows where it is. She does very well at school, but that's because she works so hard, not because she's clever. She's pretty quiet.

Jacqueline van Maarsen is supposedly my best friend, but I've never had a real friend. At first I thought Jacque would be one, but I was badly mistaken.

D.Q.[5] is a very nervous girl who's always forgetting things, so the teachers keep giving her extra homework as a punishment. She's very kind, especially to G.Z.

E.S. talks so much it isn't funny. She's always touching your hair or fiddling with your buttons when she asks you something. They say she can't stand me, but I don't care, because I don't like her much either.

Henny Mets is a nice girl with a cheerful disposition, except that she talks in a loud voice and is really childish when we're playing outside. Unfortunately, Henny has a girlfriend named Beppy who's a bad influence on her because she's dirty and vulgar.

J.R. – I could write a whole book about her. J. is a detestable, sneaky, stuck-up, two-faced gossip who thinks she's so grown-up. She's really got Jacque under her spell, and that's a shame. J. is easily offended, bursts into tears at the slightest thing and, to top it all, is a terrible show-off. Miss J. always has to be right. She's very rich, and has a wardrobe full of the most adorable dresses that are much too old for her. She thinks she's gorgeous, but she's not. J. and I can't stand each other.

Ilse Wagner is a nice girl with a cheerful disposition, but she's extremely finicky and can spend hours moaning and groaning about something. Ilse likes me a lot. She's very clever, but lazy.

Hanneli Goslar, or Lies as she's called at school, is a bit on the strange side. She's usually shy – outspoken at home, but reserved with other people. She blabs whatever you tell her to her mother. But she says what she thinks, and lately I've come to appreciate her a great deal.

Nannie van Praag-Sigaar is small, funny and sensible. I think she's nice. She's pretty clever. There isn't much else you can say about Nannie.

Eefje de Jong is, in my opinion, terrific. Though she's only twelve, she's quite the lady. She treats me like a baby. She's also very helpful, and I like her.

---

[5] Initials have been assigned at random to those persons who prefer to remain anonymous.

G.Z. is the prettiest girl in our class. She has a nice face, but is a bit stupid. I think they're going to hold her back a year, but of course I haven't told her that.

COMMENT ADDED BY ANNE AT A LATER DATE: *To my great surprise, G.Z. wasn't held back a year after all.*

And sitting next to G.Z. is the last of us twelve girls, me.

There's a lot to be said about the boys, or maybe not so much after all.

Maurice Coster is one of my many admirers, but pretty much of a pest.

Sallie Springer has a filthy mind, and rumour has it that he's gone all the way. Still, I think he's terrific, because he's very funny.

Emiel Bonewit is G.Z.'s admirer, but she doesn't care. He's pretty boring.

Rob Cohen used to be in love with me too, but I can't stand him any more. He's an obnoxious, two-faced, lying, snivelling little twit with an awfully high opinion of himself.

Max van de Velde is a farm boy from Medemblik, but a decent sort, as Margot would say.

Herman Koopman also has a filthy mind, just like Jopie de Beer, who's a terrible flirt and girl-chaser.

Leo Blom is Jopie de Beer's best friend, but has been spoiled by Jopie's dirty mind.

Albert de Mesquita came from the Montessori School and jumped a year. He's really clever.

Leo Slager came from the same school, but isn't as clever.

Ru Stoppelmon is a short, goofy boy from Almelo who transferred to this school in the middle of the year.

C.N. does whatever he's not supposed to.

Jacques Kocernoot sits behind us, next to C., and we (G. and I) laugh ourselves stupid.

Harry Schaap is the most decent boy in our class. He's nice.

Werner Joseph is nice too, but all the changes taking place lately have made him too quiet, so he seems boring.

Sam Salomon is one of those tough guys from the rough part of town. A real brat. (Admirer!)

Appie Riem is pretty Orthodox, but a brat too.

Saturday, 20 June 1942

Writing in a diary is a really strange experience for someone like me. Not only because I've never written anything before, but also because it seems to me that later on neither I nor anyone else will be interested in the musings of a thirteen-year-old schoolgirl. Oh well, it doesn't matter. I feel like writing, and I have an even greater need to get all kinds of things off my chest.

'Paper has more patience than people.' I thought of this saying on one of those days when I was feeling a little depressed and was sitting at home with my chin in my hands, bored and listless, wondering whether to stay in or go out. I finally stayed where I was, brooding. Yes, paper *does* have more patience, and since I'm not planning to let anyone else read this stiff-backed notebook grandly referred to as a 'diary', unless I should ever find a real friend, it probably won't make a bit of difference.

Now I'm back to the point that prompted me to keep a diary in the first place; I don't have a friend.

Let me put it more clearly, since no one will believe that a thirteen-year-old girl is completely alone in the world. And I'm not. I have loving parents and a sixteen-year-old sister, and there are about thirty people I can call friends. I have a throng of admirers who can't keep their adoring eyes off me and who sometimes have to resort to using a broken pocket mirror to try and catch a glimpse of me in the classroom. I have a family, loving aunts and a good home. No, on the surface I seem to have everything, except my one true friend. All I think about when I'm with friends is having a good time. I can't bring myself to talk about anything but ordinary everyday things. We don't seem to be able to get any closer, and that's the problem. Maybe it's my fault that we don't confide in each other. In any case, that's just how things are, and unfortunately they're not liable to change. This is why I've started the diary.

To enhance the image of this long-awaited friend in my imagination, I don't want to jot down the facts in this diary the way most people would do, but I want the diary to be my friend, and I'm going to call this friend *Kitty*.

Since no one would understand a word of my stories to Kitty if I were to plunge right in, I'd better provide a brief sketch of my life, much as I dislike doing so.

My father, the most adorable father I've ever seen, didn't marry my mother until he was thirty-six and she was twenty-five. My sister

Margot was born in Frankfurt am Main in Germany in 1926. I was born on 12 June 1929. I lived in Frankfurt until I was four. Because we're Jewish, my father emigrated to Holland in 1933, when he became the Managing Director of the Dutch Opekta Company, which manufactures products used in making jam. My mother, Edith Holländer Frank, went with him to Holland in September, while Margot and I were sent to Aachen to stay with our grandmother. Margot went to Holland in December, and I followed in February, when I was plonked down on the table as a birthday present for Margot.

I started right away at the Montessori nursery school. I stayed there until I was six, at which time I started in the first form. In the sixth form my teacher was Mrs Kuperus, the headmistress. At the end of the year we were both in tears as we said a heartbreaking farewell, because I'd been accepted at the Jewish Lyceum, where Margot also went to school.

Our lives were not without anxiety, since our relatives in Germany were suffering under Hitler's anti-Jewish laws. After the pogroms in 1938 my two uncles (my mother's brothers) fled Germany, finding safe refuge in North America. My elderly grandmother came to live with us. She was seventy-three years old at the time.

After May 1940 the good times were few and far between: first there was the war, then the capitulation and then the arrival of the Germans, which is when the trouble started for the Jews. Our freedom was severely restricted by a series of anti-Jewish decrees: Jews were required to wear a yellow star; Jews were required to turn in their bicycles; Jews were forbidden to use trams; Jews were forbidden to ride in cars, even their own; Jews were required to do their shopping between 3.00 and 5.00 p.m.; Jews were required to frequent only Jewish-owned barbershops and beauty salons; Jews were forbidden to be out on the streets between 8.00 p.m. and 6.00 a.m.; Jews were forbidden to go to theatres, cinemas or any other forms of entertainment; Jews were forbidden to use swimming pools, tennis courts, hockey fields or any other athletic fields; Jews were forbidden to go rowing; Jews were forbidden to take part in any athletic activity in public; Jews were forbidden to sit in their gardens or those of their friends after 8.00 p.m.; Jews were forbidden to visit Christians in their homes; Jews were required to attend Jewish schools, etc. You couldn't do this and you couldn't do that, but life went on. Jacque always said to me, 'I don't dare do anything any more, 'cause I'm afraid it's not allowed.'

In the summer of 1941 Grandma fell ill and had to have an operation, so my birthday passed with little celebration. In the summer of 1940 we didn't do much for my birthday either, since the fighting had just ended in Holland. Grandma died in January 1942. No one knows how often I think of her and still love her. This birthday celebration in 1942 was intended to make up for the others, and Grandma's candle was lit along with the rest.

The four of us are still doing well, and that brings me to the present date of 20 June 1942, and the solemn dedication of my diary.

Saturday, 20 June 1942

Dearest Kitty!

Let me get started right away; it's nice and quiet now. Father and Mother are out and Margot has gone to play ping-pong with some other young people at her friend Trees's. I've been playing a lot of ping-pong myself lately. So much that five of us girls have formed a club. It's called 'The Little Dipper Minus Two'. A really silly name, but it's based on a mistake. We wanted to give our club a special name; and because there were five of us, we came up with the idea of the Little Dipper. We thought it consisted of five stars, but we turned out to be wrong. It has seven, like the Big Dipper, which explains the 'Minus Two'. Ilse Wagner has a ping-pong set, and the Wagners let us play in their big dining-room whenever we want. Since we five ping-pong players like ice-cream, especially in the summer, and since you get hot playing ping-pong, our games usually end with a visit to the nearest ice-cream parlour that allows Jews: either Oasis or Delphi.

Source: Anne Frank (1997) *The Diary of a Young Girl*, Otto H. Frank and Mirjam Pressler (eds) Susan Massotty (tr.), London: Puffin Books, pp. 3–9.

41 from *Sidetracks: Explorations of a Romantic Biographer*

RICHARD HOLMES

Richard Holmes (b. 1945), biographer, was born in London and educated at Cambridge. He started out as a journalist, and spent nearly twenty years as a feature writer and reviewer for *The Times*, but is now widely recognised as one of the greatest modern literary biographers, specialising particularly in the Romantic period. He is Professor of Biographical Studies at the University of East Anglia. Among his best-known works are *Shelley: The pursuit* (1974), *Coleridge* (1989, 1998), and *Dr Johnson & Mr Savage* (1993). In 1985 he published *Footsteps: Adventures of a Romantic Biographer*, which combined travel, personal memoirs, and an exploration of the relationship between biographer and subject. A second volume, *Sidetracks: Explorations of a Romantic Biographer* (2000), collected various pieces on other Romantic writers, as well as the scripts of two radio plays and a short story.

To The Tempest Given

A radio-play based on Shelley's last days in Italy.

wind, storm and sea

SHELLEY

The breath whose might I have invoked in Song
Descends on me: my spirit's bark is driven
Far from the shore, far from the trembling throng
Whose sails were never to the Tempest given;
The massy earth and sphéred skies are riven!
I am born darkly, fearfully afar ...

fades to seaside, gulls, modern children on holiday

HOLMES ...Yes, my 'spirit's bark.' Shelley always loved boats. At Eton, at Oxford, on Highgate ponds it was paper boats, at Pisa a skiff. That's what brought him to San Terenzo in April 1822, a sailing holiday really, far away from the crowds, the 'trembling throng.' He rented a beach house, Casa Magni, right at the sea's edge, miles from anywhere.

It still exists: seven white-washed arches below, four white-washed rooms above, and a long open balcony directly overlooking the surf: a primitive, magical place. Shelley loved the whole set-up. He had a 24-foot yacht especially built for him at the naval dockyards up the coast at Genoa. Typically it had too much sail and too much ballast: very fast and very unstable.

SHELLEY Like Anacreon's swallow, I have left my Nile, and have taken up my summer quarters here, in a lonely house close to the sea side, surrounded by the soft and sublime scenery of the Gulph of Spezia. – I do not write. – I have lived too long near Lord

Byron and the sun has extinguished the glowworm ... We have been out now several days in our boat, the Don Juan, although we have sought in vain for an opportunity of trying her against the feluccas or other large craft in the bay: she passes the small ones as a Comet might pass the dullest planets in heaven.

HOLMES On the surface, Shelley was as happy as he'd ever been, suntanned, healthy, revelling in the outdoor life; bathing, sailing, picnicking. His clever young wife, Mary, was with him; and various friends and children packed into the four inhabitable rooms of the Casa Magni. From the various accounts they have left of these last weeks, we can discover a great deal about what was going on, especially from Mary. But it is not always easy to understand at first.

MARY Our house, Casa Magni, was close to the village of Lerici; the sea came up to the door, a steep wooded hill sheltered it from behind. The proprietor of the estate on which it was situated was insane ... The scene was of unimaginable beauty. The blue extent of the waters, the almost landlocked bay, the near castle of Lerici shutting it in to the east, and distant Porto Venere to the west, formed a picture such as one sees in Salvator Rosa's landscapes only ... But sometimes the gales and squalls surrounded the bay with foam, and the sea roared unremittingly, so that we almost fancied ourselves on board a ship.

HOLMES In reality, what was going on at Casa Magni, below the holiday surface, was very mysterious, very strange. To begin with, a small point, in May and June, one by one all their Italian servants – their cook, their nanny, their odd-job man – left them, saying the place was too remote, too peculiar. Then it became clear that Shelley's wife Mary, who had travelled as happily as a gypsy with him all over Italy for the last four years, was uneasy about this place.

MARY The sense of misfortune hung over my spirits. No words can tell you how I hated our house and the country about it. Shelley reproached me for this – his health was good and the place quite after his own heart – What could I answer? – No words could describe my feelings – the beauty of the woods made me weep and shudder ... My only moments of peace were on board that unhappy boat, when lying down with my head on his knees, I shut my eyes and felt the wind and our swift motion alone.

HOLMES Of course, the biographer has to intervene here and say that we are hearing Mary in retrospect. She may have been the cool, intellectual daughter of the philosopher William Godwin; but she was also a novelist and the author of *Frankenstein*. She was an imaginative woman, and surely her testimony was affected by the appalling series of things that subsequently occurred? Perhaps so: truth is a shimmering, uncertain element, that is refracted through time, like sunlight through shifting water. Yet there is one letter of her's, actually written at this moment, to a friend in Livorno, Leigh Hunt, who was planning to visit them after coming out especially all the way from England. In it Mary already expresses the same feelings of unease, of menacing beauty, and everything being somehow out of control. And more than that.

MARY My dear friend, I know that Shelley has some idea of persuading you to come here. I am too ill to write the reasonings, only let me entreat you, let *no persuasions* induce you to come. Selfish feelings, you may be sure, do not dictate me – but it would be complete madness to come. I wish I could write more, I wish I could break my chains and leave this dungeon.

HOLMES The idea of being held captive, of being trapped in some enchanted prison at Casa Magni, affected other members of the holiday party with Shelley. His old friend Edward Williams, who was there with his beautiful rather sporty young wife Jane, was a solid, extrovert type not given to fanciful notions. Williams had been to Eton (like Shelley), served in the navy, and then as an officer in the East India Company army. Throughout his time with the Shelleys he kept a daily Journal, in a bluff matter-of-fact manner, which nonetheless seems almost unconsciously to reflect the disturbing atmosphere of the place, and sense of imminent disaster.

WILLIAMS 4th May. Went fishing with Shelley – no sport. Returned late, a heavy swell getting up. I think if there are no tides in the Mediterranean that there are strong currents on which the moon both at the full and change has a very powerful effect.

5th May. Kept awake during the whole night by a heavy swell, which made a noise upon the beach like the discharge of heavy artillery.

7th May. In the afternoon I made an effort with Jane in the rowing boat to put to sea ... but a wave struck her on the bow while launching and almost swamped her. I landed Jane half drowned on the rocks. In the evening a heavy thunderstorm passed over – one flash of lightning over Lerici was particularly vivid. The steeple of the place has already been struck, and the inhabitants say at a time when there was not a cloud to be seen.

HOLMES But at the centre of this seascape of beauty and disturbance was always Shelley himself, acting in ways that came to seem increasingly strange, as if he was himself the eye of some invisible storm. Within a week of arriving at Casa Magni, an uncanny incident occurred.

surf

WILLIAMS After tea while walking with Shelley on the terrace and observing the effect of moonlight on the waters, he complained of being unusually nervous, and stopping short he grasped me violently by the arm and stared steadily on the white surf that broke upon the beach under our feet. Observing him sensibly affected, I demanded of him if he were in pain – but he only answered, saying 'There it is again! – there!' He recovered after some time, and declared that he saw, as plainly as then he saw me, a naked child rise from the sea, clap its hands as if in joy and smiling at him. This was a trance that it required some reasoning and philosophy entirely to wake him from, so forcibly had the vision operated on his mind.

HOLMES There can be no doubt that Williams, who did not live to correct or add to this Journal, was telling the truth as he experienced it at the time that evening on the terrace. But what did the vision mean, and who was the child? Williams himself put it down to a 'rather melancholy' conversation he had had with Shelley, probably about the very recent death of Allegra, Claire Clairmont's illegitimate child by Byron.

Source: Richard Holmes (2000) *Sidetracks: Explorations of a romantic biographer*,
London: HarperCollins, pp. 283–8.

42 from *In Ethiopia with a Mule*

DERVLA MURPHY

Dervla Murphy (b. 1931), bicyclist and travel writer, was born in County Waterford, Ireland. In 1963 she set off on her first expedition, a bicycle tour from Ireland to India. In Yugoslavia she began keeping a journal, which was later turned into her first book, *Full Tilt: Ireland to India with a bicycle* (1965), describing particularly her adventures in Persia, Pakistan and Afghanistan. In the forty years since then she has bicycled through Africa, Tibet, Siberia and the Balkans, for the most part travelling alone. She has published some twenty books based on her experiences and giving her observations of the people she meets and their cultures.

17 December

At lunch-time today I had my first meal of *injara* and *wat*. *Injara* has a bitter taste and a gritty texture; it looks and feels exactly like damp, grey foam-rubber, but is a fermented bread made from *teff*—the cereal grain peculiar to the Ethiopian highlands—and cooked in sheets about half-an-inch thick and two feet in circumference. These are double-folded and served beside one's plate of *wat*—a highly spiced stew of meat or chicken. One eats with the right hand (only), by mopping up the *wat* with the *injara*; and, as in Muslim countries, a servant pours water over one's hands before and after each meal.

During the afternoon a blessed silence enfolds sun-stricken Massawah and I slept soundly from two to five. By then it was a little less hellish outside, so I set forth to see the sights—not that there are many to see here. Visitors are forbidden to enter the grounds of the Imperial Palace and women are forbidden to enter the mosques—of which there are several, though only the new Grand Mosque looks interesting. It was built by the Emperor, presumably to placate his rebellious Eritrean Muslim subjects.[6]

[6] Throughout Ethiopian history Massawah has been important in a negative sense, for it was the highlanders' inability to hold their natural port that isolated them so momentously. At the beginning of the fifteenth century King Yeshaq took Massawah from the Muslims, who had been in possession for seven centuries, but within eighty years it had been lost again to the coastal tribes then warring against the highlanders. From 1520 to 1526 it was occupied by the Portuguese, from 1527 to 1865 by the Turks, and from 1865 to 1882 by the Egyptians. The British next took over, promising the Emperor John IV that on leaving Massawah they would return it to the highlanders. They left three years later, but their anxiety to counter French influence along the Red Sea coast led them to hand Massawah over to the Italians—for whom it was the capital of their new colony until 1897, when Asmara was built. After World War II the British again took possession and not until 1952 did Massawah, with the rest of Eritrea, become part of the Ethiopian Empire. To-day this province is a troublesome part, for many Eritreans resent being ruled from Addis Ababa, and foreign Muslim powers are busy transforming this resentment into a modern nationalistic ambition to have Eritrea declared an independent state.

In the old city, south of the port, the architecture is pure Arabic, though many of the present population have migrated from the highlands. The narrow streets of solid stone or brick houses seem full of ancient mystery and maimed beggars drag themselves through the dust while diseased dogs slink away at one's approach, looking as though they wanted to snarl but hadn't enough energy left.

18 December. Nefasit

The process of converting a cyclist into a hiker is being rather painful. Today I only walked eighteen miles, yet now I feel more tired than if I had cycled a hundred and eighteen; but this is perhaps understandable, as I'm out of training and was carrying fifty pounds from 3,000 to 6,000 feet. At the moment my shoulder muscles are fiery with pain and—despite the most comfortable of boots—three massive blisters are throbbing on each foot.

Yesterday Commander Iskander Desta of the Imperial Navy kindly suggested that I should be driven across the coastal desert strip in a naval jeep, which collected me from my *pensione* at eight o'clock this morning. The Eritrean driver spoke fluent Italian, but no English, and the dozen English-speaking cadets, who were going to spend Sunday at the 4,000-feet Embatcallo naval rest-camp, were not disposed to fraternise with the *faranj* (foreigner).

Beyond a straggle of new 'council houses' our road climbed through hillocks of red sand, scattered with small green shrubs. Then these hillocks became hills of bare rock—and all the time the high mountains were looming ahead in a blue haze, sharpening my eagerness to get among them. We passed one primitive settlement of half-a-dozen oblong huts, which is marked as a village on my map—perhaps because Coca-Cola is sold outside one of the shacks—and a few miles further on the road tackled the steep escarpment in a series of brilliantly-engineered hairpin bends.

By 10 a.m. I had been released from the truck at 3,000 feet, where mountains surrounded me on every side. Here the climate was tolerable, though for an hour or so sweat showered off me at every step; then clouds quickly piled up and a cool breeze rose. On the four-mile stretch to Ghinda I passed many other walkers—ragged, lean Muslim tribesmen, highlanders draped in *shammas* (white cotton cloaks) and skinny children herding even skinnier goats. Everyone stared at me suspiciously and only once was my greeting returned—by a tall, ebony-skinned tribesman. One doesn't resent such aloofness, since surprise is probably the main cause, but I soon stopped being so unrewardingly amiable. Already I notice a difference between cycling and walking in an unknown country; on foot one is even more sensitive to the local attitude and one feels a little less secure.

Ghinda is described in my official guide-book as 'a small resort city' to which people come to escape the cold of Asmara or the heat of Massawah. In fact it is a small town of tin-roofed hovels from which I personally would be glad to escape in any direction.

Just beyond Ghinda a squad of children advised me to avoid the main road and guided me up a steep short cut for about two miles. Later I took two other short cuts and discovered that on this loose, dry soil what looks like a reasonable climb is often an exhausting struggle. The busy Massawah–Asmara railway runs near the road and when I was attempting one short cut, up the embankment, I went sliding down on to the track just as an antiquated engine, belching clouds of black smoke, came round the corner twenty yards away. Happily this line does not cater for express trains; extermination by a steam-engine would be a prosaic ending to travels in Ethiopia. During the abrupt descent my knees had been deeply grazed and my hands torn by the thorny shrubs at which I clutched; but this was merely the initiation ceremony. When one has been injured by a country, then one really has arrived.

From Ghinda to the outskirts of Nefasit the rounded mountains and wooded gorges appear to be almost entirely uninhabited and uncultivated. Even this colonised fringe of Ethiopia feels desolate and the silence is profound. Many of the lower slopes are covered in green bushes, giant cacti and groves of tall trees; one lovely shrub blazes with flowers like the flames of a turf-fire and vividly coloured birds dart silently through the undergrowth. Around the few villages some terracing is attempted, but it looks crude and ineffective. My impression so far is of a country much more primitive, in both domestic architecture and agriculture, than any Asian region I know.

At intervals the week-end traffic passed me—Italian or American cars returning to Asmara in convoys of six or eight as a precaution against *shifta*. (There are 5,000 Americans stationed at the Kagnew Military Base near Asmara.) As another precaution two policemen sat watchfully by the roadside every five miles, leaning on antediluvian rifles. The *shifta* are said to be far better armed than the police, their foreign backers having equipped them well. Many cars stopped to offer me a lift, and soon this kindness became tiresome; it is difficult to persuade motorists that two legs can also get one there—at a later date.

The last five miles were a hell of muscular exhaustion. At every other kilometre stone I had to stop, remove my rucksack and rest briefly.

Here I'm staying in a clean Italian doss-house and being overcharged for everything by the Eritrean-born proprietress. While writing this I've got slightly drunk on a seven-and-six-penny bottle of odious vinegar called 'vino bianco'—produced by the Italians in Asmara.

19 December. Asmara

I awoke at 6.30 to see a cool, pearly dawn light on mountains that were framed in bougainvillea. The Eritrean servant indicated that *mangiare* was impossible, so by 6.50 I was on the road. After ten hours unbroken sleep my back felt surprisingly unstiff, though my feet were even more painful than I had expected.

From Nefasit the road zig-zagged towards a high pass and before I had covered four miles all my foot-blisters burst wetly. During the next two hours of weakening pain only my flask of 'emergency' brandy kept me going. It seemed reckless to use it so soon, yet this did feel like a genuine emergency. Several cars stopped to offer me tempting lifts, but I then supported a theory (since abandoned) that the quickest way to cure footsores is by walking on them.

Here the road ran level, winding from mountain to mountain, and the whole wide sweep of hills and valleys was deserted and silent. These mountains are gently curved, though steep, and despite the immense heights and depths one sees none of the expected precipices or crags.

The sky remained cloudless all day, though a cool breeze countered any sensation of excessive heat. However, the sun's ultra-violet rays are severe at this altitude and the back of my neck has been badly burned.

It takes a few days for one's system to adjust to being above 6,000 feet and as I struggled towards the 8,000 foot plateau my head was throbbing from too little oxygen and my back from too much weight, though I hardly noticed these details because of the pain of my feet. Then at last I was there—exultantly overlooking a gleaming mass of pure white cloud that concealed the lower hills. But on this exposed ridge a strong, cold wind blew dust around me in stinging whirls and pierced through my sweat-soaked shirt; so I soon began to hobble down the slight incline towards Asmara.

On the last lap I passed a big British War Cemetery and gazed into it enviously, feeling that a cemetery rather than an hotel was the obvious resting place for anyone in my condition. Fifteen minutes later I was approaching the uninspiring suburbs of Asmara and looking out for a bar. At 1.30 I found one, pushed aside a curtain of bottle-tops on strings and in a single breath ordered three beers. Since morning I had only walked fifteen miles, yet my exhaustion was so extreme that I had to be helped to remove my rucksack.

By three o'clock I had found this Italian-run *pensione* in the centre of the city, conveniently opposite the British Consulate. Sitting on the edge of my bed, I took off my boots and socks and saw the worst. It is no longer a question of blisters: with my socks I had peeled off all the skin from both soles, leaving what looks like two pounds of raw steak. Undoubtedly this is where I forget 'mind-over-matter' and sit around for some days industriously growing new skin.

20 December

This morning I hobbled over to the Consulate to ask for the name of a reliable doctor; but the Consul, Major John Bromley, is on duty in Massawah today and his Ethiopian staff were vague—though friendly and anxious to help. The next few hours were spent limping around in a daze of pain searching for sound medical advice—not that there is any shortage of doctors here, but in my insular way I distrust foreign medicinemen whose names are followed by a rearrangement of the whole alphabet. Eventually I chanced to meet a kind nurse from the Lutheran Red Sea Mission, who recommended Professor Mario Manfredonia as being Ethiopia's best doctor; but he, too, is in Massawah today, so I could only make an appointment for tomorrow morning.

Source: Dervla Murphy (1968) *In Ethiopia with a Mule*, London: John Murray, pp. 11–16.

43 from *Footsteps: Adventures of a Romantic Biographer*

RICHARD HOLMES

For biographical details, see Reading 41, p. 577.

All that night I heard footsteps: down by the river through the dark trees, or up on the moonlit road from Le Puy to Le Monastier. But I saw nothing except the stars, hanging over me where I wanted to be, with my head on a rucksack, and my rucksack on the grass, lying alone somewhere in the Massif Central of France, dreaming of the dead coming back to life again. I was eighteen.

I had started a travel-diary, teaching myself to write, and trying to find out what was happening to me, what I was feeling. I kept it simple:

> Found a wide soft dry ditch under thorn hedge between the track and the little Loire. Here lit candle once more, studied ground for red ants, then set out bed-roll with all spare clothes between me and my waterproof cloak-sheet. Soon I was gazing up at stars, thinking of all the beats and tramps and travellers *à la bette étoile* from RLS to JK. Story of snakes that are drawn to body-heat and slide into your sleeping-bag. Cicadas and strange sounds river makes at night flowing over rocks. Slept fitfully but without disturbance from man or beast, except a spider in my ear. Saw a green glow-worm like a spark.

I woke at 5 a.m. in a glowing mist, my green sleeping-bag blackened with the dew, for the whole plateau of the Velay is above two thousand feet. I made a fire with twigs gathered the night before, and set water to boil for coffee, in a *petit pois* tin with wire twisted round it as a handle. Then I went down to the Loire, here little more than a stream, and sat naked in a pool cleaning my teeth. Behind me the sun came out and the woodfire smoke turned blue. I felt rapturous and slightly mad.

I reached Le Monastier two hours later, in the local grocer's van, one of those square Citroëns like a corrugated garden privy, which smelt of camembert and apples. Monsieur Crèspy, chauffeur and patron, examined my pack and soaking bag as we jounced along through rolling uplands. Our conversation took place in a sort of no-man's land of irregular French. M. Crèspy's patois and Midi twang battled for meaning against my stonewall classroom phrases. After initial skirmishing, he adopted a firm line of attack.

'You are walking on foot?' he said, leaning back into the depths of the van with one arm and presenting me with a huge yellow pear.

'Yes, yes. I am searching for *un Ecossais*, a Scotsman, a writer, who walked on foot through all this beautiful country.'

'He is a friend of yours? You have lost him?' enquired M. Crèspy with a little frown.

'No, no. Well ... Yes. You see, I want to find him.' My chin streamed hopelessly with pear juice.

M. Crèspy nodded encouragingly: 'The pear is good, *n'est-ce pas?*'

'Yes, it is very good.'

The Citroën lurched round a bend and plunged down towards a rocky valley, broken with trees and scattered stone farmhouses, with pink tiled roofs and goats tethered in small bright pastures where the sun struck and steamed. The spire of a church, perched on the far hillside, pointed the horizon.

'There is Le Monastier. Look! Perhaps your friend is waiting for you,' said M. Crèspy with great confidence.

'No, no, I don't think so,' I said. But it was exactly what I hoped.

I rummaged in my rucksack. 'You see, here is his book. It tells the story of his walk on foot.'

M. Crèspy peered at the little brown volume, and the Citroën swung back and forth across the road, the sound of rolling fruit growing thunderous behind us. I hastily propped the book up on the dashboard, being careful not to cover the St Christophe medal or the picture of Our Lady mounted above a cone of paper flowers. I ran my finger down the sketch map on the title page: Le Monastier, Pradelles, Langogne, Notre Dame des Neiges, Montagne du Goulet, Pic de Finiels, Le Pont-de-Montvert, Florac, Gorges du Tarn, St Jean-du-Gard — to me already magic names, a litany of hills and rivers, with a lone figure striding along them, laughing, beckoning, even mocking: follow! follow!

M. Crèspy considered the map, and then my face, then the map again, and changed gear with a reflective air. 'It is far, it is far.'

'Yes,' I said, 'it is two hundred and twenty kilometres.'

M. Crèspy raised a finger from the steering wheel. 'And you, you are Scottish then?'

'No, no. I am English. My friend—that is to say, Mr Stevenson—was Scottish. He walked on foot with a donkey. He slept *à la belle étoile.*
He ...'

'Ah, *that!*' broke in M. Crèspy with a shout, taking both hands from the steering wheel, and striking his forehead. 'I understand, I understand! You are on the traces of Monsieur Robert Louis Steamson. Bravo, bravo!'

'Yes, yes, I am following his paces!'

We both laughed and the Citroën proceeded by divine guidance.

'I understand, I understand,' repeated M. Crèspy. And I believe he was the first person who ever did.

Robert Louis Stevenson came to Le Monastier in September 1878. He was twenty-seven, spoke good French, and had already spent several summers abroad; near Fontainebleau, and on the canals of Holland, paddling a canoe with a friend. The experience had produced his first book, *An Inland Voyage*, which despite its whimsical style captured an attitude to travel that enthralled me, a child of the Sixties.

> I take it, in short, that I was about as near Nirvana as would be convenient in practical life; and if this be so, I make the Buddhists my sincere compliments ... It may be best figured by supposing yourself to get dead drunk, and yet keep sober to enjoy it ... A pity to go to the expense of laudanum, when here is a better paradise for nothing! This frame of mind was the great exploit of our voyage, take it all in all. It was the farthest piece of travel accomplished.

That was the kind of travel which interested me too: as far out in Nirvana as possible. After ten years of English boarding schools, brought up by Roman Catholic monks, I was desperate to slip the leash. Free thought, free travel, free love was what I wanted. I suppose a foreign *affaire de coeur* would have been the best thing of all; and that, in a way, was what I got.

It did not immediately occur to me to wonder what Stevenson himself was doing in that remote little town 'in the French highlands'. I knew he wanted to be a writer, had published essays in the London reviews, but was still struggling to establish his independence from his family in Edinburgh. They had brought him up a strict Calvinist, an outlook which he had rejected; and they had wanted him to be an engineer. Instead he had adopted the life of a literary bohemian, was a friend of Edmund Gosse and Sidney Colvin, affected wide-brimmed hats and velvet jackets, and fled to France whenever he could.

Source: Richard Holmes (1995) *Footsteps: Adventures of a Romantic Biographer*, London: Flamingo, pp. 13–15.

44 from '"I Always Wanted You to Admire My Fasting"; or, Looking at Kafka'

PHILIP ROTH

> Philip Roth (b. 1933), novelist and short-story writer, was born in Newark, New Jersey. His grandparents were European Jews who emigrated to the United States in the nineteenth century. He studied at the University of Chicago, and went on to teach creative writing and comparative literature at Iowa, Princeton and the University of Pennsylvania. His first book, *Goodbye, Columbus* (1959) won the National Book Award for fiction, but it was his third novel, *Portnoy's Complaint* (1969), a very funny account of an adolescent's obsession with masturbation, that made Roth famous. Later works in a prolific career include a trilogy of novels in the 1980s featuring Nathan Zuckerman, an alter ego of Roth's through which he explores the relationship between a fictional character and his creator, and four books – *The Facts* (1988), *Deception* (1990), *Patrimony* (1991), and *Operation Shylock* (1993) – in which he questions, mischievously and unsettlingly, the boundaries between autobiography and fiction.

1942. I AM NINE; my Hebrew school teacher, Dr. Kafka, is fifty-nine. To the little boys who must attend his 'four-to-five' class each afternoon, he is known—in part because of his remote and melancholy foreignness, but largely because we vent on him our resentment at having to learn an ancient calligraphy at the very hour we should be out screaming our heads off on the ballfield—he is known as Dr. Kishka. Named, I confess, by me. His sour breath, spiced with intestinal juices by five in the afternoon, makes the Yiddish word for 'insides' particularly telling, I think. Cruel, yes, but in truth I would have cut out my tongue had I ever imagined the name would become legend. A coddled child, I do not yet think of myself as persuasive, nor, quite yet, as a literary force in the world. My jokes don't hurt, how could they, I'm so adorable. And if you don't believe me, just ask my family and the teachers in school. Already at nine, one foot in Harvard, the other in the Catskills. Little Borscht Belt comic that I am outside the classroom, I amuse my friends Schlossman and Ratner on the dark walk home from Hebrew school with an imitation of Kishka, his precise and finicky professorial manner, his German accent, his cough, his gloom. 'Doctor *Kishka!*' cries Schlossman, and hurls himself savagely against the newsstand that belongs to the candy store owner whom Schlossman drives just a little crazier each night. 'Doctor Franz—Doctor Franz—Doctor Franz—*Kishka!*' screams Ratner, and my chubby little friend who lives upstairs from me on nothing but chocolate milk and Mallomars does not stop laughing until, as is his wont (his mother has asked me 'to keep an eye on him' for just this reason), he wets his pants. Schlossman takes the occasion of Ratner's humiliation to pull the little boy's paper out of his notebook and wave it in the air—it is the assignment Dr. Kafka has just returned to us, graded; we were told to make up an alphabet of our own, out of straight lines and curved lines and dots. 'That is all an alphabet is,' he had explained. 'That is all Hebrew is. That is all English is. Straight lines and curved lines and dots.' Ratner's alphabet, for which he received a C, looks like twenty-six skulls strung in a row. I received my A for a curlicued alphabet inspired largely (as Dr. Kafka would seem to have surmised from his comment at the top of the page) by the number eight. Schlossman received an F for forgetting even to do it—and a lot he seems to care, too. He is content—he is *overjoyed*—with things as they are. Just waving a piece of paper in the air, and screaming, '*Kishka! Kishka!*' makes him deliriously happy. We should all be so lucky.

At home, alone in the glow of my goose-necked 'desk' lamp (plugged after dinner into an outlet in the kitchen, my study) the vision of our refugee teacher, sticklike in a fraying three-piece blue suit, is no longer very funny—particularly after the entire beginner's Hebrew class, of which I am the most studious member, takes the name 'Kishka' to its heart. My guilt awakens redemptive fantasies of heroism. I have them often about 'the Jews in Europe.' I must save him. If not me, who? The demonic Schlossman? The babyish Ratner? And if not now, when? For I have learned in the ensuing weeks that Dr. Kafka lives in 'a room' in the house of an elderly Jewish lady on the shabby lower stretch of Avon Avenue, where the trolley still runs, and the poorest of Newark's Negroes shuffle meekly up and down the street, for all they seem to know still back in Mississippi. A *room*. And *there*! My family's apartment is no palace, but it is ours at least, so long as we pay the thirty-eight-fifty a month in rent; and though our neighbors are not rich, they refuse to be poor and they refuse to be meek. Tears of shame and sorrow in my eyes, I rush into the living room to tell my parents what I have heard (though not that I heard it during a quick game of 'aces up' played a minute before class against the synagogue's rear wall—worse, played directly beneath a stained glass window embossed with the names of the dead): 'My Hebrew teacher lives in a *room*.'

Source: Philip Roth (1973) "'I Always Wanted You to Admire My Fasting"; or, Looking at Kafka', *American Review*, no. 17, pp. 114–16.

45 from *Aké: The Years of Childhood*

WOLE SOYINKA

Wole Soyinka (b. 1934), playwright, poet and novelist, was born in Abeokuta, near Ibadan in western Nigeria, at that time a British colony. He was educated first at Ibadan, and then at the University of Leeds. During his six years in England, he began to write plays, and worked at the Royal Court Theatre, London. He returned to Nigeria and founded a theatre company which performed his plays. Because of his political views and his attacks on corruption and oppression, he was imprisoned in 1967 for nearly two years. One of his best-known plays, *Madmen and Specialists* (1970) was written shortly after his release. He has published about twenty works, including drama, novels, poetry, a volume of autobiography, and criticism. *Aké: The Years of Childhood* was published in 1981. In 1986 he became the first African writer to win the Nobel Prize for Literature.

One morning *The News* reported that a ship had blown up in the harbour taking some of its crew with it. The explosion had rocked the island, blown out windows and shaken off roofs. The lagoon was in flames and Lagosians lined the edges of the lagoon, marvelling at the strange omen—tall fires leaping frenziedly on the surface of water. Hitler was really coming close. No one however appeared to be very certain what to do when he finally appeared.

There was one exception: Paa Adatan. Every morning, Paa Adatan appeared in front of Wild Christian's shop opposite the Aafin, before whose walls he passed the entire day. Strapped to his waist was a long cutlass in its scabbard, and belts of amulets. A small Hausa knife, also in its sheath, was secured to his left arm above the elbow and on his fingers were blackened twisted wire and copper rings—we knew they were of different kinds—*onde*, *akaraba* and others. If Paa Adatan slapped an opponent with one of his hands, that man would fall at his feet and foam at the mouth. The other hand was reserved for situations where he was outnumbered. It only required that Paa Adatan slap one or more of his attackers and they would fall to fighting among themselves. The belt of amulets ensured of course that any bullet would be deflected from him, returning to hit the marksman at the very spot on his body where he had thought to hit the immortal warrior of Adatan.

Paa Adatan patrolled the Aafin area, furious that no one would take him into the Army and send him to confront Hitler, personally, and end the war once and for all.

'Ah, Mama Wole, this English people just wan' the glory for den self. Den no wan' blackman to win dis war and finish off dat non-sense-yeye Hitler one time! Now look them. Hitler dey bombing us for Lagos already and they no fit defend we.' He spat his red kola-nut juice on the ground, raging.

'When dey come Mama, dem go know say there be black man medicine. I go pile dem corpse alongside the wall of dis palace, dem go know say we done dey fight war here, long time before dey know wetin be war for den foolish land. Oh er ... Mama,' he rummaged deep in the pouches of his clothing, 'Mama Wole, I forget bring my purse enh, look, big man like myself, I forget my purse for house. And I no chop at all at all since morning time ...'

A penny changed hands, Paa Adatan saluted, drew out his sword and drew a line on the ground around the shop frontage. 'Dat na in case they come while I dey chop my eba for buka. If they try cross this line, guns go turn to broom for dem hand. Dem go begin dey sweeping dis very ground till I come back. Make dem try am make I see.'

I followed Paa Adatan once to watch him at breakfast. The foodseller already knew what he wanted and set before him four leaf-wrapped mounds of eba, lots of stew and one solitary piece of meat which sat like a half-submerged island in the middle of the stew. Paa Adatan left the meat untouched until he had demolished this prodigious amount of eba, each morsel larger than anything I could eat for an entire meal. Halfway through, the stew had dried up. Paa Adatan hemmed and hawed, but the woman took no notice. Finally,

'Hm. Iyawo.'

Silence.

'Iyawo.'

The food-seller spun round angrily. 'You want to ruin me. Everyday the same thing. If everybody swallowed the stew the way you do, how do you think a food-seller can make a living from selling eba?'

'Ah, no vex for me Iyawo. But na Win-de-war amount of stew you give me today.'

She spun round on her stool, ladle ready filled, and slopped its contents into his dish. 'Only na you dey complain. Same thing every day.'

'Good bless you, god bless you. Na dis bastard Hitler. When war finish you go see. You go see me as I am, a man of myself.'

The woman sniffed, accustomed to the promise. Paa Adatan set to, finished the remaining mounds, then held up the piece of meat and suddenly threw it into his mouth, snatching at it with his teeth like a dog at whom a lump of raw meat had been thrown. His jaw and neck muscles tensed as he chewed on the meat, banged on the low table and issued his challenge:

'Let him come! Make him step anywhere near this palace of Alake and that is how I go take in head for my mouth and bite am off.'

He rose, adjusted the rope which strung his trousers and turned to leave.

'By the way Iyawo, make you no worry for dem if den come, I don taking your buka for my protection—Aafin, de shop of Headmaster in wife, Centenary Hall, my friend the barber in shop and that cigarette shop of Iya Aniwura. If any of Hitler man come near any of you, he will smell pepper. Tell them na dis me Papa Adatan talk am!'

Head erect, chest defiant, he resumed his patrol.

One day, a convoy of army trucks stopped by the road, just in front of the row of shops which included ours. Instantly children and women fled in all directions, mothers snatching up their and others' toddlers who happened to be by. The men retreated into shops and doorways and peeped out, prepared for the worst, ready to run or beg for their lives. These were not the regular soldiers who were stationed at Lafenwa barracks. They were the notorious 'Bote', recognizable by their caps. They were said to come from the Congo, and were reputed wild and lawless. People claimed that they descended on shops, took what they needed and left without paying, abducted women and children—raping the former and eating the latter. To call a man Bote became an unpardonable insult; to await their approach was the height of folly.

I was in the shop with Wild Christian who of course had no interest in the Botes' reputation. As every other shop in the vicinity had either shut its doors or been abandoned, they made for ours and asked to purchase the items they required—biscuits, cigarettes, tinned foods, bottled drinks and sweets. I climbed up to take down jars from the shelves, handed them down to Wild Christian. Suddenly I heard a sound which could only be defined as the roar of a dozen outraged lions. Through the space between the soldiers' heads and the top of the wide door I saw the figure of Paa Adatan, his face transfigured by a set, do-or-die expression. He was naked to the waist, his usual bulbous trousers had been pulled up from the calves and tucked into his trouser-band. In one hand I beheld the drawn sword, in the other, a *sẹrẹ*[7] into which he muttered, then waved it round in a slow circle before him.

The soldiers turned, stared, and looked at one another.

Wild Christian had heard and recognized the cause of the commotion but was paying it no heed.

Paa Adatan cursed them. 'Bastards! Beasts of no nation! Bote Banza. You no better pass Hitler. Commot for that shop make you fight like men!'

The soldiers did not appear to understand a word, but the gestures could not be mistaken. They whispered among themselves in their strange language, raised their eyebrows and shrugged their shoulders. Then they turned back into the shop and continued with their purchases. Three or four sat on the pavement before the shop and watched.

Wild Christian, her view blocked by the soldiers, could not see Paa Adatan at all. At the intensification of Paa Adatan's curses, she grew worried, asked me what was happening.

'He is dancing now,' I reported.

Paa Adatan had indeed begun a war-dance. He sang at the top of his voice,

Ogun Hitila d' Aké
Eni la o pa Bote[8]

Some of the soldiers stayed on to watch him while others continued to buy up every eatable item in the shop. Wild Christian inflated the prices by at least twice what she normally charged, but they did not mind at all. On the contrary, they even gave me a packet of their own biscuits which were thick, sweet and crunchy. We spoke in sign language throughout, with plenty of smiling, shrugging and hand-waving.

---

[7] A mini-gourd with magical powers.

[8] Hitler's war arrives in Aké,
   Today we shall kill these Bote.

The trouble began when they attempted to leave. Paa Adatan stopped singing, drew a line across the ground and dared them to step over it. He himself retreated some way back from the line, leapt up and made a wild rush at the line, sword outstretched, came to an abrupt stop at the line—on one leg—rocked his body for some moments on the leg, spun round and returned to starting-point from where he repeated the process over and over again.

The soldiers were now bewildered. Wild Christian finally pushed her way out, remonstrated with Paa Adatan.

'Enough Paa, enough! They are our friends. You are stopping them from going to fight Hitler.'

'Dey be Bote,' Paa Adatan replied. 'They and Hitler na the same. Look them. Cowards!' He shook his *sere* at them. 'Put down those goods wey you tief or I go give you message take go Hitler.'

It was all over a short while later. Two of the soldiers left in the trucks had crept up behind Paa Adatan. They seized his arms from behind and disarmed him both of sword and *sere*, pinioned his arms to his sides. Paa Adatan fought back like the true warrior he was. He threw them off, fought through the wave of bodies that engulfed him, bore them to the ground with him and continued to struggle. No blows appeared to be struck, it was all wrestling, and a titanic struggle it proved. Paa Adatan fought like one who knew that the entire safety of Aké resided in his arms, legs and torso. He was a rugged terrain which had to be captured, then secured tree by tree, hill by hill, boulder by boulder. They sat on each limb, breathing and perspiring heavily, shouting orders and curses in their strange language. Then they brought some rope and bound him. Even then, he did not give in.

The soldiers then stood in a circle, wiping off perspiration and watching him. They marvelled, shook their heads, looked for some explanation from all the faces that had emerged one by one from shops, windows, nooks and corners after Paa Adatan had begun his act. No one however could speak to them, though some nodded affirmation when a soldier turned to the watchers, touched a finger to his head and raised his eyebrows.

Paa Adatan, in his bonds, struggled to a sitting position, looked at his captors and shook his head.

'O ma se o.[9] The glory of Egbaland is lay low inside dust.'

---

[9] How pitiful!

Some *ogboni* were now seen rushing from the palace, having heard of the incident. Their appearance seemed to convey to the soldiers some semblance of authority so, with signs and gestures, they transferred all responsibility for Paa Adatan to them, handed over his sword and *ṣẹrẹ* and climbed back into their lorries and drove off.

A debate then began. Should the police be called? Was it safe to untie Paa Adatan? Should he be transferred to the Mental Hospital at Aro? They argued at the top of their voices while Paa Adatan sat in his bonds, impassive.

Finally, Wild Christian had had enough. She left her shop and calling on me to help her we began to untie Paa Adatan's bonds. There were immediate cries of fear and protest but we ignored them. One of the men made to restrain her physically. She rose, drew up her body to its fullest height and dared him to touch her just once more. I bristled to her side and called the man names which would have earned me an immediate slap from Wild Christian in other circumstances. An ogboni chief intervened however, told the man off and himself completed the task of loosening the remaining knots in the ropes.

Paa Adatan, freed, rose slowly. The crowd retreated several steps. He stretched out his hand for his sword and replaced it in his scabbard. Next he took his *ṣẹrẹ*, dropped it on the ground and crushed it with his heel. The explosion was loud; it startled the watchers who moved even further back, frightened. He walked slowly away. He moved with a sad, quiet dignity. He walked in the direction of Iporo, vanished bit by bit as the road dipped downwards before it turned sharply away, round the Centenary Hall. I never saw him again.

Source: Wole Soyinka (2000) *Aké: The Years of Childhood*, London: Methuen, pp. 110–15.

46 from *Bad Blood*

LORNA SAGE

Lorna Sage (1943–2001), literary critic and author, was born in North Wales. When she was sixteen she became pregnant, but was able to continue her education, winning a scholarship to study English at Durham University. She was subsequently appointed a lecturer at the University of East Anglia, and spent the rest of her career there, becoming Professor of English Literature in

1994. Among her academic books were studies of Angela Carter (1994) and *The Cambridge Guide to Women's Writing in English*, which she edited in 1999. Her autobiography, *Bad Blood* (2000), won the Whitbread Biography Prize in January 2000. Sage died later the same month, having suffered from emphysema for many years.

Hanmer's pretty mere, the sloping fields that surrounded us, and the hedges overgrown with hawthorn, honeysuckle and dog roses that fringed the lanes, might as well have been a cunning mirage as far as Grandma was concerned. They did nothing to alleviate the lousy desert that made up her picture of village life. She lived like a prisoner, an urban refugee self-immured behind the vicarage's bars and shutters. None of my new school friends were allowed in the house. You could get into the vicarage garden via the side yard, or by climbing over the walls, and that was the way we did it. The whole thing was clandestine, the other children weren't supposed to be really *there* at all, any more than that picturesque backdrop of lake and trees and cows. Meanwhile, insulated and apart, vicarage life went on. In the church, in bars, in books (Grandpa) or in a scented bedroom fug of dreams of home in South Wales (Grandma). That is of Tonypandy in the Rhondda, which rhymed with yonder, but with its Welsh 'd's softened into 'th', so that it seemed the essence of elsewhere.

Her Welsh accent was foreign – sing-song, insidious, unctuous, converting easily to menace. Asthma lent a breathy vehemence to her curses and when she laughed she'd fall into wheezing fits that required a sniff of smelling-salts. She had a repertoire of mysterious private catchphrases that always sent her off. If anyone asked what was the time, she'd retort 'just struck an elephant!' and cackle triumphantly. Then, 'Dew, Dew,' she'd mutter as she got her breath back – or that's what it sounded like – meaning 'Deary me' or 'Well, well', shaking her head. That 'ew' sound was ubiquitous with her. She pronounced 'you' as 'ew', puckering up her small mouth as if to savour the nice or nasty taste you represented.

She had lost her teeth and could make a most ghoulish face by arranging the false set, gums and all, outside her lips, in a voracious grin. This clownish act didn't conceal her real hunger, however. She projected want. During the days of rationing she craved sugar. Its shortage must have postponed some of the worst ravages of the diabetes that martyred her later, for once the stuff was available again she couldn't resist it at all. She was soft and slightly powdery to the touch, as though she'd been dusted all over with icing sugar like a sponge cake.

She shared her Edwardian generation's genteel contempt for sunburn and freckles, and thanks to her nocturnal habits her skin was eerily pale. And just as she maintained that soap and water were too harsh for this delicate skin of hers, so she insisted that she couldn't chew or digest gristly, fibrous meals with meat and vegetables, but must live on thin bread and butter with the crusts cut off if she couldn't have tarts and buns. This, she'd repeat to me, was what little girls were made of, sugar and spice and all things nice – and I knew she was thinking of the sticky blondness of butter icing. Her ill-health had aged her into a child again in a way: a fat doll tottering on tiny swollen feet. But in her head she'd never been anything else, she still lived in the Rhondda in her mother's house, with her sister Katie. So powerful was the aura of longing surrounding the place that it *ought*, by rights, to have been entirely fantastical, or at best only a memory. But no. True, her mother was long dead, but home actually still existed.

In the summer holidays we went there to visit, Grandma, my mother and me, leaving Grandpa behind. (This was called 'letting him stew in his own juice'.) South Wales was an entirely female country in our family mythology, despite the mines and miners. A female place, an urban place and a place all indoors. Going there was like sinking into fantasy for all these reasons – and for one special reason above all, which was that home was a shop and we lived over it, and when we were there all the money horrors were magically suspended. Life was unfallen, prelapsarian, as though paying for things hadn't yet been invented. When you wanted a chop or a teacake you just went and helped yourself without even having to cross the street. It was a self-sufficient kingdom, or almost: a general stores that stocked everything from tin trays to oranges to sausages to sides of beef and cigarettes, with a special line in Lyons cakes, and when I was small I could entirely sympathise with Grandma in her resentment at having been persuaded to swap this blissful set-up for the vicarage and the dilapidations. Life at 'Hereford Stores' – named for her mother's native town – was her ideal of luxury and gentility, the source of her unshakeable conviction of social superiority to everyone in Hanmer.

Her sense of what class amounted to was remarkably pure and precise, in its South Wales way. Owning a business in a community where virtually everyone else went down the pit for wages *would* have seemed, in her youth, thoroughly posh. And the simple fact of *not working* when all around you were either slaving away or – worse – out of work would have been sufficient to mark you out as a 'lady'. What could be grander than lounging around upstairs, nibbling at the stock when the fancy took you, brushing out your curls? She and Katie would still spend hour upon hour getting ready to go out – to Cardiff, or to Pontypridd, to some teashop, or to the pictures – recapturing the world of their girlhood, before men and money had turned real.

Katie was in her forties and had never married. She too was very plump and a bit breathless, but her hair was still red, her teeth were her own and her laugh had a tuneful trill to it, so that she tended on the face of things to bear out Grandma's belief that you were better off without men. There *was* a shadowy man on the premises – their elder brother Stan – but he didn't really count, because (after, so they said, a dashing, brilliant youth) he'd had a colossal breakdown and was never quite right again. Now, in his fifties, he was seedy and skinny, with a faraway gleam in his eye, due to stubbornly wearing his mother's spectacles instead of getting some of his own. Stan hardly dented the atmosphere of scent and vanishing cream and talc I thought of as Hereford Stores. He slipped through it sideways like a ghost. There were two other brothers, but they'd long ago left home and were thought about as outcasts: elderly Tom, who looked after the butchery part of the business was a pariah because he lived with a housekeeper, who was not very secretly his mistress, and thus belonged to the same vicious male sect as Grandpa; and Danny was talked about in the past tense as though he was dead, because he had actually had the gall to set up a shop of his own in another valley. So the magic circle of sweet, stale dreams stayed intact, up the crooked stairs over the old double-fronted store, with their family name, 'Thomas', fading over the door.

The house was overheated with high-quality, jet-black, sparkling coal, swapped for groceries with the miners who got it for perks. There was a big old range in the kitchen, which was behind the shop on the ground floor in point of truthful topography, although imaginatively speaking it was upstairs. Here a serial tea party like the Mad Hatter's was in full swing all day and every day except Sunday, when Katie would ceremoniously roast a joint of meat (picked out by Tom) and get very red in the face. Otherwise we lived on Grandma's favourite diet of bread and butter, toasted teacakes, scones, sponges and so on, eked out with tinned fruit and condensed milk. It was understood that cooking, cleaning and washing-up were properly the duties of a 'skivvy', which is glossed by the *OED* as a maid-of-all-work (usually *derogatory*) – first example 1902, so very exactly a Grandma word, she'd have been ten in 1902 – but if you didn't happen to have one then you tried to get through as little crockery as possible, for instance, by hanging on to your cup all day, just giving it a cursory rinse once in a while. South Wales habits accounted for a good proportion of vicarage dirt I suppose: certainly it would have been very difficult to wash clothes, dishes or oneself with any regularity or thoroughness there, since the taps mostly seemed to be rusted up in disused outhouses in the yard and the skivvies who'd once upon a time carried water upstairs for bedroom washbasins were no more. Still, somehow, in the Rhondda we never seemed so shamingly grubby as when we were in Hanmer. And the housework that spelled such unending, ineffectual drudgery for my mother in the vicarage simply wasn't done, for the most part, and nobody much cared.

Hanmer hemmed us in and threatened to expose our secret squalor, whereas neighbours in Tonypandy's steep, jerry-built streets seemed to have lost interest in the ways of Hereford Stores. Katie and Stan gossiped with customers and this functioned as a kind of insulation – a protective barrier of chat within which their eccentricities were contained, unquestioned. They no longer had a social life otherwise and, having quarrelled with their relations, they lived as they liked. There was something pleasurable and even thrilling about this, at a time when advertising and women's magazines were so venomously clean-cut and conformist in their versions of how to be. You were supposed to cringe inwardly when you saw those Persil ads: a little boy's head swivelling on his neck as another boy, the one with the Persil-bright shirt, strides proudly by. 'Persil washes whiter – *and it shows*!' Competitive cleanliness. Hereford Stores sold soap powder all right, and the miners' wives scrubbed away on their washboards and competed with each other in the whiteness of their lace curtains and doilies and antimacassars (an endless battle, in that atmosphere) but Grandma and Katie scorned it all. They were heretics, they wouldn't play by the rules. If society wouldn't supply them with skivvies they were damned if they were going to slave away.

Source: Lorna Sage (2000) *Bad Blood*, London: Fourth Estate, pp. 31–6.

PART 5

Going public

47 from 'Through a Tangle of Branches: Reworking the poem'

REBECCA LUCE-KAPLER

Rebecca Luce-Kapler (b. 1954), poet, fiction writer and university teacher, was born and brought up in Alberta, Canada. She spent ten years working as a school teacher, before moving to Kingston, Ontario, to teach language and literacy at Queen's University Faculty of Education. Her work has been widely published in literary journals, and she is the author of two books, *The Gardens Where She Dreams* (2003) and *Writing With, Through, and Beyond the Text: An ecology of language* (2004), as well as many scholarly articles on the teaching of creative writing, especially poetry.

Rewriting seems to begin with a stepping back, a cooling off after the first heat of spilling our thoughts onto the page. I need a chance to clear my vision and to move away from my initial deep attachment to my words. Friedman (1994) tells the story about attending a poetry reading at a coffeehouse where a woman announced to the audience, 'I wrote this poem this afternoon. ... I hope I can read it before my throat closes up' (p. 76). The poem, Friedman says, was about loneliness and lying in bed at night with the heart pounding:

> She read it in a soft, breathy voice, and when she was done she looked up. We applauded politely. She blinked, then rose stiffly, as if her stomach were full of splintered glass, the disappointment palpable about her as she returned to her folding chair. Watching her I thought, I hope to God I'm different, although I suspected I was not. (p. 76)

What feels so forceful when one writes, Friedman continues, is not always forceful when it is read. Enraptured with my work, I may be unaware of the faults and inconsistencies that cause my readers or listeners to pause or stumble. Initially, I may write for myself, but in the rewriting I must remember that I also write for others, so I return to the text and position myself as reader rather than creator this time. I read, searching for the possibilities that present themselves: What images are evoked? What metaphors are suggested? What universal meaning reverberates through the words? But these questions require time for the emotional distance between ourselves and the text to grow. I think of the occasions when I have rushed students into presenting writing that has not had the luxury of distance. For them, the work still felt too close to their immediate feelings and thus was deeply personal and often private. No wonder they asked how I could assign a mark to something so intimate and so integral to their experience. A junior highschool student who was a subject in my master's research (1994) explained how he had learned to write 'schoolly' as a way of dividing the 'real writing' he enjoyed at home from the assigned work of the classroom. There often is not enough time given in schools for waiting, knowing that you will return to the writing, that such time is necessary to revision. Writers need that time: time to move from the one who originated the writing to the one who will discover its achieved version (Plumly, 1992, p. 244). The vision needs to clear for a re-vision.

Source: Marla Morris, Mary Aswell Doll and William F. Pinar (eds) (1999) *How We Work*, New York: Peter Lang, pp. 158–9.

48 from *'Putting Coyolxauhqui Together: A creative process'*

GLORIA ANZALDÚA

Gloria Anzaldúa (1942–2004), poet, writer and cultural theorist, was born in Jesus Maria of the Valley, Texas. Her family were Mexican immigrant field-workers, and she had to work in the family fields throughout her education. She taught for many years in schools, and published three books for children, before becoming a university teacher of creative writing. In 1981 she co-edited a prize-winning collection, *This Bridge Called My Back: Writings by radical women of color*, but her most famous work was *Borderlands: The new mestiza* (1987), a combination of Spanish and English poetry, personal memoir, and analysis of the condition of women, and particularly lesbians, in Latino and white American culture. It was selected as one of the Best Books of 1987 by the

The mournful sounds of the foghorn and rain drumming on the roof accompany the pecking of fingers on keyboard. You reacquaint yourself with the text's overall structure, pinpoint the major renovations, examine the linchpin holding it together.

The questions you're concerned with at this stage are: Does the piece possess coordination among parts, a balanced proportion, and a varying pace that maintains interest? Will the reader find pleasure in the imagery and language and be satisfied by the form? Is spending time in your company worth the reader's time?

After re-envisioning *la historia* and finding out what it really is about, you draw up a rough timetable for the next revision stage; you list the sections and specifics of what you're going to do. You do the first read-through silently. You work on the large chunks, saving the detailed work for later revisions. You repeatedly cut and rearrange, shape and focus the material. You input the changes and tackle the repetitions and abstractions—your major literary vices. You throw out whole sections, paragraphs, and sentences; you expand others.

Source: Marla Morris, Mary Aswell Doll and William F. Pinar (eds) (1999) *How We Work*, New York: Peter Lang, pp. 253–4.

49 from *'Redrafting and Editing'*

JENNY NEWMAN

Jenny Newman, novelist and teacher of creative writing, was educated at Liverpool University. She is Reader in Creative Writing at Liverpool John Moores University. Her short fiction has appeared in a number of literary magazines, and she has published two novels, *Going In* (1994) and *Life Class* (1999). She has edited *The Faber Book of Seductions* (1988), and co-edited *Women Talk Sex: Autobiographical writing on sex, sexuality and sexual identity* (1992). She is also co-editor of a very successful guide for creative writers, *The Writer's Workbook* (2000), and co-editor of *Contemporary British and Irish Novelists: An introduction through interviews* (2004).

Revising for Meaning

This is the most involving, demanding and important form of revision, and may be partly a question of trusting your intuition. Contrary to popular belief, the meaning of what you write is not necessarily something you start with; nor does it always pop fully formed into your first draft. Flannery O'Connor is only one of many who talk about the process of writing as an act of discovery. Meaning may take shape over several drafts; or you may, halfway through, have a nagging sense that something has been left unsaid, without knowing quite what it is. Raymond Carver feels that his revisions take him slowly into the heart of what the story is about. 'If the writing cannot be made as good as it is within us to make it, then why do it? In the end, the satisfaction of having done our best, and the proof of that labour, is the one thing we can take into the grave.' Revision, he believes, is about refusing to settle for less than the best you can do.

Finding your window

When you think you have finished, ask yourself the question, 'What is my poem, script or story about?' And then ask yourself, 'What is it really about?' If you cannot respond briefly and lucidly, it may be a sign that you need to spend more time clarifying your subject matter to yourself. Do as Stanley Elkin suggests, and 'after five or six drafts, write what [your] story means in one sentence. Then use that sentence to cut, revise, add, adjust, or change the next drafts. Use that sentence as a filter, or a window, to the whole piece.'

Revising for Character

The novelist Sue Gee says that character is all. Certainly readers and viewers like vigorous, well-drawn story people. Often this stage in revision means listening to your misgivings. You may sense, for instance, that your characters are not as compelling as they could be, but be unable to see why. This section is *not* a formula for when you write, or to be taken as proof that your story is lacking; it is simply a series of points for you to ponder.

If your heroine obstinately refuses to come to life, you may not have clarified what she wants. And have you got a good antagonist to stop her getting it? Consider giving her a detailed past, even if it does not all appear in the script or the story. Knowing a person's history alters your understanding of who she is today. Imagine your response to a loudmouth at a party – until you hear that she has just come from three years in solitary confinement.

Young writers in particular are prone to set their dramas in student flats. Why not give your character some kind of employment? You could base it on a job of your own, or research a likely career (books on work make compelling reading) or else hang around somebody else's workplace, taking notes (see Chapter 1, 'Observation and discovery'). Your character's work can shape his perceptions, and give you a store of unusual metaphors for his vision of experience.

Many writers secretly feel that their characters are their slaves. Nevertheless, to the reader the characters must look as though they are driving the action. Do your characters wait like puppets to be jerked into life, or do they quarrel with each other, fall in love, gossip behind each other's backs, try and stop each other from getting what they want, from a variety of motives, good and bad? When you are redrafting, scrutinize them all in terms of function: protagonist, antagonist, lover, child, stepmother, victim, or a bit of local colour. Have they all got something to do? If they double up, can they be cut? Or, alternatively, is there a character missing?

Few stories or scripts have space to develop every character, so many writers depend on stereotypes (the unflappable nurse, the bossy teacher) for the walk-on roles that the viewer or reader needs to recognize quickly. But if your main character is a dumb body builder, or a wily East End barrow boy, your reader may feel that she knows him already, and lose her wish to read on. You may, of course, enjoy overturning such stereotypes, as Anita Brookner does through her novelist-heroine in *Hotel du Lac*.

Whether the character is major or minor, check that the dialogue is taut and well-constructed, and that it serves a purpose besides conveying information. Try and give all your characters distinct voices and speech patterns. And do not call your two main characters Harry and Henry. Distinctive names beginning with different letters will help your reader keep track of who is who.

Revising for Pace

There is no one way to pace a piece of writing. Chekhov suggested that you write a beginning, middle and end, then cut the beginning and the end. Dangerous advice, perhaps – but if you have read Chekhov's stories you may see some of its advantages. Many script writers have likewise proposed that you enter your scene as late as possible, and leave it as early as you can, as has the short story writer Raymond Carver ('Get in, get out. Don't linger. Go on'). When you revisit that crucial beginning, ask yourself if your story starts too slowly. In the first draft, openings are often just 'throat-clearing' and can be scrapped at a later stage; or else they can be redrafted, or even written at the very end.

If you sense that the structure sags in the middle, ask if the line through your story is clear. If in doubt, try writing it out in one paragraph, and see if anything has been left out. Is the conflict and tension sustained? Do you have the right balance between dialogue and action? Scripts, novels and short stories can all be ruined by too many 'talking heads'. List your main plot points and check that they are in the right order (i.e. going from smaller to larger, with cause followed by effect). Do they hinge on a need or desire in the mind of your central character? Is there enough at stake?

You can always tighten a story by 'putting a clock on it' – think of *High Noon* or *Silence of the Lambs* or any other film or book which kept you on the edge of your seat with its race against time. Such plots are not weighed down by too much flashback, especially early on; nor are there too many subplots to detract from the main action. Yet every reader or viewer needs the occasional breather. Fiction writers know many methods – such as description, or the use of retrospect – of slowing the pace. Even the tensest film script should be spiked with scenes which vary the rhythm, by focusing, for example, on atmosphere or character development.

Every piece of writing has its own momentum, and after the struggle to get started, and plot the middle, you may find that the last third is down-hill all the way. This is why it is tempting to rush. But the stronger the story, the more your reader or viewer will feel cheated if you skimp on the turning point and resolution. Ask yourself if anything has changed. Most importantly, has your protagonist learnt something, whether pleasing or painful?

Placing the final full stop is always a delicate matter. If the ending feels hurried, ask yourself if the climax comes out of nowhere, or is it brought about by your main character? Does it have an internal logic, following on from your previous plot points?

On the other hand, if your finale seems flat, see if you have written past your ending, and given your reader not one but two conclusions.

Revising for Style

The poet and the scriptwriter are opposites. The poet redrafts in solitude, and can make the amendments which please him, down to the last semicolon. If a poem is altered without his permission by, say, a magazine editor, he will have a right to complain. A poet may not be paid much, but over his work he reigns supreme.

A writer for a television soap is part of a team. For her, revision can mean letting a script go: to script editors who prune and alter it, to producers, directors and eventually to actors. Writing for TV is not a solitary but a collaborative act.

Yet these diverse writers share one key belief: that each word counts. This is why both must revise ruthlessly. For the poet, the medium's intensity means that he must weigh every word, test every image, scrutinize his use of metre and his line endings. The short story writer too may take as much care as the poet. The screenwriter, on the other hand, may not share such scrupulous attention to detail; yet she is up against limits of time, space and the production business, where every word costs money, and must therefore have maximum impact. Both kinds of writer must learn how to 'murder their darlings'.

Few writers in any medium find that good style happens by accident: it develops little by little from your first rough notes to your final version. Jeanette Winterson uses the analogy of the acrobat: years of practice go into one single, seemingly effortless movement. Your goal is not to make writing effortless, but to make it look effortless. Underline your first interesting line or sentence. If it is not the first one, or very near it, why not?

Surplus words and phrases are not just an extra your reader can choose to discard. They detract from your whole style, and leech the life even from those words that are well chosen.

In particular, watch out for creative minefields:

■ overkill, such as lists of adjectives; or laying on so many details that you lessen credibility. Chekhov believed it was an insult to over-describe; the writer should give just enough detail to evoke the reader's knowledge of life. Elmore Leonard says, 'I try to leave out the parts that people skip', which is another way of saying that in writing less often means more. Sometimes you need the guts to cut.

- showing off at your reader's expense. Aim at being straightforward and exact, rather than too high-flown.

- predictable noun-adjective combinations such as 'bitter pill' or 'clear blue sky'.

- overuse of adverbs. A strong, expressive verb, such as 'drift', 'mooch' or 'slouch' may be more telling than 'walk slowly'. Or, rather than *telling* us that your hero reads incessantly, *show* us his red-rimmed eyes.

- redundant words, as in the following phrases: 'appreciate in value', 'rack and ruin', 'hope for the future', 'I personally'. Compile your own list of surplus expressions.

- fussy, overcomplicated punctuation.

- meaningless terms such as 'in point of fact', 'at the end of the day' and 'lo and behold'.

- weak intensifiers such as very, really, extremely and exceptionally.

- overworked similes ('green as grass') and metaphors ('dyed in the wool').

- misattributions, such as 'she clutched the receiver in one hand, while with the other she nibbled a sandwich' (with the tiny teeth in her palm?).

Source: Jenny Newman, Edmund Cusick and Aileen La Tourette (eds) (2000) *The Writer's Workbook*, London: Arnold, pp. 163–7. Endnote references have been omitted from this extract.

50 from *The Art of Fiction*

DAVID LODGE

David Lodge (b. 1935), novelist and literary critic, was born in Dulwich, south London, and educated at a Catholic school and University College London. He spent most of his career at the University of Birmingham, becoming Professor of Modern English Literature in 1976. He is the author of eleven novels, including a trilogy of satirical accounts of campus life in *Changing Places* (1975), *Small World* (1984), and *Nice Work* (1988), and has also written for the theatre and television, including adapting some of his own novels for the screen. He has won many awards, including Whitbread Book of the Year for *How Far Can You Go?* (1980). Among his many critical studies are *The Language of Fiction* (1966), *The Novelist at the Crossroads* (1971), and *The Art of Fiction* (1992), a collection of articles first published in the *Independent on Sunday*.

In the fall the war was always there, but we did not go to it any more. It was cold in the fall in Milan and the dark came very early. Then the electric lights came on, and it was pleasant along the streets looking in the windows. There was much game hanging outside the shops, and the snow powdered in the fur of the foxes and the wind blew their tails. The deer hung stiff and heavy and empty, and small birds blew in the wind and the wind turned their feathers. It was a cold fall and the wind came down from the mountains.

We were all at the hospital every afternoon, and there were different ways of walking across the town through the dusk to the hospital. Two of the ways were alongside canals, but they were long. Always, though, you crossed a bridge across a canal to enter the hospital. There was a choice of three bridges. On one of them a woman sold roasted chestnuts. It was warm, standing in front of her charcoal fire, and the chestnuts were warm afterward in your pocket. The hospital was very old and very beautiful, and you entered through a gate and walked across a courtyard and out a gate on the other side. There were usually funerals starting from the courtyard. Beyond the old hospital were the new brick pavilions, and there we met every afternoon and were all very polite and interested in what was the matter, and sat in the machines that were to make so much difference.

ERNEST HEMINGWAY 'In Another Country' (1927)

If you have the time and inclination, get some coloured pens or pencils and draw a ring round the words that occur more than once in the first paragraph of Hemingway's story, a different colour for each word, and join them up. You will reveal a complex pattern of verbal chains linking words of two kinds: those with referential meaning, *fall, cold, dark, wind, blew*, which we can call lexical words, and articles, prepositions and conjunctions like *the, of, in, and*, which we can call grammatical words.

It is almost impossible to write English without the repetition of grammatical words, so normally we don't notice it as such, but you can't fail to notice the extraordinary number of '*ands*' in this short paragraph. This is a symptom of its very repetitive syntax, stringing together declarative statements without subordinating one to another. The repetition of the lexical words is less evenly distributed, clustering at the beginning and end of the paragraph.

Lexical and grammatical repetition on this scale would probably receive a black mark in a school 'composition', and quite rightly. The traditional model of good literary prose requires 'elegant variation': if you have to refer to something more than once, you should try to find alternative ways of describing it; and you should give your syntax the same kind of variety. [...]

Hemingway, however, rejected traditional rhetoric, for reasons that were partly literary and partly philosophical. He thought that 'fine writing' falsified experience, and strove to 'put down what really happened in action, what the actual things were which produced the emotion that you experienced' by using simple, denotative language purged of stylistic decoration.

It looks easy, but of course it isn't. The words are simple but their arrangement is not. There are many possible ways of arranging the words of the first sentence, but the one chosen by Hemingway splits the phrase 'go to war' in two, implying an as yet unexplained tension in the persona of the narrator, a mixture of relief and irony. As we soon learn, he and his companions are soldiers wounded while fighting on the Italian side in World War I, now recuperating, but conscious that the war which nearly killed them may have made their lives not worth living anyway. It is a story about trauma, and how men cope with it, or fail to cope. The unspoken word which is a key to all the repeated words in the text is 'death'.

The American word for autumn, *fall*, carries in it a reminder of the death of vegetation, and echoes the conventional phrase for those who die in battle, 'the fallen'. Its juxtaposition with *cold* and *dark* in the second sentence strengthens these associations. The brightly lit shops seem to offer some distraction (an effect heightened by the fact that there is no lexical repetition in this sentence) but the narrator's attention quickly focuses on the game hanging outside the shops, further emblems of death. The description of the snow powdering in their fur, and the wind ruffling their feathers, is literal and exact, but tightens the association of *fall, cold, dark, wind, blew*, with death. Three of the repeated words come together for the first time in the last sentence with a poetic effect of closure: 'It was a cold fall and the wind came down from the mountains.' The mountains are where the war is going on. Wind, so often a symbol of life and spirit in religious and Romantic writing, is here associated with lifelessness. God is very dead in these early stories of Hemingway. The hero has learned from the trauma of combat to distrust metaphysics as well as rhetoric. He trusts only his senses, and sees experience in starkly polarized terms: cold/warm, light/dark, life/death.

The incantatory rhythms and repetitions persist in the second paragraph. It would have been easy to find elegant alternatives for 'hospital', or simply to have used the pronoun 'it' occasionally; but the hospital is the centre of the soldiers' lives, their daily place of pilgrimage, the repository of their hopes and fears, and the repetition of the word is therefore expressive. It is possible to vary the route by which the hospital is reached, but the terminus is always the same. There is a choice of bridges, but always you have to cross a canal (a faint suggestion of the river Styx in the underworld, perhaps). The narrator prefers the bridge where he can buy roasted chestnuts, warm in the pocket like the promise of life – except that Hemingway doesn't use that simile, he merely implies it; just as in the first paragraph he manages to make his description of the season as emotionally powerful as any example of the pathetic fallacy [...] without using a metaphor. The line between charged simplicity and mannered monotony is a fine one, and Hemingway didn't always stay on the right side of it, but in his early work he forged an entirely original style for his times.

Needless to say, repetition is not necessarily linked to a bleakly positivist, anti-metaphysical representation of life such as we find in Hemingway. It is also a characteristic feature of religious and mystical writing, and is used by novelists whose work tends in that direction – D. H. Lawrence, for instance. The language of the opening chapter of *The Rainbow*, evoking a lost agrarian way of life, echoes the verbal repetition and syntactical parallelism of the Old Testament:

> The young corn waved and was silken, and the lustre slid along the limbs of the men who saw it. They took the udder of the cows, the cows yielded milk and pulsed against the hands of the men, the pulse of the blood of the teats of the cows beat into the pulse of the hands of the men.

Repetition is also a favourite device of orators and preachers, roles that Charles Dickens often adopted in his authorial persona. This, for instance, is the conclusion to his chapter describing the death of Jo, the destitute crossing-sweeper, in *Bleak House*:

Dead, your Majesty. Dead, my lords and gentlemen. Dead, Right
Reverends and Wrong Reverends of every order. Dead, men and
women, born with Heavenly compassion in your hearts. And
dying thus around us every day.

And of course repetition can be funny, as in this passage from
Martin Amis's *Money*:

> Intriguingly enough, the only way I can make Selina actually *want*
> to go to bed with me is by not wanting to go to bed with her. It
> never fails. It really puts her in the mood. The trouble is, when I
> don't want to go to bed with her (and it does happen), I don't
> want to go to bed with her. When does it happen? When don't I
> want to go to bed with her? When she wants to go to bed with
> me. I like going to bed with her when going to bed with me is the
> last thing she wants. She nearly always does go to bed with me, if
> I shout at her a lot or threaten her or give her enough money.

It hardly needs to be pointed out that the frustrations and
contradictions of the narrator's sexual relationship with Selina are
rendered all the more comic and ironic by the repetition of the phrase
'go to bed with' for which any number of alternatives were available. (If
you doubt that, try rewriting the passage using elegant variation.) The
final sentence also illustrates another important type of repetition: the
recurrence of a thematic keyword throughout an entire novel – in this
case, 'money'. It is 'money' not 'go to bed' that occupies the crucially
important last-word space in the paragraph I have just quoted. Thus one
kind of repetition, belonging to the macro-level of the text, functions as
variation on the micro-level.

Source: David Lodge (1992) *The Art of Fiction: Illustrated from classic and modern texts*,
London: Penguin Books, pp. 89–93.

51 from *Steering the Craft*

URSULA K. LE GUIN

Ursula K. Le Guin (b. 1929), novelist and poet, was born and grew up in
Berkeley, California. She studied at Radcliffe College and Columbia
University. Since 1958 she has lived in Portland, Oregon. A prolific and

varied writer, she has published twenty novels, six books of poetry, eleven books for children, four collections of essays, and four volumes of translation. She is perhaps best known for her best-selling *Earthsea* trilogy of fantasy works (1968, 1972, 1973), and for her award-winning science-fiction novels, *The Left Hand of Darkness* (1969) and *The Dispossessed* (1974). She teaches creative writing, and her annual workshops in Oregon provided the impetus for her book on writing narrative, *Steering the Craft* (1998).

A Terrible Thing To Do

Take one of [your] longer narrative exercises — any one that went over 400 words — and *cut it by half.*

If none of the exercises is suitable, take any piece of narrative prose you have ever written, 400–1000 words, and do this terrible thing to it.

This doesn't mean cutting a little bit here and there, snipping and pruning — though that's part of it. It means counting the words and reducing them to *half that many*, while keeping the narrative clear and the sensory impact vivid, not replacing specifics by generalities, and never using the word 'somehow.'

If there's dialogue in your piece, cut any long speech or long conversation in half just as implacably.

This kind of cutting is something most professional writers have to do at one time or another. Just for that reason it's good practice. But it's also a real act of self-discipline. It's enlightening. Forced to weigh your words, you find out which are the styrofoam and which are the heavy gold. Severe cutting intensifies your style, forcing you both to crowd and to leap.

Unless you are unusually sparing with your words, or wise and experienced enough to cut as you write, revision will almost always involve some cutting of repetitions, unnecessary explanations, and so on. Consider using revision consciously as a time to consider what *could* go out if it *had* to.

This inevitably includes some of your favorite, most beautiful and admirable sentences and passages. You are allowed to cry or moan softly while you cut them.

Anton Chekhov gave some advice about revising a story: first, he said, throw out the first three pages. As a young writer I figured that if anybody knew about short stories, it was Chekhov, so I tried taking his advice. I really hoped he was wrong, but of course he was right. It depends on the length of the story, naturally; if it's very short, you can only throw out the first three paragraphs. But there are few first drafts to which Chekhov's Razor doesn't apply. Starting a story, we all tend to circle around, explain a lot of stuff, set things up that don't need to be set up. Then we find our way and get going, and *the story begins* ... very often just about on page 3.

In revision, as a rough rule, if the beginning can be cut, cut it. And if any passage sticks out in some way, leaves the main trajectory, could possibly come out — take it out and see what the story looks like that way. Often a cut that seemed sure to leave a terrible hole joins up without a seam. It's as if the story, the work itself, has a shape it's trying to achieve, and will take that shape if you'll only clear away the verbiage.

Source: Ursula K. Le Guin (1998) *Steering the Craft: Exercises and discussions on story writing for the lone navigator or the mutinous crew*, Portland, Oregon: The Eighth Mountain Press, pp.147–8.

52 from *English Grammar*

B. A. PHYTHIAN

B[rian] A[rthur] Phythian (1932–1993), British lexicographer and grammarian. He is best known for his *Concise Dictionary of English Slang and Colloquialisms* (1976) and his *Concise Dictionary of English Idioms* (1986), both of which went through several editions, and for his works of grammar, *English Grammar* (1980), and *Correct English* (1988). He also produced 'Concise Dictionaries' of *Correct English* (1979), *Foreign Expressions* (1982), *Confusables* (1989), and *New Words* (1996, completed by Richard Cox).

Possession

Examine these sentences:

The passengers were becoming impatient.

The passenger's ticket was invalid.

The passengers' waiting–room was full.

In the first sentence, *passengers* is the straightforward plural of the noun *passenger*, and denotes that more than one passenger was becoming impatient. In the second sentence, the word *passenger's* indicates that the ticket belonged to one passenger. In the third sentence, *passengers'* denotes that the waiting-room was for more than one passenger. The forms *passenger's* and *passengers'* denote ownership or possession: these forms are described grammatically as being in the *possessive* (or *genitive*) *case*.

The normal way of expressing possession is by the use of the *apostrophe*, a raised comma ('), though there are other ways, e.g.

The ticket *of the passenger* was invalid.

The waiting-room *for passengers* was full.

The general rule is to add -'s to singular words, and an apostrophe without the -s to plural words:

The boy's hand was hurt (i.e. the hand of one *boy*).

The shop sells boys' clothes (i.e. clothes for *boys*).

The lady's face was red with exertion.

Ladies' fashions have changed little this year.

But there is one very important exception to this rule: if a plural noun does not end in -s, the possessive is formed by adding -'s, even though the word is plural. Thus: *children's games, women's liberation, policemen's responsibilities*.

Which is correct: *men's trousers* or *mens' trousers*? The meaning is *trousers for men*; the operative noun is *men*; it does not end in -s, so the possessive is formed in the normal way by adding -'s; *men's trousers* is therefore correct.

There is an occasional complication in the case of proper nouns ending in -s, such as *Charles, Dickens, James*. If it is necessary to use such words in the possessive, either form of the possessive is correct, i.e.

Charles' reign *or* Charles's reign

Dickens' novels *or* Dickens's novels

St James' life *or* St James's life

The simpler version, using the apostrophe without the -s, is usually preferred. Likewise, note that *for goodness' sake* is irregularly punctuated, on the grounds that people do not normally say *for goodness's sake* with three consecutive -s sounds.

Exercise 16

Write out the following, putting one word in the possessive case (e.g. The leg of the dog – The dog's leg):

1. The reach of a man. 2. The best friend of a boy. 3. The den of lions. 4. The achievements of men. 5. Clothes of women. 6. The lid of the box. 7. The sleeves of the dress. 8. The cost of the dresses.

Exercise 17

The following examples of the possessive case are in the singular. Put them into the plural:

1. The boy's possessions. 2. The child's hobbies. 3. The country's exports. 4. Man's aspirations. 5. The sheep's safety. 6. A woman's place. 7. The team's results. 8. The army's exercises.

[...]

The full stop

The full stop (.) is used at the end of a sentence, and each new sentence begins with a capital letter (see below). A question mark or an exclamation mark, both of which are dealt with later in this chapter, may be used instead of a full stop where appropriate.

The full stop (sometimes called *the period*) is also used to indicate an abbreviation. An abbreviation may be

(*a*) a shortened name: *S. N. P. Brackenden*

(*b*) a shortened title: *The Revd. S. N. P. Brackenden, H.M. Government*

(*c*) initial letters standing instead of words: *U.S.A., M.A., R.A.F., M.P.*

(*d*) any shortened word: *Feb. 3, St. Jude*

It is now common, however, to omit full stops after *Mr*, *Mrs* and *Dr*, and also after well-known abbreviations that are used almost as frequently as the words they signify, such as the ones in (*c*) above. Many newspapers, in fact, now omit all full stops from abbreviations.

If an abbreviation ends a sentence, one full stop is sufficient to signify both the abbreviation and the end of the sentence.

Exercise 225

How many abbreviations can you add to the list in (*c*) above?

Exercise 226

Insert full stops where needed.

Swift defined a good style as the use of proper words in proper places the proper places will vary considerably according to degrees of emphasis usage has left many parts of the sentence relatively free and these we can vary to suit our purpose the poet Coleridge laid much stress on the importance of word order he defined poetry as 'the best words in the best order' he asserted that there is in the words of the greatest poets 'a reason not only for every word but for the position of every word' in the well-ordered sentence the hearer or the reader will receive no jolt or check Herbert Spencer observed that things which are to be thought of together must be mentioned as closely as possible together naturally we place together such words as are more closely associated in meaning we say *a big brown dog* rather than *a brown big dog*, *a handsome young man* and not *a young handsome man*, and *a kind old gardener*, not *an old kind gardener* so too we place together those phrases which are most closely associated in our minds 'Delighted to make your acquaintance' we say upon being introduced, not, as in German, 'Delighted your acquaintance to make'.

(*Simeon Potter: Adapted.*)

The comma

Perhaps the most common error in the writing of English is to use a comma in order to separate sentences. A comma *cannot* be so used, and the following are incorrect:

I am returning the electricity bill you sent me, it is incorrect.

We arrived here yesterday, the weather is perfect.

None of the photographs came out, the camera was broken.

Full stops (or their equivalent, as described in later sections) should have been used in place of commas, or the sentences should have been linked in some way, e.g. by inserting *because* before *it* in the first sentence.

The comma is used

(*a*) to mark off a phrase or clause, or occasionally a word, when the sense demands a slight pause:

Women are, for the most part, more interested in clothes than men are.

The British Constitution, as everyone knows, has been shaped by retaining old forms and putting them to new uses.

However, many writers prefer complexity to simplicity.

(*b*) to separate words (occasionally phrases or clauses) in a list:

The guests included ambassadors, envoys, consuls and other representatives of the diplomatic service.

A comma is unnecessary before *and* at the end of a list, but it is not incorrect and may be needed for emphasis or to avoid ambiguity.

(*c*) when an inversion of the normal order is used for emphasis:

He surveyed the damage grimly.

but

Grimly, he surveyed the damage.

(*d*) before a direct quotation:

An anonymous diplomat once wrote, 'If you take trouble in the use of words you are bound to clarify the thought you wish to convey.'

(*e*) on any occasion where its presence helps the reader. But remember what has been said about the importance of words and word order, rather than of punctuation, as a means of expressing what you have to say. If you write

She arrived with her husband and two cats in a basket.

you may decide that you have committed an unfortunate ambiguity, and decide to clarify by adding a comma:

She arrived with her husband, and two cats in a basket.

Better to have avoided the ambiguity in the first place by a more careful choice of words:

She arrived with her husband and with two cats in a basket.

Another example:

It can be mended perhaps with a screwdriver.

may mean

It can be mended, perhaps with a screwdriver.

(which means that it can be mended), or the meaning may be

It can be mended perhaps, with a screwdriver.

(which means that there is some doubt about whether it can be mended). There is no ambiguity in

It can perhaps be mended with a screwdriver.

or

It can be mended if you use a screwdriver.

Exercise 227

Write out the following, inserting commas and full stops, remember that to insert a comma where it is not required is as incorrect as to omit one where it is required.

(*a*) Sir Boyle Roche who is credited with some incredible statements is reported to have said 'Single misfortunes never come alone and the greatest misfortune is generally followed by a much greater one'.

(*b*) Since the war of 1939–45 and partly because of it there has arisen a Do–It–Yourself cult affecting not only the practicalities of life but also its embellishments and enhancements and consolations: music and the arts literature and the drama all show an undermining by the levelling process those for whom 'anything goes' have yet to learn that ultimately for them nothing goes lacking a worth-while ambition a compulsive aspiration a genuine integrity they are easily satisfied with mediocrity for them the speech of an illiterate is preferable to that of an educated cultured person subtlety and suppleness distinction and variety eloquence and ease clarity of phrasing and perspicacity of sentence all these are suspect for they imply superiority of mind and spirit no wonder mediocrity flourishes in literature and indeed at all levels of writing for its own vehicle language has been slowed down by the dull and the indifferent anyone who believes in civilisation must find it difficult to approve and impossible to abet one of the surest means of destroying it to degrade language is finally to degrade civilisation

(Eric Partridge: Adapted)

The colon

The colon (:) is stronger than the comma or semi-colon (see below) but weaker than the full stop. Some writers do without it altogether, but it has several valuable uses:

(*a*) at the end of a main clause when what follows is an amplification:

The system has three drawbacks: it is too expensive, it takes too much time, and no–one understands it.

A full stop would have been possible after *drawback*, but what follows is sufficiently closely linked to *The system has three drawbacks* to justify the less sharp separation provided by the colon. A comma would have been wrong, however. Why?

(*b*) to introduce a quotation, as the colon does after *amplification* in the previous paragraph, and as it is used frequently in similar circumstances throughout this book.

(*c*) to introduce a list:

> Dickens wrote a number of important novels: *Bleak House, Oliver Twist, David Copperfield* and *Hard Times*.

A comma would not have been strong enough here, though one could have said

> Dickens wrote a number of important novels, including *Bleak House, Oliver Twist ....*

where the sense requires no pause, and therefore no punctuation, before *Bleak House*.

The semi-colon

Like the colon, and unlike the comma, the semi-colon is a stop rather than a pause, but not as complete or heavy a stop as the full stop. The semi-colon is used to break up long sentences; it relates clauses or sentences which have too strong a relationship to be separated by full stops. What follows and precedes a semicolon must be a grammatically complete sentence. In other words, the semi-colon is an alternative to the full stop when the writer wishes to link, rather than separate, what follows and what has preceded. A semi-colon should not be used to mark off mere phrases and subordinate clauses (for which a comma suffices); it should mark off sentence-equivalents.

> The crematorium charges are not excessive; they have not risen for ten years.

Here, the semi-colon links two simple sentences. A full stop could have been used; alternatively, the sentences could have been linked to a conjunction such as *and*. It would not have been incorrect to use a colon on the grounds that the second statement amplifies or explains the first. The semi-colon is correctly used to link two sentences which have a common topic.

> The story is told of a man who had been suffering from insomnia for many years; no-one could find a cure. Finally, his friends hit upon a plan which succeeded perfectly: he was given a job as a night-watchman, told to stay awake at all costs, and was found asleep within the hour.

The semi-colon is used to link the first (complex) sentence and the following (simple) one which is closely related to it. The colon after *succeeded perfectly* indicates that the nature of the success is about to be described. Commas mark off the final three clauses; all of them have the same subject (*he*) and the commas provide the link.

Exercise 228

Punctuate the following. Each one is a single sentence.

1. Many English river-names are Celtic Avon Severn Thames Trent and Wye

2. The subjects of the play are love marriage separation and divorce

3. All was peaceful in the park ducks waddled lovers strolled children played old men slept and a few rowers plied their oars lazily

4. The company has been making bricks for a hundred years its expertise is thus very considerable

5. There was a sharp frost in the air it cut the nose and lungs you could feel your eyes water in the darkness

The question mark and exclamation mark

(*a*) The question mark (?) is used at the end of a sentence when a direct question is being asked; a direct question is one in which the words are phrased as an actual question:

What will they think of next?

Has anyone a match, please?

Can you tell me where the nearest telephone-box is?

Single words are sometimes used as questions:

How? When? Where? Who? Why?

Note the differences between the direct questions above and

I wonder what they will think of next.

I asked if anyone had a match.

I enquired where the nearest telephone-box was.

These are not direct questions, because they do not consist of the actual words used when asking the questions. These sentences, therefore, should not have question marks.

(*b*) The exclamation mark (!) is used to indicate a surprised tone of voice, and to punctuate exclamations (see Chapter 1).

> Good heavens! We've won!

Do not use exclamation marks excessively, certainly not in formal writing. There is room for them in letters to friends, and in works of fiction, provided that one does not lapse into the habit, frequently found in children's comics, of using them extravagantly:

> Wow!!! What?!

In this connexion, a word should be said about the use of underlining. There is a strong temptation to underline a word or phrase for emphasis, perhaps following the royal precedent of Queen Victoria, who in her letters used underlining extensively whenever she felt strongly about something – which was very often. Underlining for emphasis can become a habit; if over-used it merely suggests petulance or high blood-pressure. Used sparingly, it can draw urgent attention to something by its very unexpectedness, but the correct choice and arrangement of words are the best means of being emphatic.

The dash

The dash (–) is often too carelessly used in English instead of the comma – and often instead of most other punctuation as well.

> Its correct uses are

(*a*) to introduce and conclude an expression (phrase, clause or sentence) introduced into a sentence by way of explanation or comment:

> The ghost – so local rumour has it – walks the moors between Okehampton and Tavistock.

Brackets are sometimes used as an alternative, when a writer wants to slip something in unobtrusively without disturbing his flow, and uses brackets to suggest that the words within brackets are subordinate to the main sense of what he is saying:

> A number of defensive walls are linked together to form the Great Wall of China (the only man-made object visible from the moon) after the country was unified.

Brackets (sometimes called *a parenthesis*) could have been replaced by dashes or commas here, though commas would have brought a rather irrelevant piece of information too strongly into the main sense of the sentence.

(*b*) towards the end of a sentence, indicating an anticipatory pause before a conclusion, explanation or surprise:

The book is what every publisher dreams of – a best-seller.

(*c*) at the end of a sentence which is left uncompleted. This device is often found in works of fiction when a speaker is interrupted by another speaker or by something that happens:

'If you can't trust me –'

'It's not that I can't trust you. It's just that –'

The argument was interrupted by a shout from outside.

Some writers prefer three dots (...), however, in such circumstances.

(*d*) after a colon, to introduce a quotation or list (:–). This use is now seldom found, because the colon can do the work unaided.

Avoid over-use of the dash, especially as a parenthesis. Too many interruptions to the flow of sentences can irritate the reader; parentheses can often be worked into the main structure of sentences with a little forethought and without resort to dashes and brackets. The dash has legitimate functions, as we have seen, but it offers temptations, especially the temptation to launch into a sentence without thinking what one is going to say, secure in the knowledge that afterthoughts can always be stuck in with the help of dashes.

Quotation marks

Quotation marks ('...'), sometimes called *inverted commas*, are used to denote that a speaker's or writer's actual words are being used:

'That's true,' said Bernard.

The Prime Minister said, 'Prospects are good.'

There is no unanimous agreement about the placing of punctuation, but the above examples show widespread practice. Note that *That's true* is a whole sentence, but a comma follows it; if the words had been a question or an exclamation, a question mark or exclamation mark would have been correct. Sometimes a direct quotation is interrupted by *he said* or some similar expression; note the punctuation in

'She's bought a trampoline,' said Betty, 'so that she can practise every day!'

'Betty's not joking,' said Eva. 'What's more, do you know that she keeps the trampoline in the greenhouse?'

There is a comma after *Betty* because the second part of the quotation continues the sentence begun in the first part. There is a full stop after Eva, however, because the quotation continues with a new sentence. This explains the small *s* of *so* in the first quotation and the capital *W* of *What's* in the second. Note too that it is customary to begin a new paragraph before and after each speech.

The words within inverted commas in the above illustration are called *direct speech*.

Should it be necessary to use a quotation within a quotation, double inverted commas ("...") may be used.

Inverted commas are usually used to punctuate the title of a book, play, film, etc.:

It's many years since I read 'Wuthering Heights'.

The apostrophe

The use of the apostrophe (') to indicate possession has already been described in Chapter 2.

The apostrophe is also used to indicate a letter or letters omitted:

don't (do not), shan't (shall not), it's (it is), won't (will not), can't (cannot), I'll (I will)

Capital letters

These should be used for

(*a*) the beginning of every sentence,

(*b*) the beginning of sentences quoted in inverted commas, as described in section 8,

(*c*) the beginning of each line of poetry, though much modern poetry does not follow this convention,

(*d*) proper nouns (see Chapter 2),

Rome, Napoleon, Parliament

and some adjectives formed from some of them,

Roman, Napoleonic

but not all,

He hopes for a parliamentary career.

(*e*) names of deities:

God, Buddha, Allah

(*f*) the important words in titles of books, plays, etc.

(*g*) days of the week, months of the year and special festivals or events:

Sunday, December, Easter, the Trooping of the Colour.

(*h*) the personal pronoun *I*, but not *me*. Pronouns referring to God are given capital letters in Scripture, theological works, etc.

(*i*) the poetical device known as *personification*, when abstractions are referred to as people:

To that high capital, where kingly Death
Keeps his pale court in beauty and decay,
He came.

Exercise 229

Insert the appropriate punctuation.

1. Would you please pass the salt and pepper.

2. What a strange-looking building

3. They phoned to ask if we could help

4. It wont cost much to replace or so he says

5. Youll never guess what the price is £17

6. The guide-book a handsomely produced volume incidentally describes the library ceiling as the finest in Europe

7. He doesnt understand why it wont start

8. I met a young american in oxford street on monday he told me hed seen all the productions of the royal shakespeare company since easter and liked coriolanus best

Answers to exercises

Exercise 16

1. a man's reach 2. a boy's best friend 3. the lions' den 4. men's achievements 5. women's clothes 6. the box's lid 7. the dress's sleeves 8. the dresses' cost

Exercise 17

1. The boys' possessions 2. The children's hobbies 3. The countries' exports 4. Men's aspirations 5. the sheep's safety (no change: *sheep* is the same in singular and plural) 6. Women's place 7. The teams' results 8. The armies' exercises

   [...]

Exercise 225

Common ones include B.B.C., T.U.C., C.B.I., H.M.S., E.E.C., A.A., U. N., C.I.D., B.A., F.B.I., I.Q. Most dictionaries list the most frequently used ones.

Exercise 226

in proper places.	emphasis.	purpose.
word order.	the best order'.	every word'.
check.	possible together.	in meaning.
kind gardener.	our minds.	

Exercise 227

(*a*) Commas after *Roche, statements, said, alone*. Full stop after *one*.

(*b*) Commas after *45* (optional), *it* (optional), *cult* (optional), *arts, drama*. Full stop after *process*. Commas after *ultimately, them*. Full stop after *nothing goes*. Commas after *ambition, aspiration, integrity*. Full stop after *mediocrity*. Commas after *for them* (optional), *educated*. Full stop after *person*. Commas after *suppleness, variety, ease, sentence, suspect*. Full stop after *spirit*. Commas before and after *indeed* (optional), after *writing, vehicle, language.* Full stop after *indifferent*. Commas after *approve, abet.* Full stops after *destroying it* and *civilisation.*

Exercise 228

1. Many English river-names are Celtic: Avon, Severn, Thames, Trent and Wye.

2. The subjects of the play are love, marriage, separation, and divorce.

   (Comma optional after *separation*, but it helps to climax the sentence in a way unnecessary in the previous sentence.)

3. All was peaceful in the park: ducks waddled, lovers strolled, children played, old men slept, and a few rowers plied their oars lazily.

   (Semi-colons would not have been wrong in place of commas, but the heavier punctuation of semi-colons would have produced an unwanted jerky effect.)

4. The company has been making bricks for a hundred years; its expertise is thus very considerable.

5. There was a sharp frost in the air; it cut the nose and lungs; you could feel your eyes water in the darkness. (Commas were sufficient for the list of short clauses in (3), but the longer clauses in this sentence require stronger punctuation, and there is not the same sense of having a list.)

Exercise 229

1. ... salt and pepper?

2. ... building!

3. ... could help.

4. It won't cost much to replace – or so he says. (Or comma after *replace*.)

5. You'll never guess what the price is – £17! (Or full stop after *is*.)

6. The guide-book (a handsomely produced volume, incidentally) describes ... Europe. (Commas or dashes would serve instead of brackets.)

7. He doesn't understand why it won't start.

8. I met a young American in Oxford Street on Monday. He told me he had seen all the productions of the Royal Shakespeare Company since Easter, and liked 'Coriolanus' best.

Source: B.A. Phythian (1980) *English Grammar*, London: Hodder & Stoughton, pp. 16–18, 202–13, 219, 279–80.

53 from *MHRA Style Guide*

Group A   General

Number	Instruction	Textual mark	Marginal mark	Notes
A1	Correction is concluded	None	/	Make after each correction
A2	Leave unchanged	------ under characters to remain	(✓)	
A3	Remove extraneous marks	Encircle marks to be removed	✕	e.g. film or paper edges visible between lines on bromide or diazo proofs
A3.1	Push down spacing material which has risen and printed between words or lines	Encircle blemish	⊥	
A4	Refer to appropriate authority anything of doubtful accuracy	Encircle word(s) affected	(?)	

Group B   Deletion, insertion and substitution

B1	Insert in text the matter indicated in the margin	⋏	New matter followed by ⋏	Identical to B2
B2	Insert additional matter identified by a letter in a diamond	⋏	⋏ Followed by for example ⟨A⟩	The additional copy should be supplied with the corresponding letter marked on it in a diamond e.g. ⟨A⟩
B3	Delete	/ through character(s) or ├───┤ through words to be deleted	♂	
B4	Delete and close up	⌒ / through character or ├───┤ through characters e.g. charac⌃ter charac⌣ter	⌢♂	

PROOF CORRECTION   69

Number	Instruction	Textual mark	Marginal mark	Notes
B5	Substitute character or substitute part of one or more word(s)	/ through character or ├────────┤ through word(s)	New character or new word(s)	
B6	Wrong fount. Replace by character(s) of correct fount	Encircle character(s) to be changed	⊗	
B6.1	Change damaged character(s)	Encircle character(s) to be changed	✕	This mark is identical to A3
B7	Set in or change to italic	_____ under character(s) to be set or changed	⊔	Where space does not permit textual marks encircle the affected area instead
B8	Set in or change to capital letters	≡≡≡ under character(s) to be set or changed	≡	
B9	Set in or change to small capital letters	≡≡≡ under character(s) to be set or changed	═	
B9.1	Set in or change to capital letters for initial letters and small capital letters for the rest of the words	≡ under initial letters and ≡≡ under rest of the word(s)	≡	
B10	Set in or change to bold type	∿∿∿ under character(s) to be set or changed	∿	
B11	Set in or change to bold italic type	∿∿∿ under character(s) to be set or changed	⊔∿	
B12	Change capital letters to lower case letters	Encircle character(s) to be changed	≢	For use when B5 is inappropriate

Number	Instruction	Textual mark		Marginal mark	Notes
B12.1	Change small capital letters to lower case letters	Encircle character(s) to be changed		╪	For use when B5 is inappropriate
B13	Change italic to upright type	Encircle character(s) to be changed		⊔	
B14	Invert type	Encircle character to be inverted		↺	
B15	Substitute or insert character in 'superior' position	/	through character	⌐ under character	
		or ∧	where required	e.g. ⌐2	
B16	Substitute or insert character in 'inferior' position	/	through character	L over character	
		or ∧	where required	e.g. L2	
B17	Substitute ligature e.g. ffi for separate letters	├───┤ through characters affected		◡ e.g. ffi	
B17.1	Substitute separate letters for ligature	├───┤		Write out separate letters	
B18	Substitute or insert full stop or decimal point	/	through character	⊙	
		or ∧	where required		
B18.1	Substitute or insert colon	/	through character	⊙	
		or ∧	where required		
B18.2	Substitute or insert semi-colon	/	through character	;	
		or ∧	where required		

PROOF CORRECTION   71

Number	Instruction	Textual mark		Marginal mark	Notes
B18.3	Substitute or insert comma	/	through character	〝	
		or ⋀	where required		
B18.4	Substitute or insert apostrophe	/	through character	⁊	
		or ⋀	where required		
B18.5	Substitute or insert single quotation marks	/	through character	⁊ and/or ⁊	
		or ⋀	where required		
B18.6	Substitute or insert double quotation marks	/	through character	⁊ and/or ⁊	
		or ⋀	where required		
B19	Substitute or insert ellipsis	/	through character	• • •	
		or ⋀	where required		
B20	Substitute or insert leader dots	/	through character	(• • •)	Give the measure of the leader when necessary
		or ⋀	where required		
B21	Substitute or insert hyphen	/	through character	⊢–⊣	
		or ⋀	where required		
B22	Substitute or insert rule	/	through character	⊢—⊣	Give the size of the rule in the marginal mark e.g.
		⋀	where required		⊢1 em⊣ ⊢4 mm⊣

72   MHRA STYLE GUIDE

Number	Instruction	Textual mark	Marginal mark	Notes
B23	Substitute or insert oblique	/ through character or ⅄ where required	(/)	

Group C Positioning and spacing

Number	Instruction	Textual mark	Marginal mark	Notes
C1	Start new paragraph			
C2	Run on (no new paragraph)			
C3	Transpose characters or words	between characters or words, numbered when necessary		
C4	Transpose a number of characters or words	3 2 1	1 2 3	To be used when the sequence cannot be clearly indicated by the use of C3. The vertical strokes are made through the characters or words to be transposed and numbered in the correct sequence
C5	Transpose lines			
C6	Transpose a number of lines		——— 3 ——— 2 ——— 1	To be used when the sequence cannot be clearly indicated by C5. Rules extend from the margin into the text with each line to be transplanted numbered in the correct sequence
C7.	Centre	enclosing matter to be centred	[ ]	
C8	Indent			Give the amount of the indent in the marginal mark

PROOF CORRECTION   73

Number	Instruction	Textual mark	Marginal mark	Notes
C9	Cancel indent			
C10	Set line justified to specified measure	and/or		Give the exact dimensions when necessary
C11	Set column justified to specified measure			Give the exact dimensions when necessary
C12	Move matter specified distance to the right	enclosing matter to be moved to the right		Give the exact dimensions when necessary
C13	Move matter specified distance to the left	enclosing matter to be moved to the left		Give the exact dimensions when necessary
C14	Take over character(s), word(s) or line to next line, column or page			The textual mark surrounds the matter to be taken over and extends into the margin
C15	Take back character(s), word(s), or line to previous line, column or page			The textual mark surrounds the matter to be taken back and extends into the margin
C16	Raise matter	over matter to be raised / under matter to be raised		Give the exact dimensions when necessary. (Use C28 for insertion of space between lines or paragraphs in text)
C17	Lower matter	over matter to be lowered / under matter to be lowered		Give the exact dimensions when necessary. (Use C29 for reduction of space between lines or paragraphs in text)
C18	Move matter to position indicated	Enclose matter to be moved and indicate new position		Give the exact dimensions when necessary

74   MHRA STYLE GUIDE

Number	Instruction	Textual mark	Marginal mark	Notes
C19	Correct vertical alignment	‖ ‖	‖ ‖	
C20	Correct horizontal alignment	Single line above and below misaligned matter e.g. <u>misaligned</u>	—— ——	The marginal mark is placed level with the head and foot of the relevant line
C21	Close up. Delete space between characters or words	linking ⌒⌄ characters	⌒⌄	
C22	Insert space between characters	| between characters affected	Y	Give the size of the space to be inserted when necessary
C23	Insert space between words	Y between words affected	Y	Give the size of the space to be inserted when necessary
C24	Reduce space between characters	| between characters affected	⌃	Give the amount by which the space is to be reduced when necessary
C25	Reduce space between words	⌃ between words affected	⌃	Give amount by which the space is to be reduced when necessary
C26	Make space appear equal between characters or words	| between characters or words affected	⅄	
C27	Close up to normal interline spacing	(each side of column linking lines)		The textual marks extend into the margin

PROOF CORRECTION 75

Number	Instruction	Textual mark	Marginal mark	Notes
C28	Insert space between lines or paragraphs		or	The marginal mark extends between the lines of text. Give the size of the space to be inserted when necessary
C29	Reduce space between lines or paragraphs		or	The marginal mark extends between the lines of text. Give the amount by which the space is to be reduced when necessary

MARKS TO BE MADE ON PROOF, OR PROOFS, AFTER READING

MARK	MEANING
'Revise' (and signature)	Correct and submit another proof.
'Revise and make up' (and signature)	Correct and submit another proof in page form.
'Revise and press' (and signature)	Make final corrections and print off without submitting another proof.
'Press' (and signature)	No correction necessary. The work may be printed.

Source: *MHRA Style Guide: A handbook for authors, editors, and writers of theses* (2002), London: Modern Humanities Research Association, pp. 68–75.

54 from *How to Publish Your Poetry*

PETER FINCH

Peter Finch, poet, critic and literary entrepreneur, grew up in Cardiff. He has published over twenty books of poetry, working in both traditional and experimental forms, and is well known as a performer of his works at literary festivals and in schools. He is the author of a number of works of advice to writers about getting published, the best known of which is *How to Publish Your Poetry* (fourth edition, 1998), and of two books of historical, topographical and fictional material about Cardiff. He is now Chief Executive of the Academi, the Welsh National Literature Promotion Agency and Society for Writers.

Opportunities for poets

In many ways Cyberspace is a mirror of the conventional world. The electronic replicates the real. There are on-line books, magazines, historical and contemporary archives, scandal sheets, comics, games, films, reference works, and news services. Many dedicate themselves entirely to poetry. They also change almost as fast as the systems they run on. The Internet is enormously volatile. Addresses and providers move here at a much higher rate than they do elsewhere. [...]

Journals

On-line magazines range from those which mirror their print-based cousins (and in some cases are simply direct copies) to completely innovative, interactive compilations which mix sound and action with the text. The Net is no static place. It can provide movement, video, sound and user-defined typeface along with actual text. Some mags (e-zines, on-line journals, call them what you will) offer playable recordings of their poets performing, others give space for readers to add criticism. Most use the hyper-link, a method of moving instantly from one section of the site to another (or even somewhere else) by clicking the computer's mouse. The difference between on-line and print-based magazines becomes more apparent when you discover that what you get when you call them up is not simply the current issue but access to the entire back catalogue. All searchable, storable (put them on your hard drive, onto a floppy disk, print copies out) and, best of all, free. It is possible to restrict access by requiring users to enter a password. This happens with some news and business services along with the *Which* archive, all of whom require payment before allowing access [...] but I've yet to see this applied to verse.

Geography dissolves on-line. America is no further and no more costly to access than Britain. One of the great mags, *Isibongo*, is based in South Africa. It's just as easy to read as our own Derbyshire market leader, Sean Woodward's *Living Poets* or Mary Buechler's Sacramento *Poetic Express*. In fact, half the time, the user has no idea precisely where the site being accessed is physically based. Place ceases to matter, language takes over.

How do you contribute? Send your poems by e-mail, no sae needed. A few brave journals will accept work by snail mail from the not yet connected (*New Hope International* insists on this method) although most prefer to deal electronically. On-line mag editors hate rekeying, it goes against the grain. Opinions differ as to the validity of reusing material already published conventionally. If you are going to contribute work which has knocked around the real world then you should at least acknowledge this fact. And as ever keep a record of what you send. The sheer speed and ease of using computers to do your mailing for you usually means you forget what went where and when.

Cyberspace is huge. Some of the sites which list on-line journals, such as the *American Resources For Poets* or *Yahoo's Poetry Page* seem to go on for days. Starting your own mag is easy – frictionless, Gates calls it – and size presents few difficulties. Standards are therefore pretty variable. Not only are the UK's computer literate newbies up there but America, Canada and Australia's, too.

Competitions

Naturally there is an on-line variant to the more traditional 'send five pounds and your best shot' contests. Some actively canvas entries from the unconnected and offer Net publication as the prize. For some poets this will no doubt be sufficient reward. Others accept on-line entries and choose their winners by asking readers to vote – again on-line. Once set up, contemporary software usually allows the entire process to run automatically. The selling point for all these competitions is the enormous audience supposedly sitting around out there in front of their screens. The potential certainly is large – 40 or 50 million users already connected and with more joining every day. Yet how many actually bother to access poetry remains debatable. Still, 22,500 visitors to the *Poetic Express* site every quarter is a few more than the number of *Poetry Review* readers (5,000 per issue). *Poetic Express*'s competitions are free. Readers vote for the best poem on the site.

Books

If you tire of contributing to the Web sites of others then start your own. A whole collection of verse on-line, the equivalent of a conventional book, will present relatively little difficulty. Most Internet Service Providers (ISPs) now offer an amount of free Web space as part of the subscription. This means that with the aid of some Web authoring software (*HotMetal Pro, FrontPage*) or a handbook on *Hyper-Text Mark-Up Language* (html) you can put your work on-line. *HTML* is the not-too-complex computer language in which Web pages are written. For a good introduction try MacBride's *Teach Yourself HTML* or Elizabeth Castro's *HTML For The World Wide Web*. Hosting your own *home page* (your own Web site) is certainly not beyond anyone capable of using conventional computer word-processing packages. In fact if you run Microsoft's *Word* you'll find the readily available *Word Internet Assistant* add-on will do the job for you. If you'd like to see the kind of thing that's possible have a look at poet and singer Labi Siffre's home page, or for that matter my own, *The Peter Finch Archive*. If you are reticent get a fan to set up a site devoted to your works. This has happened to David Gascoyne, to J H Prynne, Benjamin Zephaniah and others. Otherwise go to it on your own. The trick is not so much getting the poems up there but attracting visitors. Most of the standard Internet primers offer basic advice. Try Angus J Kennedy's *The Internet and World Wide Web – The Rough Guide* (Penguin). Check with your ISP – there's loads of free, up-to-the-minute advice actually on the Net. If you have a recording of yourself doing your stuff then get one-jump ahead. Put that up on your site too.

Groups

To reduce the poet's traditional feeling of isolation the Net presents a number of opportunities. World-wide poets, once they've got over the stunning breadth of Net facilities, are usually hard to shut up. E-mail – the almost-instantaneous and far too easy-to-use equivalent of conventional letter post – provides one vehicle. Here bands of poets circulate their work, their criticisms and their views of world literature. Join a group (no cost, just ask) and you'll find a daily delivery of e-mails in your in-box. Some groups are moderated which means that contributions are filtered by a controlling individual although most are free-for-alls. Discussion can range from the moronic to the stimulating. *The British and Irish Poets Group* established by Ric Caddel and *Cyber Poets* set up by Peter Howard are two worth looking at. But check how many writers are involved. The larger the membership the harder it is for single individuals to make a mark.

A variant on e-mail discussion groups are Usenet Newsgroups. Newsgroups run through their own dedicated software (provided by your ISP as part of your subscription) and are open to contributions from anyone anywhere. To join in you *subscribe*. This does not mean parting with money but simply ticking a box. Articles are delivered to your browser for consumption. If you want to contribute then type it up, click a button and it's done. The principle poetry newsgroups, *rec. arts.poems* and *alt.arts.poetry.comments*, offer pretty varied fare. By their world-wide nature they tend to be American dominated and standards of contribution are not always that high. But they are places where you can get an instant reaction to your latest poem and where you can offer your views on the work of others.

Tools and resources

The Net offers a multitude of these. There are on-line spell-checkers (in many languages), thesauri, an anagram creator, a rhyming dictionary. The archives of universities (particularly in America) offer the great poetry of the past in comprehensive quantity. Down-load facsimile editions of *The Germ* (the first ever poetry magazine from 1850) or hear Seamus Heaney recite. Read the complete works of Blake, find out what powered the Beat generation, discover how Hardy worked, check the roots of modern verse. Not only can you find the texts themselves but entire critical apparatuses, historical contexts, biographies, bibliographies, portraits, names of lovers, typical daily menus and shoe sizes for most of the great poets of the world. You can access information on poetry readings or check at the British Council for data on literature festivals. Students seem to revel in posting their dissertations. Archives want their knowledge made available to everyone. Interested in a particular style? Haiku? Visual poetry? Traditional forms? They've all got their sites.

You'll also find that conventional publishers, bookshops and libraries are all busy establishing their own pages. You'd like to see the work of a specific bard? In print or not someone on-line should be able to either sell you it or offer it on loan.

How to find them

Internet *search engines* are vast, free-to-use, on-line databases which allow users to track down their interests by either key word or subject type. The big ones, such as *Yahoo, InfoSeek, Web Crawler, Excite, AltaVista* and *Lycos* hold billions of records. To use them you need to be specific in your request. I tried keying 'poetry' in to *AltaVista* and got 149,529 results. Much easier is to log onto one of a number of poetry resource sites which run clickable lists of relevant pages. The UK Poetry Society, The Poetry Library and *Poetry Review*'s 'web watcher' Peter Howard's home page are worth consulting. Howard's page in particular should lead you to everywhere you could possibly want to go. The Poetry Society of America's *Resources For Poets* is also a useful source. Other places with desirable listings include the UK *Society of Authors, The League of Canadian Poets, The Academy of American Poets, Poetry On the Web* and Inkspot's *Resources*.

Source: Peter Finch (1998) *How To Publish Your Poetry*, London: Allison and Busby, pp. 99–103.

55 from *Inside Book Publishing*

GILES CLARK

Giles Clark (b. 1954), adviser on co-publishing at the Open University, was educated at Berkhamsted Grammar School and University College London. He joined the Open University as an editorial trainee, becoming a course editor and then the University's agent in its collaborations with publishers. A commission by the Society of Young Publishers to carry out research into the workings of the publishing industry led to the publication in 1988 of his book *Inside Book Publishing*. It has since gone through several editions, been translated into German, and is a set text on courses on publishing in the UK and elsewhere.

Unsolicited ideas and manuscripts

Hopeful authors bombard all publishers with unsolicited manuscripts and book proposals. Consumer firms, which may reject over 99%, may wish to direct them to agents or may employ part-time readers who sort through the 'slush' pile, write reports on possible ones and refer them to the editors. Most academic theses, too, sent direct to editors are unpublishable as they stand, but a fraction can be turned into monographs. It is very unlikely that an unsolicited textbook manuscript would be structured commercially, but occasionally unsolicited ideas can be developed.

The decision to publish

Many factors influence an editor's decision to pursue a new project, including:

- Suitability for list. A title has to fit the style and aims of the list for which it is known (or sometimes branded) so that it is compatible with the firm's particular marketing systems. Furthermore, editors assessing new titles with other titles are concerned with the list's overall balance, direction and degree of innovation.

- Author assessment. The author's qualifications, motivation and time available to write the book, public standing, reliability to deliver on time, and responsiveness to suggestions.

- Unique sales proposition (USP). What makes this book different from others or special (e.g. top author, new subject treatment, first illustrated book, differentiated by price)? What are the special marketing opportunities on which the book could be promoted (e.g. author celebrity, publicity angles, especially consumer books)?

- Market. Understanding the main audience for which the book is intended, who would buy it, the possible take-up at home and overseas. (The sales records on the author's previous books or those of similar books may be used as a guide.) Sometimes the rights sales potential is assessed (e.g. licensed book club, US rights).

- Competition. The title's USPs and advantages compared with the firm's own and competitors' books (e.g. especially text-books and reference titles).

- Frontlist/backlist potential. Is the book expected to have a short life on the frontlist, or does it have potential to endure on the backlist thus ameliorating the vagaries of the frontlist?

- Investment and return. How much time and money needs to be expended on acquiring the book (such as the size of advance expected by the agent) and on developing and marketing it through to publication, in relation to its expected earnings and profitability? Would its earning power justify its place on the list?

- Risk and innovation. What are the external factors at play affecting the risk investment, such as the timing of publication in relation to optimum time to publish, the link to events and their perceived popularity, and the actions of competitors? What are the downside risks if the expectations are not realized? To what extent is the project experimental in terms of taking on a new author, or publishing in a new area or format (print or electronic), or price? Without taking risks and innovating, the publisher is overtaken by competitors.

- Content. The editor's judgement on the quality and appropriateness of the content is aided by others. Fiction editors may use junior editors, or external readers, to supply plot synopses or to offer first or second opinions. Non-fiction editors may ask specialist external readers to comment on specialist titles. Other publishers rely heavily on experts (e.g. teachers, academics, professionals) sometimes worldwide to comment by e-mail on material initially, during or after the book has been written. (All these external readers are paid small fees and remain mostly anonymous to the author.)

■ Book's physical appearance and price. The editor envisages a proposed title's desirable physical form (e.g. its word length, illustration content, size, binding style and production quality), the likely cost and the price range within which it could be sold.

Some ideas are rejected, especially on unfavourable reports; some authors are asked to re-submit in the light of editors' suggestions; others are pursued. An editor cannot offer a contract without the agreement of the senior management. Editors sound out and lobby senior colleagues, such as the marketing and sales managers, over possible prices and sales forecasts and the production manager over the production costs. The editor prepares a publishing proposal form (circulated) which covers the scope of the book, its form, its market and competition, readers' reports, publication date, reasons for publication etc. Additionally, a financial statement sets the expected sales revenue against the costs of producing the book and those of author's royalties to give the hoped-for profit margin – provided the book sells out. Different combinations of prices and sales forecasts, and of print-run production costs and of royalties, may be tried. Many publishers hold formal meetings at which the main departmental directors hear editors' proposals – most get through, but some are referred back or rejected.

The editor, given the go-ahead, negotiates the contract with the author or agent (agents present their own contracts weighted in the author's favour), agrees or invents the book's title (important for sales success), and on commissioned books ensures that the author appreciates what is expected (e.g. content, length, deadline). There may be an optimum publication date which would maximize sales (e.g. a consumer book that is topical or published for the Christmas market; or textbooks of which bound copies are needed for inspection by teachers ideally around the new year to secure autumn adoptions in the northern hemisphere and April–June for the southern). Some authors submit chapters for comment; others deliver the complete manuscript on time or later, an inherent trait of many authors (or never). The manuscript is checked for length, completeness and quality (may be again externally reviewed), may be returned or accepted and is then handed down the line. The book is costed again.

Editors brief and liaise with junior editors, designers, production, promotion and sales staff and may write the blurb (the first twenty words of which must grip the reader). Although editors have no managerial control over other departments, they endeavour to ensure their books receive due attention. The editors may present their books to the publisher's sales force at the regular sales conferences.

Some editors, especially those involved with complex and highly, illustrated books, or major textbook projects involving supplementary material and new media, get very involved in the product research and development stages.

At the page-proof stage, the book's published price is fixed, as well as the number of copies to be printed and bound. The number printed may be less or more than the number envisaged at the outset.

The editors' involvement with re-pricing, reprinting, pulping or remaindering decisions varies from firm to firm. In some, the sales director is the dominant force.

Skills

No editor can simply sit back and expect marketable ideas and authors to flow in. Building contacts and opportunities takes initiative and quick-footed detective work to identify the sources of books, the best authors and ideas. Editors need to be creative in that they encourage and develop received ideas or initiate ideas themselves and match them to authors. Inevitably these lead up false trails, so editors have to be agile enough to hunt the front-runners, ruthless enough to weed out the wrong projects and to dump unprofitable authors, and tough enough to withstand this highly exposed position within the publishing house.

Profitable publishing depends on a perception of trends in markets and timing (good editors pre-empt competitors – in textbook publishing the lead time can easily be three years); constant vigilance, inquisitiveness and receptivity to new ideas; and responsiveness to changing needs. In specialist fields it involves asking experts the right questions, being able to talk to them intelligently for at least some minutes and being aware of their personal prejudices, professional jealousies and ideological positions. The skill lies in choosing the right advisers/readers – and assessing the assessors.

The consumer book editors, who face great difficulty in ascertaining market needs, base their judgements on a combination of experience of what sells, having a finger on the pulse, and intuition. Backing one's own hunches takes considerable audacity and confidence.

Fundamental to book and author selection is the editor's ability to assess the quality of the proposal and of the author's writing and purpose. This critical faculty (underpinned by skills in speed reading and sampling sections of writing) develops from experience and intuitive discernment. Editors should be able to contribute to structural improvements, and in specialist areas appear to the author not merely as a cipher for expert readers' comments.

The authors, who supply the raw material on which the success of the enterprise is founded, are engaged in long spells of isolation when writing with little else to draw on but experience, knowledge and imagination. In their books rest their dreams and hopes. In their eyes the editor is exclusive to them; to the editor an author is one of many. Authors expect editors to represent their interests in-house, to get things done and so judge editors on their in-house clout. Conversely editors must represent the best interests of the publisher to authors – at times a fine juggling act. Most authors are extremely sensitive about their work and the way it is published. Good editors persuade authors to write, foster author loyalty to the house, and nudge and encourage them in certain directions. Major skills lie in deciding when an author will appreciate intervention and its form, and in conveying constructive opinions honestly without damaging author self-confidence. Authors need encouragement, reassurance and praise – that, and the editor's diplomacy, are vital. Those authors who rely on their books for income (unlike teachers, academics etc.) centre their whole life around their writing. To some, an editor becomes inseparable from their private lives.

Editors need a knowledge of production methods (limitations and costs) and new media opportunities and of contracts; the skill to negotiate with authors, agents and others; and the appreciation of the inter-relationships between costs and revenues, and the risk factors involved. They deploy politicking and manipulative skills (especially during the publishing proposal stage) and their infectious enthusiasm, selling and persuasive skills, used to promote the book's fortunes within the house, get communicated to the outside world.

Source: Giles Clark (2001) *Inside Book Publishing*, London and New York: Routledge, pp. 85–9.

Acknowledgements

Grateful acknowledgement is made to the following sources for permission to reproduce material within this book.

Workbook

Page 40: Bashô, 'Morning Dew', in Hardy, J. (ed.), 2002, *Haiku, Poetry Ancient and Modern*, MQ Publications.

Page 40: Bashô, 'A Chestnut Falls', in Washington, P. (ed.), 2003, *Haiku*, Everyman Pocket Library.

Page 40: Hall, H., 'Cat', by kind permission of the author.

Pages 51–2: Heaney, S. (1980) 'Death of a Naturalist', *Collected Poems 1965–1975*, Faber & Faber.

Pages 60–1: 'The Captain of the 1964 Top of the Form Team' is taken from 'Mean Time' by Carol Ann Duffy published by Anvil Press Poetry in 1993.

Pages 182–3: Lochhead, L. (1984) 'Dreaming Frankenstein', *Dreaming Frankenstein and Collected Poems*, Polygon Books.

Pages 187–8: Auden, W. H. (1968) 'Age of Anxiety', *The Longer Collected Poems*, Faber & Faber.

Page 189: Boran, P. (1999) *The Portable Creative Writing Workshop*, Salmon Publishing Ltd.

Page 196: Bhatt, S., 'Sherdi', in Paterson D. and Simic, C. (eds), *New British Poetry*, Carcanet Press Limited.

Pages 198–9: Shapcott, J. (1992) 'The Mad Cow Talks Back', *Phrase Book*, Faber & Faber.

Pages 201–2: 'A Peculiar Suicide' from *Selected Poems* by Matthew Sweeney, published by Secker & Warburg. Reprinted by permission of The Random House Group Ltd.

Page 204: 'The Nine Muses', www.cosmolis.com

Pages 208–10: Pablo Neruda, 'Oda a la sal' poem belonging to the work *Tercer Libro De Las Odas*, © Fundación Pablo Neruda, 1957.

Page 212: Armitage, S. (2002) 'Nutshell', *The Universal Home Doctor*, Faber & Faber.

Page 215: MacCraig, N. (1985) 'Summer Farm', *Collected Poems*, Polygon Books.

Pages 217–19: Raine, C. (1984) 'A Free Translation', *Rich*, David Goodwin Associates.

Pages 220–1: Selima Hill (2002), *Portrait of My Lover as a Horse*, Bloodaxe Books.

Page 228: 'Leaving Inishmore' from *Selected Poems* by Michael Longley, published by Jonathan Cape. Reprinted by permission of The Random House Group Ltd and by kind permission of Michael Longley.

Pages 231–2: Muldoon, P. (1983) *Quoof*, Faber & Faber

Page 235: Copyright © 1957 and 1958 by Ogden Nash, Reprinted by permission of Curtis Brown Ltd. and Andre Deutsch. All rights reserved.

Page 242–3: Jamie, K. (1994) 'Mr and Mrs Scotland are Dead', *The Queen of Sheba*, Bloodaxe Books Ltd.

Page 248: Brendan Kennelly (2003) *Martial Art*, Bloodaxe Books.

Page 249: G. W. Robinson (trans), *Wang Wei: Poems*, © G. W. Robinson, 1973, London, page 31. Reproduced by permission of Penguin Books Ltd.

Page 249: Stryk, L.(trans), *On Love and Barley: Haiku of Bashô*, © Lucien Stryk, 1985, London, page 75. Reproduced by permission of Penguin Books Ltd;

Page 251: Morgan, E. (1990) 'Glasgow Sonnets, (i)', *Collected Poems*, Carcanet Press Limited.

Page 251: Brown, E. (1996) 'XLIII', *Maiden Speech*, Bloodaxe Books Ltd.

Pages 260–3: Graham, W. S., 'Johann Joachim Quantz's Five Lessons', in Francis, M. (ed.) (2004) *New Collected Poems*, Faber & Faber.

Page 277: Huxley, A., 'Fifth Philosopher's Song', in Allott, K. (ed.) (1962) *The Penguin Book of Contemporary Verse*.

Pages 286–7: from *Paula* by Isabel Allende and trans. by Margaret Sayers Peden. Copyright © 1994 by Isabel Allende. Translation copyright © 1995 by HarperCollins Publishers. Reprinted by permission of HarperCollins Publishers Inc.

Page 287: Lewisohn, M. (2002) *Funny Peculiar – The True Story of Benny Hill*, Sidgwick and Jackson.

Page 316: The Society of Authors as the Literary Representative of the Estate of Virginia Woolf.

Pages 352–3: 'Long Distance' from *Selected Poems: Harrison* by Tony Harrison (Penguin Books, 1984, 1987, 1989, 1995). Copyright © Tony Harrison, 1984.

Pages 353–4: from *The Wellspring* by Sharon Olds © 1996 by Sharon Olds. Used by permission of Alfred A. Knopf, a division of Random House, Inc.

Readings

Reading 1: from *Fires* by Raymond Carver, published by Harvill Press. Reprinted by permission of The Random House Group Ltd / Copyright © 1968 Raymond Carver. Reproduced by permission of the author c/o Rogers, Coleridge & White Ltd., 20 Powis Mews, London W11 1JN.

Reading 3: Somerset Maugham, W. (1949) *A Writer's Notebook*, reproduced by permission of A. P.Watt Ltd on behalf of The Royal Literary Fund.

Reading 4: Brande, D. (1983) *Becoming a Writer*, Abner Stein.

Reading 7: Glaister, L. (2001) 'Memory: The True Key To Real Imagining' in Bell, J. and Magrs, P. (eds), *The Creative Writing Coursebook*, Macmillan.

Reading 8: from Perry Donna, *Backtalk: Women Writers Speak Out*, Copyright © 1993 by Donna Perry. Reprinted by permission of Rutgers University Press.

Reading 9: from *Cal* by Bernard MacLaverty, published by Jonathan Cape. Copyright © 1983 Bernard MacLaverty. Reprinted by permission of The Random House Group Ltd. and by permission of the author c/o Rogers, Coleridge & White Ltd., 20 Powis Mews, London W11 1JN.

Reading 10: Kluge, P. F.(1996) *Biggest Elvis*, Penguin Group (USA) Inc.

Reading 12: Erdrich, L. (1986) *The Beet Queen*, Pavanne/Pan Books Ltd.

Reading 13: from *Age of Iron* by J. M. Coetzee, published by Secker and Warburg, reprinted by permission of The Random House Group Ltd.

Reading 14: Barker, P., *Another World*, London 1998, pp 130–32, reproduced by permission of Penguin Books Ltd./ Aitken & Stone Ltd.

Reading 15: Hemingway, E. (1993) 'The Doctor and the Doctor's Wife', from *The Essential Hemingway*, published by Jonathan Cape. Reprinted by permission of The Random House Group Ltd.

Reading 16: Lott, T. (2002) *Rumours of a Hurricane*, © Tim Lott, 2002. Reproduced by permission of Penguin Books Ltd and David Godwin Associates.

Reading 18: 'Girl' from *At the Bottom of the River*, Jamaica Kincaid, copyright © 1978, 1979, 1982, 1983 by Jamaica Kincaid by Pan Books Ltd. London and by Farrar Straus and Giraux, Inc, USA.

Reading 19: Copyright© 1997 *Rick Moody*. Reproduced by permission of the author c/o Rogers, Coleridge & White Ltd., 20 Powis Mews, London W11 1JN.

Reading 20: Excerpt from *Oxygen*, copyright © Andrew Miller 2001, reprinted by permission of Harcourt, Inc. and Hodder Headline.

Reading 21: Clarke, L. (2001) 'Going the Last Inch: Some Thoughts on Showing and Telling' in Bell, J. and Magrs, P. (eds), *The Creative Writing Coursebook*, Macmillan.

Reading 22: From *Little Tales of Misogyny* by Patricia Highsmith. First published in German as *Kleine Geschichten* for Weiberfeinde in a translation by W. E. Richartz. Copyright 1975 by Diogenes Verlag AG Zurich. Original English text first published in Great Britain 1977. Copyright 1977 by Diogenes Verlag AG Zurich. First published as a Norton paperback 2002. Used by permission of W. W. Norton & Company, Inc., Diogenes Verlag AG Zurich and Bloomsbury Publishing plc.

Reading 25: from *What We Talk About When We Talk About Love* by Raymond Carver, copyright © 1981 by Raymond Carver. Used by permission of Alfred A. Knopf, a division of Random House, Inc. Reprinted by permission of International Creative Management, Inc. Copyright © 1981–1988 by Raymond Carver, 1989–present by Tess Gallagher.

Reading 26: Copyright © Georgina Hammick, 1992, by kind permission of the artist and The Sayle Literary Agency.

Reading 43: Homes, R., *Footsteps – Adventures of a Romantic Biographer*, reprinted by permission of HarperCollins Publishers Ltd and David Godwin Associates, © Holmes, R., 1985.

Reading 44: Roth, P. (2001) *Reading Myself and Others*, Vintage.

Reading 45: Soyinka, W. (1981) *Aké – The Years of Childhood*, Methuen Publishing Limited and Melanie Jackson Agency, LLC.

Reading 46: Sage, L. (2000), *Bad Blood*, reprinted by permission of HarperCollins Publishers Ltd. and William Morrow. © Lorna Sage 2000.

Reading 49: Newman, J. (2000) *The Writer's Workbook*, copyright © 2000 Jenny Newman, Reproduced by permission of the author and Edward Arnold.

Reading 50: Curtis Brown on behalf of David Lodge, *The Art of Fiction*, Copyright © David Lodge 1992.

Reading 52: Phythian, B. A. (1980) *English Grammar*, Hodder Education.

Reading 53: *MHRA Style Guide* (2002), BSI Standards.

Reading 54: Finch, P. (1998) *How to Publish Poetry*, © Peter Finch.

Reading 55: Clark, G., 'Finding and developing the books', in *Inside Book Publishing*, Routledge, 1988, pp 85–9, www.tandf.co.uk & www.eBookstore.tandf.co.uk

Every effort has been made to contact copyright holders. If any have been inadvertently overlooked the publishers will be pleased to make the necessary arrangements at the first opportunity.

Index